FOUNDATIONS OF DATA EXCHANGE

The problem of exchanging data between different databases with different schemas is an area of immense importance. Consequently data exchange has been one of the most active research topics in databases over the past decade. Foundational questions related to data exchange largely revolve around three key problems: how to build target solutions; how to answer queries over target solutions; and how to manipulate schema mappings themselves? The last question is also known under the name "metadata management", since mappings represent metadata, rather than data in the database.

In this book the authors summarize the key developments of a decade of research. Part I introduces the problem of data exchange via examples, both relational and XML; Part II deals with exchanging relational data; Part III focuses on exchanging XML data; and Part IV covers metadata management.

MARCELO ARENAS is an Associate Professor at the Department of Computer Science at the Pontificia Universidad Catolica de Chile. He received his Ph.D. from the University of Toronto in 2005. His research interests are in different aspects of database theory, such as expressive power of query languages, database semantics, inconsistency handling, database design, XML databases, data exchange, metadata management and database aspects of the Semantic Web. He has received an IBM Ph.D. Fellowship (2004), seven best paper awards (PODS 2003, PODS 2005, ISWC 2006, ICDT 2010, ESWC 2011, PODS 2011 and WWW 2012) and an ACM-SIGMOD Dissertation Award Honorable Mention in 2006 for his Ph.D. dissertation "Design Principles for XML Data". He has served on multiple program committees, and since 2009 he has been participating as an invited expert in the World Wide Web Consortium.

PABLO BARCELÓ is an Assistant Professor in the Department of Computer Science at the University of Chile. He received his Ph.D. from the University of Toronto in 2006. His main research interest is in the area of Foundations of Data Management, in particular, query languages, data exchange, incomplete databases, and, recently, graph databases. He has served on program committees of some of the major conferences in database theory and the theoretical aspects of Computer Science (PODS, ICDT, CIKM, STACS, SIGMOD).

LEONID LIBKIN is Professor of Foundations of Data Management in the School of Informatics at the University of Edinburgh. He was previously a Professor at the University of Toronto and a member of research staff at Bell Laboratories in Murray Hill. He received his PhD from the University of Pennsylvania in 1994. His main research interests are in the areas of data management and applications of logic in computer science. He has written four books and over 150 technical papers. He was the recipient of a Marie Curie Chair Award from the EU in 2006, and won four best paper awards. He has chaired programme committees of major database conferences (ACM PODS, ICDT) and was the conference chair of the 2010 Federated Logic Conference. He has given many invited conference talks and has served on multiple program committees and editorial boards. He is an ACM fellow and a fellow of the Royal Society of Edinburgh.

FILIP MURLAK is assistant professor at the Faculty of Mathematics, Informatics, and Mechanics at the University of Warsaw, Poland. Previously he was research fellow at the University of Edinburgh. He received his PhD from the University of Warsaw in 2008. His main research areas are automata theory and semi-structured data. He was the recipient of the best paper award at ICALP 2006, the Witold Lipski Prize for young researchers in 2008, and the Homing Plus scholarship from the Foundation for Polish Science in 2010. He was co-chair of MFCS 2011 and served on program committees of several database and theoretical computer science conferences.

FOUNDATIONS OF DATA EXCHANGE

MARCELO ARENAS

Pontificia Universidad Católica de Chile

PABLO BARCELÓ

Universidad de Chile

LEONID LIBKIN

University of Edinburgh

FILIP MURLAK

Uniwersytet Warszawski, Poland

CAMBRIDGE
UNIVERSITY PRESS

CAMBRIDGE
UNIVERSITY PRESS

University Printing House, Cambridge CB2 8BS, United Kingdom

Published in the United States of America by Cambridge University Press, New York

Cambridge University Press is part of the University of Cambridge.

It furthers the University's mission by disseminating knowledge in the pursuit of education, learning and research at the highest international levels of excellence.

www.cambridge.org
Information on this title: www.cambridge.org/9781107016163

First published 2014

Printed in the United Kingdom by CPI Group Ltd, Croydon CR0 4YY

A catalogue record for this publication is available from the British Library

Library of Congress Cataloguing in Publication data

ISBN 978-1-107-01616-3 Hardback

Contents

Preface

Data exchange, as the name suggests, is the problem of exchanging data between different databases that have different schemas. One often needs to exchange data between existing legacy databases, whose schemas cannot be easily modified, and thus one needs to specify rules for translating data from one database to the other. These rules are known as schema mappings. Once a source database and a schema mapping are given, one needs to transfer data to the target, i.e., construct a target database. And once the target database is constructed, one needs to answer queries against it.

This problem is quite old; it has been studied, and systems have been built, but it was done in a rather ad hoc way. A systematic study of the problem of data exchange commenced with the 2003 paper "Data exchange: semantics and query answering" by Fagin, Kolaitis, Miller, and Popa, published in the proceedings of the International Conference on Database Theory. A large number of followup papers appeared, and for a while data exchange was one of the most active research topics in databases. Foundational questions related to data exchange largely revolved around three key problems:

1. how to build a target solution;
2. how to answer queries over target solutions; and
3. how to manipulate schema mappings themselves.

The last question is also known under the name of metadata management, since mappings represent metadata, rather than data in the database.

This book summarizes the key developments of the decade of research in the area of data exchange. It is organized into four parts.

In Part One, the problem of data exchange is introduced via examples, both relational and XML. We present key definitions: of schema mappings, of solutions (possible target instances), and of query answering and rewriting. We also describe some background material on relational databases, query languages, incomplete data, complexity theory, and automata theory (that will be required in the study of XML data exchange).

Part Two deals with exchanging relational data. We start by looking at the problem of checking if solutions, or possible target instances, exist. In general, the problem may even be undecidable, so we look at restrictions on schema mappings to guarantee not only decidability but also tractability of the problem of building solutions. Under one restriction, called weak acyclicity, particularly nice solutions can be constructed efficiently. These are called universal solutions, and they are particularly well suited for query answering in data exchange. It turns out that a given source may have many targets compatible with it, and thus we use the semantics of certain answers, i.e., answers true in all compatible targets. It is those answers that can be efficiently found in universal solutions. Universal solutions themselves are not unique, and we look at two types of these, the canonical universal solution, and the core, that have particularly nice properties. We also look at alternative ways of defining the semantics of query answering in data exchange.

Part Three deals with exchanging XML data. It mimics the developments of Part Two, but there are crucial differences between XML and relations. In particular, the complexity of many basic tasks increases in the XML case, and one needs different types of restrictions for keeping the complexity manageable. We identify those, particularly by placing restrictions on schemas, as it is their complexity that affects data exchange problems most. We also look at answering two types of queries: XML-to-relations, and XML-to-XML. Finally, we show how to perform XML data exchange tasks using relational data exchange engines.

Part Four deals with metadata management, i.e., handling schema mappings themselves. We deal with their static analysis, in particular, the consistency (or satisfiability) problem and the simplification problem. We study schema evolution described by means of operations on mappings. Two key operations one needs are composition of mappings and inverting mappings, and we provide a detailed study of both.

Each part of the book comes with a summary, bibliographic comments, and exercises.

A much shorter draft of this book was published in the Morgan & Claypool Synthesis series under the title *"Relational and XML Data Exchange"* in 2010. While working on that short version, and on the full draft, as well as on papers that are reflected in this book, we benefited from comments and critical remarks from our colleagues. We would like to thank Shunichi Amano, Mikołaj Bojańczyk, Rada Chirkova, Wojtek Czerwiński, Claire David, Ronald Fagin, Wenfei Fan, Amélie Gheerbrant, Andre Hernich, Phokion Kolaitis, Maurizio Lenzerini, Katja Losemann, Wim Martens, Jorge Pérez, Juan Reutter, Cristian Riveros, Miguel Romero, Nicole Schweikardt, Thomas Schwentick, and Cristina Sirangelo. We are also grateful to Tamer Özsu and Diane Cerra for convincing us to write the short Morgan & Claypool version of the book, and to David Tranah at Cambridge University Press for persuading us to turn it into a proper book, and for his patience and assistance.

Santiago, Edinburgh, Warsaw   M.A., P.B., L.L., F.M.

PART ONE
GETTING STARTED

1
Data exchange by example

Data exchange is the problem of finding an instance of a target schema, given an instance of a source schema and a specification of the relationship between the source and the target. Such a target instance should correctly represent information from the source instance under the constraints imposed by the target schema, and should allow one to evaluate queries on the target instance in a way that is semantically consistent with the source data.

Data exchange is an old problem that re-emerged as an active research topic recently due to the increased need for exchange of data in various formats, often in e-business applications.

The general setting of data exchange is this:

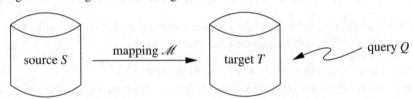

We have fixed source and target schemas, an instance S of the source schema, and a mapping $\mathcal{M}$ that specifies the relationship between the source and the target schemas. The goal is to construct an instance T of the target schema, based on the source and the mapping, and answer queries against the target data in a way consistent with the source data.

The goal of this introductory chapter is to make precise some of the key notions of data exchange: schema mappings, solutions, source-to-target dependencies, and certain answers. We do it by means of an example we present in the next section.

1.1 A data exchange example

Suppose we want to create a database containing three relations:

- ROUTES(flight#,source,destination)
  This relation has information about routes served by several airlines: it has a flight# attribute (e.g., AF406 or KLM1276), as well as source and destination attributes (e.g., Paris and Santiago for AF406).

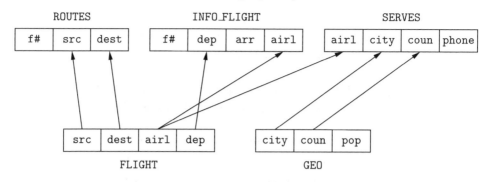

Figure 1.1 Schema mapping: a simple graphical representation

- INFO_FLIGHT(flight#,departure_time,arrival_time,airline)
  This relation provides additional information about the flight: departure and arrival times, as well as the name of an airline.
- SERVES(airline,city,country,phone)
  This relation has information about cities served by airlines: for example, it may have a tuple (*AirFrance, Santiago, Chile, 5550000*), indicating that Air France serves Santiago, Chile, and its office there can be reached at 555-0000.

We do not start from scratch: there is a source database available from which we can transfer information. This source database has two relations:

- FLIGHT(source,destination,airline,departure)
  This relation contains information about flights, although not all the information needed in the target. We only have source, destination, and airline (but no flight number), and departure time (but no arrival time).
- GEO(city,country,population)
  This relation has some basic geographical information: cities, countries where they are located, and their population.

As the first step of moving the data from the source database into our target, we have to specify a *schema mapping*, a set of relationships between the two schemas. We can start with a simple graphical representation of such a mapping shown in Figure 1.1. The arrows in such a graphical representation show the relationship between attributes in different schemas.

But simple connections between attributes are not enough. For example, when we create records in ROUTES and INFO_FLIGHT based on a record in FLIGHT, we need to ensure that the values of the flight# attribute (abbreviated as f# in the figure) are the same. This is indicated by a curved line connecting these attributes. Likewise, when we populate table SERVES, we only want to include cities which appear in table FLIGHT – this is indicated by the line connecting attributes in tables GEO and FLIGHT.

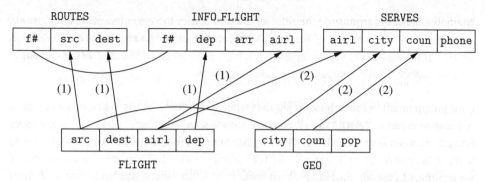

Figure 1.2 Schema mapping: a proper graphical representation

Furthermore, there are several *rules* in a mapping that help us populate the target database. In this example, we can distinguish two rules. One uses table FLIGHT to populate ROUTES and INFO_FLIGHT, and the other uses both FLIGHT and GEO to populate SERVES. So in addition we annotate arrows with names or numbers of rules that they are used in. Such a revised representation is shown in Figure 1.2.

While it might be easy for someone understanding source and target schemas to produce a graphical representation of the mapping, we need to translate it into a formal specification. Let us look at the first rule which says:

whenever we have a tuple (src,dest,airl,dep) *in relation* FLIGHT, *we must have a tuple in* ROUTES *that has* src *and* dest *as the values of the second and the third attributes, and a tuple in* INFO_FLIGHT *that has* dep *and* airl *as the second and the fourth attributes.*

Formally, this can be written as:

$$\text{FLIGHT(src,dest,airl,dep)} \longrightarrow$$
$$\text{ROUTES(\_,src,dest), INFO\_FLIGHT(\_,dep,\_,airl).}$$

This is not fully satisfactory: indeed, as we lose information that the flight numbers must be the same; hence, we need to explicitly mention the names of all the variables, and produce the following rule:

$$\text{FLIGHT(src,dest,airl,dep)} \longrightarrow$$
$$\text{ROUTES(f\#,src,dest), INFO\_FLIGHT(f\#,dep,arr,airl).}$$

What is the meaning of such a rule? In particular, what are those variables that appear in the target specification without being mentioned in the source part? What the mapping says is that values for these variables must *exist* in the target, in other words, the following must be satisfied:

$$\text{FLIGHT(src,dest,airl,dep)} \longrightarrow$$
$$\exists \text{f\#} \, \exists \text{arr} \, \big(\, \text{ROUTES(f\#,src,dest)}$$
$$\land \, \text{INFO\_FLIGHT(f\#,dep,arr,airl)} \big).$$

To complete the description of the rule, we need to clarify the role of variables `src`, `dest`, `airl` and `dep`. The meaning of the rule is that *for every* tuple (`src`,`dest`,`airl`,`dep`) in table `FLIGHT` we have to create tuples in relations `ROUTES` and `INFO_FLIGHT` of the target schema. Hence, finally, the meaning of the first rule is:

$$\forall \texttt{src}\ \forall \texttt{dest}\ \forall \texttt{airl}\ \forall \texttt{dep}\ \Big(\texttt{FLIGHT(src,dest,airl,dep)} \longrightarrow$$
$$\exists \texttt{f\#}\ \exists \texttt{arr}\ \big(\ \texttt{ROUTES(f\#,src,dest)}$$
$$\land\ \texttt{INFO\_FLIGHT(f\#,dep,arr,airl)}\ \big)\Big).$$

Note that this is a query written in relational calculus, without free variables. In other words, it is a sentence of first-order logic, over the vocabulary including both source and target relations. The meaning of this sentence is as follows: given a source S, a target instance we construct is such that together, S and T satisfy this sentence.

We now move to the second rule. Unlike the first, it looks at two tuples in the source: (`src`,`dest`,`airl`,`dep`) in `FLIGHT` and (`city`,`country`,`popul`) in `GEO`. If they satisfy the join condition `city=scr`, then a tuple needs to be inserted in the target relation `SERVES`:

$$\texttt{FLIGHT(src,dest,airl,dep), GEO(city,country,popul), city=src}$$
$$\longrightarrow \texttt{SERVES(airl,city,country,phone)}.$$

As with the first rule, the actual meaning of this rule is obtained by explicitly quantifying the variables involved:

$$\forall \texttt{city}\ \forall \texttt{dest}\ \forall \texttt{airl}\ \forall \texttt{dep}\ \forall \texttt{country}\ \forall \texttt{popul}\ \Big($$
$$\texttt{FLIGHT(city,dest,airl,dep)} \land \texttt{GEO(city,country,popul)} \longrightarrow$$
$$\exists \texttt{phone SERVES(airl,city,country,phone)}\Big).$$

We can also have a similar rule in which the destination city is moved in the `SERVES` table in the target:

$$\forall \texttt{city}\ \forall \texttt{dest}\ \forall \texttt{airl}\ \forall \texttt{dep}\ \forall \texttt{country}\ \forall \texttt{popul}\ \Big($$
$$\texttt{FLIGHT(src,city,airl,dep)} \land \texttt{GEO(city,country,popul)} \longrightarrow$$
$$\exists \texttt{phone SERVES(airl,city,country,phone)}\Big).$$

These rules together form what we call a *schema mapping*: a collection of rules that specify the relationship between the source and the target. When we write them, we actually often omit universal quantifiers $\forall$, as they can be reconstructed by the following rule:

- every variable mentioned in one of the source relations is quantified universally.

With these conventions, we arrive at the schema mapping $\mathscr{M}$, shown in Figure 1.3.

Now, what does it mean to have a target instance, given a source instance and a mapping? Since mappings are logical sentences, we want target instances to satisfy these sentences, with respect to the source. More precisely, note that mappings viewed as logical sentences

```
(1)   FLIGHT(src,dest,airl,dep) ⟶
             ∃f# ∃arr (   ROUTES(f#,src,dest)
                          ∧ INFO_FLIGHT(f#,dep,arr,airl))


(2)   FLIGHT(city,dest,airl,dep) ∧ GEO(city,country,popul)
             ⟶ ∃phone SERVES(airl,city,country,phone)


(3)   FLIGHT(src,city,airl,dep) ∧ GEO(city,country,popul)
             ⟶ ∃phone SERVES(airl,city,country,phone)
```

Figure 1.3 A schema mapping

mention both source and target schemas. So possible target instances T for a given source S must satisfy the following condition:

For each condition φ of the mapping $\mathcal{M}$, the pair (S, T) satisfies φ.

We call such instances T *solutions for S under $\mathcal{M}$*. Look, for example, at our mapping $\mathcal{M}$, and assume that the source S has a tuple *(Paris, Santiago, AirFrance*, 2320) in FLIGHT. Then every solution T for S under $\mathcal{M}$ must have tuples

$$(x, Paris, Santiago) \quad \text{in} \quad \text{ROUTES and}$$
$$(x, 2320, y, AirFrance) \quad \text{in} \quad \text{INFO\_FLIGHT}$$

for some values x and y, interpreted as flight number and arrival time. The mapping says nothing about these values: they may be real values (constants), e.g., (406, *Paris, Santiago*), or *nulls*, indicating that we lack this information at present. We shall normally use the symbol $\bot$ to denote nulls, so a common way to populate the target would be with tuples $(\bot, Paris, Santiago)$ and $(\bot, 2320, \bot', AirFrance)$. Note that the first attributes of both tuples, while being unknown, are nonetheless the same. This situation is referred to as having *marked nulls*, or *naïve* nulls, as they are used in naïve tables, studied extensively in connection with incomplete information in relational databases. At the same time, we know nothing about the other null $\bot'$ used: nothing prevents it from being different from $\bot$ but nothing tells us that it should be.

Note that already this simple example leads to a crucial observation that makes the data exchange problem interesting: *solutions are not unique*. In fact, there could be infinitely many solutions: we can use different marked nulls, or can instantiate them with different values.

If solutions are not unique, how can we answer queries? Consider, for example, a Boolean (yes/no) query *"Is there a flight from Paris to Santiago that arrives before 10am?"*. The answer to this query has to be "no", even though in some solutions we shall have tuples with arrival time before 10am. However, in others, in particular in the one with null values, the comparison with 10am will not evaluate to true, and thus we have to return "no" as the answer.

On the other hand, the answer to the query *"Is there a flight from Paris to Santiago?"* is "yes", as the tuple including Paris and Santiago will be in every solution. Intuitively, what we want to do in query answering in data exchange is to return answers that will be true in every solution. These are called *certain answers*; we shall define them formally shortly.

XML data exchange

Before outlining the key tasks in data exchange, we briefly look at the XML representation of the above problem. XML is a flexible data format for storing and exchanging data on the Web. XML documents are essentially trees that can represent data organized in a way more complex than the usual relational databases. But each relational database can be encoded as an XML document; a portion of our example database, representing information about the Paris–Santiago flight and information about Santiago, is shown in the picture below.

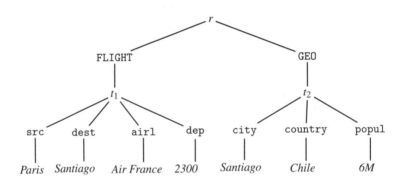

The tree has a root r with two children, corresponding to relations FLIGHT and GEO. Each of these has several children, labeled t_1 and t_2, respectively, corresponding to tuples in the relations. We show one tuple in each relation in the example. Each t_1-node has four children that correspond to the attributes of FLIGHT and each t_2-node has three children, with attributes of GEO. Finally, each of the attribute nodes has a child holding the value of the attribute.

To reformulate a rule in a schema mapping in this language, we show how portions of trees are restructured. Consider, for example, the rule

$$\text{FLIGHT(city,dest,airl,dep)} \land \text{GEO(city,country,popul)} \longrightarrow$$
$$\exists \text{phone SERVES(airl,city,country,phone)}$$

We restate it in the XML context as follows:

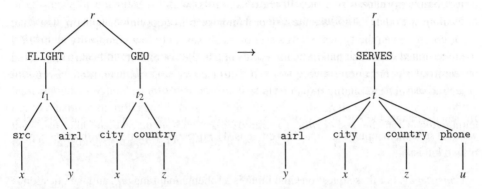

That is, if we have tuples in FLIGHT and GEO that agree on the values of the source and city attributes, we grab the values of the airline and country attributes, invent a new value u for phone and create a tuple in relation SERVES.

The rules of XML schema mappings are thus represented via *tree patterns*. Essentially, they say that if a certain pattern occurs in a source document, some other pattern, obtained by its restructuring, must occur in the target.

This view of XML schema mappings is not surprising if we note that in our relational examples, the rules are obtained by using a relational pattern – i.e., a conjunction of source atoms – and rearranging them as a conjunction of target atoms. Conjunctions of atoms are natural analogs of tree patterns. Indeed, the pattern on the right-hand side of the above rule, for example, can be viewed as the conjunction of the statements about existence of the following edge relations: between the root and a node labeled SERVES, between that node and a node labeled t, between the t-node and nodes labeled airl, city, country, and phone, respectively, and between those nodes and nodes carrying attribute values y, x, z, and u.

Of course we shall see when we describe XML data exchange that patterns could be significantly more complicated: they need not be simple translations of relational atoms. In fact one can use more complicated forms of navigation such as the horizontal ordering of siblings in a document, or the descendant relation. But for now our goal was to introduce the idea of tree patterns by means of a straightforward translation of a relational example.

1.2 Overview of the main tasks in data exchange

The key tasks in many database applications can be roughly split into two groups:

1. *Static analysis.* This mostly involves dealing with schemas; for example, the classical relational database problems such as dependency implication and normalization fall into this category. Typically, the input one considers is (relatively) small, e.g., a schema or a set of constraints. Therefore, somewhat higher complexity bounds are normally toler-

ated: for example, many problems related to reasoning about dependencies are complete for complexity classes such as NP, or CONP, or PSPACE.

2. *Dealing with data.* These are the key problems such as querying or updating the data. Of course, given the typically large size of databases, only low-complexity algorithms are tolerated when one handles data. For example, the complexity of evaluating a fixed relational algebra query is very low (AC^0, to be precise), and even more expressive languages such as Datalog stay in PTIME.

In data exchange, the key tasks too can be split into two groups. For static analysis tasks, we treat schema mappings as first-class citizens. The questions one deals with are generally of two kinds:

- *Consistency.* For these questions, the input is a schema mapping $\mathcal{M}$, and the question is whether it makes sense: for example, whether there exists a source S that has a solution under $\mathcal{M}$, or whether all sources of a given schema have solutions. These analyses are important for ruling out "bad" mappings that are unlikely to be useful in data exchange.
- *Operations on mappings.* Suppose we have a mapping $\mathcal{M}$ from a source schema $\mathbf{R_s}$ to a target schema $\mathbf{R_t}$, and another mapping $\mathcal{M}'$ that uses $\mathbf{R_t}$ as the source schema and maps it into a schema $\mathbf{R_u}$. Can we combine these mappings into one, the composition of the two, $\mathcal{M} \circ \mathcal{M}'$, which maps $\mathbf{R_s}$ to $\mathbf{R_u}$? Or can we invert a mapping, and find a mapping $\mathcal{M}^{-1}$ from $\mathbf{R_t}$ into $\mathbf{R_s}$, that undoes the transformation performed by $\mathcal{M}$ and recovers as much original information about the source as possible? These questions arise when one considers schema evolution: as schemas evolve, so do the mappings between them. And once we understand when and how we can construct mappings such as $\mathcal{M} \circ \mathcal{M}'$ or $\mathcal{M}^{-1}$, we need to understand their properties with respect to the "existence of solutions" problem.

Tasks involving data are generally of two kinds.

- *Materializing target instances.* Suppose we have a schema mapping $\mathcal{M}$ and a source instance S. Which target instance do we materialize? As we already saw, there could be many – perhaps infinitely many – target instances which are solutions for S under $\mathcal{M}$. Choosing one we should think of three criteria:
  1. it should faithfully represent the information from the source, under the constraints imposed by the mapping;
  2. it should not contain (too much) redundant information;
  3. the computational cost of constructing the solution should be reasonable.
- *Query answering.* Ultimately, we want to answer queries against the target schema. As we explained, due the existence of multiple solutions, we need to answer them in a way that is consistent with the source data. So if we have a materialized target T and a query Q, we need to find a way of evaluating it to produce the set of certain answers. As we shall see, sometimes computing $Q(T)$ does *not* give us certain answers, so we may need to change Q into another query Q' and then evaluate Q' on a chosen solution to get the

desired answer. The complexity of this task will also depend on a class of queries to which Q belongs. We shall see that for some classes, constructing Q' is easy, while for others Q' must come from languages much more expressive (and harder to evaluate) than SQL, and for some, it may not even exist.

1.3 Data exchange vs data integration

We comment briefly on the connections between data exchange and the closely related field of data integration. In a typical scenario of (virtual) data integration we have one or more *local* sources, as well as a *global* schema, and a specification of the relationship between the local schemas and the global schema, i.e., a mapping. The data resides at the local level, but the user wants to query a virtual database of the global schema. Thus, superficially, a data integration system can be seen as a data exchange system: we view all local sources as a single database of a local (source) schema, and, under a given mapping, want to query a database of global schema (target). Moreover, as in both cases the target, or the global schema database, is not unique, the semantics of query answering is provided by certain answers.

The key difference between data exchange and virtual data integration is in the treatment of target (global schema) data, and in the type of data used for query answering. In virtual data integration, we *do not* materialize a database of the global schema. Instead, we rewrite a given query Q over the global schema into queries over the sources so that their results would either compute, or approximate in the best way, the answer to Q. That is, the target is not materialized, and source data is used for query answering.

In data exchange, on the other hand, we *do* materialize the target. Of course there could be many target instances, but we choose to materialize one of them, and then use it to answer queries Q. We may choose to run the same query Q, or rewrite it into a different one, but we do run queries on the materialized target. That is, in data exchange, the target is materialized, and it is that materialized target data that is used for query answering.

2

Theoretical background

The goal of this chapter is to introduce some of the basic concepts that will be used throughout the book. We describe the relational data model, including languages and integrity constraints for relational databases, as well as the fundamental concepts related to handling of incomplete information. We also talk about ways of measuring the complexity of various computational tasks that occur in the database context. Finally, we recall some basic facts about finite automata; these will be used extensively in connection with XML data.

2.1 Relational database model

In the relational database model, data is organized in relations, and is described by means of a *relational schema*. Informally, we have seen such schemas already in the examples of the previous chapter. Formally, a relational schema $\mathbf{R}$ is a finite sequence $\langle U_1, \ldots, U_m \rangle$ of relation symbols, with each U_i having a fixed arity $n_i > 0$. For example, the target relational schema considered in the introduction has three relations: ROUTES of arity 3, INFO_FLIGHT of arity 4, and SERVES, also of arity 4.

An instance of a schema contains a relation, or a table, for each relation symbol. For example, the following is a possible relation for ROUTES:

flight#	source	destination
AF406	Paris	Santiago
KLM1276	Edinburgh	Amsterdam
KLM1365	Amsterdam	Warsaw
AF5148	Paris	Edinburgh

Formally, we assume a domain of possible values D (such as *AF406* or *Paris*). Recall that a k-ary relation over D is a subset of $D^k = D \times \cdots \times D$, the product of k copies of

D. An *instance S* of schema $\mathbf{R} = \langle U_1, \ldots, U_m \rangle$ assigns to each relation symbol U_i, where $1 \le i \le m$, a finite n_i-ary relation U_i^S. Recall that n_i is the arity of U_i.

The *domain* of instance *S*, denoted by DOM(*S*), is the set of all elements that occur in the relations U_i^S. It is often convenient to define instances by simply listing the tuples attached to the corresponding relation symbols. Further, sometimes we use the notation $U(\bar{t}) \in S$ instead of $\bar{t} \in U^S$, and call $U(\bar{t})$ a *fact* of *S*. For instance, FLIGHT(*Paris, Santiago, AirFrance*, 2320) is an example of a fact.

Given instances *S* and *S'* of **R**, we write $S \subseteq S'$ if instance *S* is contained in instance *S'*; that is, if $U_i^S \subseteq U_i^{S'}$ for every $i \in \{1, \ldots, m\}$.

The size of instance *S* is denoted by $\|S\|$. It is measured as the sum of the sizes of all relations in *S*. The size of each relation is the total number of values stored in that relation; that is, the product of the number of tuples and the arity of the relation. In the example of a relation above, we measure its size as 12, since it has four tuples, and has arity 3.

Integrity constraints We often consider relational schemas with *integrity constraints*, which are conditions that instances of such schemas must satisfy. The most commonly used constraints in databases are functional dependencies (and a special case of those: keys), and inclusion dependencies (and a special case of functional and inclusion dependencies: foreign keys). Schema mappings, as we saw, are given by constraints that relate instances of two schemas. These will be studied in detail in the book; for now we review the most common database constraints.

A *functional dependency* states that a set of attributes *X* uniquely determines another set of attributes *Y*; a key states that a set of attributes uniquely determines the tuple. For example, it is reasonable to assume that `flight#` is a key of ROUTES, which one may write as a logical sentence

$$\forall f \forall s \forall d \forall s' \forall d' \left(\text{ROUTES}(f,s,d) \wedge \text{ROUTES}(f,s',d') \ \rightarrow \ (s=s') \wedge (d=d') \right).$$

An inclusion dependency states that a value of an attribute (or values of a set of attributes) occurring in one relation must occur in another relation as well. For example, we may expect each flight number appearing in INFO_FLIGHT to appear in ROUTES as well: this is expressed as a logical sentence

$$\forall f \forall d \forall a \forall a' \left(\text{INFO\_FLIGHT}(f,d,a,a') \ \rightarrow \ \exists s \exists d' \, \text{ROUTES}(f,s,d') \right).$$

Foreign keys are simply a combination of an inclusion dependency and a key constraint: by combining the above inclusion dependency with the constraint that `flight#` is a key for ROUTES, we get a foreign key constraint INFO_FLIGHT[flight#] $\subseteq_{\text{FK}}$ ROUTES[flight#], stating that each value of flight number in INFO_FLIGHT occurs in ROUTES, and that this value is an identifier for the tuple in ROUTES.

2.2 Query languages

We now give a brief overview of the standard relational query languages such as relational calculus, relational algebra, and their fragments.

Relational calculus

This is another name for first-order predicate logic, abbreviated as FO. Its formulae, over a schema **R** with relation names $\langle U_1, \ldots, U_m \rangle$, are built inductively, using the rules presented below. We assume a (countably infinite) set of variables, typically denoted by lowercase letters such as $x, y, z, \ldots$, sometimes with subscripts and superscripts. We now define both formulae of relational calculus, and their *free variables*.

- If U_i is a relation in the schema, and $\bar{t} = (t_1, \ldots, t_{n_i})$ is a tuple of the same length as the arity of U_i so that each t_j is either a variable, or a constant from the domain, then $U_i(\bar{t})$ is a formula.

  Its free variables are exactly the variables present in $\bar{t}$.

- If each of t_1, t_2 is either a variable, or a constant from the domain, then $t_1 = t_2$ is a formula. Its free variables are exactly the variables among t_1 and t_2. For example, $x = 5$ is a formula with free variable x, while $x = y$ is a formula with free variables x and y.

  Formulae of the two kinds described above are called *atomic formulae*.

- If φ and ψ are formulae, then both $\varphi \vee \psi$ and $\varphi \wedge \psi$ are formulae. Their free variables include all the free variables of φ and ψ.

- If φ is a formula, then $\neg\varphi$ is a formula. Its free variables coincide with the free variables of φ.

- If φ is a formula and x is a variable, then both $\exists x\ \varphi$ and $\forall x\ \varphi$ are formulae. Their free variables include all the free variables of φ except the variable x.

If we have a formula φ whose free variables are $\bar{x} = (x_1, \ldots, x_n)$, we shall write $\varphi(\bar{x})$ or $\varphi(x_1, \ldots, x_n)$.

We next define the semantics of relational calculus queries. Assume that we have an instance S, in which each predicate U_i of arity n_i is interpreted as an n_i-ary relation U_i^S. For each formula $\varphi(x_1, \ldots, x_n)$ and a mapping σ from a set of variables including $x_1, \ldots, x_n$ to $\text{DOM}(S)$ we define the notion of

$$(S, \sigma) \models \varphi(\bar{x}),$$

saying that $\varphi(\bar{x})$ is true when variables $x_1, \ldots, x_n$ are interpreted as $\sigma(x_1), \ldots, \sigma(x_n) \in \text{DOM}(S)$. Then the output of a query $\varphi(x_1, \ldots, x_n)$ on the instance S is

$$\varphi(S) = \left\{ \left(\sigma(x_1), \ldots, \sigma(x_n)\right) \mid (S, \sigma) \models \varphi(\bar{x}) \right\}.$$

We now define $(S, \sigma) \models \varphi(\bar{x})$ inductively. For atomic formulae, we have:

- $(S, \sigma) \models (t_1 = t_2)$ iff $\sigma(t_1) = \sigma(t_2)$.
- $(S, \sigma) \models U_i(t_1, \ldots, t_{n_i})$ iff $\left(\sigma(t_1), \ldots, \sigma(t_{n_i})\right) \in U_i^S$.

In these first two rules, one of the t_i's could be a constant c. In that case, we make the assumption that $\sigma(c) = c$.

The remaining rules are as follows:

- $(S, \sigma) \models \varphi \vee \psi$ iff $(S, \sigma) \models \varphi$ or $(S, \sigma) \models \psi$.
- $(S, \sigma) \models \varphi \wedge \psi$ iff $(S, \sigma) \models \varphi$ and $(S, \sigma) \models \psi$.
- $(S, \sigma) \models \neg\varphi$ iff $(S, \sigma) \models \varphi$ is false.
- $(S, \sigma) \models \exists x \, \varphi$ iff $(S, \sigma[c/x]) \models \varphi$ for some $c \in \text{DOM}(S)$. Here $\sigma[c/x]$ coincides with σ on all variables except x, on which its value is defined to be c.
- $(S, \sigma) \models \forall x \, \varphi$ iff $(S, \sigma[c/x]) \models \varphi$ for all $c \in \text{DOM}(S)$.

In general, not all of the connectives are required. Due to the standard equivalences:

$$\varphi \vee \psi \quad \leftrightarrow \quad \neg(\neg\varphi \wedge \neg\psi)$$
$$\forall x \, \varphi \quad \leftrightarrow \quad \neg\exists x \, \neg\varphi$$

conjunction, negation, and existential quantification are sufficient to express all relational calculus queries.

As an example, consider a query $\varphi(x)$ below:

$$\exists y \exists y' \exists z \exists z' \left(\text{ROUTES}(y, x, z) \wedge \text{ROUTES}(y', z', x) \right), \tag{2.1}$$

asking for cities that appear as both a source and a destination in table ROUTES. In the example shown earlier, the answer to this query will include Edinburgh and Amsterdam.

A note on Boolean queries   We shall sometimes deal with Boolean queries, or queries returning `true` or `false`. Normally we assume that the output of any relational query is a relation, and the same must hold for Boolean queries. We represent the Boolean values `true` and `false` by means of relations of arity 0, i.e., containing tuples with no attributes. There is only one such tuple, namely the empty tuple, which we denote by (). Hence, there are only two possible relations of arity zero:

$$\emptyset \quad \text{and} \quad \{()\};$$

that is, the empty set, and the set containing the empty tuple. We shall associate the empty set with `false`, and the set containing the empty tuple with `true`.

Relational algebra

Although we mainly deal with logical formalisms in this book, we now briefly review relational algebra – the standard procedural counterpart of relational calculus. Each expression of relational algebra, when applied to a database instance, produces a relation of some arity $n \geq 0$. In general, we assume that attributes of an n-ary relation are named as $1, \ldots, n$.

Relational algebra has the following five operations.

- *Projection.* This operation is applied to a single n-ary relation and only keeps some of the columns. More precisely, if $i_1, \ldots, i_k$ is a set of numbers between 1 and n, and U is an n-ary relation, then $\pi_{i_1,\ldots,i_k}(U)$ is a k-ary relation defined as follows:

$$\pi_{i_1,\ldots,i_k}(U) = \{(c_{i_1},\ldots,c_{i_k}) \mid (c_1,\ldots,c_n) \in U\}.$$

- *Selection.* This operation is applied to a single n-ary relation and only keeps tuples that satisfy some conditions. The basic conditions are of the form $i = j$ or $i = c$; these are true in a tuple $(c_1,\ldots,c_n)$ if $c_i = c_j$ or $c_i = c$, respectively. A condition is a conjunction of basic conditions. Given such a condition θ, the selection operation σ_θ is defined as

$$\sigma_\theta(U) = \{(c_1,\ldots,c_n) \in U \mid (c_1,\ldots,c_n) \text{ satisfies } \theta\}.$$

- *Cartesian product.* This is the standard Cartesian product that takes an n-ary relation U and an m-ary relation U' and produces an $n + m$-ary relation

$$U \times U' = \left\{(c_1,\ldots,c_n,c_{n+1},\ldots,c_{n+m}) \,\middle|\, \begin{array}{l} (c_1,\ldots,c_n) \in U \\ (c_{n+1},\ldots,c_{n+m}) \in U' \end{array}\right\}.$$

- *Union.* This is the union $U \cup U'$ of two relations of the same arity.
- *Difference.* Again, this operation is applied to relations of the same arity: $U - U'$ has tuples that occur in U but do not occur in U'.

Relational algebra is a procedural language: its queries transform data, to obtain answers to queries written declaratively. For example, the declarative query (2.1), written in logical notation, is equivalent to the following relational algebra query:

$$\pi_2\big(\sigma_{2=6}(R \times R)\big).$$

By taking the product $R \times R$, we create a relation with six attributes. If we look at the logical query, the variable x occurs in positions 2 and 6, so we must ensure they are equal. Then only variable x is kept in the output.

The operation obtained by taking the product of two relations, and then selecting tuples that satisfy some condition – typically equality of attributes – is usually referred to as a *join*. For example, $\sigma_{2=6}(R \times R)$ is a join of two copies of R.

The classical result of database theory states that relational calculus and relational algebra queries are equivalent: that is, for each relational calculus query there exists an equivalent relational algebra query, and vice versa. That is, declarative queries written in relational calculus have procedural implementation in relational algebra.

Conjunctive queries

This is an extremely important subclass of relational calculus/algebra queries. They are the basic building block for most queries run by relational DBMSs, and they play a special role in data exchange.

Formally, conjunctive queries are defined as the $\exists, \wedge$-fragment of relational calculus:

that is, disjunction, negation, and universal quantification are not allowed. Hence, they are queries of the form

$$\varphi(\bar{x}) \;=\; \exists \bar{y} \left(\alpha_1(\bar{z}_1) \wedge \ldots \wedge \alpha_m(\bar{z}_m) \right), \tag{2.2}$$

where:

- each α_i is an atomic relational formula, i.e., a formula of the form $U(\bar{z}_i)$, where U is a relation symbol, and
- $\bar{z}_i$ is a tuple of variables and constants, with all the variables coming from $\bar{x}$ and $\bar{y}$.

For example, the query (2.1) is a conjunctive query.

Conjunctive queries can be translated into the fragment of relational algebra that contains only the operations of projection (π), selection (σ), and Cartesian product ($\times$). One sometimes refers to this fragment as select-project-join queries. Conversely, every query in the $\{\pi, \sigma, \times\}$-fragment of relational algebra is a conjunctive query.

Conjunctive queries also correspond to the basic fragment of SQL, namely to queries of the form SELECT-FROM-WHERE, in which the WHERE clause contains a conjunction of equalities.

A related class we consider consists of *unions of conjunctive queries*. As the name suggests, these are queries of the form $Q_1 \cup \cdots \cup Q_m$, where all the Q_i's are conjunctive queries. In other words, they are the queries expressible in the $\{\pi, \sigma, \times, \cup\}$-fragment of relational algebra. Since these are queries without the difference operation, they are also sometimes referred to as queries in the positive fragment of relational algebra. From the calculus perspective, they can be expressed in the $\{\exists, \wedge, \vee\}$-fragment of FO (i.e., no negation, no universal quantification).

There are several important properties of conjunctive queries and their unions that we shall use throughout the book. One of them is monotonicity. If Q is a conjunctive query, or a union of conjunctive queries, then

$$S \subseteq S' \;\Rightarrow\; Q(S) \subseteq Q(S').$$

Another useful property is that containment and equivalence of conjunctive queries are decidable. We say that a query Q is *contained* in a query Q', written as $Q \subseteq Q'$, if $Q(S) \subseteq Q'(S)$ for every instance S. Queries are equivalent if $Q(S) = Q'(S)$ for every instance S.

To explain why containment is decidable for conjunctive queries, we introduce key notions of *tableaux* and their *homomorphisms*. These notions will be central for us in the book.

Suppose we have a conjunctive query of the form (2.2). Its *tableau* is a pair $(T_\varphi, \bar{x})$, where T_φ is a relational database containing essentially the atoms $\alpha_i(\bar{z}_i)$. For example, for the conjunctive query in (2.1), the tableau will contain two facts: ROUTES(y, x, z) and ROUTES(y', z', x).

Given two tableaux $(T, \bar{x})$ and $(T', \bar{x})$, a *homomorphism* between them is a map $h :$ DOM$(T) \to$ DOM(T') satisfying two conditions:

1. $h(x) = x$ for every x that occurs in $\bar{x}$; and
2. if $U(\bar{t})$ is a fact in T, then $U(h(\bar{t}))$ is a fact in T'.

If $\bar{x}$ is clear from the context, we say that h is simply a homomorphism from T to T'.

Consider an example of two conjunctive queries:

$$
\begin{aligned}
Q_1(x,y) &= \exists z \left(U_1(x,z) \wedge U_2(y,z,x) \right) \\
Q_2(x,y) &= \exists z \exists w \exists r \left(U_1(x,z) \wedge U_1(v,w) \wedge U_2(y,z,x) \wedge U_2(r,w,v) \right).
\end{aligned}
$$

The tableau for the first contains the facts $U_1(x,z)$ and $U_2(y,z,x)$; the tableau for the second in addition contains the facts $U_1(v,w)$ and $U_2(r,w,v)$. One can then see that the map given by:

$$
\begin{array}{ccccccc}
h(v) &=& x & \quad h(w) &=& z & \quad h(r) &=& y \\
h(x) &=& x & \quad h(y) &=& y & \quad h(z) &=& z
\end{array}
$$

is a homomorphism from T_{Q_2} to T_{Q_1}, as it preserves the free variables x and y, and sends $U_1(v,w)$ into $U_1(x,z)$ and $U_2(r,w,v)$ into $U_2(y,z,x)$.

The importance of homomorphisms comes from the fact that they allow one to test conjunctive queries for containment. Namely, if we have two conjunctive queries $Q(\bar{x})$ and $Q'(\bar{x})$ with tableaux $(T_Q, \bar{x})$ and $(T_{Q'}, \bar{x})$, then

$$
Q \subseteq Q' \quad \Leftrightarrow \quad \text{there is a homomorphism } h : T_{Q'} \to T_Q.
$$

Note that the direction of the homomorphism is opposite to the direction of containment. For the above examples of queries Q_1 and Q_2, we have both a homomorphism $T_{Q_2} \to T_{Q_1}$ and a homomorphism $T_{Q_1} \to T_{Q_2}$ (the identity), which implies $Q_1 = Q_2$.

2.3 Incomplete data

We have seen in earlier examples that target instances may contain *incomplete information*. Typically, incomplete information in databases is modeled by having two disjoint and infinite sets of values that populate instances:

- the set of *constants*, denoted by CONST, and
- the set of *nulls*, or variables, denoted by VAR.

In general the domain of an instance is a subset of CONST ∪ VAR (although we shall assume that domains of source instances are always contained in CONST). We usually denote constants by lowercase letters $a, b, c, \ldots$ (or mention specific constants such as numbers or strings), while nulls are denoted by symbols $\perp, \perp_1, \perp_2$, etc.

Incomplete relational instances over CONST ∪ VAR are usually called *naïve* databases. Note that a null $\perp \in$ VAR can appear multiple times in such an instance. If each null $\perp \in$ VAR appears at most once, we speak of *Codd* databases. If we talk about single relations, it is common to refer to them as naïve tables and Codd tables. For example, the instance

$$S_1: \quad \begin{array}{ccc} 1 & 2 & \bot_1 \\ \hline \bot_2 & \bot_1 & 3 \\ \hline \bot_3 & 5 & 1 \end{array} \qquad (2.3)$$

is a naïve table: the null $\bot_1$ occurs twice. On the other hand, the instance

$$S_2: \quad \begin{array}{ccc} 1 & 2 & \bot_1 \\ \hline \bot_2 & \bot_3 & 3 \end{array} \qquad (2.4)$$

is a Codd table, since each null occurs just once.

The semantics of an incomplete instance S is the set of *complete* instances (i.e., instances without nulls) it can represent. These are defined via homomorphisms. We write $\text{CONST}(S)$ and $\text{VAR}(S)$ for the sets of constants and nulls, respectively, that occur in S. For example, in the instance S_1 above (2.3), we have $\text{CONST}(S_1) = \{1,2,3,5\}$ and $\text{VAR}(S_1) = \{\bot_1, \bot_2, \bot_3\}$.

A *homomorphism* $h : S \to S'$ between two database instances of the same schema is a map

$$h : \text{VAR}(S) \to \text{CONST}(S') \cup \text{VAR}(S')$$

such that, for every relation symbol U, if the fact $U(\bar{t})$ is in S, then the fact $U(h(\bar{t}))$ is in S'. In defining $h(\bar{t})$, we extend h to constants by letting $h(c) = c$ for every $c \in \text{CONST}$.

The semantics of an incomplete database instance S, denoted by $Rep(S)$, is then defined as the set of complete databases S' such that there is a homomorphism $h : S \to S'$. That is,

$$Rep(S) = \{S' \text{ with } \text{DOM}(S') \subset \text{CONST} \mid \exists \text{ homomorphism } h : S \to S'\}.$$

For example, given the incomplete database S_1 in (2.3), the instance

$$S': \quad \begin{array}{ccc} 1 & 2 & 4 \\ \hline 3 & 4 & 3 \\ \hline 5 & 5 & 1 \\ \hline 3 & 7 & 8 \end{array}$$

is in $Rep(S_1)$, as witnessed by the homomorphism $h(\bot_1) = 4$, $h(\bot_2) = 3$, and $h(\bot_3) = 5$.

Certain answers and naïve evaluation   Given an incomplete database S and a query Q, one normally tries to compute *certain answers*, i.e., answers that are true regardless of the interpretation of nulls. These are defined as

$$certain(Q,S) = \bigcap \{Q(S') \mid S' \in Rep(S)\}.$$

Recall that when Q is a Boolean (true/false) query, we associate true with the set containing the empty tuple, and false with the empty set. Then the above definition says that for a Boolean query, $certain(Q,S)$ is true iff Q is true in every S' from $Rep(S)$.

The problem of computing certain answers is not solvable algorithmically for all FO queries. However, it is solvable efficiently (essentially, with the standard query evaluation techniques) for unions of conjunctive queries. This is done by *naïve evaluation*, defined as follows.

If we have a query Q and a database instance S with nulls, define $Q_{\text{naïve}}(S)$ as the result of a two-step process:

1. first, evaluate Q as if nulls were values (e.g., $\bot = \bot$ is true but $\bot = \bot'$ or $\bot = c$ for a constant c are false); and

2. second, eliminate tuples containing nulls from the result.

As an example, consider the instance below:

$$U_1: \quad \begin{array}{|c c|} \hline 1 & \bot \\ \hline 2 & \bot' \\ \hline \end{array} \qquad U_2: \quad \begin{array}{|c c c|} \hline \bot & 4 & \bot' \\ \hline \bot' & 5 & 6 \\ \hline \end{array}$$

and the query

$$Q(x,y,z) = \exists v \left(U_1(x,v) \wedge U_2(v,y,z) \right).$$

The first step of evaluating Q naïvely results in a table

$$\begin{array}{|c c c|} \hline 1 & 4 & \bot' \\ \hline 2 & 5 & 6 \\ \hline \end{array}$$

In the second step, the tuple $(1,4,\bot')$ is eliminated, as it contains a null. The end result has one tuple, (2,5,6).

For general queries, naïve evaluation need not coincide with certain answers. However, if Q is a conjunctive query, or a union of conjunctive queries, then

$$certain(Q,S) = Q_{\text{naïve}}(S).$$

This result is essentially optimal, as every larger subclass of relational calculus will contain a query for which naïve evaluation will fail to compute certain answers.

Properties of homomorphisms Using homomorphisms is essential for establishing properties of conjunctive queries. We have already seen that containment of conjunctive queries can be formulated in terms of the existence of homomorphisms between their tableaux. Notice that tableaux are nothing but naïve tables with some distinguished variables.

Another important property concerns the interaction of homomorphisms with certain answers. Suppose we have two instances S and S' of the same schema, a homomorphism $h : S \to S'$, and a conjunctive query Q. Then

$$certain(Q, S) \subseteq certain(Q, S').$$

The reason for this is that conjunctive queries are *preserved* under homomorphisms. That is, if $\bar{a}$ is a tuple of constants and $\bar{a}$ is in $Q(S)$, then $\bar{a}$ also belongs to $Q(S')$. Indeed, if Q is of the form $\exists \bar{y} \; \alpha(\bar{x}, \bar{y})$, and $\bar{a} \in Q(S)$, it means that $\alpha(\bar{a}, \bar{b})$ is true in S for some tuple $\bar{b}$ that may contain both constants and nulls. But then by the definition of homomorphisms, $\alpha(\bar{a}, h(\bar{b}))$ is true in $Q(S')$, implying $\bar{a} \in Q(S')$.

This preservation property applies to unions of conjunctive queries as well, and will be used in designing algorithms for query answering in data exchange.

2.4 Complexity classes

For most computational tasks we encounter in the book, we need to establish whether they are solvable algorithmically and, if the answer is positive, what type of computational resources are required. The former, of course, is the *decidability* question for a given problem; the latter is the question of its *computational complexity*. Complexity is typically measured in terms of the membership of a problem in a complexity class, and, ideally, *completeness* for a complexity class. Completeness means that the problem is as hard as any problem in a given class, which tells us that resources demanded by problems in that class are really needed to solve the problem at hand.

Membership of a problem in a complexity class is established by providing an algorithm that uses resources allowed by the complexity class. Resources are measured in terms of either *time* or *space* required by the computation, as well as the type of computation (deterministic or nondeterministic). Completeness (or undecidability) is established by reducing from problems already known to be complete for the class.

We now provide basic information about the complexity classes we use, as well as the prototypical complete problems to be used in reductions.

Definitions of complexity classes

The classes we consider are defined in terms of:

- time or space requirements; that is, problems requiring $O(f(n))$ time or space, for a class of functions f, and
- deterministic or nondeterministic mode of computation.

We consider Turing machines as a computational model, so $O(f(n))$ refers to the number of steps made by the machine on an input of size n (for time complexity), or the number of cells used by the machine (for space complexity).

The main classes we look at are described below. Note that these are intuitive definitions; formal definitions can be found in multiple complexity theory texts, some of which are mentioned in the bibliographic comments.

- PTIME, the class of polynomial-time solvable problems, by deterministic computation. That is, the running time is $O(n^k)$ for some fixed k.
- NP, the class of polynomial-time solvable problems, but by *nondeterministic computation*. The standard way of thinking about this class is as follows: for problems in NP, one can guess a solution (of polynomial size), and check in deterministic polynomial time if this solution to the problem works.
- CONP, the class of problems whose complement is in NP. That is, if we have a problem which, given an input, has to check if some statement is true about it, and we know that the complexity of this problem is in NP, then the complexity of the problem that has to check if the same statement is false is in CONP.
- Levels of the polynomial hierarchy: we shall need two of them, Σ_2^p and Π_2^p. The former is the class of problems that can be solved by an NP algorithm that has access to oracles (i.e., procedure calls) for other problems in NP. The class Π_2^p has the same relationship with Σ_2^p as CONP with NP: it is the class of complements of problems in Σ_2^p.
- PSPACE, the class of problems that require polynomial space (with deterministic Turing machines). It is known that with polynomial space nondeterminism comes for free. That is, if NPSPACE is defined as the class of problems solved by nondeterministic Turing machines requiring polynomial space, then PSPACE=NPSPACE.
- EXPTIME and EXPSPACE, the classes of problems requiring exponential time or space, i.e., time or space of the order of $2^{O(n^k)}$, with a deterministic Turing machine. As with PSPACE, nondeterminism comes for free in EXPSPACE, i.e., EXPSPACE=NEXPSPACE.
- NEXPTIME, the nondeterministic analog of EXPTIME.
- LOGSPACE and NLOGSPACE, classes of problems requiring space of the order of $O(\log n)$, deterministic and nondeterministic, respectively (for those classes, it is not known whether they coincide).
- AC^0, the class of problems admitting "very fast" parallel algorithms. We shall not define it precisely, but the intuitive idea is that problems in this class can be solved in parallel in *constant time* if one has access to polynomially many processors. All queries in relational calculus have this complexity.

The class PTIME is normally used as a tractability boundary. Problems inside PTIME are referred to as tractable, and problems outside as intractable. The following inclusions are known inside PTIME:

$$\text{AC}^0 \subsetneq \text{LOGSPACE} \subseteq \text{NLOGSPACE} \subseteq \text{PTIME}.$$

The first inclusion is known to be strict; the strictness of others are big open problems in complexity theory. Between PTIME and PSPACE we have the following inclusions:

$$\text{PTIME} \subseteq \left\{ \begin{array}{c} \text{NP} \\ \text{CONP} \end{array} \right\} \subseteq \left\{ \begin{array}{c} \Sigma_2^p \\ \Pi_2^p \end{array} \right\} \subseteq \text{PSPACE}.$$

None of the inclusions is known to be strict, nor is it known whether the classes listed in the curly brackets coincide. Again, all of these are big open problems in complexity, including the famous PTIME vs NP question. It is conjectured that PTIME $\neq$ NP; in fact, it is generally believed that practical algorithms for NP-complete problems will run in exponential time in the worst case.

Above PSPACE we have the following:

$$\text{PSPACE} \subseteq \text{EXPTIME} \subseteq \text{NEXPTIME} \subseteq \text{EXPSPACE}.$$

Again, none of the inclusions is known to be strict, although we know that PSPACE $\subsetneq$ EXPSPACE. It is also generally assumed that there are problems in NEXPTIME that are harder than the problems in EXPTIME, and thus, for all practical purposes, probably require double-exponential time (i.e., time of the order of $2^{2^{n^k}}$).

Complete problems

For each complexity (at least among those we consider here), some problems play a special role in that they are *hard* for those classes. Namely, if we have an algorithm for solving such a hard problem P, we can have an algorithm for solving every problem P' in the class. This is achieved by reducing P' to P, typically by means of a polynomial-time algorithm. That is, one has a polynomial-time algorithm that may include some calls to the subroutine solving P, and this algorithm solves P'. If the problem P both belongs to some complexity class and is hard for it, then we call it a *complete* problem for the class. One typically refers to these problems such as NP-complete, PSPACE-complete, etc.

In most cases, one uses polynomial-time reductions, but quite often it suffices to use reductions expressed in very simple languages. For example, many reductions can be expressed in FO. In fact, for classes inside PTIME, reductions must be expressible in a simple language, and for those classes we normally assume that they are FO-expressible.

If we know that a problem is complete for a class, it tells us that it is as hard to solve as any other problem in the class. Hence, it gives us a good estimate of how much computational resources one needs. For example, if a problem is NP-complete, then in all likelihood one needs an exponential-time algorithm to find a practical solution to the problem.

To establish completeness of some problem P of interest in a complexity class C, it suffices to take a known complete problem P_c for C and do the following:

- first, show that P is in C (this step is often quite easy), and
- second, reduce from P_c to P, i.e., show that if we have an algorithm for solving P, then we have an algorithm for solving P_c. Such a reduction must be done in polynomial time for classes above PTIME, and in FO for other classes we consider here.

We now give samples of complete problems for various classes. Others will be cited in proofs later in the book, when we need them.

NP-*complete problems* The quintessential NP-complete problem is *satisfiability* for Boolean formulae, or SAT. The input is a Boolean formula over variables $x_1, \ldots, x_n$, typically in CNF. The question is whether the formula is satisfiable, that is, whether there exists an assignment of values 0 or 1 to each variable x_i, for $1 \leq i \leq n$, that make the Boolean formula true.

Consider, for example, the formula

$$(x_1 \vee \neg x_2 \vee \neg x_3) \wedge (\neg x_1 \vee x_2 \vee \neg x_3) \wedge (\neg x_1 \vee x_2 \vee x_3).$$

It is satisfiable by the following assignment: $x_1 = 0, x_2 = 0, x_3 = 1$.

Some restrictions of SAT remain NP-complete, for example, the problem 3-SAT, which asks for satisfiability of Boolean formulae in CNF in which each clause contains at most three literals (like the formula above).

Many NP-complete problems are related to graphs. Consider, for example, the *k-colorability* problem. The input to the problem is an undirected graph $G = \langle V, E \rangle$ with vertices V and edges E. The question is whether the set of vertices can be partitioned into k sets, $V = C_1 \cup \cdots \cup C_k$, where all the C_i's are disjoint, so that for each edge $(x, y) \in E$, the vertices x and y are in different sets C_i and C_j. One can think of these sets as assigning colors 1 through k. Then the vertices of each edge must be colored by different colors.

The *k*-colorability problem is NP-complete for every $k \geq 3$ (and is solvable in polynomial time for $k = 2$).

Note that for both SAT and *k*-colorability, showing their membership in NP is easy by guessing the solution. In the case of SAT, one guesses an assignment of 0 or 1 to the variables, in the case of colorability, one guesses an assignment of colors to vertices. It is then easy to check, in deterministic polynomial time, whether these are proper solutions (i.e., a satisfying assignment, or a coloring).

Each NP-complete problem gives rise to a CONP-complete problem which is simply its complement. The following are examples of CONP-complete problems: asking if a Boolean formula is *un*satisfiable (i.e., *every* assignment makes it false), and if a graph is not *k*-colorable for $k \geq 3$ (i.e., for *every* assignment of colors at least one edge has both vertices colored with the same color).

Problems complete for PSPACE, Σ_2^p, *and* Π_2^p The canonical complete problems are variants of SAT, but this with quantifiers in front of the Boolean formula. These problems are referred to as *quantified satisfiability problems*, or QSAT. In general, an instance of QSAT is a formula of the form

$$\forall \bar{x}_1 \exists \bar{x}_2 \forall \bar{x}_3 \exists \bar{x}_4 \ldots \; \alpha(\bar{x}_1, \bar{x}_2, \bar{x}_3, \bar{x}_4, \ldots)$$

or

$$\exists \bar{x}_1 \forall \bar{x}_2 \exists \bar{x}_3 \forall \bar{x}_4 \ldots \; \alpha(\bar{x}_1, \bar{x}_2, \bar{x}_3, \bar{x}_4, \ldots),$$

where $\alpha(\bar{x}_1, \bar{x}_2, \bar{x}_3, \bar{x}_4, \ldots)$ is a Boolean formula. For example,

$$\exists(x_1, x_2)\forall x_3 (x_1 \vee \neg x_2 \vee \neg x_3) \wedge (\neg x_1 \vee x_2 \vee \neg x_3) \wedge (\neg x_1 \vee x_2 \vee x_3)$$

is an instance of QSAT. The question is whether the formula is true. In the above example, the answer is yes: if $x_1 = x_2 = 0$, then the propositional formula is true for both $x_3 = 0$ and $x_3 = 1$.

The problem QSAT is PSPACE-complete. Moreover, its variations give rise to complete problems for lower classes: if the quantifier prefix is $\exists \bar{x}_1 \forall \bar{x}_2$, then it is Σ_2^p-complete, and if the prefix is $\forall \bar{x}_1 \exists \bar{x}_2$, then it is Π_2^p-complete.

Complete problems for other classes For LOGSPACE and NLOGSPACE, canonical complete problems are related to graph reachability. Consider *directed* graphs $G = \langle V, E \rangle$, where the edge $(x, y) \in E$ indicates a directed edge that goes from x to y. The problem of checking, for a given directed graph G and a pair of nodes s and t, whether there is a path from s to t, is NLOGSPACE-complete. A path is a sequence $s = x_0, x_1, x_2, \ldots, x_k = t$ such that each (x_i, x_{i+1}) is an edge in E, for $i < k$. The problem of checking whether there is a deterministic path is LOGSPACE-complete. A path is deterministic if each (x_i, x_{i+1}) is the only outgoing edge from x_i, for $i < k$.

For NEXPTIME, the standard complete problem is satisfiability for the Bernays–Schönfinkel class of FO formulae. These are FO formulae of the form $\exists \bar{x} \forall \bar{y} \; \varphi(\bar{x}, \bar{y})$, where φ is quantifier-free (i.e., a Boolean combination of atomic formulae). It is known that such a formula is satisfiable if and only if it is satisfiable in some finite structure. Checking whether there exists a finite structure making this formula true is NEXPTIME-complete.

Another example of an NEXPTIME-complete problem is the following version of the tiling problem. Given a set of k tiles, and compatibility relations $H, V \subseteq \{1, \ldots, k\} \times \{1, \ldots, k\}$, we say that the $n \times n$ square can be tiled if there is a map $f : \{0, \ldots, n\} \times \{0, \ldots, n\} \to \{1, \ldots, k\}$ that satisfies both vertical and horizontal compatibility conditions:

- $(f(i, j), f(i+1, j)) \in H$ for all $i < n$ and $j \leq n$;
- $(f(i, j), f(i, j+1)) \in V$ for all $i \leq n$ and $j < n$.

Given relations H and V, and a number n given in *binary*, checking whether the $n \times n$ square can be tiled is NEXPTIME-complete. It is important that n is given in binary: under the unary representation of n, the problem is NP-complete.

Undecidability Several problems we consider in the book will be shown to be undecidable; that is, no algorithms exist for solving them. The classical undecidable problem used in reductions is the *halting problem*: given a (suitable encoding of a) Turing machine M and an input w, does M halt on w? In fact, all nontrivial properties of Turing machines are undecidable, for example, whether the Turing machine M halts on the empty input.

In our undecidability proofs we shall use more complex computational models for which halting/termination of computation is undecidable as well. Those will be introduced when we need them.

Data and combined complexity

When we deal with database-motivated questions, it is important to specify precisely what is viewed as an input to a problem. Consider, for now, query evaluation. A typical formulation of this problem is as follows:

PROBLEM:	QUERY EVALUATION
INPUT:	A query Q, a database D, a tuple $\bar{t}$.
QUESTION:	Does $\bar{t}$ belong to $Q(D)$?

We refer to the complexity of this problem as the *combined complexity* of query evaluation, as both the query Q, and the data – D and $\bar{t}$ – are included in the input.

In the database setting, however, queries are typically very small compared to data. Hence, it makes sense to measure the complexity in terms of the data: this is what we often are interested in. This is captured by the following modification of the query evaluation problem:

PROBLEM:	QUERY EVALUATION(Q)
INPUT:	A database D, a tuple $\bar{t}$.
QUESTION:	Does $\bar{t}$ belong to $Q(D)$?

We refer to the complexity of this problem as the *data complexity* of query evaluation, since the input consists only of data.

The two complexities can be dramatically different. For example:

- For relational calculus (i.e., FO), the combined complexity is PSPACE-complete, while the data complexity is in AC^0.

- For conjunctive queries (and their unions), the combined complexity is NP-complete, while the data complexity is in AC^0.

In fact, it is very common to have an exponential gap between data and combined complexities. To give an intuitive explanation of where it comes from, one can see that a query evaluation algorithm runs, very roughly, in time $\|D\|^{O(\|Q\|)}$, where $\|Q\|$ refers to the size of Q. Thus, for a fixed Q, it is polynomial, but when Q is a part of the input, it takes exponential time. A careful implementation of this naïve algorithm results in PSPACE complexity. For conjunctive queries of the form $\exists \bar{x}\ \alpha$, one needs to guess witnesses for the existential quantifiers, and then check if they make the formula α true, which gives an NP algorithm.

When we consider problems related to data exchange, the input generally will be split into two parts: the data part, involving instances (source and target), and the nondata part, involving schema mappings and queries. If only data is viewed as the input, we shall be talking about data complexity; if mappings and queries are part of the input as well, we shall be talking about combined complexity.

2.5 Basics of automata theory

In the last part of the book, where we deal with XML data exchange, we shall need some basic facts about automata on words and trees. Most of the notions of schemas for XML are automata-based; since XML documents themselves are modeled as labeled unranked trees, automata that one uses are those that run on such trees. In this section we review the basics of automata on words, and on binary trees. Automata on XML trees will be defined in the last part of the book.

If Σ is a finite alphabet, then Σ^* stands for the set of all finite words over Σ. We let ε denote the empty word. A *nondeterministic finite automaton (NFA)* is a tuple $\mathscr{A} = (Q, \Sigma, q_0, F, \delta)$, where

- Q is a finite set of states, with the initial state $q_0 \in Q$ and the set of final states $F \subseteq Q$, and
- $\delta : Q \times \Sigma \to 2^Q$ is the transition function.

Given a word $w = a_0 a_1 \ldots a_{n-1}$ of length n over Σ, a *run* of $\mathscr{A}$ on w is a function $\rho : \{0, \ldots, n-1\} \to Q$ such that:

1. $\rho(0) \in \delta(q_0, a_0)$; and
2. $\rho(i+1) \in \delta(\rho(i), a_{i+1})$ for $0 < i < n-1$.

A run shows in which state the automaton can be after reading each letter a_i of w. It starts in q_0 and, whenever it is in state q and reads letter a, it moves to a state in $\delta(q, a)$. Note that there could be more than one run of an NFA on a string.

A run is *accepting* if $\rho(n-1) \in F$, i.e., if it ends in a final state. A word w is *accepted* by $\mathscr{A}$ if there exists an accepting run of $\mathscr{A}$ on w. The set of all words accepted by $\mathscr{A}$ is the language accepted by the automaton, denoted by $\mathscr{L}(\mathscr{A})$. Languages arising in this way are called *regular*.

There is another familiar way of specifying regular languages, namely by means of regular expressions. These are defined by the grammar:

$$e, e' := \emptyset \mid \varepsilon \mid a, a \in \Sigma \mid e \cdot e' \mid e \cup e' \mid e^*.$$

These will be used in some XML schema specifications (DTDs). We assume that the reader is familiar with regular expressions. A regular expression can be converted into an equivalent automaton in polynomial time.

There are some standard decision problems related to NFAs. One of them is nonemptiness: given $\mathscr{A}$, is $\mathscr{L}(\mathscr{A}) \neq \emptyset$? That is, does $\mathscr{A}$ accept at least one word? This problem is known to be NLOGSPACE-complete (and thus solvable in polynomial time). At the other end, one can ask whether the automaton is universal, i.e., $\mathscr{L}(\mathscr{A}) = \Sigma^*$. This problem is PSPACE-complete (and thus it is very unlikely to be solvable in polynomial time). The problem of checking, for two automata $\mathscr{A}_1$ and $\mathscr{A}_2$, whether $\mathscr{L}(\mathscr{A}_1) \subseteq \mathscr{L}(\mathscr{A}_2)$ is also PSPACE-complete.

Automata can run not only on words but also on trees. We now briefly review automata on binary trees. A binary tree domain D is a subset of $\{0,1\}^*$ that, together with each $w \in D$, contains all its prefixes (including ε), and such that for each $w \in D$, either both $w \cdot 0$ and $w \cdot 1$ are in D, or none of them is. These define the nodes of a tree, as is shown in the picture below:

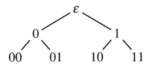

A tree over Σ is then a pair $T = (D, \lambda)$, where D is a binary tree domain and $\lambda : D \to \Sigma$ is a labeling function. A *nondeterministic (bottom-up) tree automaton (NTA)* is defined as a tuple $\mathscr{A} = (Q, \Sigma, q_0, F, \delta)$, where the only difference with the definition of an NFA is that the transition function is $\delta : Q \times Q \times \Sigma \to 2^Q$. The intuition behind this transition function is that if states q and q' are already assigned to left and right children of a node v labeled a, then any state from $\delta(q, q', a)$ can be assigned to v.

Formally, a run of $\mathscr{A}$ on a tree $T = (D, \lambda)$ is a function $\rho : D \to Q$ such that:

- if v is a leaf and $\lambda(v) = a$, then $\rho(v) \in \delta(q_0, q_0, a)$, and
- if v has children v_0, v_1 and $\lambda(v) = a$, then $\rho(v) \in \delta(\rho(v_0), \rho(v_1), a)$.

A run is accepting if $\rho(\varepsilon) \in F$. With this, the notions of trees accepted by $\mathscr{A}$ and the language $\mathscr{L}(\mathscr{A})$ are defined as before.

The same questions we considered for word automata can be asked about tree automata. Nonemptiness, i.e., checking whether $\mathscr{L}(\mathscr{A}) \neq \emptyset$, is solvable in polynomial time, and is in fact PTIME-complete. The universality problem, i.e., checking whether every tree is accepted by $\mathscr{A}$, is EXPTIME-complete. The containment problem for two tree automata is EXPTIME-complete as well.

3

Data exchange: key definitions

In this chapter we present formal definitions of the key data exchange concepts that will be used throughout the book:

- schema mappings and source-to-target dependencies;
- solutions, and the semantics of mappings; and
- query answering and query rewriting in data exchange.

3.1 Schema mappings

Let $\mathbf{R}$ be a relational schema. By $\text{INST}(\mathbf{R})$ we denote the set of all database instances over $\mathbf{R}$. As described in Section 2.3, domains of instances come from two disjoint and infinite sets of values:

- the set CONST of *constants*, and
- the set VAR of *nulls*, or variables, denoted by VAR.

We normally use the symbol $\perp$ (with subscripts or superscripts) to denote nulls, and lowercase letters or specific values to denote constants.

Domains of instances will combine constants and nulls, i.e., they will come from $\text{CONST} \cup \text{VAR}$. Most of the time (but not always) we assume that domains of source instances come from CONST only.

The three essential components of a schema mapping are:

- a *source schema* $\mathbf{R_s}$,
- a *target schema* $\mathbf{R_t}$, and
- a set Σ_{st} of *source-to-target dependencies*, or *stds*.

Source-to-target dependencies are typically logical sentences over $\mathbf{R_s}$ and $\mathbf{R_t}$. We have seen a number of examples in Chapter 1, for instance:

$$\forall \text{src}\, \forall \text{dest}\, \forall \text{airl}\, \forall \text{dep}\, \Big(\text{FLIGHT}(\text{src},\text{dest},\text{airl},\text{dep}) \longrightarrow$$
$$\exists \text{f\#}\, \exists \text{arr}\, \Big(\text{ROUTES}(\text{f\#},\text{src},\text{dest})$$
$$\wedge \text{INFO\_FLIGHT}(\text{f\#},\text{dep},\text{arr},\text{airl}) \Big) \Big).$$

$\mathbf{R_s}$:	FLIGHT$(\cdot,\cdot,\cdot,\cdot)$, GEO$(\cdot,\cdot,\cdot)$
$\mathbf{R_t}$:	ROUTES$(\cdot,\cdot,\cdot)$, INFO_FLIGHT$(\cdot,\cdot,\cdot,\cdot)$, SERVES$(\cdot,\cdot,\cdot,\cdot)$

(Σ_{st})	FLIGHT(src,dest,airl,dep) $\longrightarrow$
	$\exists$f# $\exists$arr $($ ROUTES(f#,src,dest)
	$\wedge$ INFO_FLIGHT(f#,dep,arr,airl)$)$
(Σ_{st})	FLIGHT(city,dest,airl,dep) $\wedge$ GEO(city,country,popul)
	$\longrightarrow$ $\exists$phone SERVES(airl,city,country,phone)
(Σ_{st})	FLIGHT(src,city,airl,dep) $\wedge$ GEO(city,country,popul)
	$\longrightarrow$ $\exists$phone SERVES(airl,city,country,phone)

(Σ_t)	$\forall$f#$\forall$s$\forall$d$\forall$s$'\forall$d$'$ ROUTES(f#,s,d) $\wedge$ ROUTES(f#,s',d') $\rightarrow$
	$s = s' \wedge d = d'$
(Σ_t)	$\forall$f#$\forall$s$\forall$d ROUTES(f#,s,d) $\rightarrow$
	$\exists a \exists a' \exists d'$ INFO_FLIGHT(f#,d',a,a')

Figure 3.1 A complete schema mapping $\mathcal{M} = (\mathbf{R_s}, \mathbf{R_t}, \Sigma_{st}, \Sigma_t)$

In addition, one might impose constraints on target instances, for example, keys and foreign keys, or other database integrity constraints. Let Σ_t be a set of such constraints, expressed by logical sentences over $\mathbf{R_t}$.

A **schema mapping** is then defined as a quadruple

$$\mathcal{M} = (\mathbf{R_s}, \mathbf{R_t}, \Sigma_{st}, \Sigma_t),$$

or just $\mathcal{M} = (\mathbf{R_s}, \mathbf{R_t}, \Sigma_{st})$, when there are no target constraints.

An example of a schema mapping was shown in Figure 1.3 on page 7. That schema had no target constraints. If one expands it with the rules stating that f# is a key for ROUTES and f# occurring in INFO_FLIGHT is a foreign key referencing ROUTES, one would arrive at the complete schema mapping shown in Figure 3.1.

3.2 Solutions

Now assume that S is a *source instance*, i.e., a database instance over $\mathbf{R_s}$. Then a target instance T is called a **solution for S under $\mathcal{M}$** if and only if S and T together satisfy all the stds in Σ_{st}, and T satisfies all the constraints in Σ_t. That is, T is a solution for S under $\mathcal{M}$ if

$$(S,T) \models \Sigma_{st} \text{ and } T \models \Sigma_t.$$

For mappings without target constraints, we only require $(S,T) \models \Sigma_{st}$.

As an example, consider an instance with the following tuples:

$$\text{FLIGHT } (\textit{Paris, Santiago, AirFrance, 2320})$$
$$\text{GEO } (\textit{Santiago, Chile, 5.3M}).$$

Then the following is a solution:

$$\text{ROUTES}(\bot_1, \textit{Paris, Santiago})$$
$$\text{INFO\_FLIGHT}(\bot_1, 2320, \bot_2, \textit{AirFrance})$$
$$\text{SERVES}(\textit{AirFrance, Santiago, Chile}, \bot_3).$$

The **set of all solutions** for S under $\mathcal{M}$ is denoted by $\text{SOL}_{\mathcal{M}}(S)$:

$$\text{SOL}_{\mathcal{M}}(S) = \{ T \in \text{INST}(\mathbf{R_t}) \mid (S,T) \models \Sigma_{st} \text{ and } T \models \Sigma_t \}.$$

It shall often be convenient for us to view the semantics of a schema mapping as a binary relation, containing source–target pairs that it relates. In fact, when we deal with metadata management, we often view mappings this way. Thus, the **semantics of a mapping** $\mathcal{M}$ is a binary relation $[\![\mathcal{M}]\!]$ between $\text{INST}(\mathbf{R_s})$ and $\text{INST}(\mathbf{R_t})$ (i.e., $[\![\mathcal{M}]\!] \subseteq \text{INST}(\mathbf{R_s}) \times \text{INST}(\mathbf{R_t})$) defined as

$$[\![\mathcal{M}]\!] = \left\{ (S,T) \;\middle|\; \begin{array}{l} S \in \text{INST}(\mathbf{R_s}), \\ T \in \text{INST}(\mathbf{R_t}), \\ T \in \text{SOL}_{\mathcal{M}}(S) \end{array} \right\}.$$

3.3 Query answering and rewriting

Given a query Q over the target schema $\mathbf{R_t}$, the notion of query answering is that of certain answers, which are true in all solutions for a given source instance S, and thus do not depend on a particular target instance that is materialized.

Thus, **certain answers** are defined as

$$\textit{certain}_{\mathcal{M}}(Q,S) = \bigcap_{T \in \text{SOL}_{\mathcal{M}}(S)} Q(T).$$

However, one needs to compute $\textit{certain}_{\mathcal{M}}(Q,S)$ using just one specific materialized solution, say T_0. In general, there is no reason why simply running Q on T_0 and computing $Q(T_0)$ would yield $\textit{certain}_{\mathcal{M}}(Q,S)$. Thus, instead one tries to find another query Q' that, over the materialized target T_0, computes $certain_{\mathscr{M}}(Q,S)$. This query Q' is called a **rewriting of Q over T_0**; then

$$Q'(T_0) = certain_{\mathscr{M}}(Q,S).$$

When we have such a materialized solution T_0 and a rewriting Q' for each query Q we want to pose, we have the answer to the two key questions of data exchange. First, we know which solution to materialize – it is T_0. Second, we know how to answer queries – compute the rewriting Q' of Q and apply it to T_0.

3.4 Bibliographic comments

Data exchange, also known as data translation, is a very old problem that arises in many tasks where data must be transferred between independent applications (Housel et al., 1977). Examples of data exchange problems appeared in the literature over 30 years ago. But as the need for data exchange increased over the years (Bernstein, 2003), research prototypes appeared and made their way into commercial database products. An early motivating example for much of research on data exchange was IBM's Clio system, described by Miller et al. (2001) and Fagin et al. (2009). The theory was lagging behind until the paper by Fagin et al. (2005a) which presented the widely accepted theoretical model of data exchange. It developed the basis of the theory of data exchange, by identifying the key problems and looking into materializing target instances and answering queries.

Within a year or two of the publication of the conference version of this paper, data exchange grew into a dominant subject in the database theory literature, with many papers published in conferences such as PODS, SIGMOD, VLDB, ICDT, etc. By now there are several papers presenting surveys of various aspects of relational data exchange and schema mappings (Kolaitis, 2005; Bernstein and Melnik, 2007; Barceló, 2009), and a short book dealing with both relational and XML data exchange by Arenas et al. (2010b). In addition to the Clio system mentioned early, a new open-source system called ++Spicy has recently been released, see the paper by Marnette et al. (2011). Much more extensive bibliographic comments will be provided in the subsequent chapters.

The subject of data integration has also received much attention, see, for example, the keynote by Haas (2007), the tutorial by Lenzerini (2002), and the comprehensive survey by Doan et al. (2012). Relationships between data exchange and integration have also been explored (Giacomo et al., 2007).

For additional background information on relational databases, complexity classes, and automata the reader is referred to standard textbooks, for example, the books by Abiteboul et al. (1995); Ullman (1988); Hopcroft and Ullman (1979); Papadimitriou (1994); Garey and Johnson (1979); Garcia-Molina et al. (2001); and Sipser (1997).

PART TWO
RELATIONAL DATA EXCHANGE

4

The problem of relational data exchange

The goal of this chapter is to introduce the key definitions for relational data exchange, as well as the key problems that we are going to study – checking whether a solution exists, constructing solutions with good properties, and using such solutions for query answering.

4.1 Key definitions

We start by revisiting the data exchange example presented in Chapter 1.

Example 4.1   In the example seen in Chapter 1, we used the mapping $\mathcal{M} = (\mathbf{R_s}, \mathbf{R_t}, \Sigma_{st})$ in which:

(1) The source schema $\mathbf{R_s}$ consists of the ternary relation

$$\text{GEO(city,country,population)}$$

and the 4-ary relation

$$\text{FLIGHT(source,destination,airline,departure)}.$$

(2) The target schema $\mathbf{R_t}$ consists of the ternary relation

$$\text{ROUTES(flight\#,source,destination)}$$

and the 4-ary relations

$$\text{INFO\_FLIGHT(flight\#,departure\_time,arrival\_time,airline)}$$
$$\text{and}$$
$$\text{SERVES(airline,city,country,phone).}$$

(3) Σ_{st} consists of the following source-to-target dependencies:

```
FLIGHT(src,dest,airl,dep) ⟶
        ∃f#∃arr (ROUTES(f#,src,dest) ∧
                     INFO_FLIGHT(f#,dep,arr,airl))

FLIGHT(city,dest,airl,dep) ∧ GEO(city,country,popul) ⟶
        ∃phone SERVES(airl,city,country,phone)

FLIGHT(src,city,airl,dep) ∧ GEO(city,country,popul) ⟶
        ∃phone SERVES(airl,city,country,phone).
```

The source-to-target dependencies guide the construction of target instances. For example, given the source instance

$$S = \{\text{FLIGHT}(Paris, Santiago, AirFrance, 2320)\},$$

one possible target instance – a solution – is the instance T below:

$$\{\text{ROUTES}(\bot_1, Paris, Santiago), \text{INFO\_FLIGHT}(\bot_1, 2320, \bot_2, AirFrance)\},$$

where $\bot_1, \bot_2$ are null values.   □

To reiterate, in data exchange we have source and target schemas, and constraints that relate them. These constitute relational schema mappings defined below.

Definition 4.2 (Relational mappings)   A *relational mapping* $\mathscr{M}$ is a tuple $(\mathbf{R_s}, \mathbf{R_t}, \Sigma_{st}, \Sigma_t)$, where:

- $\mathbf{R_s}$ and $\mathbf{R_t}$ are relational schemas – $\mathbf{R_s}$ is called the *source* schema, $\mathbf{R_t}$ is called the *target* schema;
- Σ_{st} is a finite set of *source-to-target* dependencies (i.e., dependencies over the relations in $\mathbf{R_s}$ and $\mathbf{R_t}$);
- Σ_t is a finite set of *target* dependencies (i.e., dependencies over $\mathbf{R_t}$).

If the set Σ_t is empty, i.e., there are no target dependencies, we write $\mathscr{M} = (\mathbf{R_s}, \mathbf{R_t}, \Sigma_{st})$.   □

We always assume that $\mathbf{R_s}$ and $\mathbf{R_t}$ do not have any relation names in common. If both use the same relation name R, we simply rename R as R' in the target schema.

The intuition behind the different components of these mappings is as follows:

- Source-to-target dependencies in Σ_{st} are a tool for specifying conditions on the source that entail a condition that must be satisfied by the target. Thinking operationally, one can view them as a tool for specifying how source data gets translated into target data.
- The translated data must satisfy usual database constraints. This is represented by means of the target dependencies in Σ_t.

Source instances – that is, instances of $\mathbf{R_s}$ – are assumed to take values from the domain CONST, usually referred to as constants. On the other hand, target instances – that is, instances of $\mathbf{R_t}$ – may use both constants from CONST and null values, or nulls from the set

VAR. That is, they are instances over CONST ∪ VAR. Source instances are usually denoted $S, S_1, S_2, \ldots$, while target instances are denoted $T, T_1, T_2, \ldots$.

Instances like

$$\{\texttt{ROUTES}(\bot_1, Paris, Santiago), \texttt{INFO\_FLIGHT}(\bot_1, 2320, \bot_2, AirFrance)\},$$

in the above example are *solutions*: they satisfy all the dependencies in the mapping for a given source instance. That is, given a source instance S over CONST, a target instance T over CONST ∪ VAR is a *solution for S under $\mathscr{M}$*, if (S,T) satisfies every sentence in Σ_{st} and T satisfies every sentence in Σ_t. In symbols, $(S,T) \models \Sigma_{st}$ and $T \models \Sigma_t$. When $\mathscr{M}$ is clear from the context, we call simply call T a solution for S. As before, the set of solutions for instance S will be denoted by $\text{SOL}_{\mathscr{M}}(S)$.

The notion $(S,T) \models \Sigma_{st}$ from the above definition is formally stated as follows. If the source schema $\mathbf{R_s}$ contains relation symbols $U_1, \ldots, U_m$ and the target schema $\mathbf{R_t}$ contains relation symbols $W_1, \ldots, W_n$ (with no relation symbols in common), then $\langle \mathbf{R_s}, \mathbf{R_t} \rangle$ refers to the schema with relation symbols $U_1, \ldots, U_m, W_1, \ldots, W_n$. If S is an instance of $\mathbf{R_s}$ and T is an instance of $\mathbf{R_t}$, then (S,T) denotes an instance of $\langle \mathbf{R_s}, \mathbf{R_t} \rangle$ in which every relation symbol U_i is interpreted as U_i^S and every relation symbol W_j is interpreted as W_j^T, for each $1 \le i \le m$ and $1 \le j \le n$.

The general definition of relational schema mappings does not put restrictions on the type of source-to-target dependencies one can use. Admitting arbitrary dependencies however easily leads to undecidability of some fundamental problems, such as checking for the existence of solutions. Thus, it is customary to impose restrictions on classes of mappings $\mathscr{M}$ that guarantee efficient algorithms for the key computational tasks associated with data exchange.

The standard restrictions used in data exchange are as follows: constraints used in Σ_{st} are *tuple-generating dependencies* (which generalize inclusion dependencies), and constraints in Σ_t are either tuple-generating dependencies or *equality-generating dependencies* (which generalize functional dependencies). More precisely:

- Σ_{st} consists of a set of *source-to-target tuple-generating dependencies (st-tgds)* of the form

$$\forall \bar{x} \forall \bar{y} (\varphi_s(\bar{x}, \bar{y}) \rightarrow \exists \bar{z} \, \psi_t(\bar{x}, \bar{z})),$$

  where $\varphi_s(\bar{x}, \bar{y})$ and $\psi_t(\bar{x}, \bar{z})$ are conjunctions of atomic formulae in $\mathbf{R_s}$ and $\mathbf{R_t}$, respectively; and
- Σ_t is the union of a set of *tuple-generating dependencies (tgds)*, i.e., dependencies of the form

$$\forall \bar{x} \forall \bar{y} (\varphi(\bar{x}, \bar{y}) \rightarrow \exists \bar{z} \, \psi(\bar{x}, \bar{z})),$$

  where $\varphi(\bar{x}, \bar{y})$ and $\psi(\bar{x}, \bar{z})$ are conjunctions of atomic formulae in $\mathbf{R_t}$, and a set of *equality-generating dependencies (egds)*, i.e., dependencies of the form

$$\forall \bar{x} (\varphi(\bar{x}) \rightarrow x_i = x_j),$$

where $\varphi(\bar{x})$ is a conjunction of atomic formulae in $\mathbf{R_t}$, and x_i, x_j are variables among those in $\bar{x}$.

One can observe that the mapping we used in Chapter 1 follows this pattern. Equality-generating dependencies generalize functional dependencies, and in particular keys. Tuple-generating dependencies generalize inclusion constraints. For example, if we have a binary relation R_1, then the fact that the first attribute is a key is expressed by an egd $\forall x \forall y \forall y'\, (R_1(x,y) \wedge R_1(x,y') \rightarrow y = y')$. The fact that each element of a set R_2 occurs as the first attribute of R_1 is expressed by a tgd $\forall x\, R_2(x) \rightarrow \exists y\, R_1(x,y)$. Together these two constraints form a foreign key.

For the sake of simplicity, we usually omit universal quantification in front of st-tgds, tgds, and egds. Notice, in addition, that each (st-)tgd $\varphi(\bar{x},\bar{y}) \rightarrow \exists \bar{z}\, \psi(\bar{x},\bar{z})$ is logically equivalent to the formula $(\exists \bar{y}\, \varphi(\bar{x},\bar{y})) \rightarrow (\exists \bar{z}\, \psi(\bar{x},\bar{z}))$. Thus, when we use the notation $\theta(\bar{x}) \rightarrow \exists \bar{z}\, \psi(\bar{x},\bar{z})$ for a (st-)tgd, we assume that $\theta(\bar{x})$ is a formula of the form $\exists \bar{y}\, \varphi(\bar{x},\bar{y})$, where $\varphi(\bar{x},\bar{y})$ is a conjunction of atomic formulae.

Tgds without existential quantification on the right-hand side, i.e., of the form $\forall \bar{x} \forall \bar{y}(\varphi(\bar{x},\bar{y}) \rightarrow \psi(\bar{x}))$, are called *full*.

From now on, and unless stated otherwise, we assume all relational mappings to be of the restricted form specified above. Such mappings are not restrictive from the database point of view. Indeed, tuple-generating dependencies together with equality-generating dependencies precisely capture the class of *embedded* dependencies. And the latter class contains all relevant dependencies that appear in relational databases; in particular, it contains functional and inclusion dependencies, among others.

LAV *and* GAV *mappings*

There are two classes of data exchange mappings, called *Local-As-View* (LAV) and *Global-As-View* (GAV) mappings, that we will often use. Both classes have their origin in the field of data integration, but have proved to be of interest for data exchange as well. Let $\mathcal{M} = (\mathbf{R_s}, \mathbf{R_t}, \Sigma_{st})$ be a relational mapping without target dependencies. Then:

1. $\mathcal{M}$ is a LAV mapping if Σ_{st} consists of LAV st-tgds of the form:

$$\forall \bar{x}(U(\bar{x}) \rightarrow \exists \bar{z}\, \varphi_t(\bar{x},\bar{z})),$$

   where U is a relation symbol in $\mathbf{R_s}$. That is, to generate tuples in the target, one needs a single source fact. In Example 4.1, the first rule is of this shape.
2. $\mathcal{M}$ is a GAV mapping if Σ_{st} consists of GAV st-tgds of the form:

$$\forall \bar{x}(\varphi_s(\bar{x}) \rightarrow U(\bar{x})),$$

   where U is a relation symbol in $\mathbf{R_t}$. That is, conjunctive query views over the source define single facts in the target.

Both GAV and LAV mappings – as well as mappings defined by full (st-)tgds – will be useful for us in two different ways. First, sometimes restricting our attention to one of these classes leads to better complexity bounds for the problem we study. Second, it is sometimes possible to show that the computational complexity of a data exchange problem is hard even if restricted to mappings in one of these classes. This will indicate that such problems are inherently very hard.

4.2 Key problems

As we mentioned in Chapter 3, one of the key goals in data exchange is to materialize a solution that reflects as accurately as possible the given source instance. But before we do so, we need to ask ourselves if it is possible in principle. And once we have materialized a solution, we need to use it for query answering. These considerations give rise to three problems we shall study in this chapter – the existence of solutions, materialization of solutions, and query answering.

Existence of solutions

We now look again at the mapping $\mathcal{M}$ from Example 4.1. Under this mapping, *every* source instance has a solution under $\mathcal{M}$. In fact, since the st-tgds do not completely specify the target, solutions are not necessarily unique and, indeed, there are infinitely many of them for each source instance.

For the source instance $S = \{\text{FLIGHT}(\textit{Paris, Santiago, AirFrance}, 2320)\}$ from the example, we saw one possible solution

$$T \quad = \quad \{\text{ROUTES}(\bot_1, \textit{Paris, Santiago}), \text{INFO\_FLIGHT}(\bot_1, 2320, \bot_2, \textit{AirFrance})\}.$$

But others are possible too, for instance

$$T' \quad = \quad \{\text{ROUTES}(\bot_1, \textit{Paris, Santiago}), \text{INFO\_FLIGHT}(\bot_1, 2320, \bot_1, \textit{AirFrance})\},$$

or even a solution with no nulls:

$$T'' = \{\text{ROUTES}(\textit{AF}406, \textit{Paris, Santiago}),$$

$$\text{INFO\_FLIGHT}(\textit{AF}406, 2320, 920, \textit{AirFrance})\}.$$

On the other hand, assume that $\mathcal{M}'$ is the extension of $\mathcal{M}$ with the target dependency (an egd) stating that src is a key in ROUTES(f#,src,dest). Then it is no longer true that every source instance has a solution under $\mathcal{M}'$. Indeed, consider a source instance

$$S = \{\text{FLIGHT}(\textit{Paris, Santiago, AirFrance}, 2320),$$

$$\text{FLIGHT}(\textit{Paris, Rio, TAM}, 1720)\}.$$

We can see that the first st-tgd in Σ_{st} implies that there are facts of the form ROUTES(x, *Paris, Santiago*) and ROUTES(y, *Paris, Rio*) in every solution T for S. But these tuples violate the key constraint. Hence, S has no solutions under $\mathcal{M}'$.

This suggests that to materialize a target solution for a given source instance, at the very least we need to be able to determine whether a solution exists at all. This is the problem of existence of solutions.

PROBLEM:	SOLEXISTENCE$_{\mathcal{M}}$.
INPUT:	A source instance S.
QUESTION:	Is there a solution for S under $\mathcal{M}$?

We study the existence of solutions problem in Chapter 5. We show in Section 5.2 that the problem is undecidable in general, but that it becomes decidable – and, actually, tractable – for a relevant class of mappings: those with a *weakly acyclic* set of tgds, as defined in Section 5.4. In order to prove this, we show, in Section 5.3, how to construct solutions using the well-known *chase* procedure.

Notice that in the definition of the problem of existence of solutions the mapping $\mathcal{M}$ is assumed to be *fixed* – that is, the complexity is measured in terms of the size of the source instance. This corresponds to the *data complexity* of the problem. In Section 5.5 we also study its combined complexity; that is, the complexity when both the source instance and the mapping are given as input.

Materializing target instances

Once we know that solutions exist, we need to construct one. The problem, explained in Chapter 1, is that usually there is more than just one solution; in fact, as we just saw, typically there are infinitely many of them. Thus, we need compute one that reflects accurately the source data and does not contain too much redundant information. Intuitively, this means that we want to compute solutions that are more *general* than any other solution. The following example illustrates the notion of a solution being more general than others.

Example 4.3   Again we refer to the setting of Example 4.1, and three possible solutions T, T', and T'', shown on page 39. Intuitively, it appears that T' and T'' are less general than T. This is because T' assumes that the values that witness the existentially quantified variables f# and arr, in the first st-tgd of Σ_{st}, are the same, while T'' assumes that these variables are witnessed by the constants $AF406$ and 920, respectively. On the other hand, solution T contains exactly what the specification requires. Thus, it seems natural to say that one would like to materialize a solution like T rather than solution T' or T'', as T is more accurate with respect to S (under $\mathcal{M}$) than T' and T'' are.   □

More general solutions in data exchange are identified with *universal* solutions. We will see in the following chapters that universal solutions have a number of good properties in terms of representing other solutions, as well as answers to queries. In general, however, the existence of solutions does not imply the existence of universal solutions, and the problem of existence of universal solutions is undecidable. We show these results in Section 6.2, but later, in Section 6.3, we show that for the same class of mappings for which the existence of solutions becomes tractable (that is, those with a weakly acyclic set of tgds), the unpleasant problems just mentioned disappear. For this class of mappings, the existence of solutions always coincides with the existence of universal solutions, and, therefore, the problem of existence of universal solutions is tractable. Furthermore, if a solution exists, then a particular universal solution – called *canonical* universal solution – can be materialized in polynomial time.

Finally, in Section 6.4 we address the problem of computing the *smallest* universal solution, which can be understood as the problem of computing a universal solution with the least amount of redundant information. Smallest universal solutions are shown to be unique (up to renaming of nulls) and to coincide with the graph-theoretic notion of the *core* of the universal solutions. The smallest universal solution can always be computed in polynomial time for mappings with a weakly acyclic set of tgds.

Computing certain answers

Once a target instance is materialized, we need to answer queries against it. Recall that in the context of data exchange, we are interested in computing the certain answers of a query. That is, if $\mathcal{M} = (\mathbf{R_s}, \mathbf{R_t}, \Sigma_t, \Sigma_{st})$ is a relational mapping, Q is a query in some query language over the target schema $\mathbf{R_t}$, and S is a source instance, we want to find *certain answers of Q with respect to S under $\mathcal{M}$* defined as

$$ certain_{\mathcal{M}}(Q, S) = \bigcap \{Q(T) \mid T \in \text{SOL}_{\mathcal{M}}(S)\}. $$

Example 4.4 (Examples 4.1 and 4.3 continued)   Consider again the source instance

$$ S = \{\text{FLIGHT}(Paris, Santiago, AirFrance, 2320)\}. $$

The certain answers of the query $Q = \text{ROUTES}(x, y, z)$ with respect to S is the empty set. This is because if a tuple belongs to the certain answers of Q it can only be formed by constants, and there is no fact of the form $\text{ROUTES}(a, b, c)$, for $a, b, c \in \text{CONST}$, such that $\text{ROUTES}(a, b, c) \in T$.

On the other hand, it is not hard to see that $certain_{\mathcal{M}}(Q', S) = \{(Paris, Santiago)\}$, for $Q' = \exists x \text{ROUTES}(x, y, z)$. Indeed, every solution for S must contain a fact of the form $\text{ROUTES}(x, Paris, Santiago)$, and, thus, it must satisfy the query $\exists x \text{ROUTES}(x, Paris, Santiago)$. □

Given a mapping $\mathcal{M}$ and a query Q over $\mathbf{R_t}$, the problem of computing certain answers for Q under $\mathcal{M}$ is defined as follows:

PROBLEM:	CERTAIN$_{\mathcal{M}}(Q)$.
INPUT:	A source instance S and a tuple $\bar{t}$ of elements from S.
QUESTION:	Does $\bar{t}$ belong to $certain_{\mathcal{M}}(Q, S)$?

We study query answering in Chapter 7. We start by showing in Section 7.1 that computing certain answers of FO queries is an undecidable problem, even when we deal with relational mappings without target dependencies. This implies the need for restrictions on query languages, which we study next. In Section 7.2 we show that the query answering problem becomes tractable for conjunctive queries over the class of mappings with a weakly acyclic set of tgds, i.e., those for which the existence of (universal) solutions can be checked in polynomial time.

Unfortunately, this positive result cannot be extended much further, since we show in Section 7.3 that adding a very restricted kind of negation to conjunctive queries leads to intractability, even in the absence of target dependencies. In Section 7.4 we partially tackle this problem, and develop a language that at the same time adds a limited form of negation to conjunctive queries, can express interesting data exchange properties, and retains the good properties of conjunctive queries for data exchange. Later, in Sections 7.5 and 7.6 we study the notion of query rewriting – that is, when the certain answers of a query Q can be obtained by posing a (perhaps different) query Q' over a materialized target instance. We develop techniques that help us decide when a query admits a rewriting in some query language.

Finally, in Chapter 8, we study alternative semantics for data exchange. These semantics are not based on the class of all solutions, as the certain answers semantics defined above, but rather on subclasses of suitably chosen preferred solutions. For instance, Section 8.1 develops a semantics based only on the set of universal solutions. Sections 8.2 and 8.3 are devoted to the study of a closed-world semantics that, unlike the other semantics, does not allow solutions to be open for adding new facts. Since neither the closed-world nor the open-world semantics are completely satisfactory in some scenarios, we study in Section 8.4 a *clopen* semantics that tries to combine the best of both worlds.

5

Existence of solutions

Before we address the problem of materializing target instances, we need to address a more basic problem, that is, whether solutions exist in the first place. As we already mentioned, the most general version of this problem is undecidable. To obtain decidability – and, as it turns out, tractability as well – one has to restrict the class of relational mappings. We show that there is a simple syntactic restriction that only depends on the class of tgds used in target constraints Σ_t and that guarantees these good properties. In order to obtain tractability for this syntactic class we make use of the well-known chase procedure, which was first developed in the early 1980s as a tool for checking the implication of data dependencies.

5.1 The problem and easy cases

Recall that in this chapter we study the problem of existence of solutions in data exchange, defined as follows:

PROBLEM:	SOLEXISTENCE$_\mathcal{M}$.
INPUT:	A source instance S.
QUESTION:	Is there a solution for S under $\mathcal{M}$?

We start by analyzing some easy cases of the problem, and show the following.

- In the absence of target dependencies the problem is trivial for mappings specified by st-tgds: every source instance has a solution.
- If we use more powerful mappings, in which source-to-target constraints are specified by arbitrary FO sentences, then the problem is undecidable.

Relational mappings without target dependencies

We now consider relational mappings of the form $\mathcal{M} = (\mathbf{R_s}, \mathbf{R_t}, \Sigma_{st})$, i.e., mappings without target dependencies, in which all dependencies in Σ_{st} are st-tgds. In this case, the problem of the existence of solutions becomes trivial, that is, every source instance has a solution (in fact, infinitely many of them). Furthermore, for each source instance S, a solution T for S can be constructed in polynomial time. In fact, it is the same procedure that we used in the last chapter to produce a solution T on page 39 for the instance S from Example 4.1.

Proposition 5.1 *Let $\mathscr{M} = (\mathbf{R_s}, \mathbf{R_t}, \Sigma_{st})$ be a relational mapping, where Σ_{st} consists of a finite set of st-tgds. Then every source instance S has infinitely many solutions under $\mathscr{M}$. Moreover, at least one solution for S can be constructed in polynomial time.*

Proof We first define a procedure that takes as input a source instance S and computes a solution T for S. For each st-tgd in Σ_{st} of the form:

$$\varphi(\bar{x}) \rightarrow \exists \bar{w} \left(R_1(\bar{x}_1, \bar{w}_1) \wedge \cdots \wedge R_k(\bar{x}_k, \bar{w}_k) \right),$$

where $\bar{x}$ and $\bar{w}$ are the tuples of variables that appear in the $\bar{x}_i$'s and the $\bar{w}_i$'s, for $1 \leq i \leq k$, and for each tuple $\bar{a}$ from $\mathrm{DOM}(S)$ of length $|\bar{x}|$ such that $S \models \varphi(\bar{a})$, choose a tuple $\bar{\perp}$ of length $|\bar{w}|$ of fresh distinct null values over VAR. Then populate each relation R_i, $1 \leq i \leq k$, with tuples $(\pi_{\bar{x}_i}(\bar{a}), \pi_{\bar{w}_i}(\bar{\perp}))$, where $\pi_{\bar{x}_i}(\bar{a})$ refers to the components of $\bar{a}$ that occur in the positions of $\bar{x}_i$, and likewise for $\pi_{\bar{w}_i}(\bar{\perp})$. It is easy to see that the resulting target instance T is a solution for S under $\mathscr{M}$, as the process ensures that every st-tgd is satisfied. Moreover, each target instance T' that extends T with new tuples is also a solution for S. Thus, every source instance S admits infinitely many solutions. Finally, since $\mathscr{M}$ is fixed, the process of constructing T is done in polynomial time in $\|S\|$, since computing sets of tuples $\bar{a}$ such that $S \models \varphi(\bar{a})$ can be done in polynomial time. $\square$

Relational mappings defined in FO

We mentioned in Section 4.1 that admitting arbitrary expressive power for specifying dependencies in data exchange easily leads to undecidability of the problem of existence of solutions. The next result confirms this, even for relational mappings with no target dependencies, and just a single source-to-target dependency given by an FO sentence.

Proposition 5.2 *There exists a relational mapping $\mathscr{M} = (\mathbf{R_s}, \mathbf{R_t}, \Sigma_{st})$, where Σ_{st} consists of a single FO dependency over the symbols in $\mathbf{R_s}$ and $\mathbf{R_t}$, such that the problem $\mathrm{SOLEXISTENCE}_{\mathscr{M}}$ is undecidable.*

This result confirms the fact that relational mappings have to be restricted in order to become useful for data exchange purposes. A possible proof of Proposition 5.2 goes by a rather tedious codification of the halting problem for Turing machines. We postpone the proof, however, because in the next section we show a stronger result, with a much more concise and elegant proof, that immediately implies the above.

5.2 Undecidability for st-tgds and target constraints

The fact that arbitrary expressive power of source-to-target dependencies destroys decidability of the most basic data exchange problem was one of the reasons why in Section 4.1 we decided to impose a restriction that mappings be of the form $\mathscr{M} = (\mathbf{R_s}, \mathbf{R_t}, \Sigma_{st}, \Sigma_t)$, where Σ_{st} consists of a finite set of st-tgds and Σ_t consists of a finite set of tgds and egds.

So a natural question then is: does this restriction guarantee decidability of the problem of existence of solutions? It turns out that it is still insufficient for decidability, let alone efficiency.

Theorem 5.3 *There exists a relational mapping $\mathcal{M} = (\mathbf{R_s}, \mathbf{R_t}, \Sigma_{st}, \Sigma_t)$, such that the problem* SOLEXISTENCE$_\mathcal{M}$ *is undecidable.*

Before proving Theorem 5.3, note that it immediately implies Proposition 5.2. Indeed, if SOLEXISTENCE$_\mathcal{M}$ is undecidable, where $\mathcal{M} = (\mathbf{R_s}, \mathbf{R_t}, \Sigma_{st}, \Sigma_t)$, Σ_{st} consists of a finite set of st-tgds, and Σ_t consists of a finite set of tgds and egds, then SOLEXISTENCE$_{\mathcal{M}'}$ is also undecidable, where $\mathcal{M}' = (\mathbf{R_s}, \mathbf{R_t}, \Sigma'_{st})$ and Σ'_{st} consists of the single FO dependency φ_{st} over $\langle \mathbf{R_s}, \mathbf{R_t} \rangle$ that expresses the conjunction of all dependencies in $\Sigma_{st} \cup \Sigma_t$.

Proof of Theorem 5.3 We reduce from the embedding problem for finite semigroups (explained below), which is known to be undecidable.

Recall that a finite semigroup is an algebra $\mathbf{A} = (A, f)$, where A is a finite nonempty set and f is an associative binary function on A. Let $\mathbf{B} = (B, g)$ be a partial finite algebra; i.e., B is a finite nonempty set and g is a partial function from $B \times B$ to B. Then $\mathbf{B}$ is *embeddable* in the finite semigroup $\mathbf{A} = (A, f)$ if and only if $B \subseteq A$ and f is an extension of g, that is, whenever $g(a, a')$ is defined, we have that $g(a, a') = f(a, a')$. The *embedding* problem for finite semigroups is as follows: given a finite partial algebra $\mathbf{B} = (B, g)$, is $\mathbf{B}$ embeddable in some finite semigroup?

We construct a relational mapping $\mathcal{M} = (\mathbf{R_s}, \mathbf{R_t}, \Sigma_{st}, \Sigma_t)$ such that the embedding problem for finite semigroups is reducible to the problem of existence of solutions for $\mathcal{M}$. The mapping $\mathcal{M}$ is constructed as follows:

- $\mathbf{R_s}$ consists of a ternary relation symbol U, and $\mathbf{R_t}$ consists of a ternary relation symbol V. Intuitively, these encode the graphs of binary functions.
- $\Sigma_{st} = \{U(x, y, z) \rightarrow V(x, y, z)\}$; that is, the content of relation U in a source instance S is directly copied into relation V in any target instance that is a solution for S.
- Σ_t consists of one egd and two tgds. An egd

$$V(x, y, z) \wedge V(x, y, z') \rightarrow z = z'$$

asserts that V encodes a function. A tgd

$$V(x, y, u) \wedge V(y, z, v) \wedge V(u, z, w) \rightarrow V(x, v, w)$$

asserts that the function encoded by V is associative. Finally, a tgd

$$V(x_1, x_2, x_3) \wedge V(y_1, y_2, y_3) \rightarrow \bigwedge_{1 \leq i, j \leq 3} \exists z_{ij} V(x_i, y_j, z_{ij})$$

states that the function encoded by V is total. Indeed, this tgd says that if two elements a and b appear in the interpretation of V, then there must be an element c such that $V(a, b, c)$ holds.

Let $\mathbf{B} = (B, g)$ be a finite partial algebra. Consider the source instance $S_\mathbf{B} = \{U(a, b, c) \mid g(a, b) = c\}$. It is clear that $\mathbf{B}$ is embeddable in the class of finite semigroups if and only if $S_\mathbf{B}$ has a solution under $\mathcal{M}$. This shows that the existence of solutions problem for $\mathcal{M}$ is undecidable. $\qquad \square$

Thus, the existence of solutions problem is undecidable over arbitrary relational mappings given by st-tgds. This suggests that we should further restrict the class of dependencies allowed in mappings, in such a way that checking the existence of solutions is a decidable (ideally, tractable) problem. Before presenting such a class, we describe the main algorithmic tool used in data exchange for checking the existence of solutions and for building them – the well-known chase procedure.

5.3 The chase

The chase was originally designed for reasoning about the implication problem for data dependencies. In data exchange, the chase is used as a tool for constructing a solution for a given source instance. In fact, it constructs a solution with very good properties, as we will see in the next chapter.

The basic idea behind the chase can be described as follows. It starts with a source instance S, and then triggers every dependency in $\Sigma_{st} \cup \Sigma_t$, as long as this process is applicable. In doing so, the chase may fail (if firing an egd forces two constants to be equal) or it may never terminate (for instance, in some cases when the set of tgds is *cyclic*). Notice that, in a way, we already applied the chase procedure in the proof of Proposition 5.1.

Before defining it formally, we illustrate it with an example.

Example 5.4 Let $\mathcal{M} = (\mathbf{R_s}, \mathbf{R_t}, \Sigma_{st}, \Sigma_t)$ be a mapping such that:

- the source schema consists of a binary relation E;
- the target schema consists of binary relations G and L;
- Σ_{st} consists of the st-tgd $\varphi = E(x,y) \rightarrow G(x,y)$;
- Σ_t consists of the tgd $\theta_1 = G(x,y) \rightarrow \exists z L(y,z)$.

Let S be the source instance $E(a,b)$. The chase procedure starts with the empty target T and keeps firing rules while some of the constraints are violated. This is done as follows.

1. We start with $S = \{E(a,b)\}$ and $T_0 = \emptyset$. Then (S,T_0) violates the st-tgd φ. The chase procedure uses this constraint to populate the target with the fact $G(a,b)$.
2. Now $T_1 = \{G(a,b)\}$ and $(S,T_1) \models \varphi$. However, $(S,T_1) \not\models \theta_1$, since the relation L is still empty. This triggers the application of θ_1, which results in adding a fact $L(b,\bot)$ to the target, where $\bot$ is a fresh null value.
3. Now $T_2 = \{G(a,b), L(b,\bot)\}$, and no dependency is violated. Thus, the chase *successfully terminates*, and T_2 is a solution for S.

We now modify target constraints and assume that Σ_t' contains θ_1 and a new tgd $\theta_2 = L(x,y) \rightarrow \exists z G(y,z)$. The beginning of the chase procedure is the same as before, but it does not stop at step 3 as before, since $(S,T_2) \not\models \theta_2$. The chase continues as follows.

4. A fact $G(\bot, \bot_1)$ is added to the target to satisfy θ_2. Here again $\bot_1$ is a new null value.
5. Now $T_3 = \{G(a,b), G(\bot, \bot_1), L(b,\bot)\}$ violates θ_1. So we have to add a new fact $L(\bot_1, \bot_2)$, where $\bot_2$ is a fresh null value.

6. Now $T_4 = \{G(a,b), G(\perp, \perp_1), L(b, \perp), L(\perp_1, \perp_2)\}$ violates θ_2, so a new fact $G(\perp_2, \perp_3)$ must be added. And the process now continues indefinitely.

In this case, the chase *does not terminate*. Notice that it does not imply the lack of solutions for S; in fact, $T = \{G(a,b), L(b,a)\}$ is a solution for S. Nontermination simply says that the chase procedure cannot compute a solution.

Finally, consider a Σ_t'' that contains a single egd $\alpha = G(x,y) \to x = y$. Then, after the first step when it constructs T_1, the chase *fails*, since the fact $G(a,b)$, and the egd α implies that two distinct constants a and b are equal. Notice that, in this case, S has no solution. $\square$

We now formally define the chase procedure, and explain how its three possible outcomes – successful termination, nontermination, and failure – are interpreted in terms of the existence of data exchange solutions.

We first define the notion of a *chase step* for an instance S. We distinguish between two kinds of chase steps – tgd steps and egd steps.

(tgd) Let d be a tgd of the form $\varphi(\bar{x}) \to \exists \bar{y} \psi(\bar{x}, \bar{y})$, such that for some tuple $\bar{a}$ of elements in $\textsc{Dom}(S)$ it is the case that $\varphi(\bar{a})$ holds in S, where $|\bar{a}| = |\bar{x}|$. Then the *result of applying d to S with $\bar{a}$* is the instance S' that extends S with every fact $R(\bar{c})$ that belongs to $\psi(\bar{a}, \bar{\perp})$, where $\bar{\perp}$ is a tuple of fresh distinct values in $\textsc{Var}$ such that $|\bar{\perp}| = |\bar{y}|$.

In that case we write $S \xrightarrow{d, \bar{a}} S'$.

(egd) Let d be an egd of the form $\varphi(x_1, \ldots, x_n) \to x_i = x_j$. Assume that there is a tuple $\bar{a} = (a_1, \ldots, a_n)$ of elements of $\textsc{Dom}(S)$ such that $\varphi(\bar{a})$ holds in S, and $a_i \neq a_j$. Then:

- if both a_i and a_j are constants, the *result of applying d to S with $\bar{a}$* is "failure", which is denoted by $S \xrightarrow{d, \bar{a}} \texttt{fail}$;
- otherwise, the *result of applying d to S with $\bar{a}$* is the instance S' obtained as follows:

  1. if one of a_i, a_j is a constant and the other is a null, then S' is obtained from S by replacing the null with the constant everywhere;
  2. if both a_i and a_j are nulls, then S' is obtained from S by replacing a_i with a_j everywhere.

In both cases we write $S \xrightarrow{d, \bar{a}} S'$. Note that in the second step we arbitrarily choose whether to replace a_i by a_j or a_j to a_i, but, up to renaming of nulls, this will not affect the result.

With the notion of chase step we can now define a chase sequence.

Definition 5.5 (Chase)   Let Σ be a set of tgds and egds and S an instance.

- A chase *sequence* for S under Σ is a sequence

$$S_i \xrightarrow{d_i, \bar{a}_i} S_{i+1} \quad (i \geq 0)$$

of chase steps such that

(i) $S_0 = S$,
(ii) each d_i is a dependency in Σ, and
(iii) for each distinct $i, j \geq 0$, it is the case that $(d_i, \bar{a}_i) \neq (d_j, \bar{a}_j)$ (that is, $d_i \neq d_j$ or $\bar{a}_i \neq \bar{a}_j$). This technical condition simply ensures that chase sequences consist of different chase steps.

- A *finite* chase sequence for S under Σ is a chase sequence

$$S_i \xrightarrow{d_i, \bar{a}_i} S_{i+1} \quad (0 \leq i < m)$$

for S under Σ. We call S_m its *result*.

- If $S_m = \texttt{fail}$, we refer to this sequence as a *failing* chase sequence.
- If no chase step can be applied to S_m with the dependencies in Σ, we refer to it as a *successful* chase sequence. Technically, this means the following: there is no dependency d in Σ, tuple $\bar{a}$ in S_m and instance S' such that $S_m \xrightarrow{d, \bar{a}} S'$ and $(d, \bar{a}) \neq (d_i, \bar{a}_i)$ for every $0 \leq i \leq m - 1$. □

In principle there could be different results of the chase, as we have to make some arbitrary choices: for example, if an egd equates nulls $\perp$ and $\perp'$, we can either replace $\perp$ by $\perp'$, or $\perp'$ by $\perp$. These choices are rather innocuous, as they produce *isomorphic* instances, i.e., instances that are equal up to a renaming of the nulls. There is, however, a more important choice we make when constructing a chase sequence: that is the order in which the egds and tgds are applied. We show in Chapter 6 that this choice is relevant. In particular, we show in Section 6.3 that the result of the chase is not always unique, i.e., that two different chase sequences may yield different results.

The chase in data exchange

We now explain how chase can be used in data exchange. Let $\mathcal{M}$ be a relational mapping and S a source instance. A *chase sequence for S under $\mathcal{M}$* is defined as a chase sequence for $(S, \emptyset)$ under $\Sigma_{st} \cup \Sigma_t$. Since in data exchange we are interested in materializing a target instance, the result (S, T) of a successful chase sequence for S under $\mathcal{M}$ is usually identified with the target instance T.

The following proposition justifies the application of the chase as a tool for checking for the existence of solutions in data exchange.

Proposition 5.6 *Let $\mathcal{M}$ be a mapping and S a source instance. If there is a successful chase sequence for S under $\mathcal{M}$ with result T, then T is a solution for S. On the other hand, if there exists a failing chase sequence for S under $\mathcal{M}$, then S has no solution.*

Notice that, by definition, any result of a successful chase sequence for S under $\mathcal{M}$ must be an instance of the form T where T is a solution for S. But not only that, the proposition tells us that if there exists a failing chase sequence for S under $\mathcal{M}$, then all of its chase sequences are failing, which further implies that S has no solutions under $\mathcal{M}$. We skip the proof of Proposition 5.6, since in Section 6.2 (Theorem 6.7) we will prove a more general result.

Example 5.7 (Example 4.1 continued)   It is clear that there is a unique successful chase sequence for S under $\mathscr{M}$, and that its result is T shown on page 39. Thus, from Proposition 5.6, T is a solution for S. $\qquad\square$

But the chase as a tool for data exchange has one drawback: nothing can be concluded about the existence of solutions in the case when the chase does not terminate. Thus, we now concentrate on conditions that guarantee chase termination.

5.4 Weak acyclicity of target constraints

As we have seen, the main problem with the application of the chase is nontermination. This happens, for instance, when the set of tgds permits an infinite sequence of null creation during the chase (as in the second case of Example 5.4). So a natural idea is to restrict target constraints to make such an infinite sequence of null creation impossible.

We now do precisely this, and restrict the shape of tgds to prevent such behavior, and obtain a meaningful class of mappings for which the chase is not only guaranteed to terminate, but does it in polynomially many steps.

We first provide some intuition behind the restriction. Recall Example 5.4, in which we had a single target tgd $\theta_1 = G(x,y) \to \exists z \, L(y,z)$. In that example, the tgd was fired to create new tuples in relation L based on tuples in relation G, and once it was done, the chase terminated. However, when we extended the set of constraints with the tgd $\theta_2 = L(x,y) \to \exists z \, G(y,z)$, we entered a cycle: each fact in G created a fact in L, which then created a fact in G, which created a fact in L, and so on.

Thus, we need to avoid cycles. To enforce this syntactically, note that in our example, θ_1 says that L depends on G, and θ_2 says that G depends on L. So, we break cycles of this kind. Formally, we do it as follows.

Assume that Σ is a set of tgds over $\mathbf{R_t}$. We construct the *simple dependency graph* of Σ as follows. The nodes (positions) of the graph are all pairs (R,i), where R is a relation symbol in $\mathbf{R_t}$ of arity n and $1 \le i \le n$. Then we add edges as follows. For every tgd $\forall \bar{x} \forall \bar{y} \, (\varphi(\bar{x}, \bar{y}) \to \exists \bar{z} \, \psi(\bar{x}, \bar{z}))$ in Σ, and for every variable x mentioned in $\bar{x}$ that occurs in the ith position (attribute) of relation R in φ, add an edge from (R,i) to (T,j) if the variable that occurs in the jth position of relation T in ψ is:

- x itself, or
- an existentially quantified variable z (that corresponds to the introduction of a new value).

Definition 5.8 (Acyclicity)   We say that a set Σ of tgds is *acyclic* if its simple dependency graph has no cycles. $\qquad\square$

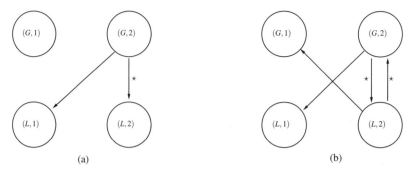

Figure 5.1 Dependency graphs of (a) $\{\theta_1\}$ and (b) $\{\theta_1, \theta_2\}$.

Look at the example in Figure 5.1 (for now, ignore the $\star$ annotation of some of the edges). The graph in the left part of the figure corresponds to θ_1, and it has no cycles; the graph in the right part of the figure corresponds to $\{\theta_1, \theta_2\}$, and it has a cycle. So intuitively, the notion of acyclicity does the job prohibiting nonterminating chase.

We will see that the chase will terminate, and do so in polynomially many steps, if the set of target tgds is acyclic. But in fact we will do more. The notion of acyclicity could be too restrictive sometimes (although it does arise in several examples; for instance we shall see it again when we deal with XML data exchange by means of relational representations).

If we look at the definition of the simple dependency graph, we see that there are two kinds of edges, and only the second kind, to an existentially quantified variable, actually creates a new value in the target instance. So it seems that all we need to do is to forbid cycles involving such value-creating edges, and this will be enough to rule out infinite chase sequences.

We now modify the definition of a graph of a set of tgds. If Σ is a set of tgds over $\mathbf{R_t}$, its *dependency graph* has the same nodes as before, and two kinds of edges: usual ones, and edges with a special label $\star$. For every tgd $\forall \bar{x} \forall \bar{y} (\varphi(\bar{x}, \bar{y}) \to \exists \bar{z}\, \psi(\bar{x}, \bar{z}))$ in Σ, and for every variable x mentioned in $\bar{x}$ that occurs in the ith position of relation R in φ, we add an edge from (R, i) to (T, j) if the variable that occurs in the jth position of relation T in ψ is:

- x itself, or
- an existentially quantified variable z; in this case, the edge from (R, i) to (T, j) that we add is labeled $\star$.

Definition 5.9 (Weak acyclicity)   A set Σ of tgds is *weakly acyclic* if the dependency graph of Σ does not have a cycle going through an edge labeled $\star$. $\square$

Example 5.10 (Example 5.4 continued)   Returning to Figure 5.1, we see that it depicts dependency graphs of $\{\theta_1\}$ (which is weakly acyclic), and $\{\theta_1, \theta_2\}$ (which is not). $\square$

Of course every acyclic set of tgds is weakly acyclic too, as the edges in the dependency graph and the simple dependency graph are the same: the only difference is that in the dependency graph, some edges are annotated with $\star$. Another interesting class of weakly acyclic sets of tgds includes sets of tgds without existential quantification in the right-hand side, i.e., full tgds.

We now prove that the chase always terminates for mappings with a weakly acyclic sets of tgds. Moreover, in this case the chase for S terminates after polynomially many steps.

Theorem 5.11 *Let $\mathcal{M} = (\mathbf{R_s}, \mathbf{R_t}, \Sigma_{st}, \Sigma_t)$ be a fixed relational mapping, such that Σ_t is the union of a set of egds and a weakly acyclic set of tgds. Then there exists a polynomial p such that the length of every chase sequence for a source instance S under $\mathcal{M}$ is bounded by $p(\|S\|)$.*

Proof For the sake of simplicity we prove the theorem in the absence of egds. The addition of egds does not change the argument of the proof in any fundamental way.

First of all, with each node (V, i) in the dependency graph of Σ_t we associate its *rank*, denoted by $\mathrm{rank}(V, i)$, which is the maximum number of special edges in any path in the dependency graph G of Σ_t that ends in (V, i). Since Σ_t is weakly acyclic, the rank of each node in G is finite. Moreover, it is clear that the maximum rank r of a node in G is bounded by the number m of nodes in G itself. Notice that m (and, thus, r) is a constant, since it corresponds to the total number of attributes in the schema $\mathbf{R_t}$ (which is assumed to be fixed).

Let us partition the nodes of G into sets $N_0, N_1, \ldots, N_r$ such that (V, i) belongs to N_j if and only if $\mathrm{rank}(V, i) = j$, for $0 \leq j \leq r$. To prove the theorem, we need the following technical result.

Claim 5.12 *For each $0 \leq j \leq r$, there exists a polynomial p_j such that the following holds. Let T be a target instance and T' be any target instance that is obtained from T by a sequence of chase steps using the tgds in Σ_t. Then the number of distinct elements (i.e., constants and nulls) that occur in T' at positions that are restricted to be in N_j is bounded by $p_j(\|T\|)$.*

First we show how the theorem can be proved from Claim 5.12. It follows easily from the proof of Proposition 5.1 that there is a polynomial p', which depends only on $\mathcal{M}$, such that if T is the result of any chase sequence for S under Σ_{st}, then $\|T\|$ is bounded by $p'(\|S\|)$. Furthermore, it follows from Claim 5.12 that there exists a polynomial p'', which depends only on $\mathcal{M}$, such that the maximum number of elements that occur in the result T' of a chase sequence for T under Σ_t, at a single position, is bounded by $p''(\|T\|)$. Thus, the total number of tuples that can exist in one relation in T' is at most $p''(\|T\|)^m$ (since each relation symbol in $\mathbf{R_t}$ can have arity at most m). Thus, the total number of tuples in T' is bounded by $\|\mathcal{M}\| \cdot p''(\|T\|)^m$. This is polynomial in $\|T\|$, since $\mathcal{M}$ is fixed. Furthermore, each chase step that uses a tgd adds at least one tuple. Thus, the length of any chase sequence c for a source instance S under $\mathcal{M}$ is bounded by $\|\mathcal{M}\| \cdot p''(p'(\|S\|))^m$. This is because c is a sequence of chase steps that are obtained by either applying an std in Σ_{st} to the source instance S, or a tgd in Σ_t to the facts that have already been added to the target. Hence we can take $p(x)$ to be the polynomial $\|\mathscr{M}\| \cdot p''(p'(x))^m$. This completes the proof of Theorem 5.11 assuming Claim 5.12.

To finish the proof of Theorem 5.11 we prove Claim 5.12. We do this by induction on j.

Base case: We consider positions (V,A) in N_0. These are positions for which no incoming path has a special edge. This means that no new values are created in those positions, and, thus, that the number of elements in each $(V,A) \in N_0$ is at most $\|T\|$. Since this is true for each (V,A) in N_0, we can take $p_0(x) = x$.

Inductive case: There are three different ways by which an element may appear in T' at a position in N_j. First, there may be values that were already there in T, of which there are at most $\|T\|$. Second, there may be values that are copied by a chase step from a position in N_i, with $j \neq i$. And third, there may be elements that are generated as new values (i.e., nulls) during a chase step.

We first count the number of distinct elements that can be copied to positions in N_j from positions in N_i with $i \neq j$. This means that there exists a nonspecial edge from a position in N_i to a position in N_j. Notice first that this can only happen if $i < j$. Indeed, assume otherwise. Then there exists a nonspecial edge from a position (V,A) in N_i to a position (U,B) in N_j with $i > j$. But then there is a path in G ending at (U,B) that has i special edges. This contradicts the fact that $\mathrm{rank}(U,B) = j < i$. We can conclude then that the number of distinct elements that can be copied to positions in N_j from positions in N_i, with $i \neq j$, is bounded by the polynomial $q(\|T\|) = \sum_{i=0}^{j-1} p_i(\|T\|)$.

Let us count now the number of new values (i.e., nulls) that can be generated at positions in N_j by the chase steps. This can only be done by using a special edge going from a position in N_i, with $i < j$, to a position in N_j. We know that the number of distinct values that appear at positions belonging to the N_i's such that $i < j$ is bounded by the polynomial $q(\|T\|) = \sum_{i=0}^{j-1} p_i(\|T\|)$. Let (V,A) be a position in N_j, and let e be the maximum number of special edges that enter a node in G (we know that e is a constant, as it only depends on $\mathscr{M}$). Then for every choice of e values in $\bigcup_{i=0}^{j-1} N_i$ (one value for each special edge that can enter a position) and for every dependency in Σ_t there is at most one new value that can be generated at position (V,A). Thus, the maximum number of new values that can be generated during a chase step in (V,A) is at most $\|\mathscr{M}\| \cdot q(\|T\|)^e$. We conclude that the maximum number of distinct values that can be generated at a position in N_j is at most $q'(\|T\|) = \|\mathscr{M}\|^2 \cdot q(\|T\|)^e$, which is polynomial, since $\mathscr{M}$ and e are fixed.

Putting this all together, we can define the polynomial $p_i(x)$ as $x + q(x) + q'(x)$. This finishes the proof of the claim and the theorem. $\qquad \square$

The theorem above shows that the class of mappings with a weakly acyclic set of tgds is well behaved with respect to data exchange. Indeed, as an immediate corollary to Proposition 5.6 (which states that the result of the chase is always a solution) and Theorem 5.11, we obtain that the problem of existence of solutions for mappings with a weakly acyclic set of tgds is tractable. But not only that, we also see that for every source instance that has solution, a particular solution can be materialized in polynomial time.

Corollary 5.13 *Let $\mathcal{M} = (\mathbf{R_s}, \mathbf{R_t}, \Sigma_{st}, \Sigma_t)$ be a relational mapping, such that Σ_t is the union of a set of egds and a weakly acyclic set of tgds. Then* SOLEXISTENCE$_{\mathcal{M}}$ *can be solved in* PTIME. *Furthermore, if a solution for a source instance S exists, a particular solution can be computed in polynomial time.*

Summary

In summary, the following holds for the problem of existence of solutions in relational data exchange.

- For arbitrary relational mappings defined by (st)-tgds and egds the problem is undecidable.

- For the class of relational mappings $\mathcal{M} = (\mathbf{R_s}, \mathbf{R_t}, \Sigma_{st}, \Sigma_t)$ such that Σ_t consists of a set of egds and a weakly acyclic set of tgds, the problem becomes decidable (using the chase), and, indeed, tractable.

- For the latter class of mappings, if a source instance S has a solution, then a particular solution T for S can be computed in polynomial time.

We prove later, in Section 6.3, that the class of mappings with a weakly acyclic set of tgds enjoys further desirable properties. We will see that for each source instance S with at least one solution, a particular *universal* solution for S (that is, a solution for S that is more general than any other) can be efficiently constructed.

5.5 Complexity of the problem

We have seen that one can efficiently (in polynomial time) test whether solutions exist for a given source instance if target constraints use a weakly acyclic set of tgds. But can we do better than this? For instance, is it possible to prove that the problem is not only tractable but, also, that it can be solved in some *parallelizable* class like NLOGSPACE or NC^1? We give a negative answer to this question, at least under widely held complexity-theoretical assumptions. We state, in particular, that this problem can be PTIME-complete, and, thus, it can be considered to be inherently sequential. Moreover, we obtain this lower bound for fairly simple mappings that contain only egds and full (st-)tgds. The proof of the next proposition is left as an exercise (Exercise 9.3).

Proposition 5.14 *There exists a mapping $\mathcal{M} = (\mathbf{R_s}, \mathbf{R_t}, \Sigma_{st}, \Sigma_t)$, such that:*

- *Σ_{st} consists of a set of full st-tgds;*
- *Σ_t consists of a set of full tgds and egds;*

for which the problem SOLEXISTENCE$_{\mathcal{M}}$ *is* PTIME-*complete.*

Combined complexity

Until now, the complexity analysis of the problem of checking for the existence of solutions has been carried out under the assumption that the mapping is fixed. In other words, we looked at the *data complexity* of the problem. However, while data complexity makes sense in a lot of data exchange scenarios, a more refined complexity analysis should consider both source instances and mappings as the input. This corresponds to the combined complexity of the problem, which we study next.

PROBLEM:	SOLEXISTENCE.
INPUT:	A relational mapping $\mathscr{M} = (\mathbf{R_s}, \mathbf{R_t}, \Sigma_{st}, \Sigma_t)$ and a source instance S.
QUESTION:	Does there exist a solution for S under $\mathscr{M}$?

We study this problem for the class of mappings $\mathscr{M} = (\mathbf{R_s}, \mathbf{R_t}, \Sigma_{st}, \Sigma_t)$ such that Σ_t consists of a set of egds and a weakly-acyclic set of tgds. This is because for them, as we know, the existence of solutions problem is decidable (indeed, even if $\mathscr{M}$ is not considered to be fixed).

Let $\mathscr{M} = (\mathbf{R_s}, \mathbf{R_t}, \Sigma_{st}, \Sigma_t)$ be a mapping such that Σ_t consists of a set of edgs and a weakly acyclic set of tgds. A close inspection of the proof of Theorem 5.11 shows that the length of every chase sequence for a source instance S under $\mathscr{M}$ is bounded by $\|S\|^{O(\|\mathscr{M}\|)}$. This provides us with an EXPTIME (exponential time) upper bound for the combined complexity of the problem of existence of solutions. Furthermore, this bound is tight even for restricted classes of mappings.

Theorem 5.15 *The problem* SOLEXISTENCE *is* EXPTIME-*complete, if restricted to the class of mappings* $\mathscr{M} = (\mathbf{R_s}, \mathbf{R_t}, \Sigma_{st}, \Sigma_t)$ *such that* Σ_t *consists of a set of egds and a weakly acyclic set of tgds.*

Moreover, the problem remains EXPTIME-*hard even if restricted to the class of mappings such that* Σ_{st} *consists of a set of full st-tgds and* Σ_t *consists of a set of egds and a set of full tgds.*

Proof We only prove the lower bound, since we already sketched the proof of the upper bound. We provide a reduction from the complement of the problem of checking whether a fact $R(c_1, \dots, c_k)$ belongs to the evaluation of a DATALOG program Π over an instance S, which is known to be EXPTIME-hard. (The reader not familiar with datalog can find the definition of DATALOG in Section 7.4.)

Based on the fact $R(c_1, \dots, c_k)$, the program Π, and the instance S, we construct a mapping $\mathscr{M} = (\mathbf{R_s}, \mathbf{R_t}, \Sigma_{st}, \Sigma_t)$ and a source instance S' as follows:

- $\mathbf{R_s}$ consists of all the extensional and intensional relation symbols $U_1, \dots, U_m$ mentioned in Π, plus a new symbol W of arity $k+1$;
- $\mathbf{R_t}$ is a copy of $\mathbf{R_s}$. That is, $\mathbf{R_t}$ consists of relation symbols $U'_1, \dots, U'_m$ and W', where the arities are the same as in $\mathbf{R_s}$;

- Σ_{st} contains full st-tgds that copy source relations into target relations: $U_i(\bar{x}) \to U_i'(\bar{x})$, for $1 \le i \le m$, and $W(x_1, \ldots, x_k, x_{k+1}) \to W'(x_1, \ldots, x_k, x_{k+1})$;
- Σ_t consists of the following:
  - For each rule $U_{i_{t+1}}(\bar{x}_{t+1}) \leftarrow U_{i_1}(\bar{x}_1), \ldots, U_{i_t}(\bar{x}_t)$ in Π, the full tgd $U_{i_1}'(\bar{x}_1) \wedge \cdots \wedge U_{i_t}'(\bar{x}_t) \to U_{i_{t+1}}'(\bar{x}_{t+1})$; and
  - the egd $R'(x_1, \ldots, x_k) \wedge W'(x_1, \ldots, x_k, x_{k+1}) \to x_1 = x_{k+1}$ (recall that R is one of the intensional predicates);
- the source instance S' is populated with the facts in S plus the fact $W(c_1, \ldots, c_k, d)$, where d is a fresh constant that does not occur elsewhere in S.

Clearly, $\mathscr{M}$ and S' can be constructed in polynomial time from $R(c_1, \ldots, c_k)$, Π and S. Since all tgds are full, we have a weakly acyclic set of tgds. In addition, $R(c_1, \ldots, c_k)$ belongs to the evaluation of Π over S iff S' has no solution. Indeed, assume first that $R(c_1, \ldots, c_k)$ belongs to the evaluation of Π over S. Then chasing S' with $\Sigma_{st} \cup \Sigma_t$ will produce the fact $R'(c_1, \ldots, c_k)$. But then the egd $R'(x_1, \ldots, x_k) \wedge W'(x_1, \ldots, x_k, x_{k+1}) \to x_1 = x_{k+1}$ is triggered with this fact and $W'(c_1, \ldots, c_k, d)$, which implies that the chase fails. Assume, on the other hand, that S' has no solution. Since we have a weakly acyclic set of tgds, this implies that the chase fails. The only way that this can happen is that the egd is triggered with $R'(c_1, \ldots, c_k)$ and $W'(c_1, \ldots, c_k, d)$. But this implies that $R(c_1, \ldots, c_k)$ belongs to the evaluation of Π over S. □

We conclude that there is a *provable* gap between the combined and the data complexity of the problem of checking for the existence of solutions in data exchange, even for mappings whose target dependencies consist of egds and weakly acyclic sets of tgds.

6

Good solutions

As we know by now, solutions in data exchange are not unique; indeed, if a source instance has a solution under a relational mapping $\mathcal{M}$, then it has infinitely many of them. But if many solutions exist, which one should we materialize? To answer this question, we must be able to distinguish *good* solutions from others. As we already mentioned in Section 4.2, good solutions in data exchange are usually identified with the most general solutions (see Example 4.3), which in turn can be characterized as the *universal* solutions. We will see in this chapter that universal solutions admit different equivalent characterizations.

The existence of solutions does not in general imply the existence of universal solutions (in fact, checking whether universal solutions exist is an undecidable problem). However, this negative theoretical result does not pose serious problems in data exchange. Recall from the previous chapter that the class of mappings $\mathcal{M} = (\mathbf{R_s}, \mathbf{R_t}, \Sigma_{st}, \Sigma_t)$, such that Σ_t consists of a set of egds and a weakly acyclic set of tgds, is particularly well-behaved for data exchange. Indeed, for this class the existence of solutions – that is undecidable in general – can be checked in polynomial time, and, in case a solution exists, at least one solution can be efficiently computed. We will see in this chapter that for this class, the existence of solutions implies the existence of universal solutions. Furthermore, when one exists, it can be efficiently computed. The reason behind these good properties is that the result of a successful chase sequence for a source instance with Σ_{st} and Σ_t is always a universal solution. Hence, the class of mappings that behaves well with respect to checking for the existence of solutions also behaves well if one wants to materialize solutions with good properties.

We will see in Chapter 7 that universal solutions are also crucial for the task of query answering in data exchange. In particular, all the positive properties of universal solutions we show in this chapter will be later used to obtain efficient query evaluation algorithms for relevant fragments of the relational algebra in a data exchange scenario.

6.1 Universal solutions

How do we formally define the notion that a solution is as general as any other solution? To do so, recall that a solution T is in general an instance with nulls. Such an instance represents complete instances T' (without nulls) such that there is a homomorphism $h : T \to T'$. The set of such instances is denoted by $Rep(T)$ (see Section 2.3).

There appear to be three different ways to state that a solution T is more general than other solutions, explained below.

1. Solutions that describe all others: A most general solution T must describe the set of all other complete solutions, i.e., every complete solution must be represented by T:

UnivSol$_1$(T): $\qquad \{T' \in \text{SOL}_{\mathcal{M}}(S) \mid T' \text{ is over CONST}\} \subseteq Rep(T).$

2. Solutions that are as general as others: A seemingly slightly weaker condition says that if a solution T is universal, it cannot describe fewer complete instances than another solution, i.e.

UnivSol$_2$(T): $\qquad Rep(T') \subseteq Rep(T) \text{ for every } T' \in \text{SOL}_{\mathcal{M}}(S).$

3. Solutions that map homomorphically into others: This more technical, and yet very convenient definition, is inspired by the algebraic notion of a universal object, that has a homomorphism into every object in a class. Recall that a homomorphism $h : T \to T'$ is a mapping from the domain of T into the domain of T', that is the identity on constants, and such that $\bar{t} = (t_1, \dots, t_n) \in W^T$ implies $h(\bar{t}) = (h(t_1), \dots, h(t_n))$ is in $W^{T'}$ for all W in $\mathbf{R_t}$. Our third condition then is:

UnivSol$_3$(T): $\qquad$ there is a homomorphism $h : T \to T'$ for each $T' \in \text{SOL}_{\mathcal{M}}(S).$

So, which definition should we adopt? It turns out that we can take any one, as they are equivalent.

Proposition 6.1 *If $\mathcal{M} = (\mathbf{R_s}, \mathbf{R_t}, \Sigma_{st}, \Sigma_t)$ is a mapping, and T is a solution for some source instance S, then conditions* **UnivSol$_1$(T)**, **UnivSol$_2$(T)** *and* **UnivSol$_3$(T)** *are equivalent.*

Proof We first observe the following. Let $T' \in \text{SOL}_{\mathcal{M}}(S)$, and let $\perp_1, \dots, \perp_n$ enumerate the nulls in $\text{DOM}(T')$. Then clearly any instance T'_c that can be obtained from T' by replacing each $\perp_i$ with a distinct constant c_i $(1 \le i \le n)$, such that c_i does not appear in T', belongs to $Rep(T')$. We prove below that it also belongs to $\text{SOL}_{\mathcal{M}}(S)$.

Assume otherwise; that is, $T'_c \notin \text{SOL}_{\mathcal{M}}(S)$. Then $T'_c \not\models \Sigma_t$. Suppose first that T'_c violates a tgd of the form $\varphi(\bar{x}) \to \exists \bar{y} \psi(\bar{x}, \bar{y})$ in Σ_t. That is, assume that there exists a tuple $\bar{a}$ of elements in $\text{DOM}(T'_c)$ such that $|\bar{x}| = |\bar{a}|$, $T'_c \models \varphi(\bar{a})$, but $T'_c \not\models \exists \bar{y} \psi(\bar{a}, \bar{y})$. Let $\bar{a}'$ be the tuple of elements in $\text{DOM}(T')$ that is obtained from $\bar{a}$ by replacing each occurrence of c_i with $\perp_i$, for $i \le n$. Then it is not hard to see that $T' \models \varphi(\bar{a}')$ and $T' \not\models \exists \bar{y} \psi(\bar{a}', \bar{y})$. This is because both $\varphi(\bar{x})$ and $\exists \bar{y} \psi(\bar{x}, \bar{y})$ are conjunctive queries, which are closed under homomorphisms, and there is a one-to-one homomorphism from T' into T'_c that sends each $\perp_i$ to a distinct constant c_i $(1 \le i \le n)$ that does not occur in T' or in Σ_t. But this contradicts the fact that $T' \in \text{SOL}_{\mathcal{M}}(S)$. The case when T'_c violates an egd in Σ_t is completely analogous. With this observation, we can now easily prove the proposition.

UnivSol$_1$ $(T) \Rightarrow$ **UnivSol$_2$**(T). Assume T' is an arbitrary solution. Let $\bot_1, \ldots, \bot_m$ enumerate the nulls in $\text{DOM}(T')$, and let T'_c be as defined above. Since $T'_c \in \text{SOL}_{\mathcal{M}}(S)$ and does not contain nulls, it must be the case by **UnivSol$_1$**(T) that $T'_c \in Rep(T)$. Take a homomorphism h witnessing $T'_c \in Rep(T)$ and change it into a mapping h' from $\text{DOM}(T)$ into $\text{DOM}(T')$ by setting $h'(\bot) = \bot_i$ whenever $h(\bot) = c_i$, and otherwise letting h' coincide with h. Then clearly h' is a homomorphism from T to T'.

Take an arbitrary $T'' \in Rep(T')$, and let h'' be a homomorphism from T' in T''. Then $h'' \circ h'$ is a homomorphism from T into T'', and, thus, $T'' \in Rep(T)$.

UnivSol$_2$ $(T) \Rightarrow$ **UnivSol$_3$**(T). Assume $T' \in \text{SOL}_{\mathcal{M}}(S)$. Let $\bot_1, \ldots, \bot_m$ enumerate the nulls in $\text{DOM}(T')$, and let T'_c be as defined above. Then $T'_c \in Rep(T')$ and hence, by **UnivSol$_2$**(T), $T'_c \in Rep(T)$. Take a homomorphism h witnessing $T'_c \in Rep(T)$ and change it into a mapping h' from $\text{DOM}(T)$ into $\text{DOM}(T')$ by setting $h'(\bot) = \bot_i$ whenever $h(\bot) = c_i$, and otherwise letting h' coincide with h. Then clearly h' is a homomorphism from T to T'.

UnivSol$_3$ $(T) \Rightarrow$ **UnivSol$_1$**(T). Let T' be an arbitrary instance in $\text{SOL}_{\mathcal{M}}(S)$ that does not contain nulls. Then, by **UnivSol$_3$**(T), there is a homomorphism h from T into T'. But this immediately implies that $T' \in Rep(T)$. This completes the proof of the proposition. $\square$

Proposition 6.1 justifies the following definition.

Definition 6.2 (Universal solutions)   Given a mapping $\mathcal{M}$, a solution T for S under $\mathcal{M}$ is a *universal* solution if one of **UnivSol$_i$**(T), for $i = 1, 2, 3$, is satisfied (and hence all are satisfied). $\square$

Most commonly in the proofs one uses the condition that for every solution T' for S, there exists a homomorphism $h : T \to T'$.

Example 6.3 (Example 4.3 continued)   Neither solution T' nor T'' in Example 4.3 is universal. In fact, there is no homomorphism $h : T' \to T$; otherwise

$$h((\bot_1, 2320, \bot_1, AirFrance)) = (\bot_1, 2320, \bot_2, AirFrance),$$

and, thus, $h(\bot_1) = \bot_1$ and $h(\bot_1) = \bot_2$, which is impossible. Moreover, there is no homomorphism $h : T'' \to T$; otherwise

$$h((AF406, 2320, 920, AirFrance)) = (\bot_1, 2320, \bot_2, AirFrance),$$

and, thus, $h(AF406) = \bot_1$ and $h(920) = \bot_2$, which is impossible too, because a homomorphism must be the identity on constants. On the other hand, it can be seen that T is a universal solution. $\square$

As we will see in the following sections, universal solutions have several good properties that make them the preferred data exchange solutions. Unfortunately, universal solutions are not a general phenomenon. Indeed, we show in the next section that there is a mapping

$\mathcal{M}$ and a source instance S, such that S has at least one solution under $\mathcal{M}$ but has no universal solutions. This immediately turns our attention to the problem of the existence of universal solutions. We prove in the next section that for arbitrary relational mappings this problem is undecidable. After that we return to the good class of mappings, and show that universal solutions behave well for them.

6.2 Existence of universal solutions

The fact that there are source instances that have solutions but not universal solutions was already implicit in Example 5.4.

Example 6.4 (Example 5.4 continued)   Consider again the mapping in which Σ_{st} consists of the st-tgd $E(x,y) \to G(x,y)$ and $\Sigma_t = \{\theta_1, \theta_2\}$, where:

$$\theta_1 := G(x,y) \to \exists z L(y,z),$$
$$\theta_2 := L(x,y) \to \exists z G(y,z).$$

Let $S = \{E(a,b)\}$ be a source instance. Then clearly $T = \{G(a,b), L(b,a)\}$ is a solution for S. We prove next that S does not have universal solutions.

Assume for the sake of contradiction that there is a universal solution T for S. Then, due to the presence of θ_1 and θ_2, there must be an infinite sequence of the form

$$G(a,b), L(b,v_1), G(v_1,v_2), L(v_2,v_3), G(v_3,v_4), \dots$$

of facts in T. But since T is finite and satisfies θ_1 and θ_2, it must be the case that:

- $v_{2i-1} = a$ or $v_{2i} = b$, for some $i \geq 1$, or
- $v_{2i} = v_{2j}$, for some $1 \leq i < j$, or
- $v_{2i-1} = v_{2j-1}$, for some $1 \leq i < j$.

We show that each of these cases leads to a contradiction.

Assume first that $v_{2i-1} = a$, for some $i \geq 1$. Consider the instance

$$T' := \{G(a,b), L(b,c_1), G(c_1,c_2), L(c_2,c_3), G(c_3,c_4), \dots,$$

$$L(c_{j-1},c_j), G(c_j,c_{j-1})\},$$

where all the c_ℓ's are distinct constants not appearing in T and $2i < j$. Clearly $T' \in \text{SOL}_{\mathcal{M}}(S)$, and since T is universal there is a homomorphism h from T into T'. But then it is easy to see that $h(v_\ell) = c_\ell$ for each $1 \leq \ell \leq 2j$, which implies that $h(v_{2i-1}) = c_{2i-1}$. However, this is a contradiction since $h(v_{2i-1}) = h(a) = a$ and $c_{2i-1} \neq a$. The remaining cases, that is, when either $v_{2i} = b$, for some $i \geq 1$, or $v_{2i} = v_{2j}$ or $v_{2i-1} = v_{2j-1}$, for some $1 \leq i < j$, are similar and are left as an exercise to the reader. $\qquad\square$

The previous example immediately raises the question of whether the existence of universal solutions problem, as defined below, is a decidable problem.

PROBLEM:	UNISOLEXISTENCE$_{\mathscr{M}}$.
INPUT:	A source instance S.
QUESTION:	Is there a universal solution for S under $\mathscr{M}$?

Like the existence of solutions, this problem is undecidable for arbitrary relational mappings.

Theorem 6.5 *There exists a relational mapping $\mathscr{M} = (\mathbf{R_s}, \mathbf{R_t}, \Sigma_{st}, \Sigma_t)$, such that the problem* UNISOLEXISTENCE$_{\mathscr{M}}$ *is undecidable.*

Note that Theorem 6.5 does *not* follow from (the proof of) Theorem 5.3, that is, from the undecidability of the problem of existence of solutions. Indeed, it is easy to see that for the mapping $\mathscr{M}$ used in that proof, the existence of solutions does not necessarily coincide with the existence of universal solutions. Nor does Theorem 5.3 follow from the proof of Theorem 6.5. This is because for the mapping $\mathscr{M}$ that we construct in the proof below, the problem of existence of solutions is trivial, as every source instance has a solution.

Proof of Theorem 6.5 This time we provide a generic reduction from the halting problem for single-tape deterministic Turing machines that never move their head to the left of the initial position. In particular, this means that we can assume without loss of generality that the tape is infinite only to the right. Clearly, the halting problem for this class of Turing machines is undecidable. We construct a mapping $\mathscr{M}$ such that source instances encode Turing machines and universal solutions encode halting computations of Turing machines on the empty input.

Let $\mathscr{A} = (Q, A, \delta, q_0, F)$ be a single-tape deterministic Turing machine that never moves its head to the left of the initial position, where:

- Q is a finite set of states,
- A is the tape alphabet that contains a distinguished blank symbol that we denote by #,
- $\delta : (Q \setminus F) \times A \to Q \times A \times \{\text{left}, \text{right}\}$ is the (total) transition function,
- $q_0 \in Q$ is the initial state,
- and $F \subseteq Q$ is the set of final states.

Notice that we assume without loss of generality that final states are terminal, i.e. when the machine enters an accepting state it halts, and that those are the only halting states. We encode $\mathscr{A}$ as an instance $S(\mathscr{A})$ over the source schema $\mathbf{R_s} = \{\Delta, \text{Init}, \text{Zero}, \text{One}, \text{Blank}, \text{Left}, \text{Right}\}$, where Δ is a 5-ary relation symbol and the rest of the symbols in $\mathbf{R_s}$ are unary. We define $S(\mathscr{A})$ as follows:

- $\Delta^{S(\mathscr{A})}$ consists of all the tuples (q, a, q', a', d) $(q, q' \in Q, a, a' \in A, d \in \{\text{left}, \text{right}\})$ such that $\delta(q, a) = (q', a', d)$; that is, $\Delta^{S(\mathscr{A})}$ encodes the transition graph of δ.
- $\text{Init}^{S(\mathscr{A})}$ contains only the initial state q_0.
- $\text{Zero}^{S(\mathscr{A})}$ contains only the constant 0, $\text{One}^{S(\mathscr{A})}$ contains only the constant 1, $\text{Blank}^{S(\mathscr{A})}$ contains only the symbol #, $\text{Left}^{S(\mathscr{A})}$ contains only the direction left, and, finally, $\text{Right}^{S(\mathscr{A})}$ contains only the direction right.

We now define a target schema $\mathbf{R_t}$ such that instances of $\mathbf{R_t}$ describe finite computations of Turing machines. But first we need to introduce some terminology.

A *computation* of $\mathscr{A}$ is a sequence $(c_0, c_1, \ldots, c_n)$ of *configurations*, $n \geq 1$, such that:

1. c_0 is the *initial* configuration, and
2. for each $i < n$, c_{i+1} is the *successor* configuration of c_i.

The computation is *halting* if c_n is a halting configuration. As will become clear after we define configurations, $\mathscr{A}$ halts on the empty input if and only if there is a halting computation of $\mathscr{A}$.

Each configuration c_j, for $0 \leq j \leq n$, can be represented as a tuple $(q_j, i_j, \bar{a}_j) \in Q \times \mathbb{N} \times A^{j+2}$, where:

- q_j represents the state of $\mathscr{A}$ in c_j,
- i_j represents the position of the head of $\mathscr{A}$ in c_j (which can be assumed to be a nonnegative integer since the head never moves to the left of the initial position), and
- $\bar{a}_j$ is the tuple $(a_{j,0}, \ldots, a_{j,j+1})$, where $a_{j,\ell}$ represents the symbol that appears in position ℓ, for $0 \leq \ell \leq j+1$, in c_j. Since $\mathscr{A}$ can visit at most j positions in j steps, we can assume that all the remaining positions contain the blank symbol #.

The initial configuration is $(q_0, 0, (\#, \#))$. The configuration $c_{j+1} = (q_{j+1}, i_{j+1}, \bar{a}_{j+1})$ is the successor of the configuration $c_j = (q_j, i_j, \bar{a}_j)$ if the following holds (assuming $\bar{a}_j = (a_{j,0}, \ldots, a_{j,j+1})$):

- $\delta(q_j, a_{j,i_j}) = (q_{j+1}, a', d)$,
- $\bar{a}_{j+1} = (a_{j,0}, \ldots, a_{j,i_j-1}, a', a_{j,i_j+1}, \ldots, a_{j,j+1}, \#)$, and
- if $d = \text{right}$, then $i_{j+1} = i_j + 1$, otherwise $i_{j+1} = i_j - 1$.

A configuration is halting if it is of the form $(q, i, \bar{a})$ for some $q \in F$. Thus, a halting configuration has no successor configuration.

Let $\bar{c} = (c_0, c_1, \ldots, c_n)$ be a computation of $\mathscr{A}$. Assume that $c_j = (q_j, i_j, \bar{a}_j = (a_{j,0}, \ldots, a_{j,j+1}))$ for each $0 \leq j \leq n$. We represent $\bar{c}$ as a target instance $T(\mathscr{A}, \bar{c})$ over a schema $\mathbf{R_t}$ that contains the binary relation symbol Steps and the ternary relation symbols Positions, Config and Symbols. The instance $T(\mathscr{A}, \bar{c})$ is defined as follows:

- The domain $\text{DOM}(T(\mathscr{A}, \bar{c}))$ of $T(\mathscr{A}, \bar{c})$ consists of elements $u_0, v_0, u_1, v_1, \ldots, u_n, v_n, v_{n+1}$, where (i) u_0 and v_0 are set to be the constant 0 and v_1 is set to be the constant 1, and (ii) $u_1, u_2, v_2, \ldots, u_n, v_n, v_{n+1}$ are distinct elements in VAR. Intuitively, $u_0, \ldots, u_n$ encode the configuration steps and $v_0, \ldots, v_{n+1}$ encode the tape positions.
- The interpretation of Steps is the successor relation in the set of configuration steps; namely, $\text{Steps}^{T(\mathscr{A}, \bar{c})} = \{(u_j, u_{j+1}) \mid 0 \leq j \leq n-1\}$.
- The interpretation of Positions is the successor relation on the set of positions for each configuration; namely, $\text{Positions}^{T(\mathscr{A}, \bar{c})} = \{(u_j, v_\ell, v_{\ell+1}) \mid 0 \leq j \leq n, 0 \leq \ell \leq j\}$.

- The interpretation of Config contains the information about the state and the position of the head in each configuration; namely, $\text{Config}^{T(\mathscr{A},\bar{c})} = \{(u_j, q_j, v_{i_j}) \mid 0 \leq j \leq n\}$.
- Finally, the interpretation of Symbols contains the information about the symbol present at each position that is relevant for a configuration; namely, $\text{Symbols}^{T(\mathscr{A},\bar{c})} = \{(u_j, a_{j,\ell}, v_\ell) \mid 0 \leq j \leq n, 0 \leq \ell \leq j+1\}$.

Our goal is to construct a set $\Sigma_{st} \cup \Sigma_t$ of (st)-tgds that check whether $\bar{c}$ is a halting computation of $\mathscr{A}$. However, in order to be able to do that we need to enhance the target instance $T(\mathscr{A}, \bar{c})$ with new relations. We extend $\mathbf{R_t}$ with new relation symbols Left, Right, Blank, $\hat{\Delta}$, LeftCopy, RightCopy and End – such that Left, Right, Blank are unary, $\hat{\Delta}$ is 5-ary, LeftCopy and RightCopy are ternary, and End is binary – and interpret them as follows:

- $\hat{\text{Left}}^{T(\mathscr{A},\bar{c})}$, $\hat{\text{Right}}^{T(\mathscr{A},\bar{c})}$ and $\hat{\text{Blank}}^{T(\mathscr{A},\bar{c})}$ are simply copies of $\text{Left}^{S(\mathscr{A})}$, $\text{Right}^{S(\mathscr{A})}$ and $\text{Blank}^{S(\mathscr{A})}$, respectively. That is, $\hat{\text{Left}}^{T(\mathscr{A},\bar{c})}$ contains only the direction left, $\hat{\text{Right}}^{T(\mathscr{A},\bar{c})}$ contains only the direction right, and, finally, $\hat{\text{Blank}}^{T(\mathscr{A},\bar{c})}$ contains only the symbol #.
- $\hat{\Delta}^{T(\mathscr{A},\bar{c})}$ is simply a copy of $\Delta^{S(\mathscr{A})}$, that is, $\hat{\Delta}^{T(\mathscr{A},\bar{c})}$ encodes the transition graph of δ.
- $\text{LeftCopy}^{T(\mathscr{A},\bar{c})}$ is defined as $\{(u_{j+1}, u_j, v_\ell) \mid 0 \leq j \leq n-1, 0 \leq \ell \leq i_j\}$, and will be used to verify that configurations c_j and c_{j+1} coincide in all positions that are strictly to the left of position i_j.
- $\text{RightCopy}^{T(\mathscr{A},\bar{c})}$ is defined as $\{(u_{j+1}, u_j, v_\ell) \mid 0 \leq j \leq n-1, i_j \leq \ell \leq j+1\}$, and will be used to verify that configurations c_j and c_{j+1} coincide in all positions that are strictly to the right of position i_j.
- $\text{End}^{T(\mathscr{A},\bar{c})}$ is defined as $\{(u_j, v_{j+1}) \mid 0 \leq j \leq n\}$, and marks the last position that is relevant for a configuration.

We are now ready to define $\Sigma_{st} \cup \Sigma_t$. First of all, Σ_{st} contains the full st-tgds:

$$\text{Left}(x) \rightarrow \hat{\text{Left}}(x)$$
$$\text{Right}(x) \rightarrow \hat{\text{Right}}(x)$$
$$\text{Blank}(x) \rightarrow \hat{\text{Blank}}(x)$$
$$\Delta(q, a, q', a', d) \rightarrow \hat{\Delta}(q, a, q', a', d),$$

that simply "copy" tuples in Left, Right, Blank and Δ into $\hat{\text{Left}}$, $\hat{\text{Right}}$, $\hat{\text{Blank}}$ and $\hat{\Delta}$, respectively. Second, Σ_{st} contains the full st-tgd:

$$\text{Init}(x) \wedge \text{Zero}(y) \wedge \text{One}(z) \wedge \text{Blank}(w) \rightarrow$$
$$\text{Config}(y, x, y) \wedge \text{Symbols}(y, y, w) \wedge$$
$$\text{Symbols}(y, z, w) \wedge \text{Positions}(y, y, z) \wedge \text{End}(y, z).$$

Notice that this st-tgd implies that any solution for $S(\mathscr{A})$ must contain the tuples $\text{Config}(0, q_0, 0)$, $\text{Symbols}(0, \#, 0)$, $\text{Symbols}(0, \#, 1)$, $\text{Positions}(0, 0, 1)$ and $\text{End}(0, 1)$, which encode the initial configuration of $\mathscr{A}$.

In order to simulate transitions of $\mathscr{A}$ we need to include two tgds in Σ_t. These are defined as:

$$\varphi_{\text{left}}(t,q,q',a,a',p,p') \rightarrow \exists t' \psi(t,t',q',a,a',p,p')$$
$$\varphi_{\text{right}}(t,q,q',a,a',p,p') \rightarrow \exists t' \psi(t,t',q',a,a',p,p'),$$

where the formula φ_{left} is defined as:

$$\mathsf{Config}(t,q,p) \wedge \mathsf{Symbols}(t,a,p) \wedge \mathsf{Positions}(t,p',p) \wedge \hat{\Delta}(q,a,q',a',d) \wedge \hat{\mathsf{Left}}(d),$$

the formula φ_{right} is defined as:

$$\mathsf{Config}(t,q,p) \wedge \mathsf{Symbols}(t,a,p) \wedge \mathsf{Positions}(t,p,p') \wedge \hat{\Delta}(q,a,q',a',d) \wedge \hat{\mathsf{Right}}(d),$$

and the formula ψ is defined as:

$$\mathsf{Steps}(t,t') \wedge \mathsf{Config}(t',q',p') \wedge \mathsf{Symbols}(t',a',p) \wedge$$
$$\mathsf{LeftCopy}(t',t,p) \wedge \mathsf{RightCopy}(t',t,p).$$

Intuitively, φ_{left} (resp. φ_{right}) states that a transition from the configuration c_t in step t to its successor configuration $c_{t'}$ in step t' is possible by moving the head of the Turing machine to the left (resp. right). On the other hand, ψ populates the initial part of configuration $c_{t'}$ and establishes the link between the configurations c_t and $c_{t'}$.

Afterwards, we need to extend Σ_t with two new tgds that check that if c_t and $c_{t'}$ are successor configurations then they coincide in all unmodified positions:

1. $\mathsf{LeftCopy}(t',t,p) \wedge \mathsf{Positions}(t,p',p) \wedge \mathsf{Symbols}(t,a,p') \rightarrow$
   $\mathsf{LeftCopy}(t',t,p') \wedge \mathsf{Positions}(t',p',p) \wedge \mathsf{Symbols}(t',a,p').$
2. $\mathsf{RightCopy}(t',t,p) \wedge \mathsf{Positions}(t,p,p') \wedge \mathsf{Symbols}(t,a,p') \rightarrow$
   $\mathsf{RightCopy}(t',t,p') \wedge \mathsf{Positions}(t',p,p') \wedge \mathsf{Symbols}(t',a,p').$

Notice that these tgds also check that the positions from c_t occur in the same order in $c_{t'}$.

Finally, we extend Σ_t with the tgd:

$$\mathsf{Steps}(t,t') \wedge \mathsf{End}(t,p) \wedge \hat{\mathsf{Blank}}(x) \rightarrow$$
$$\exists p' \big(\mathsf{Positions}(t',p,p') \wedge \mathsf{Symbols}(t',x,p') \wedge \mathsf{End}(t',p') \big).$$

This tgd extends $c_{t'}$ with a new position at the right-end of the tape, puts the blank symbol in it, and declares it to be the last relevant position for $c_{t'}$.

Let $\mathscr{M} = (\mathbf{R_s}, \mathbf{R_t}, \Sigma_{st}, \Sigma_t)$, where $\mathbf{R_s}$, $\mathbf{R_t}$, Σ_{st} and Σ_t are as defined above. We show that $\mathscr{A}$ halts on the empty input if and only if $S(\mathscr{A})$ has a universal solution under $\mathscr{M}$. In order to prove this, we use the following claim that directly relates source instance $S(\mathscr{A})$ with target instance $T(\mathscr{A},\bar{c})$, assuming that $\bar{c}$ is a computation of $\mathscr{A}$.

Claim 6.6 *For every computation $\bar{c} = (c_0, \ldots, c_n)$ of $\mathscr{A}$ it is the case that $T(\mathscr{A},\bar{c})$ is the result of some finite chase sequence for $S(\mathscr{A})$ under $\mathscr{M}$.*

Claim 6.6 can be easily proved by induction on n, and is left as an exercise for the reader. Using Claim 6.6 and Theorem 6.7 in Section 6.3 (showing that the result of a successful chase sequence for a source instance is always a universal solution) we conclude that if $\mathscr{A}$ halts on the empty input then $S(\mathscr{A})$ has a universal solution under $\mathscr{M}$. Indeed, let $\bar{c}$ be a halting computation of $\mathscr{A}$. Then Claim 6.6 implies that $T(\mathscr{A},\bar{c})$ is the result of a finite chase sequence for $S(\mathscr{A})$ under $\mathscr{M}$. By inspecting the tgds in Σ_t, it is easy to see that $T(\mathscr{A},\bar{c})$ violates none of them, and hence this chase sequence is successful. Using Theorem 6.7 we conclude that $T(\mathscr{A},\bar{c})$ is a universal solution for $S(\mathscr{A})$ under $\mathscr{M}$.

We now prove the opposite direction; that is, if $S(\mathscr{A})$ has a universal solution under $\mathscr{M}$, then $\mathscr{A}$ halts on the empty input. Assume, for the sake of contradiction, that T is a universal solution for $S(\mathscr{A})$ under $\mathscr{M}$, but $\mathscr{A}$ does not halt on the empty input. Let n be the largest integer such that there are pairwise distinct values $u'_0, u'_1, \ldots, u'_n$ that satisfy the following: $u'_0 = 0$ and $(u'_i, u'_{i+1}) \in \mathsf{Steps}^T$, for each $0 \le i \le n-1$. Since $\mathscr{A}$ does not halt on the empty input there is a computation $\bar{c} = (c_0, c_1, \ldots, c_n)$ of $\mathscr{A}$ such that c_n is not final. From Claim 6.6, there is a finite chase sequence for $S(\mathscr{A})$ under $\mathscr{M}$ with result $T(\mathscr{A},\bar{c})$.

It can be proved (by repeatedly applying Lemma 6.8 in Section 6.3) that there is a homomorphism $h : T(\mathscr{A},\bar{c}) \to T$. Recall that $\mathsf{Steps}^{T(\mathscr{A},\bar{c})} = \{(u_j, u_{j+1}) \mid 0 \le j \le n\}$. But then it must be the case that $(h(u_j), h(u_{j+1})) \in \mathsf{Steps}^T$, for each $0 \le j \le n$. Notice that by the choice of n, it must be the case that $h(u_k) = h(u_\ell)$, for some $0 \le k < \ell \le n+1$.

We now extend $T(\mathscr{A},\bar{c})$ to a target instance T' by adding the following tuples:

- (u_{n+1}, u_{n+1}) to Steps.
- $(u_{n+1}, v_p, v_{p'})$ to Positions, for each $0 \le p, p' \le n+2$.
- (u_{n+1}, q, v_p) to Config, for each $0 \le p \le n+2$ and $q \in Q$.
- (u_{n+1}, a, v_p) to Symbols, for each $0 \le p \le n+2$ and $a \in A$.
- (u_{n+1}, v_p, v_p) to LeftCopy and RightCopy, for each $0 \le p \le n+2$.
- (u_{n+1}, v_p) to End, for each $0 \le p \le n+2$.

It is not hard to see, by inspecting the tgds in Σ_t, that T' violates none of them, and hence T' is a solution for $S(\mathscr{A})$ under $\mathscr{M}$. Since T is a universal solution for $S(\mathscr{A})$ under $\mathscr{M}$, there is a homomorphism $h' : T \to T'$.

We next prove the following property: $h'(h(u_j)) = u_j$ for each $0 \le j \le n+1$. The proof is by induction on j. For $j = 0$ this is trivial, since u_0 is the constant 0 and homomorphisms preserve constants. Assuming the statement holds for $0, \ldots, j$, we prove it for $j+1$. Since $h : T(\mathscr{A},\bar{c}) \to T$ is a homomorphism and $(u_j, u_{j+1}) \in \mathsf{Steps}^{T(\mathscr{A},\bar{c})}$, we have $(h(u_j), h(u_{j+1})) \in \mathsf{Steps}^T$. Since $h' : T \to T'$ is also a homomorphism, we get $(h'(h(u_j)), h'(h(u_{j+1}))) \in \mathsf{Steps}^{T'}$. By the induction hypothesis, we know $h'(h(u_j)) = u_j$. Furthermore, the only tuple of the form $(u_j, \cdot)$ in $\mathsf{Steps}^{T'}$ is (u_j, u_{j+1}). This implies that $h'(h(u_{j+1})) = u_{j+1}$, which finishes the inductive proof.

Recall that $u_0, u_1, \ldots, u_{n+1}$ are pairwise distinct elements. Thus, since $h'(h(u_j)) = u_j$, for each $0 \le j \le n+1$, it must be the case that $h(u_0), h(u_1), \ldots, h(u_{n+1})$ are also pairwise distinct elements. But this is a contradiction since we stated above that for some $1 \le k <$

$\ell \leq n+1$ it must be the case that $h(u_k) = h(u_\ell)$. We conclude that T is not a universal solution for $S(\mathscr{A})$ under $\mathscr{M}$, which also finishes the proof of the theorem. $\qquad\square$

Do we have to interpret the previous undecidability result as a serious drawback? Not really. Indeed, as we proved in Theorem 5.3, even the conceptually more basic problem of the existence of arbitrary solutions in data exchange is undecidable. Recall that in order to recover decidability in that case, we had to further restrict the class of mappings to those with a weakly acyclic set of tgds.

Thus, what the results in this section really suggest is that it is necessary to impose extra conditions on mappings if one wants to ensure that the following two conditions are satisfied:

(C1) The existence of solutions implies the existence of universal solutions.

(C2) The problem of checking for the existence of universal solutions is not only decidable, but also tractable.

Furthermore, since we are interested in materializing a good solution for a source instance, we should also add the following desirable requirement:

(C3) If solutions exist for a source instance S, one must be able to construct some universal solution in polynomial time.

We study these requirements in the next section. In particular, we show that the mappings with a weakly acyclic set of tgds also behave well with respect to universal solutions, as they satisfy the three good properties described above. (Notice, in particular, that the mappings used in Example 6.4 and in the proof of Theorem 6.5 are not weakly acyclic.) But before doing so, we show the strong connection between the chase and the class of universal solutions.

6.3 Canonical universal solution and chase

We first prove an important result that relates the notion of the chase to the class of universal solutions. It states that the result of a successful chase sequence, if it exists, is not only a solution but also a universal solution. Moreover, if the chase fails for a source instance S, then no solutions for S exist.

Theorem 6.7 *Let $\mathscr{M} = (\mathbf{R_s}, \mathbf{R_t}, \Sigma_{st}, \Sigma_t)$ be a mapping and S a source instance. If there is a successful chase sequence for S under $\mathscr{M}$ with result T, then T is a universal solution for S. On the other hand, if there exists a failing chase sequence for S under $\mathscr{M}$, then S has no solution.*

Proof In order to prove the theorem we need the following technical, but rather intuitive lemma. The proof is left as an exercise.

Lemma 6.8 *Let $S_1 \xrightarrow{d,\bar{a}} S_2$ be a chase step, where $S_2 \neq \mathtt{fail}$. Assume that S_3 is an instance* *that satisfies the dependency d and such that there is a homomorphism from S_1 into S_3. Then there exists a homomorphism from S_2 into S_3.*

We now prove the theorem. Assume first that (S,T) is the result of a successful chase sequence for S under $\mathscr{M}$. Then T is a solution for S. We show next that it is also a universal solution. Let T' be an arbitrary solution for S. Thus, (S,T') satisfies every dependency in $\Sigma_{st} \cup \Sigma_t$. Furthermore, the identity mapping is a homomorphism from $(S,\emptyset)$ into (S,T'). Applying Lemma 6.8 at each step of the chase sequence with result (S,T), we conclude that there exists a homomorphism $h : (S,T) \to (S,T')$. In fact, h is also a homomorphism from T into T'.

Next, assume that there is a failing chase sequence for S under $\mathscr{M}$, and that the last chase step in that sequence is $(S,T) \xrightarrow{d,\bar{a}} \texttt{fail}$. Thus, d is an egd of the form $\varphi(x_1,\ldots,x_m) \to x_i = x_j$, the formula $\varphi(\bar{a})$ holds in (S,T) for some tuple $\bar{a} = (a_1,\ldots,a_m)$, and a_i and a_j are distinct constants. Suppose that S has a solution T'. As above, using Lemma 6.8, we see that there is a homomorphism h from T to T'. Thus, $\varphi(h(\bar{a}))$ holds in T' (since conjunctive queries are preserved under homomorphisms), but $h(a_i) = a_i$ and $h(a_j) = a_j$ are distinct constants. This contradicts the fact that T' satisfies d. □

The result of a successful chase sequence for a source instance S is usually called a *canonical* universal solution for S. As the following example shows, canonical universal solutions are not unique up to isomorphism, since the order in which tgds and egds are applied in a chase sequence may yield different results.

Example 6.9   Let $\mathscr{M} = (\mathbf{R_s}, \mathbf{R_t}, \Sigma_{st}, \Sigma_t)$ be a mapping, such that $\mathbf{R_s}$ consists of the single unary relation P, $\mathbf{R_t}$ consists of two binary relations, E and F, the set Σ_{st} consists of the st-tgd:

$$P(x) \to \exists z \exists w (E(x,z) \wedge E(x,w)),$$

and the set Σ_t consists of the following tgd and egd:

$$E(x,y) \to \exists z F(y,z),$$
$$E(x,y) \wedge E(x,y') \to y = y'.$$

Consider the source instance $S = \{P(a)\}$. We have to start by applying the st-tgd. This populates the target with the instance $T = \{E(a,\perp_1), E(a,\perp_2)\}$. At this point, we have two possible choices. Either we apply the tgd or the egd in Σ_t, since both of them are violated. We show that these choices lead to different chase results.

- Suppose that we apply the tgd first to each one of the tuples in T. Then T is extended with facts $F(\perp_1,\perp_3)$ and $F(\perp_2,\perp_4)$. The resulting instance violates the egd, and hence this has to be applied. The application of the egd equates nulls $\perp_1$ and $\perp_2$, which yields a target instance:

$$T_1 = \{E(a,\perp_1), F(\perp_1,\perp_3), F(\perp_1,\perp_4)\}.$$

This target instance violates no dependency in Σ_t, and, therefore, is the result of a successful chase sequence for S. We conclude that T_1 is a canonical universal solution for S under $\mathcal{M}$.

- Suppose, on the other hand, that it is the egd that is applied first on T. Then nulls $\perp_1$ and $\perp_2$ are equated, which yields a target instance $T' = \{E(a, \perp_1)\}$. Afterwards, we apply the tgd and obtain the target instance:

$$T_2 = \{E(a, \perp_1), F(\perp_1, \perp_2)\}.$$

This instance does not violate any dependency in Σ_t, and hence it is another canonical universal solution for S under $\mathcal{M}$.

Clearly, T_1 and T_2 are not isomorphic, which shows that S does not have a unique canonical universal solution up to isomorphism. □

Although canonical solutions are not necessarily unique, this cannot be considered as a serious drawback. Indeed, Theorem 6.7 states that no matter which one of them we materialize, the result will be equally useful for data exchange purposes (since any result of a successful chase sequence is a universal solution). In some restricted cases, however, it will be important to have a unique canonical universal solution. As the following simple proposition shows, this is always the case when mappings contain no tgds in Σ_t. The proof is left as an exercise for the reader.

Proposition 6.10 *Let $\mathcal{M} = (\mathbf{R_s}, \mathbf{R_t}, \Sigma_{st}, \Sigma_t)$ be a mapping such that Σ_t consists only of egds. Then every source instance S has a unique canonical universal solution T (up to a renaming of nulls) under $\mathcal{M}$.*

Each time that all canonical universal solutions are isomorphic for a source instance S, we will talk about *the* canonical universal solution for S.

Canonical universal solutions and weak acyclicity

Recall that at the end of Section 6.2 we introduced the desiderata for good solutions in data exchange, in the form of three properties **(C1)**, **(C2)**, and **(C3)**: these state that the existence of solutions must imply the existence of universal solutions, which can be tested algorithmically, and that some universal solution could be built in polynomial time. We can now conclude that the class of mappings with weakly acyclic sets of tgds satisfies these conditions. Indeed, we obtain the following as an immediate corollary to Theorems 6.7 and 5.11.

Corollary 6.11 *Let $\mathcal{M} = (\mathbf{R_s}, \mathbf{R_t}, \Sigma_{st}, \Sigma_t)$ be a relational mapping, such that Σ_t is the union of a set of egds and a weakly acyclic set of tgds. Then* UNISOLEXISTENCE$_{\mathcal{M}}$ *can be solved in* PTIME. *Furthermore, if solutions for a source instance S exist, then universal solutions exist, and a canonical universal solution for S can be computed in polynomial time.*

Summary

In summary, the following holds for the problem of existence of universal solutions in relational data exchange:

- For arbitrary relational mappings defined by (st)-tgds and egds the problem is undecidable. Moreover, the existence of solutions does not necessarily imply the existence of universal solutions.
- For the class of relational mappings $\mathcal{M} = (\mathbf{R_s}, \mathbf{R_t}, \Sigma_{st}, \Sigma_t)$ such that Σ_t consists of a set of egds and a weakly acyclic set of tgds, the problem becomes decidable (using the chase procedure), and, indeed, tractable. In addition, the existence of solutions implies the existence of universal solutions.
- For the latter class of mappings, and in the case when a source instance S has solutions, a canonical universal solution T for S can be computed in polynomial time.

6.4 The core

We start this section with an example.

Example 6.12 (Example 4.1 continued)   Consider the source instance

$$S = \{\text{FLIGHT}(Paris, Amsterdam, KLM, 1410),$$
$$\text{FLIGHT}(Paris, Amsterdam, KLM, 2230),$$
$$\text{GEO}(Paris, France, 2M)\}.$$

There are no target constraints, so the chase computes the canonical universal solution T for S:

$$\{\text{ROUTES}(\perp_1, Paris, Amsterdam), \text{ROUTES}(\perp_3, Paris, Amsterdam),$$
$$\text{INFO\_FLIGHT}(\perp_1, 1410, \perp_2, KLM), \text{INFO\_FLIGHT}(\perp_3, 2230, \perp_4, KLM),$$
$$\text{SERVES}(KLM, Paris, France, \perp_5), \text{SERVES}(KLM, Paris, France, \perp_6)\}.$$

Now consider the instance T^* obtained from T by removing the tuple SERVES$(KLM, Paris, France, \perp_6)$. Then T^* is also a solution for S, and, moreover, there are homomorphisms $h : T \to T^*$ (that is the identity on every element except $\perp_6$, where h takes value $\perp_5$) and $h^* : T^* \to T$ (simply because T^* is contained in T). It follows therefore that T^* is also a universal solution for S.   □

We can draw an interesting conclusion from this example: among all possible universal solutions, the canonical universal solution is not necessarily the smallest, as T^* is strictly contained in T. Moreover, in the example, T^* is actually the smallest universal solution (up to isomorphism).

The first natural question is whether there is always a unique smallest universal solution. As we will see later, this question has a positive answer. It can be argued that this smallest universal solution is the "best" universal solution – since it is the most economical one in terms of size – and hence that it should be the preferred one at the moment of materializing a solution. On the other hand, we will see that there are additional costs involved in constructing such a solution. For now our goal is to characterize the smallest solutions in data exchange.

It turns out that such smallest universal solutions happen to be the *cores* of universal solutions. The notion of a *core* originated and played an important role in graph theory. Here we present it for arbitrary instances. Recall that if we have two instances T and T', then T' is a *subinstance* of T if $V^{T'} \subseteq V^T$ for every relation symbol V used in T. In that case we write $T' \subseteq T$. If at least one of the inclusions $V^{T'} \subseteq V^T$ is proper, i.e., $V^{T'} \subset V^T$, then T' is a *proper subinstance* of T, and we write $T' \subset T$.

Definition 6.13 (Core)   Let T be a target instance with values in $\text{CONST} \cup \text{VAR}$, and let T' be a subinstance of T. Then T' is a *core* of T if there is a homomorphism from T to T', but there is no homomorphism from T to a proper subinstance of T'.   □

Recall that homomorphisms only act on nulls from VAR, i.e., they are always the identity on constants from CONST.

The proposition below lists some well-known facts about cores.

Proposition 6.14   *1. Every instance has a core.*
2. All cores of a given instance are isomorphic, i.e., the same up to a renaming of nulls.
3. Two instances are homomorphically equivalent if and only if their cores are isomorphic.
4. If T' is the core of the instance T, then there is a homomorphism $h : T \to T'$ such that $h(v) = v$ for each element $v \in \text{DOM}(T')$.

The first two items in Proposition 6.14 mean that we can talk about *the* core of an instance. To give an intuition, for instance, behind the second fact, assume that T_1 and T_2 are cores of T, and that $h_i : T \to T_i$ are homomorphisms, for $i = 1, 2$. Then h_1 restricted to T_2 cannot map it to a subinstance of T_1, for otherwise $h_1 \circ h_2$ would be a homomorphism from T to a subinstance of the core T_1. Likewise, h_2 restricted to T_1 cannot map it to a subinstance of T_2. Hence, these restrictions are one-to-one homomorphisms between T_1 and T_2. From here it is easy to derive that T_1 and T_2 are isomorphic.

The next result summarizes some of the good properties of cores in data exchange.

Theorem 6.15   *Let $\mathcal{M} = (\mathbf{R}_s, \mathbf{R}_t, \Sigma_{st}, \Sigma_t)$ be a mapping, such that Σ_{st} consists of a set of st-tgds and Σ_t consists of a set of tgds and egds.*

1. If S is a source instance and T is a solution for S, then the core of T is also a solution for S.
2. If S is a source instance and T is a universal solution for S, then the core of T is also a universal solution for S.
3. If S is a source instance for which a universal solution exists, then all universal solutions have the same core (up to renaming of nulls), and the core of an arbitrary universal solution is precisely the smallest universal solution.

Proof   We start by proving the first item. Assume that T' is the core of T. We prove that (S, T') satisfies every dependency in $\Sigma_{st} \cup \Sigma_t$. Take an arbitrary st-tgd $\varphi_s(\bar{x}) \to \exists \bar{y} \psi_t(\bar{x}, \bar{y}) \in \Sigma_{st}$ and assume that $S \models \varphi_s(\bar{a})$, for some tuple $\bar{a}$ of elements in $\text{DOM}(S)$ such that $|\bar{a}| = |\bar{x}|$. Since T is a solution for S it must be the case that $T \models \psi_t(\bar{a}, \bar{b})$, for some tuple $\bar{b}$ of elements in $\text{DOM}(T)$ such that $|\bar{b}| = |\bar{y}|$. But T' is the core of T, and, therefore, there is a homomorphism $h : T \to T'$. Notice that $h(\bar{a}) = \bar{a}$, since each element in $\bar{a}$ is a constant. As conjunctive queries are preserved under homomorphisms, we conclude that $T' \models \psi_t(\bar{a}, h(\bar{b}))$. Thus, $T' \models \exists \bar{y} \psi_t(\bar{a}, \bar{y})$, and hence (S, T') satisfies the st-tgd.

Next, take an arbitrary tgd $\varphi(\bar{x}) \to \exists \bar{y} \psi(\bar{x}, \bar{y}) \in \Sigma_t$ and assume that $T' \models \varphi(\bar{a})$, for some tuple $\bar{a}$ of elements in $\text{DOM}(T')$ such that $|\bar{a}| = |\bar{x}|$. Since T' is a subinstance of T, it must be the case that $T \models \varphi(\bar{a})$, and, therefore, since T is a solution for S, that $T \models \psi(\bar{a}, \bar{b})$ for some tuple $\bar{b}$ of elements in $\text{DOM}(T)$ such that $|\bar{b}| = |\bar{y}|$. From Proposition 6.14 it follows that there is a homomorphism $h : T \to T'$ such that $h(v) = v$ for each element v in $\text{DOM}(T')$. In particular, $h(\bar{a}) = \bar{a}$, since $\bar{a}$ is a tuple of elements in $\text{DOM}(T')$. This implies that $T' \models \psi(\bar{a}, h(\bar{b}))$, and, therefore, that $T' \models \exists \bar{y} \psi(\bar{a}, \bar{y})$. We conclude that T' satisfies the tgd.

Finally, take an arbitrary egd $\varphi(\bar{x}) \to x_i = x_j \in \Sigma_t$ and assume that $T' \models \varphi(\bar{a})$, for some tuple $\bar{a}$ of elements in $\text{DOM}(T')$ such that $|\bar{a}| = |\bar{x}|$. As in the previous case, we conclude that $T \models \varphi(\bar{a})$, and, therefore, since T is a solution for S, that $a_i = a_j$. Hence, T' also satisfies the egd, and, therefore, T' is a solution for S.

The second part of the proposition follows easily from the facts that the core of T is a solution for S and that there is a homomorphism h from T into any other solution (and, thus, h is also a homomorphism from the core of T into such solution).

The third part follows easily from the properties of the core stated in Proposition 6.14. Indeed, universal solutions are by definition homomorphically equivalent, and, thus, from the third part of Proposition 6.14, they all have the same core up to renaming of nulls. Furthermore, the core T^* of the universal solutions is the smallest universal solution. Assume, to the contrary, that there is a universal solution T' for S of smaller size. But then T^* must be isomorphic to the core of T', which contradicts the fact that T' is of smaller size than T^*. $\square$

Example 6.16 (Example 6.12 continued)   The solution T^* is the core of the universal solutions for S, since there is a homomorphism from T to T^* but there is no homomorphism from T^* to a proper subinstance of itself. $\square$

In conclusion, the core of the universal solutions has good properties for data exchange. This naturally raises the question about the computability of the core. As we have mentioned, the chase yields a universal solution that is not necessarily the core of the universal solutions, so different techniques have to be applied in order to compute the core.

Computing the core

It is well known that computing the core of an arbitrary graph is a computationally intractable problem. Indeed, we know that a graph G is 3-colorable if and only if there is a homomorphism from G to K_3, the clique of size 3. Thus, G is 3-colorable if and only if the core of the disjoint union of G and K_3 is K_3 itself. This shows that there is a polynomial time reduction from the problem of 3-colorability to the problem of computing the core of a graph. It follows that the latter is NP-hard. In fact, checking if a *fixed* graph G_0 is the core of an input graph G is an NP-complete problem; if both G and G_0 are inputs, then the complexity is even higher (more precisely, in the class DP, studied in complexity theory).

However, in data exchange we are interested in computing the core of a universal solution and not of an arbitrary instance. And the intractability of the general problem does not mean bad news in our case. In fact, we are about to see that computing the core of the universal solutions under the class of mappings with a weakly acyclic set of tgds is a tractable problem.

Let us consider first a simple class of relational mappings: those without tgds. Then there is a simple greedy algorithm that computes the core of the universal solutions (under the assumption that universal solutions exist, i.e., that the chase does not fail). Moreover, it does so in polynomial time. The algorithm COMPUTECORE($\mathcal{M}$) for a mapping $\mathcal{M} = (\mathbf{R_s}, \mathbf{R_t}, \Sigma_{st}, \Sigma_t)$ without tgds in Σ_t is shown below.

Algorithm 6.1 COMPUTECORE($\mathcal{M}$)

Require: A source instance S

Ensure: If S has a universal solution under $\mathcal{M}$, then T^* is a target instance that is a core for S. Otherwise, $T^* = \mathtt{fail}$

1: let T be the result of a successful chase sequence for S under $\mathcal{M}$
2: **if** $T = \mathtt{fail}$ **then**
3:     $T^* = \mathtt{fail}$
4: **else**
5:     $T^* := T$
6:     **for all** fact $R(\bar{a})$ in T^* **do**
7:        let $T^{*,-}$ be an instance obtained from T^* by removing fact $R(\bar{a})$
8:        **if** $(S, T^{*,-})$ satisfies Σ_{st} **then**
9:           $T^* := T^{*,-}$
10:        **end if**
11:     **end for**
12: **end if**

Theorem 6.17 *Let $\mathcal{M} = (\mathbf{R_s}, \mathbf{R_t}, \Sigma_{st}, \Sigma_t)$ be a mapping without tgds in Σ_t. If the chase computing the canonical universal solution does not fail, then* COMPUTECORE($\mathcal{M}$) *outputs the core of the universal solutions for S. Furthermore, this algorithm runs in polynomial time in the size of S.*

Proof It is clear that the algorithm runs in polynomial time in the size of S, since computing T is done in polynomial time, and checking whether $T^{*,-}$ is a solution for S can be done in polynomial time as well.

We show next that it outputs the core if the chase computing the canonical universal solution does not fail. Assume that T is the result of a successful chase sequence for S under $\mathcal{M}$. We first show that each instance T^* that is obtained from T inside the **for** loop in lines (6-10) is a universal solution for S. By definition, $(S, T^*) \models \Sigma_{st}$. Since T^* is a subinstance of T and T satisfies each egd in Σ_t, we have that $T^* \models \Sigma_t$. Thus, T^* is a solution for S. Finally, T^* is a subinstance of T, and, therefore, there is a homomorphism from T^* into any other solution. This proves that T^* is also a universal solution for S.

Assume now that T^* is the result of COMPUTECORE($\mathcal{M}$) for S. We prove next that T^* is the core of the universal solutions for S. As we have just proved, T^* is a universal solution and hence it contains a copy T_0 of the core of the universal solutions as a subinstance. It follows from Theorem 6.15 that $T_0 \in \text{SOL}_{\mathcal{M}}(S)$. Assume now, for the sake of contradiction, that $T_0 \neq T^*$ and hence that there is a fact $R(\bar{t}) \in T^* \setminus T_0$. Thus, $T^* \setminus \{R(\bar{t})\}$ is a solution for S (because it contains T_0), and hence it satisfies Σ_{st}. This implies that the result of the algorithm could not have been T^*. This is our desired contradiction. $\qquad\square$

Unfortunately, the algorithm described above cannot be easily adapted to more complex mappings that have both tgds and egds among target constraints. Indeed, a crucial assumption in the previous algorithm is that whenever an instance satisfies an egd, then every subinstance of it also satisfies it. However, this assumption fails for tgds. For example, the instance $T = \{U(a), V(a)\}$ satisfies the tgd $U(x) \rightarrow V(x)$, but removing the fact $V(a)$ yields an instance that does not satisfy it. In fact, if the previous greedy algorithm is applied directly to mappings in which Σ_t contains at least one tgd, then the resulting instance may fail to be a solution.

Thus, more sophisticated techniques need to be developed if one wants to compute cores of universal solutions in polynomial time in the presence of tgds. Unfortunately, no simple adaptation of the previous greedy algorithm is known to solve this problem. Hence different techniques have to be developed, which are based on the *blocks method* that is described below.

Let us assume for the time being that we deal with mappings without target dependencies. The blocks method relies on the following observation. If T is the canonical universal solution of a source instance S with respect to a set of st-tgds Σ_{st}, then the *Gaifman* graph of the nulls of T consists of a set of connected components (blocks) of size bounded by a constant c that depends only on the mapping (which we assume to be fixed). By the Gaifman graph of nulls of T we mean the graph whose nodes are the nulls of T, such that two nulls $\perp_1, \perp_2$ are adjacent if and only if there is a tuple in some relation of T that mentions both $\perp_1$ and $\perp_2$.

A crucial observation is that checking whether there is a homomorphism from T into an arbitrary instance T' can be done in polynomial time. The justification is that this problem boils down to the problem of checking whether each block of T has a homomorphism into T'. The latter can be solved in polynomial time since the size of each block is bounded by c – hence there are polynomially many candidates for such a homomorphism. It follows that computing the core of the canonical universal solution T can be done in polynomial time. Indeed, it suffices to check whether there is a homomorphism $h : T \rightarrow T$ such that the size of the image of T under h is strictly less than the size of T. Then we replace T by $h(T)$, and iteratively continue this process until reaching a fixed-point.

The blocks method was also extended to the case when Σ_t consists of a set of egds. There is an extra difficulty in this case. The property mentioned above, the bounded block-size in the Gaifman graph of the canonical universal solution T of a source instance S, is no longer true in the presence of egds. This is because the chase, when applied to egds, can equate nulls from different blocks, and thus, create blocks of nulls of larger and larger size.

This problem is solved by a surprising rigidity lemma stating the following. Let T be the canonical universal solution for a source instance with respect to a set of st-tgds Σ_{st}, and let T' be the target instance obtained from T by chasing with the egds in Σ_t. Then if two nulls $\perp_1$ and $\perp_2$ in different blocks of T are replaced by the same null $\perp$ in T', then the null $\perp$ is *rigid*. That is, if $h : T' \rightarrow T'$ is a homomorphism then $h(\perp) = \perp$, and thus, T' has the bounded block-size property if we treat those nulls as constants.

The situation is much more complex in the presence of tgds. This is because the canonical universal solution T for a source instance S does not have the bounded block-size property, and in addition, it is no longer true that equated nulls are rigid. A refined version of the blocks method has been developed; it was used to show that computing cores of universal solutions for mappings whose set of target dependencies consists of egds and a weakly acyclic set of tgds can be done in polynomial time.

Theorem 6.18 *Let $\mathcal{M} = (\mathbf{R_s}, \mathbf{R_t}, \Sigma_{st}, \Sigma_t)$ be a fixed relational mapping, such that Σ_t consists of a set of egds and a weakly acyclic set of tgds. There is a polynomial-time algorithm that, for every source instance S, checks whether a solution for S exists, and if that is the case, computes the core of the universal solutions for S.*

The proof of this result, which is based on the notion of hypertree decompositions, is technically quite involved and goes beyond the scope of this book.

Summary

In summary, the core is a universal solution that has several good properties for data exchange purposes: it is unique up to isomorphism, it is the smallest universal solution, and it can be computed in polynomial time for mappings with a weakly acyclic set of tgds.

However, the choice of a solution to materialize does not boil down exclusively to the size of such a solution. After all, we materialize solutions to answer queries; in addition, we should also consider the cost of building a solution. We have already seen that it is costlier to build the core than the canonical universal solution (as building the latter is the first step in building the core). In addition, we shall see in the next chapter that although the core and the canonical universal solution are indistinguishable with respect to some basic query answering tasks, the canonical universal solution behaves better than the core when handling more expressive query languages.

We conclude that there is a tradeoff in deciding which solution – canonical universal or core – to materialize:

- the core allows the most compact materialization among all possible universal solutions; however,
- there are additional computational costs, and it is not as flexible when it comes to query answering.

7

Query answering and rewriting

In data exchange, we are interested in computing certain answers to a query. However, we do not yet know when such a computation is feasible. The goal of the chapter is to answer this question.

The bad news is that the problem of computing certain answers for relational calculus (equivalently, relational algebra or FO) queries is undecidable, even in the absence of target dependencies. But the good news is that the problem becomes decidable, and, indeed, tractable, for unions of conjunctive queries over mappings with a weakly acyclic set of tgds. Conjunctive queries, as was already mentioned several times, play a very important role and are very common, and mappings with weakly acyclic sets of tgds, as we have seen, are the ones behaving particularly well when it comes to materializing solutions.

The positive result, however, breaks down when we extend conjunctive queries with inequalities. But we can still find a meaningful class of queries capable of expressing interesting properties in the data exchange context that extends conjunctive queries with a limited amount of negation and shares most of their good properties for data exchange.

Finally, we study the notion of query rewriting, i.e., when certain answers to a query Q can be computed by posing a possibly different query Q' over a materialized solution. Such rewritings are easy for unions of conjunctive queries; our study concentrates on rewritings of relational algebra queries. We compare rewritings over different solutions, and develop easily applicable tools that determine when rewritings are not possible.

7.1 Answering relational calculus queries

In this chapter we are interested in the problem of computing certain answers for a relational mapping $\mathcal{M}$ and a query Q over $\mathbf{R_t}$. Recall that a mapping $\mathcal{M}$ is a tuple $(\mathbf{R_s}, \mathbf{R_t}, \Sigma_{st}, \Sigma_t)$, where $\mathbf{R_s}$ is the source schema, $\mathbf{R_t}$ is the target schema, Σ_{st} is the set of source-to-target dependencies, and Σ_t is the set of target dependencies. Given a source instance S, certain answers to Q are defined as $certain_{\mathcal{M}}(Q,S) = \bigcap\{Q(T) \mid T \in \text{SOL}_{\mathcal{M}}(S)\}$.

The problem we study is formulated as follows.

PROBLEM:	CERTAIN $_{\mathcal{M}}(Q)$.
INPUT:	A source instance S and a tuple $\bar{t}$ of elements in DOM(S).
QUESTION:	Is $\bar{t} \in certain_{\mathcal{M}}(Q,S)$?

Since finding certain answers involves computing the intersection of a (potentially) infinite number of sets, this strongly suggests that computing certain answers of arbitrary relational calculus (equivalently, relational algebra or FO) queries is an undecidable problem. Indeed, this is the case even in the absence of target dependencies.

Proposition 7.1 *There exists an FO-query Q and a mapping $\mathcal{M} = (\mathbf{R_s}, \mathbf{R_t}, \Sigma_{st})$, such that* CERTAIN $_{\mathcal{M}}(Q)$ *is undecidable.*

Proof Recall from Theorem 5.3 that there exists a mapping $\mathcal{M}' = (\mathbf{R_s}, \mathbf{R_t}, \Sigma_{st}, \Sigma_t)$ such that SOLEXISTENCE $_{\mathcal{M}'}$ is undecidable. Let Q' be the Boolean FO-query that is obtained by taking the conjunction of all dependencies in Σ_t and let $\mathcal{M}$ be the mapping $(\mathbf{R_s}, \mathbf{R_t}, \Sigma_{st})$, i.e., $\mathcal{M}'$ without the target dependencies. Let $Q = \neg Q'$. Then for every source instance S, we have

$$\begin{aligned} certain_{\mathcal{M}}(Q,S) = \texttt{false} \;&\Leftrightarrow\; \exists T : T \in \text{SOL}_{\mathcal{M}}(S) \text{ and } T \not\models Q \\ &\Leftrightarrow\; \exists T : T \in \text{SOL}_{\mathcal{M}}(S) \text{ and } T \models Q' \\ &\Leftrightarrow\; \exists T : T \in \text{SOL}_{\mathcal{M}'}(S). \end{aligned}$$

This proves that CERTAIN $_{\mathcal{M}}(Q)$ is undecidable. $\qquad\square$

Notice that although the mapping $\mathcal{M}$ used in the proof of Proposition 7.1 is quite simple (it does not even have target dependencies), the FO query Q is not. Indeed, Q corresponds to the negation of a conjunction of a finite number of tgds and egds, and, therefore, it is equivalent to an FO-query of the form $\exists^* \forall^* \psi$, where ψ is quantifier-free. This result does not preclude, however, the existence of simpler but yet practically relevant classes of queries for which the problem of computing certain answers is decidable, and even tractable. We prove in the next section that this is indeed the case for the class of unions of conjunctive queries.

7.2 Answering conjunctive queries

Recall that a *conjunctive* query is an FO formula of the form $\exists \bar{x}\, \varphi(\bar{x}, \bar{y})$, where $\varphi(\bar{x}, \bar{y})$ is a conjunction of atoms. Equivalently, it is a query expressed in the selection-projection-join fragment of relational algebra. Unions of conjunctive queries are thus the queries expressed by the operations of selection, projection, join, and union of relational algebra.

Our next result shows that some of the most common SQL queries – namely, unions of conjunctive queries – can be efficiently answered in data exchange scenarios involving the same kind of mappings that give us good algorithms for materializing solutions. The proof of this result shows that universal solutions are crucial to query answering in data exchange.

Theorem 7.2 *Let $\mathcal{M} = (\mathbf{R_s}, \mathbf{R_t}, \Sigma_{st}, \Sigma_t)$ be a mapping, such that Σ_t consists of a set of egds and a weakly acyclic set of tgds, and let Q be a union of conjunctive queries. Then* CERTAIN$_\mathcal{M}(Q)$ *can be solved in* PTIME.

Theorem 7.2 can be easily proved in a way that also produces an algorithm for computing certain answers. Namely, we can show that

$$certain_\mathcal{M}(Q,S) = Q_{\text{naïve}}(T), \tag{7.1}$$

when Q is a union of conjunctive queries and T is an arbitrary universal solution. Recall that $Q_{\text{naïve}}(T)$ is the naïve evaluation of Q over T, as described in Section 2.3. That is, one first treats nulls as if they were values, evaluates Q, and then removes tuples containing nulls from the result.

This can be easily shown when we put together the following facts.

1. For the class of mappings in Theorem 7.2, it is the case that if a source instance S has at least one solution, then a universal solution T for S can be computed in polynomial time (Corollary 6.11).
2. If T is a universal solution for a source instance S, then there is a homomorphism $h : T \to T'$ for every $T' \in \text{SOL}_\mathcal{M}(S)$. But (unions of) conjunctive queries are preserved under homomorphisms. Hence, if $\bar{t}$ is a tuple not containing nulls in $Q(T)$, then it also belongs to $Q(T')$. Thus,

$$\text{null-free tuples in } Q(T) \subseteq \bigcap_{T' \in \text{SOL}_\mathcal{M}(S)} \text{null-free tuples in } Q(T').$$

The other inclusion is true since T itself is a solution, and hence we have the equality above. Now note that the right-hand side is $certain_\mathcal{M}(Q,S)$, since certain answers could not contain any nulls, and the left-hand side is $Q_{\text{naïve}}(T)$ by definition. Thus, we have proved (7.1).
3. FO-queries, and in particular, unions of conjunctive queries, have polynomial time data complexity (as explained in Section 2.4). Hence, computing $Q_{\text{naïve}}(T)$ is done in polynomial time, as well as computing T itself.

Thus, in order to compute the certain answers of a union of conjunctive queries Q with respect to a source instance S, one can use the algorithm COMPUTECERTAINANSWERS$(Q,\mathcal{M})$ shown below. Note that in the algorithm one can use any universal solution. For example, if we compute the core instead of the canonical universal solution, the output of the algorithm is still the set of certain answers.

In summary, conjunctive queries form a very good class for data exchange as their certain answers can always be obtained in polynomial time by means of naïve evaluation over a materialized universal solution. A natural question at this point is whether this positive behavior extends to other interesting classes of queries. For instance, conjunctive queries

---

Algorithm 7.1 COMPUTECERTAINANSWERS($Q,\mathcal{M}$)

Require: A source instance S

Ensure: If $\text{SOL}_{\mathcal{M}}(S) \neq \emptyset$, then CA is the set of certain answers for Q over S under $\mathcal{M}$.
Otherwise, $CA = \texttt{fail}$

1: let T be the result of a successful chase sequence of S under $\mathcal{M}$
2: **if** $T = \texttt{fail}$ **then**
3:     $CA := \texttt{fail}$
4: **else**
5:     $CA := Q_{\text{naïve}}(T)$
6: **end if**

---

keep us in the realm of the positive while most database query languages are equipped
with negation. What happens if we extend conjunctive queries with a restricted form of
negation? Do we retain the good properties mentioned above? We deal with this problem
in the next section.

7.3 Conjunctive queries with inequalities

In the previous section we raised the following question: What happens in the data exchange context if we extend conjunctive queries with a restricted form of negation? We
study this problem for a particular class of queries, namely, conjunctive queries with *inequalities*. This class of queries is of practical importance, and corresponds to a natural and
common subclass of SQL queries, namely those that have conjunctions of equalities and
inequalities in the `where` clause.

Formally, a conjunctive query with inequalities is an FO-query of the form $\varphi(\bar{x}) = \exists \bar{y} \psi(\bar{x}, \bar{y})$, where $\psi(\bar{x}, \bar{y})$ is a conjunction of

- atomic relational formulae, and
- inequalities of the form $z_1 \neq z_2$, where the variables z_1 and z_2 come from $\bar{x}$ and $\bar{y}$.

We impose a simple safety condition that every variable that appears in an inequality must
also appear in a relational atom. For example,

$$\varphi(x,z) = \exists y \exists y' \left(\text{ROUTES}(y,x,z) \wedge \text{ROUTES}(y',x,z) \wedge y \neq y' \right) \tag{7.2}$$

is a conjunctive query with one inequality that asks for pairs (a,b) of cities such that there
is more than one flight from a to b.

Thus, conjunctive queries with inequalities are capable of expressing interesting and
natural properties of data. Now we would like to see how they behave in data exchange. For
instance, is it true that certain answers to a conjunctive query with inequalities Q coincide
with the naïve evaluation of Q over some universal solution? The following simple example
shows that with inequalities, naïve evaluation fails.

Example 7.3 (Example 4.1 continued)   Consider the source instance

$$S = \{\text{FLIGHT}(Paris, Santiago, AirFrance, 2320),$$

$$\text{FLIGHT}(Paris, Santiago, LAN, 2200)\}.$$

Notice that every universal solution for S under $\mathscr{M}$ must contain as a subinstance a copy of the following target instance T:

$$\{\text{ROUTES}(\perp_1, Paris, Santiago), \text{INFO\_FLIGHT}(\perp_1, 2320, \perp_2, AirFrance)$$

$$\text{ROUTES}(\perp_3, Paris, Santiago), \text{INFO\_FLIGHT}(\perp_3, 2200, \perp_4, LAN)\}.$$

It is not hard to see that T is a canonical universal solution for S.

The FO-query $\varphi(x, z)$ in (7.2) must return the pair $(Paris, Santiago)$ over any universal solution for S. On the other hand, the certain answer of $\varphi(x, z)$ over S is the empty set. This is because T' defined as

$$\{\text{ROUTES}(\perp_1, Paris, Santiago), \text{INFO\_FLIGHT}(\perp_1, 2320, \perp_2, AirFrance),$$

$$\text{INFO\_FLIGHT}(\perp_1, 2200, \perp_2, LAN)\}$$

is a solution for S and $\varphi(x, z)$ returns the empty set when evaluated over it. (Notice that T' is *not* a universal solution for S as there is no homomorphism from T' into T). Intuitively, this means that the set of solutions for S does not imply that there is more than one flight from *Paris* to *Santiago* in the target. $\quad\square$

Thus, certain answers of conjunctive queries with inequalities cannot be obtained by naïve evaluation over a materialized universal solution. However, this does not exclude the possibility that certain answers to conjunctive queries with inequalities can be efficiently computed.

We show next that this is unfortunately not the case. In particular, we prove that the problem of computing certain answers for the class of conjunctive queries with inequalities remains decidable, but it can be intractable even in the absence of target dependencies.

Theorem 7.4 1. *Let $\mathscr{M}$ be a mapping such that Σ_t consists of a set of egds and a weakly acyclic set of tgds, and let Q be a union of conjunctive queries with inequalities. Then* CERTAIN$_{\mathscr{M}}(Q)$ *is in* CONP.

2. *There is a Boolean conjunctive query Q with inequalities and a* LAV *mapping $\mathscr{M}$, such that* CERTAIN$_{\mathscr{M}}(Q)$ *is* CONP-*hard.*

Proof We first prove 1. We show that if there is a solution T for a source instance S such that $\bar{t} \notin Q(T)$, then there is a solution T' of polynomial size such that $\bar{t} \notin Q(T')$. Suppose that T is a solution for S such that $\bar{t} \notin Q(T)$. Let T_{can} be a canonical universal solution for S. (Notice that T_{can} exists since S has at least one solution). Then there is a homomorphism $h : T_{\text{can}} \to T$. We denote by $h(T_{\text{can}})$ the homomorphic image of T under h. It is not hard to prove that $h(T_{\text{can}})$ is a solution for S. Furthermore, $h(T_{\text{can}})$ is of polynomial size in $\|S\|$ (since T_{can} is also of polynomial size in $\|S\|$). We claim that $\bar{t} \notin Q(h(T_{\text{can}}))$.

Assume otherwise; then $\bar{t} \in Q(h(T_{can}))$. But $h(T_{can})$ is a subinstance of T, and, therefore, since unions of conjunctive queries with inequalities are *monotone* (i.e., if $\bar{t} \in Q(T_1)$ then $\bar{t} \in Q(T_2)$, for every T_2 such that T_1 is a subinstance of T_2), it is the case that $\bar{t}$ also belongs to $Q(T)$, which is a contradiction.

With this observation, it is easy to construct a CONP algorithm for the problem of certain answers of Q and $\mathcal{M}$. In fact, a CONP algorithm for checking $\bar{t} \in certain_{\mathcal{M}}(Q,S)$ is the same as an NP algorithm for checking $\bar{t} \notin certain_{\mathcal{M}}(Q,S)$. By the above observation, for the latter it simply suffices to guess a polynomial-size instance T and check, in polynomial time, that T is a solution, and that $\bar{t} \notin Q(T)$.

We now prove 2. The LAV mapping $\mathcal{M} = (\mathbf{R_s}, \mathbf{R_t}, \Sigma_{st})$ is as follows. The source schema $\mathbf{R_s}$ consists of two relations: a binary relation P and a ternary relation R. The target schema $\mathbf{R_t}$ also consists of two relations: a binary relation U and a ternary relation V. The set Σ_{st} contains the following source-to-target dependencies:

$$P(x,y) \rightarrow \exists z(U(x,z) \wedge U(y,z))$$
$$R(x,y,z) \rightarrow V(x,y,z).$$

The Boolean query Q is defined as:

$$\exists x_1 \exists y_1 \exists x_2 \exists y_2 \exists x_3 \exists y_3 (V(x_1,x_2,x_3) \wedge U(x_1,y_1) \wedge$$
$$U(x_2,y_2) \wedge U(x_3,y_3) \wedge x_1 \neq y_1 \wedge x_2 \neq y_2 \wedge x_3 \neq y_3).$$

Next we show that CERTAIN$_{\mathcal{M}}(Q)$ is CONP-hard.

The CONP-hardness is established from a reduction from 3SAT to the complement of the problem of certain answers for Q and $\mathcal{M}$. More precisely, for every 3CNF propositional formula φ, we construct in polynomial time an instance S_φ of $\mathbf{R_s}$ such that φ is satisfiable iff $certain_{\mathcal{M}}(Q,S_\varphi) = \texttt{false}$.

Given a propositional formula $\varphi \equiv \bigwedge_{1 \leq j \leq m} C_j$ in 3CNF, where each C_j is a clause, let S_φ be the following source instance:

- The interpretation of P in S_φ contains the pair $(q, \neg q)$, for each propositional variable q mentioned in φ; and
- the interpretation of R in S_φ contains all tuples (α, β, γ) such that for some $1 \leq j \leq m$ it is the case that $C_j = (\alpha \vee \beta \vee \gamma)$.

Clearly, S_φ can be constructed in polynomial time from φ.

It is not hard to see that the unique canonical universal solution T for S_φ is as follows, where we denote by $\perp_q$ the null generated by applying the st-tgd $P(x,y) \rightarrow \exists z(U(x,z) \wedge U(y,z))$ to $P(q, \neg q)$:

- The interpretation of the relation U in T contains the tuples $(q, \perp_q)$ and $(\neg q, \perp_q)$, for each propositional variable q mentioned in φ; and
- the interpretation of the relation V in T is just a copy of the interpretation of the relation R in S_φ.

We leave it as a simple exercise to the reader to prove that φ is satisfiable iff $certain_{\mathscr{M}}(Q, S_\varphi) = \texttt{false}$. This finishes the proof of the theorem. □

Notice that the query Q constructed in the proof of the previous theorem contains exactly three inequalities. But this can be strengthened, as there is a Boolean conjunctive query Q with exactly two inequalities and a LAV mapping $\mathscr{M}$ such that CERTAIN$_{\mathscr{M}}(Q)$ is CONP-hard. We leave the proof of this fact as an interesting exercise for the reader. For the class of (unions of) conjunctive queries with at most one inequality per disjunct, the certain answers can be computed in polynomial time. We explain how this can be done in the next section.

Summary

Summing up, conjunctive queries with inequalities do not retain the good properties of unions of conjunctive queries for data exchange. In particular, while the problem of computing certain answers for conjunctive queries with inequalities remains decidable, it becomes intractable even in the absence of target dependencies. However, this still leaves open the question of whether the class of unions of conjunctive queries can be extended with a limited amount of negation in such a way that:

1. The extension preserves the good properties of conjunctive queries for data exchange; and
2. it also allows expressing relevant data exchange properties.

We show how to construct such language in the next section.

7.4 Tractable query answering with negation

So far we have seen the following examples of the behavior of query answering in data exchange:

- Good behavior, as observed for unions of conjunctive queries: certain answers to them can be found efficiently by running naïve evaluation over the canonical solution (in fact, over an arbitrary universal solution). This is based on the key fact that

$$certain(Q, T) = Q_{\text{naïve}}(T) \tag{7.3}$$

for all instances T, when Q is a union of conjunctive queries.
- Bad behavior, as for arbitrary relational algebra queries: for them, no algorithm in general can compute $certain_{\mathscr{M}}(Q, S)$.
- Moderately bad behavior, as for unions of conjunctive queries with inequalities: for them, $certain_{\mathscr{M}}(Q, S)$ can be computed, but the computation is intractable.

What we look for now is examples of *moderately good behavior*: that is, certain answers can be efficiently computed, but not necessarily by naïve evaluation. We first do this search within the realm of relational algebra, and then leave it and move to more expressive languages such as DATALOG.

Tractable query answering within relational algebra

We now give an example of moderately good behavior within relational algebra: we show that for some relational algebra queries, certain answers $certain_{\mathcal{M}}(Q,S)$ can be computed efficiently, but not by naïve evaluation; in fact, not even by any query that itself is expressible in relational algebra.

Recall that a *conjunctive query with negated atoms* is an FO formula of the form $\exists \bar{x}\alpha(\bar{x},\bar{y})$, where $\alpha(\bar{x},\bar{y})$ is a conjunction of atoms and negated atoms (that is, inequalities of the form $x \neq y$ or negated relational atoms of the form $\neg R(\bar{x})$). Again, as a safety condition we impose the constraint that each variable that appears in the query appears in at least one nonnegated atom.

Theorem 7.5 *There is a* LAV *mapping* $\mathcal{M} = (\mathbf{R_s}, \mathbf{R_t}, \Sigma_{st})$ *without target dependencies and a union of conjunctive queries with negated atoms Q such that:*

1. *$certain_{\mathcal{M}}(Q,S)$ can be computed in polynomial time; and*
2. *there is no relational algebra query Q' such that $Q'(T) = certain_{\mathcal{M}}(Q,S)$, where T is the canonical universal solution.*

In particular, in this case $certain_{\mathcal{M}}(Q,S)$ cannot be computed by naïve evaluation on the canonical solution.

Proof Consider the LAV mapping $\mathcal{M} = (\mathbf{R_s}, \mathbf{R_t}, \Sigma_{st})$ such that $\mathbf{R_s}$ consists of a binary relation E and unary relations A and B, $\mathbf{R_t}$ consists of a binary relation G and unary relations P and R, and Σ_{st} consists of the following st-tgds:

$$E(x,y) \rightarrow G(x,y)$$
$$A(x) \rightarrow P(x)$$
$$B(x) \rightarrow R(x).$$

Notice that if S is a source instance, then the canonical universal solution T for S is such that $E^S = G^T$, $A^S = P^T$ and $B^S = R^T$.

Let Q be the following query over $\mathbf{R_t}$:

$$\exists x \exists y\, (P(x) \wedge R(y) \wedge G(x,y)) \vee \exists x \exists y \exists z\, (G(x,z) \wedge G(z,y) \wedge \neg G(x,y)).$$

This is a union of conjunctive queries with a single negated relational atom and no inequalities. It is also a Boolean query. We show next that for every source instance S, the certain answers $certain_{\mathcal{M}}(Q,S)$ are true if and only if there exist elements a,b in $\text{DOM}(T)$ such that a belongs to P^T, b belongs to R^T and (a,b) belongs to the transitive closure of the relation G^T. Or equivalently, $certain_{\mathcal{M}}(Q,S) = \texttt{true}$ if and only if there exist elements a,b in $\text{DOM}(S)$ such that a belongs to A^S, b belongs to B^S and (a,b) belongs to the transitive closure of the relation E^S.

Assume first that there exist elements a,b in $\text{DOM}(T)$ such that a belongs to P^T, b belongs to R^T and (a,b) belongs to the transitive closure of the relation G^T. Let T_1 be an arbitrary solution of S. We prove that Q holds in T_1, and hence that $certain_{\mathcal{M}}(Q,S) = \texttt{true}$.

We consider two cases. Suppose first that there is a pair (c,d) of elements in $\text{DOM}(T_1)$ such that $(c,d) \notin G^{T_1}$ and for some element $e \in \text{DOM}(T_1)$ it is the case that both (c,e) and (e,d) are in G^{T_1}. Then clearly, $T_1 \models \exists x \exists y \exists z (G(x,z) \wedge G(z,y) \wedge \neg G(x,y))$, and, thus, $T_1 \models Q$. Suppose, on the other hand, that this is not the case. Then G^{T_1} contains its own transitive closure. Moreover, $G^T \subseteq G^{T_1}$, since T_1 is a solution for S, and hence from the previous observation the transitive closure of G^T is also contained in G^{T_1}. We conclude that $(a,b) \in G^{T_1}$, and, therefore, $T_1 \models \exists x \exists y (P(x) \wedge R(y) \wedge G(x,y))$ (and hence $T_1 \models Q$).

Assume, on the other hand, that for every pair (a,b) in the transitive closure of G^T it is the case that either $a \notin P^T$ or $b \notin R^T$. Consider the target instance T_1 that extends T by adding to the interpretation of G every tuple in the transitive closure of G^T. It is clear then that $T_1 \not\models Q$. Indeed, $T_1 \not\models \exists x \exists y (P(x) \wedge R(y) \wedge G(x,y))$ because G^{T_1} coincides with transitive closure of G^T and hence there is no pair (a,b) in G^{T_1} such that both $a \in P^{T_1}$ and $b \in R^{T_1}$. Moreover, $T_1 \not\models \exists x \exists y \exists z (G(x,z) \wedge G(z,y) \wedge \neg G(x,y))$ because G^{T_1} coincides with its own transitive closure. We conclude that $certain_{\mathcal{M}}(Q,S) = \texttt{false}$.

Since transitive closure is polynomial-time computable, we have proved the first statement of the theorem. Moreover, it is well known that there is no FO (i.e., relational algebra) query that expresses the transitive closure of a graph, which shows the second statement of the theorem. $\qquad\square$

The example used in the above proof also shows that negated relational atoms add expressive power to the class of unions of conjunctive queries in the context of data exchange, as they express interesting data exchange properties (e.g., transitive closure) that go way beyond the ones that can be expressed by means of relational algebra queries.

Tractable query answering beyond relational algebra

To retain good properties of query answering in data exchange beyond relational algebra, ideally we should start with the language for which naïve evaluation computes certain answers (i.e., (7.3) holds), and then extend it with a limited form of negation. It is known that the class of unions of conjunctive queries is not the only language that satisfies (7.3); in fact, queries expressible in DATALOG, the recursive extension of the class of unions of conjunctive queries are also such, and they have polynomial time data too. (For the reader who is not familiar with DATALOG, we review its syntax and semantics later in this section). Thus, DATALOG retains several of the good properties of unions of conjunctive queries for data exchange purposes. In particular, certain answers to a DATALOG program Π over a source instance S can be computed efficiently by first materializing a canonical universal solution T for S, and then evaluating Π over T.

However, as we proved in Theorem 7.4, adding an unrestricted form of negation to DATALOG (or even to the class of conjunctive queries) easily yields to intractability of the problem of computing certain answers (even for mappings without target dependencies). Despite this negative result, it can still be shown that there is a natural way to add negation to DATALOG while keeping all of the good properties of this language for data exchange. In order to define this language, we assume that the target schema $\mathbf{R_t}$ is enriched with a way to distinguish constants from nulls. That is, we assume that there is a unary relation symbol $\mathbf{C}$, such that for every target instance T the interpretation of $\mathbf{C}$ in T is precisely the set of constants in the domain of T. This is a very realistic assumption: practical languages allow testing for nulls (e.g., the IS NULL condition in SQL; its negation thus defines constants).

Definition 7.6 (DATALOG$^{\mathbf{C}(\neq)}$ programs)   A *constant-inequality* DATALOG *rule* is one of the form:

$$S(\bar{x}) \leftarrow S_1(\bar{x}_1), \ldots, S_\ell(\bar{x}_\ell), \mathbf{C}(y_1), \ldots, \mathbf{C}(y_m), u_1 \neq v_1, \ldots, u_n \neq v_n, \qquad (7.4)$$

such that:

(1) $S, S_1, \ldots, S_\ell$ are (not necessarily distinct) relation symbols,
(2) every variable in $\bar{x}$ is mentioned in some tuple $\bar{x}_i$, for $1 \leq i \leq \ell$,
(3) every variable y_j, for $1 \leq j \leq m$, is mentioned in some tuple $\bar{x}_i$, for $1 \leq i \leq \ell$,
(4) every variable u_j and every variable v_j, for $1 \leq j \leq n$, is equal to some variable y_i, for $1 \leq i \leq m$.

A *constant-inequality* DATALOG *program* (DATALOG$^{\mathbf{C}(\neq)}$ program) Π is a finite set of constant-inequality DATALOG rules. A DATALOG program is a DATALOG$^{\mathbf{C}(\neq)}$ program without inequalities.   □

That is, DATALOG$^{\mathbf{C}(\neq)}$ programs are just the usual DATALOG programs enriched with inequalities which can only be checked for constants, and not nulls. This is syntactically enforced by condition (4) in the definition of a DATALOG$^{\mathbf{C}(\neq)}$ rule: if the inequality $x \neq y$ appears in a DATALOG$^{\mathbf{C}(\neq)}$ rule, then the atoms $\mathbf{C}(x)$ and $\mathbf{C}(y)$, binding x and y to the set of constants, must also appear in it.

The following is an example of a constant-inequality DATALOG program:

$$R(x,y) \leftarrow T(x,z), S(z,y), \mathbf{C}(x), \mathbf{C}(z), x \neq z$$
$$S(x) \leftarrow U(x,u,v,w), \mathbf{C}(u), \mathbf{C}(v), u \neq v.$$

For a rule of the form (7.4), we say that $S(\bar{x})$ is its head. The set of predicates of a DATALOG$^{\mathbf{C}(\neq)}$ program Π, denoted by $Pred(\Pi)$, is the set of predicate symbols mentioned in Π, while the set of intensional predicates of Π, denoted by $IPred(\Pi)$, is the set of predicates symbols $R \in Pred(\Pi)$ such that $R(\bar{x})$ appears as the head of some rule of Π.

Fix a DATALOG$^{\mathbf{C}(\neq)}$ program Π and let I be a database instance of the relational schema $Pred(\Pi)$. Then $\mathscr{T}(I)$ is an instance of $Pred(\Pi)$ such that for every $R \in Pred(\Pi)$ and every tuple $\bar{t}$, it holds that $\bar{t} \in R^{\mathscr{T}(I)}$ if and only if there exists a rule

$$R(\bar{x}) \leftarrow R_1(\bar{x}_1), \ldots, R_\ell(\bar{x}_\ell), \mathbf{C}(y_1), \ldots, \mathbf{C}(y_m), u_1 \neq v_1, \ldots, u_n \neq v_n$$

in Π and a variable assignment σ such that:

1. $\sigma(\bar{x}) = \bar{t}$,
2. $\sigma(\bar{x}_i) \in R_i^I$, for every $1 \leq i \leq \ell$,

3. $\sigma(y_i)$ is a constant, for every $1 \leq i \leq m$, and

4. $\sigma(u_i) \neq \sigma(v_i)$, for every $1 \leq i \leq n$.

The operator $\mathscr{T}$ is used to define the semantics of constant-inequality Datalog programs. More precisely, define

- $\mathscr{T}_{\Pi}^0(I) := I$, and
- $\mathscr{T}_{\Pi}^{n+1}(I) := \mathscr{T}(\mathscr{T}_{\Pi}^n(I)) \cup \mathscr{T}_{\Pi}^n(I)$, for every $n \geq 0$.

Then the evaluation of Π over I is defined as $\mathscr{T}_{\Pi}^{\infty}(I) = \bigcup_{n \geq 0} \mathscr{T}_{\Pi}^n(I)$.

A constant-inequality Datalog program Π is said to be defined over a relational schema $\mathbf{R}$ if $\mathbf{R} = Pred(\Pi) - IPred(\Pi)$ and $\text{ANSWER} \in IPred(\Pi)$. Intuitively, ANSWER is a distinguished predicate that is used to define the evaluation of a $\text{DATALOG}^{C(\neq)}$ program over an instance. Given an instance I of $\mathbf{R}$ and a tuple $\bar{t}$ in $\text{DOM}(I)^n$, where n is the arity of ANSWER, we say that $\bar{t} \in \Pi(I)$ if $\bar{t} \in \text{ANSWER}^{\mathscr{T}_{\Pi}^{\infty}(I_0)}$, where I_0 is the extension of I defined as: $R^{I_0} = R^I$ for $R \in \mathbf{R}$ and $R^{I_0} = \emptyset$ for $R \in IPred(\Pi)$.

Computing certain answers of $\text{DATALOG}^{C(\neq)}$ programs

The reason that explains why certain answers of unions of conjunctive queries can be obtained by means of naïve evaluation is that these queries are preserved under homomorphisms. Recall that this means that if Q is a union of conjunctive queries over $\mathbf{R_t}$, and T and T' are two target instances such that there is a homomorphism from T to T', then a tuple $\bar{a}$ of constants that belongs to the evaluation of Q over T also belongs to the evaluation of Q over T'.

It is well-known that DATALOG programs are also preserved under homomorphisms, and, therefore, that their certain answers can be obtained by means of naïve evaluation. Unfortunately, extending DATALOG programs (or even conjunctive queries) with inequalities destroys preservation under homomorphisms. For example, assume that we have an instance T that only contains the fact $R(a, \bot)$, where $a \in \text{CONST}$ and $\bot \in \text{VAR}$. Let Q be the following conjunctive query with one inequality: $\exists x \exists y (R(x,y) \wedge x \neq y)$. Clearly, $T \models Q$ but $T' \not\models Q$, where T' is the homomorphic image of T witnessed by the homomorphism $h(\bot) = a$.

But as we mentioned before, the homomorphisms in data exchange are not arbitrary; they are the identity on the constants. Thus, given that inequalities are witnessed by constants in $\text{DATALOG}^{C(\neq)}$ programs, we have that these programs are preserved under homomorphisms. From this we conclude that the certain answers of a $\text{DATALOG}^{C(\neq)}$ program Π can be computed by directly evaluating Π over a universal solution and then discarding those tuples that contain nulls. Since the data complexity of evaluating $\text{DATALOG}^{C(\neq)}$ programs is in PTIME, we conclude the following:

Proposition 7.7 *Let $\mathscr{M} = (\mathbf{R_s}, \mathbf{R_t}, \Sigma_{st}, \Sigma_t)$ be a mapping such that Σ_t consists of a set of egds and a weakly acyclic set of tgds, and let Π be a $\text{DATALOG}^{C(\neq)}$ program over $\mathbf{R_t}$. Then $\text{CERTAIN}_{\mathscr{M}}(\Pi)$ can be solved in PTIME.*

Expressive power of $\text{DATALOG}^{\text{C}(\neq)}$ programs

With respect to the expressive power of $\text{DATALOG}^{\text{C}(\neq)}$ programs, it is possible to prove that they are capable of subsuming, in terms of certain answers, the class of unions of conjunctive queries with at most one negated atom per disjunct (in the absence of target dependencies).

Theorem 7.8 *Let $\mathcal{M} = (\mathbf{R_s}, \mathbf{R_t}, \Sigma_{st})$ be a mapping and let Q be a union of conjunctive queries with at most one inequality or negated relational atom per disjunct. Then there exists a $\text{DATALOG}^{\text{C}(\neq)}$ program Π_Q such that for every source instance S, $certain_{\mathcal{M}}(Q,S) = certain_{\mathcal{M}}(\Pi_Q, S)$.*

It immediately follows that computing certain answers for this class of queries is tractable:

Corollary 7.9 *Let $\mathcal{M} = (\mathbf{R_s}, \mathbf{R_t}, \Sigma_{st})$ be a relational mapping and let Q be a union of conjunctive queries with at most one inequality or negated relational atom per disjunct. Then $\text{CERTAIN}_{\mathcal{M}}(Q)$ can be solved in PTIME.*

The proof of Theorem 7.8, although not too difficult, is quite technical. For our purposes it will be sufficient to illustrate the basic ideas behind this proof with an example.

Example 7.10 Let $\mathcal{M} = (\mathbf{R_s}, \mathbf{R_t}, \Sigma_{st})$ be a LAV mapping such that $\mathbf{R_s}$ consists of a unary relation A and binary relations B and C, and $\mathbf{R_t}$ consists of a unary relation U and a binary relation V. Let Σ_{st} consist of the following st-tgds:

$$A(x) \rightarrow U(x)$$
$$B(x,y) \rightarrow V(x,y)$$
$$C(x,y) \rightarrow \exists z (V(x,z) \wedge V(z,y) \wedge U(z)).$$

Let Q be the following Boolean conjunctive query with one inequality:

$$\exists x \exists y \exists z (V(x,z) \wedge V(z,y) \wedge U(x) \wedge U(y) \wedge x \neq y).$$

We construct a $\text{DATALOG}^{\text{C}(\neq)}$ program Π_Q such that $certain_{\mathcal{M}}(Q,S) = certain_{\mathcal{M}}(\Pi_Q, S)$, for every source instance S. The set of intensional predicates of the $\text{DATALOG}^{\text{C}(\neq)}$ program Π_Q consists of the unary predicate U', the binary predicate V', the unary predicate DOM, and the distinguished 0-ary predicate ANSWER. The program Π_Q over $\mathbf{R_t}$ is defined as follows.

- First, the program collects in $\text{DOM}(x)$ all the elements that belong to the domain of the instance of $\mathbf{R_t}$ where Π_Q is evaluated:

$$\text{DOM}(x) \leftarrow V(x,y) \tag{7.5}$$
$$\text{DOM}(x) \leftarrow V(y,x) \tag{7.6}$$
$$\text{DOM}(x) \leftarrow U(x). \tag{7.7}$$

- Second, the program Π_Q includes the following rules that formalize the idea that $\text{EQUAL}(x,y)$ holds if x and y are the same elements:

$$\text{EQUAL}(x,x) \leftarrow \text{DOM}(x) \tag{7.8}$$

$$\text{EQUAL}(x,y) \leftarrow \text{EQUAL}(y,x) \tag{7.9}$$

$$\text{EQUAL}(x,y) \leftarrow \text{EQUAL}(x,z), \text{EQUAL}(z,y). \tag{7.10}$$

Notice that we cannot simply use the rule $\text{EQUAL}(x,x) \leftarrow$ to say that EQUAL is reflexive, as $\text{DATALOG}^{\text{C}(\neq)}$ programs are *safe*, i.e., every variable that appears in the head of a rule also has to appear in its body.

- Third, Π_Q includes the rules:

$$U'(x) \leftarrow U(x) \tag{7.11}$$

$$V'(x,y) \leftarrow V(x,y) \tag{7.12}$$

$$U'(x) \leftarrow U'(u), \text{EQUAL}(u,x) \tag{7.13}$$

$$V'(x,y) \leftarrow V'(u,v), \text{EQUAL}(u,x), \text{EQUAL}(v,y). \tag{7.14}$$

Intuitively, the first two rules create in U' and V' a copy of U and V, respectively. This allows us to work with copies of U and V as intensional predicates. The last two rules replace equal elements in the interpretation of U' and V'.

- Fourth, Π_Q includes the following rule representing the query Q:

$$\text{EQUAL}(x,y) \leftarrow V'(x,z) \wedge V'(z,y) \wedge U'(x) \wedge U'(y). \tag{7.15}$$

Intuitively, this rule says that if the certain answer of Q is false, then for every tuple (a,b,c) of elements such that the pairs (a,b) and (b,c) belong to the interpretation of V', and the elements a and c belong to the interpretation of U', it must be the case that $a = c$.

- Finally, Π_Q includes one rule for collecting the answer to Q:

$$\text{ANSWER} \leftarrow \text{EQUAL}(x,y), \text{C}(x), \text{C}(y), x \neq y. \tag{7.16}$$

Intuitively, rule (7.16) says that if in the process of evaluating Π_Q, two distinct constants a and b are declared to be equal ($\text{EQUAL}(a,b)$ holds), then the certain answer to Q is true. Notice that this rule makes use of constant-inequalities.

We show the application of the program with an example. Let $S = \{A(a), A(b), B(a,c), B(d,b), C(c,d)\}$ be a source instance. It is not hard to see that the canonical universal solution T for S is of the form

$$\{U(a), U(b), U(\bot), V(a,c), V(c,\bot), V(\bot,d), V(d,b)\},$$

where $\bot$ is a null. Recall that $certain_{\mathcal{M}}(\Pi_Q, S) = \Pi_Q(T)$, and hence it is sufficient for us to study the evaluation of Π_Q over T.

First, by applying rules (7.11) and (7.12) we can conclude that $U'(a)$, $U'(b)$, $U'(\bot)$, $V'(a,c)$, $V'(c,\bot)$, $V'(\bot,d)$ and $V'(d,b)$ hold in T. Therefore, we obtain by using rule

(7.15) with different assignments that $\text{EQUAL}(a, \perp)$ and $\text{EQUAL}(\perp, b)$ hold in T. Notice that this rule is trying to prove that $certain_{\mathscr{M}}(Q, S) = \texttt{false}$, and hence it forces $\perp$ to be equal to a and to b. Now by using rule (7.10), we obtain that $\text{EQUAL}(a, b)$ holds in T. But this cannot be the case since a and b are distinct constants and, thus, rule (7.16) is used to conclude that $certain_{\mathscr{M}}(Q, S) = \texttt{true}$. Note that this conclusion is correct. Indeed, if T' is an arbitrary solution for S, then there exists a homomorphism $h : T \to T'$. Given that a and b are distinct constants, we have that $a \neq h(\perp)$ or $b \neq h(\perp)$. It follows that there are elements $w_1, w_2, w_3 \in \text{DOM}(T')$ such that (w_1, w_2) and (w_2, w_3) belong to $V^{T'}$, $w_1, w_3 \in U^{T'}$ and $w_1 \neq w_3$. Thus, we conclude that $certain_{\mathscr{M}}(Q, S) = \texttt{true}$.

It is now an easy exercise to show that $certain_{\mathscr{M}}(Q, S) = certain_{\mathscr{M}}(\Pi_Q, S)$, for every source instance S.   □

The $\text{DATALOG}^{\mathbf{C}(\neq)}$ program Π_Q shown in the previous example made use of constant-inequalities. It is not hard to prove that constant-inequalities are, indeed, necessary in this case. That is, there is no DATALOG program Π such that $certain_{\mathscr{M}}(Q, S) = certain_{\mathscr{M}}(\Pi, S)$, for every source instance S. We leave this as an exercise to the reader.

Notice that all the results in this section have been established for mappings without target dependencies. It is easy to see that Theorem 7.8 remains true when mappings are allowed to contain egds in Σ_t. This implies that certain answers of unions of conjunctive queries, with at most one negated atom per disjunct, can be computed in polynomial time for relational mappings $(\mathbf{R_s}, \mathbf{R_t}, \Sigma_{st}, \Sigma_t)$ such that Σ_t consists of a set of egds. It can also be proved, by using slightly different techniques based on a refinement of the chase procedure, that the latter result remains true even for mappings that allow in Σ_t a set of egds and a weakly acyclic set of tgds.

7.5 Rewritability over special solutions

Recall that a very desirable property for query answering in data exchange is to be able to compute certain answer to queries over a materialized solution. The query that one evaluates over a materialized solution is not necessarily the original query Q, but rather a query Q' obtained from Q, or, in other words, a *rewriting* of Q. The key property of such a rewriting Q' is that, for each given source S and materialized target T, we have

$$certain_{\mathscr{M}}(Q, S) = Q'(T). \tag{7.17}$$

Comparing this with (7.1), we see that $Q_{\text{naïve}}$ was a rewriting for unions of conjunctive queries, over universal solutions.

In general, the rewriting Q' of a query Q need not be a query in the same language as Q. But usually, one looks for rewritings in languages with polynomial time data complexity (e.g., relational algebra or, equivalently, FO). In this chapter we deal with FO-rewritings.

We now define the notion of rewritings precisely. For that, we continue using the unary predicate $\mathbf{C}$ that distinguishes constants in target instances. The extension of the target schema $\mathbf{R_t}$ with this predicate $\mathbf{C}$ is denoted by $\mathbf{R_t^C}$. For the rest of this section, we only deal with mappings without target dependencies (in particular, for avoiding the problem of the existence of universal solutions).

Definition 7.11 (Rewritings)   Let $\mathcal{M} = (\mathbf{R_s}, \mathbf{R_t}, \Sigma_{st})$ be a mapping and Q a query over the target schema $\mathbf{R_t}$. We say that Q is FO-*rewritable over the canonical universal solution (respectively, the core) under* $\mathcal{M}$, if there is an FO-query Q' over $\mathbf{R_t^C}$ such that

$$certain_{\mathcal{M}}(Q,S) = Q'(T),$$

for every source instance S with canonical universal solution (respectively, core) T.   □

The following facts are known about FO-rewritings in data exchange.

- Unions of conjunctive queries are FO-rewritable under any mapping $\mathcal{M}$, both over the canonical universal solution and the core. Indeed, we have seen that the rewriting of a union of conjunctive queries $Q(x_1,\ldots,x_m)$ is the query $Q_{\text{naïve}}$, which is obtained by evaluating Q and only keeping tuples without nulls. It can therefore be expressed as

$$Q(x_1,\ldots,x_m) \wedge \mathbf{C}(x_1) \wedge \cdots \wedge \mathbf{C}(x_m).$$

  Notice that this rewriting is a union of conjunctive queries as well, is independent of the mapping, and can be constructed in linear time from $Q(x_1,\ldots,x_m)$.
- There exists a union of conjunctive queries with negated atoms, Q, and a LAV mapping $\mathcal{M}$, such that Q is not FO-rewritable under $\mathcal{M}$ over the canonical universal solution. We gave an example in the proof of Theorem 7.5.
- There exists a Boolean conjunctive query Q with a single inequality and a LAV mapping $\mathcal{M}$, such that Q is not FO-rewritable under $\mathcal{M}$, both over the canonical universal solution and over the core. The proof of this fact is left as an exercise to the reader. We prove a closely related result in the next section (Proposition 7.16).

The previous two observations naturally raise the following question: Is the problem of checking whether an FO-query admits an FO-rewriting over the canonical universal solution (or the core) decidable? Unfortunately, the answer is negative.

Proposition 7.12   *The problem of checking, for a relational mapping* $\mathcal{M} = (\mathbf{R_s}, \mathbf{R_t}, \Sigma_{st})$ *and an* FO-*query Q over $\mathbf{R_t}$, whether Q is* FO-*rewritable over the canonical universal solution or over the core under* $\mathcal{M}$, *is undecidable.*

Proof   In order to prove the proposition we need the concept of a *domain-independent* query. We avoid the formal definition but take advantage of one of the more important properties of a domain-independent query Q over schema $\mathbf{R}$: If K' is an instance of a schema $\mathbf{R}'$ that extends $\mathbf{R}$ and K is the restriction of K' to the relation symbols in $\mathbf{R}$, then $Q(K) = Q(K')$. Intuitively, this means that the evaluation of Q is independent of the interpretation of the relation symbols that are not mentioned in Q. An example of a query that is not domain-independent is $\forall x(\neg Q(x) \rightarrow R(x))$.

It follows from Trakhtenbrot's theorem that the following problem is undecidable: Given a domain-independent Boolean FO formula φ over schema $\mathbf{R}$, is there an instance K of

R such that $K \models \varphi$? In order to prove the proposition, we reduce this problem to the complement of the problem of checking whether a Boolean FO formula admits an FO-rewriting over the canonical universal solution or the core. That is, we show that for each schema **R** and domain-independent Boolean FO formula φ over **R**, one can compute a relational mapping $\mathscr{M} = (\mathbf{R_s}, \mathbf{R_t}, \Sigma_{st})$ and a Boolean FO formula θ over $\mathbf{R_t}$ such that the following two facts are equivalent:

1. There is an instance K of **R** such that $K \models \varphi$.
2. θ is *not* FO-rewritable over the canonical universal solution (respectively, the core) under $\mathscr{M}$.

Take an arbitrary schema **R** and a domain-independent Boolean FO formula φ over **R**. We show how to construct $\mathscr{M}$ and θ from φ and **R**. First of all, we prove in the following section (Proposition 7.16) that there is a relational mapping $\mathscr{M}' = (\mathbf{R}'_s, \mathbf{R}'_t, \Sigma'_{st})$ and a domain-independent Boolean FO formula ψ_{nr}, such that ψ_{nr} is FO-rewritable neither over the canonical universal solution nor over the core under $\mathscr{M}'$. Without loss of generality we assume that $\mathbf{R}'_s$ and **R** contain no relation symbols in common. With the help of $\mathscr{M}'$ and ψ_{nr} we can construct $\mathscr{M} = (\mathbf{R_s}, \mathbf{R_t}, \Sigma_{st})$ and θ as follows:

- $\mathbf{R_s}$ consists of all the relation symbols that are either in **R** or in $\mathbf{R}'_s$ (recall that **R** and $\mathbf{R}'_s$ are assumed to be disjoint).
- $\mathbf{R_t}$ consists of all the relation symbols that are either in $\mathbf{R}'$ or in $\mathbf{R}'_t$, where $\mathbf{R}'$ is a disjoint copy of **R**; that is, if $\mathbf{R} = \{R_1, \dots, R_n\}$ then $\mathbf{R}' = \{R'_1, \dots, R'_n\}$ and R_i and R'_i have the same arity. Further, we assume without loss of generality that $\mathbf{R}'$ has no relation symbols in common with either $\mathbf{R}'_t$ or $\mathbf{R}'_s$.
- Σ_{st} is defined as

$$\Sigma'_{st} \cup \{R_i(\bar{x}) \rightarrow R'_i(\bar{x}) \mid 1 \leq i \leq n\}.$$

That is, Σ_{st} consists of the st-tgds in Σ'_{st}, that relate source relation symbols in $\mathbf{R}'_s$ with target relation symbols in $\mathbf{R}'_t$ in a way that is consistent with $\mathscr{M}'$, plus a set of *copying* st-tgds that transfer the source content of each relation symbol in **R** into the corresponding target relation symbol in $\mathbf{R}'$.

- Finally, θ is defined as $\varphi' \rightarrow \psi_{nr}$, where φ' is the Boolean FO formula over $\mathbf{R}'$ that is obtained from φ by replacing each occurrence of the relation symbol R_i with R'_i, for every $1 \leq i \leq n$.

We prove next that there exists an instance K of **R** such that $K \models \varphi$ if and only if θ is not rewritable over the canonical universal solution (respectively, over the core) under $\mathscr{M}$.

Assume first that for every instance K of **R** it is the case that $K \not\models \varphi$. Then for every source instance S of $\mathbf{R_s}$, and solution T for S under $\mathscr{M}$, we have $T \not\models \varphi'$. Assume otherwise. Then the restriction T' of T to the relation symbols in $\mathbf{R}'$ also satisfies φ' (since φ' is domain-independent), and, therefore, the instance K of **R** that is obtained from T' by setting R_j^K to coincide with the interpretation of R'_j in T', for each $1 \leq j \leq n$, satisfies φ, which is a contradiction. This implies that θ is FO-rewritable over the canonical universal solution and over the core simply by the Boolean constant `true`.

The proof of the converse is postponed until the next section as we need to develop some additional techniques, based on locality, for showing it. The proof will be given at the very end of Section 7.5. □

Despite this undecidability result, we can state some sufficient conditions for *non-rewritability* of queries that allow us to exclude some classes of relational algebra queries as not easily answerable in the data exchange scenario, This will be done in the next section.

Rewritability: canonical universal solution vs the core

What is the relationship between rewritability over the canonical universal solution, and over the core? It turns out that the class of queries rewritable over the core is strictly smaller than the class of queries rewritable over the canonical universal solution, as long as mappings do not contain target constraints.

Theorem 7.13 *For mappings without target dependencies Σ_t, the following hold:*

1. *Every* FO-*query Q that is* FO-*rewritable over the core is also rewritable over the canonical universal solution.*
2. *There is a mapping $\mathcal{M}$ and an* FO-*query Q that is* FO-*rewritable over the canonical universal solution but not over the core.*

Thus, as we mentioned before, there is the following trade-off in choosing the canonical universal solution or the core as the preferred solution in data exchange:

- the core allows the most compact materialization among all possible universal solutions; however,
- this comes at the cost of losing the capability for FO-rewriting of some queries.

The proof of Theorem 7.13 depends on nontrivial model theoretical properties of cores and canonical universal solutions that go beyond the scope of the book.

7.6 Non-rewritability tool: locality

Locality is a standard tool in the study of logical expressibility, for instance, in relational calculus (FO) and some of its extensions. Here we use it to answer questions about the expressive power of FO-rewritings in data exchange. In particular, we develop a simple locality tool that helps determine when a target query does *not* admit an FO-rewriting over the solutions we have studied so far. But first we need to introduce the necessary terminology for studying local properties of data.

The *Gaifman graph $\mathcal{G}(S)$* of an instance S of **R** is the graph whose nodes are the elements of $\text{DOM}(S)$, and such that there exists an edge between a and b in $\mathcal{G}(S)$ iff a and b belong to the same tuple of a relation R^S, for some $R \in \mathbf{R}$. For example, if H is an undirected graph, then $\mathscr{G}(H)$ is H itself; if H' is a directed graph, then $\mathscr{G}(H')$ is its underlying undirected graph.

The distance between two elements a and b in S, denoted by $\Delta_S(a,b)$ (or $\Delta(a,b)$, if S is understood), is the distance between them in $\mathscr{G}(S)$. If $\bar{a}$ is a tuple of elements in $\text{DOM}(S)$, we define $\Delta(\bar{a},b)$ as the minimum value of $\Delta(a,b)$ where a is an element of $\bar{a}$.

Given a tuple $\bar{a} = (a_1, \ldots, a_m) \in \text{DOM}(S)^m$, we define the instance $N_d^S(\bar{a})$, called the *d-neighborhood of $\bar{a}$ in S*, as the restriction of S to the elements at distance at most d from $\bar{a}$, with the members of $\bar{a}$ treated as distinguished elements. That is, if two neighborhoods $N_d^{S_1}(\bar{a})$ and $N_d^{S_2}(\bar{b})$ are isomorphic (written as $N_d^{S_1}(\bar{a}) \cong N_d^{S_2}(\bar{b})$), then there is an isomorphism $f : N_d^{S_1}(\bar{a}) \to N_d^{S_2}(\bar{b})$ such that $f(a_i) = b_i$, for $1 \leq i \leq m$.

Next we define when two tuples in different instances are locally indistinguishable. Let S_1 and S_2 be two instances of the same schema, and $\bar{a}$ in $\text{DOM}(S_1)$ and $\bar{b}$ in $\text{DOM}(S_2)$ be two m-tuples. We write $(S_1, \bar{a}) \leftrightarrows_d (S_2, \bar{b})$ if there is a bijection $f : \text{DOM}(S_1) \to \text{DOM}(S_2)$ such that $N_d^{S_1}(\bar{a}c) \cong N_d^{S_2}(\bar{b}f(c))$ for every $c \in \text{DOM}(S_1)$. The $\leftrightarrows_d$ relation expresses, in a sense, the notion that locally two structures look the same, with respect to a certain bijection f. In particular, f sends each element c into $f(c)$ that has the same neighborhood.

It is important in the development of our locality tool to understand when the semantics of a target query in data exchange depends only on the local character of the source data. In order to do this, we introduce next the concept of *local source-dependence* that relates notions of locality over source instances with certain answers for target queries. Intuitively, a target query Q is locally source-dependent if the fact that tuples $\bar{a}$ and $\bar{b}$ of constants in source instance S_1 and S_2, respectively, are locally indistinguishable, implies that $\bar{a}$ and $\bar{b}$ cannot be distinguished by computing certain answers to Q over S_1 and S_2. Formally:

Definition 7.14 (Locally source-dependent queries)   Given a relational mapping $\mathscr{M} = (\mathbf{R_s}, \mathbf{R_t}, \Sigma_{st})$ and an m-ary query Q over $\mathbf{R_t}$, where $m \geq 0$, we say that Q is *locally source-dependent* under $\mathscr{M}$ if there is a $d \geq 0$ such that for every two source instances S_1 and S_2 and for every $\bar{a} \in \text{DOM}(S_1)^m$ and $\bar{b} \in \text{DOM}(S_2)^m$,

if $(S_1, \bar{a}) \leftrightarrows_d (S_2, \bar{b})$ then

$$(\bar{a} \in certain_{\mathscr{M}}(Q, S_1) \quad \Leftrightarrow \quad \bar{b} \in certain_{\mathscr{M}}(Q, S_2)). \qquad \square$$

The main result of this section states that this notion applies to all queries that are FO-rewritable over the canonical universal solution or over the core.

Theorem 7.15   *Let $\mathscr{M} = (\mathbf{R_s}, \mathbf{R_t}, \Sigma_{st})$ be a relational mapping and Q a query over $\mathbf{R_t}$. Assume that Q is FO-rewritable over the canonical universal solution or over the core. Then Q is locally source-dependent under $\mathscr{M}$.*

The proof of this result is technically involved, and again depends on model-theoretical properties of canonical universal solutions and cores (as in the case of the proof of Theorem 7.13). More interesting for us is the fact that this theorem is a powerful tool for proving non-rewritability results for target FO-queries. We explain how to obtain these inexpressibility results below.

Let $\mathcal{M} = (\mathbf{R_s}, \mathbf{R_t}, \Sigma_{st})$ be a relational mapping. Assume that we want to show that an m-ary query Q over $\mathbf{R_t}$ ($m \geq 0$) is FO-rewritable neither over the core, nor over the canonical universal solution, under $\mathcal{M}$. According to Theorem 7.13, for that it is enough to prove that Q is not locally source-dependent under $\mathcal{M}$. And in order to do this it is sufficient to construct for every $d \geq 0$ two source instances S_1 and S_2 and two m-tuples $\bar{a}$ and $\bar{b}$ of constants in $\text{DOM}(S_1)$ and $\text{DOM}(S_2)$, respectively, such that:

- $(S_1, \bar{a}) \leftrightarrows_d (S_2, \bar{b})$, and
- $\bar{a} \in certain_{\mathcal{M}}(Q, S_1)$ but $\bar{b} \notin certain_{\mathcal{M}}(Q, S_2)$.

Even simpler, in the case of Boolean queries Q, we know that Q is *not* FO-rewritable (over the core or the canonical universal solution) if, for every $d \geq 0$, we can find two instances S_1, S_2 such that:

- $S_1 \leftrightarrows_d S_2$, and
- $certain_{\mathcal{M}}(Q, S_1) \neq certain_{\mathcal{M}}(Q, S_2)$.

We now apply this methodology to prove non-rewritability results for FO-queries under extremely simple relational mappings. We call a relational mapping $\mathcal{M} = (\mathbf{R_s}, \mathbf{R_t}, \Sigma_{st})$ *copying* if $\mathbf{R_s}$ and $\mathbf{R_t}$ are two copies of the same schema; that is, $\mathbf{R_s} = \{R_1, \ldots, R_n\}$, $\mathbf{R_t} = \{R'_1, \ldots, R'_n\}$, and R_i and R'_i have the same arity, and

$$\Sigma_{st} = \{R_i(\bar{x}) \to R'_i(\bar{x}) \mid 1 \leq i \leq n\}.$$

Note that a copying mapping is both LAV and GAV. Informally, these mappings simply "copy" the source data into the target.

We now look at the existence of FO-rewritings for the class of unions of conjunctive queries with at most one negated relational atom per disjunct. We know, from Theorem 7.8, that each one of these queries admits a rewriting over an arbitrary universal solution in DATALOG$^{C(\neq)}$. Some of these queries, of course, admit FO-rewritings (e.g., if no negated atom are present). But this is not a general phenomenon, even under copying mappings.

Proposition 7.16 *There exists a copying relational mapping $\mathcal{M} = (\mathbf{R_s}, \mathbf{R_t}, \Sigma_{st})$ and a Boolean FO query Q over $\mathbf{R_t}$ such that:*

1. *Q is the union of a conjunctive query and a conjunctive query with a single negated atom; and*

2. *Q is not rewritable over the canonical universal solution, nor over the core, under $\mathcal{M}$.*

Proof We use exactly the same mapping and query as in the proof of Theorem 7.5. That is, $\mathcal{M} = (\mathbf{R_s}, \mathbf{R_t}, \Sigma_{st})$ is the relational mapping such that $\mathbf{R_s}$ consists of a binary relation E and unary relations A and B, $\mathbf{R_t}$ consists of a binary relation G and unary relations P and

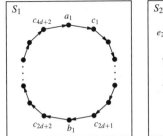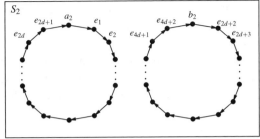

Figure 7.1 Instances S_1 and S_2 of Proposition 7.16.

R, and Σ_{st} consists of the st-tgds:

$$E(x,y) \rightarrow G(x,y)$$
$$A(x) \rightarrow P(x)$$
$$B(x) \rightarrow R(x).$$

Clearly, $\mathscr{M}$ is copying. The query Q over $\mathbf{R_t}$ is defined as:

$$\exists x \exists y \, (P(x) \wedge R(y) \wedge G(x,y)) \vee \exists x \exists y \exists z \, (G(x,z) \wedge G(z,y) \wedge \neg G(x,y)).$$

This is the union of a conjunctive query and a conjunctive query with a single negated relational atom. We prove next that Q is rewritable neither over the canonical universal solution nor over the core under $\mathscr{M}$.

Assume otherwise. We prove below that Q is not locally source-dependent under $\mathscr{M}$, which directly contradicts Theorem 7.15. Recall that for this we need to construct, for every $d \geq 0$, two source instances S_1 and S_2 such that $S_1 \leftrightarrows_d S_2$ but $certain_{\mathscr{M}}(Q,S_1) \neq certain_{\mathscr{M}}(Q,S_2)$.

Define source instances S_1 and S_2 as shown in Figure 7.1: E^{S_1} is a cycle of length $4d+4$ with elements

$$a_1,b_1,c_1,c_2,\ldots,c_{4d+2},$$

E^{S_2} is the disjoint union of two cycles of length $2d+d$, the first one with elements

$$a_2,e_1,\ldots,e_{2d+1},$$

and the second one with elements

$$b_2,e_{2d+2},\ldots,e_{4d+2},$$

$A^{S_1} = \{a_1\}$, $A^{S_2} = \{a_2\}$, $B^{S_1} = \{b_1\}$ and $B^{S_2} = \{b_2\}$. Let $f : \text{DOM}(S_1) \rightarrow \text{DOM}(S_2)$ be defined as $f(a_1) = a_2$, $f(b_1) = b_2$ and

$$\begin{cases} f(c_i) = e_i & \text{if } 1 \le i \le d+1 \text{ or } 2d+2 \le i \le 3d+2 \\ f(c_i) = e_{2d+1+i} & \text{if } d+2 \le i \le 2d+1 \\ f(c_i) = e_{i-2d-1} & \text{if } 3d+3 \le i \le 4d+2. \end{cases}$$

Clearly, f is a bijection from $\text{DOM}(S_1)$ into $\text{DOM}(S_2)$. Furthermore, a simple case analysis proves that for every $v \in \text{DOM}(S_1)$ it is the case that $N_d^{S_1}(v) \cong N_d^{S_2}(f(v))$. This implies that $S_1 \leftrightarrows_d S_2$. However, we prove below that $certain_{\mathscr{M}}(Q,S_1) = \text{true}$ while $certain_{\mathscr{M}}(Q,S_2) = \text{false}$.

Let us consider first S_1. Let T_1 be the canonical universal solution for S_1. Notice that T_1 is just a "copy" of S_1 over the target; that is, $E^{S_1} = G^{T_1}$, $A^{S_1} = P^{T_1}$ and $B^{S_1} = R^{T_1}$. Let T_1' be an arbitrary solution for S_1 that does not satisfy the second disjunct $\exists x \exists y \exists z (G(x,z) \wedge G(z,y) \wedge \neg G(x,y))$ of Q. Then it must be the case that the transitive closure of G^{T_1} is contained in $G^{T_1'}$, and hence that T_1' satisfies the first disjunct $\exists x \exists y (P(x) \wedge R(y) \wedge G(x,y))$ of Q. This is because $a_1 \in P^{T_1'}$, $b_1 \in R^{T_1'}$ and (a_1,b_1) belongs to the transitive closure of G^{T_1}. We conclude that $certain_{\mathscr{M}}(Q,S_1) = \text{true}$.

Let us consider now S_2. Again, the canonical universal solution T_2 for S_2 is a "copy" of S_2 over the target. Let T_2' be the solution for S_2 that is obtained from T_2 by extending the interpretation of G with every tuple that belongs to the transitive closure of G^{T_2}. Then clearly $T_2' \not\models \exists x \exists y \exists z (G(x,z) \wedge G(z,y) \wedge \neg G(x,y))$. Moreover, since a_2 is the only element in T_2' that belongs to the interpretation of P, and b_2 is the only element in T_2' that belongs to the interpretation of R, and a_2 and b_2 belong to different connected components of the graph induced by G^{T_2}, it is the case that $T_2' \not\models \exists x \exists y (P(x) \wedge R(y) \wedge G(x,y))$. We conclude that $T_2' \not\models Q$, and hence that $certain_{\mathscr{M}}(Q,S_2) = \text{false}$. □

With the help of the locality tool, we can now conclude the proof of Proposition 7.12, since now we have techniques for showing non-rewritability of queries. It can be easily shown that the query used in the proof of the previous proposition is domain-independent. Thus, if $\mathscr{M}' = (\mathbf{R}_s', \mathbf{R}_t', \Sigma_{st}')$ and ψ_{nr} are, respectively, the mapping and FO-query used in the proof of the previous proposition, we have that the following holds. The domain-independent Boolean FO-query ψ_{nr} over $\mathbf{R}_t'$ is not FO-rewritable over the canonical universal solution, nor over the core, under $\mathscr{M}'$. (The reasons why we use the names $\mathscr{M}'$ and ψ_{nr} will become clear below.)

Recall what we need to complete the proof of Proposition 7.12. Assume that φ is a domain-independent Boolean FO-query over schema $\mathbf{R}$ (disjoint from $\mathbf{R}_s'$ and $\mathbf{R}_t'$), such that for at least some instance K of $\mathbf{R}$ it is the case that $K \models \varphi$. Let $\mathbf{R}'$ be a "copy" of $\mathbf{R}$, that is in particular disjoint from $\mathbf{R}$, $\mathbf{R}_s'$ and $\mathbf{R}_t'$. Then $\varphi' \to \psi_{nr}$ is not FO-rewritable over the canonical universal solution, nor over the core, under $\mathscr{M} = (\mathbf{R}_s, \mathbf{R}_t, \Sigma_{st})$, where φ' is the "translation" of φ into $\mathbf{R}'$ and $\mathscr{M}$ is the relational mapping that is constructed inside the proof of Proposition 7.12 for $\mathbf{R}$ and $\mathscr{M}'$. That is, (1) φ' is obtained from φ by replacing each occurrence of the relation symbol R in $\mathbf{R}$ with its "copy" R' in $\mathbf{R}'$, (2) $\mathbf{R}_s$ is the disjoint union of $\mathbf{R}$ and $\mathbf{R}'_s$, (3) $\mathbf{R}_t$ is the disjoint union of $\mathbf{R}'$ and $\mathbf{R}_t$, and (4) Σ_{st} consists of the st-tgds in Σ_{st} plus a set of copying st-tgds from $\mathbf{R}$ into $\mathbf{R}'$.

To prove that $\varphi' \to \psi_{nr}$ is not FO-rewritable over the canonical universal solution, nor over the core, we need to show, of course, that it is not locally source-dependent. In the present case, for each $d \geq 0$ we construct source instances S'_1 and S'_2 such that:

- The restriction of both S'_1 and S'_2 to schema $\mathbf{R}$ corresponds to the instance K, and
- the restriction of S'_i, for $i = 1$ or $i = 2$, to $\mathbf{R}_s$ corresponds to the instance S_i used in the proof of Proposition 7.16.

It is easy to see that $S'_1 \leftrightarrows_d S'_2$. This is because S'_i, for $i = 1$ or $i = 2$, essentially consists of the disjoint union of S_i and K, and we know from the proof of Proposition 7.16 that $S_1 \leftrightarrows_d S_2$. We show below that $certain_{\mathcal{M}}(\varphi' \to \psi_{nr}, S'_1) \neq certain_{\mathcal{M}}(\varphi' \to \psi_{nr}, S'_2)$.

Let us consider first S'_1. Consider an arbitrary solution T'_1 for S'_1 under $\mathcal{M}$. Then the restriction T_1 of T'_1 to the relation symbols in $\mathbf{R}'_t$ is a solution for S_1 under $\mathcal{M}'$. But then, since $certain_{\mathcal{M}'}(\psi_{nr}, S_1) = \texttt{true}$, it must be the case that $T_1 \models \psi_{nr}$. Since ψ_{nr} is domain-independent, it follows that $T'_1 \models \psi_{nr}$. We conclude that $certain_{\mathcal{M}}(\varphi' \to \psi_{nr}, S'_1) = \texttt{true}$.

Let us consider now S'_2. Since $certain_{\mathcal{M}'}(\psi_{nr}, S_2) = \texttt{false}$, there exists a solution T_2 for S_2 under $\mathcal{M}'$ such that $T_2 \not\models \psi_{nr}$. Consider now the instance T'_2 of schema $\mathbf{R}_t$ that consists of the disjoint union of T_2 (over schema $\mathbf{R}'_t$) and a "copy" of K (over schema $\mathbf{R}'$). Clearly, T'_2 is a solution for S'_2 under $\mathcal{M}$. The restriction of T'_2 to the relation symbols in $\mathbf{R}'_t$ (which is T_2) does not satisfy ψ_{nr}. But since ψ_{nr} is domain-independent, we also have $T'_2 \not\models \psi_{nr}$. Furthermore, the restriction of T'_2 to $\mathbf{R}$ is a "copy" of K, which satisfies φ. Since φ is a domain-independent query over $\mathbf{R}$, it must be the case that $T'_2 \models \varphi$. We conclude that $T'_2 \models \varphi \wedge \neg \psi_{nr}$, and hence that $certain_{\mathcal{M}}(\varphi \to \psi_{nr}, S'_2) = \texttt{false}$. This completes the proof of Proposition 7.12 from the previous section.

8

Alternative semantics

So far, our default semantics for answering queries in data exchange was the certain answers semantics. But is it always right to use it? After all, we have seen that even in the simplest possible, *copying* mappings, that essentially say "copy the source to the target", some relational algebra queries cannot be answered (see Proposition 7.16 in Section 7.6). This is rather counter-intuitive behavior: one should expect that, in a copying mapping, relations simply change name but not content, and queries should be answerable over a copy of the source.

The standard certain answers semantics presents us with a host of problems:

- some queries are not rewritable even under the simplest mappings;
- computing answers to relational algebra queries is in general an undecidable problem; and
- computing certain answers could be intractable even for very simple and practically relevant classes of queries (e.g., conjunctive queries with inequalities, or SQL queries admitting inequalities in the `where` clause, as shown in Theorem 7.4).

Should we always follow the certain answers semantics? Is it really sacred in data exchange? Or perhaps we can find an alternative data exchange semantics that avoids the problems we listed above?

In a way, there is no fully satisfactory answer to these questions. Every semantics one presents is going to work well in some scenarios, and exhibit problems in others, and thus the choice of the semantics depends on the precise interpretation of what the mapping rules actually mean. But alternative semantics have been proposed, and we present several here that attempt to solve the problems above.

Each of these semantics follows the same idea as certain answers semantics, but *restricts the space of solutions*. That is, they are defined as

$$certain_{\mathcal{M}}^{good}(Q, S) = \bigcap \{Q(T) \mid T \text{ is a "good" solution for } S\}, \qquad (8.1)$$

where "good" somehow determines the preferred solutions in data exchange.

The first of these takes "good" to be universal solutions, which, as we stated in Chapter 6, are the preferred solutions in data exchange. This semantics offers good complexity bounds for query answering over a big class of FO queries, but unfortunately does not solve some of the simplest anomalies.

The second semantics is based on the notion of a *closed-world assumption* that forbids data exchange solutions to be enlarged with facts that are not implied by the source instance and the mapping. That is, "good" solutions are those that populate targets with only as much information as needed to satisfy constraints of mappings. The third semantics is less rigid than the closed-world semantics: it explicitly specifies which attributes are interpreted under the closed-world, and which under the open-world assumptions. These semantics do solve many of the anomalies that appear in data exchange, but unfortunately shares the usual certain answers semantics problems related to intractability of query answering.

Again, it is fair to say that there is no single semantics that solves all the problems in data exchange. But by presenting at least three alternatives to the usual certain answers semantics, we give the reader a few options to choose the semantics that achieves the right balance between the desired expressiveness of queries in data exchange and the efficiency of query evaluation.

8.1 Universal solutions semantics

The first alternative semantics that we present takes the view that universal solutions are the preferred ones in data exchange, and equates "good" in (8.1) with being universal. Thus, for a given query Q, it looks for tuples present in the answer to Q on every *universal* solution, as opposed to every solution. Formally, this semantics is defined as follows.

Definition 8.1 (Universal certain answers)   Let $\mathcal{M}$ be a mapping, Q a query over $\mathbf{R_t}$ and S a source instance. We define the set of *universal certain answers of Q with respect to S under $\mathcal{M}$* (or simply the universal certain answers of Q with respect to S, if $\mathcal{M}$ is clear from the context), as:

$$certain^u_{\mathcal{M}}(Q,S) \ = \ \bigcap \{Q(T) \mid T \text{ is a universal solution for } S\}. \qquad \square$$

Since computing certain answers for a union of conjunctive queries can be done by posing the query over an arbitrary universal solution, we conclude the following:

Proposition 8.2   *If $\mathcal{M}$ is a mapping and Q is a union of conjunctive queries over $\mathbf{R_t}$, then $certain_{\mathcal{M}}(Q,S) = certain^u_{\mathcal{M}}(Q,S)$ for every source instance S.*

However, Proposition 8.2 does not even extend to conjunctive queries with inequalities, as shown in the following example.

Example 8.3   Consider the mapping $\mathcal{M} = (\mathbf{R_s}, \mathbf{R_t}, \Sigma_{st})$ such that Σ_{st} consists of the following st-tgd:

$$R(x,y) \rightarrow \exists z P(x,y,z).$$

That is, R is a binary relation symbol in $\mathbf{R_s}$ and P is a ternary relation symbol in $\mathbf{R_t}$.

Let S be the source instance $\{R(a,b)\}$. Then the universal certain answer of the query

$Q = \exists x \exists y \exists z (P(x,y,z) \wedge x \neq z)$ with respect to S is true, since every universal solution T for S must contain a fact of the form $P(a,b,\bot)$, where $\bot$ is a value in VAR. On the other hand, $certain_{\mathcal{M}}(Q,S) = $ false since $T = \{P(a,b,a)\}$ is a solution for S. Notice that T is not a universal solution for S. □

Query answering under universal solutions semantics

Recall from Theorem 7.2 that certain answers for unions of conjunctive queries can be computed in polynomial time, if the set of target dependencies consists of a set of egds and a weakly acyclic set of tgds. Proposition 8.2 then says that the same is true for universal certain answers. But what can we say about universal certain answers for more expressive relational calculus queries?

First of all, for all of relational calculus, the problem of computing universal certain answers of FO queries is still undecidable, just as the problem of computing the usual certain answers. Indeed, we can just mimic the proof of Proposition 7.1 that shows the result for the usual certain answers. In that proof we constructed, from each relational mapping $\mathcal{M}$, a relational mapping $\mathcal{M}'$ without target dependencies and an FO query Q such that for every source instance S the following holds:

$$certain_{\mathcal{M}'}(Q,S) = \text{false} \iff S \text{ has a solution under } \mathcal{M}.$$

Using exactly the same construction we can prove that for every source instance S, we have:

$$certain^{u}_{\mathcal{M}'}(Q,S) = \text{false} \iff S \text{ has a } universal \text{ solution under } \mathcal{M}.$$

Now using Theorem 6.5 which says that there exists a relational mapping for which the problem of checking for the existence of universal solutions is undecidable, we obtain the following:

Proposition 8.4 *There exists a Boolean* FO *query Q over $\mathbf{R_t}$ and a mapping $\mathcal{M} = (\mathbf{R_s}, \mathbf{R_t}, \Sigma_{st})$, such that the following problem is undecidable: Given a source instance S, is* $certain^{u}_{\mathcal{M}}(Q,S) = $ true?

Summing up, so far we know the following with respect to the complexity of the problem of computing universal certain answers of relational calculus queries:

- For unions of conjunctive queries it is *tractable*, since in this case universal certain answers coincide with the usual certain answers.
- For FO queries, it is *undecidable*, since the problem can be reduced to checking the existence of universal solutions.

But, of course, there is a wide range of interesting classes of relational calculus queries between these two extremes. We now demonstrate that some of these classes lead to efficient query answering algorithms under the universal certain answers semantics, which will be in sharp contrast with the case of the standard certain answers semantics.

Recall from Theorem 7.4 that computing certain answers to conjunctive queries with inequalities is an intractable problem. But Example 8.3 above showed that for this class of queries, the usual certain answers need not coincide with the universal certain answers. This suggests that it may still be possible to compute universal certain answers for conjunctive queries with inequalities in polynomial time. We will actually state a much stronger result in Theorem 8.5: under the universal certain answers semantics, we have tractability of query answering for a big and practically relevant class of FO queries that extends unions of conjunctive queries.

Roughly, an *existential* FO query is given by an FO formula of the form $\exists \bar{y} \varphi(\bar{x}, \bar{y})$, where $\varphi(\bar{x}, \bar{y})$ is a quantifier-free formula in disjunctive normal form satisfying a safety condition. More precisely, it is given by a formula of the form

$$\psi(\bar{x}) = \exists \bar{y} \bigvee_i \bigwedge_j \alpha_{ij},$$

where

- each α_{ij} is either an atomic formula, or the negation of an atomic formula;
- the free variables of each α_{ij} come from $\bar{x}, \bar{y}$; and
- (safety condition) if α_{ij} is a negated atom, i.e., of the form $\neg R(\bar{z})$, then each variable in $\bar{z}$ must occur in some formula $\alpha_{ij'}$ which is a nonnegated atom.

For example, both unions of conjunctive queries, and unions of conjunctive queries with inequalities and negated atoms satisfy these three conditions.

Existential formulae ψ are known to be monotone in the following sense. If I' is an *induced sub-instance* of I and $\bar{t}$ belongs to the evaluation of ψ over I', then $\bar{t}$ belongs to the evaluation of ψ over I. Recall that an induced sub-instance I' of an instance I is given by a set $A \subseteq \text{DOM}(I)$; it contains exactly all the tuples of I whose elements come from A.

Since every universal solution contains a copy of the core as an induced sub-instance, we conclude that the problem of computing the universal certain answers for an existential FO query ψ boils down to evaluating ψ over the core of the universal solutions, discarding all tuples that contain nulls. Thus, in order to compute the universal certain answers of an existential Q with respect to a source instance S, one can use the following procedure.

Recall from Theorem 6.18 that the core of the universal solutions can be computed in polynomial time for every mapping whose sets of target dependencies consists of a set of egds and a weakly acyclic set of tgds. Furthermore, existential queries are FO queries and thus have polynomial time data complexity. Putting these two things together we obtain the following positive result.

Theorem 8.5 *Let $\mathcal{M} = (\mathbf{R_s}, \mathbf{R_t}, \Sigma_{st}, \Sigma_t)$ be a relational mapping such that Σ_t consists of a set of egds and a weakly acyclic set of tgds, and let Q be an existential query over $\mathbf{R_t}$. Then the algorithm* COMPUTEUNIVERSALCERTAINANSWERS$(Q, \mathcal{M})$ *correctly computes universal certain answers of Q with respect to a source S under $\mathcal{M}$ in polynomial time.*

Algorithm 8.1 COMPUTEUNIVERSALCERTAINANSWERS($Q, \mathcal{M}$)

Require: A source instance S

Ensure: If $\text{SOL}_{\mathcal{M}}(S) \neq \emptyset$, then CUA is the set of universal certain answers for Q over S under $\mathcal{M}$. Otherwise, $CUA = \texttt{fail}$

1: let T be the result of COMPUTECORE($\mathcal{M}$) over S

2: **if** $T = \texttt{fail}$ **then**

3:     $CUA := \texttt{fail}$

4: **else**

5:     $CUA := Q_{\text{naïve}}(T)$

6: **end if**

Notice that this is in sharp contrast with Theorem 7.4 which showed that even for very simple existential FO queries (namely, conjunctive queries with inequalities) the problem of computing certain answers could become intractable. Theorem 8.5 also shows that the universal certain answers semantics solves one of the main problems with the usual data exchange semantics that we mentioned at the beginning of the chapter; namely, it permits efficient query answering for a big and practically relevant class of queries that goes well beyond the class of (unions of) conjunctive queries.

Since the semantics based on the set of universal solutions behaves relatively well with respect to the complexity of computing certain answers of FO queries, it is natural to ask whether it also avoids some of the anomalies of query answering mentioned at the beginning of the chapter.

The simplest of the anomalies was stated in Proposition 7.16: there is a copying mapping $\mathcal{M}$ and an FO query Q such that Q is not FO-rewritable over the canonical universal solution. The query Q used in the proof of that proposition was existential. We can now state a partial positive result: for existential queries, the universal certain answers semantics avoids those "copying" anomalies.

Corollary 8.6 *Let $\mathcal{M} = (\mathbf{R_s}, \mathbf{R_t}, \Sigma_{st})$ be a copying mapping and Q an existential query over $\mathbf{R_t}$. Then for every source instance S it is the case that $\text{certain}^u_{\mathcal{M}}(Q, S) = Q(T)$, where T is the canonical universal solution for S under $\mathcal{M}$ (that is, T is the "copy" of S that is obtained by renaming each relation symbol in $\mathbf{R_s}$ into its corresponding relation symbol in $\mathbf{R_t}$).*

For the proof, we observe that universal certain answers of an existential query Q can be obtained by naïve evaluation of Q over the core of the universal solutions. But in copying mappings, the canonical universal solution always coincides with its core (and is just a copy of the source).

However, the counter-intuitive behavior of the certain answers semantics in copying mappings can still be witnessed when we leave the class of existential queries and deal with arbitrary relational calculus queries. In fact, if certain answers to a query Q with respect to a source instance S under a copying mapping do not coincide with the evaluation of Q

over the canonical universal solution T for S (that is, over the "copy" of S that is obtained by renaming each relation symbol in $\mathbf{R_s}$ into its corresponding relation symbol in $\mathbf{R_t}$), we may have an anomaly. The following example shows that the universal certain answers semantics presents this kind of counter-intuitive behavior, even for simple FO queries.

Example 8.7   Consider the copying mapping $\mathcal{M} = (\mathbf{R_s}, \mathbf{R_t}, \Sigma_{st})$ such that Σ_{st} consists of the following st-tgd:

$$P(x,y) \rightarrow P'(x,y).$$

Let $S = \{P(a,b)\}$ be a source instance and Q be the Boolean FO query that asks whether the interpretation of the target relation P' contains exactly one tuple. That is,

$$Q := \exists x \exists y \big(P'(x,y) \wedge \forall x_1 \forall y_1 (P'(x_1,y_1) \rightarrow x = x_1 \wedge y = y_1) \big).$$

Clearly, the query Q holds over the canonical universal solution $T = \{P'(a,b)\}$ for S under $\mathcal{M}$. On the other hand, $certain^u_{\mathcal{M}}(Q,S) = \texttt{false}$, since it is easy to see that the target instance $T' = \{P'(a,b), P'(\perp_1, \perp_2)\}$, where $\perp_1, \perp_2$ are distinct null values, is also a universal solution for S under $\mathcal{M}$, and Q does not hold in T'. $\square$

Summary

We have seen the following behavior of the universal solution semantics:

- Computing universal certain answers for arbitrary relational calculus queries is an undecidable problem, even in the absence of target dependencies.
- There is a large and practically relevant class of FO queries (namely, the class of existential queries), for which query answering under the universal solution semantics can be efficiently solved. Moreover, some of the query answering anomalies disappear for queries in this class.
- However, the new semantics continues to exhibit counter-intuitive behavior when applied to arbitrary FO queries, even in the simplest copying mappings.

In the next section we study a different semantics, based on the idea of a closed-world assumption, that solves all the query answering anomalies we have seen so far and presents good decidability properties for query answering.

8.2 Closed-world semantics

Both the usual and the universal certain answers semantics are based on the *open-world assumption*, or *OWA*. Under this assumption, solutions in $\text{SOL}_{\mathcal{M}}(S)$ are open to adding new facts. That is, if T is a solution, then all extensions of T are solutions as well. Under the universal solution semantics, if T is a universal solution, then all its extensions which are universal must be accounted for when one computes query answers.

All the query answering anomalies we have seen so far arise because of this openness: one can see that in all the examples, we exploit this fact in an essential way. But if we look, for example, at copying settings, then one expects, intuitively, the target to be a copy of the source rather than an extension of a copy, which OWA permits.

To capture this intuition, we propose a different semantics. It is based not on the OWA, but rather on the *closed-world assumption*, or CWA. Under the CWA semantics, solutions are closed for adding any new facts which are not implied by the source instance and the mapping. Since data exchange is about transferring data from source to target, then, intuitively, the semantics for the data exchange problem should be based on the exchanged data only, and not on data that can be later added to the instances. In other words, the semantics should be based on those solutions that contain no more than what is needed to satisfy the specification.

Defining such CWA solutions is not as straightforward as defining solutions under the OWA. The definition in fact is quite different in spirit. Note that the definition of OWA-solutions is declarative: they are instances T such that S and T together satisfy the constraints of the mapping. In contrast, the definition of CWA solutions is *procedural*: it explains how to construct T from S using the mapping and nothing else.

This procedural definition relies on a notion of a justification for a tuple with nulls that may appear in the target. We will present this definition later, but for the time being we shall use a precise *characterization* of solutions under the CWA as our working definition. This characterization is easy to state. For the sake of simplicity, in this section we only deal with mappings without target dependencies. We will later extend the study of the CWA semantics to mappings with target dependencies in Section 8.3.

Recall that an instance T' is a *homomorphic image* of T if there is a homomorphism $h : T \to T'$ such that $h(T)$ – the instance obtained from T by replacing each null $\perp$ by $h(\perp)$ – is exactly T'.

Definition 8.8 (Working definition of CWA solutions)   Let $\mathcal{M} = (\mathbf{R_s}, \mathbf{R_t}, \Sigma_{st})$ be a mapping, S a source instance and T a solution for S. Then T is a CWA *solution* for S if

• T is a universal solution for S, and
• T is a homomorphic image of the canonical universal solution for S.

We denote the set of CWA solutions for S under $\mathcal{M}$ by $\mathrm{SOL}_{\mathcal{M}}^{\mathrm{CWA}}(S)$.   □

The definition makes sense since canonical universal solutions are unique when mappings have no target dependencies (see Proposition 6.10).

If $\mathcal{M}$ is a copying mapping and S is a source instance, then $\mathrm{SOL}_{\mathcal{M}}^{\mathrm{CWA}}(S)$ contains a copy of S and nothing else (since the canonical universal solution is a copy of S and thus the only homomorphism defined on it is the identity). Of course, this observation will be crucial when we later show that a semantics based on the CWA solutions solves query answering anomalies of the OWA.

Note also that the core of the universal solutions is a CWA solution (since, by definition, it is a homomorphic image of the canonical universal solution, and by Proposition 6.15 it is also a universal solution). Moreover, every CWA solution contains the core (since it is universal).

We illustrate the concept of CWA solutions with the following example.

Example 8.9   Consider the mapping $\mathcal{M} = (\mathbf{R_s}, \mathbf{R_t}, \Sigma_{st})$ such that Σ_{st} consists of the following st-tgds:

$$R(x,y) \to \exists z \exists w (P(x,y,z) \wedge U(w,z))$$
$$N(x,y) \to \exists u P(x,y,u).$$

Let S be the source instance $\{R(a,b), N(a,b)\}$. Then, with respect to S, both its canonical universal solution $T = \{P(a,b,\perp_1), P(a,b,\perp_2), U(\perp_3,\perp_1)\}$ and the core of its universal solutions $T' = \{P(a,b,\perp_1), U(\perp_3,\perp_1)\}$ are CWA solutions.

On the other hand, the solution $T_1 = \{P(a,b,\perp_1), U(\perp_1,\perp_1)\}$ is not a CWA solution, simply because it is not a universal solution for S (as there is no homomorphism from T_1 into T). The solution $T_2 = \{P(a,b,\perp_1), P(a,b,\perp_2), P(a,b,\perp_4), U(\perp_3,\perp_1)\}$ is a universal solution for S that is not a homomorphic image of T. Thus, T_2 is not a CWA solution.   □

To connect the definition of CWA solutions with a proper intuition behind the CWA, we will show that these are the solutions that "satisfy" the requirements below (once we properly formalize them):

(A1) Each fact in the solution is *justified* by the source instance and the st-tgds in Σ_{st}.

(A2) *Justifications* for facts are not overused; that is, justifications for facts do not justify more facts than necessary.

(A3) Each "statement" that holds in the solution can be explained by the contents of the source instance and the st-tgds in Σ_{st} only.

We now formalize these requirements. Start with requirement (A1). Consider a mapping $\mathcal{M} = (\mathbf{R_s}, \mathbf{R_t}, \Sigma_{st})$ and a source instance S. A *justification* in S under $\mathcal{M}$ is a tuple of the form $(\sigma, \bar{a})$, where:

- σ is an st-tgd in Σ_{st} of the form $\varphi(\bar{x}) \to \exists \bar{y} \psi(\bar{x}, \bar{y})$, and
- $\bar{a}$ is a tuple of elements in $\text{DOM}(S)$ such that $|\bar{a}| = |\bar{x}|$ and $S \models \varphi(\bar{a})$.

This justification states that any solution T for S under $\mathcal{M}$ must satisfy $\exists \bar{y} \psi(\bar{a}, \bar{y})$. Intuitively, it can be used to *justify* any fact $P(\bar{u})$ that appears in $\psi(\bar{a}, \bar{w})$, where $\bar{w}$ is a tuple of elements in $\text{DOM}(T)$ such that $|\bar{w}| = |\bar{y}|$. If that is the case, we say that the justification $(\sigma, \bar{a})$ is *suitable* for $P(\bar{u})$.

Let T be a solution for S under $\mathcal{M}$. Then the first requirement can be properly formalized as follows:

(A1) Each fact in T can be assigned to some suitable justification in S under $\mathcal{M}$.

In other words, we require that for each fact $P(\bar{v})$ in T there is:

- a justification $(\sigma, \bar{a})$ in S, with σ of the form $\varphi(\bar{x}) \to \exists \bar{y} \psi(\bar{x}, \bar{y})$, and
- an assignment $v : \text{VAR}(\bar{y}) \to \text{DOM}(T)$ where $\text{VAR}(\bar{y})$ is the set of variables mentioned in $\bar{y}$,

such that $T \models \psi(\bar{a}, v(\bar{y}))$ and $P(\bar{v})$ appears in $\psi(\bar{a}, v(\bar{y}))$.

We now move to requirement (A2). Intuitively, it asks that justifications should not be overused. That is, each justification $(\sigma, \bar{a})$ in S under $\mathcal{M}$ must be suitable for the facts in $\psi(\bar{a}, \bar{w})$ for *at most one* tuple $\bar{w}$. Let $\mathscr{J}_{\mathcal{M}}^S$ be the set of justifications in S under $\mathcal{M}$. Let T be a solution for S under $\mathcal{M}$. Then we can formally define the second requirement as follows:

(A2) For every justification $j = (\sigma, \bar{a})$ in $\mathscr{J}_{\mathcal{M}}^S$ with σ of the form $\varphi(\bar{x}) \to \exists \bar{y} \psi(\bar{x}, \bar{y})$, it is the case that there exists *exactly one tuple* $\bar{v}_j$ of elements in $\mathrm{DOM}(T)$ such that $(\sigma, \bar{a})$ is suitable for the facts in $\psi(\bar{a}, \bar{v}_j)$.

By combining with (A1), we obtain that T is the union of the facts in $\psi(\bar{a}, \bar{v}_j)$, as $j = (\sigma, \bar{a})$ ranges over all justifications in $\mathscr{J}_{\mathcal{M}}^S$ and σ is of the form $\varphi(\bar{x}) \to \exists \bar{y} \psi(\bar{x}, \bar{y})$.

Before formalizing requirement (A3), we define a useful notion of CWA *presolutions*; intuitively, these are solutions that satisfy requirements (A1) and (A2).

Let $\mathcal{M} = (\mathbf{R_s}, \mathbf{R_t}, \Sigma_{st})$ be a mapping and S a source instance. Also let $\mathscr{K}_{\mathcal{M}}^S$ be the set of all pairs of the form (j, z), where:

- $j = (\sigma, \bar{a})$ is a justification in $\mathscr{J}_{\mathcal{M}}^S$ with $\sigma = \varphi(\bar{x}) \to \exists \bar{y} \psi(\bar{x}, \bar{y})$, and
- z is a variable in $\bar{y}$.

Consider an assignment $\alpha : \mathscr{K}_{\mathcal{M}}^S \to \mathrm{CONST} \cup \mathrm{VAR}$. We define $\mathscr{B}_\alpha(j)$ to be $\psi(\bar{a}, \alpha(\bar{y}))$, where $\alpha(\bar{y})$ is the tuple of elements in $\mathrm{CONST} \cup \mathrm{VAR}$ that is obtained from $\bar{y}$ by replacing each variable z mentioned in $\bar{y}$ with $\alpha(j, z)$.

Definition 8.10 (CWA presolutions) A CWA *presolution* for source instance S under mapping $\mathcal{M} = (\mathbf{R_s}, \mathbf{R_t}, \Sigma_{st})$ is a target instance T over $\mathbf{R_t}$ such that

$$ T = \bigcup_{j \in \mathscr{J}_{\mathcal{M}}^S} \mathscr{B}_\alpha(j), $$

for some assignment $\alpha : \mathscr{K}_{\mathcal{M}}^S \to \mathrm{CONST} \cup \mathrm{VAR}$. $\qquad \square$

We illustrate this definition with an example:

Example 8.11 Let us consider a mapping $\mathcal{M} = (\mathbf{R_s}, \mathbf{R_t}, \Sigma_{st})$ such that Σ_{st} consists of the st-tgd

$$ \sigma := P(x, y) \to \exists z \exists w (R(x, z) \wedge R(y, w)), $$

and a source instance $S = \{P(a, b)\}$. Then $\mathscr{J}_{\mathcal{M}}^S$ consists of the single justification $j = (\sigma, (a, b))$. Thus, $\mathscr{K}_{\mathcal{M}}^S = \{(j, z), (j, w)\}$.

The canonical universal solution for S is $T = \{R(a, \perp_1), R(b, \perp_2)\}$, where $\perp_1$ and $\perp_2$ are distinct nulls. It is not hard to see that T is a CWA presolution for S under $\mathcal{M}$. Indeed, this is witnessed by the mapping $\alpha : \mathscr{K}_{\mathcal{M}}^S \to \mathrm{CONST} \cup \mathrm{VAR}$ such that $\alpha(j, z) = \perp_1$ and $\alpha(j, w) = \perp_2$. In the same way, the target instance $T_1 = \{R(a, c), R(b, d)\}$ is a CWA presolution for S, as witnessed by the mapping $\alpha : \mathscr{K}_{\mathcal{M}}^S \to \mathrm{CONST} \cup \mathrm{VAR}$ such that $\alpha(j, z) = c$ and $\alpha(j, w) =$

d. Also, the target instance $T_2 = \{R(a, \bot), R(b, \bot)\}$, where $\bot \in \text{VAR}$, is a CWA presolution for S, as witnessed by the mapping $\alpha : \mathcal{K}^S_{\mathcal{M}} \to \text{CONST} \cup \text{VAR}$ such that $\alpha(j, z) = \alpha(j, w) = \bot$.

Notice that although both T_1 and T_2 are solutions for S, none of them is a *universal* solution for S under $\mathcal{M}$. This shows that the notions of CWA presolutions and CWA solutions do not coincide. $\qquad \square$

By abstracting from the previous example, one can easily conclude that the canonical universal solution T for a source instance S is also a CWA presolution for S under $\mathcal{M}$. This is witnessed by some assignment $\alpha_{\text{can}} : \mathcal{K}^S_{\mathcal{M}} \to \text{CONST} \cup \text{VAR}$ that assigns a distinct null value to each pair $(j, z) \in \mathcal{K}^S_{\mathcal{M}}$. Indeed, it is not hard to see that in this case the result of the chase for S under $\mathcal{M}$ is always a target instance that is isomorphic to $\bigcup_{j \in \mathcal{J}^S_{\mathcal{M}}} \mathcal{B}_{\alpha_{\text{can}}}(j)$.

We now relate the notions of CWA solutions and CWA presolutions, showing, as the names suggest, that every solution is a presolution.

Proposition 8.12 *Let $\mathcal{M} = (\mathbf{R_s}, \mathbf{R_t}, \Sigma_{st})$ be a mapping, S a source instance and T a target instance in $\text{SOL}^{\text{CWA}}_{\mathcal{M}}(S)$. Then T is a CWA presolution for S under $\mathcal{M}$.*

Proof Since T is a CWA solution, it is, in particular, a homomorphic image of the canonical universal solution T_{can} for S. Let $h : T_{\text{can}} \to T$ be the homomorphism that witnesses this fact. Recall that we can assume that T_{can} is of the form $\bigcup_{j \in \mathcal{J}^S_{\mathcal{M}}} \mathcal{B}_{\alpha_{\text{can}}}(j)$, where $\alpha_{\text{can}} : \mathcal{K}^S_{\mathcal{M}} \to \text{CONST} \cup \text{VAR}$ is a mapping that assigns a distinct null value to each pair (j, z) in $\mathcal{K}^S_{\mathcal{M}}$. But then T is of the form $\bigcup_{j \in \mathcal{J}^S_{\mathcal{M}}} \mathcal{B}_{\alpha}(j)$, where $\alpha : \mathcal{K}^S_{\mathcal{M}} \to \text{CONST} \cup \text{VAR}$ is defined as $\alpha(j, z) = h \circ \alpha_{\text{can}}(j, z)$, for each pair $(j, z) \in \mathcal{K}^S_{\mathcal{M}}$. This implies that T is a CWA presolution, as is witnessed by the mapping $\alpha : \mathcal{K}^S_{\mathcal{M}} \to \text{CONST} \cup \text{VAR}$. $\qquad \square$

On the other hand, the converse of Proposition 8.12 is not true, as it was already shown in Example 8.11. That is, there are CWA presolutions that are not CWA solutions. The intuition is that CWA presolutions can still make true some "statements" that are not necessarily implied by the source instance and the st-tgds in Σ_{st}. For instance, CWA presolution T_1 in Example 8.11 tells us that the fact $R(a, c)$ is true. However, this is clearly not a logical consequence of the source instance and the st-tgd. In the same way, CWA presolution T_2 in Example 8.11 tells us that the "statement" $\exists x R(a, x) \land R(c, x)$ is true. But again, this does not follow from S and Σ_{st}. With this idea in mind, we can finally define requirement (A3), which ensures that such "invented" statements do not appear in our solutions. But more important, this last requirement will allow us to connect our definition of CWA solution with a proper intuition behind the CWA.

Let $\mathcal{M} = (\mathbf{R_s}, \mathbf{R_t}, \Sigma_{st})$ be a mapping. A *statement* over $\mathcal{M}$ is a Boolean conjunctive query over the target schema $\mathbf{R_t}$. Recall that the intuition behind requirement (A3) is that every statement in a CWA solution T for a source instance S must logically follow from S and the st-tgds in Σ_{st}. We formally define this as follows:

(A3) Every statement that holds in T also holds in every solution T' for S under $\mathcal{M}$.

We can now characterize the CWA solutions as those CWA presolutions that satisfy this last requirement. This finally allows us to connect the CWA solutions with a proper intuition behind the CWA. This is done in the next theorem, which states that the following two sets of solutions are the same:

- Those that satisfy our initial semantic definition of CWA solution (Definition 8.8); that is, those universal solutions that are also homomorphic images of the canonical universal solution; and
- those that satisfy requirements (A1)-(A2)-(A3), which properly capture the intuition behind the CWA.

Theorem 8.13 *Let* $\mathcal{M} = (\mathbf{R_s}, \mathbf{R_t}, \Sigma_{st})$ *be a mapping and* S *a source instance. Then* $\text{SOL}_{\mathcal{M}}^{\text{CWA}}(S)$ *is the set of* CWA *presolutions for* S *under* $\mathcal{M}$ *that satisfy the requirement* (A3) *formalized above.*

Proof Assume first that a target instance T belongs to $\text{SOL}_{\mathcal{M}}^{\text{CWA}}(S)$. We proved in Proposition 8.12 that T is a CWA presolution. We prove next that it also satisfies (A3). Indeed, let Q be a statement over $\mathcal{M}$ (that is, a Boolean conjunctive query over $\mathbf{R_t}$) that holds in T. Also, let T' be an arbitrary solution for S. We show that Q holds in T'. Indeed, since $T \in \text{SOL}_{\mathcal{M}}^{\text{CWA}}(S)$, it is by definition a universal solution for S. Thus, there exists a homomorphism $h : T \to T'$. But conjunctive queries are preserved under homomorphisms, and hence Q holds in T'.

Assume, on the other hand, that T is a CWA presolution for S that satisfies (A3). We prove first that T is a universal solution for S under $\mathcal{M}$. Take the Boolean conjunctive query Q_T that has T as its tableaux. Clearly, $T \models Q_T$, and hence $T' \models Q_T$ for each solution T' for S under $\mathcal{M}$ (because T satisfies (A3)). But the latter holds if and only if there exists a homomorphism $h : T \to T'$. This shows that T has homomorphisms into every possible solution and, therefore, that T is a universal solution for S.

We prove next that T is a homomorphic image of the canonical universal solution T_{can} for S under $\mathcal{M}$. Since T is a CWA presolution, it is the case that $T = \bigcup_{j \in \mathcal{J}_{\mathcal{M}}^S} \mathcal{B}_\alpha(j)$ for some assignment $\alpha : \mathcal{K}_{\mathcal{M}}^S \to \text{CONST} \cup \text{VAR}$. Recall that T_{can} is also a CWA presolution, and that this is witnessed by some assignment $\alpha_{\text{can}} : \mathcal{K}_{\mathcal{M}}^S \to \text{CONST} \cup \text{VAR}$ that sends each pair (j, z) in $\mathcal{K}_{\mathcal{M}}^S$ into a distinct null value. But then it is not hard to see that T is the homomorphic image of T_{can} under homomorphism h defined as follows. Let $\perp$ be a null value in $\text{DOM}(T_{\text{can}})$. Then $\perp = \alpha_{\text{can}}(j, z)$, for some pair $(j, z) \in \mathcal{K}_{\mathcal{M}}^S$. We set $h(\perp)$ to be $\alpha(j, z)$. $\qquad\square$

Query answering under CWA

Under both the usual certain answers and the universal certain answers semantics, we apply queries Q to solutions as if solutions were ordinary relational instances without nulls. More precisely, we treated nulls as ordinary database values. As we have mentioned earlier, this corresponds to the naïve evaluation of queries, which leads to a naïve semantics. But the dangers of treating nulls in this way have been known for a long time. The key drawback of the naïve semantics is that, while it does compute certain answers of unions of conjunctive queries, it fails to do so for any proper extension of this class of queries (see Section 2.3). Therefore, it is not strange that beyond the class of positive queries, the certain answers semantics exhibits a counter-intuitive behavior.

Thus, to define a CWA semantics that avoids as many anomalies as possible, we need to keep in mind that target instances in data exchange are tables with nulls. In particular, we need to make use of the techniques that have been developed for handling this kind of tables, and that were introduced in Section 2.3. Those techniques, however, only apply to the OWA, and hence we need to adjust them now for the case of the CWA.

Recall that the semantics of an instance T with nulls is given by the set $Rep(T)$ of complete instances that are *represented* by T. An instance T' without nulls belongs to $Rep(T)$ if there is a homomorphism $h : T \to T'$. Notice that the previous definition leaves complete instances represented by T open for adding new facts. The reason is that instances T' in $Rep(T)$ may contain tuples that do not belong to the homomorphic image of T in T'. But this certainly does not go well with our goal of having a semantics based on the CWA. Hence we need to refine the previous notion, and define the set of complete instances represented by T *under the* CWA. This is what we do next.

As expected, an instance T with nulls represents, under the CWA, the set $Rep_{CWA}(T)$ of complete instances that are homomorphic images of T. Notice that in this way, under the CWA, we no longer let instances be open for adding new tuples. Moreover, the sizes of instances in $Rep_{CWA}(T)$ do not exceed the size of T itself (contrary to $Rep(T)$, which contains instances of arbitrarily large sizes).

In order to evaluate a query Q over an incomplete instance T, the standard approach is to compute the set:

$$\Box Q(T) \;=\; \bigcap \{Q(D) \mid D \in Rep_{CWA}(T)\}.$$

This set is usually called the certain answers of Q with respect to T under the CWA in the incomplete information literature, but we prefer to represent it by $\Box Q(T)$ here, in order to avoid confusion with the certain answers as defined for data exchange. Note that in general this set may be different from $\bigcap \{Q(D) \mid D \in Rep(T)\}$; however, if Q is a union of conjunctive queries, it does not matter whether Rep or Rep_{CWA} is used.

We now define the notion of query answering under the CWA.

Definition 8.14 (CWA certain answers)   Let $\mathcal{M} = (\mathbf{R_s}, \mathbf{R_t}, \Sigma_{st})$ be a mapping, Q a query over $\mathbf{R_t}$, and S a source instance. Then the CWA *certain answers* of Q with respect to S under $\mathcal{M}$, denoted by $certain_{\mathcal{M}}^{CWA}(Q,S)$, is the set of tuples that would be in $Q(D)$ for every CWA solution T and every $D \in Rep_{CWA}(T)$. That is:

$$certain_{\mathcal{M}}^{CWA}(Q,S) \;=\; \bigcap \{\Box Q(T) \mid T \in \mathrm{SOL}_{\mathcal{M}}^{CWA}(S)\}. \qquad \Box$$

We illustrate the definition with an example.

Example 8.15 (Example 8.11 continued)   We use again the source instance $S = \{P(a,b)\}$

with the canonical universal solution $T = \{R(a, \perp_1), R(b, \perp_2)\}$, where $\perp_1$ and $\perp_2$ are distinct nulls. Consider the following Boolean query over $\mathbf{R_t}$:

$$Q := \exists x \left(R(a,x) \wedge \forall y (R(a,y) \rightarrow x = y) \right).$$

That is, Q checks whether there is exactly one tuple of the form $R(a, \cdot)$ in a solution. Then it is not hard to see that $certain_{\mathcal{M}}^{\text{CWA}}(Q,S) = \text{true}$. Indeed, every CWA solution T' for S is a homomorphic image of T, and hence it contains exactly one tuple of the form $R(a, \cdot)$. This implies that also each complete instance D in $Rep_{\text{CWA}}(T')$ contains exactly one tuple of that form (since D is a homomorphic image of T'). That is, $certain_{\mathcal{M}}^{\text{CWA}}(Q,S) = \bigcap \{ \square Q(T) \mid T \in \text{SOL}_{\mathcal{M}}^{\text{CWA}}(S) \} = \text{true}$. □

We now show that computing CWA certain answers reduces to query answering over an incomplete instance and, unlike in the OWA case, this works for *all* queries. Let $\mathcal{M} = (\mathbf{R_s}, \mathbf{R_t}, \Sigma_{st})$ be a mapping, S a source instance and T the canonical universal solution for S under $\mathcal{M}$. Then the CWA certain answers of Q with respect to S can be simply computed as $\square Q(T)$. That is, the CWA certain answers coincide with those answers that are true in every complete instance that belongs to $Rep_{\text{CWA}}(T)$.

Theorem 8.16 *Let $\mathcal{M} = (\mathbf{R_s}, \mathbf{R_t}, \Sigma_{st})$ be a mapping and Q an arbitrary query over $\mathbf{R_t}$. Then*

$$certain_{\mathcal{M}}^{\text{CWA}}(Q,S) = \square Q(T),$$

for every source instance S with canonical universal solution T.

Proof The proof follows from the following two observations, where T' is an arbitrary CWA solution for S:

- First, it is the case that $Rep_{\text{CWA}}(T') \subseteq Rep_{\text{CWA}}(T)$. Indeed, assume that $D \in Rep_{\text{CWA}}(T')$. Then D is a homomorphic image of T'. By definition, T' is a homomorphic image of T. We conclude that D is also a homomorphic image of T, and hence that $D \in Rep_{\text{CWA}}(T)$.
- Second, for every query Q, it is the case that $\square Q(T) \subseteq \square Q(T')$. Indeed, assume that the tuple $\bar{a}$ belongs to $\square Q(T)$. That is, $\bar{a}$ belongs to the evaluation of Q over each $D \in Rep_{\text{CWA}}(T)$. But from the previous observation it also follows that $\bar{a}$ belongs to the evaluation of Q over each $D \in Rep_{\text{CWA}}(T')$. We conclude that $\bar{a}$ belongs to $\square Q(T')$.

We prove the theorem now. Clearly, $certain_{\mathcal{M}}^{\text{CWA}}(Q,S) \subseteq \square Q(T)$ since T is a CWA solution for S. The opposite direction is proved as follows. From the second observation above we obtain that $\square Q(T) \subseteq \square Q(T')$ for every CWA solution T' for S. But then:

$$\square Q(T) \subseteq \bigcap \{ \square Q(T') \mid T' \text{ is a CWA solution for } S \}.$$

We conclude that $\square Q(T) \subseteq certain_{\mathcal{M}}^{\text{CWA}}(Q,S)$. This finishes the proof of the theorem. □

Thus, the problem of finding certain answers under CWA boils down to the problem of evaluating queries over incomplete databases (which happen to be canonical universal solutions). This allows us to make two important observations:

- Returning to our initial example with copying mappings, we can see that under such a mapping $\mathcal{M}$, the only CWA solution for an instance S is a copy of S itself. Hence, $certain^{CWA}_{\mathcal{M}}(Q,S) = Q(S)$, as expected. This shows that the CWA semantics solves all the query answering anomalies of our two previous semantics, at least under copying mappings.

- The key difference between certain answers under the OWA and under the CWA is that the latter are always computable, for all relational calculus queries, and many more. Recall that under the OWA, we may have FO queries for which finding certain answers is an undecidable problem. But Theorem 8.16 states that under the CWA, certain answers are computable for all relational calculus queries simply due to the fact that the sizes of instances in $Rep_{CWA}(T)$, for the canonical universal solution T, do not exceed the size of T itself.

From the last remark we easily obtain that computing CWA certain answers of FO queries is not only decidable, but it can be solved in CONP.

Proposition 8.17 *Let $\mathcal{M} = (\mathbf{R_s}, \mathbf{R_t}, \Sigma_{st})$ be a mapping and Q an FO query over $\mathbf{R_t}$. Then the following problem can be solved in* CONP: *Given a source instance S, and a tuple $\bar{a}$, is $\bar{a}$ in $certain^{CWA}_{\mathcal{M}}(Q,S)$?*

Proof Assume for the sake of simplicity that Q is Boolean. Otherwise we use essentially the same argument. We can use the following NP algorithm to check that $certain^{CWA}_{\mathcal{M}}(Q,S) = \texttt{false}$:

1. Compute in polynomial time the canonical universal solution T for S.
2. Guess a polynomial size instance T' in $Rep_{CWA}(T)$.
3. Check in polynomial time that Q does not hold in T'.

Since a CONP algorithm for checking whether $certain^{CWA}_{\mathcal{M}}(Q,S) = \texttt{true}$ is the same as an NP algorithm for checking whether $certain^{CWA}_{\mathcal{M}}(Q,S) = \texttt{false}$, this proves the proposition. □

The notions of certain answers under the CWA and the OWA are different, and in fact it is easy to construct explicit examples. Let $\mathbf{R_s}$ contain a unary predicate U, and $\mathbf{R_t}$ contain a unary predicate U'. Assume that we have one st-tgd $U(x) \rightarrow \exists z U'(z)$, and let S be the source instance containing only $U(a)$. Then the only CWA solution (up to renaming of nulls) is the instance $U'(\bot)$. However, for an arbitrary collection of nulls $\bot_1, \ldots, \bot_n$, the instance $U'(\bot_1), \ldots, U'(\bot_n)$ is a universal solution. Hence, if we take the Boolean query $Q = \forall x \forall y \, (U'(x) \wedge U'(y) \rightarrow x = y)$, then $certain^{CWA}_{\mathcal{M}}(Q,S) = \texttt{true}$ while $certain_{\mathcal{M}}(Q,S) = certain^u_{\mathcal{M}}(Q,S) = \texttt{false}$.

The previous example shows that there is a mapping $\mathcal{M}$ and an FO query Q such that $certain^{CWA}_{\mathcal{M}}(Q,S) \neq certain_{\mathcal{M}}(Q,S)$ for some source instance S. On the other hand, there is an interesting class of queries for which the semantics based on CWA coincides with the usual semantics. This is the class of existential queries.

Proposition 8.18 *Let $\mathcal{M} = (\mathbf{R_s}, \mathbf{R_t}, \Sigma_{st})$ be a mapping and Q an existential query over $\mathbf{R_t}$. Then for every source instance S, $certain_{\mathcal{M}}^{CWA}(Q,S) = certain_{\mathcal{M}}(Q,S)$.*

Proof For the sake of simplicity, assume that Q is Boolean. For arbitrary queries we use exactly the same argument. Clearly, every instance in $Rep_{CWA}(T)$, where T is a CWA solution for S under $\mathcal{M}$, is also a solution for S. Thus, $certain_{\mathcal{M}}(Q,S) = \texttt{true}$ implies $certain_{\mathcal{M}}^{CWA}(Q,S) = \texttt{true}$. Next we prove the opposite direction.

Assume, for the sake of contradiction, that $certain_{\mathcal{M}}^{CWA}(Q,S) = \texttt{true}$ but $certain_{\mathcal{M}}(Q,S) = \texttt{false}$. Then there exists a solution T for S where Q does not hold. But it is easy to see then that Q neither holds in the solution T' for S that is obtained from T by simultaneously replacing each null in $\textsc{Dom}(T)$ with a distinct constant that appears neither in T nor in Q. Let T_{can} be the canonical universal solution for S under $\mathcal{M}$. By definition, there is a homomorphism $h : T_{can} \to T'$. Let T_1 be the homomorphic image of T_{can} under h. Then $T_1 \in Rep_{CWA}(T_{can})$. Furthermore, Q does not hold in T_1. In fact, since Q is an existential query it is also monotone. This implies that if $T_1 \models Q$ then $T' \models Q$, which would be a contradiction. Hence, there is an instance in $Rep_{CWA}(T_{can})$ over which Q does not hold. We conclude that $certain_{\mathcal{M}}^{CWA}(Q,S) = \texttt{false}$, which is a contradiction. $\square$

By combining Proposition 8.18 and results on query answering under the usual certain answers semantics from Chapter 7, we obtain the following:

Corollary 8.19 *1. Let $\mathcal{M} = (\mathbf{R_s}, \mathbf{R_t}, \Sigma_{st})$ be a mapping and Q a union of conjunctive queries over $\mathbf{R_t}$. Then the following problem can be solved in polynomial time: Given a source instance S, compute $certain_{\mathcal{M}}^{CWA}(Q,S)$.*
2. There exists a mapping $\mathcal{M} = (\mathbf{R_s}, \mathbf{R_t}, \Sigma_{st})$ and a Boolean conjunctive query Q with inequalities over $\mathbf{R_t}$, such that the following problem is $\textsc{CONP}$-complete: Given a source instance S, is $certain_{\mathcal{M}}^{CWA}(Q,S) = \texttt{true}$?

That is, the CWA semantics shares with the usual certain answers semantics the problem of intractability of query answering for nonpositive queries.

Summary

We can summarize the query answering behavior of the semantics based on CWA certain answers as follows:

- The semantics eliminates the anomalies of the usual certain answers semantics, at least under copying mappings.
- Computing CWA certain answers of arbitrary relational calculus queries is a decidable problem that belongs to the class $\textsc{CONP}$.
- Computing CWA certain answers of (unions of) conjunctive queries can be done in polynomial time, but extending this class with inequalities immediately leads to intractability.

8.3 Closed-world semantics and target constraints

So far we considered CWA data exchange in the absence of target dependencies. Here we extend it to general mappings with egds and tgds. The basic idea is to characterize the class of solutions that satisfy requirements (A1), (A2) and (A3), as formalized in the previous section, under mappings that have target dependencies.

Unlike the case without target dependencies, for the class of mappings with target constraints it is not so simple to provide a characterization of the class of CWA solutions in the spirit of Definition 8.8 (which states that CWA solutions are precisely the universal solutions that are homomorphic images of the canonical universal solution). Hence, we present a more procedural version now. This version continues the idea from the previous section that facts and true statements in CWA solutions must be justified (but not overjustified) by the source instance and the dependencies only. However, in this case it will be necessary to consider not just the dependencies in Σ_{st} but also those in Σ_t. As expected, involving dependencies in Σ_t has an associated cost in the technical complexity of the definition. The procedural characterization of CWA solutions under target dependencies that we provide in this section is based on a suitably "controlled" modification of the chase.

Our initial goal is to redefine the notion of CWA presolution in the presence of target dependencies; that is, those solutions that satisfy the requirements:

(A1) Each fact in the solution is justified by the source instance and the st-tgds in $\Sigma_{st} \cup \Sigma_t$.
(A2) Justifications for facts are not overused; that is, justifications for facts do not justify more facts than necessary.

Let us start with requirement (A1). Informally, a fact in a solution T for S under $\mathcal{M} = (\mathbf{R_s}, \mathbf{R_t}, \Sigma_{st}, \Sigma_t)$ is justified, if either:

- It can be obtained from S by applying an st-tgd in Σ_{st}, or .
- it can be obtained by applying a tgd in Σ_t to already justified facts.

We have not yet considered egds; these will be incorporated later.

One has to be careful with "cyclic" justifications: for instance, a tgd $\varphi(\bar{x}) \to \exists \bar{y} \psi(\bar{x}, \bar{y})$ together with a tuple $\bar{a}$ such that $|\bar{a}| = |\bar{x}|$ may be used to justify facts in $\psi(\bar{a}, \bar{v})$, while, at the same time, another tgd may use the atoms in $\psi(\bar{a}, \bar{v})$ to justify the atoms in $\varphi(\bar{a})$. In order to avoid this problem, we make use of a "controlled" version of the chase, in which each tgd can only be applied to facts already obtained by another tgd in the chase sequence.

As in the case with no target dependencies, in order to satisfy requirement (A2) we force every (st-)tgd $\varphi(\bar{x}) \to \exists \bar{y} \psi(\bar{x}, \bar{y})$ in $\Sigma_{st} \cup \Sigma_t$ to be applied at most once with each tuple $\bar{a}$ such that $|\bar{a}| = |\bar{x}|$. We formalize these intuitions below.

We start by redefining the notion of justification in the new setting. Let $\mathcal{M} = (\mathbf{R_s}, \mathbf{R_t}, \Sigma_{st}, \Sigma_t)$ be a mapping, where Σ_t consists of a set of tgds only, and S a source instance. That is, for the time being we do not consider egds, although we will incorporate them later. A *potential* justification under $\mathcal{M}$ is a tuple of the form $(\sigma, \bar{a})$, where σ is an st-tgd in Σ_{st} or a tgd in Σ_t of the form $\varphi(\bar{x}) \to \exists \bar{y} \psi(\bar{x}, \bar{y})$, and $\bar{a}$ is a tuple of elements in $\text{CONST} \cup \text{VAR}$ such that $|\bar{a}| = |\bar{x}|$. Notice that a potential justification differs from a justification, as defined in the previous section, since $\varphi(\bar{a})$ does not need to be satisfied. Intuitively, $(\sigma, \bar{a})$ is used to justify any tuple in $\psi(\bar{a}, \bar{v})$, provided the atoms in $\varphi(\bar{a})$ are already justified.

By slightly abusing notation, we denote by $\mathscr{J}_{\mathscr{M}}$ the set of all potential justifications under $\mathscr{M}$, and by $\mathscr{K}_{\mathscr{M}}$ the set of all pairs of the form (j,z), where:

- $j = (\sigma, \bar{a})$ is a potential justification in $\mathscr{J}_{\mathscr{M}}$ with $\sigma = \varphi(\bar{x}) \to \exists \bar{y} \psi(\bar{x}, \bar{y})$, and
- z is a variable in $\bar{y}$.

As we did before, we assign values to the existentially quantified variables of (st-)tgds by a mapping $\alpha : \mathscr{K}_{\mathscr{M}} \to \text{CONST} \cup \text{VAR}$. For each $j = (\sigma, \bar{a})$ in $\mathscr{J}_{\mathscr{M}}$ with σ of the form $\varphi(\bar{x}) \to \exists \bar{y} \psi(\bar{x}, \bar{y})$, let $\mathscr{B}_{\alpha}(j) := \psi(\bar{a}, \alpha(\bar{y}))$, where $\alpha(\bar{y})$ is obtained from $\bar{y}$ by replacing each variable z in $\bar{y}$ with $\alpha(j,z)$.

The α-*chase*, for $\alpha : \mathscr{K}_{\mathscr{M}} \to \text{CONST} \cup \text{VAR}$, corresponds to the following "controlled" modification of the standard chase procedure (as defined in Section 5.3):

1. An α-*chase sequence for S under* $\mathscr{M}$ is a (finite or infinite) sequence $S_0, S_1, \ldots$ of instances such that: (i) $S_0 = S$; and (ii) for each $i \geq 0$ it is the case that S_{i+1} is the result of applying to S_i an α-*chase step* given by a tgd σ in $\Sigma_{st} \cup \Sigma_t$ as follows:

    Let σ be a tgd in $\Sigma_{st} \cup \Sigma_t$ of the form $\varphi(\bar{x}) \to \exists \bar{y} \psi(\bar{x}, \bar{y})$. Then σ can be applied to instance S_i, if there is a tuple $\bar{a}$ of elements in $\text{DOM}(S_i)$ with $|\bar{a}| = |\bar{x}|$ such that $S_i \models \varphi(\bar{a})$, and if $j = (\sigma, \bar{a})$ then there is at least one atom in $\mathscr{B}_{\alpha}(j)$ that does not belong to S_i. The *result* of this application is the instance S that extends S_i with every fact in $\mathscr{B}_{\alpha}(j)$.

3. An α-chase sequence for S under $\mathscr{M}$ is *successful*, if it is finite and it cannot be extended to a longer α-chase sequence for S under $\mathscr{M}$. That is, if S_m is the last instance in the sequence then no tgd in $\Sigma_{st} \cup \Sigma_t$ can be further applied to S_m. If this is the case, we call S_m the *result* of the α-chase sequence. As usual, we identify this result with its restriction to the relation symbols in $\mathbf{R_t}$.

It is easy to prove that, in the absence of egds, the usual chase for a source instance S under $\mathscr{M}$ always coincides with the α-chase, when $\alpha : \mathscr{K}_{\mathscr{M}} \to \text{CONST} \cup \text{VAR}$ is the mapping that assigns a distinct null value to each pair (j,z) in $\mathscr{K}_{\mathscr{M}}$. That is, we can see the α-chase as a *refinement* of the chase previously defined in Section 5.3. Nevertheless, there is a big difference in motivation between the two variations of chase. While the usual chase is applied in data exchange to compute a universal solution, we use the α-chase to show that all facts in a solution satisfy the requirements (A1) and (A2) formalized in the previous section.

As in the case without target dependencies, in order to define CWA solutions it will be convenient to introduce the notion of CWA presolutions. Notice that at this point we again include the egds.

Definition 8.20 (CWA presolutions with target dependencies)   Let $\mathscr{M} = (\mathbf{R_s}, \mathbf{R_t}, \Sigma_{st}, \Sigma_t)$ be a mapping, where Σ_t consists of a set of tgds and egds. If S is a source instance, then T is a CWA *presolution* for S under $\mathscr{M}$ if (i) T is a solution for S, and (ii) T is the result of an α-chase sequence for S under $\mathscr{M}$, for some $\alpha : \mathscr{K}_{\mathscr{M}} \to \text{CONST} \cup \text{VAR}$.   □

The reason why we impose the condition that a CWA presolution is also a solution for S is to make sure that the result of the α-chase does satisfy the egds in Σ_t. We leave it as an exercise for the reader to verify that when $\Sigma_t = \emptyset$ this definition coincides with Definition 8.10, which defines CWA presolutions in the absence of target dependencies.

We illustrate the concept of CWA presolution with the following example.

Example 8.21   Consider the mapping $\mathscr{M}$ such that the source schema consists of the unary relation P and the target schema consists of the ternary relations E and F. Assume that Σ_{st} consists of the st-tgd σ_1 and Σ_t consists of the tgd σ_2, where:

$$\sigma_1 = P(x) \to \exists z_1 \exists z_2 \exists z_3 \exists z_4 (E(x, z_1, z_3) \wedge E(x, z_2, z_4))$$
$$\sigma_2 = E(x, x_1, y) \wedge E(x, x_2, y) \to F(x, x_1, x_2).$$

For the source instance $S = \{P(a)\}$ the following three target instances are CWA presolutions:

$$T_1 = \{E(a, \bot_1, \bot_3), E(a, \bot_2, \bot_4), F(a, \bot_1, \bot_1), F(a, \bot_2, \bot_2)\}$$
$$T_2 = \{E(a, \bot_1, \bot_3), E(a, \bot_2, \bot_3), F(a, \bot_1, \bot_1),$$
$$F(a, \bot_2, \bot_2), F(a, \bot_1, \bot_2), F(a, \bot_2, \bot_1)\}$$
$$T_3 = \{E(a, b, \bot_3), E(a, \bot_2, \bot_4), F(a, b, b), F(a, \bot_2, \bot_2)\}.$$

This is because for each $1 \leq i \leq 3$ it is the case that T_i is a solution for S that is the result of the α_i-chase that satisfies the following (among other things that are not relevant for the final result):

- $\alpha_1(\sigma_1, z_j) = \bot_j$, for each $1 \leq j \leq 4$.
- $\alpha_2(\sigma_1, z_j) = \bot_j$, for each $1 \leq j \leq 3$, and $\alpha_2(\sigma_1, z_4) = \alpha_2(\sigma_1, z_3)$.
- $\alpha_3(\sigma_1, z_1) = b$ and $\alpha_3(\sigma_1, z_j) = \bot_j$, for each $2 \leq j \leq 4$.

Notice that, in particular, T_1 is the canonical universal solution for S.   □

We are finally in the position of defining CWA solutions in the presence of target dependencies. As in the case without target dependencies, these are the CWA presolutions T for S that satisfy the requirement:

(A3) Every statement that holds in T also holds in every solution T' for S.

Definition 8.22 (CWA solutions with target dependencies)   Let $\mathscr{M} = (\mathbf{R_s}, \mathbf{R_t}, \Sigma_{st}, \Sigma_{st})$ be a mapping, where Σ_t consists of a set of tgds and egds. If S is a source instance, then T is a CWA *solution* for S under $\mathscr{M}$ if (i) T is a CWA presolution for S, and (ii) T satisfies requirement (A3) formalized above.

As before, we denote by $\text{SOL}_{\mathcal{M}}^{\text{CWA}}(S)$ the set of CWA solutions for S under $\mathcal{M}$. □

It is not hard to prove that this definition coincides with Definition 8.8 when $\Sigma_t = \emptyset$.

Interestingly enough, it is possible to provide a simple characterization of the CWA presolutions that are also CWA solutions. The proof is left as an exercise for the reader.

Proposition 8.23 *Let $\mathcal{M} = (\mathbf{R_s}, \mathbf{R_t}, \Sigma_{st}, \Sigma_{st})$ be a mapping, where Σ_t consists of a set of tgds and egds, and S a source instance. Then for every target instance T, the following are equivalent:*

1. *$T \in \text{SOL}_{\mathcal{M}}^{\text{CWA}}(S)$.*
2. *T is a CWA presolution and a universal solution for S under $\mathcal{M}$.*

The previous characterization is useful, as it can be applied to identify which solutions are also CWA solutions.

Example 8.24 (Example 8.21 continued) Target instances T_1 and T_2 belong to $\text{SOL}_{\mathcal{M}}^{\text{CWA}}(S)$, since it is not hard to see that they are at the same time CWA presolutions and universal solutions for S under $\mathcal{M}$. Indeed, T_1 is simply the result of the usual chase (and, hence, it is universal) and T_2 has a homomorphism h into T_1 (h is the identity in every element except $\bot_2$, where it takes value $\bot_1$). This implies that T_2 has a homomorphism into every solution, and, therefore, that it is a universal solution.

On the other hand, the CWA presolution T_3 does not belong to $\text{SOL}_{\mathcal{M}}^{\text{CWA}}(S)$, simply because it is not a universal solution for S (as there is no homomorphism from T_3 to T_1). □

We now prove an important proposition that shows that the core is always a CWA solution:

Proposition 8.25 *Let $\mathcal{M} = (\mathbf{R_s}, \mathbf{R_t}, \Sigma_{st}, \Sigma_t)$ be a mapping and S be a source instance such that at least one universal solution for S under $\mathcal{M}$ exists. Assume that T is the core of the universal solutions for S under $\mathcal{M}$. Then $T \in \text{SOL}_{\mathcal{M}}^{\text{CWA}}(S)$.*

Proof We know from Proposition 6.15 that T is a universal solution. Hence, Proposition 8.23 tells us that we only need to show that T is the result of an α-chase sequence, for some $\alpha : \mathcal{K}_{\mathcal{M}} \to \text{CONST} \cup \text{VAR}$.

We start by inductively constructing partial mappings $\alpha_i : \mathcal{K}_{\mathcal{M}} \to \text{CONST} \cup \text{VAR}$ and sequences $\mathcal{C}_i = (L_1, \ldots, L_i)$ of instances of $\langle \mathbf{R_s}, \mathbf{R_t} \rangle$ such that:

- $\mathcal{C}_i$ is an α_i'-chase sequence for S under $\mathcal{M}$, for each $\alpha_i' : \mathcal{K}_{\mathcal{M}} \to \text{CONST} \cup \text{VAR}$ that *extends* α_i; that is, α_i' coincides with α_i on every element of $\mathcal{K}_{\mathcal{M}}$ for which α_i is defined, and
- $L_i \subseteq S \cup T$.

We define $\alpha_0 : \mathcal{K}_{\mathcal{M}} \to \text{CONST} \cup \text{VAR}$ as the partial mapping that is undefined on each element of $\mathcal{K}_{\mathcal{M}}$, and $\mathcal{C}_0 = (L_0)$, where $L_0 := S$. Clearly, $L_0 \subseteq S \cup T$ and $\mathcal{C}_0$ is an α_0'-chase sequence for S under $\mathcal{M}$, for each $\alpha_0' : \mathcal{K}_{\mathcal{M}} \to \text{CONST} \cup \text{VAR}$ that extends α_0.

Assume, for the inductive case, that $\alpha_i : \mathcal{K}_{\mathcal{M}} \to \text{CONST} \cup \text{VAR}$ and $\mathcal{C}_i = (L_0, \ldots, L_i)$ are, respectively, a partial mapping and a sequence of instances over $\langle \mathbf{R_s}, \mathbf{R_t} \rangle$ that satisfy the hypothesis. That is, (1) $\mathscr{C}_i$ is an α_i'-chase sequence for S under $\mathscr{M}$, for each $\alpha_i' : \mathscr{K}_\mathscr{M} \to$ CONST $\cup$ VAR that extends α_i, and (2) $L_i \subseteq S \cup T$. If $L_i \models \Sigma_{st} \cup \Sigma_t$, then the inductive construction simply stops. Otherwise, we construct from α_i and $\mathscr{C}_i$ a partial mapping $\alpha_{i+1} :$ $\mathscr{K}_\mathscr{M} \to$ CONST $\cup$ VAR and a sequence $\mathscr{C}_{i+1} = (L_1, \ldots, L_i, L_{i+1})$ of instances of $\langle \mathbf{R_s}, \mathbf{R_t} \rangle$ as follows.

Since $L_i \not\models \Sigma_{st} \cup \Sigma_t$ there must be a dependency $\sigma \in \Sigma_{st} \cup \Sigma_t$ such that $L_i \not\models \sigma$. Notice that since $L_i \subseteq S \cup T$, the dependency σ cannot be an egd (otherwise, $T \not\models \sigma$, which is a contradiction since T is a solution for S). Thus, σ is an (st)-tgd.

Assume without loss of generality that

$$\sigma \ = \ \varphi(\bar{x}) \to \exists \bar{y} \psi(\bar{x}, \bar{y}),$$

where $\bar{y} = (y_1, \ldots, y_k)$. Thus, (1) $L_i \models \varphi(\bar{a})$ for some tuple $\bar{a}$ of elements in CONST $\cup$ VAR such that $|\bar{a}| = |\bar{x}|$, and (2) $L_i \not\models \psi(\bar{a}, \bar{v})$ for every tuple $\bar{v}$ of elements in CONST $\cup$ VAR such that $|\bar{v}| = |\bar{y}|$. Since $L_i \subseteq S \cup T$ it is the case that $T \models \varphi(\bar{a})$. But T is a solution for S, and hence $T \models \psi(\bar{a}, \bar{w})$ for some tuple $\bar{w}$ of elements in CONST $\cup$ VAR such that $|\bar{w}| = |\bar{y}|$.

Assuming $\bar{w} = (w_1, \ldots, w_k)$, we define the partial mapping $\alpha_{i+1} : \mathscr{K}_\mathscr{M} \to$ CONST $\cup$ VAR as follows. Let (j, z) be a pair in $\mathscr{K}_\mathscr{M}$. Then:

$$\alpha_{i+1}(j, z) \ = \ \begin{cases} w_\ell, & \text{if } j = (\sigma, \bar{a}) \text{ and } z = y_\ell, \text{ for } 1 \leq \ell \leq k \\ \alpha_i(j, z), & \text{if } j \neq (\sigma, \bar{a}) \text{ and } \alpha_i(j, z) \text{ is defined} \\ \text{undefined}, & \text{otherwise.} \end{cases}$$

Now we let $\mathscr{C}_{i+1}$ be $(L_1, \ldots, L_i, L_{i+1})$, where $L_{i+1} := L_i \cup \mathscr{B}_{\alpha_{i+1}}(\sigma, \bar{a})$. That is, L_{i+1} extends L_i with every atom in $\psi(\bar{a}, \bar{w})$. Notice that by the induction hypothesis and the choice of $\bar{w}$, we can immediately conclude L_{i+1} is contained in $S \cup T$. From the induction hypothesis it also easily follows that $\mathscr{C}_{i+1}$ is an α_{i+1}'-chase sequence for S under $\mathscr{M}$, for each $\alpha_{i+1}' :$ $\mathscr{K}_\mathscr{M} \to$ CONST $\cup$ VAR that extends α_{i+1}.

Since T is finite and each α_i-application of a tgd produces at least one new atom, we conclude that the iterative construction of α_i and $\mathscr{C}_i$ as described above stops after some number $i \geq 0$ of atoms (in fact $i \leq |\text{DOM}(T)|^k$ for some k that only depends on the mapping). In particular, if $\mathscr{C}_i = (L_1, \ldots, L_i)$ then $L_i \models \Sigma_{st} \cup \Sigma_t$ and $L_i \subseteq S \cup T$. In order to finish the proof it will be sufficient to prove the following: (1) L_i is the result of a successful α-chase sequence for S under $\mathscr{M}$, for some mapping $\alpha : \mathscr{K}_\mathscr{M} \to$ CONST $\cup$ VAR, and (2) if T' is the restriction of L_i to the relation symbols in $\mathbf{R_t}$, then $T' = T$. We prove this below.

First, we know that L_i is the result of a successful α-chase sequence, for each mapping $\alpha : \mathscr{K}_\mathscr{M} \to$ CONST $\cup$ VAR that extends α_{i+1}. This proves (1). Second, $L_i \models \Sigma_{st} \cup \Sigma_t$, and hence T' is a solution for S under $\mathscr{M}$. It follows that there exists a homomorphism from T into T', since T is a universal solution for S. Since $L_i \subseteq S \cup T$, we have $T' \subseteq T$. It follows that $T' = T$; otherwise there would be a homomorphism from T into a proper subinstance of itself, which contradicts the fact that T is a core. This proves (2). $\qquad \square$

Recall that in the absence of target dependencies the canonical universal solution was, in a sense, the "maximal" element of the class of CWA solutions, since every other CWA solution was a homomorphic image of it. Example 8.21 shows that this property is no longer true in the presence of target dependencies. In particular, T_2 is a CWA solution that is not a homomorphic image of the canonical universal solution T_1 for S.

The observation that CWA solutions are not necessarily homomorphic images of the canonical universal solution (if the latter exists) is particularly important, as it will affect query answering in a significant way. In fact, we will see later that it implies that in the presence of target dependencies it is no longer true that for every FO query Q, the set of CWA certain answers coincides with $\Box Q(T)$, for each source instance S with canonical universal solution T.

But perhaps there is a different target instance that satisfies the role of being the "maximal" element of the class of CWA solutions in the presence of target dependencies (that is, a CWA solution such that any other CWA solution is a homomorphic image of it)? And, if a unique maximal element does not exist, perhaps there are polynomially many of them?

However, this is not the case, as source instances may generate an exponential number of "maximal" elements in the class of CWA solutions. This holds even for the case of mappings such that Σ_t consists of a set of egds and a weakly acyclic set of tgds. We leave the proof of this fact as an interesting exercise for the reader.

Proposition 8.26 *There exists a mapping $\mathcal{M} = (\mathbf{R_s}, \mathbf{R_t}, \Sigma_{st}, \Sigma_t)$, such that Σ_t consists of a set of egds and a weakly acyclic set of tgds, with the following property. For every positive integer n, there exists a source instance S and distinct CWA solutions $T_1, T_2, \ldots, T_{2^n}$ for S under $\mathcal{M}$ such that:*

- *the instance S contains $2n$ tuples, and*
- *each solution $T \in \mathrm{SOL}_{\mathcal{M}}^{\mathrm{CWA}}(S)$ is the homomorphic image of exactly one T_i, for $1 \leq i \leq 2^n$.*

Existence of CWA solutions and target dependencies

In the presence of target dependencies the existence of CWA solutions is not a trivial problem. Indeed, it can be proved that it is equivalent to the existence of universal solutions.

Theorem 8.27 *For every mapping $\mathcal{M} = (\mathbf{R_s}, \mathbf{R_t}, \Sigma_{st}, \Sigma_t)$ and source instance S, the following are equivalent:*

- $\mathrm{SOL}_{\mathcal{M}}^{\mathrm{CWA}}(S) \neq \emptyset$.
- *There exists a universal solution for S under $\mathcal{M}$.*

Proof Clearly, if $\mathrm{SOL}_{\mathcal{M}}^{\mathrm{CWA}}(S) \neq \emptyset$ then there exists a universal solution for S under $\mathcal{M}$ (since each CWA solution is, by Proposition 8.23, a universal solution). Assume, on the other hand, that T is a universal solution for S under $\mathcal{M}$. Take the core T' of T. Then it follows from Proposition 8.25 that $T' \in \mathrm{SOL}_{\mathcal{M}}^{\mathrm{CWA}}(S)$. □

Since we already have a good understanding of when the problem of existence of universal solutions is decidable (and even tractable) from Chapter 6, we can now state the following result about the complexity of existence of CWA solutions under $\mathcal{M}$. The input to this problem is a source S; the question is whether $\text{SOL}_{\mathcal{M}}^{\text{CWA}}(S) \neq \emptyset$.

Corollary 8.28 *1. There is a mapping $\mathcal{M} = (\mathbf{R_s}, \mathbf{R_t}, \Sigma_{st}, \Sigma_t)$ such that the existence of CWA solutions under $\mathcal{M}$ problem is undecidable.*

2. Let $\mathcal{M} = (\mathbf{R_s}, \mathbf{R_t}, \Sigma_{st}, \Sigma_t)$ be a mapping, where Σ_t consists of a set of egds and a weakly acyclic set of tgds. Then the existence of CWA solutions under $\mathcal{M}$ problem can be solved in polynomial time.

Query answering under CWA and target dependencies

Recall that in the absence of target dependencies we defined the set of CWA certain answers of target query Q for source instance S under mapping $\mathcal{M} = (\mathbf{R_s}, \mathbf{R_t}, \Sigma_{st})$ as:

$$certain_{\mathcal{M}}^{\text{CWA}}(Q, S) = \bigcap\{\Box Q(T) \mid T \in \text{SOL}_{\mathcal{M}}^{\text{CWA}}(S)\},$$

where $\Box Q(T) = \bigcap\{Q(D) \mid D \in Rep_{\text{CWA}}(T)\}$. Recall also that in the absence of target dependencies, $Rep_{\text{CWA}}(T)$ was defined as the set of complete instances represented by T under the CWA; that is, those complete instances that were homomorphic images of T. Notice, in particular, that in this case if T was a solution then each instance T' represented by T was also a solution.

But is the latter fact also true in the presence of target dependencies? The answer is negative, as shown by the following example. Consider an incomplete instance $T = \{P(\perp_1, \perp_2)\}$ and a tgd $P(x, x) \rightarrow R(x)$. Then clearly T satisfies the tgd. But, on the other hand, its homomorphic image $T' = \{P(a, a)\}$ does not satisfy it. Thus, in order to be semantically sound, we need to redefine the notion of $Rep_{\text{CWA}}(T)$ when there is a set of egds and tgds Σ_t that needs to be satisfied. In particular, we define the set of instances represented by T with respect to Σ_t under the CWA, denoted by $Rep_{\text{CWA}}^{\Sigma_t}(T)$, as the one that consists of each complete instance that is a homomorphic image of T and satisfies Σ_t.

In the same way, we define

$$\Box_{\Sigma_t} Q(T) := \bigcap\{Q(D) \mid D \in Rep_{\text{CWA}}^{\Sigma_t}(T)\},$$

and the set of CWA certain answers of target query Q for source instance S under mapping $\mathcal{M} = (\mathbf{R_s}, \mathbf{R_t}, \Sigma_{st}, \Sigma_t)$ as:

$$certain_{\mathcal{M}}^{\text{CWA}}(Q, S) = \bigcap\{\Box_{\Sigma_t} Q(T) \mid T \in \text{SOL}_{\mathcal{M}}^{\text{CWA}}(S)\}.$$

We will see later some examples of the application of this semantics.

Our first observation is that the problem of computing CWA certain answers of FO queries is undecidable in the presence of target dependencies, even for mappings with a weakly acyclic set of tgds. Recall that, on the other hand, for mappings without target dependencies the problem is decidable.

Proposition 8.29 *There exists a mapping $\mathcal{M} = (\mathbf{R_s}, \mathbf{R_t}, \Sigma_{st}, \Sigma_t)$, such that Σ_t consists of a set of egds and a weakly acyclic set of tgds, and a Boolean FO query Q over $\mathbf{R_t}$, for which* *the following problem is undecidable: Given a source instance S, is* $certain_{\mathscr{M}}^{CWA}(Q,S) =$ true?

One would expect, as in the case of Propositions 7.1 and 8.4, that the previous fact follows directly from the undecidability of the problem of existence of CWA solutions (Corollary 8.28). Unfortunately, this is not the case. The reason is that the CWA semantics is given not by the CWA solutions themselves, but by the complete instances represented by them. Proving Proposition 8.29 is left as an exercise for the reader.

Recall that, in the absence of target dependencies, we used the following fact to show that the problem of computing CWA certain answers of any FO query Q is decidable:

$$certain_{\mathscr{M}}^{CWA}(Q,S) = \Box Q(T),$$

for each source instance S with canonical universal solution T. Indeed, this fact states that computing CWA certain answers of an FO query Q is equivalent to taking the intersection of the evaluation of Q over every complete instance D that is represented by the canonical universal solution under the CWA. Since there is only a finite number of such complete instances D, it follows that computing CWA certain answers in this case is decidable.

But as Proposition 8.29 states, in the presence of target dependencies the problem of computing CWA certain answers of FO queries is no longer decidable. And, furthermore, as the following example shows, the property that $certain_{\mathscr{M}}^{CWA}(Q,S) = \Box_{\Sigma_t}Q(T)$, for each source instance S with canonical universal solution T, no longer holds when Σ_t contains some dependencies .

Example 8.30 (Example 8.21 continued)   Recall that

$$T_1 = \{E(a,\bot_1,\bot_3), E(a,\bot_2,\bot_4), F(a,\bot_1,\bot_1), F(a,\bot_2,\bot_2)\}$$

is the canonical universal solution for $S = \{P(a)\}$. Consider the Boolean FO query Q that asks whether there are at most two tuples of the form $F(a,\cdot,\cdot)$ in a solution. Then clearly every complete instance in $Rep_{CWA}^{\Sigma_t}(T)$ satisfies Q, and, therefore, $\Box_{\Sigma_t}Q(T_1) =$ true.

On the other hand, it is not hard to see that $certain_{\mathscr{M}}^{CWA}(Q,S) =$ false. Indeed, recall that the solution

$$T_2 = \{E(a,\bot_1,\bot_3), E(a,\bot_2,\bot_3), F(a,\bot_1,\bot_1),$$
$$F(a,\bot_2,\bot_2), F(a,\bot_1,\bot_2), F(a,\bot_2,\bot_1)\}$$

belongs to $SOL_{\mathscr{M}}^{CWA}(S)$. The instance

$$\{E(a,a,c), E(a,b,c), F(a,a,a), F(a,b,b), F(a,a,b), F(a,b,a)\}$$

belongs to $Rep_{CWA}^{\Sigma_t}(T_2)$ and does not satisfy Q. ☐

Is there any other mechanism by which we can prove decidability, in the presence of target dependencies, of the problem of query answering under the CWA for an interesting class of FO queries? Recall that in the case without target dependencies we were able to prove that the CWA semantics coincides with the usual certain answers semantics for the class of existential queries (Proposition 8.18). If this was also the case in the presence of target dependencies, then it would allow us to transfer all the results we know about query answering under the usual semantics into the present setting. However, the next example shows that this property fails already for the class of conjunctive queries with inequalities under mappings with a weakly acyclic set of tgds in Σ_t.

Example 8.31 Let $\mathcal{M} = (\mathbf{R_s}, \mathbf{R_t}, \Sigma_{st}, \Sigma_t)$ be the mapping such that Σ_{st} consists of the st-tgd:

$$P(x,y) \rightarrow \exists u \exists v R(u,v),$$

and Σ_t consists of the tgd:

$$R(x,x) \rightarrow S(x).$$

Consider source instance $S = \{P(a,a)\}$. It is not hard to prove that the only CWA solution for S in this case is $T = \{R(\bot_1, \bot_2)\}$, where $\bot_1$ and $\bot_2$ are distinct nulls. Notice, in particular, that the target instance $T' = \{R(\bot, \bot), S(\bot)\}$ is a CWA presolution for S (since it is clearly a solution for S and the result of an α-chase), but not a CWA solution (simply because it is not a universal solution for S).

Moreover, each $D \in Rep_{\mathrm{CWA}}^{\Sigma_t}(T)$ is of the form $\{R(b,c)\}$, where b and c are distinct constants. In fact, instances of the form $\{R(b,b)\}$ cannot belong to $Rep_{\mathrm{CWA}}^{\Sigma_t}(T)$ because they violate Σ_t. This implies that if $Q = \exists x \exists y (R(x,y) \wedge x \neq y)$ then $certain_{\mathcal{M}}^{\mathrm{CWA}}(Q,S) = \mathtt{true}$. On the other hand, $certain_{\mathcal{M}}(Q,S) = \mathtt{false}$, since the solution $T_1 = \{R(a,a), S(a)\}$ for S does not satisfy Q. $\qquad\square$

Interestingly enough, we can still recover the equivalence in one important case, namely for unions of conjunctive queries under mappings with a weakly acyclic set of tgds. This will allow us to transfer the good behavior of this class of queries under the usual semantics into the present setting. The following is left as an exercise.

Proposition 8.32 *Let $\mathcal{M} = (\mathbf{R_s}, \mathbf{R_t}, \Sigma_{st}, \Sigma_t)$ be a mapping such that Σ_t consists of a set of egds and a weakly acyclic set of tgds, and assume that Q is a union of conjunctive queries over $\mathbf{R_t}$. Then for every source instance S it is the case that $certain_{\mathcal{M}}^{\mathrm{CWA}}(Q,S) = certain_{\mathcal{M}}(Q,S)$.*

Notice that the reason why we need to restrict the statement of the proposition to mappings with a weakly acyclic set of tgds, is that in this way we can be sure that the existence of solutions coincides with the existence of universal solutions, and hence, from Theorem 8.27, also with the existence of CWA solutions.

By combining Proposition 8.32 and what we know about computing certain answers of unions of conjunctive queries from Chapter 7, we obtain the following important corollary:

Corollary 8.33 *Let $\mathcal{M} = (\mathbf{R_s}, \mathbf{R_t}, \Sigma_{st}, \Sigma_t)$ be a mapping such that Σ_t consists of a set of egds and a weakly acyclic set of tgds, and assume that Q is a union of conjunctive queries over $\mathbf{R_t}$. Then the data complexity of computing certain answers, i.e., computing $certain_{\mathcal{M}}^{\mathrm{CWA}}(Q,S)$, is polynomial.*

On the other hand, we know from Corollary 8.19 that the problem of computing CWA certain answers for Boolean conjunctive queries with inequalities is CONP-hard, even in the absence of target dependencies.

Summary

We can summarize the query answering behavior of the CWA semantics, in the presence of target dependencies, as follows:

- Computing CWA certain answers of arbitrary relational calculus queries is an undecidable problem.
- Computing CWA certain answers of (unions of) conjunctive queries can be done in polynomial time, under mappings with a weakly acyclic set of tgds, but extending this class with inequalities immediately leads to intractability (even in the absence of target dependencies).

8.4 Clopen-world semantics

We have seen that the closed-world semantics lets us avoid some of the problems that arise under the open-world semantics of data exchange solutions. But is the closed-world semantics free of problems itself? It is not, as the following example shows.

Suppose the source schema has a relation Papers(paper#,title) with the list of papers, say submitted to a journal, so that the id of each paper and its title are recorded. Suppose that in the target we have a relation Assignments(paper#,reviewer), with assignments of papers to reviewers. The natural st-tgd in this case is

$$\text{Papers}(x,y) \rightarrow \exists z \, \text{Assignments}(x,z).$$

But now assume that paper# is a key for S, and consider the target query asking whether every paper has exactly one reviewer. Under the CWA semantics, the certain answer to this query is *true*. This is because of the minimalistic CWA, which creates just one (paper#,reviewer) tuple for each paper id.

This is clearly unsatisfactory, but it also suggests that some attributes in a mapping may correspond to the CWA, while others correspond to the OWA. In the case of the reviewer attribute, it is clear that the intention is not to limit it to having a single value for each paper.

We capture this intuition by *annotating* variables in the target part of the mapping with *cl* or *op*, depending on whether they correspond to the closed- or open-world semantics. For instance, in the above example, we shall use an annotated st-tgd:

$$\text{Papers}(x,y) \rightarrow \exists z \, \text{Assignments}(x^{cl}, z^{op})$$

saying that for each submitted paper, several tuples can be created in the target: they will all have the same paper id, since x is annotated as *cl*, but reviewer names can be different, since z is annotated as *op*.

Formally, an annotation for a mapping $\mathcal{M}$ is a function α that maps every position of a variable in a target atom into cl or op. We refer to the pair $(\mathcal{M}, \alpha)$ as an *annotated mapping*.

To define the notion of a canonical solution under an annotated mapping, we need to consider annotated instances: these are instances in which every constant or null is labeled with cl or op. The semantics of such an instance T is a set $Rep(T)$ on instances over CONST obtained as follows: after applying a valuation v to T, any tuple $(\dots, a^{op}, \dots)$ in $v(T)$ can be replicated arbitrarily many times with $(\dots, b, \dots)$, for $b \in$ CONST. For example, $Rep(\{(a^{cl}, \bot^{op})\})$ contains all binary relations whose projection on the first attribute is $\{a\}$, and $Rep(\{(a^{cl}, \bot^{cl})\})$ contains all one-tuple relations $\{(a, b)\}$ with $b \in$ CONST.

Now suppose we have a source instance S and an annotated mapping $(\mathcal{M}, \alpha)$. These generate the *annotated canonical universal solution* $\mathrm{CANSOL}_{(\mathcal{M}, \alpha)}(S)$ in the same way as the usual mapping will generate the canonical universal solution except that now we have an annotated instance. For example, if we have a tuple (#1,'Data exchange') in relation *Papers*, the first st-tgd in the mapping will produce a tuple $(\#1^{cl}, \bot^{op})$ in relation *Assignment*.

The first observation is that the two extreme cases of annotated mappings correspond precisely to the open-world and the closed-world semantics we have seen earlier. Let $(\mathcal{M}, op)$ (respectively, $(\mathcal{M}, cl)$) stand for the mapping $\mathcal{M}$ in which every position is annotated op (respectively, cl). Then, for each source instance S we have

- $\mathrm{SOL}_{\mathcal{M}}(S) = Rep(\mathrm{CANSOL}_{(\mathcal{M}, op)}(S))$;
- $\mathrm{SOL}_{\mathcal{M}}^{\mathrm{CWA}}(S) = Rep(\mathrm{CANSOL}_{(\mathcal{M}, cl)}(S))$.

Annotated solutions can be defined in a way similar to the CWA solutions, using the notion of justification. Since we consider settings without target constraints, we can obtain their algebraic characterization: annotated solutions T for S under $(\mathcal{M}, \alpha)$ are homomorphic images of $\mathrm{CANSOL}_{(\mathcal{M}, \alpha)}(S)$ so that there is a homomorphism from T into an *expansion* of $\mathrm{CANSOL}_{(\mathcal{M}, \alpha)}(S)$. An expansion of the annotated instance $\mathrm{CANSOL}_{(\mathcal{M}, \alpha)}(S)$ is obtained by expanding op-annotated elements; that is, every tuple in the expansion must agree with some tuple in the instance on all cl-annotated attributes.

With this, we have some expected properties of annotated solutions:

- $Rep(\mathrm{CANSOL}_{(\mathcal{M}, \alpha)}(S))$ is precisely the set of all annotated solutions under $(\mathcal{M}, \alpha)$;
- if α' is obtained from α by changing some cl annotations to op, then each annotated solution under $(\mathcal{M}, \alpha)$ is an annotated solution under $(\mathcal{M}, \alpha')$.

Given an annotated mapping $(\mathcal{M}, \alpha)$ and a query Q over the target schema, we define

$$certain_{(\mathcal{M}, \alpha)}(Q, S) = \bigcap \{Q(D) \mid D \in Rep(T) \text{ where } T \text{ is an } (\mathcal{M}, \alpha)\text{-solution}\}.$$

For unions of conjunctive queries, this notion coincides with those we have seen.

Proposition 8.34 *If $\mathcal{M}$ is a mapping, Q is a union of conjunctive queries, S is a source instance, and α is an arbitrary annotation, then*

$$certain_{\mathcal{M}}(Q, S) = certain_{\mathcal{M}}^{\mathrm{CWA}}(Q, S) = certain_{(\mathcal{M}, \alpha)}(Q, S).$$

What about more general queries, say FO queries? We know that in the case of CWA, we can always answer them (and the complexity is CONP-complete). In the case of OWA, finding certain answers is an undecidable problem. Annotated mappings give us some additional cases, compared to OWA, when query answering is decidable.

The parameter that we use is the following:

- $\#_{op}(\mathcal{M}, \alpha)$ – the maximum number of open positions per atom in an st-tgd in the annotated mapping.

In our example, the value of $\#_{op}(\mathcal{M}, \alpha)$ is 1, as no st-tgd uses more than one open position.

Theorem 8.35 *The data complexity of finding certain answers for* FO *queries under annotated mappings is as follows:*

1. *in* CONP *if* $\#_{op}(\mathcal{M}, \alpha) = 0$ *(which is the* CWA *case);*
2. *decidable (in* CONEXPTIME*) if* $\#_{op}(\mathcal{M}, \alpha) = 1$.
3. *undecidable for some mappings* $(\mathcal{M}, \alpha)$ *with* $\#_{op}(\mathcal{M}, \alpha) > 1$.

Thus, if more than one position in a rule is marked *op*, query answering behaves like in OWA. With no *op* positions, we have the CWA case. The new intermediate case is one open annotation per rule, and there we retain decidability of query answering.

9

Endnotes to Part Two

9.1 Summary

- Without putting restrictions on schema mappings, all the key computational tasks are undecidable in data exchange. Hence, one usually deals with the mappings in which:

  1. the relationship between the source and the target schemas is specified by source-to-target tuple generating dependencies (st-tgds), and
  2. the target constraints are tuple-generating and equality-generating dependencies (tgds and egds).

- Even in this setting, the problem of checking whether a given source admits a solution is undecidable. Hence, one usually imposes a further acyclicity condition on the target constraints.

- With this condition (called weak acyclicity), solutions – if they exist – can be constructed in polynomial time by the chase procedure. If the chase fails, it means that there are no solutions.

- Solutions constructed by the chase are more general than others – they are so-called universal solutions. There are several equivalent ways of stating that a solution is more general than others. The result of the chase is usually referred to as the canonical universal solution.

- There is a unique minimal universal solution, called the core. It can be constructed in polynomial time under the weak acyclicity assumption, although the algorithm is quite complicated. A simpler algorithm exists if target constraints contain only egds.

- Certain answers for arbitrary conjunctive queries Q (or unions of conjunctive queries) can be found if one has an arbitrary universal solution: this is done by means of answering another query, the rewriting of Q, over the solution.

- Finding certain answers for arbitrary FO (relational algebra) queries is an undecidable problem in general. But useful restrictions guaranteeing decidability, and even tractability, can be found if one limits the amount of negation allowed in queries. In some cases, tractable query answering extends even to fragments of Datalog.

- Any relational calculus query that is rewritable over the core is rewritable over the canonical universal solution, but not vice versa. Also, there is a simple condition that lets one test whether a query is not rewritable over those solutions.

9.2 Bibliographic comments

The basics of data exchange were described by Fagin et al. (2005a). That paper presented the notions of schema mappings as we use them, adapted the chase procedure to the data exchange setting, and introduced universal solutions (using the definition based on homomorphisms). The choice of schema mappings one normally considers in data exchange was justified by ten Cate and Kolaitis (2009). Complexity of the key tasks associated with data exchange, such as the existence of (universal) solutions, was studied by Kolaitis et al. (2006).

The central notion of weak acyclicity was first formulated by Deutsch and Popa, and later independently used by Fagin et al. (2005a), and Deutsch and Tannen (2003). Given the role of chase in data exchange, finding conditions for its termination is an active research topic. Recent results show that chase can be pushed beyond weak acyclicity (Deutsch et al., 2008; Marnette, 2009; Meier et al., 2009).

The notion of core originates in graph theory (Hell and Nešetřil, 1992). Its usefulness in data exchange was shown by Fagin et al. (2005c), who gave the simple algorithm for computing cores. The polynomial-time algorithm for the general case was developed by Gottlob and Nash (2008).

The algorithm for answering conjunctive queries based on naïve evaluation (Imieliński and Lipski, 1984) was given by Fagin et al. (2005a). It was already shown by Fagin et al. (2005a) that the extension of the algorithm for all of FO is impossible. In the case of unions of conjunctive queries with inequalities, they showed that finding certain answers remains tractable with one inequality per disjunct; however, Mądry (2005) showed that with two inequalities per disjunct, query answering becomes CONP-complete. Extensions to Datalog with predicates for constant and inequalities are by Arenas et al. (2011c).

The notions of rewritings over the core and the canonical universal solution were studied by Fagin et al. (2005a,c). The result showing the exact relationship between them is by Arenas et al. (2013). The notion of being locally source-dependent, and its applications in proving that some queries are not rewritable, comes from the work of Arenas et al. (2013) as well. An alternative notion of locality for schema mappings based on conjunctive queries was studied by Fagin and Kolaitis (2012).

It was also shown by Arenas et al. (2013) that query answering in data exchange may exhibit unnatural behavior. It was argued by Libkin (2006a) that this is due to the openness of solutions to adding new facts. The closed world semantics was proposed in that paper too and later extended to schemas with target constraints by Hernich and Schweikardt (2007); these semantics avoid some of the unwanted behavior noticed by Arenas et al. (2013). A combined account of the closed world semantics is given by Hernich et al. (2011), who also presented a version of chase that led to easy proofs of some older results by Deutsch et al. (2008). The clopen semantics was proposed by Libkin and Sirangelo (2011); further extensions are given by Afrati and Kolaitis (2008), who considered aggregate queries in a data exchange scenario, and Hernich (2011), who dealt with a relaxed version of closed-world semantics.

We briefly mention some other extensions that have not been treated in detail in this part. First, we viewed data exchange as unidirectional (from source to target); an extension of schema mappings that works in a bidirectional way (peer data exchange) was given by Fuxman et al. (2006). Giacomo et al. (2007) proposed a setting that reconciled peer data exchange with both data exchange and data integration settings. Approximate data exchange settings, which do not require targets to follow all constraints precisely, were proposed by de Rougemont and Vieilleribière (2007). Data exchange in a probabilistic setting was studied by Fagin et al. (2010). Techniques for implementing general data exchange using mappings without target constraints are studied by Marnette et al. (2010). Practical aspects of computing cores are discussed in Mecca et al. (2009) and ten Cate et al. (2009). Learning schema mapping from data exchange examples is studied in ten Cate et al. (2012).

9.3 Exercises

1. Find the exact complexity of computing the canonical universal solution. Also prove that the canonical universal solution can be constructed in DLOGSPACE if the mapping is fixed.

2. Show that the set of tgds constructed in the proof of Theorem 5.3 is not weakly acyclic.

3. (Source: Deutsch et al. (2008))

    In this exercise we prove that efficient chase procedures can be pushed beyond weak acyclicity. Let $d_1 := \varphi_1(\bar{x}_1) \to \exists \bar{y}_1 \psi_1(\bar{x}_1, \bar{y}_1)$ and $d_2 := \varphi_2(\bar{x}_2) \to \exists \bar{y}_2 \psi_2(\bar{x}_2, \bar{y}_2)$ be tgds over the schema $\mathbf{R}$. Then d_1 *triggers* d_2 if there are instances T_1 and T_2 over $\mathbf{R}$, and tuples $\bar{a} \in \text{DOM}(T_1)^{|\bar{x}_1|}$ and $\bar{b} \in \text{DOM}(T_2)^{|\bar{x}_2|}$, respectively, such that:

    - either some element of $\bar{b}$ does not belong to $\text{DOM}(T_1)$, or $T_1 \models \varphi_2(\bar{b}) \to \exists \bar{y}_2 \psi_2(\bar{b}, \bar{y}_2)$. That is, d_2 is not applicable in T_2 for tuple $\bar{b}$;

    - $T_1 \xrightarrow{d_1, \bar{a}} T_2$, i.e., T_2 is obtained from T_1 by applying a chase step on d_1 with tuple $\bar{a}$; and

    - $T_2 \models \varphi_2(\bar{b}) \wedge \neg \exists \bar{y}_2 \psi_2(\bar{b}, \bar{y}_2)$, i.e., T_2 violates d_2, and this is witnessed by tuple $\bar{b}$.

    Let Σ be a set of tgds. We define the *chase graph* of Σ as the undirected graph whose nodes are the tgds in Σ and such that there is an edge between tgds d_1 and d_2 if and only if d_1 triggers d_2. The set Σ is *stratified* if the set of constraints in every cycle of its chase graph is weakly acyclic.

    (i) Prove that the notion of stratification properly extends the notion of weak acyclicity. That is, prove that each weakly acyclic set of tgds is stratified, but there is a stratified set of tgds that is not weakly acyclic.

    (ii) Prove that the chase is guaranteed to terminate, in at most polynomially many steps, for stratified sets of tgds. That is, prove that there exists a polynomial p such that the length of every chase sequence for an instance T under a stratified set of tgds is bounded by $p(\|T\|)$.

4. (Source: Arenas et al. (2011c))

   Prove the following stronger version of Theorem 5.14. There exists a LAV mapping $\mathcal{M} = (\mathbf{R_s}, \mathbf{R_t}, \Sigma_{st}, \Sigma_t)$, such that Σ_t consists of a single egd, and the problem of checking for the existence of solutions under $\mathcal{M}$ is PTIME-complete.

5. (Source: Kolaitis et al. (2006))

   Prove that there exist *fixed* source and target schemas $\mathbf{R_s}$ and $\mathbf{R_t}$ such that SOLEXISTENCE restricted to mappings of the form $(\mathbf{R_s}, \mathbf{R_t}, \Sigma_{st}, \Sigma_t)$, where Σ_t consists only of egds, is EXPTIME-hard.

6. Complete the proof of Theorem 6.5 by proving Claim 6.6.

7. Prove Lemma 6.8 stated as follows. Let $S_1 \xrightarrow{d,\bar{a}} S_2$ be a chase step, where $S_2 \neq \texttt{fail}$. Assume that S_3 is an instance that satisfies the dependency d and such that there is a homomorphism from S_1 into S_3. Then there exists a homomorphism from S_2 into S_3.

8. Prove Proposition 6.10, i.e., show that if $\mathcal{M} = (\mathbf{R_s}, \mathbf{R_t}, \Sigma_{st}, \Sigma_t)$ is a mapping such that Σ_t consists only of egds, then every source instance S has a unique canonical universal solution T (up to a renaming of nulls) under $\mathcal{M}$.

9. Show that in general cores cannot be constructed as canonical solutions of a modified mapping. That is, give an example of a schema mapping $\mathcal{M}$ without target constraints for which there is no mapping $\mathcal{M}'$ (also without target constraints) satisfying the condition that for every source S, the canonical universal solution for S under $\mathcal{M}'$ is the core for S under $\mathcal{M}$.

10. (Source: Gottlob and Nash (2008))

    Prove Theorem 6.18 stated as follows. Let $\mathcal{M} = (\mathbf{R_s}, \mathbf{R_t}, \Sigma_{st}, \Sigma_t)$ be a fixed relational mapping, such that Σ_t consists of a set of egds and a weakly acyclic set of tgds. There is a polynomial-time algorithm that, for every source instance S, checks whether a solution for S exists, and if that is the case, computes the core of the universal solutions for S.

11. Give an example of a relational algebra query that is not a union of conjunctive queries such that its certain answers cannot be computed by naïve evaluation. In fact, even a stronger statement is true: if Q is a Boolean relational calculus, i.e., FO, query, and its certain answers can be computed by naïve evaluation, then Q is equivalent to a union of conjunctive queries.

12. Show that certain answers for DATALOG queries can be computed in exactly the same was as for conjunctive queries. Namely, if Q is a DATALOG query, S is a source instance, and T is a universal solution for S, then $certain_{\mathcal{M}}(Q,S) = Q_{\text{naïve}}(T)$.

13. Complete the proof of Theorem 7.4 by showing that φ is satisfiable iff $certain_{\mathcal{M}}(Q, S_\varphi) = \texttt{false}$.

14. (Source: Mądry (2005))

    Show that there exists a Boolean conjunctive query Q with two inequalities and a LAV mapping $\mathcal{M}$, such that CERTAIN$_{\mathcal{M}}(Q)$ is CONP-complete.

15. (Source: Arenas et al. (2011c))

    In this exercise we prove that one can efficiently compute certain answers to conjunctive queries with two inequalities, by assuming some syntactic restrictions on queries.

Furthermore, those restrictions are, in a sense, optimal, since by lifting any one of them the problem becomes intractable.

Let $\mathcal{M} = (\mathbf{R_s}, \mathbf{R_t}, \Sigma_{st})$ be a mapping. Then for every n-ary relation symbol T in $\mathbf{R_t}$, we say that the i-th attribute of T $(1 \leq i \leq n)$ *can be nullified* under $\mathcal{M}$, if there is an st-tgd α in Σ_{st} such that the i-th attribute of T is existentially quantified in the right-hand side of α. Notice that for each mapping $\mathcal{M}$ and source instance S, if the i-th attribute of T cannot be nullified under $\mathcal{M}$, then for every tuple $T(c_1, \ldots, c_n)$ in the canonical universal solution for S, it holds that c_i is a constant. Moreover, if Q is a conjunctive query with inequalities over $\mathbf{R_t}$ and x is a variable in Q, then we say that x *can be nullified* under Q and $\mathcal{M}$, if x appears in Q as the i-th attribute of a target relation T, and the i-th attribute of T can be nullified under $\mathcal{M}$.

Let Q be a conjunctive query with two inequalities over a target schema $\mathbf{R_t}$. Assume that the quantifier free part of Q is of the form $\varphi(x_1, \ldots, x_m) \wedge u_1 \neq v_1 \wedge u_2 \neq v_2$, where φ is a conjunction of relational atoms over $\mathbf{R_t}$ and u_1, v_1, u_2 and v_2 are all mentioned in the set of variables $x_1, \ldots, x_m$. Then:

- Q has *almost constant inequalities* under $\mathcal{M}$, if u_1 or v_1 cannot be nullified under Q and $\mathcal{M}$, and u_2 or v_2 cannot be nullified under Q and $\mathcal{M}$. Intuitively, this means that to satisfy Q in the canonical universal solution of a source instance, one can only make comparisons of the form $c \neq \bot$ and $c \neq c'$, where c, c' are constants and $\bot$ is a null value.

- Q has *constant joins* under $\mathcal{M}$, if for every variable x that appears at least twice in φ, the variable x cannot be nullified under Q and $\mathcal{M}$. Intuitively, this means that to satisfy Q in the canonical universal solution of a source instance, one can only use constant values when joining relations.

Prove that the two syntactic restrictions mentioned above yield tractable computation of certain answers for conjunctive queries with two inequalities, at least in the absence of target dependencies. That is, let $\mathcal{M} = (\mathbf{R_s}, \mathbf{R_t}, \Sigma_{st})$ be a mapping without target dependencies, and let Q be a conjunctive query with two inequalities. Then CERTAIN$_\mathcal{M}(Q)$ can be solved in polynomial time, if Q has constant joins and almost constant inequalities.

Then prove that by lifting any of the two syntactic restrictions the problem becomes intractable, even under LAV mappings. That is, prove that there exists Boolean conjunctive query Q with two inequalities, such that Q does not have almost constant inequalities (or does not have constant joins), and a LAV mapping $\mathcal{M}$, such that CERTAIN$_\mathcal{M}(Q)$ is CONP-complete.

16. (Source: Arenas et al. (2011c))

Prove the following stronger version of Theorem 7.8. Let $\mathcal{M} = (\mathbf{R_s}, \mathbf{R_t}, \Sigma_{st}, \Sigma_t)$ be a mapping such that Σ_t consists of a set of egds, and let Q be a union of conjunctive queries with at most one inequality or negated relational atom per disjunct. Then there exists a DATALOG$^{C(\neq)}$ program Π_Q such that for every source instance S, $certain_\mathcal{M}(Q, S) = certain_\mathcal{M}(\Pi_Q, S)$.

17. Give an example of a query Q, which is a union of conjunctive queries with at most one negated atom or inequality per disjunct, and a mapping $\mathcal{M}$, such that there is no DATALOG program Π satisfying $certain_{\mathcal{M}}(Q,S) = certain_{\mathcal{M}}(\Pi,S)$ for every source instance S.

18. (Source: Fagin et al. (2005a))

   Let $\mathcal{M} = (\mathbf{R_s}, \mathbf{R_t}, \Sigma_{st}, \Sigma_t)$ be a mapping such that Σ_t consists of a set of egds and a weakly acyclic set of tgds, and let Q be a union of conjunctive queries with at most one inequality or negated relational atom per disjunct. Prove that CERTAIN$_{\mathcal{M}}(Q)$ can be solved in PTIME.

19. (Source: Arenas et al. (2011c))

   In this exercise we analyze the combined complexity of computing certain answers to conjunctive queries with inequalities, under mappings without target dependencies. Define CERTAIN$(CQ^{\neq})$ as the problem of, given a mapping $\mathcal{M} = (\mathbf{R_s}, \mathbf{R_t}, \Sigma_{st})$, without target dependencies, a Boolean conjunctive query with inequalities Q, and a source instance S, determine whether $certain_{\mathcal{M}}(Q,S) = \text{true}$. Prove that CERTAIN$(CQ^{\neq})$ can be solved in CONEXPTIME, and that it is CONEXPTIME-hard even for conjunctive queries with two inequalities.

20. Show that there exists a Boolean conjunctive query Q with a single inequality and a LAV mapping $\mathcal{M}$, such that Q is not FO-rewritable under $\mathcal{M}$, both over the canonical universal solution and the core.

21. (Source: Arenas et al. (2013))

   Consider the following statement which essentially says that small neighborhoods are preserved in data exchange. Given a mapping $\mathcal{M}$ without target constraints, for each number $r \geq 0$ there is a number $d \geq 0$ so that the following holds:

   - if S is a source instance and $\bar{a}, \bar{b}$ two tuples of elements of S such that $N_d^S(\bar{a}) \cong N_d^S(\bar{b})$, then $N_d^T(\bar{a}) \cong N_d^T(\bar{b})$, when T is the canonical universal solution for S.

   Show that this is true if $\mathcal{M}$ is a LAV mapping. Also give an example of a GAV mapping which makes the statement above false.

22. (Source: Arenas et al. (2013))

   Show that there exists a mapping $\mathcal{M} = (\mathbf{R_s}, \mathbf{R_t}, \Sigma_{st})$ and an FO query Q such that Q is FO-rewritable over the canonical universal solution under $\mathcal{M}$, but it is not rewritable over the core.

23. Prove Proposition 8.23. That is, let $\mathcal{M} = (\mathbf{R_s}, \mathbf{R_t}, \Sigma_{st}, \Sigma_{st})$ be a mapping, where Σ_t consists of a set of tgds and egds, and S a source instance. Then for every target instance T, the following are equivalent:

   (i) $T \in \text{SOL}_{\mathcal{M}}^{\text{CWA}}(S)$.

   (ii) T is a CWA-presolution and a universal solution for S under $\mathcal{M}$.

24. Show that Proposition 8.26 is witnessed by the following example. The source schema contains a binary relation E, and the target schema contains two ternary relations R_1 and R_2. The only st-tgd is $R(x,y) \to \exists z \exists z'\, R_1(x,z,z')$, and the only target tgd is

$R_1(x,u,y) \wedge R_1(x,v,y) \rightarrow R_2(x,u,v)$. Then the $2n$-tuple instance S producing exponentially many maximal CWA-solutions is $\{E(i,a), E(i,b) \mid 1 \leq i \leq n\}$.

25. Prove Proposition 8.29, i.e., there exists a mapping $\mathscr{M} = (\mathbf{R_s}, \mathbf{R_t}, \Sigma_{st}, \Sigma_t)$, such that Σ_t consists of a set of egds and a weakly acyclic set of tgds, and a Boolean FO query Q over $\mathbf{R_t}$, for which the following problem is undecidable: Given a source instance S, is $certain_{\mathscr{M}}^{\mathrm{CWA}}(Q, S) = \mathtt{true}$?

26. Prove Proposition 8.32: Let $\mathscr{M} = (\mathbf{R_s}, \mathbf{R_t}, \Sigma_{st}, \Sigma_t)$ be a mapping such that Σ_t consists of a set of egds and a weakly acyclic set of tgds, and assume that Q is a union of conjunctive queries over $\mathbf{R_t}$. Then for every source instance S it is the case that $certain_{\mathscr{M}}^{\mathrm{CWA}}(Q, S) = certain_{\mathscr{M}}(Q, S)$.

27. (Source: Hernich et al. (2011))

    Prove that there exists a mapping $\mathscr{M} = (\mathbf{R_s}, \mathbf{R_t}, \Sigma_{st}, \Sigma_t)$ such that Σ_t consists of a set of egds and a weakly acyclic set of tgds, and a Boolean conjunctive query with a single inequality Q over $\mathbf{R_t}$, such that the following problem is CONP-complete: Given a source instance S, is $certain_{\mathscr{M}}^{\mathrm{CWA}}(Q, S) = \mathtt{true}$?

28. Show that for annotated mappings, we have $certain_{(\mathscr{M}, \alpha)}(Q, S) = \bigcap \{Q(D) \mid D \in Rep(\mathrm{CANSOL}_{(\mathscr{M}, \alpha)}(S))\}$ for arbitrary queries, and give a proof of Proposition 8.34.

29. (Source: Libkin and Sirangelo (2011))

    Prove that there exists an annotated mapping $(\mathscr{M}, \alpha)$ with $\#_{op}(\mathscr{M}, \alpha) = 1$ and an FO query Q such that data complexity of finding $certain_{(\mathscr{M}, \alpha)}(Q, S)$ is CONEXPTIME-complete.

30. (Source: Arenas et al. (2011b))

    A usual assumption in data exchange is that the domain of a source instance consists exclusively of constants. On the other hand, target instances are allowed to contain null values, and, in fact, universal solutions require those null values in order to capture the whole space of solutions. However, this naturally raises the question of what happens if we need to further exchange those instances with null values? What is the right semantics for data exchange in this case, and how is it possible to represent universal instances for source instances with nulls?

    Let $\mathscr{M} = (\mathbf{R_s}, \mathbf{R_t}, \Sigma_{st})$ be a mapping without target dependencies. Assume that S is a source instance with nulls, i.e., S is a naïve database over $\mathbf{R_s}$. Then a naïve database T over $\mathbf{R_t}$ is a universal *representative* for S under $\mathscr{M}$ if

$$Rep(T) = \bigcup_{S' \in Rep(S)} \mathrm{SOL}_{\mathscr{M}}(S').$$

    Hence, analogously to the case when source instances contain no nulls, a universal representative T defines the whole space of solutions for a source instance S. The difference in this case is that S itself represents an infinite set of source instances without nulls, and therefore T must represent the space of solutions for each one of them.

    Prove the following:

- If S is a source instance without nulls, then the set of universal representatives for S coincides with the set of universal solutions for S.

- There exists a mapping $\mathcal{M} = (\mathbf{R_s}, \mathbf{R_t}, \Sigma_{st})$ and a naïve database over $\mathbf{R_s}$, such that no naïve database over $\mathbf{R_t}$ is a universal representative for S under $\mathcal{M}$.

- The latter result states that naïve databases are not expressive enough to act as universal representatives in data exchange when source instances contain null values. Here we present an extension of the class of naïve databases, called *conditional databases* (see Abiteboul et al. (1995); Imieliński and Lipski (1984)), that allows defining universal representatives for source instances given as naïve databases (and, in fact, even for source instances given as conditional databases).

  A *conditional database* T extends a naïve database with a *condition* ρ_t attached to each fact $t \in T$. Each such condition is a Boolean combination of formulae of the form $x = y$ with $x, y \in \text{CONST} \cup \text{VAR}$. Given a valuation $v : \text{VAR} \cup \text{CONST} \to \text{CONST}$ that is the identity on CONST, we denote by $v(T)$ the instance that is obtained from T by replacing each fact $W(u_1, \ldots, u_n)$ in T with $W(v(u_1), \ldots, v(u_n))$, and then removing the resulting facts of the form $v(t)$ such that v does not satisfy ρ_t (in the usual sense). The set $Rep(T)$ is defined as all those instances T', without nulls, such that $v(T) \subseteq T'$, for some mapping $v : \text{VAR} \cup \text{CONST} \to \text{CONST}$ that is the identity on CONST.

  As before, a conditional database T over $\mathbf{R_t}$ is a universal representative for conditional database S over $\mathbf{R_s}$ under $\mathcal{M}$, if

  $$Rep(T) = \bigcup_{S' \in Rep(S)} \text{SOL}_{\mathcal{M}}(S').$$

  Prove that for every mapping $\mathcal{M} = (\mathbf{R_s}, \mathbf{R_t}, \Sigma_{st})$ and conditional database S over $\mathbf{R_s}$, there is a conditional database T over $\mathbf{R_t}$ that is a universal representative for S under $\mathcal{M}$. Moreover, prove that the same property holds if one restricts to the case of *positive* conditional databases, which are obtained by disallowing the use of negation in the conditions attached to the facts in conditional databases. Thus, we say that conditional databases, and positive conditional databases, form a *strong representation system* for the class of mappings specified by st-tgds (this problem has also been studied by Grahne and Onet (2012)).

31. In this exercise, you will provide another justification for the mapping languages used in this book, which is inspired by the notion of instance-completeness that was used to justify relational languages. More precisely, say that a pair (S, T) of instances is *admissible* if: (1) the schemas of S and T are disjoint, (2) every constant mentioned in T is also mentioned in S, and (3) every isomorphism from S to itself (which is not necessarily the identity on constants) can be extended to an isomorphism from T to itself. Moreover, say that a class $\mathscr{C}$ of mappings is *instance-complete* if for every admissible pair (S, T), there exists a mapping $\mathcal{M} \in \mathscr{C}$ such that T is a universal solution for S under $\mathcal{M}$. In this exercise, you have to prove that the class of mappings defined by finite sets of st-tgds including inequalities in the source formulae is instance-complete.

PART THREE
XML DATA EXCHANGE

10

The problem of XML data exchange

In this chapter we shall study data exchange for XML documents. XML itself was invented as a standard for data exchange on the Web, albeit under a different interpretation of the term "data exchange". In the Web context, it typically refers to a common, flexible format that everyone agrees on, and that, therefore, facilitates the transfer of data between different sites and applications. When we speak of data exchange, we mean transforming databases under different schemas with respect to schema mapping rules, and querying the exchanged data.

10.1 XML documents and schemas

In this section we review the basic definitions regarding XML. Note that a simple example was already shown in Chapter 1. XML documents have a *hierarchical* structure, usually abstracted as a tree. An example is shown in Figure 10.1. This document contains information about rulers of European countries. Its structure is represented by a labeled tree; in this example, the labels are europe, country, and ruler. In the XML context, these are referred to as *element types*. We assume that the labels come from a finite labeling alphabet and correspond, roughly, to relation names from the classical relational setting.

The root of the tree is labeled europe, and it has two children that are labeled country. These have *data values*, given in parentheses: the first one is *Scotland*, and the second one is *England*. Each country in turn has a set of rulers. That is, the children of each country node are labeled ruler, and have associated data values assigned to them, for example, *James V*. These data values come from a potentially infinite set (e.g., of strings, or numbers). We also assume that, in general, children of each node are *ordered*; normally this order is interpreted as going from left to right in the picture. That is, *James V* is the first child of the *Scotland* node, and *Charles I* is the last. In our example, this corresponds to the chronological order.

In general, a node may have more than one data value. We assume, under the analogy between node labels and relation names, that each node has some *attributes* that store data values associated with it.

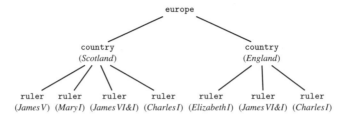

Figure 10.1 An XML tree: an example

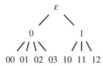

Figure 10.2 Unranked tree domain for the XML tree in Figure 10.1

XML documents: definition

To define XML documents, we need to specify both their *structure* and the *data* they carry. The structure, as we already mentioned, comes in the shape of a tree. Unlike binary trees (considered, for example, in Section 2.5), trees describing XML documents may have internal nodes with different numbers of children. For example, in the document shown in Figure 10.1, the root has two children, the *Scotland* node has four, and the *England* node has three. We refer to such trees as *unranked trees*.

We describe the nodes of the tree by paths to them from the root . For example, the *Mary I* node is the second child of the first child of the root, hence we describe it by the sequence 01. Note that we start numbering children from 0, i.e., the first child is numbered 0, the second is numbered 1, and so on. The node corresponding to *Charles I* as the ruler of England is the third child of the second child of the root, hence we describe it by the sequence 12. In general each node is a sequence of natural numbers, i.e., a string over $\mathbb{N}$. If we have such a node $s = i_1 i_2 \ldots i_k$, then all its prefixes $i_1 \ldots i_m$ for $m < k$ are nodes of the tree as well, as they lie on the path from the root to s. Furthermore, if $s \cdot i$ is a node in a tree, then so is $s \cdot j$ for $j < i$: that is, if there is, say, a third child of a node, there must be the first and the second as well. This leads to the following definition.

Definition 10.1 (Unranked tree domain)   An *unranked tree domain* is a finite set $U \subseteq \mathbb{N}^*$ of strings of natural numbers that contains with each element all its prefixes (i.e., is prefix closed) and such that $s \cdot i \in U$ implies $s \cdot j \in U$ for all $i, j \in \mathbb{N}$ satisfying $j < i$.

The unranked tree domain of the tree from Figure 10.1 is shown in Figure 10.2.

With this, we can formally define XML documents over a given labeling alphabet (i.e., the set of element types) and a set of attributes as follows.

Definition 10.2 (XML trees)   Given a labeling alphabet Γ of element types and a set of

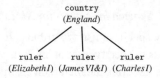

Figure 10.3 A subtree of the XML tree form Figure 10.1

attributes *Att*, *XML trees (documents)* over Γ and *Att* are structures

$$T = (U, \downarrow, \rightarrow, lab, (\rho_a)_{a \in Att}),$$

where

- U is an unranked tree domain;
- $\downarrow$ is the binary *child* relation on U, i.e., $s \downarrow s \cdot i$ whenever both s and $s \cdot i$ are in U;
- $\rightarrow$ is the binary *next-sibling* relation, i.e., $s \cdot i \rightarrow s \cdot (i+1)$ whenever both $s \cdot i$ and $s \cdot (i+1)$ are in U;
- $lab : U \rightarrow \Gamma$ is the labeling function; and
- each ρ_a is a partial function from U to V, the fixed domain of attribute values, or *data values*, that gives the values of attribute a for all the nodes in U where it is defined.

Consider again the document shown in Figure 10.1. It has 10 nodes, as depicted in Figure 10.2. The root is always ε, the empty string, the children of the root are 0 and 1, both labeled country, the children of 0 are $00, 01, 02$, and 03, and the children of 1 are $10, 11$, and 12, all of which are labeled ruler. If we assume that both country and ruler have an attribute @name defined for them, then the values of this attribute, assigned by the function $\rho_{@name}$, are as shown in the figure, e.g., $\rho_{@name}(03) = Charles\ I$.

Very often we will need to talk about parts of XML trees. A most basic part is the *subtree* rooted at some given node. For example, the subtree of the document in Figure 10.1 rooted at node 1 is the tree shown in Figure 10.3. Formally, we define subtrees as follows.

Definition 10.3 Let $T = (U, \downarrow, \rightarrow, lab, (\rho_a)_{a \in Att})$ be an XML tree and let $v \in U$ be its node. The *subtree of T rooted at v* is the XML tree

$$T.v = \left(v^{-1}U, \downarrow^{T.v}, \rightarrow^{T.v}, lab^{T.v}, (\rho_a^{T.v})_{a \in Att}\right)$$

where

- $v^{-1}U = \{w \mid vw \in U\}$ is the set of all words in U having v as a prefix;
- $\downarrow^{T.v}$ and $\rightarrow^{T.v}$ are the child and sibling relations restricted to $v^{-1}U$, and
- $lab^{T.v}(w)$ and $\rho_a^{T.v}$ are inherited from lab and ρ_a in T, i.e., $lab^{T.v}(w) = lab(vw)$, and $\rho_a^{T.v}(w) = \rho_a(vw)$.

Observe that the definition assures that the subtree is an XML tree, i.e., its root is ε, the root's children are $0, 1, \ldots, k$, etc. For example, the node storing the value *Charles I* is 12 in the original document, but in the subtree it is 2.

Schema languages for XML

Relational schemas essentially specify a list of attributes (columns) for every relation. In the case of XML one also needs to specify a set of attributes for each label. This, however, is insufficient, as schemas must describe the hierarchical structure of XML documents too.

To see how this can be done, let us revisit again the example in Figure 10.1. If we look at the root and read the labels of its children, from left to right, then we get a string country country. If we look at the *Scotland* node and read the labels of its children, then we see a string ruler ruler ruler ruler. It is a common approach to describe schemas in terms of the allowed strings obtained in this way. The simplest such schemas are *Document Type Definitions*, or *DTDs*. They put restrictions on strings of labels in terms of regular languages they belong to.

For example, the tree from Figure 10.1 conforms to the DTD below:

$$\begin{array}{llll} \text{europe} & \rightarrow & \text{country}^* & \text{country}: @\text{name} \\ \text{country} & \rightarrow & \text{ruler}^* & \text{ruler}: @\text{name} \end{array}$$

The first column restricts regular expressions of strings of labels. It says that labels of children of a europe node must come from the language country*, i.e., be a sequence of country labels, and that labels of children of a country node must come from the language ruler*. The right column gives a list of attributes: in this case, the attribute @name is defined for country and ruler nodes. Formally, DTDs are defined as follows.

Definition 10.4 (DTDs)   A *DTD D* over an alphabet Γ with a distinguished symbol r (for the root) and a set of attributes *Att* is a triple (P_D, A_D, r) where:

- P_D is a mapping from Γ to regular expressions over $\Gamma - \{r\}$, which one typically writes as productions $\ell \rightarrow e$ if $P_D(\ell) = e$.
- A_D is a mapping $A_D : \Gamma \rightarrow 2^{Att}$ that assigns a (possibly empty) set of attributes to each element type.

The size of D, written as $\|D\|$, is the total length of all used regular expressions, plus $|Att|$.

Leaf nodes do not have any children; for instance, ruler nodes are such. Technically, it means that they have an *empty string* of children. For them, DTDs will have rules like ruler $\rightarrow \varepsilon$; however, we usually omit them when we describe DTDs. So, if there is no rule of the form $\ell \rightarrow e$ in the description of a DTD, we assume that $\ell \rightarrow \varepsilon$.

We always assume, for notational convenience, that attributes of a node (if there are several of them) come in some order. This is the same as in the relational case: attributes in tuples come in some order so we can write $R(a_1, \ldots, a_n)$. Likewise, we shall describe an ℓ-labeled tree node with n attributes as $\ell(a_1, \ldots, a_n)$.

A tree T *conforms to a DTD* $D = (P_D, A_D, r)$, written as $T \models D$, if:

1. its root is labeled r;
2. for each node labeled ℓ, the labels of its children, read left-to-right, form a string in the language of $P_D(\ell)$; and

3. the set of attributes for each node labeled ℓ is $A_D(\ell)$.

In particular, if an ℓ-labeled node is a leaf in a tree T that conforms to D, then the empty string ε must belong to the language $P_D(\ell)$.

We shall often deal with a very common subclass of DTDs based on simple regular expressions. Examples of such simple expressions are country* and ruler*, or for example, book · chapter*, or book · author* · publisher?, where ℓ? is an abbreviation for $\ell|\varepsilon$ (i.e., an optional element). Formally, these are defined as follows.

Definition 10.5 A DTD D is *nested-relational* if two conditions are satisfied:

- Every production in it is of the form

$$\ell \rightarrow \hat{\ell}_1 \cdot \ldots \cdot \hat{\ell}_m,$$

  where all the ℓ_i's are distinct labels from Γ and each $\hat{\ell}_i$ is either ℓ_i, or ℓ_i^*, or ℓ_i^+, or $\ell_i? = \ell_i|\varepsilon$.
- The DTD D is not recursive, i.e., there are no cycles in the graph in which we put a directed edge from ℓ to all the ℓ_i's for each production above.

The DTD used in our example in this section is nested-relational. In fact, empirical studies show that these are very common in practice, and cover many, if not most, real-world DTDs. As we will see shortly, many computational problems become easier for them.

Automata and schemas

There are specification languages which are richer than DTDs. In those languages (e.g., XML Schema, or RelaxNG), one can specify more general *regular* properties of trees. For example, one can define the string of labels of children of a node based on the whole path to the node from the root, not just its label. In general, all these languages are captured by the power of automata for trees.

We have explained how automata operate on binary trees (see Section 2.5). In such trees, each non leaf node has exactly two children, so transition functions are of the form $Q \times Q \times \Gamma \rightarrow 2^Q$ and define possible states of a node, based on its label and the states of its two children. In the case of unranked trees, we do not know a priori how many children a node would have. Instead of introducing a separate transition function $\delta_n : Q^n \times \Gamma \rightarrow 2^Q$ for nodes with n children, these automata are defined with a different transition function, that assigns regular languages of *states* to states and labels.

Definition 10.6 An *unranked nondeterministic finite tree automaton* (UNFTA) on unranked node-labeled trees over alphabet Γ is defined as $\mathscr{A} = (Q, \Gamma, F, \delta)$ where

- Q is the set of states,
- $F \subseteq Q$ is the set of final, or accepting states, and
- $\delta : Q \times \Gamma \rightarrow 2^{Q^*}$ is the transition function such that $\delta(q, a)$ is a regular language over the set of states Q, for every $q \in Q$ and $a \in \Gamma$.

Given an unranked tree T, a *run* of $\mathscr{A}$ on T is a function $\rho_{\mathscr{A}} : T \to Q$ that assigns states to nodes. This function must satisfy the following condition:

- if s is a node with label a and children $s_1, \ldots, s_n$ ordered by the sibling relation as $s_1 \to \cdots \to s_n$, then the word $\rho_{\mathscr{A}}(s_1) \ldots \rho_{\mathscr{A}}(s_n)$ over Q must be in the language $\delta(\rho_{\mathscr{A}}(s), a)$.

Note that if s is a leaf, this condition states that a run can assign a state q to s only if the empty string ε is in $\delta(q,a)$.

A run is *accepting* if it assigns an accepting state to the root, i.e., $\rho_{\mathscr{A}}(\varepsilon) \in F$. A tree T is *accepted by* $\mathscr{A}$ if there is an accepting run. The *language recognized by* $\mathscr{A}$, denoted by $L(\mathscr{A})$, is the set of trees accepted by $\mathscr{A}$.

The standard representation of UNFTAs uses NFAs for transitions: δ maps pairs state-letter to NFAs over Q. We will call these NFAs *horizontal automata*. Assuming this representation, the size of $\mathscr{A}$, written as $\|\mathscr{A}\|$, is the number of states plus the total size of the horizontal automata (number of states plus the size of transition relation). It is known that testing nonemptiness and testing membership can be done in polynomial time, in the size of the automaton. An automaton is (bottom-up) deterministic if for each label $\ell \in \Gamma$, the languages $\delta(q, \ell)$ are pairwise disjoint for q ranging over all states of the automaton. Note that in this case each tree admits at most one run. For such automata we assume that all transitions are represented by DFAs, and refer to them as UFTA(DFA).

A *(regular) schema* $\mathscr{S}$ over the set of element types Γ and the set of attributes *Att* consists of an UNFTA $\mathscr{A}$ over Γ and a mapping $A_{\mathscr{S}} : \Gamma \to 2^{Att}$ that assigns a (possibly empty) set of attributes to each element type. The size $\|\mathscr{S}\|$ is $\|\mathscr{A}\|$ plus $|Att|$. A tree T conforms to such a schema if it is accepted by $\mathscr{A}$ and the set of attributes of each ℓ-labeled node is $A_{\mathscr{S}}(\ell)$. Testing conformance to a schema can be done in polynomial time, even if the schema is counted as a part of the input.

DTDs can be seen as a restricted form of regular schemas. A DTD $D = (P_D, A_D, r)$ over Γ and *Att* can be presented as $\mathscr{S}_D = (\mathscr{A}_D, A_D)$, where $\mathscr{A}_D = (Q, F, \delta)$ is an UNFTA defined as follows:

- the set of states Q is $\{q_a \mid a \in \Gamma\}$;
- the set of final states F is $\{q_r\}$;
- the transition function is defined as follows: $\delta(q_\ell, \ell)$ is the language of the regular expression $P_D(\ell)$, with each letter a replaced by q_a, and $\delta(q_\ell, \ell') = \emptyset$ for $\ell \neq \ell'$.

Then the set of trees that conform to D is exactly the set of trees that conform to $\mathscr{S}_D$.

Coming back to our example, the labeling alphabet consists of `europe`, `country`, and `ruler`. The automaton will have three states: q_{europe}, q_{country}, and q_{ruler}; the state q_{europe} is the only final state. The transitions are as follows:

$$\begin{aligned}
\delta(q_{\text{europe}}, \texttt{europe}) &= q_{\text{country}}^* \\
\delta(q_{\text{country}}, \texttt{country}) &= q_{\text{ruler}}^* \\
\delta(q_{\text{ruler}}, \texttt{ruler}) &= \varepsilon.
\end{aligned}$$

For all other combinations (q, a), we have $\delta(q, a) = \emptyset$.

10.2 Key problems of XML data exchange

The main tasks of XML data exchange are similar to those in relational data exchange. Static analysis tasks, dealing with schemas and mappings only, involve consistency issues and operations on mappings like composing and inverting. We discuss them in PART FOUR. In the current part we focus on the tasks that deal also with data, that is, XML documents. Among these the following are the most prominent ones.

- *Materializing target instances (solutions)*. Given a source document, one needs to restructure it under the target schema following the rules specified by a mapping. In the XML context, the target schema (DTD or XML schema) imposes complex conditions on the structure of the solution. One of the consequences is that schema mappings are often *over specified*. As a result of this, for some source instances there are no solutions. One needs to be able to verify that a mapping admits a solution for a given source document and, if it does, build one.
- *Query answering*. Usually, schema mappings are also hugely *under specified*, giving rise to many possible choices for the target document. Nevertheless, queries should be answered in a way that depends only on the content of the source document and not on particular choices made when a target instance is constructed. For queries that return sets of tuples this is guaranteed by declaring correct only these tuples that are returned for each solution (so-called *certain answers*). For queries that return XML documents, the notion of correct answers is based on common properties of the answers returned on all solutions.

  For some mappings, the choices in the solution building process can be made in a harmless way so that no facts are invented: the solution only satisfies properties enforced by the dependencies in the mappings and the target schema. This guarantees correctness of the answer returned by a query. We will see classes of mappings for which such solutions can be obtained and queries can be answered effectively. For other classes, we will have finite representations of all possible choices that can be examined to determine correct answers.

Why not use relational techniques?

All of PART TWO was about developing techniques for relational data exchange. So, why can we not just use them for XML? After all, XML documents are special relational structures, and in fact there are many ways of storing XML documents in relations.

The answer to this question is that relational and XML data exchange techniques are largely incompatible. This is due to the fact that restrictions imposed by XML schemas and XML source-to-target dependencies are much more complex than their relational counterparts, due to the more complex hierarchical structure of XML documents. Many of them cannot even be expressed as relational calculus constraints over relational translations of XML, making the previously developed techniques inapplicable.

That said, we can, and will make use of relational techniques. We do so in two ways.

First, some of the lower bounds for various XML data exchange problems are already witnessed in the relational case. Since relational databases can be represented as particularly simple XML documents, every now and then we shall obtain lower bounds for free. Second, we shall see that under some restrictions, XML data exchange can be performed by translating XML into relations and then using relational techniques. However, for that to happen, restrictions need to be imposed both on schemas and on schema mappings.

11

Patterns and mappings

XML schema mappings are expressed in terms of *tree patterns*, a simple query language for XML trees that plays the role analogous to that of conjunctive queries for relational databases. In this chapter we define the syntax and semantics of tree patterns, introduce a classification based on the features they use, and determine the complexity of basic computational problems. Then we do the same for XML schema mappings.

11.1 Tree patterns: classification and complexity

In XML trees information can be represented by means of data values, as well as the structure of the tree. Let us return to the example shown in Figure 10.1. The edge between the node storing *Scotland* and the node storing *Mary I* represents the fact that Mary I ruled Scotland. The value *Charles I* appearing twice informs us that Charles I ruled both Scotland and England. The node storing *Mary I* coming directly after the node storing *James V* corresponds to the fact that Mary I succeeded James V on the throne of Scotland. This already suggests the querying features needed to extract information from XML trees: *child*, *next sibling*, and their transitive closures: *descendant, following sibling*. We call these four features *axes*. It is also necessary to compare data values stored in different nodes.

In the light of PART TWO, a natural query language for XML trees is the family of conjunctive queries over XML trees viewed as databases over two sorts of objects: tree nodes, and data values. Relations in such representations include child, next sibling, and relations associating attribute values with nodes.

To avoid the syntactically unpleasant formalism of two-sorted structures, conjunctive queries on trees are best formalized by means of tree patterns with variables for attribute values. Nodes are described by formulae $\ell(\bar{x})$, where ℓ is either a label or the wildcard _, and $\bar{x}$ is a tuple of variables corresponding to the attributes of the node (possibly empty). For each node, a list of its children and descendants is specified, together with (perhaps partial) information on their order.

For instance, the pattern on the left of Figure 11.1 expresses that y succeeded ruler x in some country; the solid edges of the tree express the child relation, and the solid arrow denotes the next-sibling relation. The middle patterns simply says that x is a ruler; the dashed edge expresses the descendant relation. The pattern on the right expresses that x

Figure 11.1 Examples of tree patterns

ruled in two different countries; the dashed arrow denotes the following sibling relation between two `country` nodes.

Definition 11.1 (Pattern syntax)   Tree patterns are given by the following grammar:

$$
\begin{array}{rcll}
\pi & := & \ell(\bar{x})[\lambda] \mid \ell(\bar{x}) & \text{(patterns)} \\
\lambda & := & \mu \mid //\pi \mid \lambda, \lambda & \text{(sets)} \\
\mu & := & \pi \mid \pi \to \mu \mid \pi \to^+ \mu & \text{(sequences)}
\end{array}
$$

We write $\pi(\bar{x})$ to indicate that $\bar{x}$ is the list of all the variables used in π. By $\|\pi\|$ we denote the size of π, i.e., the length of its syntactic representation.

The intuition behind this syntax is as follows:

- a pattern is either $\ell(\bar{x})$, describing a node labeled ℓ with attributes $\bar{x}$, or it is $\ell(\bar{x})[\lambda]$, describing a node and part of the subtree rooted at this node (given by λ);
- sets λ have as their elements either sequences μ rooted one level down (e.g., like the `ruler`→`ruler` sequence below the `country` node in the leftmost pattern in Figure 11.1), or single patterns which are rooted an arbitrary nonzero number of levels down ($//\pi$);
- sequences describe patterns rooted at the same level and connections between them: those could be next-sibling ($\to$) or following-sibling ($\to^+$) connections.

Before giving the formal semantics, we show how the patterns from Figure 11.1 can now be written in this syntax:

$$
\begin{aligned}
\pi_1(x,y) &= \texttt{europe}[\texttt{country}[\texttt{ruler}(x) \to \texttt{ruler}(y)]], \\
\pi_2(x) &= \texttt{europe}[//\texttt{ruler}(x)], \\
\pi_3(x) &= \texttt{europe}[\texttt{country}[\texttt{ruler}(x)] \to^+ \texttt{country}[\texttt{ruler}(x)]].
\end{aligned}
$$

We shall use abbreviations:
$$
\begin{aligned}
\ell(\bar{x})/\pi &\quad \text{for} \quad \ell(\bar{x})[\pi], \text{ and} \\
\ell(\bar{x})//\pi &\quad \text{for} \quad \ell(\bar{x})[//\pi]
\end{aligned}
$$
to write patterns more compactly. For instance, the patterns above can be briefly written as

$$
\begin{aligned}
\pi_1(x,y) &= \texttt{europe}/\texttt{country}[\texttt{ruler}(x) \to \texttt{ruler}(y)], \\
\pi_2(x) &= \texttt{europe}//\texttt{ruler}(x), \\
\pi_3(x) &= \texttt{europe}[\texttt{country}/\texttt{ruler}(x) \to^+ \texttt{country}/\texttt{ruler}(x)].
\end{aligned}
$$

To define the semantics of patterns, we introduce relations $\downarrow^+$ and $\rightarrow^+$ which are transitive closures of $\downarrow$ and $\rightarrow$. That is, $\downarrow^+$ is the descendant relation, and $\rightarrow^+$ is the following-sibling relation. Formally, we have $s \downarrow^+ s \cdot s'$, whenever s' is a nonempty string, and $s \cdot i \rightarrow^+ s \cdot j$ whenever $i < j$. With this, we are ready to introduce the semantics of patterns.

Definition 11.2 (Pattern semantics)   The semantics of patterns is formally defined by means of the relation $(T,s) \models \pi(\bar{a})$, saying that $\pi(\bar{x})$ is satisfied in a node s of a tree T when its variables $\bar{x}$ are interpreted as $\bar{a}$. It is defined inductively as follows:

$(T,s) \models \ell(\bar{a})$	iff	s is labeled by ℓ (or $\ell = \_$) and $\bar{a}$ is the tuple of attributes of s (or is empty);
$(T,s) \models \ell(\bar{a})[\lambda_1, \lambda_2]$	iff	$(T,s) \models \ell(\bar{a})[\lambda_1]$ and $(T,s) \models \ell(\bar{a})[\lambda_2]$;
$(T,s) \models \ell(\bar{a})[\mu]$	iff	$(T,s) \models \ell(\bar{a})$ and $(T,s') \models \mu$ for some s' with $s \downarrow s'$;
$(T,s) \models \ell(\bar{a})[//\pi]$	iff	$(T,s) \models \ell(\bar{a})$ and $(T,s') \models \pi$ for some s' with $s \downarrow^+ s'$;
$(T,s) \models \pi \rightarrow \mu$	iff	$(T,s) \models \pi$ and $(T,s') \models \mu$ for some s' with $s \rightarrow s'$;
$(T,s) \models \pi \rightarrow^+ \mu$	iff	$(T,s) \models \pi$ and $(T,s') \models \mu$ for some s' with $s \rightarrow^+ s'$.

Patterns are witnessed at the root: for a tree T and a pattern π, we write

$$T \models \pi(\bar{a})$$

if $(T,\varepsilon) \models \pi(\bar{a})$. We also define

$$\pi(T) = \{\bar{a} \mid T \models \pi(\bar{a})\}$$

and write $T \models \pi$ if $\pi(T)$ is not empty.

If T is the tree from Figure 10.1, then

$$\pi_1(T) = \{(James\ V, Mary\ I), (Mary\ I, James\ VI\ \&\ I),$$
$$(James\ VI\ \&\ I, Charles\ I), (Elizabeth\ I, James\ VI\ \&\ I)\},$$
$$\pi_2(T) = \{James\ V, Mary\ I, James\ VI\ \&\ I, Charles\ I, Elizabeth\ I\},$$
$$\pi_3(T) = \{James\ VI\ \&\ I, Charles\ I\}.$$

Note that witnessing patterns at the root is not a restriction since we have descendant $//$ in the language, and can thus express satisfaction of a pattern in an arbitrary node of a tree. Also note that "sets" in tree patterns are literally sets, i.e., the listed subpatterns do not have to be witnessed by distinct nodes. That is, for a node satisfying $\ell(\bar{a})[\lambda_1, \lambda_2]$, the nodes witnessing λ_1 are not necessarily distinct from the ones witnessing λ_2. For instance, the pattern $r[\_, a]$ is witnessed by a tree with an r-labeled root and a single a-labeled child, as that child witnesses both $\_$ and a.

Observe that the patterns can already express equalities between data values by simply repeating variables, e.g., pattern π_3 uses the variable x twice. Inequalities have to be added explicitly. To keep the setting uniform, we also allow explicit equalities.

Definition 11.3 *Generalized tree patterns* are expressions of the form

$$\pi(x_1, x_2, \ldots, x_n) \wedge \alpha(x_1, x_2, \ldots, x_{n+m}),$$

where $\pi(x_1, x_2, \ldots, x_n)$ is a tree pattern and $\alpha(x_1, x_2, \ldots, x_{n+m})$ is a conjunction of equalities and inequalities among variables $x_1, x_2, \ldots, x_{n+m}$. The semantics is naturally extended:

$$T \models \pi(\bar{a}) \wedge \alpha(\bar{a}, \bar{b}) \quad \text{iff} \quad T \models \pi(\bar{a}) \text{ and } \alpha(\bar{a}, \bar{b}) \text{ holds.}$$

For example the pattern

$$\texttt{europe}[\texttt{country}[\texttt{ruler}(y) \rightarrow \texttt{ruler}(x)],$$
$$\texttt{country}[\texttt{ruler}(z) \rightarrow \texttt{ruler}(x)]] \wedge y \neq z$$

expresses the fact that x succeeded two different rulers, y and z.

From now on, whenever we write *pattern*, we mean *generalized tree pattern*. We refer to the non-generalized tree patterns as *pure patterns*.

A pattern $\varphi(\bar{x}) = \pi(x_1, x_2, \ldots, x_n) \wedge \alpha(x_1, x_2, \ldots, x_{n+m})$ satisfies the *safety condition* if for each variable x there is a sequence of equalities in α connecting x to a variable used in π. In other words, either x is used in π, or we have a sequence of equalities $x = x_{i_0}$, $x_{i_0} = x_{i_1}, \ldots, x_{i_{k-1}} = x_{i_k}$ in α such that x_{i_k} is used in π. Note that all pure patterns have this property.

The safety condition guarantees that for each finite tree there are only finitely many tuples for which the pattern is satisfied. Without it, we would have to be prepared to handle infinite answers. Therefore, from now on we assume that all patterns satisfy the safety condition.

Where is the conjunction?

We are going to use patterns as analogs of conjunctive queries when we define XML schema mappings. However, one key feature of conjunctive queries appears to be missing from patterns – namely, the conjunction itself!

The syntax of patterns can be trivially extended with conjunction: if π_1 and π_2 are patterns, then so is $\pi_1 \wedge \pi_2$. The semantics of conjunction is the natural one: given patterns $\pi_1(\bar{x}, \bar{y})$ and $\pi_2(\bar{x}, \bar{z})$, where $\bar{x}, \bar{y}, \bar{z}$ are disjoint tuples of variables, we have

$$(T, v) \models (\pi_1 \wedge \pi_2)(\bar{a}, \bar{b}, \bar{c}) \quad \text{if and only if} \quad (T, v) \models \pi_1(\bar{a}, \bar{b}) \text{ and } (T, v) \models \pi_2(\bar{a}, \bar{c}).$$

The reason why we do not include explicit conjunction into the definition of patterns is that patterns are already *closed under conjunction*. That is, for each $\pi_1(\bar{x}, \bar{y})$ and $\pi_2(\bar{x}, \bar{z})$, there exists a pattern $\pi(\bar{x}, \bar{y}, \bar{z})$ such that for each tree T and each node v, for all tuples $\bar{a}, \bar{b}, \bar{c}$,

$$(T, v) \models \pi(\bar{a}, \bar{b}, \bar{c}) \quad \text{if and only if} \quad (T, v) \models (\pi_1 \wedge \pi_2)(\bar{a}, \bar{b}, \bar{c}).$$

The conjunction of the form $\ell[\lambda_1] \wedge \ell[\lambda_2]$ can be expressed by $\ell[\lambda_1, \lambda_2]$, e.g.,

$$r/\texttt{country}(x)/\texttt{ruler}(y) \quad \wedge \quad r/\texttt{country}(x')/\texttt{ruler}(y)$$

can be expressed as

$$r[\texttt{country}(x)/\texttt{ruler}(y), \texttt{country}(x')/\texttt{ruler}(y)].$$

The conjunction

$$\texttt{country}(x)/\texttt{ruler}(y) \quad \wedge \quad \texttt{country}(x')[\texttt{ruler}(y') \to \texttt{ruler}(y'')]$$

needs to be expressed as

$$\texttt{country}(x)[\texttt{ruler}(y), \texttt{ruler}(y') \to \texttt{ruler}(y'')] \wedge x = x'.$$

The equality $x = x'$ explicitly expresses the fact that the variables x and x' are always equal to the attribute value of the common node where the patterns are matched.

In general, the conjunction

$$\ell_1(\bar{x})[\lambda_1] \wedge \alpha_1 \quad \wedge \quad \ell_2(\bar{y})[\lambda_1] \wedge \alpha_2$$

can be expressed as

$$\ell_1(\bar{x})[\lambda_1, \lambda_2] \wedge \alpha_1 \wedge \alpha_2 \wedge x_1 = y_1 \wedge x_2 = y_2 \wedge \cdots \wedge x_n = y_n,$$

if only $\ell_1(\bar{x})$ and $\ell_2(\bar{y})$ are *compatible*, i.e., $\ell_1 = \ell_2$ or $\ell_1 = \_$ or $\ell_2 = \_$, and $\bar{x} = x_1, x_2, \ldots, x_n$, $\bar{y} = y_1, y_2, \ldots, y_n$. If $\ell_1(\bar{x})$ and $\ell_2(\bar{y})$ are not compatible, the conjunction is always false. To express this we allow a special pattern $\bot$, which can be seen as a new element type, never allowed by the schema.

Classification of patterns

In our analysis we often consider patterns with a restricted set of available axes and comparisons. We denote classes of patterns by $\Pi(\sigma)$, where σ is a signature indicating which axes and comparisons are present. Specifically, we can choose from having the following features (including navigational axes and comparisons):

- $\downarrow$ (child),
- $\downarrow^+$ (descendant),
- $\to$ (next-sibling),
- $\to^+$ (following-sibling),
- $\_$ (wildcard),
- $=$ (equality), and
- $\neq$ (inequality).

We now explain what it means to say that patterns use these features. All our patterns will use the simple child navigation (as it corresponds to $\ell(\bar{x})[\lambda]$). If a subpattern of the form $//\pi$ is present, then a pattern uses descendant. If a sequence of the form $\mu_1 \to \mu_2$ is present, then a pattern uses next-sibling. If a sequence of the form $\mu_1 \to^+ \mu_2$ is present, then a pattern uses following-sibling. If we have a subpattern of the form $\_(\bar{x})[\lambda]$, then a wildcard is used in a pattern. For patterns not using the wildcard, only $\ell(\bar{x})$ with $\ell \in \Gamma$ are allowed.

Equality and inequality require some additional explanation. Having $\neq$ in σ means that we can use conjuncts of the form $x \neq y$ in the patterns; having $=$ in σ means that we can use explicit equalities $x = y$ in patterns, as well as reuse variables. If $=$ is not in σ, we are only allowed to reuse variables in inequalities (if $\neq$ is in σ) or nowhere at all.

For instance, $\Pi(\downarrow)$ is the class of patterns only using the child axis. Patterns in this class can be described as follows:

- if ℓ is a label in Γ, then $\ell(\bar{x})$ is a pattern in $\Pi(\downarrow)$; and
- if $\pi_1, \ldots, \pi_m$ are patterns in $\Pi(\downarrow)$, then so is $\ell(\bar{x})[\pi_1, \ldots, \pi_m]$.

The class $\Pi(\downarrow, \downarrow^+, \rightarrow, \rightarrow^+, \_, =, \neq)$ describes all (generalized) patterns.

To save space, we often write:

- $\Downarrow$ for the triple $(\downarrow, \downarrow^+, \_)$,
- $\Rightarrow$ for the triple $(\rightarrow, \rightarrow^+, \_)$, and
- $\sim$ for the pair $(=, \neq)$.

For example, the class of all patterns is $\Pi(\Downarrow, \Rightarrow, \sim)$.

Semantics of patterns via homomorphisms

We now present a different way of defining the semantics of patterns that resembles the semantics of conjunctive queries. One way of checking if, for a relational database D and a conjunctive query $Q(\bar{x})$, we have $\bar{a} \in Q(D)$ is to check whether we have a *homomorphism* from the tableau $(T_Q, \bar{x})$ of Q into $(D, \bar{a})$. Or, equivalently, we want to see if there is a homomorphism h from T_Q to D such that $h(\bar{x}) = \bar{a}$.

We now apply the same approach to patterns. First, we need an analog of the notion of tableau for patterns: that is, we need to view patterns as structures. Indeed, a pure tree pattern can be seen as a tree-like structure

$$S_\pi = (U, \downarrow, \downarrow^+, \rightarrow, \rightarrow^+, lab, \pi, \rho),$$

where U is the set of (occurrences of) subpatterns of π of the form $\ell(\bar{x})[\lambda]$, with lab and ρ naturally defined as:

- $lab(\ell(\bar{x})[\lambda]) = \ell$;
- $\rho(\ell(\bar{x})[\lambda]) = \bar{x}$.

Other relations are defined as follows:

- the relation $\downarrow$ contains all pairs $\pi_1, \pi_2 \in U$ such that the set under the head of π_1 contains a list that contains π_2, i.e., $\pi_1 = \ell(\bar{x})[\lambda, \mu \rightsquigarrow \pi_2 \rightsquigarrow \mu', \lambda']$, where $\rightsquigarrow$ is $\rightarrow$ or $\rightarrow^+$, and all $\lambda, \lambda', \mu, \mu'$ can be empty;
- $(\pi_1, \pi_2) \in \downarrow^+$ iff $\pi_1 = \ell(\bar{x})[\lambda, //\pi_2, \lambda']$;

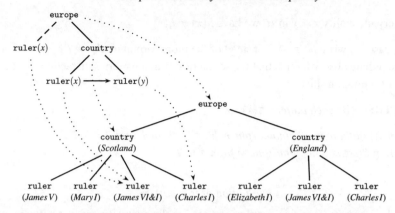

Figure 11.2 A homomorphism from a pattern to an XML tree

- $(\pi_1, \pi_2) \in \to$ iff π contains (syntactically) $\pi_1 \to \pi_2$; and
- $(\pi_1, \pi_2) \in \to^+$ iff π contains $\pi_1 \to^+ \pi_2$.

For instance, for $\pi = \texttt{europe}[\texttt{country}[\texttt{ruler}(x)] \to^+ \texttt{country}[\texttt{ruler}(x)]]$ shown in Figure 11.1, S_π has five nodes: u corresponding to the whole pattern, v_1, v_2 corresponding to the two occurrences of $\texttt{country}[\texttt{ruler}(x)]$, and w_1, w_2 corresponding to the two occurrences of $\texttt{ruler}(x)$. The relations are given as follows: $\downarrow = \{(u, v_i), (v_i, w_i) \mid i = 1, 2\}$, $\downarrow^+ = \{(u, v_i), (v_i, w_i), (u, w_i) \mid i = 1, 2\}$, and $\to = \to^+ = \{(v_1, v_2)\}$.

Under this interpretation, there exists a natural notion of homomorphism.

Definition 11.4 Let π be a *pure pattern* with $S_\pi = (U, \downarrow, \downarrow^+, \to, \to^+, lab, \pi, \rho)$, and let $T = (U^T, \downarrow^T, \to^T, lab^T, (\rho_a^T)_{a \in Att})$. A *homomorphism* $h \colon S_\pi \to T$ is a function that maps U into U^T and the variables of π into the domain of attribute values V such that for all $\pi_1, \pi_2 \in U$

- the root of π is mapped to the root of T, i.e., $h(\pi) = \varepsilon$;
- the labeling is preserved, i.e., if $lab(\pi_1) \neq \_$, then $lab(\pi_1) = lab^T(h(\pi_1))$;
- for every $\diamond \in \{\downarrow, \downarrow^+, \to, \to^+\}$, if $\pi_1 \diamond \pi_2$ in S_π, then $h(\pi_1) \diamond h(\pi_2)$ in T;
- if $\rho(\pi_1) = \bar{x}$ then $h(\pi_1)$ stores the tuple $h(\bar{x})$, i.e., $h(\pi_1)$ is a node with attributes $a_1, a_2, \dots, a_k$ and $h(x_i) = \rho_{a_i}^T(h(\pi_1))$ where $\bar{x} = (x_1, x_2, \dots, x_k)$.

Note that while in T the relations $\downarrow^+$ and $\to^+$ are externally defined as transitive closures of $\downarrow$ and $\to$, in S_π they are built-in relations. In fact, in S_π it is true that $\downarrow \cap \downarrow^+ = \emptyset$ and $\to \cap \to^+ = \emptyset$ but all four relations can be extended in such a way that the structure becomes a proper tree. An example of a homomorphism is given in Figure 11.2.

For $h \colon S_\pi \to T$, we say that h is a *homomorphism from π to T*. For a generalized pattern $\pi = \pi_0 \wedge \alpha$, a homomorphism from π to T is a homomorphism $h \colon S_{\pi_0} \to T$ extended to all variables used in α in such a way that

- for every equality $x = y$ in α, we have $h(x) = h(y)$;

- for every inequality $x \neq y$ in α, we have $h(x) \neq h(y)$.

In either case we write $h : \pi \to T$ instead of the more formal $h : S_\pi \to T$.

An immediate observation is that the semantics of tree pattern satisfaction can be stated in terms of homomorphisms:

Lemma 11.5 *For each pattern* $\pi(\bar{x})$

1. $T \models \pi(\bar{a})$ *iff there is a homomorphism* $h : \pi \to T$ *such that* $\bar{a} = h(\bar{x})$;
2. $T \models \pi$ *iff there is a homomorphism from* π *to* T.

Evaluation of tree patterns

We now look at basic decision problems related to the evaluation of tree patterns, as well as their satisfiability. We start with evaluating tree patterns, formulated as follows.

PROBLEM:	PATTERNEVAL.
INPUT:	A tree pattern π, a tree T, a tuple $\bar{a}$.
QUESTION:	Does $T \models \pi(\bar{a})$?

The problem PATTERNEVAL corresponds to the combined complexity of pattern evaluation. For each fixed pattern π, we have a problem PATTERNEVAL(π), whose input consists only of T and $\bar{a}$, with the question whether $T \models \pi(\bar{a})$. This corresponds to data complexity of pattern evaluation.

Since patterns are essentially conjunctive queries over trees, the data complexity is in LOGSPACE (and the bound cannot be lowered in general, since transitive closures of $\downarrow$ and $\to$ may have to be computed). And since they are tree structured conjunctive queries, the combined complexity is tractable as well. More precisely, we have:

Proposition 11.6 *The problem* PATTERNEVAL(π) *is in* LOGSPACE *for each pattern* π; *moreover, there exist patterns* π *so that* PATTERNEVAL(π) *is* LOGSPACE-*complete. The problem* PATTERNEVAL *is solvable in* PTIME.

Proof Take a tree pattern $\pi(\bar{x})$, a tuple $\bar{a}$, and a tree T. Checking that $T \models \pi(\bar{a})$ can be done in PTIME by a bottom-up evaluation of the subpatterns of $\pi(\bar{a})$, i.e., the pattern $\pi(\bar{x})$ with variables $\bar{x}$ evaluated according to $\bar{a}$. The idea is to annotate each node v with a set $\Phi(v)$ of the subformulae of $\pi(\bar{a})$ satisfied in v. More precisely, if v is a leaf labeled with σ and storing a tuple $\bar{b}$, let $\Phi(v)$ contain all subpatterns of $\pi(\bar{a})$ of the form $\sigma'(\bar{b})$, with $\sigma' \in \{\sigma, \_\}$. If v is an internal node labeled with σ, having children $v_1, v_2, \ldots, v_k$, and storing a tuple b, let $\Phi(v)$ contain all subpatterns of $\pi(\bar{a})$ of the form $\sigma'(\bar{b})[\lambda_1, \lambda_2, \ldots, \lambda_p]$ satisfying

- $\sigma' \in \{\sigma, \_\}$,
- for each $\lambda_i = //\pi_1$ there exists a node v_j such that $//\pi_1 \in \Phi(v_j)$ or $\pi_1 \in \Phi(v_j)$,
- for each $\lambda_i = \pi_1 \leadsto_1 \pi_2 \leadsto_2 \ldots \leadsto_{r-1} \pi_r$ there exists a sequence $1 \leq n_1 < n_2 < \ldots < n_r \leq k$ such that $\pi_j \in \Phi(v_{n_j})$, and if $\leadsto_j = \to$ then $n_{j+1} = n_j + 1$ for all j,

and all subpatterns of $\pi(\bar{a})$ of the form $//\pi_1$ satisfying $\pi_1 \in \Phi(v_j)$ or $//\pi_1 \in \Phi(v_j)$ for some j. The answer is "yes" iff $\pi(\bar{a}) \in \Phi(\varepsilon)$, where ε is the root of the tree.

Let us now consider the data complexity. Tree patterns can be viewed as first-order queries over signature extended with descendant and following-sibling, and so can be evaluated in LOGSPACE provided we can evaluate descendant and following-sibling tests in LOGSPACE. This can be done since the next-sibling relation graph has outgoing degree at most one, and for the child relation graph the same holds if we only reverse edges. LOGSPACE-hardness follows from the hardness of reachability over successor relations; hence even evaluating $r[a \rightarrow^+ b]$ over a tree of height 1 is LOGSPACE-hard. $\qquad\square$

Satisfiability of tree patterns

The satisfiability problem for tree patterns is about finding a tree that satisfies a pattern. The input consists of a schema $\mathscr{S}$ (a tree automaton or a DTD) and a pattern $\pi(\bar{x})$; the problem is to check whether there is a tree T that conforms to $\mathscr{S}$ and has a match for π (i.e., $T \models \pi$). That is, the problem is formulated as follows:

PROBLEM:	PATTERNSAT.
INPUT:	A schema $\mathscr{S}$, a tree pattern π.
QUESTION:	Is there a tree T that conforms to $\mathscr{S}$ and has a match for π?

We are now going to pinpoint the exact complexity of this problem.

Theorem 11.7 *The problem* PATTERNSAT *is* NP-*complete.*

Furthermore, it remains NP-*complete even if the schema is given as a DTD, and the pattern comes from* $\Pi(\downarrow, \_)$ *and has no free variables.*

Proof We start with the upper bound. We are going to show that there exists a small witness for satisfiability. This witness, however, cannot be a tree that conforms to $\mathscr{S}$ and satisfies π, simply because even the smallest tree that conforms to $\mathscr{S}$ can be exponential in the size of $\mathscr{S}$ (see Exercise 16.3). However, to check that a tree T conforms to $\mathscr{S}$ and satisfies π, we do not need the whole tree, but only a portion of it that happens to be polynomial in the sizes of $\mathscr{S}$ and π. We define it now.

Definition 11.8 (Support) The *support* of a homomorphism $h : \pi \rightarrow T$, denoted supp h, is the subtree of T obtained by keeping only nodes that have a descendant in the range of h, or one of their sibling does.

For example, consider a tree pattern $r[//a, //b/c, //e]$. This pattern is satisfied by a tree T given in Figure 11.3(a) with the obvious homomorphism h which appropriately assigns subformulae to the encircled nodes. To obtain supp h, we start with the range of h, then we add all ancestors of these nodes, and finally all siblings of all previously added nodes. The result is shown in Figure 11.3(b).

Note that together with each node included in the support we also include all its siblings. As we shall see shortly, this is convenient if we want to check if a given support can be extended to a tree conforming to the schema.

Patterns and mappings

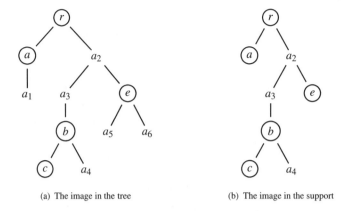

(a) The image in the tree   (b) The image in the support

Figure 11.3 A homomorphism from $r[//a, //b/c, //e]$ into a tree and its support

It turns out that for satisfiable patterns one can always find a tree and a homomorphism with a polynomial support.

Lemma 11.9 *For each pattern $\pi(\bar{x})$ and tuple $\bar{a}$ such that $\pi(\bar{a})$ is satisfiable with respect to a regular schema $\mathscr{S}$, there exists a homomorphism h from π to some T conforming to $\mathscr{S}$ such that $h(\bar{x}) = \bar{a}$ and $|\mathrm{supp}\, h| \leq 12\|\pi\| \cdot \|\mathscr{S}\|^2$.*

Proof Take an arbitrary T conforming to $\mathscr{S}$ and satisfying $\pi(\bar{a})$. Let h be a homomorphism from π to T such that $h(\bar{x}) = \bar{a}$. Divide the nodes of $\mathrm{supp}\, h$ into four categories: the nodes from the image of h are *red*, the nodes that are not red and have more than one child that is an ancestor of a red node (or is red itself) are *green*, the others are *yellow* if they are ancestors of red nodes, and *blue* otherwise. For example, in Figure 11.3(b) the encircled nodes are red, a_2 is green, a_3 is yellow, and a_4 is blue (colors are not shown in the figure). Let N_{red}, N_{green}, N_{yellow}, and N_{blue} be the numbers of red, green, yellow, and blue nodes.

By definition, $N_{\mathrm{red}} \leq \|\pi\|$. Also $N_{\mathrm{green}} \leq \|\pi\|$: when going bottom-up, each green node decreases the number of subtrees containing a red node by at least one, and since in the root we arrive with one subtree containing a red node, $N_{\mathrm{green}} \leq N_{\mathrm{red}}$.

We now show by a pumping argument that the length of yellow paths in $\mathrm{supp}\, h$ can be bounded by the number of states in the UNFTA $\mathscr{A}$ underlying $\mathscr{S}$. Let ρ be an accepting run of $\mathscr{A}$ on T. If a yellow path is longer than the number of states of $\mathscr{A}$, by the pigeonhole principle, it contains two nodes v, w such that $\rho(v) = \rho(w)$. Modify T by replacing $T.v$ (the subtree rooted at v) with $T.w$. The run ρ can be easily transformed into an accepting run of $\mathscr{A}$ over the modified T, and h can be similarly transformed into a homomorphism to the modified tree.

Analogously, the length of blue sequences of siblings in $\mathrm{supp}\, h$ can be bounded by the maximal number of states in the horizontal automata of $\mathscr{A}$ (which can also be bounded by $\|\mathscr{S}\|$). Indeed, suppose that a sequence $v_1, v_2, \ldots, v_n$ of blue siblings is longer. Let v be the parent of the v_i's. Fix an accepting run of the corresponding horizontal automaton over the sequence of states of $\mathscr{A}$ in the children of v. By the pigeon-hole principle there exist nodes $v_i, v_j, i < j$, that are assigned the same state in this run. If we remove from T the subtrees rooted in $v_i, v_{i+1}, \ldots, v_{j-1}$, the resulting tree is also accepted by $\mathscr{A}$ and the homomorphism h can be naturally adjusted.

The number of (maximal) yellow paths is at most $N_{\text{red}} + N_{\text{green}}$. Hence there are at most $2\|\pi\| \cdot \|\mathscr{S}\|$ yellow nodes. Since all blue nodes are siblings of nodes of other colors, the number of (maximal) blue sequences of siblings is at most $2(N_{\text{red}} + N_{\text{green}} + N_{\text{yellow}}) \leq 4\|\pi\| \cdot (\|\mathscr{S}\| + 1)$ and so $N_{\text{blue}} \leq 4\|\pi\| \cdot (\|\mathscr{S}\| + 1)\|\mathscr{S}\|$. Altogether we have at most $2\|\pi\|(\|\mathscr{S}\| + 1)(2\|\mathscr{S}\| + 1) \leq 12\|\pi\| \cdot \|\mathscr{S}\|^2$ nodes. □

We now can prove the NP upper bound. Let π and $\mathscr{S}$ be the given pattern and schema. By Lemma 11.9, if π is satisfiable, there exists a homomorphism into a tree conforming to $\mathscr{S}$, with a polynomial support. To decide satisfiability first guess a polynomial support together with a partial run of the UNFTA underlying $\mathscr{S}$ (a consistent labeling with states) and a homomorphism. Verifying the homomorphism takes time polynomial in the size of the formula and the support (which is also polynomial in the size of the formula). Verifying that the support is actually a restriction of a tree conforming to $\mathscr{S}$ requires a consistency check which amounts to checking if a given word is in the language defined by a given NFA (checking correctness of the guessed labeling), and checking if the language defined by a given UNFTA is non-empty (providing subtrees to be rooted in the yellow nodes). Both these checks can be done in polynomial time.

To get NP-hardness, we do a standard 3CNF SAT reduction. In fact, we only use patterns from $\Pi(\downarrow, \_)$ without variables. Take a formula $\psi = \bigwedge_{j=1}^{k} Z_j^1 \vee Z_j^2 \vee Z_j^3$ with $Z_j^i \in \{x_1, x_2, \ldots, x_n, \bar{x}_1, \bar{x}_2, \ldots, \bar{x}_n\}$. Consider a DTD D (without attributes)

$$r \to x_1 x_2 \cdots x_n$$
$$x_i \to \{C_j \mid \exists \ell Z_j^\ell = x_i\} | \{C_j \mid \exists \ell Z_j^\ell = \bar{x}_i\} \qquad\qquad 1 \leq i \leq n$$

over the alphabet $\{x_1, x_2, \ldots, x_n, C_1, C_2, \ldots, C_k\}$. In the second rule, interpret each set as a concatenation of all its elements. (The order in which the elements are concatenated does not matter.)

The labels C_j are intended to correspond to $Z_j^1 \vee Z_j^2 \vee Z_j^3$. Each tree conforming to D encodes a valuation of all variables x_i: for each x_i it stores either all conjuncts made true by assigning 1 to x_i, or all conjuncts made true by assigning 0 to x_i.

The satisfiability of ψ is equivalent to the satisfiability of the pattern $r[\_/C_1, \_/C_2, \ldots, \_/C_k]$ with respect to D. □

11.2 XML schema mappings and their complexity

XML schema mappings resemble relational mappings a lot. Like before, each mapping consists of a source schema, a target schema, and a set of source-to-target tuple generating dependencies relating the two schemas. In the XML context, relational schemas are naturally replaced by regular schemas and dependencies use patterns instead of conjunctive queries.

Definition 11.10 (XML schema mapping) An *XML schema mapping* is a triple $\mathcal{M} = (\mathcal{S}_s, \mathcal{S}_t, \Sigma_{st})$, where $\mathcal{S}_s$ is the source schema, $\mathcal{S}_t$ is the target schema, and Σ_{st} is a set of st-tgds of the form

$$\pi(\bar{x}, \bar{y}) \;\to\; \exists \bar{z}\, \pi'(\bar{x}, \bar{z})$$

where π and π' are (generalized) patterns and π satisfies the safety condition (see page 146).

Definition 11.11 (Semantics of mappings) Let $\mathcal{M} = (\mathcal{S}_s, \mathcal{S}_t, \Sigma_{st})$ be an XML schema mapping. Given a tree S that conforms to $\mathcal{S}_s$ (a *source instance*) and a tree T that conforms to $\mathcal{S}_t$ (a *target instance*), we say that T is a *solution* for S under $\mathcal{M}$ if (S, T) satisfy all the st-tgds from Σ_{st}, i.e., for every st-tgd $\pi(\bar{x}, \bar{y}) \to \exists \bar{z}\, \pi'(\bar{x}, \bar{z})$ in Σ_{st},

$$S \models \pi(\bar{a}, \bar{b}) \;\implies\; T \models \pi'(\bar{a}, \bar{c}) \text{ for some tuple of data values } \bar{c}.$$

We denote the set of all solutions under $\mathcal{M}$ for S by $\mathrm{SOL}_{\mathcal{M}}(S)$.

The *semantics* of $\mathcal{M}$ is defined as a binary relation

$$[\![\mathcal{M}]\!] = \left\{ (S, T) \mid S \models \mathcal{S}_s,\; T \models \mathcal{S}_t,\; T \in \mathrm{SOL}_{\mathcal{M}}(S) \right\}.$$

Just like for relational databases (see Section 2.3), the domain of data values V allowed in the attributes of XML trees is partitioned into two disjoint and infinite sets:

- the set CONST of *constants*, and
- the set VAR of *nulls*, or variables.

We use the symbol $\perp$ (with subscripts or superscripts) to denote nulls, and lowercase letters or specific values to denote constants. Most of the time we shall assume that source trees take data values from CONST only. In target trees we use VAR for attribute values that are not specified by the dependencies.

Example 11.12 Let $\mathcal{S}_s$ be the familiar DTD

$$
\begin{array}{ll}
\texttt{europe} \;\to\; \texttt{country}^* & \texttt{country} : \texttt{@name} \\
\texttt{country} \;\to\; \texttt{ruler}^* & \texttt{ruler} : \texttt{@name}
\end{array}
$$

and let $\mathcal{S}_t$ be

$$
\begin{array}{ll}
\texttt{rulers} \;\to\; \texttt{ruler}^* & \texttt{ruler} : \texttt{@name} \\
\texttt{ruler} \;\to\; \texttt{successor} & \texttt{successor} : \texttt{@name}
\end{array}
$$

Assuming the rulers are stored in chronological order on the source side, a natural schema mapping $\mathcal{M}$ might be defined with the following st-tgd:

$$\texttt{europe}[\texttt{ruler}(x) \to \texttt{ruler}(y)] \;\longrightarrow\; \texttt{rulers/ruler}(x)/\texttt{successor}(y).$$

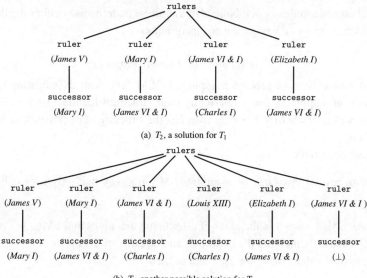

(a) T_2, a solution for T_1

(b) T_3, another possible solution for T_1

Figure 11.4 Solutions for T_1 under $\mathscr{M}$

A natural solution for T_1 in Figure 10.1 is the tree T_2 in Figure 11.4(a). As we already know, every tree obtained from T_2 by adding new children with arbitrary data values, or by permuting the existing children, is also a solution for T_1. For instance, T_3 in Figure 11.4(b) is as good a solution for T_1 as any. On the other hand, according to the schema, each ruler node should only have one successor child. So, merging the two *James VI & I* nodes in T_3 would not give a solution.

The XML mappings we have just defined naturally generalize the usual relational mappings. If we have relational schemas $\mathbf{R_s}$ and $\mathbf{R_t}$, they can be represented as regular schemas $\mathscr{S}_s$ and $\mathscr{S}_t$: for example, for $\mathbf{R_s} = \{S_1(A,B), S_2(C,D)\}$, the schema $\mathscr{S}_s$ is the following DTD

$$r \to s_1 s_2$$
$$s_1 \to t_1^* \qquad\qquad t_1 : @A, @B$$
$$s_2 \to t_2^* \qquad\qquad t_2 : @C, @D.$$

Then each conjunctive query over a relational schema is easily translated into a pattern over the corresponding DTD together with some equality constraints. For example, the query $Q(x,y,z) = S_1(x,y) \wedge S_2(y,z)$ will be translated into

$$r[s_1/t_1(x,y_1), s_2/t_2(y_2,z)], \ y_1 = y_2.$$

Of course equalities can be incorporated into the pattern (i.e., by $r[s_1/t_1(x,y), s_2/t_2(y,z)]$) but as we said, we often prefer to list them separately to make classification of different types of schema mappings easier. Note also that these patterns use neither the descendant relation nor the horizontal navigation nor inequalities.

Classification of schema mappings

We shall denote classes of schema mappings by $SM^*(\sigma)$, with σ indicating features of patterns used in mappings, and $*$ restricting their structural features, such as the type of schemas they use, or whether they deal with just the structure of documents, or both structure and data.

Specifically, we write

- $SM^*(\sigma)$ to restrict any class of mappings SM^* in a way that only uses patterns from $\Pi(\sigma)$.

For instance, $SM(\Downarrow, \Rightarrow, \sim)$ is the class of all schema mappings and $SM(\downarrow, =)$ is the class of mappings that only mention the child axis and equality of data values.

As for possible values for $*$, we use three of them.

- $SM^\circ(\sigma)$ is the class of mappings in $SM(\sigma)$ where st-tgds in Σ_{st} do not mention attribute values, i.e., where all pattern formulae are of the form $\ell[\lambda]$. These will be useful for establishing hardness results, telling us that structural properties alone make certain problems infeasible.
- $SM^{dtd}(\sigma)$ is the class of mappings from $SM(\sigma)$ whose schemas are DTDs.
- $SM^{nr}(\sigma)$ is the class of *nested relational schema mappings* in $SM(\sigma)$, i.e., schema mappings whose *target* schemas are nested relational DTDs.

The class of nested relational schema mappings will play an important role in the study of XML data exchange. These mappings have particularly nice properties, especially with respect to the complexity of many computational problems. The class itself includes many important types of schema mappings. Note, for example, that under the standard XML encoding of relational databases shown earlier, relational schema mappings fall into the class $SM^{nr}(\downarrow, =)$.

Complexity of schema mappings

We now move to the complexity of schema mappings. The general *membership problem* we consider is defined as follows:

PROBLEM:	XML-SM-MEMBERSHIP.
INPUT:	A schema mapping $\mathcal{M}$, two XML trees S and T.
QUESTION:	Is (S, T) in $[\![\mathcal{M}]\!]$?

Of course this corresponds to the *combined complexity* of schema mappings. We shall also look at *data complexity*, when the mapping is fixed. That is, for each mapping $\mathcal{M}$, we look at the problem XML-SM-MEMBERSHIP($\mathcal{M}$) whose input consists only of S and T, and the question, as before, is whether $(S, T) \in [\![\mathcal{M}]\!]$.

Compared to patterns, the data complexity remains low; the combined complexity jumps to the second level of the polynomial hierarchy, but the parameter that makes it jump there is the number of variables in st-tgds. If we fix that number, even the combined complexity is tractable.

Theorem 11.13 • *The problem* XML-SM-MEMBERSHIP *is* Π_2^p*-complete. Its complexity drops to* PTIME *if the maximum number of variables per pattern is fixed.*
• *The problem* XML-SM-MEMBERSHIP($\mathcal{M}$) *is always in* LOGSPACE. *Moreover, there is a mapping* $\mathcal{M}_0$ *such that* XML-SM-MEMBERSHIP($\mathcal{M}_0$) *is* LOGSPACE-*complete.*

In other words, the combined complexity of schema mappings is Π_2^p-complete, but tractable when we fix the number of variables used in patterns; the data complexity of schema mappings is low: in LOGSPACE, and the bound cannot be lowered.

Proof We first explain the proof for data complexity. Checking if a given tree conforms to a schema amounts to verifying if the tree is accepted by the underlying UNFTA . As shown by Gottlob et al. (2005), this can be done in LOGSPACE if the size of the automaton is fixed. Let us now see how to check if S and T satisfy a single constraint $\pi(\bar{x}, \bar{y}) \rightarrow \exists \bar{z} \, \pi'(\bar{x}, \bar{z})$. Let $\bar{x} = x_1, x_2, \ldots, x_k$, $\bar{y} = y_1, y_2, \ldots, y_\ell$, and $\bar{z} = z_1, z_2, \ldots, z_m$. Let A be the set of data values used in S or T. We need to check that for each $\bar{a} \in A^k$ and each $\bar{b} \in A^\ell$ such that $S \models \pi(\bar{a}, \bar{b})$ there exists $\bar{c} \in A^m$ such that $T \models \pi'(\bar{a}, \bar{c})$. Since the numbers k, ℓ, m are fixed (as parts of the fixed mapping), the space needed for storing all three valuations is logarithmic in the size of S and T. Using Proposition 11.6 we obtain a LOGSPACE algorithm by simply iterating over all possible valuations $\bar{a}$, $\bar{b}$, and $\bar{c}$. LOGSPACE-hardness is shown in the same way as in the proof of Proposition 11.6.

We now move to combined complexity. Checking conformance to schemas can be done in PTIME. Let us concentrate on verifying the dependencies. Consider the following algorithm for the complementary problem: guess a dependency $\pi(\bar{x}, \bar{y}) \rightarrow \exists \bar{z} \, \pi'(\bar{x}, \bar{z})$ and tuples $\bar{a}$, $\bar{b}$, and check that $S \models \pi(\bar{a}, \bar{b})$ and $T \not\models \exists \bar{z} \, \pi'(\bar{a}, \bar{z})$. By Proposition 11.6, the first check is polynomial. The second check however involves a tree pattern possibly containing variables, so it can only be done in CONP. Altogether the algorithm is in Π_2^p. Hardness can be obtained via a reduction from the validity of Π_2 quantified Boolean formulae (see Exercise 16.3).

When the maximum number of variables per pattern is fixed, proceed like in the case of a fixed mapping. Since there are only polynomially many possible valuations of variables, we may iterate over all of them using the algorithm from Proposition 11.6 to check if $S \models \pi(\bar{a}, \bar{b})$ and $T \models \pi'(\bar{a}, \bar{c})$. □

12

Building solutions

One of the two fundamental aims of data exchange is to *build a solution* for a given source document. Under the complex restrictions that can be imposed on target documents by XML schemas, this task is highly nontrivial. The goal of this chapter is to describe a *polynomial-time* algorithm that builds solutions in XML data exchange. We first explain why the straightforward approach gives an exponential-time algorithm. Then we show a simple polynomial algorithm for child-based mappings between nested-relational DTDs and point out difficulties arising from the presence of sibling order and regular schemas. In the subsequent two sections we refine the algorithm to deal with them. We finally analyze the combined complexity of the solution building problem and show that, modulo some complexity-theoretic assumptions, the presented algorithm is likely to be optimal in terms of combined complexity.

12.1 Building solutions revisited

Recall the problem of building solutions. We are given an XML schema mapping $\mathcal{M} = (\mathcal{S}_s, \mathcal{S}_t, \Sigma_{st})$, where $\mathcal{S}_s$ is the source schema, $\mathcal{S}_t$ is the target schema, and Σ_{st} is a set of st-tgds. These are of the form

$$\pi(\bar{x}, \bar{y}) \;\rightarrow\; \exists \bar{z}\, \pi'(\bar{x}, \bar{z})$$

where π and π' are generalized patterns (and π is required to satisfy the safety condition). We are also given a tree T that conforms to $\mathcal{S}_s$. The goal is to construct a *solution* T' for T under $\mathcal{M}$, i.e., a tree T' that conforms to $\mathcal{S}_t$ such that the pair (T, T') satisfies all the st-tgds from Σ_{st}.

When the mapping $\mathcal{M}$ is fixed, we refer to the complexity of the problem as the data complexity of building a solution. When both $\mathcal{M}$ and T are given as inputs, we refer to the combined complexity of the problem.

Building a solution for a given source tree T with respect to a mapping $\mathcal{M}$ can be seen as a constructive version of satisfiability, i.e., finding a tree conforming to a given schema and satisfying a given pattern. Given a mapping $\mathcal{M} = (\mathcal{S}_s, \mathcal{S}_t, \Sigma_{st})$ and a source tree T

conforming to $\mathscr{S}_s$, consider the following set of partially valuated tree patterns

$$\Delta_{T,\mathscr{M}} = \{\psi(\bar{a},\bar{z}) \mid \varphi(\bar{x},\bar{y}) \rightarrow \exists \bar{z}\, \psi(\bar{x},\bar{z}) \in \Sigma_{st} \text{ and } T \models \varphi(\bar{a},\bar{b})\}.$$

We refer to elements of $\Delta_{T,\mathscr{M}}$ as *target requirements*. Then Definition 11.11 (of XML data exchange solutions) can be restated as follows. A tree T' conforming to the target schema is a solution for T if and only if it satisfies each target requirement,

$$T' \in \mathrm{SOL}_{\mathscr{M}}(T) \iff T' \models \mathscr{S}_t \text{ and } T' \models \psi(\bar{a},\bar{z}) \text{ for all } \psi(\bar{a},\bar{z}) \in \Delta_{T,\mathscr{M}}.$$

We can simplify this even further by combining all the patterns from $\Delta_{T,\mathscr{M}}$ into one. First, rename variables in $\Delta_{T,\mathscr{M}}$ so that every pattern uses disjoint sets of variables. Then, take the conjunction of all the patterns from the modified $\Delta_{T,\mathscr{M}}$ by merging all the patterns at the root,

$$\delta_{T,\mathscr{M}} = \bigwedge \Delta_{T,\mathscr{M}}.$$

Recall that we have shown in the previous chapter that patterns are closed under conjunction. Also, in the case when $\Delta_{T,\mathscr{M}}$ contains two patterns with incompatible labels in the root, set $\delta_{T,\mathscr{M}} = \bot$, where $\bot$ is a fixed pattern incompatible with the schema.

Thus, we have the following property:

Lemma 12.1 $T' \in \mathrm{SOL}_{\mathscr{M}}(T) \iff T' \models \mathscr{S}_t \text{ and } T' \models \delta_{T,\mathscr{M}}.$

In other words, building a solution for T amounts to finding a tree T' with two properties:

$$
\begin{array}{ll}
1. & T' \text{ conforms to the target schema, and} \\
2. & T' \text{ satisfies the pattern } \delta_{T,\mathscr{M}}.
\end{array}
\tag{12.1}
$$

Hence, building a solution in XML data exchange amounts, according to (12.1), to building a tree accepted by a tree automaton (serving as an abstraction of a schema) and satisfying a tree pattern.

12.2 A simple exhaustive search algorithm

We now provide a simple algorithm searching for a tree T' satisfying (12.1). The main idea is as follows:

- If there is a tree satisfying conditions (12.1), there is one whose size, and the size of the set of possible data values it uses, is bounded by some function of the size of the schema mapping and the source tree.
- We can then simply search over all such trees, checking if a solution is found.

The bounds in this naïve algorithm will be exponential, but we shall see later how to lower them. To establish such bounds, we need three results, putting restrictions on:

- sizes of trees accepted by a tree automaton;

- sizes of trees accepted by a tree automaton and at the same time satisfying a tree pattern; and
- sets of data values that appear in trees satisfying (12.1).

We establish these bounds in the next three lemmas, and then use them to provide an exhaustive search algorithm for building solutions. We begin with the case with no pattern, i.e., only a tree automaton providing restrictions on trees.

Lemma 12.2 *Let $\mathscr{A}$ be an UNFTA. If $L(\mathscr{A})$ is nonempty, it contains a tree of height and branching bounded by $\|\mathscr{A}\|$.*

Proof Let Q be the set of states of $\mathscr{A}$. Suppose $L(\mathscr{A})$ is nonempty and let $T \in L(\mathscr{A})$. Fix an accepting run ρ of $\mathscr{A}$ on T. If the height of T is larger then $|Q|$, by the pigeon-hole principle, T contains two nodes v, w such that w is a descendant of v and $\rho(v) = \rho(w)$. Modify T by replacing $T.v$ (the subtree rooted at v) with $T.w$. The run ρ can be easily transformed into an accepting run of $\mathscr{A}$ over the modified T. Repeating this operation as long as needed, we obtain a tree of height at most $|Q|$ accepted by $\mathscr{A}$.

Similarly, we can bound the branching. Let v be a node with children $v_1, v_2, \ldots, v_n$, where n is greater than the maximum of the numbers of states of the vertical automata. Fix a witnessing accepting run of the corresponding horizontal automaton. Again one can find two children, v_i and v_j, $i < j$, that are labeled with the same state of the the horizontal automaton. If we remove from T the subtrees rooted in $v_i, v_{i+1}, \ldots, v_{j-1}$, the resulting tree is also accepted by $\mathscr{A}$. Repeating this operation we obtain an accepted tree whose height and branching are bounded by $\|\mathscr{A}\|$.   □

From Lemma 12.2 it follows immediately that for each regular schema $\mathscr{S}$ there is an exponential-size tree conforming to $\mathscr{S}$, or there is no conforming tree at all. This is also true if we restrict to trees satisfying a given pattern.

Lemma 12.3 *For a regular schema $\mathscr{S}$ over Γ, a pattern $\pi(\bar{x})$, and a tuple of data values $\bar{a}$, either there exists a tree T of size at most $12 \cdot \|\pi\| \cdot \|\mathscr{S}\|^{2+\|\mathscr{S}\|}$ such that $T \models \mathscr{S}$ and $T \models \pi(\bar{a})$, or no tree conforming to $\mathscr{S}$ satisfies $\pi(\bar{a})$.*

Proof By Lemma 11.9, for each pattern π satisfiable with respect to a schema $\mathscr{S}$ over Γ, there exists a homomorphism from π to some T conforming to $\mathscr{S}$ satisfying $|\text{supp}\,h| \leq 12 \cdot \|\pi\| \cdot \|\mathscr{S}\|^2$. Let us take such a tree T and homomorphism h. Let $\mathscr{A}$ be the UNFTA underlying schema $\mathscr{S}$. Fix an accepting run ρ of $\mathscr{A}$ on T and take a node v of T that is a leaf in $\text{supp}\,h$. It is easy to see that if we replace $T.v$ with any XML tree T' such that the root of T' is labeled with $lab_T(v)$ and there is a run of $\mathscr{A}$ on T' that assigns state $\rho(v)$ to the root, we get a tree conforming to $\mathscr{S}$ and satisfying $\pi(\bar{a})$. Observe that the set of such trees can be recognized by an automaton of size bounded by $\|\mathscr{S}\|$: it is enough to change the initial state of $\mathscr{A}$ to $\rho(v)$ and modify the transition relation by setting $\delta(\rho(v), \ell) = \emptyset$ for all $\ell \neq lab_T(v)$. Consequently, by Lemma 12.2, we can assume that for each leaf v in $\text{supp}\,h$ the subtree $T.v$ has size at most $\|\mathscr{S}\|^{\|\mathscr{S}\|}$. The total number of nodes in T is then bounded by $|\text{supp}\,h| \cdot \|\mathscr{S}\|^{\|\mathscr{S}\|}$, which proves the lemma.   □

The bound on the size does not immediately give a bound on the number of trees we need to consider, because there are infinitely many ways to fill the attributes with data values. We now show that one can restrict to data values used in the source tree and a small set of *nulls*, representing the values invented to fill in the unspecified attributes on the target side.

Lemma 12.4 *For each XML tree T, pattern $\pi(\bar{x}, \bar{y})$ and tuple of values $\bar{a}$, such that $T \models \pi(\bar{a}, \bar{y})$, there exists a tree T' with the same tree structure as T but storing only data values used in $\bar{a}$ or taken from the set $\{\perp_0, \perp_1, \ldots, \perp_{|\bar{y}|}\}$, such that $T' \models \pi(\bar{a}, \bar{y})$.*

Proof Suppose that $T \models \pi(\bar{a}, \bar{b})$ for some tuple of values $\bar{b}$ and let h be the witnessing homomorphism. Let A, B be the sets of values used in $\bar{a}$ and $\bar{b}$, respectively. There exists an injection

$$f : A \cup B \to A \cup \{\perp_1, \perp_2, \ldots, \perp_{|\bar{y}|}\}$$

such that $f(a) = a$ for all $a \in A$. Let $\bar{c}$ be the tuple $(f(b_1), f(b_2), \ldots, f(b_{|y|}))$ and let T' be obtained by replacing each data value d in T with $f(d)$ if $d \in A \cup B$, and with $\perp_0$ otherwise. Note the nodes in the image of h can only store data values from $A \cup B$. Hence, h witnesses that $T' \models \pi(\bar{a}, \bar{c})$. □

Combining the bounds, we obtain a simple algorithm for constructive satisfiability (Algorithm 12.1). Checking conformance to a schema can be done in polynomial time. By

---

Algorithm 12.1 Constructive satisfiability by exhaustive search

Require: $\mathscr{S}$ is a regular schema over Γ, $\pi(\bar{x}, \bar{y})$ is a pattern, $\bar{a}$ is a tuple of values
$\quad n := 12 \cdot \|\pi\| \cdot \|\mathscr{S}\|^{2+\|\mathscr{S}\|}$
$\quad D := \{d \mid d \text{ is used in } \bar{a}\} \cup \{\perp_0, \perp_1, \ldots, \perp_{|\bar{y}|}\}$
$\quad$ **for all** trees T of size at most n and data values in D **and all** tuples $\bar{b}$ from D **do**
$\quad\quad$ **if** $T \models \mathscr{S}$ and $T \models \pi(\bar{a}, \bar{b})$ **then return** T
$\quad$ **end for**
$\quad$ **if no** T **found return** '$\pi(\bar{a}, \bar{y})$ is not satisfiable with respect to $\mathscr{S}$'

Proposition 11.6, evaluation of the patterns also takes only polynomial time. Hence, each iteration of the loop takes time polynomial in n, and the number of iterations is exponential in n. For a fixed schema $\mathscr{S}$ this gives a single exponential algorithm.

To compute a solution for a given source tree T with respect to a fixed mapping $\mathscr{M}$, we simply apply Algorithm 12.1 to the pattern $\delta_{T,\mathscr{M}}$ and the schema $\mathscr{S}_t$. Since $\mathscr{M}$ is fixed, the size of $\delta_{T,\mathscr{M}}$ is polynomial, and the whole procedure is single exponential. Summing up, we have the following.

Theorem 12.5 *Algorithm 12.1 correctly computes a solution for a source tree T under a schema mapping $\mathscr{M}$ (if there is one). Its data complexity is single-exponential.*

The brute force algorithm for constructive satisfiability described above cannot be significantly improved unless $\text{NP} = \text{PTIME}$. Indeed, constructing a tree satisfying a given pattern is clearly at least as hard as deciding if it exists, which constitutes the satisfiability problem. If the schema is part of the input, the satisfiability problem is NP-hard by Theorem 11.7. It is not difficult to find fixed schemas for which the problem is NP-hard (see Exercise 16.3). This means that if we want a polynomial solution-building procedure, reduction to constructive satisfiability is not enough.

12.3 Nested-relational DTDs

As we learned in the previous section, the approach via a single pattern combining all the target requirements leads to an inefficient algorithm. In this section we introduce a different approach: instead of combining the requirements and then trying to find a solution satisfying the obtained pattern, we first find *partial* solutions for all target requirements, and then try to combine the solutions. We first implement this general recipe in a simple setting of $SM^{nr}(\Downarrow, \sim)$, i.e., mappings with nested-relational DTDs using only vertical navigation, and identify difficulties arising in the general case.

Definition 12.6 (Partial solution)   Let $\mathcal{M}$ be mapping and T a source tree. A *partial solution* for a target requirement $\psi(\bar{a}, \bar{z}) \in \Delta_{T, \mathcal{M}}$ is a tree that conforms to the target schema of $\mathcal{M}$ and satisfies $\psi(\bar{a}, \bar{b})$ for some tuple $\bar{b}$.

The first step of the recipe is easy. Since the target side patterns are bounded by the size of the mapping, the partial solutions for all target requirements can be constructed in polynomial time by Lemma 12.3 if the mapping is fixed. The difficult part is to combine the partial solutions into one tree that satisfies all target side patterns.

Let us begin with an example. Consider the schema $r \to ab^*$
with $a, b : @attr$ and two trees

$$S = r[a(1), b(2)], \qquad T = r[a(1), b(3)].$$

A natural combination of S and T is

$$S \oplus T = r[a(1), b(2), b(3)].$$

Clearly $S \oplus T$ contains all nodes of S and T, and more generally, $S \oplus T$ satisfies all patterns from $SM^{nr}(\Downarrow, \sim)$ that are satisfied by S or T.

Note that not all nodes of S and T are treated in the same way. The nodes $b(2)$ and $b(3)$ are put separately in $S \oplus T$, but the $a(1)$-nodes and r-nodes from S and T are merged together. This seems the only reasonable thing to do, but it is only possible under certain assumptions: the nodes can be put separately only if the schema allows it, and they can be merged only if they store the same data value. For instance, if we take $r[a(3), b(3)]$ instead of T, the trees cannot be combined. Likewise for D replaced with $r \to ab$.

This gives rise to the following strategy: if the schema allows it, put both nodes, otherwise merge the nodes. But how do we distinguish the nodes that must be merged? For nested-relational DTDs they can be identified easily.

Definition 12.7 Fix a DTD D over Γ. For a node v in a tree conforming to T we can consider the *label sequence* $\sigma_1 \sigma_2 \ldots \sigma_n$ that is read on the downward path from the root to v. We say that the label sequence is *unambiguous* if for all i, the symbol σ_{i+1} occurs in the production for σ_i as σ_{i+1}? or σ_{i+1}.

If σ_{i+1} occurred as σ_{i+1}^* or σ_{i+1}^+ in the production for σ_i, then a σ_i-labeled node could have had many different children labeled σ_{i+1}, and there would be some ambiguity regarding the appearance of a σ_{i+1}-labeled node as its child. If, however, σ_{i+1} occurs as σ_{i+1}? or σ_{i+1} in the production for σ_i, then the position of a σ_{i+1}-labeled child of a σ_i-labeled node is unambiguous.

Note that in every tree conforming to D

- nodes with unambiguous label sequences form a subtree which contains a root;
- there is at most one node with any given unambiguous label sequence (there may be none if σ_{i+1} occurs in the production for σ_i as σ_{i+1}? for some i).

The second property implies that nodes with the same unambiguous label sequence taken from S and T always need to be merged. It turns out that all other nodes can be put into $S \oplus T$ without merging.

Thus, the partial solutions we are constructing need to store the same data values in nodes with the same unambiguous label sequences, which means that they are all extensions of a single XML tree containing all unambiguous label sequences. It is possible that some of these sequences correspond to nodes optional in the schema and are not required by the patterns, but adding them does not spoil the partial solution.

The idea of the algorithm is then to guess this tree, construct partial solutions extending it, and then combine them. The manipulations on parts of trees performed by the algorithm are most easily described in terms of forests and contexts.

Definition 12.8 A *forest* is a sequence of trees. We write $F + G$ for the concatenation of forests F and G.

A *multicontext* C over an alphabet Γ is a tree over $\Gamma \cup \{\circ\}$ such that $\circ$-labeled nodes have at most one child. The nodes labeled with $\circ$ are called *ports*. A *context* is a multicontext with a single port, which is additionally required to be a leaf. A leaf port u can be *substituted* with a forest F, which means that in the sequence of the children of u's parent, u is replaced by the roots of F. An internal port u can be substituted with a context C' with one port u': first the subtree rooted at u's only child is substituted at u', then the obtained tree is substituted at u.

For a context C and a forest F we write $C \cdot F$ to denote the tree obtained by substituting the unique port of C with F. If we use a context D instead of the forest F, the result of the substitution is a context as well. More generally, for a multicontext M with leaf ports only, say $u_1, u_2, \ldots, u_m$, we write $M(T_1, T_2, \ldots, T_m)$ for the tree obtained by substituting T_i at u_i, for $1 \leq i \leq m$.

Instead of the subtree containing all unambiguous label sequences, it is convenient to

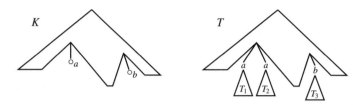

Figure 12.1 A *D-kind K* and a tree $T \in L(K)$. The trees T_1, T_2 have label a in the root and conform to D_a; T_3 has label b in the root and conforms to D_b.

work with a multicontext, called a *kind*, that contains this tree and has a port wherever new nodes can be added according to the DTD. For the sake of uniformity, in the definition of kind we assume that whenever the DTD contains a rule $\tau \to \ldots \sigma^+ \ldots$, each τ-node in the kind has one σ-child.

Definition 12.9   For a nested-relational DTD D over Γ, a *D-kind K* is any XML tree conforming to the DTD $\widehat{D}$ over $\Gamma \cup \{\circ_\sigma \mid \sigma \in \Gamma\}$ obtained by replacing for each σ, each occurrence of σ? with σ, each occurrence of σ^* by $\circ_\sigma$, and each occurrence of σ^+ by $\sigma \cdot \circ_\sigma$, where the fresh labels $\circ_\sigma$ have no attributes and their productions are $\circ_\sigma \to \varepsilon$.

Note that for a nested-relational DTD D, all D-kinds are identical up to data values.

For a kind we define a set of trees that can be obtained from it by substitutions at ports, according to the additional information provided by the label of the port.

Definition 12.10   Let D be a nested-relational DTD and let D_σ stand for the DTD obtained from D by changing the root symbol to σ. An XML tree T *agrees* with a *D-kind K* if T can be obtained from K by substituting at each port labeled with $\circ_\sigma$ a forest (possibly empty) consisting of trees conforming to the DTD D_σ. By $L(K)$ we denote the set of XML trees that agree with K.

An illustration of these notions is given in Figure 12.1. The tree T shown in the figure is obtained from K by substituting $T_1 + T_2$ at the port labeled with $\circ_a$ and T_3 at the port labeled with $\circ_b$.

Directly from the definition we get that for every nested-relational DTD D,

$$\{T \mid T \models D\} = \bigcup \{L(K) \mid K \text{ is a } D\text{-kind}\}. \tag{12.2}$$

Note that for each $T \in L(K)$ there exists a *witnessing substitution*: a sequence of forests and contexts T_u, with u ranging over the ports of K, such that substituting each u in K with T_u we obtain T. It is easy to check that T_u is unique (Exercise 16.3). The combining operation can be described as follows.

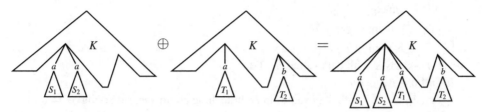

Figure 12.2 The operation ⊕ on trees from $L(K)$

Definition 12.11 Let K be a D-kind for some nested-relational DTD D. For trees T and S in $L(K)$, define $T \oplus S \in L(K)$ as the tree obtained by substituting at each port u in K the forest $S_u + T_u$. Since the operation is associative, we will skip the parentheses and write $T_1 \oplus T_2 \oplus \cdots \oplus T_n$ for $T_1, T_2, \ldots, T_n \in L(K)$.

An illustration of the operation ⊕ is given in Figure 12.2.

We now need to check that if we start with a set of partial solutions for all valuations of target patterns, the operation ⊕ gives a complete solution. We prove a more general fact.

Lemma 12.12 *For all $T_1, T_2, \ldots, T_n \in L(K)$ and every $\pi \in \Pi(\Downarrow, \sim)$,*

$$T_1 \oplus T_2 \oplus \cdots \oplus T_n \models \pi(\bar{a}) \quad \text{whenever} \quad T_i \models \pi(\bar{a}) \text{ for some } i.$$

Proof For all i, $T_1 \oplus T_2 \oplus \cdots \oplus T_n$ subsumes T_i, i.e., T_i is a subtree of $T_1 \oplus T_2 \oplus \cdots \oplus T_n$ containing the root. In particular, there exists an unordered homomorphism from T_i to $T_1 \oplus T_2 \oplus \cdots \oplus T_n$. This means that for all $\pi \in \Pi(\Downarrow, \sim)$, whenever $T_i \models \pi(\bar{a})$, it also holds that $T_1 \oplus T_2 \oplus \cdots \oplus T_n \models \pi(\bar{a})$. □

Now that we have all the ingredients ready, it remains to put them together. This is done by Algorithm 12.2 that shows how to build solutions for mappings in $\mathrm{SM}^{\mathrm{nr}}(\Downarrow, \sim)$.

Theorem 12.13 *For each mapping $\mathcal{M} \in \mathrm{SM}^{\mathrm{nr}}(\Downarrow, \sim)$, Algorithm 12.2 computes a solution for a source tree T (or determines that it does not exist) in polynomial time.*

Proof Let D_t be the target schema of $\mathcal{M}$. By equation (12.2), if there is a solution for T, it agrees with a D_t-kind K. The size of K is at most $\ell = \|D_t\|^{\|D_t\|}$. The kind only needs to use data values from T and nulls from a set $\{\perp_1, \perp_2, \ldots, \perp_\ell\} \subseteq \{\perp_1, \perp_2, \ldots, \perp_n\}$. Hence, we can check such kinds K one by one, looking for a solution in $L(K)$.

For each $\delta(\bar{z}) \in \Delta_{T, \mathcal{M}}$ we need to find a tree $S_\delta \in L(K)$ and a tuple $\bar{c}$ such that $S \models \delta(\bar{c})$. The branching of S_δ can be bounded by $\|D_t\| + \|\delta\|$: one can safely remove each child v that is not enforced by D_t and the subtree rooted at v has empty intersection with the image of the homomorphism witnessing that $S_\delta \models \delta$. Furthermore, arguing like in Lemma 12.4

Algorithm 12.2 Building solutions for nested-relational DTDs

Require: $\mathcal{M} = (D_s, D_t, \Sigma) \in \mathrm{SM}^{\mathrm{nr}}(\Downarrow, \sim)$ and $T \models D_s$

    compute $\Delta_{T,\mathcal{M}}$

    $m := \|D_t\| + \max_{\delta \in \Delta_{T,\mathcal{M}}} \|\delta\|$

    $n := \|D_t\|^{\|D_t\|} + \max_{\delta \in \Delta_{T,\mathcal{M}}} \|\delta\|$

    $D := \{d \mid d \text{ is used in } T\} \cup \{\perp_0, \perp_1, \ldots, \perp_n\}$

    for all D_t-kinds K with data values in D **do**

        for all $\delta \in \Delta_{T,\mathcal{M}}$ **do**

            find $S_\delta \in L(K)$ with data values in D, branching at most m, satisfying $S_\delta \models \delta$

        end for

        if all S_δ found **then return** $\bigoplus_{\delta \in \Delta_{T,\mathcal{M}}} S_\delta$

    end for

    if no success for each K **return** 'T has no solution with respect to $\mathcal{M}$'

---

one shows that S_δ only needs to use data values in D. Hence, also the entries of $\bar{c}$ are taken from D. In consequence, we can look for a partial solution S_δ by exhaustive search.

If for some δ the search fails, there is no solution for T agreeing with K. If all partial solutions have been found, we can combine them with the operation $\oplus$ into a single full solution in EXPTIME, by Lemma 12.12.

For a fixed mapping, the set $\Delta_{T,\mathcal{M}}$ can be computed in polynomial time. The number of possible kinds is polynomial in $|T|$ and their size is bounded by a constant. Their correctness can be checked in time polynomial in $|K|$ and $\|D_t\|$ (independent of T). For each kind finding and combining partial solutions takes polynomial time. Hence, the whole procedure is in PTIME. $\qquad\qquad\qquad\qquad\qquad\qquad\qquad\qquad\qquad\qquad\qquad\qquad\qquad\qquad\qquad\qquad$ □

Difficulties with extension to the general case

We now give two examples which explain why extending the algorithm of this section to the general case causes problems.

Example 12.14 Consider the mapping given by

$$D_s = \{r \to ab^*\}, \qquad D_t = \{r \to c; \, c \to cb \mid a\},$$

$$\Sigma_{st} = \{r[a(x), b(y)] \longrightarrow r[//a(x), //b(y)]\},$$

where a and b have one attribute. For the source tree shown in Figure 12.3(a), partial solutions could be the trees in Figure 12.3(b). The natural combination of these partial solutions, shown in Figure 12.3(c), cannot be expressed in terms of kinds, as defined in this section. The unique a node on the target side should clearly be part of the kind, as shown in Figure 12.3(d), but under the current definition this is not allowed. In the next section, we are going to develop a more general definition of kinds, allowing internal ports into which contexts are substituted. The ports will also have much richer requirements for the forests or contexts that can be substituted, which will be essential in handling arbitrary regular schemas.

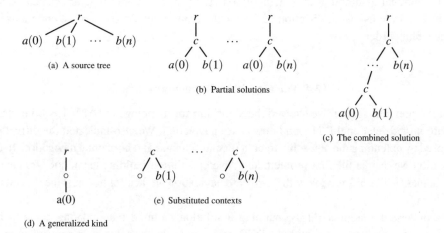

(a) A source tree

(b) Partial solutions

(c) The combined solution

(d) A generalized kind

(e) Substituted contexts

Figure 12.3 Combining partial solutions under recursive schemas

Example 12.15 Let us look at the following mapping:

$$D_s = \{ r \to (ab)^* \}, \qquad D_t = \{ r \to ab^* \},$$

$$\Sigma_{st} = \{ r[a(x) \to b(y)] \longrightarrow r[a(x) \to b(y)] \}.$$

Figures 12.4(a) and 12.4(b) show a source tree T and a possible set of partial solutions. Unless $n = 0$, these partial solutions cannot be combined into a full solution, because in fact there is no solution at all for T. This shows that extending our algorithm to mappings using sibling order requires additional requirements on kinds. Intuitively, to ensure that partial solutions can always be combined, we demand that large enough areas of the tree around each port are specified. We formalize this in terms of margins, introduced in Section 12.5. An example of a kind that allows combining solutions (for the mapping we are considering) is shown in Figure 12.4(c). Note that this kind does not provide all the partial solutions for T, and this is exactly what we need: if there is no full solution, no kind should provide all partial solutions.

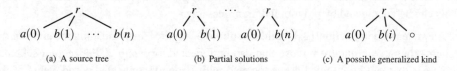

(a) A source tree

(b) Partial solutions

(c) A possible generalized kind

Figure 12.4 Combining partial solutions in the presence of sibling order

Thus there are two main challenges: complex schemas and sibling order. In the following two sections we show how to overcome them by refining the notion of kind, essentially without modifying the main algorithm. In Section 12.4 we deal with regular schemas under an additional assumption that the child axis is forbidden (under regular schemas it also causes problems), and in Section 12.5 we extend our methods to cover the child axis and the sibling order.

12.4 The algorithm for regular schemas

In the previous section we showed the algorithm for mappings in $\mathrm{SM}^{\mathrm{nr}}(\Downarrow, \sim)$, i.e., those with nested-relational DTDs and downward navigation. We also indicated the difficulties posed by extending the algorithm to both regular schemas and horizontal navigation. In this section we handle the first problem and develop solution-building techniques for regular schemas (while still staying with downward navigation, in fact, for now just the descendant relation).

For nested-relational DTDs, building a solution required manipulating contexts and forests in a way consistent with the DTD. For regular schemas it is most convenient to describe contexts and forests in terms of existing runs of the UNFTA underlying the schema.

Definition 12.16 Let p, p', p'' be states of an UNFTA $\mathscr{A}$, and let q, q' be states of one of $\mathscr{A}$'s horizontal automata. A tree T is a p-*tree* if it admits a run of $\mathscr{A}$ that assigns p to the root. A context C is a p, p'-*context* if it admits a run of $\mathscr{A}$ which assigns the state p to the port of C (formally, we add a transition $\delta(p, \circ) = \varepsilon$ to $\mathscr{A}$) and p' to the root. More generally, a multicontext M is a $p_1, p_2, \ldots, p_n$-*multicontext* if it has $n - 1$ ports $u_1, u_2, \ldots, u_{n-1}$, each of them a leaf port, and it admits a run of $\mathscr{A}$ which assigns p_i to u_i for $i = 1, 2, \ldots, n - 1$, and p_n to the root. A forest $F = S_1 S_2 \ldots S_n$ is a q, q'-*forest* if and only if there are states $p_1, p_2, \ldots, p_m$ of $\mathscr{A}$ such that S_i is a p_i-tree and there is a run of the corresponding horizontal automaton over $p_1 p_2 \ldots p_m$ starting in q and ending in q'.

Note that for the initial state q_I, the set of q_I-trees is exactly $L(\mathscr{A})$. Moreover, if T is a p-tree, and C is a p, p'-context, then $C \cdot T$ is a p'-tree. Indeed, the run over $C \cdot T$ is obtained by substituting the run over T in the run over C. Similarly, for a p', p''-context D, $D \cdot C$ is a p, p''-context, and for a q, q'-forest F and a q', q''-forest G, $F + G$ is a q, q''-forest. If M is a $p_1, p_2, \ldots, p_n$-multicontext and T_i is a p_i-tree, $M(T_1, T_2, \ldots, T_{n-1})$ is a p_n-tree.

It will be convenient to assume that all states of $\mathscr{A}$ are *productive*, in the sense that for each state p there exists a p-tree, and that all states of the horizontal automata are reachable. This can be guaranteed by polynomial preprocessing.

As we learned in Section 12.3, building solutions requires distinguishing the areas of the schema that are unique from those that can be repeated, or *pumped*. For regular schemas the areas that can be pumped are associated with strongly connected components of the underlying graphs. An NFA $\mathscr{B} = (Q, \Sigma, q_0, \delta, F)$ can be seen as a graph $G_{\mathscr{B}} = (Q, E)$, where $(p, q) \in E$ if $(p, \sigma, q) \in \delta$ for some $\sigma \in \Gamma$. With an UNFTA $\mathscr{A} = (Q, \Gamma, \delta, F)$ we can also associate a graph: let $G_{\mathscr{A}} = (Q, E)$, where $(p, p') \in E$ iff $Q^* p Q^* \cap \delta(p', \sigma)$ is nonempty for some $\sigma \in \Gamma$. We speak of strongly connected components (SCCs) of $\mathscr{B}$ or $\mathscr{A}$ meaning SCCs of $G_{\mathscr{B}}$ and $G_{\mathscr{A}}$, respectively.

The pumping properties of SCCs of $\mathscr{A}$ depend on their internal structure. We say that an SCC is *nontrivial* if it contains an edge (it might have only one vertex though). A nontrivial SCC X of $\mathscr{A}$ is *branching* if there exist $p, p_1, p_2 \in X$ such that $Q^* p_1 Q^* p_2 Q^* \cap \delta(p, \sigma)$ is nonempty for some σ. If this is not the case, X is *nonbranching*.

In the automata version of the notion of kind, which we are about to define, ports come in three flavors, corresponding to pumpable trees, contexts, and forests. The additional requirements forests or contexts that can be substituted is given in terms of the UNFTA's states.

Definition 12.17 Let $\mathscr{A}$ be an UNFTA. An $\mathscr{A}$*-kind K* is a multicontext in which each port belongs to one of the following categories:

- *p-port*, a leaf port decorated with a state p contained in a branching SCC of $\mathscr{A}$;
- p, p'*-port*, an internal port with a single child, decorated with states p, p' contained in the same nonbranching SCC of $\mathscr{A}$;
- q, q'*-port*, a leaf port decorated with states q, q' contained in the same SCC of one of $\mathscr{A}$'s horizontal automata.

By $L(K)$ we denote the set of trees that *agree* with K, i.e., can be obtained from K by *compatible substitutions*, i.e., by substituting p-trees at p-ports, p, p'-contexts at p, p'-ports, and q, q'-forests at q, q'-ports. We refer to the three kinds of ports above as *tree*, *context*, and *forest* ports.

Trees agreeing with a kind can be combined in a natural way, just like trees conforming to a nested-relational DTD. Like before, for $T \in L(K)$ there is witnessing substitution T_u, u ranging over the ports of K, such that if we substitute at each port u of K the forest or context T_u, we obtain T. Unlike for nested-relational DTDs, we cannot guarantee that there is a unique witnessing substitution (Exercise 16.3), but as we shall see in Lemma 12.19, this is not a problem. In order to combine $S, T \in L(K)$ into a single tree

$$S \oplus T \in L(K)$$

we perform the following substitutions at ports of K:

- if u is a q, q'-port u, substitute $S_u + F + T_u$ for some q', q-forest F;
- if u is a p, p'-port, substitute $S_u \cdot C \cdot T_u$ for some p', p-context C;
- if u is a p-port, substitute $M(S_u, T_u)$ for some p, p, p-multicontext M.

Multifold $\oplus$ is performed from left to right, i.e.,

$$T_1 \oplus T_2 \oplus \cdots \oplus T_n = (\ldots (T_1 \oplus T_2) \oplus \ldots) \oplus T_n.$$

The result of the operation $\oplus$ depends on the choice of F, C, M. The existence of small F, C, M is guaranteed by the following lemma. In this lemma and elsewhere we shall be talking of "single-exponential" objects (e.g., forests or multicontexts); the meaning of this is that the size of such an object is at most single-exponential in the size of the automaton that gives rise to it.

Lemma 12.18   *Let $\mathscr{A}$ be an UNFTA.*

- *For all states q, q' from the same SCC of one of $\mathscr{A}$'s horizontal automata, there exist a single exponential q, q'-forest.*
- *For all states p, p' from the same SCC of $\mathscr{A}$, there exists a single exponential p, p'-context.*
- *For all states p, p', p'' from the same branching SCC of $\mathscr{A}$, there exists a single exponential p, p', p''-multicontext.*

Proof   Assume that q, q' belong to the same SCC of a horizontal automaton $\mathscr{B}$. Then there is a sequence of states $r_1 r_2 \ldots r_m$ of $\mathscr{A}$ that admits a run of $\mathscr{B}$ starting in q' and ending in q. For each i we can find a single exponential r_i-tree S_i: branching can be bounded by the maximal number of states of the horizontal automata, and paths' lengths need not exceed the number of states of $\mathscr{A}$. Then $S_1 S_2 \ldots S_m$ is a q, q'-forest of single exponential size.

A p, p'-context can be constructed as follows. If there is an edge (p, p') in $G_{\mathscr{A}}$, then $r_1 r_2 \ldots r_k\, p\, r_{k+1} r_{k+2} \ldots r_m \in \delta(p', \sigma)$ for some σ and some states $r_1, r_2, \ldots, r_m$. Hence, $\sigma[S_1, S_2, \ldots, S_k, \circ, S_{k+1}, S_{k+2}, \ldots, S_m]$ is a p, p'-context if only S_i is an r_i-tree for all i. In the general case, let the path from p to p' in $G_{\mathscr{A}}$ be $r_1 r_2 \ldots r_m$, with $r_1 = p$, $r_m = p'$. A p, p'-context is obtained by taking $C_1 C_2 \ldots C_{m-1}$, where C_i is an r_i, r_{i+1}-context constructed like above.

If X is a branching SCC, there are $p_0, p_1, p_2 \in X$ such that $Q^* p_1 Q^* p_2 Q^* \cap \delta(p_0, \sigma)$ is nonempty for some σ. Hence, a p_1, p_2, p_0-multicontext M of exponential size can be constructed in the same way as above. To obtain a p, p', p''-multicontext for arbitrary $p, p', p'' \in X$, take $C \cdot M(C_1, C_2)$, where C_1 is a p, p_1-context, C_2 is a p', p_2-context, and C is a p_0, p-context. $\square$

Regardless of the chosen F, C, M, and the witnessing substitutions, the operation preserves satisfiability of patterns that do not use $\downarrow$, $\rightarrow$ and $\rightarrow^+$.

Lemma 12.19   *For all $T_1, T_2, \ldots, T_n \in L(K)$ and every $\pi \in \Pi(\downarrow^+, _-, \sim)$,*

$$T_1 \oplus T_2 \oplus \cdots \oplus T_n \models \pi(\bar{a}) \quad \text{whenever} \quad T_i \models \pi(\bar{a}) \text{ for some } i.$$

Proof   It is enough to observe that the operation $\oplus$ does not break the descendant relation: if a node w is a descendant of v in T_i, the corresponding nodes in $T_1 \oplus T_2 \oplus \cdots \oplus T_n$ will also be in this relation. $\square$

Based on the above lemma, we can effectively build solutions for mappings that do not use $\downarrow$, $\rightarrow$ and $\rightarrow^+$. The last missing ingredient is to show that one can cover all target trees with small kinds. Towards this end we need to distinguish kinds that produce only trees accepted by the UNFTA.

An *accepting run* of $\mathscr{A}$ over an $\mathscr{A}$-kind K must satisfy the usual conditions for ordinary nodes, and the following rules for the ports:

- each p-port is evaluated to p;
- the only child of each p, p'-port u is evaluated to p, and u evaluates to p';
- if u is a q, q'-port, the horizontal automaton arrives at u in state q and leaves in state q'.

More precisely, we assume that each port u is labeled with a unique label $\circ_u$ and we consider an accepting run of $\mathscr{A}$ extended with the following transition rules for each u:

$$\delta(p, \circ_u) = \varepsilon \qquad\qquad \text{if } u \text{ is a } p\text{-port,}$$
$$\delta(p', \circ_u) = p \qquad\qquad \text{if } u \text{ is a } p, p'\text{-port,}$$
$$\delta(p_u, \circ_u) = \varepsilon \text{ and } q, p_u \to q' \qquad\qquad \text{if } u \text{ is a } q, q'\text{-port,}$$

where p_u is a fresh state.

Thus, if a tree T is obtained from K by substituting compatible forests or contexts, an accepting run of $\mathscr{A}$ over T can be obtained by combining an accepting run over K with runs witnessing compatibility. In consequence, if K admits an accepting run of $\mathscr{A}$, then $L(K) \subseteq L(\mathscr{A})$.

Lemma 12.20 *Every $T \in L(\mathscr{A})$ agrees with some $\mathscr{A}$-kind K of branching and size bounded by $\|\mathscr{A}\|$, admitting an accepting run.*

Proof Fix an accepting run λ of $\mathscr{A}$ on T, together with witnessing runs of the horizontal automata. Prune T introducing ports as stubs according to the following rules.

First, each maximal forest such that the witnessing horizontal run in its roots stays within some (horizontal) SCC is replaced with a q, q'-port, where q, q' are the first and the last state of the corresponding fragment of the run.

Next, all maximal subtrees that evaluate to a state p, which is contained in a branching SCC of $\mathscr{A}$, are replaced with a p-port.

Finally, for each nonbranching SCCs X, consider the maximal paths of length at least 2 where the run stays in X. Since X is nonbranching, the paths are disjoint. Replace the subtree rooted at the top end of the path with a p, p'-port for suitable p, p', and under it put the subtree originally rooted at the bottom end of the path.

Note that the result of this procedure depends on the order in which the nonbranching SCCs are processed.

Let K be the resulting kind. By construction $T \in L(K)$. The bounds on the height and branching of K follow from the observation that no state and no SCC occurs more than once in a sequence of children, or a branch. □

The solution-building algorithm for $\mathrm{SM}(\downarrow^+, \_, \sim)$ is just like for the case of $\mathrm{SM}^{\mathrm{nr}}(\Downarrow, \sim)$, except that we use $\mathscr{A}$-kinds admitting an accepting run of $\mathscr{A}$ instead of D_t-kinds, where $\mathscr{A}$ is the UNFTA underlying the target schema.

Theorem 12.21 *For each mapping $\mathscr{M} \in \mathrm{SM}(\downarrow^+, \_, \sim)$, Algorithm 12.3 computes a solution for a source tree T (or determines that it does not exist) in polynomial time.*

Algorithm 12.3 Building solutions for $SM(\downarrow^+,\text{-},\sim)$
Require: $\mathcal{M} = (\mathcal{S}_s, \mathcal{S}_t, \Sigma) \in SM(\downarrow^+, \text{-}, \sim)$, $T \models \mathcal{S}_s$, and $\mathcal{S}_t = (\mathcal{A}, Attr)$
  compute $\Delta_{T,\mathcal{M}}$
  $n := \|\mathcal{A}\|^{\|\mathcal{A}\|} + \max_{\delta \in \Delta_{T,\mathcal{M}}} \|\delta\|$
  $D := \{d \mid d \text{ is used in } T\} \cup \{\perp_0, \perp_1, \dots, \perp_n\}$
  for all $\mathcal{A}$-kinds K of height and branching at most $\|\mathcal{A}\|$, data values in D, admitting an
  accepting run **do**
    for all $\delta \in \Delta_{T,\mathcal{M}}$ **do**
      find $S_\delta \in L(K)$ with data values in D and a witnessing substitution of forests and
      contexts of height and branching at most $\|\mathcal{A}\| \cdot (2 + \|\delta\|)$, satisfying $S_\delta \models \delta$
    end for
    if all S_δ found **then return** $\bigoplus_{\delta \in \Delta_{T,\mathcal{M}}} S_\delta$
  end for
  if no success for each K **return** 'T has no solution with respect to $\mathcal{M}$'

Proof Let $\mathcal{A}$ be the UNFTA underlying the target schema of $\mathcal{M}$. Lemma 12.20 guarantees that if there is a solution to T, it agrees with a kind K that admits an accepting run, and has height and branching bounded by $\|\mathcal{A}\|$. It suffices to consider kinds using data values used in T and nulls $\{\perp_1, \perp_2, \dots, \perp_\ell\}$, with $\ell = \|\mathcal{A}\|^{\|\mathcal{A}\|}$. The size of the run is linear in $|K|$ and its correctness can be checked in time polynomial in $|K|$ and $\|\mathcal{A}\|$. By Lemma 12.19, it is enough to check for each such kind if there is a partial solution for each target requirement $\delta \in \Delta_{T,\mathcal{M}}$: if we succeed, we combine the partial solutions using the operation $\oplus$. It is not difficult to give bounds on the height and branching of forest and contexts substituted at ports of K in the partial solutions. Arguing exactly like in Lemma 12.3 one shows the bound $\|\mathcal{A}\| \cdot (1 + \|\delta\|)$ for forest and tree ports. For context ports we modify the argument as follows. When a context C is substituted, one needs to take into account the existence of the port in C. It is enough to consider the port a red node in the argument of Lemma 12.3. Since the port is a leaf in C, the number of blocks of white nodes on any branch does not increase, and the bound on the height is not influenced. In the argument for the branching, the number of blocks can increase by one, which means that the bound increases by $\|\mathcal{A}\|$, resulting in $\|\mathcal{A}\| \cdot (2 + \|\delta\|)$. □

12.5 The general algorithm

Recall our journey so far:

- First, in Section 12.2, we gave a naïve exhaustive-search algorithm for building a solution; it ran in exponential time.
- Then, in Section 12.3, we described a polynomial-time algorithm for building solutions for mappings in $SM^{nr}(\Downarrow, \sim)$, i.e., those with nested-relational DTDs and downward nav-

igation. The algorithm could not, however, be straightforwardly extended to handle regular schemas and horizontal navigation.

- Then, in Section 12.4, we showed how to incorporate regular schemas, extending the polynomial-time algorithm to handle mappings in $\text{SM}(\downarrow^+, \_, \sim)$.

In this section we complete the journey by providing a polynomial-time solution-building algorithm for arbitrary mappings: we refine our techniques to cover mappings using $\downarrow$, $\rightarrow$ and $\rightarrow^+$. For such patterns Lemma 12.19 no longer holds for arbitrary kinds; for instance, the schema $r \rightarrow ab^*$, where b has a single attribute, and a kind $K = r[a, \circ]$, where the port admits any forest that is a sequence of b-nodes with no children. For each $d = 1, 2, \ldots, n$ there is a T_d in $L(K)$ that satisfies $\pi(d) = r[a \rightarrow b(d)]$, but there is no single tree in $L(K)$ satisfying $\pi(d)$ for all d.

What is wrong with our definition of kind? Recall that the intuition behind kinds is to specify completely the areas of the tree that are unique and cannot be pumped. The reason why there is no way to combine the trees T_d above is that values in the leftmost b-node are different, and they are different because the kind does not specify this data value. But this violates the idea behind the kinds: in the presence of sibling order, the leftmost b-node is clearly a unique node!

Thus for expressive patterns we cannot simply rely on SCCs of the UNFTA underlying the schema, when distinguishing between the unique and pumpable node; we also need to think of nodes that can be uniquely selected by patterns. This leads to further difficulties. In a tree conforming to the schema $r \rightarrow ab^*$, every b-node can be specified uniquely with a pattern of the form $r[a \rightarrow b \rightarrow b \rightarrow \cdots \rightarrow b(x)]$. Does this mean that we can give no bound on the size of schemas? The answer is that we can, but the bound needs to depend on the patterns used in the mapping. Intuitively, a pattern with n nodes can only specify uniquely $n - 1$ leftmost b-nodes. To guarantee an analog of Lemma 12.19, the kinds need to specify large enough areas around each port (the phenomenon described above takes place also for context ports and tree ports, and the child axis). We formalize this intuition by the notion of a margin.

Definition 12.22 For $m \in \mathbb{N}$, a run λ of an UNFTA over a kind K has *margins of size m* if there exist witnessing runs of the horizontal automata such that for each port u, the following hold:

- if u is a tree port, there is a $\downarrow$-path $v_{-m}, v_{-m+1}, \ldots, v_0$ where λ stays in the same SCC and the only port on the path is $v_0 = u$;
- if u is a context port, there is a $\downarrow$-path $v_{-m}, v_{-m+1}, \ldots, v_m$ where λ stays in the same SCC and the only port on the path is $v_0 = u$;
- if u is a q, q'-port with q, q' in an SCC X of some horizontal automaton, there is a sequence of consecutive siblings $v_{-m}, v_{-m+1}, \ldots, v_m$ where the horizontal run stays in the same SCC and the only port in the sequence is $v_0 = u$.

Before we show how to combine trees, let us observe that the set of target instances can be covered by small kinds with margins of given length.

Lemma 12.23 *For every UNFTA $\mathscr{A}$ and a tree $T \in L(\mathscr{A})$ and $m \in \mathbb{N}$ there is an $\mathscr{A}$-kind K with height and branching at most $(2m+1)\|\mathscr{A}\|$, admitting an accepting run with margins of size m, such that $T \in L(K)$.*

Proof Argue just like for Lemma 12.20, only keep margins of size m around ports: for SCCs of horizontal automata and nonbranching SCCs of $\mathscr{A}$ keep m initial and m final steps of the run within the SCC, and for branching SCCs keep the m final steps (looking bottom-up).   □

In the combining procedure, instead of the T_u's we use larger forest/contexts, encompassing the margins. Fix a run λ over K with margins of length m. For a tree $T \in L(K)$, a port u in K, and $k \leq m$, define T_u^k as an extension of T_u by k nodes along the margins, i.e., using the notation in Definition 12.22:

- if u is a p-port, let $T_u^k = T.\tilde{v}_k$;
- if u is a p, p'-port, then T_u^k is the context obtained from $T.\tilde{v}_{-k}$ by replacing $T.\tilde{v}_k$ with a port;
- if u is a q, q'-port, let $T_u^k = \sum_{i=-k}^{-1} T.\tilde{v}_i + T_u + \sum_{i=1}^{k} T.\tilde{v}_i$;

where $\tilde{v}$ denotes the node in T corresponding to v, and $T.w$ denotes the subtree of T rooted at w. In particular, $T_u^0 = T_u$.

Note that in $T \in L(K)$, then the T_u^k's need not be disjoint. This means that combining n trees one by one would result in an exponential overhead. In consequence, we have to combine them in one go by concatenating the forests or contexts replacing u in all n trees.

Fix a run λ over K with margins of size m, together with the witnessing horizontal runs, and let $T_1, T_2, \ldots, T_n \in L(K)$. For $i = 1, 2, \ldots, n$ fix a run λ_i compatible with λ, witnessing that $T_i \in L(K)$. We build

$$T_1 \oplus_m T_2 \oplus_m \cdots \oplus_m T_n \in L(K)$$

by substituting at each port u in K the following forest or context

- $F_1 + (T_1)_u^m + F_2 + (T_2)_u^m + \cdots + F_{m+1}$ if u is a forest port, or
- $C_1 \cdot (T_1)_u^m \cdot C_2 \cdot (T_2)_u^m \cdot \ldots \cdot C_{m+1}$ if u is a context port, or
- $M_1((T_1)_u^m, M_2((T_2)_u^m, \ldots M_{n-1}((T_{n-1})_u^m, (T_n)_u^m) \ldots))$ if u is a tree port,

where F_i are compatible forests, C_i are compatible contexts, and M_i are compatible multicontexts with two ports. The existence of small F_i's, C_i's, and M_i's follows from Lemma 12.18 and the fact that along the margins the runs stay within a single SCC (a branching one in the case of tree ports). In this way we obtain a tree of size at most $|K|(|T_1| + |T_2| + \cdots + |T_n| + (n+1)c)$, where c is a constant independent of the T_i's, single-exponential in $\mathscr{A}$.

Correctness of the construction is guaranteed by the following lemma.

Lemma 12.24 *Let λ be a run over K with margins of size m. For all $T_1, T_2, \ldots, T_n \in L(K)$ and every pattern π of size at most m,*

$$T_1 \oplus_m T_2 \oplus_m \cdots \oplus_m T_n \models \pi(\bar{a}) \quad \text{whenever} \quad T_i \models \pi(\bar{a}) \text{ for some } i.$$

Before giving the proof, we show how Lemmas 12.23 and 12.24 lead to a general solution-building algorithm.

Algorithm 12.4 Building solutions for $\mathrm{SM}(\Downarrow, \Rightarrow, \sim)$

Require: $\mathcal{M} = (\mathcal{S}_s, \mathcal{S}_t, \Sigma) \in \mathrm{SM}(\Downarrow, \Rightarrow, \sim)$, $T \models \mathcal{S}_s$, and $\mathcal{S}_t = (\mathcal{A}, \mathrm{Attr})$

  compute $\Delta_{T, \mathcal{M}}$

  $m := \max_{\delta \in \Delta_{T, \mathcal{M}}} \|\delta\|$

  $n := \|\mathcal{A}\|^{\|\mathcal{A}\|} + \max_{\delta \in \Delta_{T, \mathcal{M}}} \|\delta\|$

  $D := \{ d \mid d \text{ is used in } T \} \cup \{ \perp_0, \perp_1, \ldots, \perp_n \}$

  for all $\mathcal{A}$-kinds K of height and branching at most $(2m+1)\|\mathcal{A}\|$, data values in D, admitting an accepting run with margins of size m **do**

    for all $\delta \in \Delta_{T, \mathcal{M}}$ **do**

      find $S_\delta \in L(K)$ with data values in D and a witnessing substitution of forests and contexts of height and branching at most $\|\mathcal{A}\| \cdot (2 + \|\delta\|)$, satisfying $S_\delta \models \delta$

    end for

    if all S_δ found **then return** $\bigoplus_{\delta \in \Delta_{T, \mathcal{M}}} S_\delta$

  end for

  if no success for each K **return** 'T has no solution with respect to $\mathcal{M}$'

Theorem 12.25 *For each mapping $\mathcal{M} \in \mathrm{SM}(\Downarrow, \Rightarrow, \sim)$, Algorithm 12.4 computes a solution for a source tree T (or determines that it does not exist) in polynomial time.*

Proof Let m be the maximal size of target side patterns in $\mathcal{M}$. The only modification needed in the argument in Theorem 12.21 is that we only consider kinds admitting runs with margins of size m, the operation $\oplus$ is replaced by $\oplus_m$, and Lemmas 12.19 and 12.20 are replaced by Lemmas 12.24 and 12.23, respectively. $\qquad\square$

It remains to prove Lemma 12.24. From the point of view of a single T_i, the tree $T_1 \oplus_m T_2 \oplus_m \cdots \oplus_m T_n$ is obtained from T_i by extending the forests/contexts substituted at the ports, according to some rules. An *m-safe extension* of T at port u is obtained by replacing T_u with any compatible

- forest of the form $F + T_u^m + F'$, if u is a forest port;
- tree of the form $C \cdot T_u^m$, if u is a tree port;
- context of the form $C \cdot T_u^m \cdot C'$, if u is a context port.

A tree $T' \in L(K)$ is an *m-safe extension* of $T \in L(K)$ if it is obtained from T by simultaneous *m*-safe extensions at different ports.

Clearly, $T_1 \oplus_m T_2 \oplus_m \cdots \oplus_m T_n$ is a safe extension of T_i for each i, so Lemma 12.24 follows from the following fact.

Lemma 12.26   *Fix a pattern π, a natural number $m \geq \|\pi\|$, a kind K together with an extended run with margins of size m, and a tree $T \in L(K)$. For each m-safe extension T' of T*

$$T' \models \pi(\bar{a}) \text{ whenever } T \models \pi(\bar{a}).$$

Proof   Fix $\bar{a}$ such that $T \models \pi(\bar{a})$ and a witnessing homomorphism $h : \pi \to T$. We define a partition $\mathscr{V}$ of V_π, the set of π's vertices, such that a homomorphism $h' : \pi \to T'$ can be defined independently on each part as long as some simple rules are satisfied.

The areas potentially affected by the extension are the T_u's. We associate with u a set Z_u such that $T_u \subseteq Z_u \subseteq T_u^m$, where the homomorphism can be modified independently of the rest of the tree. If for some u the image of h is disjoint from T_u, take $Z_u = \emptyset$. If T_u is not disjoint from the image of h, there are three cases, depending on the type of u.

Case 1   If u is a forest port, then $T_u^m = M + T_u + N$ and since the image of h has cardinality at most $\|\pi\|$ and is not disjoint from T_u, by the pigeon-hole principle there exist roots v in M and v' in N outside of the image of h. (If there is choice, choose the ones closest to T_u.) Let Z_u be the forest of trees rooted at the sequence of siblings between v and v' (excluding v and v').

Case 2   If u is a tree port, then $T_u = M \cdot T_u$ and there exists a node v in M on the pathfrom the root to the port, closest to T_u, that is not in the image of h. Let $Z_u = T.v$.

Case 3   If u is a context port, then $T_u^m = M \cdot T_u \cdot N$, and one can find v on the path from the root to the port in M and v' on the path from the root to the port in N, closest to T_u, that are not in the image of h. Let $Z_u = T.v - T.v'$.

The sets Z_u need not be disjoint, but we can pick a pairwise disjoint subfamily $\mathscr{Z}$ covering all the sets T_u that intersect the image of h. To prove this, we first show by case analysis that for each u', u'' either $T_{u'} \subseteq Z_{u''}$, or $T_{u''} \subseteq Z_{u'}$, or $Z_{u'}$ and $Z_{u''}$ are disjoint. In fact, in all cases except the last one, $Z_{u'}$ and $Z_{u''}$ either are disjoint or one is contained in the other.

- For two forest ports, we are dealing with two forests whose roots are children of some nodes w and w'. If such forests are not disjoint, and neither is contained in a subtree of the other, then they share one of the roots. But this is impossible: two sibling ports are always separated by a margin, which must contain a node that is not in the image of h; the associated forests are disjoint because they were chosen minimal.

- For a tree port and a forest port (or a tree port), the corresponding sets are: a subtree, and a subforest whose roots are siblings. Such sets are always either disjoint, or one is contained in the other.

- For a context port and a tree port, whose corresponding sets are not disjoint and neither is contained in the other, the root of the tree must be contained in the path between the root and the port of the context. But this would mean that the margin paths of the two ports are not disjoint, which implies that the SCCs associated with the ports are the same. This leads to a contradiction, as one was assumed branching and the other nonbranching.

- For two context ports, if the contexts are not disjoint and neither is contained in the other, the root of one of them lies on the path between the root and the port of the other. Like above, in this case both ports are associated with the same SCC. Moreover, since the SCC is nonbranching, the two ports are on the same branch of K (otherwise, the two margin paths would branch). It follows that the ports are separated by a node that is not in the image of h, which guarantees disjointness of the associated contexts.

- Finally, for a context port u' and a forest port u'', we are dealing with a context $T.v - T.v'$, and a forest whose roots are children of a single node w. If such sets are not disjoint and neither is contained in the other, the node w must lie on the path between v and v' (excluding v'). The margin path around u' in K cannot contain other ports, which means that the set $T_{u''}$ is disjoint from this path. As v' lies on this path, $T_{u''}$ does not contain v'. It follows that $T_{u''} \subseteq Z_{u'}$.

To construct $\mathscr{Z}$ start with $\mathscr{Z} = \emptyset$ and for each port u make sure that T_u is covered: let $\mathscr{Z}(u) = \{Z \in \mathscr{Z} \mid Z \cap Z_u \neq \emptyset\}$; if $T_u \subseteq Z$ for some $Z \in \mathscr{Z}(u)$, then T_u is already covered and we can proceed to the next port; otherwise, by the observation above, $T_{u'} \subseteq Z_u$ for all u' such that $Z_{u'} \in \mathscr{Z}(u)$, and we replace $\mathscr{Z}$ with $\mathscr{Z} - \mathscr{Z}(u) \cup \{Z_u\}$. Let $\mathscr{V} = \{h^{-1}(Z) \mid Z \in \mathscr{Z}\} \cup \{V_\pi - h^{-1}(\bigcup \mathscr{Z})\}$ and denote $V_u = h^{-1}(Z_u)$.

Since $h^{-1}(\bigcup \mathscr{Z})$ covers all vertices of π mapped to $\bigcup_u T_u$, for $x \in V_\pi - h^{-1}(\bigcup \mathscr{Z})$, $h(x) = w$ is a vertex from the fixed area of T, and hence has its counterpart w' in T'. Let $h'(x) = w'$. Now let us see how to define h' on $V_u \in \mathscr{V}$. Since T' is a safe extension of T, the forest/context substituted at u in T' contains a copy of Z_u, which in turn contains $h(V_u)$. We define h' on V_u by transferring h from Z_u to its copy in T'. To prove that this gives a homomorphism we need to check that no relation between vertices of π is violated. We are going to show that each relation between $x \in V_u$ and $y \notin V_u$ must be witnessed by a path visiting a *critical node* in the fixed part of T induced by K, and that in T' the witnessing paths to the critical nodes exist as well. Since the critical nodes are in the fixed part, the relations between them are the same in T and in T' and the correctness of h' follows.

Suppose first that u is a forest port. Let us analyze the possible relations in π between x and y. First, we exclude some possibilities. The case $(x \downarrow y)$ is impossible, because it would mean that $h(y)$ is a child of $h(x)$, and since $h(x) \in Z_u$, it would follow that $h(y) \in Z_u$, contradicting the fact that $y \notin V_u = h^{-1}(Z_u)$. Similarly, the cases $(x \to y), (y \to x), (x \downarrow^+ y)$ are impossible. If $(y \downarrow x)$, then $h(y) = w$, the parent of v and v'. In the remaining cases, $(y \downarrow^+ x), (x \to^+ y), (y \to^+ x)$, one checks easily that the witnessing paths must visit w, v', and v, respectively. Note that w, v, v' are vertices of K and have their counterparts in T'. After transferring the image of V_u to the copy of Z_u contained in T'_u as a subforest, the child and descendant relation with w and the following-sibling relation with v, v' are preserved.

If u is a tree port, the only possible edge between $x \in V_u$ and $y \notin V_u$ is $(y \downarrow^+ x)$, and the witnessing path must visit v. Hence, the image of V_u can be transferred to the copy of Z_u contained in T'_u, without violating the existence of witnessing paths.

Finally, if u is a context port, let V_{below}, V_u, V_{above} be a partition of π's vertices into those mapped to $T.v'$, $Z_u = T.w - T.v'$, and elsewhere. The only possible edges between $x \in V_u$, $y \in V_{\text{above}}$, and $y' \in V_{\text{below}}$, are $(y \downarrow^+ x)$, $(x \downarrow^+ y')$, or $(y \downarrow^+ y')$ with the witnessing paths visiting v, v', or both of these, respectively. Consequently, we can transfer the image of V_u to the copy of Z_u contained in T'_u, preserving the existence of the witnessing paths.   □

12.6 Combined complexity of solution building

The solutions built by the algorithms from the previous sections are polynomial-size, and can be constructed in polynomial time, for each fixed mapping $\mathcal{M}$. A quick analysis of the algorithm (already done in the proofs of correctness results) shows that in terms of $\mathcal{M}$, such solutions can be of exponential size. This bound is in fact tight: the smallest tree conforming to the target schema might be exponential, and even if the schema is fixed, a simple rule like

$$r[//\_(x_1), //\_(x_2), \ldots, //\_(x_n)] \longrightarrow r/a(x_1, x_2, \ldots, x_n)$$

causes exponential blow-up.

We now investigate the bounds on the combined complexity of solution building. That is, we look at the problem of building a solution when the input consists of *both* a mapping $\mathcal{M}$ and a source tree T.

Theorem 12.27 *The combined complexity of solution building for schema mappings in* $\text{SM}(\Downarrow, \Rightarrow, \sim)$ *is in* EXPSPACE.

Proof Let us sum up the space used by Algorithm 12.4. The kinds and partial solutions considered by the algorithm have branching and height bounded by functions polynomial in the size of the mapping, and their data values come from a set single-exponential in the size of the mapping. The number of partial solutions kept in memory at the same time is bounded by the number of target requirements, i.e., $|\Delta_{T,\mathcal{M}}|$, which is at most $\|\mathcal{M}\| \cdot |T|^{\|\mathcal{M}\|}$. It follows that these objects can be stored in exponential memory.

The merging operation $\oplus_m$ uses memory polynomial in the size of the partial solutions and the kind (modulo exponential multiplicative overhead needed for the padding contexts and forests used in the operation). All other checks and operations need memory polynomial in the size of these objects.   □

Note that an EXPSPACE algorithm in general implies doubly-exponential running time (just like a PSPACE algorithm implies a single-exponential running time). To understand better the complexity of the problem, and to see whether this bound can be lowered, we consider a decision version of solution building, i.e., *solution existence*.

PROBLEM:	SOLEXISTENCE
INPUT:	Mapping $\mathcal{M}$, source tree T.
QUESTION:	Is $\mathcal{M}(T)$ nonempty?

Clearly, finding a solution is at least as hard as deciding if it exists. The following theorem implies that an algorithm for solution building with exponential combined complexity is unlikely to exist. We show that the problem is NEXPTIME-complete, even for a simple class of mapping. Just like NP-completeness implies an exponential-time algorithm (modulo some unresolved problems in complexity theory), NEXPTIME-complete is a strong indication that doubly-exponential time is required.

Theorem 12.28 SOLEXISTENCE *is* NEXPTIME-*complete. The problem remains* NEXPTIME-*hard for mappings from* $SM^{nr}(\downarrow, \_)$.

Proof To get the upper bound proceed just like in the proof of Theorem 12.25, only instead of examining every possible kind K, choose it nondeterministically, together with a witnessing run. Then, for each dependency $\pi(\bar{x}, \bar{y}) \to \exists \bar{z} \, \pi'(\bar{x}, \bar{z})$ in Σ_{st} and tuples $\bar{a}, \bar{b}$ such that $T \models \pi(\bar{a}, \bar{b})$, we need to check if there exists $T' \in L(K)$ such that $T' \models \pi'(\bar{a}, \bar{z})$. By Lemma 12.29 below, this can be done nondeterministically in polynomial time.

Lemma 12.29 *For an $\mathscr{A}$-kind K, a pattern π, and a tuple $\bar{a}$, satisfiability of $\pi(\bar{a})$ in a tree agreeing with K can be witnessed by an object polynomial in the size of π, the height and branching of K, and the size of $\mathscr{A}$.*

Proof We need to check if the ports of K can be filled in such a way that $\pi(\bar{a})$ is satisfied in the resulting tree. The contexts/forests needed might be large, but just like in the proof of Theorem 11.7 all we need is a support for the homomorphism from $\pi(\bar{a})$ to the tree. It is easy to see that the total size of the support in the substituted parts can be bounded polynomially. In particular, the number of ports involved in the realization of $\pi(\bar{a})$ is polynomial, and for the remaining ones the support is empty. A homomorphism from $\pi(\bar{a})$ into K extended with the support can also be stored in polynomial memory. Verifying the witness can be done in PTIME. □

To get the lower bound we give a reduction from the following NEXPTIME-complete problem: given a nondeterministic Turing machine M and $n \in \mathbb{N}$, does M accept the empty word in at most 2^n steps? The idea of the reduction is to encode the run of the machine in the target tree. The run will be encoded as a sequence of 2^n configurations of length 2^n. The machine M is stored in the source tree, except the (specially preprocessed) transition relation, which is encoded in the target tree. The source tree is also used to address the configurations and their cells.

We give a reduction of this problem to $SM^{nr}(\downarrow, \_, =)$. Removing $=$ from the source side is an instructive exercise (see Exercise 16.3).

Let M have the tape alphabet A with the blank symbol $\flat \in A$ and the states $q_0, q_1, \ldots, q_f$. W.l.o.g. we assume that q_f is the only final accepting state. The *extended transition relation* of M, denoted $\hat{\delta}$, describes possible transitions in a window of three consecutive tape cells. Formally, $\hat{\delta} \subseteq (\{q_0, q_1, \ldots, q_f, \perp\} \times \hat{A})^6$, where $\hat{A}$ is the set of *decorated tape symbols*, defined as $\hat{A} = \{s, s^{\triangleright}, s^{\triangleleft} \mid s \in A\}$. The symbol $\perp$ means "the head is elsewhere", $\triangleright$ marks the beginning of the tape, $\triangleleft$ marks the end of the tape (at position 2^n), and $(p_1, \sigma_1, p_2, \sigma_2, \ldots, p_6, \sigma_6) \in \hat{\delta}$ iff at most one of p_1, p_2, p_3 is not equal to $\bot$, and $p_4 \sigma_4 p_5 \sigma_5 p_6 \sigma_6$ is obtained from $p_1 \sigma_1 p_2 \sigma_2 p_3 \sigma_3$ by performing a transition of M. Note that $p_1 = p_2 = p_3 = \bot$ and $p_4 \neq \bot$ is possible as long as σ_4 is not marked with $\triangleright$. Note that $\hat{\delta}$ can be computed in polynomial time.

The source DTD is given as

$$r \to zero\ one\ q_0 q_1 \cdots q_f \bot \tau_1 \tau_2 \cdots \tau_m$$
$$zero, one \to bit$$

where $\hat{A} = \{\tau_1, \tau_2, \ldots, \tau_m\}$ and each label except r, *zero*, *one* has a single attribute. The target DTD is given as

$$r \to a_1 b_1 tr_1 tr_2 \cdots tr_d$$
$$tr_i \to tr$$
$$a_j, b_j \to a_{j+1} b_{j+1}$$
$$a_{2n}, b_{2n} \to cell$$
$$tr\colon @st_1 @sym_1 @sym_2 @sym_2 \cdots @sym_6 @sym_6$$
$$cell\colon @a_1 @a_2 \cdots @a_{2n} @st @sym$$

for $i = 1, 2, \ldots, d$, $j = 1, 2, \ldots, 2n - 1$, and $d = |\hat{\delta}|$. The *cell* nodes store in binary a configuration number and a cell number, as well as a state and a decorated tape symbol. The *tr* nodes store $\hat{\delta}$.

The source tree T is any tree conforming to the source schema storing a different data value in each node. The children of the root store data values encoding the states and tape symbols used in $\hat{\delta}$. To ensure that $\hat{\delta}$ is stored properly on the target side, for each $(p_1, \sigma_1, p_2, \sigma_2, \ldots, p_6, \sigma_6) \in \hat{\delta}$ add a dependency

$$r[p_1(u_1), \sigma_1(v_1), p_2(u_2), \sigma_2(v_2), \ldots, p_6(u_6), \sigma_6(v_6)] \longrightarrow$$
$$\longrightarrow r/_-/tr(u_1, v_1, u_2, v_2, \ldots, u_6, v_6).$$

Note that d different dependencies are introduced, so each *tr* node in the target tree contains a tuple from $\hat{\delta}$.

The data values stored in T in two *bit* nodes are used to address the configurations and their cells. This is done by means of three auxiliary patterns, $First(\bar{x})$, $Last(\bar{x})$, and $Succ(\bar{x}, \bar{y})$ with $\bar{x} = x_1, x_2, \ldots, x_n$, $\bar{y} = y_1, y_2, \ldots, y_n$, which roughly speaking implement a binary counter over n bits. In the auxiliary patterns we use disjunction, but since we are only going to apply them on the source side of dependencies, disjunction can be easily eliminated at the cost of multiplying dependencies. Formally, they are defined as:

$$First(\bar{x}) = zero\left[bit(x_1), bit(x_2), \ldots, bit(x_n)\right],$$
$$Last(\bar{x}) = one\left[bit(x_1), bit(x_2), \ldots, bit(x_n)\right],$$
$$Succ(\bar{x}, \bar{y}) = \bigvee_{i=1}^{n} \left(\bigwedge_{j=1}^{i-1} {}_{-}\left[bit(x_j), bit(y_j)\right], zero/bit(x_i) \wedge one/bit(y_i), \right.$$
$$\left. \bigwedge_{j=i+1}^{n} one/bit(x_j) \wedge zero/bit(y_j) \right).$$

Using the auxiliary patterns we ensure that the target tree encodes an accepting run of M. In the first configuration the tape is empty and the head state q_0 is over the first cell,

$$r[First(\bar{x}), First(\bar{y}), q_0(u), \flat^{\triangleright}(v)] \longrightarrow r//cell(\bar{x}, \bar{y}, u, v),$$
$$r[First(\bar{x}), Succ(\bar{z}_1, \bar{y}), Succ(\bar{y}, \bar{z}_2), \perp(u), \flat(v)] \longrightarrow r//cell(\bar{x}, \bar{y}, u, v),$$
$$r[First(\bar{x}), Last(\bar{y}), \perp(u), \flat^{\triangleleft}(v)] \longrightarrow r//cell(\bar{x}, \bar{y}, u, v).$$

Note that the valuations of $\bar{y}$ correspond to all numbers from 0 to $2^n - 1$, and thus the content of each cell of the tape is specified.

The correctness of transitions is ensured by

$$r\left[Succ(\bar{x}_0, \bar{x}_1), Succ(\bar{y}_1, \bar{y}_2), Succ(\bar{y}_2, \bar{y}_3)\right] \longrightarrow$$
$$\longrightarrow \exists \bar{u} \exists \bar{v} \, r\left[{}_{-}/tr(u_1, v_1, u_2, v_2, \ldots, u_6, v_6), \bigwedge_{i,j} //cell(\bar{x}_i, \bar{y}_j, u_{3i+j}, v_{3i+j})\right].$$

Again, $\bar{x}_0, \bar{x}_1$ range over $k, k+1$ with $0 \le k < 2^n - 1$, and y_1, y_2, y_3 range over $\ell, \ell+1, \ell+2$ with $0 \le \ell < 2^n - 2$, which means that the evolution of each three consecutive cells is checked for every step.

Finally, the machine needs to reach the accepting state (w.l.o.g. we assume that the accepting state is looping),

$$r[q_f(u)] \longrightarrow \exists \bar{x} \exists \bar{y} \exists v \, r//cell(\bar{x}, \bar{y}, u, v).$$

Note that each occurrence of $//$ above can be replaced with a sequence of $_{-}$ and $/$ symbols of suitable length.

It is straightforward to verify that M has an accepting computation of length at most 2^n if and only if T has a solution with respect to the mapping defined above. $\qquad\square$

13

Answering tuple queries

The ultimate goal of data exchange is to answer queries over the target data in a way consistent with the source data. In this chapter we focus on queries that return sets of tuples of data values. The reason for this restriction is twofold:

- first, for such queries the notion of certain answers is easy to define; and
- second, already for these queries we shall be able to identify features that need to be ruled out in order to ensure tractability of query answering.

We deal with a query language based on tree patterns, as it forms a natural analog of (unions of) conjunctive queries. We show that the problem of finding certain answers is in CONP, just like for conjunctive queries in the relational case. We then identify several features specific to XML, such as disjunction in DTDs or the horizontal order, that make the query answering problem intractable. Finally, we give a polynomial query answering algorithm that computes certain answers for unions of conjunctive queries that only use vertical navigation, restricted to schema mappings with nested-relational DTDs.

13.1 The query answering problem

Just like in the relational case, we study conjunctive queries and their unions. As we have learned, it is convenient to work with tree patterns, which have very similar expressivity to conjunctive queries. Thus, for querying XML documents we use the same language as for the dependencies: tree patterns with equalities and inequalities, to capture the analog of relational conjunctive queries (with inequalities). And, of course, we allow projection.

That is, a query Q is an expression of the form

$$\exists \bar{y} \, \pi(\bar{x}, \bar{y}),$$

where π is a (generalized) tree pattern satisfying the safety condition, i.e., each variable used in π is connected by a sequence of equalities to a variable used in the pure pattern underlying π. The semantics is defined in the standard way:

$$T \models \exists \bar{y} \, \pi(\bar{a}, \bar{y}) \quad \Leftrightarrow \quad T \models \pi(\bar{a}, \bar{b}) \text{ for some tuple } \bar{b} \text{ of attribute values.}$$

The output of the query is the set of those valuations of free variables that make the query hold true

$$Q(T) = \{\bar{a} \mid T \models \exists \bar{y}\, \pi(\bar{a}, \bar{y})\}\,.$$

This class of queries is denoted by **CTQ** (conjunctive tree queries).

Note that conjunctive queries from **CTQ** are indeed closed under conjunctions. This is because patterns are closed under conjunction, as we have seen in Section 11.1.

We also consider unions of such queries: **UCTQ** denotes the class of queries of the form

$$Q_1(\bar{x}) \cup \cdots \cup Q_m(\bar{x}),$$

where each Q_i is a query from **CTQ**. Like for schema mappings, we write **CTQ**(σ) and **UCTQ**(σ) for $\sigma \subseteq \{\downarrow, \downarrow^+, \rightarrow, \rightarrow^+, =, \neq, \_\}$ to denote the subclass of queries using only the symbols from σ. Recall that we are using abbreviations $\Downarrow$ for $(\downarrow, \downarrow^+, \_)$, $\Rightarrow$ for $(\rightarrow, \rightarrow^+, \_)$, and $\sim$ for $(=, \neq)$.

Example 13.1 Recall the mapping defined in Example 11.12 on page 154. Suppose we want to find out which rulers succeeded more than one other ruler. This can be expressed over the target schema by the following conjunctive query with inequalities MultiSucc:

$$\exists x\, \exists y\, \texttt{rulers}[\texttt{ruler}(x)/\texttt{successor}(z), \texttt{ruler}(y)/\texttt{successor}(z)] \wedge x \neq y.$$

Just like in the relational case, the query might return different answers on different solutions to a given source tree. For instance, for the source tree T_1 shown in Figure 10.1, two possible solutions are T_2 and T_3 shown in Figure 11.4. On T_2 the query MultiSucc returns {*James VI & I*}, and on T_3 the answer is {*James VI & I, Charles I*}. □

What is the right answer to a query then? Since the queries return tuples of values, we can simply adapt the *certain answers semantics* from the relational case. For a mapping $\mathcal{M}$, a query Q, and a source tree S conforming to D_s, we return the tuples which would be returned for every possible solution:

$$certain_{\mathcal{M}}(Q, S) = \bigcap \left\{ Q(T) \,\middle|\, T \text{ is a solution for } S \text{ under } \mathcal{M} \right\}.$$

The subscript $\mathcal{M}$ is omitted when it is clear from the context.

This is precisely why for now we restrict to queries that return tuples of data values: for them, it is clear how to define certain answers. For queries that can return XML documents, the definition is not so clear; we revisit the problem in the next chapter.

In our running example,

$$certain_{\mathcal{M}}(\texttt{MultiSucc}, T_1) = \{\textit{James VI \& I}\}\,.$$

Note that when Q is a Boolean query, $certain_{\mathcal{M}}(Q, S)$ is true if and only if Q is true for all the solutions.

To understand the computational resources needed to find certain answers, we focus on the following decision problem, for fixed $\mathcal{M}$ and Q:

PROBLEM:	CERTAIN$_{\mathcal{M}}(Q)$
INPUT:	Source tree S, tuple $\bar{s}$.
QUESTION:	$\bar{s} \in certain_{\mathcal{M}}(Q,S)$?

In what follows we investigate how the complexity of this problem depends on the features allowed in schemas, st-tgds and queries.

13.2 An upper bound

We have seen that in the relational case the certain answers problem for CQs with inequalities is in CONP. In the XML setting this is no longer the case: the problem can be undecidable for some mappings and queries. This happens either with mappings and queries permitting downward navigation, or child/next-sibling navigation, as long as inequalities are allowed in queries. Specifically, the following is true.

Proposition 13.2 *Let σ include either downward axes $\downarrow, \downarrow^+$, or the child and next-sibling axes $\downarrow$ and $\rightarrow$. Then there exist a mapping $\mathcal{M} \in \mathrm{SM}(\sigma)$ and a query $Q \in \mathbf{CTQ}(\sigma, \sim)$ such that* CERTAIN$_{\mathcal{M}}(Q)$ *is undecidable.*

As soon as we forbid inequalities in queries, we get the CONP upper bound back, but the proof is more involved. Below, we only give a sketch of the main ideas.

Theorem 13.3 *For every schema mapping $\mathcal{M}$ from $\mathrm{SM}(\Downarrow, \Rightarrow, \sim)$ and every query Q from* $\mathbf{UCTQ}(\Downarrow, \Rightarrow, =)$, *the problem* CERTAIN$_{\mathcal{M}}(Q)$ *is in* CONP.

Proof idea Take a query $Q \in \mathbf{UCTQ}(\Downarrow, \Rightarrow, \sim)$, an XML schema mapping $\mathcal{M} = (\mathscr{S}_s, \mathscr{S}_t, \Sigma_{st})$, and a source tree S conforming to $\mathscr{S}_s$. Without loss of generality we can assume that Q is a Boolean query.

A tree conforming to the target schema is a solution for S iff it satisfies every pattern from the following set:

$$\Delta_{S,\mathcal{M}} = \{\psi(\bar{a},\bar{z}) \mid \varphi(\bar{x},\bar{y}) \rightarrow \exists \bar{z} \, \psi(\bar{x},\bar{z}) \in \Sigma_{st} \text{ and } S \models \varphi(\bar{a},\bar{b})\}.$$

Note that for a fixed mapping the set $\Delta_{S,\mathcal{M}}$ can be computed in PTIME.

The certain answer to Q is `false` iff there exists a *counter-example* tree T such that

1. $T \models \mathscr{S}_t$,
2. $T \models \Delta_{S,\mathcal{M}}$, and
3. $T \not\models Q$.

Assume that there exists such a counter-example T. Fix a set of nodes witnessing $\Delta_{S,\mathcal{M}}$. Observe that since Q does not use $\neq$, we can assume that all the nonwitnessing nodes store unique data values. Under this assumption, we will show that we can trim most of the nonwitnessing nodes without satisfying Q, or violating $\mathscr{S}_t$, so that T becomes of polynomial size. This gives an NP algorithm for checking whether certain answers are false: simply guess a tree T of polynomial size, and check if it satisfies the three conditions of being a counter-example. This, in turn, implies that checking whether certain answers are true is in CONP.

Consider a first-order logic (FO) formula equivalent to Q, and let k be its quantifier rank, i.e., the depth of quantifier nesting. The k-type of a node is the set of all FO formulae of quantifier rank k with one free variable it satisfies. It is known that there are only finitely many nonequivalent FO formulae of any given quantifier rank. In consequence, there are only finitely many different k-types. Since k depends only on the query, we have a fixed number of k-types.

Now, roughly, for any pair u, v of nonwitnessing nodes with the same FO k-type, we cut the nodes in-between and merge u, v (provided that cutting neither removes any witnessing node nor leads to violation of the schema). Cutting this way, vertically and horizontally, we make sure all the witnesses are not too far apart, and the resulting tree has polynomial size. Since u and v above have the same k-type, it can be shown that after cutting, the tree satisfies all the same FO formulae of quantifier rank k as before; in particular, the cut tree satisfies Q iff the original tree did. □

13.3 Sources of intractability

The certain answers problem easily becomes CONP-hard. In the this section we investigate the reasons for hardness which will help us isolate a fairly expressive tractable case, that is further analyzed in the next section.

The reasons for hardness may come from three main sources: schemas, st-tgds, and queries.

Hardness due to schemas

Let us first consider schemas. It can be shown that for $\text{SM}^{\text{dtd}}(\downarrow, =)$ and $\textbf{UCTQ}(\downarrow, =)$ there is a dichotomy: if schemas (DTDs) allow enough disjunction, the problem is CONP-hard, otherwise it is polynomial. Without giving the precise (and rather technical) characteriza-tion of the class of mappings that gives hardness, we show how simple these mappings can be.

To do so, we will give examples of an XML schema mapping $\mathcal{M}$ and a Boolean query Q such that the well-known NP-complete problem 3SAT is reducible to the complement of $\text{CERTAIN}_{\mathcal{M}}(Q)$, i.e., for each 3SAT instance (a propositional formula) φ, we have

$$certain_{\mathcal{M}}(Q, S_\varphi) \text{ is } \texttt{false} \text{ iff } \varphi \text{ is satisfiable,}$$

where S_φ is a tree encoding of φ described below.

Suppose we are given a 3-CNF formula $\varphi = \bigwedge_{i=1}^{n} \bigvee_{j=1}^{3} c_{ij}$, where c_{ij} is a literal and in each clause all three literals are different. The tree encoding, S_φ, is best explained on a concrete example. A formula $(x_1 \vee \neg x_3 \vee x_4) \wedge (x_2 \vee x_3 \vee \neg x_4)$ is encoded as

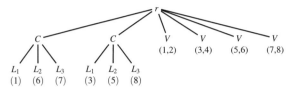

Each V node has two attribute values encoding a variable and its negation with two different values. For example $V(1,2)$ indicates that x_1 is encoded by the data value '1' and $\neg x_1$ by '2'. Also for each clause in the formula we have a C node that has three children labeled L_1, L_2, L_3. The L_i node holds the data value encoding the ith literal in the clause. In the example above, the second literal of the first clause is $\neg x_3$ and hence the data value of L_1 under the middle C node is '6'.

Let us first see that disjunction in schemas leads to intractability.

Proposition 13.4 *There is a schema mapping $\mathcal{M} \in \mathrm{SM}^{\mathrm{dtd}}(\downarrow,=)$ whose source DTD is nested-relational, the target DTD combines nested-relational rules and rules of the form $a \to b|c$, and a query $Q \in \mathbf{UCTQ}(\downarrow,=)$ so that $\mathrm{CERTAIN}_{\mathcal{M}}(Q)$ is CONP-complete.*

Proof Let D_s, the source DTD, be

$$r \to C^*V^* \qquad\qquad V: @a_1, @a_2$$
$$C \to L_1L_2L_3 \qquad\qquad L_i: @b$$

where $i = 1,2,3$. The target DTD D_t is defined as

$$r \to C^*V^* \qquad\qquad V: @a_1, @a_2$$
$$C \to L_1L_2L_3 \qquad\qquad L_i: @b$$
$$L_i \to K \mid N$$

where $i = 1,2,3$. The st-tgds Σ_{st} simply copy the tree S_φ in the target, guessing a K-node or an N-node under each L_i-node:

$$r/C[L_1(x), L_2(y), L_3(z)] \to r/C[L_1(x), L_2(y), L_3(z)],$$
$$r/V(x,y) \to r/V(x,y).$$

K means that the literal is set to `true`, N means it is set to `false`. Now we need to check that either a variable and its negation is set to `true`, or there is a clause with all literals set to `false`. This is done by the following query:

$$Q = \bigcup_{i,j} \exists x \exists y \, r\big[V(x,y), C/L_i(x)/K, C/L_j(y)/K\big] \, \cup \, r/C[L_1/N, L_2/N, L_3/N].$$

It is easy to verify that $certain_{\mathcal{M}}(Q, S_\varphi)$ is false iff φ is satisfiable.   □

Next, we show that setting a fixed number of children (greater than 1) with the same label can lead to intractability.

Proposition 13.5 *There is a schema mapping $\mathcal{M} \in \mathrm{SM}^{\mathrm{dtd}}(\downarrow,=)$ whose source DTD is nested-relational, the target DTD has nested-relational rules except one of the form $a \rightarrow bbb$, and a query $Q \in \mathbf{CTQ}(\downarrow,=)$ so that $\mathrm{CERTAIN}_{\mathcal{M}}(Q)$ is CONP-complete.*

Proof This time, the mapping itself is defined so that a solution for S_{φ} corresponds to a selection of (at least) one literal for each clause in φ. The query only asks if the selection contains a variable and its negation. Thus the existence of a solution falsifying the query implies the existence of a well-defined (partial) assignment that satisfies the formula φ.

The source DTD D_s is as in the proof of Proposition 13.4, and the target DTD D_t is:

$$r \rightarrow C^*V^* \qquad\qquad V:@a_1,@a_2$$
$$C \rightarrow LLL \qquad\qquad L:@b$$
$$L \rightarrow K?$$

The st-tgds Σ_{st} are:

$$r/C[L_1(x),L_2(y),L_3(z)] \rightarrow r/C[L(x),L(y),L(z),L/K],$$
$$r/V(x,y) \rightarrow r/V(x,y).$$

Essentially, we copy S_{φ} in the target, and with a K-child we indicate the chosen literals. As we demand that in each clause at least one literal be chosen, a solution gives a valuation satisfying the formula, provided that we have chosen consistently. This is verified by the query, which is defined as

$$\exists x \exists y\, r\big[V(x,y),C/L(x)/K,C/L(y)/K\big].$$

Clearly, the query is true if a variable and its negation are chosen. $\qquad\square$

The examples in the two propositions above involve a lot of guessing on where patterns could be put in a target tree. If the mapping is specific enough, this is not possible. In terms of schemas this restriction is well captured by the notion of nested-relational DTDs (for instance, there is no explicit disjunction). Thus, in the analysis of the remaining two parameters, st-tgds and queries, we will be assuming that schemas are given by nested-relational DTDs.

Hardness due to st-tgds

Even under nested-relational DTDs guessing can be enforced by st-tgds: allowing wild-card, descendant, or next-sibling leads to intractability.

Proposition 13.6 *There exist queries $Q_1,Q_2,Q_3 \in \mathbf{CTQ}(\downarrow,=)$ and mappings*

- *$\mathcal{M}_1 \in \mathrm{SM}^{\mathrm{nr}}(\downarrow,\_,=)$,*
- *$\mathcal{M}_2 \in \mathrm{SM}^{\mathrm{nr}}(\downarrow,\downarrow^+,=)$, and*
- *$\mathcal{M}_3 \in \mathrm{SM}^{\mathrm{nr}}(\downarrow,\rightarrow,=)$*

such that $\mathrm{CERTAIN}_{\mathcal{M}_i}(Q_i)$ is CONP-complete for $i=1,2,3$.

Proof The CONP upper bounds follow from Theorem 13.3. Below we prove the lower bound for the first claim. The proof for the second claim can be obtained by replacing $_-$ with $\downarrow^+$. The third claim is left for the reader (see Exercise 16.3).

The reduction is very similar to the one used in the proof of Proposition 13.5, only the selection of literals for each clause is done by permuting the data values in the L_i-children: we choose the literal encoded by the data value stored in L_1.

Thus, the source DTD D_s remains the same, the target DTD D_t is equal to D_s, the st-tgds Σ_{st} are

$$r/C[L_1(x), L_2(y), L_3(z)] \rightarrow r/C[\_(x), \_(y), \_(z)],$$
$$r/V(x,y) \rightarrow r/V(x,y),$$

and the query is $\exists x \exists y\, r[V(x,y), C/L_1(x), C/L_1(y)]$.

$\square$

Hardness due to queries

Let us now move to the analysis of the query language. One lesson learned from the relational case is that inequality in the query language leads to CONP-hardness. Since the usual translation from the relational setting to the XML setting produces mappings from $SM^{nr}(\downarrow, =)$, we immediately get CONP-hardness even for the simplest mappings (we have already seen that for more expressive mappings the problem may be undecidable).

Corollary 13.7 *There exist a mapping* $\mathscr{M} \in SM^{nr}(\downarrow, =)$ *and a query* $Q \in \mathbf{CTQ}(\downarrow, =, \neq)$ *such that* CERTAIN$_{\mathscr{M}}(Q)$ *is* CONP-*complete.*

Similarly, allowing any form of horizontal navigation in queries leads to intractability even for the simplest mappings.

Proposition 13.8 *There exist a schema mapping* $\mathscr{M} \in SM^{nr}(\downarrow)$, *and queries* $Q_1 \in \mathbf{CTQ}(\downarrow, \rightarrow, =)$ *and* $Q_2 \in \mathbf{CTQ}(\downarrow, \rightarrow^+, =)$, *such that both* CERTAIN$_{\mathscr{M}}(Q_1)$ *and* CERTAIN$_{\mathscr{M}}(Q_2)$ *are* CONP-*complete.*

Proof The proof is almost identical as for Proposition 13.6. The mapping uses the same D_s. The target DTD D_t is

$$r \rightarrow C^* V^* \qquad\qquad V : @a_1, @a_2$$
$$C \rightarrow L^* \qquad\qquad\quad L : @b$$

and the st-tgds Σ_{st} are

$$r/C[L_1(x), L_2(y), L_3(z)] \rightarrow r/C[L(x), L(y), L(z)],$$
$$r/V(x,y) \rightarrow r/V(x,y).$$

Intuitively, we choose the literal having more than two following siblings. Since each C node has at least three L children, clearly at least one literal is chosen for each clause. The query Q_1 is just $\exists x \exists y\, r[L(x,y), C[L(x) \rightarrow L \rightarrow L], C[L(y) \rightarrow L \rightarrow L]]$. Replacing $\rightarrow$ with $\rightarrow^+$ gives Q_2.

$\square$

We have seen that if we stick to child-based mappings, we cannot extend the query language. But perhaps we can find a more suitable class of mappings? Observe that the mapping in the proof above is very imprecise: the queries use horizontal navigation, and yet the mapping does not specify it at all. It might seem a good idea to demand more precision, for instance, by allowing only $a[b \rightarrow c]$ or $a[c \rightarrow b]$, but not $a[b,c]$. Unfortunately, the reduction above can be modified to obtain hardness for such mappings too (see Exercise 16.3). Sibling order in queries inevitably leads to intractability.

In summary, if certain answers are to be tractable, the following conditions must be imposed:

- the schemas should be simple (nested-relational),
- st-tgds should not use descendant, wildcard, nor next-sibling, and
- queries should not use horizontal navigation nor inequality.

13.4 Tractable query answering

The conclusions of the previous section indicate that, in order to have a chance to achieve tractable query answering in XML data exchange, we need to impose some restrictions:

- mappings should come from the class $\text{SM}^{\text{nr}}(\downarrow, =)$, and
- queries should come from the class $\textbf{UCTQ}(\Downarrow, =)$.

We now show that these restrictions indeed guarantee tractability of query answering.

Theorem 13.9 *For each mapping* $\mathcal{M} \in \text{SM}^{\text{nr}}(\downarrow, =)$ *and query* $Q \in \textbf{UCTQ}(\Downarrow, =)$, *the problem* CERTAIN$_{\mathcal{M}}(Q)$ *is solvable in polynomial time.*

In the rest of the section we describe the polynomial-time algorithm. The approach, just like in the relational case, is via universal solutions.

Recall that in data exchange the set of values that may appear in databases/documents is split into CONST, the set of constants (data values appearing in source documents), and VAR, the set of nulls (data values invented to fill in unspecified attributes on the target side).

In order to carry over the concept of universal solutions to the XML setting, we need the notion of homomorphisms between XML trees in which we do not care about the horizontal axes, since the mappings do not use them.

Definition 13.10 (Unordered homomorphism) For two XML trees

$$S = (U^S, \downarrow^S, \rightarrow^S, lab^S, (\rho_a^S)_{a \in Att}) \quad \text{and} \quad T = (U^T, \downarrow^T, \rightarrow^T, lab^T, (\rho_a^T)_{a \in Att}),$$

an *unordered homomorphism* $h : S \rightarrow T$ is a function mapping U^S to U^T and CONST $\cup$ VAR to CONST $\cup$ VAR such that

- h preserves the root, i.e., $h(\varepsilon) = \varepsilon$;
- h preserves the child relation, i.e., if $v \downarrow^S w$ then $h(v) \downarrow^S h(w)$;

- h preserves the labeling, i.e., $lab^S(v) = lab^T(h(v))$;
- h is the identity on CONST, i.e., $h(c) = c$ for all $c \in$ CONST;
- if v stores $\bar{t}$ then $h(v)$ stores $h(\bar{t})$, i.e., $\rho_a^T(h(v)) = h(\rho_a^S(v))$ for all $a \in Att$.

Now that we have the notion of homomorphism, universal solutions are defined just like in the relational case.

Definition 13.11 (Unordered universal solution)   A tree U is an *unordered universal solution* for a tree S under a mapping $\mathscr{M}$ if it is a solution for S, and for each other solution T there is an unordered homomorphism from U to T.

The following lemma carries over from the relational case.

Lemma 13.12   *If U is an unordered universal solution for a source tree S under a mapping $\mathscr{M}$, and $Q \in \mathbf{UCTQ}(\Downarrow, =)$, then for each tuple $\bar{a}$ of values in* CONST

$$\bar{a} \in certain_{\mathscr{M}}(Q, S) \iff \bar{a} \in Q(U).$$

Proof   One implication is obvious, as U is a solution itself. Let us focus on the other one. Take $\bar{a} \in Q(U)$. Let $\pi(\bar{x}, \bar{y})$ be a pattern such that $Q = \exists \bar{y} \, \pi(\bar{x}, \bar{y})$. Then $U \models \pi(\bar{a}, \bar{y})$. Let $h : \pi \to U$ be the witnessing homomorphism. We need to show that $T \models \pi(\bar{a}, \bar{y})$ for each solution T. By Definition 13.11, there exists a homomorphism $g : U \to T$. Since π uses no horizontal axes, the composition $h \circ g$ is a homomorphism from π to T that witnesses $T \models \pi(\bar{a}, \bar{y})$.   □

Fix a mapping $\mathscr{M} = (D_s, D_t, \Sigma_{st})$ and a source tree S. Recall the set of target requirements defined as

$$\Delta_{S, \mathscr{M}} = \{ \psi(\bar{a}, \bar{z}) \mid \varphi(\bar{x}, \bar{y}) \to \exists \bar{z} \, \psi(\bar{x}, \bar{z}) \in \Sigma_{st} \text{ and } S \models \varphi(\bar{a}, \bar{b}) \}$$

with variables renamed so that none is used in more than one pattern; the pattern $\delta_{S, \mathscr{M}}$ is obtained by taking the conjunction of all patterns from the modified $\Delta_{S, \mathscr{M}}$. By Lemma 12.1, a tree T conforming to the target schema is a solution for S if and only if $T \models \delta_{S, \mathscr{M}}$. This means that constructing a universal solution for S under the mapping $\mathscr{M} \in \mathrm{SM}^{nr}(\downarrow, =)$ amounts to finding a "universal" tree satisfying a child-only pattern π (with equalities) and conforming to a nested-relational DTD D. To this end we construct a pattern π' such that

- for every T, if $T \models D$ then $T \models \pi$ iff $T \models \pi'$,
- π' viewed as a tree conforms to D.

We construct this pattern by means of two operations: completion and merging.

We say that a pattern φ is *complete* with respect to a nested relational DTD D if each of its nodes has all the children required by the DTD. More precisely, a label τ is *missing* in a subpattern $\sigma(\bar{t})[\pi_1, \pi_2, \dots, \pi_k]$ if τ occurs in the production for σ as τ or τ^+, but no formula of the form $\tau[\lambda]$ occurs among the π_is. A pattern is complete if no label is missing in its subpatterns.

Completion simply extends the pattern with all missing labels and thus makes it complete. As the patterns use only $\downarrow$ and $=$, and DTDs are nested-relational, this can be done in a unique way. For a DTD D the operation cpl_D on pure patterns is defined inductively as

$$\text{cpl}_D\big(\sigma(\bar{t})[\pi_1, \pi_2, \ldots, \pi_k]\big) = \sigma(\bar{t})\Big[\text{cpl}_D\big(\pi_1\big), \text{cpl}_D\big(\pi_2\big), \ldots, \text{cpl}_D\big(\pi_k\big),$$

$$\text{cpl}_D\big(\tau_1(\bar{z}_1)\big), \text{cpl}_D\big(\tau_2(\bar{z}_2)\big), \ldots, \text{cpl}_D\big(\tau_m(\bar{z}_m)\big)\Big],$$

where $\tau_1, \ldots, \tau_m$ are the missing labels and $\bar{z}_1, \bar{z}_2, \ldots, \bar{z}_m$ are tuples of fresh variables. (If $\bar{t}$ is empty and σ has r attributes, replace $\bar{t}$ with a tuple of fresh variables $z_1, z_2, \ldots, z_r$.) Since D is nonrecursive, the operation terminates and returns a pattern at most single-exponential in the size of D. Note that different occurrences of τ are completed with different variables. We write $\text{cpl}_D(\pi \wedge \alpha)$ for $\text{cpl}_D(\pi) \wedge \alpha$.

It is fairly easy to see that the completed formula is equivalent to the original one.

Lemma 13.13 *Let D be a nested-relational DTD, and let π be a tree pattern. For each $T \models D$ and each $\bar{a}$*

$$T \models \pi(\bar{a}) \quad \text{iff} \quad T \models \text{cpl}_D\pi(\bar{a}, \bar{c}) \text{ for some } \bar{c}.$$

The aim of *merging* is to merge all subpatterns that are always mapped to the same node in trees conforming to the given DTD. More precisely, for a given π it produces a pattern π' such that

- π is equivalent to π' over trees conforming to D,
- π' admits an injective homomorphism into a tree conforming to D (or is not satisfiable).

Fix a nested-relational DTD D. The pattern $\text{mrg}_D(\pi)$ is built inductively, with new equalities (induced by merging nodes) added to the global set E along the way. If at some point we arrive at an inconsistency between π and D, we output an unsatisfiable pattern $\perp$. In the beginning the set E is empty.

To obtain $\text{mrg}_D(\sigma[\pi_1, \ldots, \pi_k])$ proceed as follows.

1. Return $\perp$ whenever $\pi_i = \tau(\bar{t})[\lambda]$ for some π_i and a label τ not occurring in the production for σ.
2. For each τ such that $\sigma \to \ldots \tau \ldots$ or $\sigma \to \ldots \tau? \ldots$ merge all the π_i's starting with τ:
   2a. remove all π_i's of the form $\tau(\bar{t})[\lambda]$, say, $\pi_{i_j} = \tau(\bar{t}_j)[\lambda_j]$ for $1 \leq j \leq m$,
   2b. add a single pattern $\text{mrg}_D(\tau(\bar{t}_1)[\lambda_1, \ldots, \lambda_m])$,
   2c. add to E equalities $\bar{t}_1 = \bar{t}_j$ for $2 \leq j \leq m$ (where $\bar{s} = \bar{t}$ stands for the conjunction of $s_1 = t_1, s_2 = t_2, \ldots, s_d = t_d$).
3. Replace all the remaining π_i with $\text{mrg}_D(\pi_i)$.
4. Return the obtained pattern and the equalities from E.

For a pattern with equalities $\pi \wedge \alpha$, let $\text{mrg}_D(\pi \wedge \alpha) = \text{mrg}_D(\pi) \wedge \alpha$.

Again, proving that the new formula satisfies the required properties is straightforward.

Lemma 13.14 *Let D be a nested-relational DTD, and let π be a tree pattern.*

1. For each $T \models D$ and for all $\bar{a}$

$$T \models \pi(\bar{a}) \quad \text{iff} \quad T \models \mathrm{mrg}_D\pi(\bar{a}).$$

2. If π is satisfiable with respect to D, then $\mathrm{mrg}_D(\pi)$ admits an injective homomorphism into a tree conforming to D.

The property we postulated follows.

Lemma 13.15 *Let φ be a pattern satisfiable with respect to a nested-relational DTD D.*

- *For every $T \models D$ and every $\bar{a}$*

$$T \models \varphi(\bar{a}) \quad \text{iff} \quad T \models \mathrm{mrg}_D(\mathrm{cpl}_D\varphi)(\bar{a},\bar{c}) \text{ for some } \bar{c}.$$

- *$\mathrm{mrg}_D(\mathrm{cpl}_D\varphi)$ viewed as a tree conforms to D.*

Let us now return to the construction of a universal solution. Recall the pattern $\delta_{S,\mathscr{M}}$ combining all target requirements. Define

$$\eta_{S,\mathscr{M}} = \mathrm{mrg}_{D_t}(\mathrm{cpl}_{D_t}\delta_{S,\mathscr{M}}).$$

Without loss of generality, we can assume that $\eta_{S,\mathscr{M}}$ is a pure tree pattern. Indeed, if an equality says that $v = t$, replace each occurrence of v with t, and remove this equality. If at some point we obtain an equality between two different constants, the pattern is not satisfiable and can be replaced with $\bot$.

Lemma 13.16 *For every mapping $\mathscr{M}$ from $\mathrm{SM}^{\mathrm{nr}}(\downarrow,=)$ and source tree S, the pattern $\eta_{S,\mathscr{M}}$ viewed as a tree is a universal solution (unless $\eta_{S,\mathscr{M}} = \bot$).*

Proof Suppose that $\eta_{S,\mathscr{M}} \neq \bot$ and let U be $\eta_{S,\mathscr{M}}$ viewed as a tree, with variables interpreted as new data values (nulls). Obviously $U \models \eta_{S,\mathscr{M}}$. By Lemma 13.15, $U \models \delta_{S,\mathscr{M}}$ and $U \models D_s$. Using Lemma 12.1 we conclude that U is a solution.

To show that it is universal, take some solution T. By Lemma 13.15, $T \models \eta_{S,\mathscr{M}}(\bar{z})$ and so there exists a homomorphism from $\eta_{S,\mathscr{M}}$ to T. As U and $\eta_{S,\mathscr{M}}$ are isomorphic, this gives a homomorphism from U to T, and proves universality of U. $\square$

Now we can present the polynomial-time algorithm. It works as follows:

- first, it computes $\eta_{S,\mathscr{M}}$;
- then it evaluates Q over $\eta_{S,\mathscr{M}}$; and
- finally, it removes tuples containing nulls from the result.

Its correctness is an immediate consequence of Lemmas 13.16 and 13.12.

14

XML-to-XML queries

So far we have only considered queries returning sets of tuples, but queries in practical XML languages, like XQuery, return documents, i.e., XML trees rather than sets of tuples. In this chapter we introduce a simple XML-to-XML query language and examine the challenges it brings to data exchange tasks. It turns out that the semantics of certain answers has to be reinvented, as there is no natural analog of the intersection of a set of trees. Under the new semantics, certain answers can be computed owing to the existence of finite bases for the sets of solutions. While the complexity could be high in general, for some classes of mappings the problem can be solved efficiently. Specifically, it can be solved efficiently for the same child-based mappings that led to efficient algorithms for building solutions and answering tuple queries.

14.1 XML-to-XML query language TQL

As in many functional and database query languages, including FLWR (for-let-where-return) expressions of XQuery, the key construct of the language we use is a comprehension. It is of the form

$$\text{for } \pi(\bar{x}) \text{ return } q(\bar{x})$$

where $\pi(\bar{x})$ is a pattern and $q(\bar{x})$ defines a forest. We shall formally define both the class of patterns we use and forest queries below. For now, we explain the class of queries informally, and give a few examples.

The semantics of the comprehension above is this: given an input tree T, for each tuple $\bar{a}$ such that $T \models \pi(\bar{a})$, we construct the forest $q(\bar{a})$ and take the union of all such forests as the answer to the query. To make a forest into a tree, we just put a common root above it. Forest expressions can involve subqueries as well, for example for $\pi(\bar{x})$ return $\big(\text{for } \pi'(\bar{x}, \bar{z}) \text{ return } q'(\bar{x}, \bar{z})\big)$. Then, for each $\pi(\bar{a})$ true in an input T, we construct the forest for $\pi'(\bar{a}, \bar{z})$ return $q'(\bar{a}, \bar{z})$ and take the union of these as the answer to the query over T.

Example 14.1 Consider the tree $T_{countries}$ shown in Figure 10.1, representing a set of countries with a list of subelements storing their successive rulers.

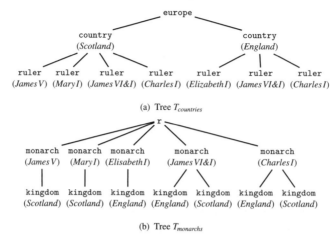

(a) Tree $T_{countries}$

(b) Tree $T_{monarchs}$

Figure 14.1 A TQL example: $T_{monarchs} = Q_2(T_{countries})$ for Q_2 in Example 14.1

Suppose that we want to list countries ruled by Charles I. This can be done with the following query Q_1:

$$\texttt{r}\big[\texttt{for europe/country}(x)/\texttt{ruler}(\textit{“Charles I”})\ \texttt{return}$$
$$\texttt{country}(x)\big].$$

The next query will involve nesting. Suppose we want to output the tree $T_{monarchs}$ given in Figure 14.1: it restructures the input by combining, for each monarch, all his/her kingdoms. The TQL query for this transformation is $Q_2 = r[q]$, where q is the following forest query:

$$\texttt{for europe//ruler}(x)\ \texttt{return}$$
$$\texttt{monarch}(x)\big[\texttt{for r/country}(y)/\texttt{ruler}(x)\ \texttt{return}$$
$$\texttt{kingdom}(y)\big].$$

As these examples indicate, patterns in queries must use constants in addition to variables. In general, we shall only use patterns with child and descendant axes, wildcard, and constants. We denote the class of such patterns by $\Pi_p(\textsc{Const}, \Downarrow, =)$ (i.e., the set of pure patterns from $\Pi(\Downarrow, =)$ that can reuse variables and use constants). Formally, these are given by the grammar below:

$$
\begin{array}{rcll}
\pi & := & \ell(\bar{x})[\lambda] \mid \ell(\bar{x}) & \text{(patterns)} \\
\lambda & := & \pi \mid //\pi \mid \lambda, \lambda & \text{(sets)}
\end{array}
\tag{14.1}
$$

where tuples $\bar{x}$ can mix both variables and constants from $\textsc{Const}$. We sometimes write $\pi(\bar{a}, \bar{x})$ to be explicit about constants and variables used in patterns; of course $\bar{a}$, $\bar{b}$, etc., will stand for tuples of constants, and $\bar{x}$, $\bar{y}$, etc., for tuples of variables.

Now we are ready to see the formal definition of TQL.

$$
\begin{array}{lll}
q(\bar{x}) & ::= & \varepsilon \\
& | & \ell(\bar{a},\bar{x}')[q'(\bar{x}'')] & \bar{x}' \text{ and } \bar{x}'' \\
& | & q'(\bar{x}'),q''(\bar{x}'') & \text{are subtuples of } \bar{x} \\
& | & \texttt{for } \pi(\bar{x},\bar{y}) \texttt{ return } q'(\bar{x},\bar{y}) & \bar{y} \text{ is disjoint from } \bar{x}
\end{array}
$$

Figure 14.2 The syntax of forest queries

Definition 14.2 A TQL query Q is an expression of the form

$$\ell(\bar{a})[q],$$

where q is a forest query without free variables. The syntax of forest queries is given in Figure 14.2; patterns in comprehensions are required to come from $\pi \in \Pi_p(\text{CONST}, \Downarrow, =)$.

For a tree T and a query $Q = \ell(\bar{a})[q]$, we define $Q(T)$ as the tree $\ell(\bar{a})[[\![q]\!]_T]$, i.e., the forest $[\![q]\!]_T$ under root $\ell(\bar{a})$.

Forest queries include the empty forest (ε), trees ($(\ell(\bar{a},\bar{x}')[q'])$), unions of forests ($q',q''$), and comprehensions (for π return q'). By a union $F \cup F'$ of forests we mean the forest obtained by putting together F and F' (i.e., it may contain more than one copy of a tree). By $\ell(\bar{a})[F]$ we mean a tree obtained by attaching a common ℓ-labeled root with values $\bar{a}$ on top of the forest F.

We next define the semantics of forest queries. Even though in the definition of TQL queries (i.e., $\ell(\bar{a})[q]$) we use forest queries q without free variables, in general one can have forest queries with free variables occurring as subqueries. For instance, the subquery of query Q_2 in Example 14.1 on page 193 has x as a free variable. Hence, we need to define semantics of forest queries with free variables too.

Specifically, if we have a forest query $q(\bar{x})$, a tree T, and a valuation $v : \bar{x} \to \text{CONST} \cup \text{VAR}$ of free variables, we define $[\![q(\bar{x})]\!]_{T,v}$ as the semantics of q in T under the valuation v. This is done by the following rules:

$$
\begin{array}{rcl}
[\![\varepsilon]\!]_{T,v} & = & \varepsilon \\
[\![\ell(\bar{a},\bar{x}')[q'(\bar{x}'')]]\!]_{T,v} & = & \ell(\bar{a},v(\bar{x}'))[[\![q']\!]_{T,v}] \\
[\![q'(\bar{x}),q''(\bar{x}'')]\!]_{T,v} & = & [\![q']\!]_{T,v} \cup [\![q'']\!]_{T,v} \\
[\![\texttt{for } \pi(\bar{x},\bar{y}) \texttt{ return } q'(\bar{x},\bar{y})]\!]_{T,v} & = & \bigcup\{[\![q']\!]_{T,(v,v')} \mid T \models \pi(v(\bar{x}),v'(\bar{y}))\}.
\end{array}
$$

In the last rule, by (v,v') we mean a valuation that acts as v on $\bar{x}$ and as v' on $\bar{y}$.

Note that according to this semantics, TQL queries can be applied not only to ground trees (i.e., trees in which all data values are constants from CONST), but also to trees with nulls, i.e., trees whose data values come from CONST $\cup$ VAR. This will provide an analog of naïve evaluation of queries.

It is easy to see that data complexity of TQL queries is polynomial.

Proposition 14.3   *For each* TQL *query Q and a tree T, computing $Q(T)$ can be done in time polynomial in the size of T.*

As we have learned, incompleteness of information cannot be avoided in data exchange: the database we query is only partly defined via source data and mappings between schemas. Semantically, an incomplete description of a database is a set $\mathscr{D}$ of completely described databases that it can represent. If we have a query Q returning sets of tuples, then certain answers are obtained by taking tuples that belong to the result no matter which complete database in $\mathscr{D}$ is used: that is, $certain(Q, \mathscr{D}) = \bigcap \{Q(D) \mid D \in \mathscr{D}\}$. But our queries return trees, rather than sets of tuples. What is a natural analog of certain answers then?

In general, we want to define $certain(Q, \mathscr{T})$ – the certain answers to a query Q returning trees over a set $\mathscr{T}$ of XML trees. This set of trees could be, for instance, a set of solutions (target instances) in data exchange. For this we need an analog of the intersection operator applied to $Q(\mathscr{T}) = \{Q(T) \mid T \in \mathscr{T}\}$. What could it be? The first idea is to take the maximal tree contained in all of trees in $Q(\mathscr{T})$. But this may fail as such a tree need not be unique: if T_1, T_2, and T_3 shown in Figure 14.3 are in $Q(\mathscr{T})$, there are three maximal trees subsumed by them shown in part (d) of the figure.

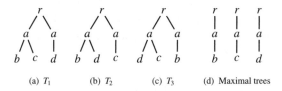

(a) T_1 (b) T_2 (c) T_3 (d) Maximal trees

Figure 14.3 Why the "maximal subsumed tree" approach fails

One might be tempted to combine these trees in (d) into one, but this is not satisfactory either. We have a choice of merging the roots, or the a-nodes, but either way the resulting tree is not subsumed by T_1, T_2 and T_3; in what sense, then, is it a certain answer? And so far we have not considered *data values*. What if in T_1, T_2, and T_3, the left a carries value "1" and the right a carries "2"? This is the situation depicted in Figure 14.4 on page 198. Then in fact, none of the three trees shown in (d) above is among the subsumed trees, and we lose the certain knowledge about the grandchildren of the root.

Thus, even in a very simple example, it is not completely clear what the natural notion of certain answers is. In the next section we develop a theory of certain answers for XML-to-XML queries, based on the concepts of theory and definition borrowed from mathematical logic.

14.2 Notion of certain answers

The idea of certain answers is to extract the maximum knowledge from answers $Q(D)$, as D ranges over some collection of databases $\mathscr{D}$. What it means precisely, depends on the *logical language* we use for expressing the knowledge. For instance, suppose we use the *language of ground conjunctive queries*: that is, conjunctions of atoms $R(\bar{a})$, where R is a relation, and $\bar{a}$ is a tuple of constants. Then $\bigcap Q(\mathscr{D})$ represents the maximum knowledge we can extract from $Q(\mathscr{D})$ with respect to this language. This is the familiar notion of certain answers.

However, if we use the more expressive *language of conjunctive queries*, we can extract additional knowledge from $Q(\mathscr{D})$. For instance, suppose $Q(\mathscr{D})$ consists of two instances:

$$\{R(a,a), R(b,c)\} \quad \text{and} \quad \{R(a,a), R(d,c)\}.$$

Then the conjunctive query $R(a,a) \wedge \exists x R(x,c)$ tells us more about $Q(\mathscr{D})$ than the intersection of the instances above, which is just $R(a,a)$. This certain knowledge about $Q(\mathscr{D})$ would be traditionally presented as a naïve table: that is, a table with variables (nulls). The naïve table corresponding to $R(a,a) \wedge \exists x R(x,c)$ is simply $\{R(a,a), R(x,c)\}$. Notice that the class of databases that satisfy $R(a,a) \wedge \exists x R(x,c)$ is not equal to $Q(\mathscr{D})$: every valuation of x in $\{R(a,a), R(x,c)\}$ gives such a database. Nevertheless, conjunctive queries are not able to extract any more knowledge about $Q(\mathscr{D})$, and thus narrow down the set of described databases. The formula $R(a,a) \wedge \exists x R(x,c)$ is as close to a definition of $Q(\mathscr{D})$ as possible within the language of conjunctive queries. Let us formalize these intuitions.

We define the notion of a *max-description* of a set $\mathscr{D}$ of databases that, in a given language, expresses the information we can infer with certainty from $\mathscr{D}$. Certain answers to queries are then a special case of max-descriptions, applied to sets $\{Q(D)\}$ as D ranges over a collection of databases.

To explain this notion, assume that $\mathscr{L}$ is a logical formalism in which we express properties of databases from $\mathscr{D}$ (e.g., conjunctive queries, or ground conjunctive queries such as $R(a,a)$). A set Φ of formulae of $\mathscr{L}$ defines a set of databases, called models of Φ and denoted $\mathrm{Mod}(\Phi)$, consisting of all databases satisfying each formula in Φ:

$$\mathrm{Mod}(\Phi) \; = \; \{D \mid D \models \varphi \text{ for every } \varphi \in \Phi\}.$$

To describe $\mathscr{D}$ fully in $\mathscr{L}$ we would need its $\mathscr{L}$-definition: a finite set Φ of $\mathscr{L}$-formulae such that $\mathscr{D} = \mathrm{Mod}(\Phi)$. This is not always achievable, so instead we settle for the next best thing, which is an $\mathscr{L}$-definition of the set of models of *certain knowledge* about $\mathscr{D}$ expressed in $\mathscr{L}$.

This certain $\mathscr{L}$-knowledge of the class $\mathscr{D}$, called $\mathscr{L}$-*theory of* $\mathscr{D}$, is the set of all formulae from $\mathscr{L}$ satisfied in all databases from $\mathscr{D}$:

$$\mathrm{Th}_{\mathscr{L}}(\mathscr{D}) \; = \; \{\varphi \in \mathscr{L} \mid D \models \varphi \text{ for every } D \in \mathscr{D}\}.$$

The most precise (finite) description of $\mathscr{D}$ we can express in $\mathscr{L}$ is a finite definition of $\mathrm{Mod}(\mathrm{Th}_{\mathscr{L}}(\mathscr{D}))$, i.e., a finite set Φ of formulae of $\mathscr{L}$ such that

$$\mathrm{Mod}(\Phi) = \mathrm{Mod}(\mathrm{Th}_{\mathscr{L}}(\mathscr{D})).$$

Let us now apply this general definition to sets $\mathscr{T}$ of XML trees. Since our setting always includes a schema, we will be making the following assumptions about such sets $\mathscr{T}$:

- all trees in them are labeled by some fixed alphabet, and
- nodes with the same label have tuples of attributes of the same length.

These assumptions can be easily avoided but we use them for now as they keep the notation simple.

A natural analog of naïve tables are trees with (reused) variables. In this role they are simply pure child-only patterns using constants and reusing variables We shall write $\Pi_p(\text{CONST},\downarrow,=)$ for such patterns. They are the same ones as those in (14.1) but without the $//\pi$ case. They will serve the role of the language $\mathscr{L}$.

Thus, for XML trees, the notions of models and theories are defined as follows. For a set of patterns B, we have

$$\text{Mod}(B) = \{T \mid T \models \pi \text{ for every } \pi \in B.$$

For a set $\mathscr{T}$ of XML trees we define its theory $\text{Th}(\mathscr{T})$ as

$$\text{Th}(\mathscr{T}) = \{\pi \in \Pi_p(\text{CONST},\downarrow,=) \mid T \models \pi \text{ for all } T \in \mathscr{T}\}.$$

This theory provides the certain knowledge (in the language $\Pi_p(\text{CONST},\downarrow,=)$) that can be extracted from $\mathscr{T}$. Max-descriptions are then the closest we can get to defining $\mathscr{T}$ in $\Pi_p(\text{CONST},\downarrow,=)$.

Definition 14.4 Let $\mathscr{T}$ be a set of XML trees. A pattern $\pi \in \Pi_p(\text{CONST},\downarrow,=)$ is a *max-description* of $\mathscr{T}$ if

$$\text{Mod}(\pi) = \text{Mod}(\text{Th}(\mathscr{T})).$$

We now illustrate the notion of max-descriptions by revisiting the example shown in Figure 14.3. A max-description for them is obtained by merging all the trees in part (d) of that figure at the root. We also asked about a modification of the example where the a-nodes carry data values, as shown in Figure 14.4. Then a max-description of $\{T_1', T_2', T_3'\}$ is the tree in part (d) of the figure. It has three occurrences of variables and preserves the certain knowledge about the grandchildren of the root.

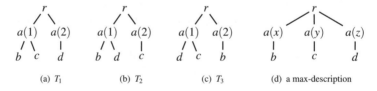

(a) T_1 (b) T_2 (c) T_3 (d) a max-description

Figure 14.4 Why max-descriptions work

Now that we understand the notion of a proper representation of certain information contained in a set of trees, we apply this notion to answering XML queries that can produce trees. Suppose we have a query Q that takes trees as inputs and returns trees. Our goal is to define certain answers to such a query over a set $\mathscr{T}$ of trees. We define such certain answers as max-descriptions of the set $Q(\mathscr{T}) = \{Q(T) \mid T \in \mathscr{T}\}$.

Definition 14.5 Given a query Q and a set $\mathcal{T}$ of trees, a pattern π is a *certain answer to Q over $\mathcal{T}$* if it is a max-description of $Q(\mathcal{T})$.

Viewed as formulae, all max-descriptions of a family $\mathcal{T}$ are equivalent. But if they are to play the role of certain answers to XML-to-XML queries, we need to view them as XML trees as well–and then they are all different. What is *the* certain answer then?

To find canonical forms of max-descriptions we need to recall the notion of homomor-phisms between XML trees and patterns. As patterns provide a syntax for trees, each pattern $\pi \in \Pi_p(\text{CONST}, \downarrow, =)$ can be viewed as a tree T_π (with variables): the tree associ-ated with $\ell(\bar{\alpha})[\pi_1, \ldots, \pi_n]$ has an ℓ-labeled root with attributes $\bar{\alpha}$ and subtrees $T_{\pi_1}, \ldots, T_{\pi_n}$, where T_ε is the empty tree. Similarly, a tree T can be viewed as a child-only pattern with constants.

Using this correspondence, we can naturally extend the notion of homomorphism be-tween patterns and trees, defined in Section 11.1, to trees with variables or equivalently child-only patterns with constants. A homomorphism maps nodes to nodes and variables to constants and variables, preserving the root, the child relation and the labeling, and if u stores a tuple $\bar{\alpha}$, then $h(u)$ stores $h(\bar{\alpha})$ (of course h extends to constants as the identity).

Recall that $T \models \pi$ iff there exists a homomorphism from π to T (Lemma 11.5). In particular, $\text{Th}(\mathcal{T})$ is the set of patterns π such that there is a homomorphism from π to every tree $T \in \mathcal{T}$. Then we have the following characterization of max-descriptions, which confirms the intuition of max-descriptions as maximum extractable information from the certain knowledge we have about $\mathcal{T}$.

Theorem 14.6 *A pattern π is a max-description of $\mathcal{T}$ iff it belongs to $\text{Th}(\mathcal{T})$ and every pattern in $\text{Th}(\mathcal{T})$ has a homomorphism into it.*

Proof Suppose that $\pi \in \text{Th}(\mathcal{T})$, and every pattern from $\text{Th}(\mathcal{T})$ has a homomorphism into π. We need to show that every tree satisfying π satisfies every pattern from $\text{Th}(\mathcal{T})$. Pick a tree T which satisfies π. By Lemma 11.5, there is a homomorphism $h : \pi \to T$. Pick a pattern π' from $\text{Th}(\mathcal{T})$. By assumption, there exists a homomorphism $h' : \pi' \to \pi$. Hence, $h \circ h' : \pi' \to T$ is a homomorphism. By Lemma 11.5, T satisfies π'.

Conversely, suppose that π is a max-description of $\mathcal{T}$. Then of course π belongs to $\text{Th}(\mathcal{T})$, and we only need to check that every pattern in $\text{Th}(\mathcal{T})$ has a homomorphism into π. Take a pattern $\pi' \in \text{Th}(\mathcal{T})$. It is obvious that π (viewed as a tree) satisfies π (viewed as a pattern). Hence, π satisfies π' as well. Then, there is a homomorphism $h : \pi' \to \pi$. □

By Theorem 14.6 every two max-descriptions π and π' of a set of trees are *homomorphi-cally equivalent*, as there are homomorphisms $\pi \to \pi'$ and $\pi' \to \pi$. This has two important consequences. The first one is that there is a natural canonical representative of all these max-descriptions: the core.

In Section 6.4 we learned that homomorphically equivalent structures have isomorphic cores. This means that all max-descriptions have the same core, which leads to the follow-ing definition.

Definition 14.7   The core of all max-descriptions of $\mathcal{T}$ is called the *core-description of* $\mathcal{T}$ and denoted by $\Box\mathcal{T}$. The *core-certain answer* to Q over $\mathcal{T}$ is $\Box Q(\mathcal{T})$.

Technically speaking, the core-description is the core of the trees associated with the max-descriptions, but we can always view it as a pattern. Furthermore, the core-description is always a max-description: being a subpattern of a max-description, $\Box\mathcal{T}$ is satisfied in every tree in $\mathcal{T}$, and since it is a homomorphic image of a max-description, every pattern from $\text{Th}(\mathcal{T})$ can be mapped into it. Thus the definition gives the canonical certain answer.

Moreover, if we restrict our attention to cores only, or equivalently, quotient the set of trees by the homomorphic equivalence , the following relation is a partial order:

$$T \leq T' \text{ if and only if there is a homomorphism from } T \text{ to } T'.$$

By Theorem 14.6 certain answers could then be defined simply as greatest lower bounds.

Corollary 14.8   *A pattern π is a max-description of $\mathcal{T}$ if it is the greatest lower bound of $\mathcal{T}$ with respect to the order $\leq$.*

The canonical certain answer comes at a certain computational cost. Recall that DP is the class of problems which amount to solving a problem in NP and a (different) problem in CONP. This class *contains* both NP and CONP; it should not be confused with NP $\cap$ CONP.

Proposition 14.9   *Checking whether π' is the core of π is in DP. Moreover, there is a fixed pattern π_0 such that checking whether π_0 is the core of π is NP-complete.*

Proof   First check if π' is a core, this is done in CONP. Then we check if there is a homomorphism from π to π', and an embedding of π' into π. Both conditions can be checked in NP.

A simple reduction from 3-colorability shows NP-hardness: let π_G be a pattern with a child $e(u,v)$ under the root for every edge of the given graph G and let π be obtained by merging π_G and $\pi' = r[e(x,y),e(y,x),e(y,z),e(z,y),e(x,z),e(z,y)]$ at the root; it is easy to see that G is 3-colorable iff π' is the core of π. $\Box$

Computing cores can be expensive, but the second consequence of homomorphic equivalence comes to the rescue: often it does not matter which certain answer we chose, because they are indistinguishable to pattern queries and TQL queries.

Proposition 14.10   *Let T_1 and T_2 be certain answers to Q over $\mathcal{T}$. Then they cannot be distinguished by TQL queries: $Q'(T_1) = Q'(T_2)$ for each $Q' \in$ TQL.*

Proof   In fact, we show more, namely that $T_1 \models \pi$ if and only if $T_2 \models \pi$ for each $\pi \in \Pi_p(\text{CONST}, \Downarrow, =)$. If $T_1 \models \pi$, there is a witnessing homomorphism $h \colon \pi \to T_1$. Since T_1 and T_2 are homomorphically equivalent, there is also a homomorphism $h' \colon T_1 \to T_2$. Composing h and h' we get a homomorphism $h' \circ h \colon \pi \to T_2$ witnessing that $T_2 \models \pi$.

The proposition now follows from this claim by induction on the structure of Q'. $\Box$

This means that if the certain answer is to be processed further within the same framework, based on tree patterns and TQL queries, our only concern should be its size.

What is then the complexity of finding a max-description, and how big can it be? In particular, how big can the smallest of them, i.e., the core-description, be?

Let $|T|$ be the number of nodes in T, and let $\|\mathcal{T}\|$ be $\sum_{T \in \mathcal{T}} |T|$. We show next that we can compute a max-description of $\mathcal{T}$ in EXPTIME in general, and in PTIME if the number of trees in $\mathcal{T}$ is fixed. Exercise 16.3 shows that even core descriptions can be exponential in the number of trees in $\mathcal{T}$.

Theorem 14.11 *Let $\mathcal{T} = \{T_1, \ldots, T_n\}$ be a finite set of XML trees. A max-description of $\mathcal{T}$ is computable in time polynomial in $\left(\frac{\|\mathcal{T}\|}{n} \right)^n$.*

Proof For simplicity assume that every node has a single attribute; extension to the general case is straightforward.

The pattern we are going to construct is a sort of consistent product of $T_1, \ldots, T_n$. Proceed as follows. For the root, labeled with r, take the sequence $(\varepsilon, \ldots, \varepsilon)$, i.e., the sequence of roots of $T_1, \ldots, T_n$. Then iteratively, under every node $(v_1, \ldots, v_n)$ put a new node $(w_1, \ldots, w_n)$ for every sequence $w_1, \ldots, w_n$ such that w_i is a child of v_i in T_i, and all w_i's are labeled with the same letter σ. Label the node σ and put a fresh variable in the attribute slot. If for some node $\bar{v} = (v_1, \ldots, v_n)$ some v_i is a leaf, $\bar{v}$ is a leaf as well.

Define $A(v_1, \ldots, v_n) = (a_1, \ldots, a_n)$ where a_i is the data value attached to the node v_i. For every node $\bar{v}$ such that $A(\bar{v}) = (c, \ldots, c)$ for a constant c, replace the variable in $\bar{v}$ with the constant c. For the remaining nodes, whenever $A(\bar{v}) = A(\bar{w})$, replace the variable in $\bar{w}$ with the variable in $\bar{v}$.

The constructed formula is clearly satisfied in every T_i. Let us see that it is indeed a max-description. Suppose that π' is satisfied in every T_i. Let h_i be a homomorphism from π' to T_i. It is easy to see that $h = (h_1, \ldots, h_n)$ is a homomorphism from π' to π.

The complexity of the algorithm is polynomial in the size of the output pattern, which is bounded by $\prod_{i=1}^n |T_i| \le \left(\frac{\|\mathcal{T}\|}{n} \right)^n$ (by the inequality between the arithmetic and the geometric means for nonnegative numbers). $\square$

14.3 Certain answers for TQL queries

When we try to compute certain answers to a query Q over a set $\mathcal{T}$ of trees, $\mathcal{T}$ is usually infinite. Hence, we need a finite representation of it. Recall also that finiteness guarantees existence of max-descriptions. Such a finite representation comes in the form of a *basis* $\mathcal{B}$ of $\mathcal{T}$, which is a set of patterns. Recall that each pattern can be viewed as a tree, so when we write $\mathcal{B} \subseteq \mathcal{T}$, we mean that for every $\pi \in \mathcal{B}$, the tree associated to π is in $\mathcal{T}$.

Definition 14.12 A *basis* for a set of trees $\mathcal{T}$ is a set of patterns $\mathcal{B} \subseteq \mathcal{T}$ such that each pattern in $\mathcal{T}$ is a model of some pattern from $\mathcal{B}$:

$$\mathcal{T} \subseteq \bigcup \{\mathrm{Mod}(\pi) \mid \pi \in \mathcal{B}\}.$$

The crucial property of a basis is that it preserves max-descriptions.

Lemma 14.13   *If $\mathscr{B}$ is a basis of $\mathscr{T}$, then the sets of max-descriptions of $\mathscr{T}$ and $\mathscr{B}$ coincide.*

Proof   Take a max-description π of $\mathscr{B}$. Since it can be mapped into every pattern from $\mathscr{B}$ and $\bigcup_{\varphi \in \mathscr{B}} \mathrm{Mod}(\varphi)$, it can also be mapped into every tree from $\mathscr{T}$. Now, take a pattern π' that can be mapped into every tree from $\mathscr{T}$. We need to show that it can be mapped into π. As $\mathscr{B} \subseteq \mathscr{T}$, π' can be mapped into every pattern from $\mathscr{B}$. By the properties of max-descriptions, π' can be mapped into π.

Conversely, assume that π is a max-description of $\mathscr{T}$. As it can be mapped into every pattern of $\mathscr{T}$, it can also be mapped into every pattern from $\mathscr{B}$. It remains to see that every pattern that can be mapped into every pattern from $\mathscr{B}$ can also be mapped into π. Pick a pattern π' that can be mapped into every pattern from $\mathscr{B}$. A pattern that can be mapped into π'' can also be mapped into every pattern from $\mathrm{Mod}(\pi'')$. Hence, π' can be mapped into every pattern from $\mathscr{T} \subseteq \bigcup_{\pi \in \mathscr{B}} \mathrm{Mod}(\pi)$. Since π is a max-description of $\mathscr{T}$, there is a homomorphism from π' to π, which ends the proof. $\square$

We say that a query Q *preserves bases* if $Q(\mathscr{B})$ is a basis of $Q(\mathscr{T})$ whenever $\mathscr{B}$ is a basis of $\mathscr{T}$. From the lemma above we immediately obtain the following.

Theorem 14.14   *If $\mathscr{T}$ is a set of trees, $\mathscr{B}$ is its basis, and Q is a query preserving bases, then certain answers to Q over $\mathscr{T}$ and over $\mathscr{B}$ coincide. In particular, $\square Q(\mathscr{T}) = \square Q(\mathscr{B})$.*

Together with Theorem 14.11, this gives a general approach to computing certain answers to queries preserving bases, shown in Algorithm 14.1.

Algorithm 14.1 Certain answers to XML-to-XML queries

Require: $\mathscr{T}$ is a recursively enumerable set of trees, Q is a query preserving bases
   compute a (small) basis $\mathscr{B}$ of $\mathscr{T}$;
   evaluate Q naïvely over elements of $\mathscr{B}$ to compute $Q(\mathscr{B})$;
   compute a max-description π of $Q(\mathscr{B})$;
   return π.

The returned max-description π is guaranteed to be a certain answer. We shall now see that this recipe can be applied to TQL.

Theorem 14.15   TQL *queries preserve bases.*

Proof   Clearly $Q(\mathscr{B}) \subseteq Q(\mathscr{T})$. It remains to check that $Q(\mathscr{T}) \subseteq \bigcup_{\pi \in Q(\mathscr{B})} \mathrm{Mod}(\pi)$. In other words, for every $T \in Q(\mathscr{T})$ we need some $\pi \in Q(\mathscr{B})$ that can be mapped into T. Let $\tilde{T}$ be a tree from $\mathscr{T}$ such that $Q(\tilde{T}) = T$. Since $\mathscr{B}$ is a basis of $\mathscr{T}$, there exists $\tilde{\pi} \in \mathscr{B}$ and a homomorphism $\tilde{h} : \tilde{\pi} \to \tilde{T}$. Let us see that $Q(\tilde{\pi})$ can be mapped into T.

We prove a more general result. Fix a homomorphism $h : S \to T$.

For each forest expression $q(\bar{x})$, and each valuation v of $\bar{x}$ into values used in S, there exists a homomorphism $\tilde{h}$: $[\![q(\bar{x})]\!]_{S,v} \to [\![q(\bar{x})]\!]_{T,h\circ v}$ coinciding with h on VAR.

We proceed by induction on $q(\bar{x})$. If $q(\bar{x}) = \varepsilon$, the claim follows trivially.

If $q(\bar{x}) = \ell(\bar{a}, \bar{x}')[q'(\bar{x}'')]$, then $[\![q(\bar{x})]\!]_{S,v} = \ell(\bar{a}, v(\bar{x}'))[[\![q'(\bar{x}'')]\!]_{S,v}]$ and $[\![q(\bar{x})]\!]_{T,h\circ v} = \ell(h \circ v(\bar{x}''))[[\![q'(\bar{x}'')]\!]_{T,h\circ v}]$, and the claim follows from the induction hypothesis.

Suppose that $q(\bar{x}) = q'(\bar{x}'), q''(\bar{x}'')$. By the induction hypothesis there exist homomorphisms h': $[\![q'(\bar{x}')]\!]_{S,v} \to [\![q'(\bar{x}')]\!]_{T,h\circ v}$ and h'': $[\![q''(\bar{x}'')]\!]_{S,v} \to [\![q''(\bar{x}'')]\!]_{T,h\circ v}$ coinciding with h on VAR. Pick a tree $U \in [\![q(\bar{x})]\!]_{S,v}$. Define h_U: $U \to [\![q(\bar{x})]\!]_{T,h\circ v}$ as $h' \upharpoonright U$ if U comes from $[\![q'(\bar{x}')]\!]_{S,v}$, and as $h'' \upharpoonright U$ if U comes from $[\![q''(\bar{x}'')]\!]_{S,v}$. Let $\tilde{h}$ be the union of h_U over all $U \in [\![q(\bar{x})]\!]_{S,v}$. Since all h_U coincide with h on VAR, $\tilde{h}$ is defined consistently. It is a homomorphism, because its restriction to every tree in the domain is a homomorphism.

Finally, let us assume that $q(\bar{x}) =$ for $\pi(\bar{a}, \bar{x}, \bar{y})$ return $q'(\bar{x}, \bar{y})$. Then

$$[\![q(\bar{x})]\!]_{S,v} = \bigcup \{ [\![q']\!]_{S,v'} \mid S \models \pi(\bar{a}, v'(\bar{x}, \bar{y})), \; v' \upharpoonright \bar{x} = v \},$$

$$[\![q(\bar{x})]\!]_{T,h\circ v} = \bigcup \{ [\![q']\!]_{T,v''} \mid T \models \pi(\bar{a}, v''(\bar{x}, \bar{y})), \; v'' \upharpoonright \bar{x} = h \circ v \}.$$

Pick a tree U from $[\![q(\bar{x})]\!]_{S,v}$. Let v' be the valuation extending v and satisfying $S \models \pi(\bar{a}, v'(\bar{x}, \bar{y}))$, such that S' comes from $[\![q']\!]_{S,v'}$. Since h: $S \to T$, it holds that $T \models \pi(h \circ v'(\bar{x}, \bar{y}))$. Moreover, $h \circ v' \upharpoonright \bar{x} = h \circ v$. Consequently, $[\![q']\!]_{T,h\circ v'}$ is a subforest of $[\![q(\bar{x})]\!]_{T,v}$. By the induction hypothesis there is a homomorphism $h_{v'}$: $[\![q']\!]_{S,v'} \to [\![q']\!]_{T,h\circ v'}$, coinciding with h on VAR. Let h_U: $U \to [\![q(\bar{x})]\!]_{T,h\circ v}$ be defined as $h_{v'} \upharpoonright U$. Let $\tilde{h}$ be the union of h_U for all $U \in [\![q(\bar{x})]\!]_{S,v}$. As all h_U are homomorphisms coinciding with h on VAR, so is $\tilde{h}$. $\qquad\square$

14.4 XML-to-XML queries in data exchange

We have shown that TQL queries preserve bases, and thus Algorithm 14.1 computes a certain answer if we can find a small finite basis. Now we would like to apply this in the data exchange context. A TQL query Q then is posed over the target schema, and we must find a certain answer to it over the set of data exchange solutions, i.e., over $\mathrm{SOL}_{\mathcal{M}}(T)$, for some source tree T and a mapping $\mathcal{M}$. For that, we need to find a finite basis $\mathcal{B}$ of $\mathrm{SOL}_{\mathcal{M}}(T)$, and then just compute a max-description of $Q(\mathcal{B})$. We know how to do the former, but how do we find bases of sets of solutions?

In general, the existence (and properties) of bases of $\mathrm{SOL}_{\mathcal{M}}(T)$ depend on the properties of mappings. Our first result shows that we can compute a finite basis $\mathcal{B}$ for $\mathrm{SOL}_{\mathcal{M}}(T)$ whenever $\mathcal{M}$ only uses vertical navigation in its pattern, and nested-relational DTDs in the target, i.e., if it is a mapping from $\mathrm{SM}^{\mathrm{nr}}(\Downarrow, =)$. Essentially, a basis is what we get when we try to compute a universal solution but cannot. The method for computing the basis will be a modification of the algorithm described in Section 13.4.

Theorem 14.16 *Given a mapping $\mathcal{M} \in \mathrm{SM}^{\mathrm{nr}}(\Downarrow, =)$ and a source tree T, one can compute a basis $\mathcal{B}$ for $\mathrm{SOL}_{\mathcal{M}}(T)$ in time single-exponential in the size of T. The size of $\mathcal{B}$ can be exponential, but the size of each pattern $\pi \in \mathcal{B}$ is polynomial in T.*

Proof   As we did before, we start with the pattern $\delta_{T,\mathcal{M}}(\bar{z})$ obtained from the set

$$\Delta_{T,\mathcal{M}} = \{\psi(\bar{a},\bar{z}) \mid \varphi(\bar{x},\bar{y}) \to \exists \bar{z}\, \psi(\bar{x},\bar{z}) \in \Sigma_{st}, T \models \varphi(\bar{a},\bar{b})\}$$

by first renaming variables so that each is used in one pattern only, and then merging all the patterns at the root. Recall that a tree conforming to the target DTD is a solution if and only if it satisfies $\delta_{T,\mathcal{M}}(\bar{a})$ for some tuple $\bar{a}$.

The next step is completing $\delta_{T,\mathcal{M}}$, i.e., adding all the nodes required by the target DTD. Before, the pattern only used the child relation, and completion could be done in a unique way. Now $//$ or $\_$ are allowed and there can be more than one way to complete a pattern. A basis should reflect all those possibilities and that is why the procedure will now compute a set of patterns corresponding to all possible choices.

The idea is to start from replacing wildcards with concrete labels and descendants with concrete paths in a way consistent with the target DTD. The algorithm processes the nodes of the patterns top-down and creates new patterns when facing a choice.

Let $\Phi = \{\delta_{T,\mathcal{M}}\}$. While Φ contains a pattern with an unprocessed node, proceed as follows. Choose a pattern $\varphi \in \Phi$ and an unprocessed node v such that the path from the root to v contains only processed nodes. Let ψ be the subpattern rooted in v and let σ be the label of its parent. If the production for σ in the target DTD is empty, simply remove φ from Φ. Otherwise, remove φ from Φ and instead add the output of the following procedure:

- if $\psi = \ell(\bar{t})[\psi_1,\ldots,\psi_k]$ and $\ell \in \Gamma$, return φ with the root of ψ marked as processed;
- if $\psi = \_(\bar{t})[\psi_1,\ldots,\psi_k]$, return the set of patterns that can be obtained from φ by replacing ψ with $\tau(\bar{t})[\psi_1,\ldots,\psi_k]$ whose root is marked as processed and τ is some label occurring in the production for σ (τ must have $|\bar{t}|$ attributes, unless $\bar{t}$ is empty);
- if $\psi = //\psi'$, return two patterns that can be obtained by replacing in φ the pattern ψ by ψ' or by $\_//\psi'$ with all nodes unmarked.

Every node is processed at most twice, and each processing introduces at most $|\Gamma|$ new patterns. The procedure terminates after at most exponentially many steps. In particular, the number of produced patterns is single-exponential. The size of each pattern is polynomial in the size of T. It is fairly easy to see that the disjunction of the obtained formulae is equivalent to $\delta_{T,M}$ (over trees conforming to the target DTD). If we now apply the original completion procedure cpl_{D_t} to each pattern in Φ, we obtain an equivalent set of complete patterns.

Finally, each of the obtained patterns needs to be merged, as described in Section 13.4. Remove $\bot$ from the set of obtained patterns. Like before, each of the remaining patterns is a solution (viewed as a tree). Together they form a basis of solutions: each solution T' satisfies the disjunctions of those patterns, so there must be a homomorphism from one of them to T'. If the obtained set of patterns is empty, the tree T has no solutions at all. $\square$

Theorem 14.16 and the recipe sketched out in the beginning of this section give us an algorithm – albeit an expensive one – for computing certain answers.

Corollary 14.17 *Given a mapping $\mathcal{M}$ in* $\mathrm{SM}^{\mathrm{nr}}(\Downarrow,=)$, *a* TQL *query Q, and tree T, one can compute certain* $_{\mathcal{M}}(Q,T)$ *in time double-exponential in the size of T.*

Exercise 16.3 shows that even core-certain answer can be exponentially large, which means there is no chance of answering queries efficiently in the general case. However, we can do this efficiently if we can efficiently build a universal solution, and we know cases when we can do so. The reason is that a universal solution constitutes a basis for all solutions.

Lemma 14.18 *If U is a universal solution for a tree T with respect to a mapping $\mathcal{M}$, then $Q(U)$ is certain* $_{\mathcal{M}}(Q,T)$ *for each $Q \in$* TQL.

Proof Let us first prove that for every universal solution U, $\{U\}$ is a basis for the set of solutions to T, $\mathrm{SOL}_{\mathcal{M}}(T)$. Obviously $\{U\} \subseteq \mathrm{SOL}_{\mathcal{M}}(T)$, so it suffices to prove that $\mathrm{SOL}_{\mathcal{M}}(T) \subseteq \mathrm{Mod}(U)$. Since U is a universal solution, for every $T' \in \mathrm{SOL}_{\mathcal{M}}(T)$ there is a homomorphism $h : U \to T'$. But this means exactly that U viewed as a pattern is satisfied in T'. In other words that $T' \in \mathrm{Mod}(U)$.

By Theorem 14.16, $\{Q(U)\}$ is a singleton basis for $Q(\mathrm{SOL}_{\mathcal{M}}(T))$, and to find the certain answer to Q with respect to T and $\mathcal{M}$ it is enough to find a max-description of $\{Q(U)\}$. For singleton sets we get a max-description for free: $Q(U)$ trivially satisfies both conditions for being a max-description of $\{Q(U)\}$. $\qquad\square$

Now using the results on the efficient building of universal solutions from Chapter 12, we show that certain answers can be efficiently found if mappings disallow the descendant relation.

Corollary 14.19 *Given a mapping $\mathcal{M}$ in* $\mathrm{SM}^{\mathrm{nr}}(\downarrow,=)$, *a* TQL *query Q, and a tree T, one can compute certain* $_{\mathcal{M}}(Q,T)$ *in time polynomial in the size of T.*

Proof In Section 13.4, we showed that for every tree T and every mapping $\mathcal{M}$ from $\mathrm{SM}^{\mathrm{nr}}(\downarrow,=)$, one can construct in polynomial time a universal solution U: it suffices to interpret the pattern $\mathrm{mrg}_{D_t}(\mathrm{cpl}_{D_t}\,\delta_{S,\mathcal{M}})$ as a tree. By Lemma 14.18, $Q(U)$ is the certain answer. By Theorem 14.3, we can compute $Q(U)$ in time polynomial in the size of U. $\quad\square$

15

XML data exchange via relations

So far we have tacitly assumed that one uses a native XML DBMS for performing data exchange tasks. However, this is not the only (and perhaps not even the most common) route: XML documents are often stored in relational DBMSs. Thus, it is natural to ask whether relational data exchange techniques, developed in PART TWO, can be used to perform XML data exchange tasks.

In XML terminology, translations from XML to relations are referred to as *shredding* of documents, whereas translations going the other way, from relations to XML, are referred to as *publishing*. Thus, to use relational technology for XML data exchange tasks, we can employ a two-step approach:

1. shred XML data into relations;
2. then apply a relational data-exchange engine (and publish the result back as an XML document if necessary).

The seems very natural, but the key question is whether it will *work correctly*. That is, are we guaranteed to have the same result as we would have gotten had we implemented a native XML data-exchange system? This is what we investigate in this chapter. It turns out that we need to impose restrictions on XML schema mappings to enable this approach, and the restrictions are similar to those we needed to ensure tractability of data exchange tasks in the previous chapters.

15.1 Translations and correctness

We now describe what we mean by correctness of translations that enable a relational data exchange system to perform XML data exchange tasks. These will be formalized as five requirements, ensuring correctness of translations of schemas, documents, queries, mappings, and certain answers.

Assume for now that that we have a translation $\sigma(\cdot)$ that can be applied to (a) XML schemas, (b) XML documents, (c) XML schema mappings, and (d) XML queries. Then the concept of *correctness* of such a translation is informally depicted in Figure 15.1.

That is, suppose we start with an XML document S and an XML schema mapping $\mathcal{M}$.

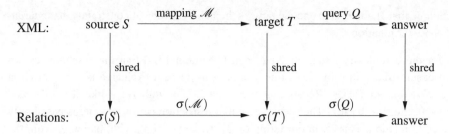

Figure 15.1 XML data exchange via relations: desiderata

In a native system, we would materialize some solution T over which we could answer queries Q.

But now we want a relational system to do the job. So we shred $\mathscr{S}$ into $\sigma(\mathscr{S})$ and then apply to $\sigma(\mathscr{S})$ the translation of the mapping $\sigma(\mathscr{M})$ to get a solution – which itself is a shredding of an XML solution – so that the answer to Q could be reconstructed from the result of the query $\sigma(Q)$ over that relational solution.

The idea seems simple and natural on the surface, but starts looking challenging once we look deeper into it. Before even attempting to show that the relational translation faithfully represents the XML data-exchange problem, we need to address the following.

- *Complexity mismatch.* Without restrictions, there *cannot be a faithful representation* of XML data exchange by a relational system. Indeed, we have seen in PART TWO that unions of conjunctive queries can be efficiently evaluated in relational data exchange, by means of constructing the canonical universal solution, and applying naïve evaluation. At the same time, we saw in Chapter 13 that answering analogs of unions of conjunctive queries in XML data exchange can be CONP-complete. So any claim that a relational data-exchange system correctly performs XML data exchange for arbitrary documents and queries is bound to be wrong. We thus need to identify the cases that can be handled by a relational system.

- *Which shredding scheme to use?* There are several, which can roughly be divided into two groups. The first group consists of shredding schemes that do not take the schema information into account (for instance, representing edge relations of the trees, or interval encodings based on associating with each node its number in pre- and post-order traversals). The second group consists of shredding schemes based on schemas for XML (e.g., variants of the inlining technique). Since in data-exchange scenarios we start with two schemas, it seems more appropriate to apply schema-based techniques.

- *Target constraints.* In relational data exchange, constraints in target schemas are required to satisfy certain acyclicity conditions (weak acyclicity, to be precise); as we have seen, without them, the chase procedure that constructs a target instance does not terminate. Constraints imposed by general XML schema specifications need not in general be even definable in relational calculus, let alone be acyclic. We thus need to find a shredding technique that enables us to encode target schemas by means of constraints that guarantee chase termination.

As for the complexity issue, we have seen (Theorem 13.9) that the essential restriction to ensure tractability of XML query answering in data exchange is the restriction to *nested-relational* DTDs. Recall that these are DTDs with rules like db $\to$ book*, book $\to$ author* subject. The second essential restriction is to use patterns based only on the child relation. That is, in our terminology, we are dealing with mappings from the class $\mathrm{SM}^{\mathrm{nr}}(\downarrow, =)$, with nested-relational DTDs and patterns using child relation and equality.

These restriction are helpful in suggesting a shredding scheme. They do not go well with schema-less representations, but match well the *inlining* scheme (which we shall define formally later). It works very well with nested-relational DTDs and child-based patterns, and generates relational schemas that only use acyclic constraints, which is perfect for data-exchange scenarios.

Desiderata for the translation

We now formulate some basic requirements for the translation σ, in order to be able to achieve our goals described in the diagram above.

Requirement 1: translation of schemas The translation $\sigma(D)$ applied to a DTD of a special form (nested-relational) produces a relational schema that has only acyclic constraints.

Requirement 2: translation of documents The translation $\sigma_D(\cdot)$ for a DTD D, applied to document T conforming to D, produces relational database $\sigma_D(T)$ of schema $\sigma(D)$.

Requirement 3: translation of queries For a DTD D, the translation $\sigma_D(Q)$ of conjunctive queries Q satisfies $\sigma_D(Q)\big(\sigma_D(T)\big) = Q(T)$. In other words, the result of $Q(T)$ can be computed by relational translations.

Requirement 4: translation of mappings For a mapping $\mathcal{M}$ between a source DTD D_s and a target DTD D_t, its translation $\sigma(\mathcal{M})$ is a mapping between $\sigma(D_s)$ and $\sigma(D_t)$ that preserves universal solutions. That is:

    (a) each σ_{D_t}-translation of a universal solution for T under $\mathcal{M}$ is a universal solution for $\sigma_{D_s}(T)$ under $\sigma(\mathcal{M})$; and

    (b) each universal solution for $\sigma_{D_s}(T)$ under $\sigma(\mathcal{M})$ contains a σ_{D_t}-translation of a universal solution of T under $\mathcal{M}$. Note that we cannot possibly require equivalence, as relational solutions are open to adding new tuples and thus cannot always be translations of trees.

Requirement 5: query answering For conjunctive queries over trees, computing the answer to Q under $\mathcal{M}$ over a source tree T is the same as computing a $\sigma(\mathcal{M})$-solution of $\sigma(T)$, followed by evaluation of $\sigma(Q)$ over that solution, as is normally done in a relational data-exchange system.

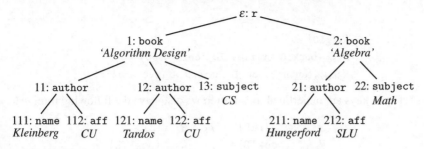

Figure 15.2 The XML tree T conforms to D

Satisfaction of these five requirements would guarantee that we have a *correct* relational translation of an XML data-exchange problem, which would guarantee correct evaluation of queries. The relational approach to XML data exchange, which we shall describe here, satisfies all these five requirements.

15.2 Translations of schemas and documents

We start by reviewing the *inlining* technique, which provides the translation satisfying **Requirements 1** and **2**. The main idea of inlining is that separate relations are created for the root and for each element type that appears under a Kleene star in the DTD, and other element types are inlined in the relations corresponding to their "nearest appropriate ancestor". Each relation for an element type has an ID attribute that is a key, as well as a "parent-ID" attribute that is a foreign key pointing to the "nearest appropriate ancestor" of that element in the document (for the root this attribute is skipped). All the attributes of a given element type in the DTD become attributes in the relation corresponding to that element type when such a relation exists, or otherwise become attributes in the relation for the "nearest appropriate ancestor" of the given element type.

Example 15.1 Consider a DTD D given by the productions

$$r \rightarrow \text{book}^*$$
$$\text{book} \rightarrow \text{author}^* \text{subject}$$
$$\text{author} \rightarrow \text{name aff}$$

$$\text{book: @title}$$
$$\text{subject: @sub}$$
$$\text{name: @nam}$$
$$\text{aff: @aff,}$$

where `aff` stands for "affiliation".

A tree T that conforms to this DTD is shown in Figure 15.2. For convenience, we also write node ids (which are strings of natural numbers, providing the path from the root to each node).

The relational schema INLSCHEMA(D) for storing XML documents that conform to D is as follows:

$R_r(\underline{\texttt{rID}})$

$R_{\text{book}}(\underline{\texttt{bookID}},\texttt{@title},\texttt{rID},\texttt{subID},\texttt{@sub})$

$R_{\text{author}}(\underline{\texttt{authID}},\texttt{bookID},\texttt{nameID},\texttt{afID},\texttt{@nam},\texttt{@aff}).$

In this schema, keys are underlined. In addition we also have the following foreign keys:

$$R_{\text{book}}(\texttt{rID}) \quad \subseteq_{FK} \quad R_r(\texttt{rID})$$
$$R_{\text{author}}(\texttt{bookID}) \quad \subseteq_{FK} \quad R_{\text{book}}(\texttt{bookID}).$$

The first relation contains just the root node. The second relation corresponds to the element book which appears under the Kleene star in D. It contains book id, as well as its attribute (title), and the id of the parent (root). In addition, book serves as the nearest appropriate ancestor for subject, so this relation also inlines the id of the subject node and its attribute @sub.

The next starred element type is author. The third relation corresponds to this element and includes its id, as well as the id of its book parent. In addition, name and aff are inlined into this relation, so ids of these elements, and their attributes, are included in R_{author} too.

We now proceed with a formal definition of the inlining shredding scheme. We first define the *nearest appropriate ancestor* for the element types used in D. Given a nested-relational DTD $D = (P_D, A_D, r)$, we define the graph of D, denoted by $G(D)$, as the graph whose nodes are element types, and where there is an edge from ℓ to ℓ' if ℓ' appears in $P_D(\ell)$. We then "mark" in $G(D)$ each element type that occurs under a Kleene star in P_D. In addition, we mark the root element type in $G(D)$. Then, for a given element type ℓ, we define the *nearest appropriate ancestor* of ℓ, denoted by $\mu(\ell)$, as the closest marked element type ℓ' in the path from the root element to ℓ in the graph $G(D)$. For example, $\mu(\text{name}) = \text{author}$ and $\mu(\text{subject}) = \text{book}$.

The inlining schema generation is formally captured by means of the procedure INLSCHEMA (Algorithm 15.1) that receives a nested-relational D and creates the inlining relational schema $inl(D)$.

Recall that to ensure good behavior of relational data exchange, we had to restrict target constraints to egds and weakly acyclic sets of tgds. In our case, all tgds will be inclusion constraints (i.e., each tgd is a part of a foreign key), and we can impose an even stronger restriction of *acyclicity*. A set F of foreign keys defines a graph $G(F)$ whose nodes are attributes, and edges are generated as follows: for each foreign key $R[A_1,\ldots,A_n] \subseteq_{FK} R'[B_1,\ldots,B_n]$, we add all the edges (A_i, B_j), for $1 \leq i, j \leq n$. Then F is acyclic if the resulting graph $G(F)$ is acyclic. If we view F as a set of tgds, then its acyclicity implies weak acyclicity as previously defined.

We call a relational schema *acyclic* if its constraints involve a set of egds, and an acyclic set of foreign keys.

The tree structure of nested-relational DTDs then implies that **Requirement 1** is satisfied.

Algorithm 15.1 INLSCHEMA(D)

Require: D is a nested relational DTD.

Ensure: $\mathbf{S}_D$ and Δ_D are the inlining relational schema $inl(D)$.

$\mathbf{S}_D := \emptyset$

$\Delta_D := \emptyset$

for all marked element types ℓ of D **do**

add to $\mathbf{S}_D$ a relation R_ℓ, with attributes

$$attr(R_\ell) = \begin{cases} id_\ell \\ A_D(\ell) \\ id_{\mu(\ell)} & | & \text{if } \ell \neq r. \\ id_{\ell'} & | & \mu(\ell') = \ell, \ \ell' \text{ is not marked,} \\ A_D(\ell') & | & \mu(\ell') = \ell, \ \ell' \text{ is not marked.} \end{cases}$$

end for

for all relations R_ℓ in $\mathbf{S}_D$ **do**

add to Δ_D the constraint stating that id_ℓ is key of R_ℓ

if $\ell \neq r$ **then**

add to Δ_D the foreign key

$$R_\ell[id_{\mu(\ell)}] \subseteq_{FK} R_{\mu(\ell)}[id_{\mu(\ell)}].$$

end if

end for

add to Δ_D the dependency (stating the uniqueness of the root)

$$\forall \bar{y} \forall \bar{z} R_r(x, \bar{y}) \wedge R_r(x', \bar{z}) \rightarrow x = x'.$$

return $(\mathbf{S}_D, \Delta_D)$

Proposition 15.2 *For every nested relational DTD D, the output of* INLSCHEMA(D) *is an acyclic relational schema.*

Shredding of XML documents We now move to the shredding procedure. Given the inlining INLSCHEMA(D) = $(\mathbf{S}_D, \Delta_D)$ of a DTD D, and an XML tree T conforming to D, we use the algorithm INLDOC to shred T into an instance of the relational schema $\mathbf{S}_D$ that satisfies the constraints in Δ_D. The algorithm basically follows the intuition behind the definition of the inlining schema: a tuple is created for each starred element, and its unstarred children and descendants, as well as parent, are inlined with its id.

Example 15.3 Recall tree T from Figure 15.2. Figure 15.3 shows relations R_{book} and R_{author} in the shredding of T.

To present the algorithm, we define the *nearest appropriate ancestor* $\mu(n)$ of a node n of an XML document T that conforms to a DTD D, as follows. Mark each node n of T such

bookID	@title	rID	subID	@sub
id_1	'Algorithm Design'	id_ε	id_{13}	CS
id_2	'Algebra'	id_ε	id_{22}	Math

(a) Relation R_{book} in INLDOC(T,D)

authID	bookID	nameID	afID	@nam	@af
id_{11}	id_1	id_{111}	id_{112}	Kleinberg	CU
id_{12}	id_1	id_{121}	id_{122}	Tardos	CU
id_{21}	id_2	id_{211}	id_{212}	Hungerford	SLU

(b) Relation R_{author} in INLDOC(T,D)

Figure 15.3 Shredding of T into INLSCHEMA(D)

that $lab(n)$ is starred in D, as well as the root of T. Then $\mu(n)$ is the closest marked node n' that belongs to the path from the root to n.

In algorithm INLDOC, and for the remainder of the chapter, we denote by id_n the relational element representing the node n of a tree T.

Algorithm 15.2 INLDOC(T,D)

Require: D is a nested relational DTD, T conforms to D.
Ensure: I is a relational instance of the schema INLSCHEMA(D).

    for all marked nodes n of T **do**
        let ℓ be the label of n;
        add to the relation R_ℓ of I a tuple that contains elements

$$\begin{cases} id_n \\ \rho_{@a}(n) & | & @a \in A_D(\ell) \\ id_{\mu(n)} & | & \text{if } \ell \neq r \\ id_{n'} & | & \mu(n') = n, n' \text{ is not marked.} \\ \rho_{@a}(n') & | & \mu(n') = n, @a \in A_D(\lambda(n')) \text{ and} \\ & & n' \text{ is not marked} \end{cases}$$

    where the identifiers and attributes values for each of the elements $id_{n'}$, $id_{\mu(n)}$ and $\rho_{@a}(n')$ coincide with the position of the attributes for $id_{\lambda(n')}$, $id_{\mu(\ell)}$ and $A_D(\lambda(n'))$ of R_ℓ.

    end for
    return I

It is then easy to verify that our **Requirement 2** is satisfied: that is, given a DTD D and an XML tree T, the instance $\text{INLDOC}(T,D)$ that corresponds to the shredding of T with respect to D always satisfies the constraints in $\text{INLSCHEMA}(D)$.

Proposition 15.4 *Let D be a DTD, and T an XML tree such that T conforms to D. Then $\text{INLDOC}(T,D)$ is an instance of the schema computed by $\text{INLSCHEMA}(D)$.*

15.3 Translations of patterns, mappings and queries

To ensure that the remaining requirements are satisfied and we can implement XML data exchange via relational translations, we need to show how to translate mappings and queries. Since both are based on patterns, we deal with patterns first; then translations of mappings and queries become easy extensions of pattern translations.

Restrictions on patterns

In addition to restrictions on DTDs, we had to impose restrictions on schema mappings to ensure tractability. Those restrictions essentially boiled down to omitting horizontal navigation, as well as the descendant axis, and not allowing wildcards. That is, patterns that we deal with in tractable XML data exchange are defined inductively as follows:

- $\ell(\bar{x})$ is a pattern, where ℓ is a label, and $\bar{x}$ is a (possibly empty) tuple of variables (listing attributes of a node);
- $\ell(\bar{x})[\pi_1,\ldots,\pi_k]$ is a pattern, where $\pi_1,\ldots,\pi_k$ are patterns, and ℓ and $\bar{x}$ are as above.

We write $\pi(\bar{x})$ to indicate that $\bar{x}$ is the tuple of all the variables used in a pattern.

As before, we shall write π_1/π_2 instead of $\pi_1[\pi_2]$. The semantics, of course, is exactly the same as in Chapter 11.

Example 15.5 Consider again the tree T from Figure 15.2, and the tree pattern

$$\pi(x,y) = \texttt{r/book}(x)/\texttt{author/name}(y).$$

This patterns finds books together with the names of their authors. The evaluation of $\pi(x,y)$ over T returns the tuples (*'Algorithm Design'*, *Tardos*), (*'Algorithm Design'*, *Kleinberg*), and (*'Algebra'*, *Hungerford*).

Given a DTD D and a tree pattern π, we say that π is *compatible* with D if there exists a tree T that conforms to D and a tuple of attribute values $\bar{a}$ such that $\pi(\bar{a})$ holds in T. Of course it only makes sense to consider compatible patterns in mappings and queries. Note that while in general, checking compatibility of patterns with DTDs is NP-complete (see Theorem 11.7), for nested-relational DTDs we consider here it can be easily done in polynomial time.

Example 15.6 (Example 15.5 continued) The pattern $\pi(x,y)$ is compatible with the DTD D we are using in our examples. On the other hand, the pattern $\pi'(x) = \texttt{r/author}(x)$ is not compatible, because no tree consistent with D can have a child of r labeled as $\texttt{author}$, nor an $\texttt{author}$-labeled node with an attribute.

Inlining patterns

The key ingredient in our algorithms is a translation of a pattern π compatible with a DTD D into a *conjunctive query* INLPATTERN(π, D) over the relational schema INLSCHEMA(D). Very roughly, it can be viewed as this:

1. View a pattern $\pi(\bar{x})$ as a tree T_π in which some attribute values could be variables.
2. Compute the relational database INLDOC(T_π, D) over the schema INLSCHEMA(D) (which may have variables as attribute values).
3. View INLDOC(T_π, D) as a tableau of a conjunctive query.

The algorithm is actually more complicated because using INLDOC "as-is" in Step 2 does not guarantee correctness (we shall explain this shortly).

Towards defining INLPATTERN properly, recall that each tree pattern $\pi(\bar{x})$ can be viewed as an XML document, which we denote by $T_{\pi(\bar{x})}$. In this document, both actual values and variables can be used as attribute values. For the sake of completeness, we recall how this is done now. The tree $T_{\ell(\bar{x})}$ is a single-node tree labeled ℓ, with $\bar{x}$ as attribute values. If π is $\ell(\bar{x})[\pi_1(\bar{x}_1), \ldots, \pi_k(\bar{x}_k)]$, then the root of T_π is labeled ℓ and has $\bar{x}$ as attribute values. It also has k children, with the subtrees rooted at them being $T_{\pi_1(\bar{x}_1)}, \ldots, T_{\pi_k(\bar{x}_k)}$.

However, even for a pattern $\pi(\bar{x})$ compatible with a DTD D, we may not be able to define its inlining as the inlining of $T_{\pi(\bar{x})}$, because $T_{\pi(\bar{x})}$ need not conform to D. For example, if a DTD has a rule $r \to ab$ and we have a pattern r/a, it is compatible with D, but $T_{r[a]}$ does not conform to D, as it is missing a b-node.

Despite this, we can still mark the nodes of $T_{\pi(\bar{x})}$ with respect to D and define the nearest appropriate ancestor exactly as it has been done previously. Intuitively, the procedure INLPATTERN shreds each node of $T_{\pi(\bar{x})}$ into a different predicate, and then joins these predicates using the nearest appropriate ancestor.

Example 15.7   The pattern

$$\pi(x, y) = r/\texttt{book}(x)/\texttt{author}/\texttt{name}(y)$$

translates into the following conjunctive query:

$$Q_\pi(x, y) = \exists id_r \exists id_b \exists id_n \exists z_1 \exists z_1 \exists z_3 \left(\begin{array}{l} R_{\texttt{r}}(id_r) \\ \wedge \quad R_{\texttt{book}}(id_b, x, id_r, z_1, z_2) \\ \wedge \quad R_{\texttt{author}}(id_a, id_b, id_n, y, z_3) \end{array} \right).$$

Next, we can state the correctness of INLPATTERN. That is, the inlining of π (which is a conjunctive query over the schema INLSCHEMA(D)), when applied to the inlining of T (which is a relational instance of the same schema), returns $\pi(T)$.

Proposition 15.8   *Given a nested relational DTD D, a pattern π compatible with D, and a tree T that conforms to D, we have*

$$\pi(T) \;=\; \text{INLPATTERN}(\pi, D)\big(\text{INLDOC}(T, D)\big).$$

Algorithm 15.3 INLPATTERN(π, D)

Require: $\pi(\bar{x})$ is a tree pattern compatible with D.

Ensure: The returned query is a conjunctive query over INLSCHEMA(D).

  for all nodes v of $T_{\pi(\bar{x})}$ of form $\ell(\bar{x}_v)$ **do**

    Construct a query $Q_v(\bar{x}_v)$ as follows

    if v is marked **then**

      Let

$$Q_v(\bar{x}_v) := \exists id_v \exists id_{\mu(v)} \exists \bar{z}\, R_\ell(id_v, \bar{x}_v, id_{\mu(v)}, \bar{z}),$$

    where $\bar{z}$ is a tuple of fresh variables, and the positions of variables id_v, $\bar{x}_v$ and $id_{\mu(v)}$ are consistent with the attributes id_ℓ, $A_D(\ell)$ and $id_{\mu(\ell)}$ respectively in $attr(R_\ell)$. If $\ell = r$, then Q_v does not use $id_{\mu(v)}$.

    else {v is not marked}

    $v' := \mu(v); \ell' := lab(v');$

    Let

$$Q_v(\bar{x}_v) := \exists id_{v'} \exists id_{\mu(v')} \exists id_v \exists \bar{z}\, R_{\ell'}(id_{v'}, id_{\mu(v')}, id_v, \bar{x}_v, \bar{z}),$$

    where $\bar{z}$ is a tuple of fresh variables, and the positions of the variables $id_{v'}$, $id_{\mu(v')}$, id_v and $\bar{x}_v$ are consistent with the attributes $id_{\ell'}$, $id_{\mu(\ell')}$, id_ℓ and $A_D(\ell)$ respectively in $attr(R_{\ell'})$. If $\ell' = r$, then Q_v does not use $id_{\mu(v')}$.

    end if

  end for

  for all nodes v of $T_{\pi(x)}$ **do**

    $Q_v(\bar{x}_v) := \exists \bar{y}_v\, \varphi(\bar{x}_v, \bar{y}_v)$

  end for

  return $\exists \bar{y} \bigwedge_{v \in T_{\pi(\bar{x})}} \varphi_v(\bar{x}_v, \bar{y}_v)$, where $\bar{y}$ has all the variables in $\bar{y}_v$'s without repetitions.

Translating conjunctive queries over trees

Now that we have a translation of patterns, we can define a translation of conjunctive queries based on them. Since our pattern language is quite limited, as we need to ensure tractability, we can define queries using explicit conjunction. That is, we deal with the class **CTQ**($\downarrow, =$) of queries which, under our restrictions, can be defined by

$$Q := \pi \mid Q \wedge Q \mid \exists x\, Q,$$

where π ranges over patterns as defined earlier. The semantics naturally extends the semantics of patterns. The output of Q on a tree T is denoted by $Q(T)$.

A query Q is *compatible* with the DTD D if every pattern used in it is compatible with D. The inlining of queries Q compatible with D is given by the simple algorithm INLQUERY. This algorithm ensures that **Requirement 3** is satisfied: that is, the answer to every query Q in **CTQ**($\downarrow, =$) can be computed by its inlining on the inlining of its input (assuming, of course, compatibility with a DTD).

Algorithm 15.4 $\text{INLQUERY}(Q, D)$

Require: Q is compatible with D.

Ensure: The returned query is a conjunctive query over $\text{INLSCHEMA}(D)$.

  if $Q = \pi$ **then**

    return $\text{INLPATTERN}(\pi, D)$

  else if $Q = Q_1 \wedge Q_2$ **then**

    return $\text{INLQUERY}(Q_1, D) \wedge \text{INLQUERY}(Q_2, D)$

  else if $Q = \exists x Q_1$ **then**

    return $\exists x \text{INLQUERY}(Q_1, D)$

  end if

Proposition 15.9 *Given a DTD D, a tree T that conforms to it, and a compatible query Q in* $\mathbf{CTQ}(\downarrow, =)$, *we have*

$$Q(T) = \text{INLQUERY}(Q, D)\big(\text{INLDOC}(T, D)\big).$$

Inlining XML schema mappings

A very similar approach can be used for inlining schema mappings: once we have inlining of patterns and DTDs, we just combine them to generate relational mappings.

Recall that we deal with schema mappings from the class $\text{SM}^{\text{nr}}(\downarrow, =)$, i.e., mappings $\mathcal{M} = (D_s, D_t, \Sigma_{st})$, where the source and target DTDs D_s and D_t are nested-relational, and Σ_{st} is a set of st-tgds of the form $\pi(\bar{x}, \bar{y}) \rightarrow \exists \bar{z} \pi'(\bar{x}, \bar{z})$ where π and π' are patterns that use only child navigation.

The following procedure generates a relational mapping $\text{INLMAP}(\mathcal{M})$ specified with a set of source-to-target tuple generating dependencies. We write $X \hookleftarrow Y$ as a shortcut for $X := X \cup Y$.

Algorithm 15.5 $\text{INLMAP}(\mathcal{M})$

Require: An XML mapping $\mathcal{M} = (D_s, D_t, \Sigma_{st})$.

Ensure: A relational mapping from $\text{INLSCHEMA}(D_s)$ to $\text{INLSCHEMA}(D_t)$.

  $\text{INLMAP}(\mathcal{M}) := \emptyset$

  for all dependencies $\pi(\bar{x}, \bar{y}) \rightarrow \exists \bar{z} \pi'(\bar{x}, \bar{z})$ in Σ_{st} **do**

    $\text{INLMAP}(\mathcal{M}) \hookleftarrow \big\{ \text{INLQUERY}(\pi, D_s)(\bar{x}, \bar{y}) \rightarrow \exists \bar{z}\, \text{INLQUERY}(\pi', D_t)(\bar{x}, \bar{z}) \big\}$

  end forreturn $\text{INLMAP}(\mathcal{M})$

This procedure ensures that **Requirement 4** holds. Recall that in part (b) of this requirement, relational universal solutions are only required to contain a shredding of an XML universal solution. This is because relational solutions are also open to adding arbitrary tuples, which need not reflect the tree structure of an XML document.

Proposition 15.10 *Let* $\mathcal{M} = (D_s, D_t, \Sigma_{st})$ *be an XML schema mapping in* $\text{SM}^{\text{nr}}(\downarrow, =)$ *and T an XML document that conforms to* D_s. *Then:*

- if T' *is a universal solution for T under $\mathcal{M}$, then its inlining* $\text{INLDOC}(T', D_t)$ *is a solution for* $\text{INLDOC}(T, D_S)$ *under* $\text{INLMAP}(\mathcal{M})$;
- *for every universal solution T' for* $\text{INLDOC}(T, D_s)$ *under* $\text{INLMAP}(\mathcal{M})$ *there exists an universal solution T'' for T under $\mathcal{M}$ such that* $\text{INLDOC}(T'', D_t)$ *is contained in T'.*

15.4 Answering XML queries using relational data exchange

Recall that for conjunctive tree queries that only use the child-relation (i.e., queries from the class $\mathbf{CTQ}(\downarrow, =)$, and for mappings that use nested-relational DTDs and child-relation only in patterns (i.e., mappings from the class $\text{SM}^{\text{nr}}(\downarrow, =)$), computing certain answers for a given source tree S is solvable in polynomial time. Thus, for the classes of mappings and queries we consider, there is no complexity mismatch between XML data exchange and relational data exchange, restricted to acyclic schemas. Indeed, translations shown here are correct with respect to query answering: that is, our **Requirement 5** is satisfied.

Proposition 15.11 *Let $\mathcal{M} = (D_s, D_t, \Sigma_{st})$ be an XML schema mapping in $\text{SM}^{\text{nr}}(\downarrow, =)$, and Q a conjunctive tree query in $\mathbf{CTQ}(\downarrow, =)$. Then, for every XML tree S that conforms to D_s, the certain answers of Q for S under $\mathcal{M}$ and the certain answers of $\text{INLQUERY}(Q, D_t)$ for $\text{INLDOC}(S, D_s)$ over $\text{INLMAP}(\mathcal{M})$ coincide:*

$$certain_{\mathcal{M}}(Q, S) = certain_{\text{INLMAP}(M)}(\text{INLQUERY}(Q, D_t), \text{INLDOC}(S, D_s)).$$

Proof Assume first that a tuple $\bar{t}$ belongs to the certain answers of a query Q over a tree S under $\mathcal{M}$. Then, clearly, $\bar{t}$ belongs to the evaluation of Q over the canonical solution $\text{CANSOL}(S)$ for S (which, in this case, is guaranteed to exist under $\mathcal{M}$). Then, by Proposition 15.9, $\bar{t}$ belongs to the evaluation of $\text{INLQUERY}(Q, D_t)$ over $\text{INLDOC}(\text{CANSOL}(S), D_t)$. Moreover, from Proposition 15.10, $\text{INLDOC}(\text{CANSOL}(S), D_t)$ is an $\text{INLMAP}(\mathcal{M})$-universal solution for $\text{INLDOC}(T, D_s)$. Hence $\bar{t}$ belongs to the certain answers of $\text{INLQUERY}(Q, D_t)$ over $\text{INLDOC}(S, D_s)$ under $\mathcal{M}$. The other direction is symmetric. ☐

The result of Proposition 15.11, combined with the standard procedure for evaluating conjunctive queries in relational data exchange, also gives us an algorithm for computing certain answers.

Combining correctness propositions, we can finally state the main correctness result.

Theorem 15.12 *For XML schema mappings $\mathcal{M}$ in $\text{SM}^{\text{nr}}(\downarrow, =)$ and conjunctive tree queries Q in $\mathbf{CTQ}(\downarrow, =)$, algorithm $\text{INLCERTANSW}(\mathcal{M}, Q)$ correctly computes certain answers $certain_{\mathcal{M}}(Q, S)$ for source documents S.*

The algorithm is illustrated in Figure 15.4, fulfilling our desiderata first outlined in Figure 15.1. It is not limited to queries considered here, and can be extended even to some XML-to-XML queries studied in the previous chapter; we refer the reader to the bibliographic comments for additional information.

Algorithm 15.6 INLCERTANSW($\mathcal{M}$,Q)

Require: S is a source document.
Ensure: The returned set of tuples is $certain_{\mathcal{M}}(Q,S)$.
  $S_r :=$ INLDOC(S,D_s)
  $\mathcal{M}_r :=$ INLMAP($\mathcal{M}$)
  $Q_r :=$ INLQUERY(Q,D_t)
  Compute the canonical universal solution T_r for S_r under $\mathcal{M}_r$.
  Compute $Q_r(T_r)$;
  Discard tuples with nulls from $Q_r(T_r)$;
  return $Q_r(T_r)$;

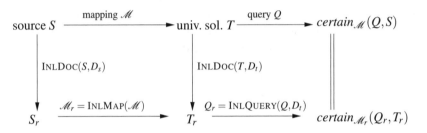

Figure 15.4 XML data exchange via relations: solution

Example 15.13 We now specify a complete XML schema mapping $\mathcal{M}$ in $SM^{nr}(\downarrow,=)$. As the source DTD D_s, we take the DTD D used in all other examples in the chapter, and as the source source tree S we take the tree in Figure 15.2. The target DTD D_t has two productions

$$r' \to \texttt{writer}^* \qquad\qquad \texttt{writer: @name}$$
$$\texttt{writer} \to \texttt{work}^* \qquad\qquad \texttt{work: @title, @year}.$$

Suppose we have a single dependency in Σ_{st}:

$$\texttt{r/book}(x)/\texttt{author/name}(y) \ \to\ \exists z\ \texttt{r'/writer}(y)/\texttt{work}(x,z),$$

restructuring book–author pairs into writer–works pairs, with a null z introduced for the unknown attribute @year. We denote $\texttt{r/book}(x)/\texttt{author/name}(y)$ by $\pi(x,y)$ and $\texttt{r'/writer}(y)/\texttt{work}(x,z)$ by $\pi'(x,y,z)$.

The inlining schema INLSCHEMA(D_t) is given by

$$R_{\texttt{r'}}(\underline{\texttt{rID}})$$
$$R_{\texttt{writer}}(\underline{\texttt{writerID}},\texttt{rID},\texttt{@name})$$
$$R_{\texttt{work}}(\underline{\texttt{workID}},\texttt{writerID},\texttt{@title},\texttt{@year})$$

with keys underlined, as well as two foreign keys: $R_{\texttt{writer}}(\texttt{rID}) \subseteq_{FK} R_{\texttt{r'}}(\texttt{rID})$ and $R_{\texttt{work}}(\texttt{writerID}) \subseteq_{FK} R_{\texttt{writer}}(\texttt{writerID})$.

The translation $S_r = \text{INLDOC}(S, D_s)$ was shown in Figures 15.3(a) and 15.3(b). To translate the mapping, we need to translate $\pi(x, y)$ and $\pi'(x, y, z)$ into conjunctive queries $Q_\pi(x, y)$ and $Q_{\pi'}(x, y, z)$; the st-tgd in $\text{INLMAP}(\mathcal{M})$ will then be

$$Q_\pi(x, y) \;\rightarrow\; \exists z \, Q_{\pi'}(x, y, z).$$

We have already shown the translation $Q_\pi(x, y)$ in Example 15.7. The translation of π' is

$$Q_{\pi'}(x, y, z) = \exists id_{r'} \exists id_{wr} \exists id_w \left(\begin{array}{c} R_{r'}(id_{r'}) \wedge R_{\text{writer}}(id_{wr}, id_{r'}, y) \wedge \\ \wedge R_{\text{work}}(id_w, id_{wr}, x, z) \end{array} \right).$$

When we apply the resulting mapping $\text{INLMAP}(\mathcal{M})$ to the instance S_r in Figures 15.3(a) and 15.3(b), we get the following canonical universal solution:

$R_{r'}$:

rId
$\perp_2$
$\perp_6$
$\perp_{10}$

R_{writer}:

writerID	rID	@name
$\perp_1$	$\perp_2$	*Kleinberg*
$\perp_5$	$\perp_6$	*Tardos*
$\perp_9$	$\perp_{10}$	*Hungerford*

R_{work}:

workID	writerID	@title	@year
$\perp_3$	$\perp_1$	*'Algorithm Design'*	$\perp_4$
$\perp_7$	$\perp_5$	*'Algorithm Design'*	$\perp_8$
$\perp_{11}$	$\perp_9$	*'Algebra'*	$\perp_{12}$

Note that this canonical universal solution does not coincide with an inlining of the canonical XML solution but rather contains one, as explained in Proposition 15.10: notice, for instance, that there are three distinct nulls in the relation for the root.

Now, if we have an XML query, for instance $Q(x) = r'/\text{writer}(x)$ asking for writer names, it will be translated into a relational query $Q_r = \text{INLQUERY}(Q, D_t)$ as follows:

$$Q_r(x) \;=\; \exists id_{r'} \exists id_{wr} \left(R_{r'}(id_{r'}) \wedge R_{\text{writer}}(id_{wr}, id_{r'}, x) \right).$$

When this query is evaluated over the canonical universal solution above (as Algorithm 15.6 prescribes), it produces the set $\{$*Kleinberg, Tardos, Hungerford*$\}$, which of course is $\text{certain}_{\mathcal{M}}(Q, S)$.

16

Endnotes to Part Three

16.1 Summary

- In XML schema mappings, analogs of st-tgds state how patterns over the source translate into patterns over the targets.

- Conditions imposed by XML schemas on the structure of target instances can contradict conditions imposed by st-tgds. This makes the existence of solutions an issue even without target dependencies.

- Testing existence and materializing solutions is tractable (for a fixed mapping).

- Query answering, even for XML analogs of relational conjunctive queries, can be intractable (CONP-complete, to be exact), and is tractable only under the following restrictions:

  1. mappings that use nested-relational DTDs and patterns with child navigation and equality comparisons only; and

  2. queries that use vertical navigation (child, descendant), wildcard, and equality comparisons.

- In this restricted case there is a polynomial-time algorithm that builds a universal solution for a given tree. Then certain answers can be computed by evaluating the query in that solution.

- For real-life XML-to-XML queries, certain answers' semantics has to be redefined. A notion of certain answers consistent with the traditional one can be built upon max-descriptions, maximally informative patterns holding in every possible answer.

- Under this semantics certain answers can be computed for mappings that use nested-relational DTDs and patterns with child and descendant navigation, wildcards, and equality.

- If schemas are assumed to be nested-relational DTDs, and mappings and queries are both based on patterns using only child and equality, certain answers can be computed via a translation to the relational case.

16.2 Bibliographic comments

There are multiple references on XML; its theoretical foundations, including the model based on unranked trees that we use here, are surveyed, for instance, in the papers by Vianu (2001); Libkin (2006b); Neven (2002); Klarlund et al. (2003), and Gou and Chirkova (2007). For basic information on tree automata, their decision problems and their complexity, see the surveys by Comon et al. (2007) and Schwentick (2007). Testing emptiness for UNFTAs with transitions represented by NFAs was shown to be polynomial by Neven (2002). LOGSPACE data complexity of testing if a given tree is accepted by an UNFTA was given by Gottlob et al. (2005).

Tree patterns as they are presented here were introduced by Arenas and Libkin (2008), and further extended with horizontal axes and data comparison by Amano et al. (2009). The patterns were introduced originally to represent conjunctive queries (Gottlob et al., 2006; Björklund et al., 2011, 2008). It should be noted however that to have the full expressive power of CQs one should allow DAG patterns, as it is done by Björklund et al. (2008). David (2008) considers a different kind of semantics based on injective homomorphisms. Expressing injective patterns as CQs requires inequality on node variables. Satisfiability and evaluation of tree patterns is essentially folklore as it appeared in many incarnations in the literature on tree patterns and XPath satisfiability (Amer-Yahia et al., 2002; Benedikt et al., 2008; Björklund et al., 2008; Hidders, 2003). The presented proof is by Amano et al. (2009).

Systematic investigation into XML data exchange was initiated by Arenas and Libkin (2008), who considered mappings based on restricted patterns disallowing horizontal navigation and data comparisons. Those features were added by Amano et al. (2009). Nested-relational DTDs were considered by Abiteboul et al. (2006), and by Arenas and Libkin (2004, 2008). Empirical studies on their usage are reported by Bex et al. (2004).

The algorithms testing existence and materializing solutions were obtained by Bojańczyk et al. (2011).

The query answering problem for child-based XML mappings was already considered by Arenas and Libkin (2008), who gave a detailed complexity analysis. The influence of sibling order and data comparisons was studied by Amano et al. (2010). Semantics of certain answers for XML-to-XML queries was originally introduced by David et al. (2010). Other studies of certain answers and incompleteness in XML include the papers by Abiteboul et al. (2006), Barceló et al. (2010), and Gheerbrant et al. (2012).

Algorithms for translating XML data exchange tasks into relational are given by Chirkova et al. (2012).

16.3 Exercises

1. Give an example of a DTD such that the smallest tree it admits is exponential.
2. Prove that the pattern satisfiability problem is NP-complete even for a fixed DTD. Hint: Use equalities and constants in the pattern.

3. Show that the problem XML-SM-MEMBERSHIP is Π_2^p-hard. Hint: Reduce the validity of Π_2 quantified Boolean formulae, i.e., formulae of the form $\forall x_1 \ldots \forall x_n \exists y_1 \ldots \exists y_m \, \varphi$ where φ is a Boolean formula over variables $x_1, \ldots, x_n, y_1, \ldots, y_m$ in conjunctive normal form and quantification ranges over *true* and *false*.

4. Prove that for a given tree T and UNFTA $\mathscr{A}$ it can be decided in PTIME if $\mathscr{A}$ accepts T. If $\mathscr{A}$ is UFTA(DFA), it can be done in LOGSPACE.

5. Prove that for a given UNFTA $\mathscr{A}$ it can be decided in PTIME if there exists a tree accepted by $\mathscr{A}$.

6. Let D be a nested-relational DTD. Show that for each XML tree T agreeing with a D-kind K there exists exactly one witnessing substitution T_u (see page 164).

7. Give an example of a tree automaton $\mathscr{A}$, an $\mathscr{A}$-kind K and a tree $T \in L(K)$ such that there is more than one witnessing substitution. Can this automaton be deterministic?

8. (Source: Bojańczyk et al. (2011))
   Show that for a fixed mapping $\mathscr{M}$, solution existence can be checked in LOGSPACE.

9. (Source: Bojańczyk et al. (2011))
   A schema $\mathscr{S}$ has depth k if each tree conforming to $\mathscr{S}$ has height at most k. Show that for mappings with the target schema of fixed depth, solution building can be done in EXPTIME, and solution existence can be tested in $\Sigma_3 P$.

10. (Source: Bojańczyk et al. (2011))
    Show that the SOLEXISTENCE problem is NEXPTIME-hard also for mappings that do not use $=$ on the source side, and for mappings that use $\downarrow^+$ but do not use $\_$. Hint: Modify the reduction in proof of Theorem 12.28.

11. (Source: Amano et al. (2010))
    Give an example of a mapping $\mathscr{M} \in \mathrm{SM}^{\mathrm{nr}}(\downarrow, \to, =)$ and a query $Q \in \mathbf{CTQ}(\downarrow, =)$ such that $\mathrm{CERTAIN}_{\mathscr{M}}(Q)$ is CONP-complete.

12. Generalize the PTIME-algorithm for certain answers so that it handles

    (a) mappings in $\mathrm{SM}^{\mathrm{nr}}(\downarrow, \to^+, =)$ and queries in $\mathbf{CTQ}(\downarrow, =)$;
    (b) mappings in $\mathrm{SM}^{\mathrm{nr}}(\downarrow, =, \neq)$ and queries in $\mathbf{CTQ}(\downarrow, =)$.

13. (Source: Amano et al. (2010))
    A mapping $\mathscr{M}$ is called $\to$-*specified* if in each target pattern, the order of the sub-patterns is completely specified by means of $\to$; e.g., $r[a \to b \to b]$ is allowed, and $r[a, b \to b]$ is not. Find a $\to$-specified mapping from $\mathrm{SM}^{\mathrm{nr}}(\downarrow, \to)$, and a query from $\mathbf{CTQ}(\downarrow, \to, =)$ such that $\mathrm{CERTAIN}_{\mathscr{M}}(Q)$ is CONP-complete. Formulate and prove a similar result for $\to^+$.

14. (Source: David et al. (2010))
    Find a family $\{\mathscr{T}_n\}_{n>0}$ of sets of XML trees such that $|\mathscr{T}_n| = n$, each tree in $\mathscr{T}_n$ has size $\mathscr{O}(n)$, but each max-description of $\mathscr{T}_n$ has size at least 2^n.

15. (Source: David et al. (2010))
    Show that there exist a family of trees $\{S_n\}_{n>0}$ with $|S_n| = \mathscr{O}(n)$, a mapping $\mathscr{M} \in \mathrm{SM}^{\mathrm{nr}}(\downarrow, \_)$, and a TQL query Q such that $\mathrm{CERTAIN}_{\mathscr{M}}(Q, S_n)$ has the size at least 2^n.

Hint: Design $\{S_n\}_{n>0}$, $\mathcal{M}$, and Q so that $Q(\text{SOL}_{\mathcal{M}}(S_n))$ behaves like the family $\mathcal{T}_n$ from Exercise 16.3.

16. (Source: David et al. (2010))

A pattern or a tree is *ground* if it uses only constants, i.e., it does not use variables/nulls. For a set of trees $\mathcal{T}$, $\text{Th}_{\text{gr}}(\mathcal{T})$ denotes the set of ground patterns that are satisfied in each tree from $\mathcal{T}$. A ground pattern π is a *ground max-description* of $\mathcal{T}$ if $\text{Mod}(\pi) = \text{Mod}(\text{Th}_{\text{gr}}(\mathcal{T}))$.

(a) Let $\text{ground}(\pi)$ be a ground pattern obtained from π by dropping all the subpatterns $\ell(\bar{a}, \bar{x})[\ldots]$ with nonempty $\bar{x}$. Show that if π is a max-description of $\mathcal{T}$, then $\text{ground}(\pi)$ is a ground max-description of $\mathcal{T}$.

(b) Show that for every nonempty set of ground trees $\mathcal{T}$, a ground max-description exists, and can be computed if $\mathcal{T}$ and $\text{Th}_{\text{gr}}(\mathcal{T})$ are recursive.

17. Show that the set of trees $\{r[a(x_1, x_2), a(x_2, x_3), \ldots, a(x_{n-1}, a_n), a(x_n, x_1)] \mid n \in \mathbb{N}\}$ has no max-description.

PART FOUR
METADATA MANAGEMENT

17
What is metadata management?

So far we have concentrated on handling data in data exchange, i.e., transforming source databases into target ones, and answering queries over them. We now look at manipulating information about schemas and schema mappings, known as *metadata*, i.e., we deal with metadata management. In this short chapter we outline the key problems that need to be addressed in the context of metadata management. These are divided into two groups of problems. The first concerns reasoning about mappings, and the second group of problems is about manipulating mappings, i.e., building new mappings from existing ones.

17.1 Reasoning about schema mappings

As we have seen, mappings are logical specifications of the relationship between schemas, both in the relational and XML scenarios. In particular, we have seen many different logical languages that are used to specify mappings. Thus, a first natural problem that one would like to study in the context of metadata management is to characterize the properties that a mapping satisfies depending on the logical formulae that are used to define it. More precisely, one would like, in the first place, to understand whether the logical formulae used to specify a mapping are excessively restrictive in the sense that no source instance admits a solution, or at least restrictive in the sense that some source instances do not admit solutions. Note that this is different from the problem of checking for the existence of solutions, studied in Chapter 5. In that problem, the input consists of both a mapping *and* an instance, and we want to see if the mapping can be applied to a particular instance. Now we are talking about just metadata management problems. That is, the input consists of a mapping alone, and we want to know, before seeing any data, whether this mapping actually makes sense. The latter could mean that it is either applicable to *some* instances, which we shall term the *consistency problem*, or it is applicable to *all* instances, which we shall term the *absolute consistency* problem. These consistency problems are studied in Chapter 18.

The second type of problems that we look at are of the following nature: we would like to understand what one can lose or gain by switching from one language to another. In particular, we want to understand what happens to the fundamental tasks such as constructing solutions or answering target queries when we switch between different logical languages that can be used to specify mappings. In Chapter 21, we shed light on these problems by providing characterizations of the most common classes of mappings in terms of the structural properties they satisfy.

17.2 Manipulating schema mappings

The second type of problems we look at in the metadata management framework (sometimes called model management) is more operational in nature. We look at operations on mappings themselves, i.e., operations that let us build new mappings from existing ones. Some operations that have been proposed include match, merge, compose and invert. Here we concentrate on composition and inversion, as these are the key operators for understanding *schema evolution*.

We now describe the intuition behind the composition operator, and show how it can be used in practice to solve some metadata management problems. Let $\mathscr{M}_{12}$ be the mapping given in Chapter 1, which is used to translate information from a source schema $\mathbf{R_1}$, consisting of relations GEO(city, country, population) and FLIGHT(source, destination, airline, departure), into a target schema $\mathbf{R_2}$, consisting of relations ROUTES(flight#, source, destination), INFO_FLIGHT(flight#, departure_time, arrival_time, airline) and SERVES(airline, city, country, phone). Mapping $\mathscr{M}_{12}$ is specified by using st-tgds:

$$FLIGHT(src, dest, airl, dep) \longrightarrow$$
$$\exists f\# \exists arr \, (ROUTES(f\#, src, dest) \wedge$$
$$INFO\_FLIGHT(f\#, dep, arr, airl))$$
$$FLIGHT(city, dest, airl, dep) \wedge GEO(city, country, popul) \longrightarrow$$
$$\exists phone \, SERVES(airl, city, country, phone)$$
$$FLIGHT(src, city, airl, dep) \wedge GEO(city, country, popul) \longrightarrow$$
$$\exists phone \, SERVES(airl, city, country, phone).$$

Assume that schema $\mathbf{R_2}$ has to be updated into a new target schema $\mathbf{R_3}$ consisting of the following relations:

- INFO_AIRLINE(airline, city, country, phone, year)
  This relation has information about cities served by airlines: for example, it may have a tuple (AirFrance, Santiago, Chile, 5550000, 1982), indicating that AirFrance serves Santiago, Chile, since 1982, and its office there can be reached at 555-0000.
- INFO_JOURNEY(flight#, source, departure_time, destination, arrival_time, airline)
  This relation has information about routes served by several airlines. For each flight, this relation stores the flight number (flight#), source, departure time, destination, arrival time and the name of the airline.

Furthermore, assume that the relationship between $\mathbf{R}_2$ and the new target schema $\mathbf{R}_3$ is given by a mapping $\mathcal{M}_{23}$ specified by the following st-tgds:

$$\text{SERVES}(\text{airl}, \text{city}, \text{country}, \text{phone}) \longrightarrow$$
$$\exists \text{year } \text{INFO\_AIRLINE}(\text{airl}, \text{city}, \text{country}, \text{phone}, \text{year})$$
$$\text{ROUTES}(\text{f\#}, \text{src}, \text{dest}) \wedge \text{INFO\_FLIGHT}(\text{f\#}, \text{dep}, \text{arr}, \text{airl}) \longrightarrow$$
$$\text{INFO\_JOURNEY}(\text{f\#}, \text{src}, \text{dep}, \text{dest}, \text{arr}, \text{airl}).$$

Given that $\mathbf{R}_2$ has to be replaced by the new target schema $\mathbf{R}_3$, the mapping $\mathcal{M}_{12}$ from schema $\mathbf{R}_1$ into schema $\mathbf{R}_2$ also has to be replaced by a new mapping $\mathcal{M}_{13}$, which specifies how to translate data from $\mathbf{R}_1$ into the new target schema $\mathbf{R}_3$. Thus, the problem in this scenario is to compute a new mapping $\mathcal{M}_{13}$ that represents the application of mapping $\mathcal{M}_{12}$ followed by the application of mapping $\mathcal{M}_{23}$. But given that mappings are binary relations from a semantic point of view, this problem corresponds to the computation of the composition of mappings $\mathcal{M}_{12}$ and $\mathcal{M}_{23}$. In fact, the composition operator for schema mappings exactly computes this, and in this particular example returns a mapping $\mathcal{M}_{13}$ specified by the following st-tgds:

$$\text{FLIGHT}(\text{src}, \text{dest}, \text{airl}, \text{dep}) \longrightarrow$$
$$\exists \text{f\#} \exists \text{arr } \text{INFO\_JOURNEY}(\text{f\#}, \text{src}, \text{dep}, \text{dest}, \text{arr}, \text{airl})$$
$$\text{FLIGHT}(\text{city}, \text{dest}, \text{airl}, \text{dep}) \wedge \text{GEO}(\text{city}, \text{country}, \text{popul}) \longrightarrow$$
$$\exists \text{phone} \exists \text{year } \text{INFO\_AIRLINE}(\text{airl}, \text{city}, \text{country}, \text{phone}, \text{year})$$
$$\text{FLIGHT}(\text{src}, \text{city}, \text{airl}, \text{dep}) \wedge \text{GEO}(\text{city}, \text{country}, \text{popul}) \longrightarrow$$
$$\exists \text{phone} \exists \text{year } \text{INFO\_AIRLINE}(\text{airl}, \text{city}, \text{country}, \text{phone}, \text{year}).$$

As we can see from this example, the composition operator is essential to handle schema evolution. If a schema evolves first from $\mathbf{R}_1$ to $\mathbf{R}_2$, as specified by a mapping $\mathcal{M}_{12}$, and then the target schema $\mathbf{R}_2$ further evolves to $\mathbf{R}_3$, as specified by a mapping $\mathcal{M}_{23}$, we do not want to create an intermediate instance of schema $\mathbf{R}_2$ to translate data structured under $\mathbf{R}_1$ into $\mathbf{R}_3$: instead we want a composition mapping $\mathcal{M}_{13}$ that translates directly from $\mathbf{R}_1$ to $\mathbf{R}_3$.

Another operator that appears in this context is the *inverse* operator. Assume that we have two schemas, $\mathbf{R}_1$ and $\mathbf{R}_2$, and a mapping $\mathcal{M}_{12}$ between them. But now suppose it is the source schema $\mathbf{R}_1$ that evolves to $\mathbf{R}_0$, and this is specified by a mapping $\mathcal{M}_{10}$. How can we now go directly from $\mathbf{R}_0$ to $\mathbf{R}_2$? The idea is to *undo* the transformation done by $\mathcal{M}_{10}$ and then apply the mapping $\mathcal{M}_{12}$. In other words, we invert the mapping $\mathcal{M}_{10}$, to get a mapping $\mathcal{M}_{10}^{-1}$ going from $\mathbf{R}_0$ to $\mathbf{R}_1$, and then compose $\mathcal{M}_{10}^{-1}$ with $\mathcal{M}_{12}$.

This explains why the operators of composition and inverse are crucial for the development of a metadata management framework. We study the composition operator in Chapter 19, and the inverse operator in Chapter 20.

18

Consistency of schema mappings

The goal of this chapter is to analyze the consistency problem for schema mappings: that is, whether a mapping can be applied to some source instance, or to all source instances, to generate a target instance. The first problem is referred to as consistency, and the second as absolute consistency. Since these problems are easily solvable for relational mappings without target dependencies, we concentrate on those problems in the XML context.

We start by proving that without comparisons of data values in st-tgds, the consistency problem is solvable in single-exponential time, and the bound cannot be improved. When comparisons are added, it quickly becomes undecidable. However, the complexity drops dramatically for nested-relational DTDs. As for absolute consistency, the problem is actually much harder to solve: a priori even decidability is not clear. We do present an algorithm, very different from the algorithm for consistency, that solves the problem with exponential space (rather than time) bounds, and look for special cases that lead to lower-complexity algorithms.

18.1 Problems statements

Consider a relational mapping $\mathcal{M} = (\mathbf{R_s}, \mathbf{R_t}, \Sigma_{st})$ specified by a finite set Σ_{st} of st-tgds. Note that the mapping does not have any target dependencies. In that case, we know that $\text{SOL}_{\mathcal{M}}(S) \neq \emptyset$ for every instance S of $\mathbf{R_s}$. In fact, assuming that $\mathcal{M}$ is fixed, we have given polynomial-time algorithms that compute, for each source instance, solutions with good properties (see Sections 6.3 and 6.4). Thus, consistency is not an issue for the class of mappings specified by st-tgds: both consistency, as we described it in Chapter 17, and absolute consistency, are trivially solvable, since the answer is simply "yes".

On the other hand, the tree model used in the case of XML data exchange gives more opportunities for expressing structural properties of data even with simple queries based on patterns. In fact, we have already seen that schemas can impose strong conditions on the structure of source and target instances, entering into complex interactions with source-to-target dependencies, which makes consistency one of the central issues in XML data exchange.

Unlike relational mappings, XML schema mappings may be inconsistent: there are mappings $\mathcal{M}$ so that $[\![\mathcal{M}]\!] = \emptyset$, i.e., no tree has a solution. In addition to consistent mappings, in which *some* trees have solutions, we would like to consider mappings in which *every* tree has a solution. These are very desirable for a variety of reasons: not only are we guaranteed to have possible target documents for every possible source, but the property is also preserved when we compose mappings (see Chapter 19).

We say that a mapping $\mathcal{M} = (\mathscr{S}_s, \mathscr{S}_t, \Sigma_{st})$ is *consistent* if it can be useful for at least some source instances. That is, a mapping is consistent if $\text{SOL}_{\mathcal{M}}(S) \neq \emptyset$ for some source instances $S \models \mathscr{S}_s$. This can be restated as $[\![\mathcal{M}]\!] \neq \emptyset$.

Recall that in Part THREE of the book we dealt with XML schema mapping classes of the form $\text{SM}(\sigma)$, where σ lists available features of the mappings, such as axes used in navigation through documents, or the possibility of using equalities and inequalities. The first key problem we consider is the one below.

PROBLEM: CONS(σ)
INPUT: A mapping $\mathcal{M} = (\mathscr{S}_s, \mathscr{S}_t, \Sigma_{st}) \in \text{SM}(\sigma)$
QUESTION: Is $\mathcal{M}$ consistent?

If we use $\text{SM}^\circ(\sigma)$ instead of $\text{SM}(\sigma)$ (i.e., if we use mappings in which attribute values are not mentioned at all), we denote the consistency problem by $\text{CONS}^\circ(\sigma)$.

A mapping $\mathcal{M}$ is *absolutely consistent* if it makes sense for *every* source tree S: each such tree has a solution under the mapping. That is, $\text{SOL}_{\mathcal{M}}(S) \neq \emptyset$ for all $S \models \mathscr{S}_s$. We then consider the problem:

PROBLEM: ABCONS(σ)
INPUT: Mapping $\mathcal{M} = (\mathscr{S}_s, \mathscr{S}_t, \Sigma_{st}) \in \text{SM}(\sigma)$
QUESTION: Is $\mathcal{M}$ absolutely consistent?

These are the two main problems studied in this chapter.

18.2 Consistency for XML

The goal of this section is to show that the behavior of the consistency problem $\text{CONS}(\sigma)$ depends heavily on σ, i.e., on the exact set of features allowed in mappings. Recall that σ may contain navigational axes $\downarrow, \rightarrow, \downarrow^+, \rightarrow^+$, as well as data comparisons $=$ and $\neq$, see Chapter 11, page 147. Recall that we abbreviate $\downarrow, \downarrow^+, \_$ as $\Downarrow$ (vertical navigation), $\rightarrow, \rightarrow^+, \_$ as $\Rightarrow$ (horizontal navigation), and $=, \neq$ as $\sim$ (data comparisons).

A brief summary of the algorithmic properties of the consistency problem is as follows:

- Without $=, \neq$ comparisons, the problem can be solved in exponential time, and this complexity cannot be lowered.
- With $=, \neq$ comparisons the problem quickly becomes undecidable.
- When schemas are restricted to be nested-relational DTDs, the complexity in general drops, but not in every single case.

Decidable cases of consistency

The main result of this section is an algorithm for solving the problem $\mathrm{CONS}(\Downarrow,\Rightarrow)$, i.e., consistency without the $=,\neq$ comparisons. The algorithm works in single-exponential time, and this time bound cannot be lowered, since the problem is EXPTIME-complete. That is, we prove the following result.

Theorem 18.1 *The problem* $\mathrm{CONS}(\Downarrow,\Rightarrow)$ *is solvable in single-exponential time, and is in fact* EXPTIME-*complete.*

The algorithm is based on using automata-theoretic tools. We already know that every schema can be encoded as an UNFTA, i.e., a nondeterministic tree automaton working on unranked trees (see Definition 10.6 on page 139). Now we are going to see how to encode a pattern as UFTA(DFA), that is, deterministic UNFTA with all transitions represented by DFAs. As UNFTAs do not look at data values at all, we cannot hope to do the same for general tree patterns; we need to assume the patterns do not talk about data values either.

Lemma 18.2 *For every pattern* π *without variables, one can compute in exponential time a UFTA(DFA)* $\mathscr{A}_\pi$ *such that* $L(\mathscr{A}_\pi) = \{T \mid T \models \pi\}$.

Proof We construct $\mathscr{A}_\pi$ by induction on the structure of π. If $\pi = \ell$ with $\ell \in \Gamma \cup \{\_\}$, the claim follows easily. Assume we have an UFTA(DFA) $\mathscr{A}_\pi = (Q,\delta,F)$ for π. To obtain $\mathscr{A}_{//\pi}$ add a fresh state f, set $\delta^{//\pi}(f,a) = Q^*(F \cup \{f\})Q^*$ for every $a \in \Gamma$ (the equivalent DFA has two states), $\delta^{//\pi}(q,a) = \delta(q,a) \cap (Q-F)^*$ for every $a \in \Gamma$, $q \in Q$ (equivalent DFAs grow by at most one state), and $F^{//\pi} = F \cup \{f\}$.

The last case is that of $\pi = \ell[\mu_1,\dots,\mu_n]$. Let us first construct an UFTA(DFA) for $\ell[\mu]$ with

$$\mu = (\pi_1 \rightsquigarrow_1 \pi_2 \rightsquigarrow_2 \cdots \rightsquigarrow_{k-1} \pi_k),$$

and $\rightsquigarrow_1, \rightsquigarrow_2, \dots, \rightsquigarrow_{k-1} \in \{\rightarrow, \rightarrow^+\}$. Let $\mathscr{A}_{\pi_j} = (Q_j,\delta_j,F_j)$ be the UFTA(DFA) constructed for π_j. The state space of $\mathscr{A}_{\ell[\mu]}$ is $Q = Q_1 \times Q_2 \times \cdots \times Q_k \times \{\top,\bot\}$. Consider the language M defined by the regular expression

$$Q^* \tilde{F}_1 \alpha_1 \tilde{F}_2 \alpha_2 \cdots \tilde{F}_{k-1} \alpha_{k-1} \tilde{F}_k Q^*,$$

where $\tilde{F}_j = \{(q_1,\dots,q_{k+1}) \in Q \mid q_j \in F_j\}$, $\alpha_i = Q^*$ if $\rightsquigarrow_i=\rightarrow^+$, and $\alpha_i = \varepsilon$ otherwise. It is not difficult to construct an NFA with $O(k)$ states recognizing M; standard determinization gives an equivalent DFA $\mathscr{B}$ with $2^{O(k)}$ states. The transition relation of $\mathscr{A}_{\ell[\mu]}$ is now defined as

$$\delta((\bar{q},s),a) = (\delta_1(q_1,a) \times \delta_2(q_2,a) \times \cdots \times \delta_k(q_k,a) \times \{\top,\bot\}) \cap K$$

where $K = M$ if $s = \top, a = \ell$ (or $\ell = \_$), and $K = Q^* - M$ otherwise. Each such transition can be represented by a product of DFAs $\mathscr{B}_1,\dots,\mathscr{B}_n$ and $\mathscr{B}$ (or its complement), where B_j are single-exponential in $\|\pi_j\|$, and $\mathscr{B}$ is single-exponential in k. Since $\|\pi\|$ is roughly $\sum_{j=1}^n \|\pi_j\|$, the size of the product DFA $\prod_{j=1}^n \|\mathscr{B}_j\| \cdot \|\mathscr{B}\|$ is single-exponential in $\|\pi\|$. The accepting states are those with $\top$ as the last component. In order to obtain an UFTA(DFA) for $\ell[\mu_1, \mu_2, \ldots, \mu_n]$ it suffices to take the product of $\mathscr{A}_{\ell[\mu_i]}$. $\qquad\qquad\square$

It is not difficult to see that the construction is asymptotically optimal (Exercise 22.3).

We can now combine the two ideas and reduce consistency of mappings to the emptiness problem. Testing emptiness can be done in polynomial time, but the UNFTA resulting from the reduction will be a product of linearly many UNFTA of exponential size, and hence will be exponential.

Proposition 18.3 CONS$^\circ(\Downarrow, \Rightarrow)$ *is* EXPTIME-*complete.*

Proof For a mapping $(\mathscr{S}_s, \mathscr{S}_t, \Sigma_{st})$ to be consistent, there must exist a pair (T_1, T_2) such that for all $\varphi \longrightarrow \psi \in \Sigma_{st}$ it holds that $T_1 \models \varphi$ implies $T_2 \models \psi$. Suppose $\Sigma_{st} = \{\varphi_i \longrightarrow \psi_i \mid i = 1, 2, \ldots, n\}$. Then the existence of such a pair is equivalent to the existence of a subset $I \subseteq \{1, 2, \ldots, n\}$ satisfying

- there exists $T_1 \models \mathscr{S}_s$ such that $T_1 \not\models \varphi_j$ for all $j \notin I$,
- there exists $T_2 \models \mathscr{S}_t$ such that $T_2 \models \psi_i$ for all $i \in I$.

This amounts to nonemptiness of the following automaton:

- $\mathscr{A}_s \times \prod_{j \notin I} \overline{\mathscr{A}_{\varphi_j}}$,
- $\mathscr{A}_t \times \prod_{j \in I} \mathscr{A}_{\psi_j}$,

where $\mathscr{A}_s$ and $\mathscr{A}_t$ are the UNFTA underlying $\mathscr{S}_s$ and $\mathscr{S}_t$. The construction of each $\mathscr{A}_\varphi$ takes exponential time. Since $\mathscr{A}_\varphi$ are deterministic, complementing them is straightforward. Testing nonemptiness of $\mathscr{A}_1 \times \cdots \times \mathscr{A}_k$ can be done in time $\mathcal{O}(|\mathscr{A}_1| \times \cdots \times |\mathscr{A}_k|)$. Hence, the overall complexity is EXPTIME.

To prove EXPTIME-hardness we provide a reduction from the nonuniversality problem for binary tree automata (NTAs). Given an NTA $\mathscr{A}$, testing if there is a tree rejected by $\mathscr{A}$ is known to be EXPTIME-hard. The idea of the encoding is that the source tree codes both an input tree and the run of the corresponding deterministic powerset automaton. The st-tgds ensure that the run is constructed properly, and that it contains only nonfinal states in the root.

Fix an NTA $\mathscr{A} = (Q, \Gamma, q_0, F, \delta)$ with $Q = \{q_0, \ldots, q_n\}$ and $\Gamma = \{a_1, \ldots, a_k\}$. Let $\mathscr{S}_s$ be given by the DTD

$$\texttt{r}, \texttt{left}, \texttt{right} \rightarrow \texttt{label}\ q_0 \ldots q_n\ (\texttt{left}\,\texttt{right} \mid \texttt{leaf})$$

$$\texttt{label} \rightarrow a_1 \mid a_2 \mid \ldots \mid a_k$$

$$q_1, q_2, \ldots, q_n \rightarrow \texttt{yes} \mid \texttt{no}$$

and $\mathscr{S}$ by $\texttt{r} \rightarrow \varepsilon$.

In every tree conforming to $\mathscr{S}_s$, the nodes labeled with $\texttt{r}$, $\texttt{left}$ and $\texttt{right}$ form a binary tree over which we run the powerset automaton. A q_i-child should lead to a yes iff the state of the powerset automaton contains q_i. This is ensured by adding for each $q_k \in \delta(a_l, q_i, q_j)$ the st-tgd

$$//_-[q_k/\texttt{no, label}/a_l, \texttt{left}/q_i/\texttt{yes, right}/q_j/\texttt{yes}] \longrightarrow \bot,$$

where $\bot$ is a fixed pattern inconsistent with $\mathscr{S}_t$, e.g. $\texttt{r}/\texttt{r}$. Similarly we enforce that every state, in which $\mathscr{A}$ can be after reading a leaf with a given label, is a yes-state:

$$//_-[q_k/\texttt{no, label}/a_l, \texttt{leaf}] \longrightarrow \bot \qquad \text{for } q_k \in \delta(a_l, q_0, q_0).$$

Finally, we check that in the root of the run only nonfinal states are present:

$$\texttt{r}/q_k/\texttt{yes} \longrightarrow \bot \qquad \text{for } q_k \in Q - F.$$

The obtained mapping is consistent iff there is a tree rejected by $\mathscr{A}$. $\qquad\square$

Now using a simple observation we can immediately extend the algorithm presented above to the case with variables, provided that data comparisons are not allowed, and conclude the proof of Theorem 18.1.

Proof of Theorem 18.1 In the absence of data comparisons we can simply "forget" about the data values. For a tree pattern π, let π° denote a tree pattern obtained from π by replacing all subformulae of the form $\ell(\bar{t})$ with ℓ, for ℓ being a label or $_-$. Let $\Sigma_{st}^\circ = \{\pi_1^\circ \longrightarrow \pi_2^\circ \mid (\pi_1 \longrightarrow \exists \bar{z}\, \pi_2) \in \Sigma_{st}\}$. It is not difficult to see that $(\mathscr{S}_s, \mathscr{S}_t, \Sigma_{st})$ is consistent iff $(\mathscr{S}_s, \mathscr{S}_t, \Sigma_{st}^\circ)$ is consistent. $\qquad\square$

Note that the complexity is relatively high, but the input to the problem consists of *metadata* only (the schemas, and dependencies between them) and not the actual data. Thus, in many cases a single-exponential bound is actually acceptable. Later we shall see how to lower it under some restrictions.

Undecidable cases of consistency

We now move to classes of schema mappings that allow comparisons of attribute values. It is common to lose decidability (or low complexity solutions) of static analysis problems once data values and their comparisons are considered. Here we witness a similar situation: having either descendant or next-sibling, together with either $=$ or $\neq$, leads to undecidability of consistency.

Theorem 18.4 *Each of the following problems is undecidable:* $\textsc{Cons}(\downarrow, \downarrow^+, =)$, $\textsc{Cons}(\downarrow, \downarrow^+, \neq)$, $\textsc{Cons}(\downarrow, \rightarrow, =)$, *and* $\textsc{Cons}(\downarrow, \rightarrow, \neq)$.

Proof We only prove undecidability of $\textsc{Cons}(\downarrow, \downarrow^+, =)$. The remaining cases are left as an exercise. We describe a reduction from the halting problem of a two-register machine, which is known to be undecidable. That is, given a two-register machine (defined below), we construct a schema mapping that is consistent iff the machine halts. Trees encoding runs of a two-register machine will be of the form:

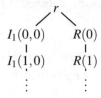

Intuitively, the left branch is meant to represent a sequence of states with data values representing registers while the right one is a sequence to represent natural numbers. We do not have any equality test against a constant (say, a natural number). So, what we really do is simulate values by the depth from the root. More concretely 0 and 1 above might as well be $\sharp$ and $\flat$. Whatever they are, we simply take the value at the zeroth level as 0 and the first level as 1, and so on. The above tree can be easily described by a DTD. To make sure it is a proper run of the given machine, we use st-tgds to check that the registers change their values according to legal transitions.

Let us now describe the reduction in detail. A two-register machine M consists of a set of states $Q = \{1, 2, \ldots, f\}$, a list of instructions $\mathcal{I} = (I_i \mid i \in Q \setminus \{f\})$ (one instruction for each state apart from the last state f), and two registers r_1 and r_2, each containing a natural number. A configuration of M is a triple (i, m, n) where $i \in Q$ and $m, n \in \mathbb{N}$ are natural numbers stored in r_1 and r_2, respectively.

An instruction of a two-register machine is either an *increment* or a *decrement*, and defines the transition relation $\to_M$ between configurations.

Increment $I_i = (r, j)$, where $i \in Q$ and r is one of r_1 and r_2. This means that M in state i increments r and goes to state j:

$$(i, m, n) \to_M \begin{cases} (j, m+1, n) & \text{if } r = r_1, \\ (j, m, n+1) & \text{if } r = r_2. \end{cases}$$

Decrement $I_i = (r, j, k)$, where $i, j, k \in Q$ and r is one of the two registers. This means that M in state i can test whether r is 0, and go to state j if it is, or decrement r and go to k if it is not. In symbols,

$$(i, m, n) \to_M \begin{cases} (j, 0, n) & \text{if } r = r_1 \text{ and } m = 0, \\ (j, m-1, n) & \text{if } r = r_1 \text{ and } m \neq 0, \\ (j, m, 0) & \text{if } r = r_2 \text{ and } n = 0, \\ (j, m, n-1) & \text{if } r = r_2 \text{ and } n \neq 0. \end{cases}$$

The initial configuration is $(1, 0, 0)$ and the final configuration is $(f, 0, 0)$. The halting problem for a two-register machine is to decide, given a two-register machine M, whether $(1, 0, 0) \to_M^* (f, 0, 0)$.

Let us now describe how to construct a mapping, which is consistent iff the given machine halts. The source DTD D_s over the alphabet $\{r, I_1, I_2, \ldots, I_f, R, \sharp\}$ is given by

$$r \rightarrow I_1 R$$
$$I_i \rightarrow I_j \qquad \text{for all } i \text{ such that } I_i = (r, j)$$
$$I_i \rightarrow I_j | I_k \quad \text{for all } i \text{ such that } I_i = (r, j, k)$$
$$R \rightarrow R | \sharp$$
$$I_f, \sharp \rightarrow \varepsilon$$

where each I_i has two attributes corresponding to the values of the registers, and R has one attribute.

The target DTD D_t is simply $\{r \rightarrow \varepsilon\}$.

As mentioned above, the sequence of R's is meant to be that of natural numbers, but what represents a number is the depth in the tree instead of a value itself. In other words, the data values are used as indices, so they must be unique. This is enforced by the following dependency

$$r//R(x)//R(x) \longrightarrow \bot.$$

Let us now deal with the left branch, which is meant to encode the run itself. We have assumed that the initial configuration is $(1,0,0)$; the constraints below exclude other situations

$$r[I_1(x,y), //R/R(x)] \longrightarrow \bot$$
$$r[I_1(x,y), //R/R(y)] \longrightarrow \bot.$$

Now, let us check that we proceed correctly. For each i such that $I_i = (r_1, j)$, we need to enforce that there is a number in the R-branch to set the value of r_1 to, and that the next configuration is indeed obtained by increasing r_1

$$r[//I_i(x,y), //R(x)/\sharp] \longrightarrow \bot$$
$$r[//I_i(x,y)/I_j(x',y'), //R(x)/R(x'')] \longrightarrow x' = x'', y' = y.$$

For each i such that $I_i = (r_1, j, k)$, we need to say: if the next state is k, then r_1 stores 0, and both registers stay the same; if the next state is j, then r_1 does not store 0, the register r_1 gets decreased, and r_2 stays the same

$$r[//I_i(x,y)/I_k(x',y'), R(x'')] \longrightarrow x = x'', x' = x, y' = y$$
$$r[//I_i(x,y)/I_j, R(x)] \longrightarrow \bot$$
$$r[//I_i(x,y)/I_j(x',y'), //R(x'')/R(x)] \longrightarrow x' = x'', y' = y.$$

For each i such that $I_i = (r_2, j)$ or $I_i = (r_2, j, k)$ we add analogous st-tgds.

Finally, we have to make sure that we end properly. In each source tree, the left branch must end with I_f, so we do not need to check that. It is enough to say that both registers are set to 0

$$r[//I_i(x,y)/\sharp, //R/R(x)] \longrightarrow \bot$$
$$r[//I_i(x,y)/\sharp, //R/R(y)] \longrightarrow \bot.$$

The obtained mapping (D_s, D_t, Σ_{st}) is consistent iff there is a halting run of the given two-register machine. Thus we have proved that $\text{CONS}(\downarrow, \downarrow^+, =)$ is undecidable. $\qquad\square$

Consistency with nested-relational DTDs

We have seen in Part III that quite a few tasks related to XML data exchange become easier computationally if the schemas are given by nested-relational DTDs (see Definition 10.5 on page 139). We start with the case of mappings that do not use $=, \neq$ comparisons. Here in the case of vertical navigation, we achieve tractability of the consistency problem. When horizontal navigation is added, the problem becomes intractable again, even with nested relational DTDs. We leave the proof of these results as an exercise (see Exercises 22.3 and 22.3).

Proposition 18.5 *For schemas restricted to nested-relational DTDs*

- $\text{CONS}(\Downarrow)$ *is solvable in polynomial (cubic) time;*
- $\text{CONS}(\Downarrow, \rightarrow)$ *is* PSPACE-*complete.*

When comparisons are allowed, the situation is somewhat similar: with vertical navigation, we recover decidability, but when horizontal navigation is added, it is lost again.

Theorem 18.6 *Under the restriction to nested-relational DTDs:*

- *the problem* $\text{CONS}(\Downarrow, \sim)$ *is* NEXPTIME-*complete;*
- *the problem* $\text{CONS}(\downarrow, \rightarrow, \sim)$ *is undecidable.*

Proof A modification of the two-register machine reduction gives the undecidability result (Exercise 22.3) and a modification of the reduction in the proof of Theorem 12.28 gives NEXPTIME-hardness already for $\text{CONS}(\downarrow, \_, =)$ (Exercise 22.3). Let us concentrate on the algorithm giving the upper bound.

Let $\mathcal{M} = (D_s, D_t, \Sigma_{st})$ be a schema mapping with the source and target schema given by nested-relational DTDs, D_s and D_t. First observe that tree pattern formulae (even with $=$ and $\neq$) are monotone in the following sense: for any tree pattern formula φ, if T' is obtained from T by erasing some subtrees and $T' \models \varphi$, then $T \models \varphi$. Roughly speaking, this allows us to consider the smallest tree conforming to the source schema. We define an operation $\circ$ on DTDs as turning each ℓ^* and $\ell?$ into ε and each ℓ^+ into ℓ. The mapping $\mathcal{M}$ is consistent iff $\mathcal{M}' = (D_s^\circ, D_t, \Sigma_{st})$ is consistent. Since disjunctions are not allowed in productions, we have only one tree conforming to D_s° (up to data values stored in the attributes). The size of this tree is at most $b_s = \|D_s\|^{\|D_s\|}$.

Suppose $S \models D_s^\circ$, and T is a solution for S. We shall trim T to obtain a single-exponential

	Arbitrary schemas	Nested-relational DTDs
CONS($\Downarrow$)	EXPTIME-complete	PTIME
CONS($\Downarrow,\Rightarrow$)	EXPTIME-complete	PSPACE-complete
CONS($\Downarrow,\sim$)	undecidable	NEXPTIME-complete
CONS($\Downarrow,\Rightarrow,\sim$)	undecidable	undecidable

Figure 18.1 Complexity of consistency problems.

solution T'. Recall that a target tree is a solution for S iff it satisfies the partially evaluated pattern $\delta_{S,\mathcal{M}'}$ combining all target requirements (Lemma 12.1). Fix a homomorphism ξ from $\delta_{S,\mathcal{M}'}$ into T. Let T' be the solution obtained from T by removing all nodes which are not enforced by ξ nor by D_t. That is, an ℓ-labeled child of an ℓ'-labeled node is removed if it has no descendant in the image of ξ, and the production for ℓ' contains ℓ^*, $\ell?$, or ℓ^+ (for ℓ^+ keep at least one ℓ-labeled child).

For each node the number of children enforced by ξ is bounded by $\|\delta_{S,\mathcal{M}'}\| \leq |\Sigma_{st}|b_s^{\|\Sigma_{st}\|}$, and the number of children enforced by D_t is at most $\|D_t\|$. As D_t is nonrecursive, the size of T' can be bounded by $b_t = (|\Sigma_{st}|b_s^{\|\Sigma_{st}\|} + \|D_t\|)^{\|D_t\|}$, which is single-exponential.

Given these bounds, the algorithm for consistency guesses some $S \models D_s^\circ$ with data values in $\{1,2,\ldots,b_s\}$, some $T \models D_t$ with branching at most $|\Sigma_{st}|b_s^{\|\Sigma_{st}\|} + \|D_t\|$ and data values in $\{1,2,\ldots,b_s+b_t\}$, and checks if S,T satisfy the st-tgds. The check need not be PTIME, but a naïve algorithm checking each st-tgd against each possible valuation requires at most $|\Sigma_{st}| \cdot (|S|+|T|)^{\|\Sigma_{st}\|}$ checks polynomial in the size of S, T, and Σ_{st}. Altogether this gives a NEXPTIME algorithm.   □

Figure 18.1 summarizes the complexity results of this section.

18.3 Absolute consistency for XML

Reasoning about the complexity of absolute consistency is significantly harder than reasoning about the consistency problem. We know that CONS($\Downarrow,\Rightarrow$) can be easily reduced to CONS$^\circ$($\Downarrow,\Rightarrow$). However, eliminating data values does not work for absolute consistency. Indeed, consider a mapping $\mathcal{M}$ with:

- a source DTD $r \to a^*$, $a \to \varepsilon$;
- a target DTD $r \to a$, $a \to \varepsilon$, with a having a single attribute in both DTDs;
- a single st-tgd $r/a(x) \longrightarrow r/a(x)$.

This mapping $\mathcal{M}$ is not absolutely consistent: take, for example, a source tree with two different values of the attribute. But stripping $\mathcal{M}$ of data values, i.e., replacing the st-tgd by $r/a \longrightarrow r/a$, makes it absolutely consistent.

Thus, we cannot use purely automata-theoretic techniques for reasoning about absolute consistency, even for vertical navigation. In fact, the above example indicates that to reason about absolute consistency even in that case, we need to reason about counts of occurrences of different data values.

Nevertheless, we start by looking at the problem $\text{ABCONS}^\circ(\Downarrow, \Rightarrow)$, i.e., checking absolute consistency of mappings $\mathcal{M}^\circ$ in which all references to attribute values have been removed. This will serve as a warm-up for other results. Besides, we see a slightly surprising behavior of the problem, as it has *lower* complexity than $\text{CONS}^\circ(\Downarrow, \Rightarrow)$.

Proposition 18.7 $\text{ABCONS}^\circ(\Downarrow, \Rightarrow)$ *is* Π_2^p-*complete.*

Proof The set of dependencies Σ_{st} is of the form $\{\pi_i \longrightarrow \pi_i'\}_{i \in I}$, where patterns have no variables. To check consistency of such a mapping, we need to check whether there exists a set $J \subseteq I$ so that $\mathscr{S}_t$ and all the π_j', $j \in J$ are satisfiable, while $\mathscr{S}_s$ together with the *negations* of π_k, $k \notin J$, are satisfiable. This makes consistency EXPTIME-complete (see Proposition 18.3). For absolute consistency, we only need to verify that there does not exist $J \subseteq I$ so that $\mathscr{S}_s$ and π_j, $j \in J$, are satisfiable but $\mathscr{S}_t$ and π_j', $j \in J$, are not. Notice that absolute consistency eliminates the need for checking satisfiability of negations of patterns. Since satisfiability of patterns in the presence of schemas is in NP, the above shows that absolute consistency of mappings $\mathcal{M}^\circ$ is in Π_2^p. Proving hardness is an instructive exercise. $\square$

Algorithm for the general case

As suggested by the example, the absolute consistency problem becomes much harder if we allow variables. Assume for a while that the mapping $\mathcal{M}$ contains a single dependency $\pi(\bar{x}, \bar{y}) \longrightarrow \exists \bar{z}\, \pi'(\bar{x}, \bar{z})$. The logical structure of the condition we need to check is:

for every source tree T
there exists a target tree T' such that
for every $\bar{a}\bar{b}$ satisfying $T \models \pi(\bar{a}, \bar{b})$
there exists $\bar{c}$ satisfying $T' \models \pi'(\bar{a}, \bar{c})$.

To turn this into an algorithm we would need to show a bound on the size of trees that need to be considered. Instead, we will try to change the order of quantifiers to the following:

for every $\bar{a}\bar{b}$ such that $\pi(\bar{a}, \bar{b})$ is satisfiable in a source tree,
there exists $\bar{c}$ such that $\pi'(\bar{a}, \bar{c})$ is satisfiable in a target tree.

The modified condition can be checked easily in Π_2^p. Indeed, what really matters is the equality type of $\bar{a}$, $\bar{b}$ and $\bar{c}$, so it is enough to choose their entries from a fixed set of linear size. Furthermore, one does not need to guess the source and target trees explicitly, it is enough to witness their existence. By Theorem 11.7, there exists a witness of polynomial size.

The algorithm that we shall present is based heavily on the ideas developed in the algorithm for building solutions in XML data exchange, see Chapter 12. In particular, we shall use the notion of a *kind*, which was central to that algorithm (see Definitions 12.9 on page 164 and 12.17 on page 169).

To justify the reordering of the quantifiers, we would need to show that for every two target trees T_1 and T_2 there is a π'-*union* tree T such that whenever $T_1 \models \pi'(\bar{a}, \bar{c})$ or $T_2 \models \pi'(\bar{a}, \bar{c})$, then $T \models \pi'(\bar{a}, \bar{c})$. As we have learned in Chapter 12, this need not be true in general, but can be guaranteed by assuming that T_1 and T_2 are of the same kind.

A single kind usually cannot provide solutions to all source trees. For instance, for $\mathcal{M} = (\{r \to a^*b^*\}, \{r \to ab^*\}, \{\pi(x) \longrightarrow \pi'(x)\})$ with $\pi(x) = \pi'(x)$, saying "there is an a-node storing x whose next sibling is a b-node", and a target kind fixes the value in the a node to some d, a tree of this kind can only be a solution for source trees that store the same d in the last a-node. Thus source documents have to be split into subsets admitting solutions of a single kind. It turns out that the latter is guaranteed by closure under π-unions, which means that we can also use kinds to split the source documents.

Based on this we reformulate the absolute consistency condition as:

for every source kind K

there exists a target kind K' such that

for every $\bar{a}\bar{b}$ such that $\pi(\bar{a}, \bar{b})$ is satisfiable in a tree of kind K,

there exists $\bar{c}$ such that $\pi'(\bar{a}, \bar{c})$ is satisfiable in a tree of kind K',

which ultimately leads to an algorithm working in exponential space.

Theorem 18.8 ABCONS($\Downarrow, \Rightarrow, \sim$) *is in* EXPSPACE.

Proof We present the algorithm as a two-round game between two players, $\forall$ and $\exists$. In each round, $\forall$ moves first. Moves are made by the choice of an object of size exponential in $\|\mathcal{M}\|$ during the first round, and polynomial in $\|\mathcal{M}\|$ during the second round. The winning condition, a polynomial time property of the moves, is defined so that $\exists$ has a winning strategy if $\mathcal{M}$ is absolutely consistent.

The existence of a strategy for $\exists$ in a game of such form can be easily tested in EXPSPACE by exhaustive search. The algorithm simply iterates over all possible (exponential-size) objects that can be played by $\forall$ and $\exists$ in the first round, and checks if $\exists$ has a winning answer for each object played by $\forall$. To test if an object Y is a winning answer to an object X, the algorithm iterates over all (polynomial-size) objects that can be played in the second round and checks if $\exists$ has a winning answer to each object played by $\forall$, which only requires testing the (polynomial) winning condition for the four objects.

Let us now describe the game. The rules reflect the reformulated absolute consistency condition: in the first round $\forall$ states what kind of tree is a counter-example to absolute consistency, while $\exists$ chooses the kind of tree that gives a solution to the purported counter-example; in the second round $\forall$ picks a tree of the declared kind and a tuple witnessing that the solutions fail, and $\exists$ tries to respond with a tree and a tuple that would prove $\forall$ wrong.

To make the rules precise, let $\mathscr{A}_s$, $\mathscr{A}_t$ be the UNFTAs underlying the source and target schemas, and let m be the maximum over the sizes of all patterns used in $\mathscr{M}$.

In the first round $\forall$ plays an $\mathscr{A}_s$-kind $K_\forall$ and an accepting run with margins of size m, such that the height and branching of K is bounded by $(2m+1)\|\mathscr{A}_s\|$. The data values used in K are to represent an equality type, so it is enough to choose them from $C = \{1, 2, \ldots, |K_\forall|\}$. The response $K_\exists$ of $\exists$ is similar except that $\mathscr{A}_s$ is replaced by $\mathscr{A}_t$, and some of the nodes can store nulls taken from a fixed set $\{\perp_1, \perp_2, \ldots, \perp_{|K_\exists|}\}$.

In the second round, $\forall$ chooses a dependency $\pi(\bar{x}, \bar{y}) \longrightarrow \exists \bar{z}\, \pi'(\bar{x}, \bar{z})$ and tuples $\bar{a}$, $\bar{b}$ (*without* nulls) together with a polynomial object witnessing that $\pi(\bar{a}, \bar{b})$ can be realized in a tree agreeing with $K_\forall$ (Lemma 12.29). The player $\exists$ then responds with a tuple $\bar{c}$ (possibly *including* nulls) and a polynomial witness that $\pi'(\bar{a}, \bar{c})$ can be realized in a tree agreeing with $K_\exists$.

A player loses if he fails to make a move complying with the rules. If all moves are made, $\exists$ wins.

Let us verify that $\exists$ has a winning strategy if and only if $\mathscr{M}$ is absolutely consistent.

If $\mathscr{M}$ is not absolutely consistent, $\forall$'s strategy in the first round is to choose an XML tree T for which no solution exists and play $K_\forall$ such that $T \in L(K_\forall)$ (see Lemma 12.23). In the second round, $\forall$ chooses an std $\pi(\bar{x}, \bar{y}) \longrightarrow \exists \bar{z}\, \pi'(\bar{x}, \bar{z})$ and tuples $\bar{a}, \bar{b}$ such that $T \models \pi(\bar{a}, \bar{b})$, but there is no $\bar{c}$ such that $\pi'(\bar{a}, \bar{c})$ can be realized in a tree agreeing with $K_\exists$. Some suitable std and $\bar{a}, \bar{b}$ exist, as otherwise for all choices of $\forall$ there would be $\bar{c}$ and a tree in $L(K_\exists)$ satisfying $\pi'(\bar{a}, \bar{c})$; by Lemma 12.24 we would then be able to combine all these trees into a tree $T' \in L(K_\exists)$ satisfying all $\pi'(\bar{a}, \bar{c})$, i.e., a solution for T.

Assume that $|\mathscr{M}|$ is absolutely consistent. $\exists$'s strategy in the first round is to choose $K_\exists$ so that for every tree agreeing with $K_\forall$ there exists a solution agreeing with $K_\exists$. In the second round, whatever $\bar{a}, \bar{b}$ was played, $\pi'(\bar{a}, \bar{c})$ can be realized in a tree from $L(K_\exists)$ for some $\bar{c}$; $\exists$'s strategy is simply to choose suitable $\bar{c}$ and a witness.

It remains to see that such $K_\exists$ can be produced, provided that $\mathscr{M}$ is absolutely consistent.

First let us see that each tree in $L(K_\forall)$ has a solution agreeing with some $K_\exists$. Let $N = ((2m+1)\|\mathscr{A}_t\|)^{(2m+1)\|\mathscr{A}_t\|}$, $T \in L(K_\forall)$ and let A be the set of data values used in T that are not elements of C. Let $A_0, A_1, \ldots, A_k$ be sets of data values such that $|A_i| = |A|$ for each i and $C, A_0, A_1, \ldots, A_k$ are pairwise disjoint. For each i fix $f_i\colon A \cup C \to A_i \cup C$ such that f_i restricted to C is the identity, and f_i restricted to A is a bijection $A \to A_i$. Let $T_i = f_i(T)$ be obtained by renaming the data values according to f_i. Since values in C are not changed, $T_i \in L(K_\forall)$ for all i. Using Lemma 12.24, we combine T_i's into a tree $T' \in L(K_\forall)$ which satisfies all the valuations of source side patterns satisfied by any of the T_i's. In particular, whenever $T \models \pi(\bar{a}, \bar{b})$, $T' \models \pi(f_i(\bar{a}), f_i(\bar{b}))$ for each i. As $\mathscr{M}$ is absolutely consistent, T' has a solution, say S'. By Lemma 12.23, S' agrees with some $\mathscr{A}_t$-kind K of height and branching bounded by $(2m+1)\|\mathscr{A}_t\|$, admitting an accepting run with margins of size m (but not necessarily using only data values from C or nulls). Since K has at most k nodes, there is i_0 such that K contains no data values from A_{i_0}. Let $f(c) = c$ for $c \in C$, $f(a) = f_{i_0}^{-1}(a)$ for $a \in A_{i_0}$, and $f(a) = \perp_a$ for all $a \notin A_{i_0} \cup C$. Then, $f(S')$ agrees with

$K_\exists = f(K)$, which only uses data values from C and nulls (not more than k of them). It is easy to check that $f(S')$ is a solution of T.

Now, assume that there is no $K_\exists$ that provides a solution for each tree agreeing with $K_\forall$. Then there exists a tree agreeing with $K_\forall$ for which there is no solution at all, contradicting absolute consistency. To see this, reason as follows. For each possible response K to $K_\forall$, let S_K be a tree agreeing with $K_\forall$ for which there is no solution agreeing with K. By Lemma 12.24 there is a tree $S \in L(K_\forall)$ such that $S \models \pi(\bar{a}, \bar{b})$ whenever one of the T_K's satisfies $\pi(\bar{a}, \bar{b})$ for every source side pattern π. That means that no $K_\exists$ provides a solution for S, which contradicts the previously proved claim. $\square$

Precise complexity

We presented the algorithm solving ABCONS as a two-round game between $\forall$ and $\exists$, in which moves are made by the choice of an object of size exponential during the first round and polynomial during the second round, and the winning condition is a polynomial-time property of these objects.

The second round of the game can be eliminated. Since the played objects are polynomial (in the size of the input), a strategy is an exponential object: it maps each object that can be played by $\forall$ to an answer of $\exists$. Thus, instead of playing the second round, $\exists$ can simply extend the object played in the first round with a winning strategy for the second round.

This means that the algorithm can be viewed as a single round game in which $\forall$ and $\exists$ play exponential-size objects and the winning condition is a polynomial-time property of these objects.

The class of problems that can be solved by such algorithms is denoted by $\Pi_2\text{EXP}$.

It is easy to see that

$$\text{NEXPTIME} \subseteq \Pi_2\text{EXP} \subseteq \text{EXPSPACE}.$$

We argued the second inclusion informally in the proof of Theorem 18.8. To justify the first inclusion, observe that a NEXPTIME algorithm can be seen as a game in which the rules tell $\forall$ to play some trivial object, and $\exists$ is supposed to play the whole accepting computation of the algorithm as a single object (it does have single-exponential size).

ABCONS happens to be complete for $\Pi_2\text{EXP}$. To show this we provide a reduction from the following $\Pi_2\text{EXP}$-complete problem:

PROBLEM:	2^n-UNIVERSALITY
INPUT:	Nondeterministic Turing machine M, number n in unary
QUESTION:	Does M accept every word of length 2^n in at most 2^n steps?

We give a reduction from 2^n-UNIVERSALITY to ABCONS for a very restricted class of mappings.

Theorem 18.9 ABCONS *is* Π_2EXP-*hard even for mappings from* SM$^{\text{dtd}}(\downarrow, \text{\_}, =)$ *using nonrecursive DTDs.*

Proof This reduction is very similar to the one in the proof of Theorem 12.28. The possible source trees will encode the input words, and the solutions will encode accepting runs as sequences of configurations. The main difficulty is that we need to copy the exponential input word to the target tree by means of polynomially many dependencies. For this purpose we use a modified mechanism of addressing the configurations and their cells, based on a linear order of length 2^n stored in the source tree.

Let an instance of 2^n-UNIVERSALITY be $n \in \mathbb{N}$ and a Turing machine M with the tape alphabet A and the blank symbol $\flat \in A$, the state space $q_0, q_1, \ldots, q_f$ and the extended transition relation $\hat{\delta}$ (see the proof of Theorem 12.28 for details). W.l.o.g. we assume that q_f is the only final accepting state.

The source DTD is given as

$$r \rightarrow ord\, q_0\, q_1\, \ldots\, q_f \perp \tau_1\, \tau_2 \cdots \tau_m$$
$$ord \rightarrow a_1\, b_1$$
$$a_i, b_i \rightarrow a_{i+1}\, b_{i+1}$$
$$a_n, b_n \rightarrow c$$
$$c \rightarrow t_1 \,|\, t_2 \,|\, \cdots \,|\, t_k$$

where $t_1, t_2, \ldots, t_k$ are the tape symbols except $\flat$, and $\tau_1, \tau_2, \ldots, \tau_m$ are the decorated tape symbols, i.e., elements of $\hat{A} = \{s, s^\flat, s^\triangleleft \mid s \in A\}$, $i = 1, 2, \ldots, n-1$ and the labels $q_0, q_1, \ldots, q_f, \perp, \tau_1, \tau_2, \ldots, \tau_m, c$ have a single attribute. The target DTD is given as

$$r \rightarrow a_1\, b_1\, tr_1\, tr_2 \cdots tr_d$$
$$tr_i \rightarrow tr$$
$$a_j, b_j \rightarrow a_{j+1}\, b_{j+1}$$
$$a_{2n}, b_{2n} \rightarrow cell$$
$$cell: @confnum\ @cellnum\ @st\ @sym$$
$$tr: @st_1\ @sym_1\ @st_2\ @sym_2 \cdots @st_6\ @sym_6$$

where $i = 1, 2, \ldots, d$, $j = 1, 2, \ldots, 2n-1$. The tr nodes store $\hat{\delta}$, the extended transition relation of M, and $d = |\hat{\delta}|$. In the *cell* nodes we store a configuration number, a cell number, a state, and a decorated tape symbol.

Assume for a while that we only need to handle source trees in which all data values are distinct. Correctness of the encoding of $\hat{\delta}$ is ensured with st-tgds

$$r[p_1(u_1), \sigma_1(v_1), p_2(u_2), \sigma_2(v_2), \ldots, p_6(u_6), \sigma_6(v_6)] \longrightarrow$$
$$\longrightarrow r/\text{\_}/tr(u_1, v_1, u_2, v_2, \ldots, u_6, v_6)$$

for each $(p_1, \sigma_1, p_2, \sigma_2, \ldots, p_6, \sigma_6) \in \hat{\delta}$.

The addressing mechanism is based on the data values stored in the c-nodes, encoding a linear order of length 2^n. With every c-node v we associate the sequence of a's and b's on the path leading from the root to v. This sequence is interpreted as a binary number (a read as 0, b read as 1), which is the position of v in the order. The auxiliary patterns take the following form:

$$First(x) = ord/a_1/a_2/\cdots/a_n/c(x),$$

$$Last(x) = ord/b_1/b_2/\cdots/b_n/c(x),$$

$$Succ(x,y) = \bigvee_{i=1}^{n} //\_[a_i/b_{i+1}/b_{i+2}/\cdots/b_n/c(x),$$

$$b_i/a_{i+1}/a_{i+2}/\cdots/a_n/c(y)],$$

$$Succ_3(x,y,z) = \bigvee_{i=1}^{n-1} //\_[a_i/b_{i+1}/b_{i+2}/\cdots/b_{n-1}[a_n/c(x),b_n/c(y)],$$

$$b_i/a_{i+1}/a_{i+2}/\cdots/a_n/c(z)] \vee$$

$$\vee \bigvee_{i=1}^{n-1} //\_[a_i/b_{i+1}/b_{i+2}/\cdots/b_n/c(x),$$

$$b_i/a_{i+1}/a_{i+2}/\cdots/a_{n-1}[a_n/c(y),b_n/c(z)]].$$

Each occurrence of $//$ above can be replaced with a sequence of $/$ and $\_$ symbols, and disjunction can be eliminated since we only use the auxiliary patterns on the source side.

To build the first configuration we copy the input word stored in the sequence of *zero* and *one* nodes with the head in the state q_0 over the first cell,

$$r[First(x), First(y)/s, q_0(u), s^{\triangleright}(v)] \longrightarrow r//Cell(x,y,u,v),$$

$$r[First(x), Succ_3(z_1,y,z_2)/s, \perp(u), s(v)] \longrightarrow r//Cell(x,y,u,v),$$

$$r[First(x), Last(y)/s, \perp(u), s^{\triangleleft}(v)] \longrightarrow r//Cell(x,y,u,v),$$

where s ranges over $A \setminus \{b\}$ and by $Succ_3(z_1,y,z_2)/s$ we mean $Succ_3(z_1,y,z_2)$ with $c(y)$ replaced with $c(y)/s$.

To make sure we encode a correct accepting run, we add

$$r[Succ(x_0,x_1), Succ_3(y_1,y_2,y_3)] \longrightarrow$$

$$\longrightarrow \exists \bar{u}\, \exists \bar{v}\, r[\_/tr(u_1,v_1,u_2,v_2,\ldots,u_6,v_6), \bigwedge_{i,j} //cell(x_i,y_j,u_{3i+j},v_{3i+j})],$$

$$r[q_f(u)] \longrightarrow \exists x \exists y \exists v\, r//cell(\bar{x},\bar{y},u,v).$$

We claim that the mapping we have just defined is absolutely consistent iff the answer to n-UNIVERSALITY is "yes". Assume that the mapping is absolutely consistent. Every input word w can be encoded in a source tree using distinct data values. An inductive argument shows that a solution to such a tree encodes an accepting run of M on w. Conversely, if the answer is "yes", for each source tree S using distinct data values, a solution is obtained from the run of M on the word encoded in the sequence of t_i-leaves of S. What if S uses some data values more than once? For a function $h : \mathbb{N} \to \mathbb{N}$ and a tree U, let $h(U)$ be the tree obtained from U by replacing each data value a with $h(a)$. Now, let S' be a tree with the structure identical as S, but using distinct data values, and let h be a function on data values such that $h(S') = S$. By the previously considered case, there is a solution T' for S'. Since our mapping does not use inequality on the target side, nor equality on the source side, $h(T')$ is a solution for $h(S') = S$. $\qquad\square$

In the reduction above we can remove disjunction from the DTDs turning them into nested-relational at the cost of allowing inequality or next-sibling on the source side. For mappings in $SM^{nr}(\downarrow, \_, =)$ one can prove NEXPTIME-hardness.

Bounded depth mappings

We have seen that absolute consistency is highly intractable even for patterns using only vertical axes and nonrecursive DTDs with very simple productions. The NEXPTIME lower bound means that for all we know, a *doubly*-exponential algorithm is required. For static reasoning that we encounter in dealing with metadata, in general it is a *single*-exponential bound that is viewed as acceptable. So the question is whether such a bound is achievable for absolute consistency under some restrictions.

In this section we show that the complexity can be lowered substantially if the height of trees is bounded by a constant. We say that a mapping $\mathscr{M}$ has *depth at most d* if the source and target schema only admit trees of height at most d.

In this case the problem falls into the polynomial hierarchy. We have seen two levels of it, Π_2^p and Σ_2^p, so far. Now we need the fourth level of it, Π_4^p. These levels are defined inductively: Σ_k^p is the class of problems solved in NP with a Σ_{k-1}^p oracle, and Π_k^p is the class of problems solved in CONP with a Σ_{k-1}^p oracle. All these classes are contained in PSPACE, and thus problems belonging to these classes can be solved in single-exponential time.

Theorem 18.10 ABCONS *for mappings of bounded depth is in Π_4^p.*

Proof We claim that the general algorithm presented in Theorem 18.8 has the desired complexity for mappings of bounded depth.

Assume that an UNFTA $\mathscr{A}$ only accepts trees of height at most d and let K be an $\mathscr{A}$-kind. Obviously K's height is at most d. Moreover, K contains no vertical ports, as otherwise arbitrarily high trees would agree with K.

It follows that, for a bounded depth mapping, the kinds played in the first round have polynomial branching and bounded depth, which means they are polynomial. In the second round, the objects played are polynomial in the size of those from the first round. As the correctness of the moves is polynomial, this gives a Π_4^p-algorithm. $\qquad\square$

A small modification of our techniques makes it possible to prove Theorem 18.10 for a more general definition of boundedness: $\mathscr{M}$ has *depth at most d* if every pattern it uses can only be realized within the initial d levels of every tree conforming to the schema.

This includes mappings using patterns starting at the root, that do not use descendants, nor child-paths of length greater than d.

We next show that ABCONS is Π_4^p-hard even for schema mappings of depth 1.

Theorem 18.11 ABCONS *is Π_4^p-hard for bounded-depth mappings, even for depth 1 mappings from* $\text{SM}^{\text{dtd}}(\downarrow,\rightarrow,=)$.

Proof We provide a reduction from TAUTOLOGY for Π_4 quantified propositional formulae. Let

$$\varphi = \forall x_1, x_2, \ldots, x_n \exists y_1, y_2, \ldots, y_n$$

$$\forall u_1, u_2, \ldots, u_n \exists v_1, v_2, \ldots, v_n \bigwedge_{i=1}^{m} X_i \vee Y_i \vee Z_i$$

with $X_i, Y_i, Z_i \in \{x_j, y_j, u_j, v_j, \bar{x}_j, \bar{y}_j, \bar{u}_j, \bar{v}_j \mid j = 1, \ldots, n\}$. Let the source schema be given by

$$r \rightarrow (a_1|a_1')(a_2|a_2')\ldots(a_n|a_n')ee,$$

where e has a single attribute, and the target schema by

$$r \rightarrow eeea_1 a_2 \ldots a_n b_1 b_2 \ldots b_n g^7,$$

where e has a single attribute, a_i and b_j have two attributes, and g has three attributes. The source tree encodes a valuation of $x_1, x_2, \ldots, x_n$, a_i means that x_i is *true*, a_i' means it is *false*. In e-positions we store values representing *true* and *false*. On the target side, we want to keep a copy of the valuation of x_i's and a guessed valuation of y_i's, except this time we use a different coding. The first attribute of the label a_i stores the value of x_i, *true* or *false*, and the second attribute stores the value of the negation of x_i. Similarly, b_i's store values of y_i's. We also want in the target word two copies of *true* and a copy of *false* arranged so as to enable a nondeterministic choice between a pair (*true, false*) or (*false, true*), as well as all triples with at least one entry *true*, stored in g-nodes, which will help us to check that each clause of φ is satisfied.

Let us now describe the st-tgds. First we make sure that values representing *true* and *false* are copied properly,

$$r[e(x) \rightarrow e(y)] \longrightarrow r[e(x) \rightarrow e(y) \rightarrow e(x)],$$

for each i translate the a_i/a_i' coding of values of x_i into true/false coding,

$$r[a_i, e(t) \rightarrow e(f)] \longrightarrow r/a_i(t, f),$$
$$r[a_i', e(t) \rightarrow e(f)] \longrightarrow r/a_i(f, t),$$

and enforce in the target tree all triples with at least one entry *true*,

$$r[e(t) \rightarrow e(f)] \longrightarrow r[g(f, f, t), g(f, t, f), \ldots, g(t, t, t)].$$

Next, we guess a value of y_i for each i,

$$r \longrightarrow r[e(x) \rightarrow e(y), b_i(x, y)],$$

and ensure that it makes the internal Π_2 part of φ true for $x_1, x_2, \ldots, x_n$ encoded in the source tree and $y_1, y_2, \ldots, y_n$ guessed in the target tree

$$r\big[e(u_1), e(u_2), \ldots, e(u_n)\big] \longrightarrow$$

$$\longrightarrow r\big[e(u_1) \to e(\bar{u}_1), e(u_2) \to e(\bar{u}_2), \ldots, e(u_n) \to e(\bar{u}_n),$$
$$e(v_1) \to e(\bar{v}_1), e(v_2) \to e(\bar{v}_2), \ldots, e(v_n) \to e(\bar{v}_n),$$
$$a_1(x_1, \bar{x}_1), a_2(x_2, \bar{x}_2), \ldots, a_n(x_n, \bar{x}_n),$$
$$b_1(y_1, \bar{y}_1), b_2(y_2, \bar{y}_2), \ldots, b_n(y_n, \bar{y}_n),$$
$$g(X_1, Y_1, Z_1), g(X_2, Y_2, Z_2), \ldots, g(X_m, Y_m, Z_m)\big]$$

(the literals X_j, Y_j, Z_j are taken from φ).

The obtained mapping is absolutely consistent iff φ is a tautology. Indeed, if the mapping is absolutely consistent, in particular it has a solution for each source tree that uses two different data values in e-positions. By construction, such trees have solutions iff φ is a tautology. If the data values in e-positions are equal, the st-tgds are satisfied trivially. $\qquad\square$

Disjunction can be eliminated from the source schema at a cost of allowing data comparisons on the source side. To achieve this, replace $(a_i \,|\, a_i')$ with a_i storing two attributes, and encode the truth value as an (in)equality of the two data values.

Tractable case

In order to guarantee tractability, stronger assumptions are required.

Theorem 18.12 ABCONS *is in* PTIME *for mappings in* $SM^{nr}(\downarrow, =)$ *without equality on the source side. Allowing equality on the source side makes the problem* CONP-*complete.*

Proof Throughout the proof we assume that each variable is used in exactly one st-tgd. Since satisfiability of $\downarrow, =$-patterns with respect to a nested relational DTD can be tested in PTIME, without loss of generality we can assume that all patterns in the mapping are satisfiable: for each $\pi \longrightarrow \pi'$, if π is not satisfiable, the st-tgd can be removed, and if π is satisfiable but π' is not, the mapping is not absolutely consistent.

Under this assumption,

$$(D_s, D_t, \{\pi_i \longrightarrow \pi_i' \mid i = 1, 2, \ldots, n\})$$

is absolutely consistent if and only if so is

$$\left(D_s, D_t, \left\{\bigwedge_{i=1}^{n} \pi_i \longrightarrow \bigwedge_{i=1}^{n} \pi_i'\right\}\right).$$

The second condition is clearly necessary. To see that it is sufficient, observe that since we disallow alternatives in schemas and inequality, the conjunctions of patterns are satisfiable, because each pattern is satisfiable on its own. Moreover, as equality is disallowed on the source side, each $T \models D_s$ can be extended to $\tilde{T} \models D_s$ satisfying all original source side patterns. Every solution for $\tilde{T}$ with respect to the modified mapping is a solution for T with respect to the original mapping, and the claim follows.

By Lemma 13.14, we replace

$$\bigwedge_{i=1}^{n} \pi_i \longrightarrow \bigwedge_{i=1}^{n} \pi_i'$$

by

$$\mathrm{mrg}_{D_s}\left(\bigwedge_{i=1}^{n} \pi_i\right) \longrightarrow \mathrm{mrg}_{D_t}\left(\bigwedge_{i=1}^{n} \pi_i'\right)$$

and get a single st-tgd $\pi(\bar{x},\bar{y}) \longrightarrow \exists \bar{z}\, \pi'(\bar{x},\bar{z})$ with equalities possibly on both sides, such that π and π' admit injective realizations.

Let $\approx_s$ be the equivalence relation on variables in π induced by equalities. We say that x_i is *unbounded on the source side* whenever for all variables $\xi \approx_s x_i$, on each path from an occurrence of ξ in π to the root of π there exist two subsequent labels ℓ, ℓ' such that ℓ occurs in the production for ℓ' in D_s as ℓ^* or ℓ^+. The relation $\approx_t$ and *unboundedness on the target side* are defined analogously.

The mapping is absolutely consistent if and only if each x_i unbounded on the source side is also unbounded on the target side and $x_i \approx_t x_j$ implies $x_i \approx_s x_j$ for all i, j (both conditions in PTIME). This follows from two simple observations: an injective realization of π or π' can easily guarantee that two variables get the same data value only if they are in the corresponding relation, $\approx_s$ or $\approx_t$; and x_i is unbounded if and only if it admits more then one value in some tree.

If equalities are allowed on the source side, first universally guess a subset of st-tgds whose source side patterns are to be satisfiable in a single tree, and then proceed like above. To show hardness, we reduce SAT to the complement of ABCONS. Fix a CNF formula $C_1 \wedge C_2 \wedge \cdots \wedge C_n$ over $\{z_1, z_2, \ldots, z_m\}$. Let the source and target DTDs be $r \to z_1\, z_2 \ldots z_m\, f\, t$ and $r \to C_0\, C_1 \ldots C_n$ where all labels except r store a single attribute. Let Σ_{st} contain the st-tgds

$$r/t(x) \longrightarrow r/C_0(x),$$
$$r/f(x) \longrightarrow r/C_n(x),$$
$$r[z_k(x), t(x)] \longrightarrow r[C_i(y), C_{i-1}(y)] \qquad \text{for all } C_i \text{ containing } z_k,$$
$$r[z_k(x), f(x)] \longrightarrow r[C_i(y), C_{i-1}(y)] \qquad \text{for all } C_i \text{ containing } \neg z_k.$$

If a valuation $z_i = b_i$ satisfies each clause, $r[z_1(b_1), z_2(b_2), \ldots, z_m(b_m), f(0), t(1)]$ has no solution. For the converse implication, observe that if some $r[z_1(b_1), z_2(b_2), \ldots, z_m(b_m), f(b_f), t(b_t)]$ has no solution, then it must hold that $b_f \neq b_t$ but the st-tgds enforce equality. Examining the st-tgds whose source side patterns were satisfied we get a partial valuation of z_i making the formula true. The remaining variables can be evaluated arbitrarily. $\qquad \square$

19

Mapping composition

In Chapter 17 we described two key operations on schema mappings: composition and inverse. These operators are needed to describe schema evolution and transformations of data according to the changing schema. In this chapter we study mapping composition. The goal of the composition operator is to generate a mapping $\mathcal{M}_{13}$ that has the same effect as applying successively two given mappings $\mathcal{M}_{12}$ and $\mathcal{M}_{23}$, provided that the target schema of $\mathcal{M}_{12}$ is the same as the source schema of $\mathcal{M}_{23}$. We shall see that in the relational case such a mapping can always be specified with st-tgds extended with second-order quantification or, equivalently, Skolem functions. In the XML case, the composition mapping can be generated only if the set of available axes is restricted.

19.1 The notion of composition and key problems

As mentioned in Chapter 17, the semantics of the composition operator can be defined in terms of the semantics of this operator for binary relations.

Definition 19.1 (Composition operator) Let $\mathcal{S}_1, \mathcal{S}_2, \mathcal{S}_3$ be relational or XML schemas. Let $\mathcal{M}_{12}$ be a mapping from $\mathcal{S}_1$ to $\mathcal{S}_2$, and $\mathcal{M}_{23}$ a mapping from $\mathcal{S}_2$ to $\mathcal{S}_3$. Then the composition of $\mathcal{M}_{12}$ and $\mathcal{M}_{23}$ is defined as

$$
[\![\mathcal{M}_{12}]\!] \circ [\![\mathcal{M}_{23}]\!] \;=\; \left\{ (S_1, S_3) \;\middle|\; \begin{array}{l} \text{there exists an instance } S_2 \text{ of schema } \mathcal{S}_2 \text{ such that} \\ (S_1, S_2) \in [\![\mathcal{M}_{12}]\!] \text{ and } (S_2, S_3) \in [\![\mathcal{M}_{23}]\!] \end{array} \right\}.
$$

For example, for the mappings $\mathcal{M}_{12}$, $\mathcal{M}_{23}$, and $\mathcal{M}_{13}$ shown in Chapter 17, $\mathcal{M}_{13}$ corresponds to the composition of $\mathcal{M}_{12}$ and $\mathcal{M}_{23}$ since $[\![\mathcal{M}_{13}]\!] = [\![\mathcal{M}_{12}]\!] \circ [\![\mathcal{M}_{23}]\!]$. It is important to notice that this example shows two mappings specified by st-tgds whose composition can also be specified by such dependencies. In contrast, the definition of the composition operator itself only defines the *semantics* of the composition and does not say anything about the existence of a *syntactic* specification of this mapping.

This motivates the first fundamental question about the composition operator, namely whether the composition of st-tgds can always be specified in the same logical language. At first glance, one may be tempted to think that the answer to this question is positive, and that the example in the introduction can be generalized to any composition of st-tgds.

However, the following example proves that this is not the case, as it shows two mappings specified by st-tgds whose composition cannot be specified by a set of such dependencies.

Example 19.2 Consider a schema R_1 consisting of one binary relation Takes, that associates a student name with a course she/he is taking, a schema R_2 consisting of a relation $Takes_1$, that is intended to be a copy of Takes, and of an additional relation symbol Student, that associates a student with a student id; and a schema R_3 consisting of a binary relation symbol Enrolled, that associates a student id with the courses this student is taking. Consider now mappings $\mathcal{M}_{12}$ and $\mathcal{M}_{23}$ specified by the following sets of st-tgds:

$$\Sigma_{12} = \{\text{Takes}(n,c) \to \text{Takes}_1(n,c), \text{Takes}(n,c) \to \exists s \, \text{Student}(n,s)\},$$
$$\Sigma_{23} = \{\text{Student}(n,s) \wedge \text{Takes}_1(n,c) \to \text{Enrolled}(s,c)\}.$$

Mapping $\mathcal{M}_{12}$ requires that a copy of every tuple in Takes must exist in $Takes_1$ and, moreover, that each student name n must be associated with some student id s in the relation Student. Mapping $\mathcal{M}_{23}$ says that if a student with name n and id s takes a course c, then (s,c) is a tuple in the relation Enrolled. Intuitively, in the composition mapping one would like to replace the name n of a student by a student id i_n, and then for each course c that is taken by n, one would like to include the tuple (i_n,c) in the table Enrolled. Unfortunately, it can be formally proved that it is not possible to express this relationship by using a set of st-tgds. In particular, an st-tgd of the form:

$$\text{Takes}(n,c) \to \exists y \, \text{Enrolled}(y,c)$$

does not express the desired relationship, as it may associate a distinct student id y to each tuple (n,c) in Takes and, thus, it may create several ids for the same student name.

Intuitively, the correct composition mapping in this case should postulate that the student id depend solely on the name, and not the course. This could, intuitively, be expressed as follows:

$$\text{Takes}(n,c) \to \text{Enrolled}(f(n),c),$$

where $f(\cdot)$ is a function associating an id with a name. This intuition will be made precise in this chapter. □

The previous example shows that st-tgds are not enough to specify the composition of st-tgd mappings. In other words, st-tgd mappings are not closed under composition. So to achieve closure under composition, we could use two approaches:

- we could restrict the class of mappings so that their compositions are expressible with st-tgds; or
- alternatively, we could extend the mapping language so that it captures compositions of st-tgd mappings.

Of course, the second approach can be taken only if the complexity of the extended class of mappings is feasible. This guides us in our search for classes of mappings closed under composition.

For relational mappings we shall follow the second approach. We shall develop a natural extension of st-tgds that has precisely the expressive power needed to specify compositions of st-tgd mappings. In contrast, for XML mappings we shall see that any such formalism would be undecidable, and we shall switch to the first approach, obtaining a restricted class of mappings closed under composition.

Since our search for the right formalism is guided by the complexity analysis of the composition problem, we need to define it properly. The complexity of the composition of mappings $\mathcal{M}_{12} = (\mathcal{S}_1, \mathcal{S}_2, \Sigma_{12})$, $\mathcal{M}_{23} = (\mathcal{S}_2, \mathcal{S}_3, \Sigma_{23})$, between relational or XML schemas, is the complexity of the following problem:

PROBLEM:	COMPOSITION$(\mathcal{M}_{12}, \mathcal{M}_{23})$
INPUT:	Instance T_1 of $\mathcal{S}_1$ and T_3 of $\mathcal{S}_3$
QUESTION:	$(T_1, T_3) \in [\![\mathcal{M}_{12}]\!] \circ [\![\mathcal{M}_{23}]\!]$?

In the following section we shall see how knowing the complexity of composition can help in finding a formalism for composing relational mappings defined by st-tgds.

19.2 Complexity of relational composition

Example 19.2 shows that in order to express the composition of mappings specified by st-tgds, one has to use a language more expressive than st-tgds. However, the example gives little information about what the right language for composition is. In fact, the composition of mappings $\mathcal{M}_{12}$ and $\mathcal{M}_{23}$ in this example can be defined in first-order logic (see Exercise 22.3):

$$\forall n \exists y \forall c \, (\texttt{Takes}(n,c) \rightarrow \texttt{Enrolled}(y,c)),$$

which may lead to the conclusion that FO is a good alternative to define the composition of mappings specified by st-tgds. However, a complexity argument shows that this conclusion is incorrect. To show this, we first need to know the complexity of COMPOSITION$(\mathcal{M}_{12}, \mathcal{M}_{23})$. The following theorem shows that it is always in NP, and can be NP-hard.

Theorem 19.3 (Complexity of composition) *For every pair of mappings $\mathcal{M}_{12}$, $\mathcal{M}_{23}$ specified by st-tgds, COMPOSITION$(\mathcal{M}_{12}, \mathcal{M}_{23})$ is in NP. Moreover, there exist mappings $\mathcal{M}_{12}^{\star}$ and $\mathcal{M}_{23}^{\star}$ specified by st-tgds such that COMPOSITION$(\mathcal{M}_{12}^{\star}, \mathcal{M}_{23}^{\star})$ is NP-complete.*

Proof The membership of COMPOSITION$(\mathcal{M}_{12}, \mathcal{M}_{23})$ in NP can be proved by showing that there exists a polynomial p (that depends on $\mathcal{M}_{12}$ and $\mathcal{M}_{23}$) such that if $(S_1, S_3) \in \mathcal{M}_{12} \circ \mathcal{M}_{23}$, then there exists an instance S_2 satisfying that $(S_1, S_2) \in \mathcal{M}_{12}$, $(S_2, S_3) \in \mathcal{M}_{23}$ and $\|S_2\| \leq p(\|S_1\| + \|S_3\|)$. We leave this proof for the reader (see Exercise 22.3), and we focus here on showing that COMPOSITION$(\mathcal{M}_{12}, \mathcal{M}_{23})$ can be NP-hard.

Let $\mathbf{R_1}$ be a schema consisting of a unary relation node and a binary relation edge, $\mathbf{R_2}$

a schema consisting of binary relations coloring and edge′, and $\mathbf{R_3}$ a schema consisting of a binary relation error and a unary relation color. Moreover, let $\mathscr{M}_{12}^\star = (\mathbf{R_1}, \mathbf{R_2}, \Sigma_{12})$ and $\mathscr{M}_{23}^\star = (\mathbf{R_2}, \mathbf{R_3}, \Sigma_{23})$, where Σ_{12} consists of the following st-tgds:

$$\text{node}(x) \rightarrow \exists y\, \text{coloring}(x,y), \tag{19.1}$$

$$\text{edge}(x,y) \rightarrow \text{edge}'(x,y),$$

and Σ_{23} consists of the following st-tgds:

$$\text{edge}'(x,y) \wedge \text{coloring}(x,u) \wedge \text{coloring}(y,u) \rightarrow \text{error}(x,y), \tag{19.2}$$

$$\text{coloring}(x,u) \rightarrow \text{color}(u). \tag{19.3}$$

Next we show that COMPOSITION($\mathscr{M}_{12}^\star, \mathscr{M}_{23}^\star$) is NP-hard by reducing from the graph 3-coloring problem. Intuitively, relations node and edge in $\mathbf{R_1}$ store a graph G, and relation edge′ in $\mathbf{R_2}$ is a copy of edge. Moreover, st-tgd (19.1) indicates that a color must be assigned to each node in the graph and, thus, relation coloring in $\mathbf{R_2}$ stores a possible coloring of graph G. Finally, st-tgd (19.3) indicates that relation color in $\mathbf{R_3}$ stores the colors used in the coloring of G, and st-tgd (19.2) indicates that error stores any incorrect assignment of colors, that is, error(x,y) holds if x, y are adjacent nodes in G and the same color is assigned to them.

Formally, let $G = (N,E)$ be a graph, and define instances S_1 of $\mathbf{R_1}$ and S_3 of $\mathbf{R_3}$ as follows:

$$\begin{aligned} \text{node}^{S_1} &= N, & \text{color}^{S_3} &= \{red, green, blue\}, \\ \text{edge}^{S_1} &= E, & \text{error}^{S_3} &= \emptyset. \end{aligned}$$

Then it holds that $(S_1, S_3) \in \mathscr{M}_{12}^\star \circ \mathscr{M}_{23}^\star$ if and only if graph G is 3-colorable. This concludes the proof of the theorem, as it shows that the graph 3-coloring problem can be reduced in polynomial time to COMPOSITION($\mathscr{M}_{12}^\star, \mathscr{M}_{23}^\star$). $\qquad\square$

Let us see now that FO is not expressive enough to define compositions of mappings defined by st-tgds. We claim that the composition of $\mathscr{M}_{12}^\star$ and $\mathscr{M}_{23}^\star$ cannot be defined by a finite set of FO formulae. Towards a contradiction, suppose that it is defined by a finite set Σ of FO formulae. Then COMPOSITION($\mathscr{M}_{12}^\star, \mathscr{M}_{23}^\star$) reduces immediately to the problem of verifying whether a pair of instances (S_1, S_3) satisfies Σ. But this means that the complexity of COMPOSITION($\mathscr{M}_{12}^\star, \mathscr{M}_{23}^\star$) is in AC^0, as the complexity of the problem of verifying whether a fixed set of FO formulae is satisfied by an instance is in this complexity class. Recall that AC^0 is the class of "constant parallel time" problems, i.e., languages that can be accepted by a family of constant-depth, unbounded-fanin circuits with AND, OR, and NOT gates. Its uniform version, which contains FO, is a subclass of LOGSPACE, and thus PTIME. By Theorem 19.3, COMPOSITION($\mathscr{M}_{12}^\star, \mathscr{M}_{23}^\star$) is NP-hard, which contradicts the well-known fact that $\text{AC}^0 \subsetneq \text{NP}$ (see Section 2.4 for a discussion about these complexity classes).

Theorem 19.3 not only shows that FO is not the right language to express the composition of mappings given by st-tgds, but also gives a good insight into what needs to be added to st-tgds to obtain a language capable of expressing the composition of such dependencies. We know that COMPOSITION($\mathcal{M}_{12}, \mathcal{M}_{23}$) is in NP. By Fagin's theorem in finite model theory, the class NP has a logical characterization as the class of problems defined in existential second-order logic, i.e., by formulae of the form $\exists R_1 \ldots \exists R_n \, \varphi$, where the R_i's range over sets or relations, and φ is an FO formula.

So it appears that some sort of second-order quantification is necessary to capture relational composition. In the following section we confirm this by presenting an extension of st-tgds with existential second-order quantification that gives rise to the *right* mapping language for dealing with the composition operator. As hinted in an earlier example in this section, the existential quantification is not over arbitrary relations but rather functions, such as, for instance, the function from student names to student ids in Example 19.2.

19.3 Extending st-tgds with second-order quantification

In the previous section, we showed that first-order logic is not expressive enough to represent the composition of mappings given by st-tgds. The bounds on the complexity of composition suggested that the existential fragment of second-order logic can be used to express the composition of this type of mappings. In this section, we go deeper into this, and show that the extension of st-tgds with existential second-order quantification is the right language for composition.

Our quantification will be over functions, like the function that associates a student id with a student name in Example 19.2. These functions will be used to build *terms* which will then be used in formulae. Recall that terms are built as follows:

- every variable is a term; and
- if f is an n-ary function symbol, and $t_1, \ldots, t_n$ are terms, then $f(t_1, \ldots, t_n)$ is a term.

For instance, if f is a unary function and g is a binary function, then $f(x)$, $f(f(x))$, $g(f(x), x)$ are all terms.

Now we are ready to define the extended class of dependencies used in mappings that are closed under composition.

Definition 19.4 Given schemas $\mathbf{R_s}$ and $\mathbf{R_t}$ with no relation symbols in common, a *second-order tuple-generating dependency from $\mathbf{R_s}$ to $\mathbf{R_t}$* (SO tgd) is a formula of the form:

$$\exists f_1 \cdots \exists f_m \left(\forall \bar{x}_1 (\varphi_1 \rightarrow \psi_1) \wedge \cdots \wedge \forall \bar{x}_n (\varphi_n \rightarrow \psi_n) \right),$$

where

1. each f_i ($1 \leq i \leq m$) is a function symbol,
2. each formula φ_i ($1 \leq i \leq n$) is a conjunction of relational atoms of the form $P(y_1, \ldots, y_k)$ and equality atoms of the form $t = t'$, where P is a k-ary relation symbol of $\mathbf{R_s}$, $y_1, \ldots, y_k$ are (not necessarily distinct) variables in $\bar{x}_i$, and t, t' are terms built from $\bar{x}_i$ and $f_1, \ldots, f_m$,

3. each formula ψ_i $(1 \le i \le n)$ is a conjunction of relational atomic formulae of the form $R(t_1, \ldots, t_\ell)$, where R is an ℓ-ary relation symbol of $\mathbf{R_t}$ and $t_1, \ldots t_\ell$ are terms built from $\bar{x}_i$ and $f_1, \ldots, f_m$, and

4. each variable in $\bar{x}_i$ $(1 \le i \le n)$ appears in some relational atom of φ_i.

Functions $f_1, \ldots, f_m$ are often referred to as *Skolem functions*. $\qquad\qquad\square$

An example of a SO tgd is the dependency $\texttt{Takes}(n,c) \rightarrow \texttt{Enrolled}(f(n),c)$, seen earlier. In the syntax of Definition 19.4 it is written as $\exists f \, \forall n, c \, (\texttt{Takes}(n,c) \rightarrow \texttt{Enrolled}(f(n),c))$.

To define the semantics of SO tgds, it is necessary to specify the semantics of the existential second-order quantifiers in these dependencies. In particular, in deciding whether $(S,T) \models \sigma$, for an SO tgd σ, what should the domain and range of the functions instantiating the existentially quantified function symbols be? The previous example clearly suggests that such functions should operate on both constants and nulls, so we always assume that a function symbol f of arity d is instantiated as a function $f^0 : (\text{CONST} \cup \text{VAR})^d \rightarrow \text{CONST} \cup \text{VAR}$. Such a function is called a *valuation* of the function symbol f.

Given a term t using variables $\bar{x}$, a tuple $\bar{a}$, and a valuation $\bar{f} = f_1^0, f_2^0, \ldots, f_n^0$ of the function symbols used in t, by $t[\bar{f}, \bar{a}]$ we denote the value obtained by evaluating the term t with variables $\bar{x}$ substituted by $\bar{a}$ and the function symbols treated as corresponding functions in $\bar{f}$. For instance, if the interpretation of the function symbol f is such that $f^0(1) = 2$ and $f^0(2) = 3$, then for the term $t = f(f(x))$ we have $t[f^0, 1] = f^0(f^0(1)) = f^0(2) = 3$.

Let I be an instance of schema $\mathbf{R}$. For a relational atom $R(t_1, \ldots, t_k)$ over $\mathbf{R}$, a valuation $\bar{f}$ of function symbols used in $t_1, \ldots, t_n$, and a valuation of variables (a tuple) $\bar{a}$ we write

$$I \models R(t_1, \ldots, t_k)[\bar{f}, \bar{a}]$$

if I contains the fact $R(b_1, b_2, \ldots, b_k)$ where $b_i = t_i[\bar{f}, \bar{a}]$. Similarly, $I \models (t_1 = t_2)[\bar{f}, \bar{a}]$ if $t_1[\bar{f}, \bar{a}] = t_2[\bar{f}, \bar{a}]$. The notation is naturally extended to conjunctions of relational atoms and equalities.

Definition 19.5 (Semantics of SO tgds) Let σ be an SO tgd from $\mathbf{R_s}$ to $\mathbf{R_t}$ given by the formula $\exists f_1 \cdots \exists f_m \left(\forall \bar{x}_1 (\varphi_1 \rightarrow \psi_1) \wedge \cdots \wedge \forall \bar{x}_n (\varphi_n \rightarrow \psi_n) \right)$, and let S be an instance of $\mathbf{R_s}$ and T an instance of $\mathbf{R_t}$. We say that (S,T) satisfies σ, denoted by $(S,T) \models \sigma$, if there exists a *witnessing valuation* of symbols $f_1, \ldots, f_m$, that is, a valuation $\bar{f}$ such that $T \models \psi_i[\bar{f}, \bar{a}]$ whenever $S \models \varphi_i[\bar{f}, \bar{a}]$ for $i = 1, 2, \ldots, n$.

Example 19.6 Let $\mathbf{R_s}$ be a source schema consisting of a unary relation P, and $\mathbf{R_t}$ a target schema consisting of a unary relation R, and σ the following SO tgd from $\mathbf{R_s}$ to $\mathbf{R_t}$:

$$\exists f \left(\forall x \, (P(x) \wedge x = f(x) \rightarrow R(x)) \right).$$

Let S be an instance of $\mathbf{R_s}$ defined as $P^S = \{a\}$, and assume that T is the empty instance of $\mathbf{R_t}$. According to the above definition, $(S,T) \models \sigma$ since a witnessing valuation of f can be any function that maps a to an element b such that $a \ne b$. On the other hand, if one is not allowed to include extra values in the range of f, then $(S,T) \not\models \sigma$, as in this case the only possible valuation of f maps a into itself since $\text{DOM}(S) \cup \text{DOM}(T) = \{a\}$. □

As shown in the previous example, the inclusion of extra values when interpreting the function symbols of an SO tgd makes a difference. But it should be noticed that the possibility of using an infinite set of extra values is not significant in the case of SO tgds, as the domain and range of the witnessing valuations can be restricted to a finite superset of $\text{DOM}(S) \cup \text{DOM}(T)$, polynomial in the size of S and T (see Exercise 22.3).

Several features of SO tgds make them the right language for composition. First, it is easy to see that every set of st-tgds can be transformed into an SO tgd. In fact, the well-known Skolemization method can be used to compute an SO tgd equivalent to a set of st-tgds. For example, the following set of st-tgds from Example 19.2:

$$\text{Takes}(n,c) \rightarrow \text{Takes}_1(n,c),$$
$$\text{Takes}(n,c) \rightarrow \exists s\, \text{Student}(n,s)$$

is equivalent to the SO tgd:

$$\exists f \Big(\forall n \forall c\, (\text{Takes}(n,c) \rightarrow \text{Takes}_1(n,c)) \wedge$$
$$\wedge \forall n \forall c\, (\text{Takes}(n,c) \rightarrow \text{Student}(n,f(n,c))) \Big).$$

Essentially, the existentially quantified variables are replaced with terms using fresh function symbols. It is very natural to just list the conjuncts of SO tgds omitting the existential second-order quantifiers and the universal first-order quantifiers. Under this convention, the SO tgd above is presented as the following set of rules:

$$\text{Takes}(n,c) \rightarrow \text{Takes}_1(n,c),$$
$$\text{Takes}(n,c) \rightarrow \text{Student}(n,f(n,c)).$$

Second, it is possible to prove that SO tgds are closed under composition. That is, given an SO tgd σ_{12} from a schema $\mathbf{R_1}$ to a schema $\mathbf{R_2}$, and an SO tgd σ_{23} from $\mathbf{R_2}$ to a schema $\mathbf{R_3}$, there exists an SO tgd σ_{13} from $\mathbf{R_1}$ to $\mathbf{R_3}$ such that $\mathcal{M}_{13} = \mathcal{M}_{12} \circ \mathcal{M}_{23}$, where $\mathcal{M}_{13}$, $\mathcal{M}_{12}$ and $\mathcal{M}_{23}$ are the mappings defined by σ_{13}, σ_{12} and σ_{23}, respectively.

Example 19.7 We show here how to compute the composition of two SO tgds by considering a variation of the mappings used in the proof of Theorem 19.3. Let $\mathbf{R_1}$ be a schema consisting of a unary relation node and a binary relation edge, $\mathbf{R_2}$ a schema consisting of binary relations coloring and edge', and $\mathbf{R_3}$ a schema consisting of unary relations error and color. Moreover, let $\mathcal{M}_{12} = (\mathbf{R_1}, \mathbf{R_2}, \Sigma_{12})$ and $\mathcal{M}_{23} = (\mathbf{R_2}, \mathbf{R_3}, \Sigma_{23})$, where Σ_{12} consists of the following st-tgds:

$$\text{node}(x) \rightarrow \exists y\, \text{coloring}(x,y),$$
$$\text{edge}(x,y) \rightarrow \text{edge}'(x,y),$$

and Σ_{23} consists of the following st-tgds:

$$\texttt{edge}'(x,y) \wedge \texttt{coloring}(x,u) \wedge \texttt{coloring}(y,u) \rightarrow \exists v\, \texttt{error}(v),$$
$$\texttt{coloring}(x,y) \rightarrow \texttt{color}(y).$$

As in the proof of Theorem 19.3, it is possible to prove that the composition of $\mathcal{M}_{12}$ and $\mathcal{M}_{23}$ can be used to encode the graph 3-coloring problem.

Consider now the SO tgds representing mappings $\mathcal{M}_{12}$ and $\mathcal{M}_{23}$. That is, let σ_{12} be the SO tgd given by the following rules:

$$\texttt{node}(x) \rightarrow \texttt{coloring}(x, f(x)),$$
$$\texttt{edge}(x,y) \rightarrow \texttt{edge}'(x,y),$$

which is equivalent to Σ_{12}, and let σ_{23} be given by

$$\texttt{edge}'(x,y) \wedge \texttt{coloring}(x,u) \wedge \texttt{coloring}(y,u) \rightarrow \texttt{error}(g(x,y,u)),$$
$$\texttt{coloring}(x,y) \rightarrow \texttt{color}(y),$$

which is equivalent to Σ_{23}.

The algorithm essentially replaces relational atoms on the source side of σ_{23} with their definitions according to σ_{12}. Some care is needed though, as σ_{12} only generates certain kinds of tuples: for instance, in $\texttt{coloring}(x, f(x))$ the second coordinate is assumed to be the result of applying f to the first coordinate. To take account of that, we include a conjunction of equalities relating the tuple of variables of the replaced atom with the tuple of terms in corresponding atom on the target side of σ_{12}. For instance, $\texttt{coloring}(x,u)$ is replaced with $\texttt{node}(x') \wedge x = x' \wedge u = f(x')$, and $\texttt{edge}'(x,y)$ is replaced by $\texttt{edge}(x'',y'') \wedge x = x'' \wedge y = y''$. Note that for each atom we rename the variables in σ_{12} to avoid conflicts. The following set of rules is obtained as a result of this process:

$$\left(\begin{array}{l} \texttt{edge}(x'',y'') \wedge x = x'' \wedge y = y'' \wedge \\ \wedge\, \texttt{node}(x') \wedge x = x' \wedge u = f(x') \wedge \\ \wedge\, \texttt{node}(y') \wedge y = y' \wedge u = f(y') \end{array} \right) \quad \rightarrow \quad \texttt{error}(g(x,y,u)),$$
$$\texttt{node}(x') \wedge x = x' \wedge y = f(x') \quad \rightarrow \quad \texttt{color}(y).$$

The above set of rules is not yet an SO tgd as it does not satisfy condition (4) in the definition of SO tgds: variables x, y, u originally used in the relational atoms on the source side of σ_{23} are not used in relational atoms (on the source side) any more. As a final step, the algorithm eliminates all such variables. This is achieved by replacing these variables by the terms they are equal to according to the newly introduced equalities. More precisely, in the first rule the equalities $x = x''$, $y = y''$ and $u = f(x')$ are removed and all occurrences of x, y, u are replaced by $x'', y'', f(x')$ respectively, and similarly in the second rule. The first rule can be further simplified by eliminating variables x'' and y'' in the same way. The algorithm returns the following SO tgd:

$$\texttt{edge}(x',y') \wedge \texttt{node}(x') \wedge \texttt{node}(y') \wedge f(x') = f(y') \;\rightarrow\; \texttt{error}(g(x',y',f(x'))),$$
$$\texttt{node}(x') \;\rightarrow\; \texttt{color}(f(x')).$$

It can be proved that σ_{13} defines the composition of the mappings specified by σ_{12} and σ_{23}. To see why this is the case, we show how σ_{13} can be used to represent the graph 3-coloring problem. It is easy to see that σ_{13} is equivalent to the following SO tgd:

$$\texttt{edge}(x,y) \wedge \texttt{node}(x) \wedge \texttt{node}(y) \wedge f(x) = f(y) \;\rightarrow\; \texttt{error}(h(x,y)),$$
$$\texttt{node}(x) \;\rightarrow\; \texttt{color}(f(x))$$

which is obtained by renaming the variables x', y' to x, y and defining the function $h(x,y)$ as $g(x,y,f(y))$. Furthermore, relations node and edge store a graph G, $f(a)$ is the color assigned to a node a of G, and error stores any incorrect assignment of colors, that is, $\texttt{error}(h(a,b))$ holds if a, b are adjacent nodes in G and the same color is assigned to them (which corresponds to the condition $f(a) = f(b)$). □

The following theorem shows that the composition algorithm presented in the previous example can be generalized to any pair of SO tgds.

Theorem 19.8 (Closure under composition of SO tgds) *Let $\mathcal{M}_{12}$ and $\mathcal{M}_{23}$ be mappings specified by SO tgds. There exists a mapping $\mathcal{M}_{13}$ specified by an SO tgd equivalent to the composition of $\mathcal{M}_{12}$ and $\mathcal{M}_{23}$. Moreover, there exists an exponential-time algorithm that computes a mapping $\mathcal{M}_{13}$ for given $\mathcal{M}_{12}$ and $\mathcal{M}_{23}$.*

Algorithm 19.1 computes the composition. We write $\|\varphi\|$ for the number of atoms in φ and $X \hookleftarrow Y$ for $X := X \cup Y$. We use π, π' for conjunctions of relational atoms, and α, β for conjunctions of equalities. Under this convention, rules of SO tgds can be presented as

$$\pi \wedge \alpha \longrightarrow \pi'.$$

A *homomorphism* h from π to π' is a function mapping variables of π to terms such that $h(\pi)$ is a conjunction of some atoms of π'. In this case we write briefly $h \colon \pi \to \pi'$.

Without loss of generality we can assume that on the source side variables are only reused in equalities: each additional occurrence of a variable x in a relational atom on the source side should be replaced with a fresh variable x' and equality $x = x'$ should be added to the source side of the rule.

Let $(\mathbf{R}_1, \mathbf{R}_3, \Sigma_{13})$ be the mapping computed by Algorithm 19.1 for the input mappings $\mathcal{M}_{12} = (\mathbf{R}_1, \mathbf{R}_2, \Sigma_{12})$ and $\mathcal{M}_{23} = (\mathbf{R}_2, \mathbf{R}_3, \Sigma_{23})$. Observe that the algorithm does not introduce any new function symbols. The following lemmas show that Algorithm 19.1 is correct.

Lemma 19.9 *If $(S_1, S_2) \in [\![\mathcal{M}_{12}]\!]$ and $(S_2, S_3) \in [\![\mathcal{M}_{23}]\!]$ with a witnessing valuation of function symbols $\bar{f}$, then $(S_1, S_3) \in [\![\mathcal{M}_{13}]\!]$ with the same witnessing valuation $\bar{f}$.*

Algorithm 19.1 Composing relational schema mappings

Require: on the source side variables are reused only in equalities

$\Sigma_{13} := \emptyset$

$m := \max_{(\varphi \to \psi) \in \Sigma_{23}} \|\varphi\|$

for all $\varphi_1 \longrightarrow \pi_1, \; \varphi_2 \longrightarrow \pi_2, \; \ldots, \; \varphi_k \longrightarrow \pi_k \; \in \Sigma_{12}, k \leq m$ **do**

    {in case of repetitions, rename variables}

    $\rho := \pi_1 \wedge \cdots \wedge \pi_k$

    for all $\pi \wedge \alpha \longrightarrow \pi' \in \Sigma_{23}$ **and all** homomorphisms $h \colon \pi \to \rho$ **do**

        $\Sigma_{13} \hookleftarrow \left\{ \varphi_1 \wedge \cdots \wedge \varphi_k \wedge h(\alpha) \longrightarrow h(\pi') \right\}$

    end for

end for

return Σ_{13}

Proof Each constraint in Σ_{13} is of the form

$$\varphi_1 \wedge \cdots \wedge \varphi_k \wedge h(\alpha) \longrightarrow h(\psi),$$

where $\varphi_1 \longrightarrow \pi_1, \; \varphi_2 \longrightarrow \pi_2, \; \ldots, \; \varphi_k \longrightarrow \pi_k \in \Sigma_{12}$ and $\pi \wedge \alpha \longrightarrow \pi' \in \Sigma_{23}$, and h is a homomorphism from π into $\pi_1 \wedge \cdots \wedge \pi_k$. Pick $\bar{a}$ such that $S_1 \models \varphi_1 \wedge \cdots \wedge \varphi_k \wedge h(\alpha)[\bar{f}, \bar{a}]$. Then $S_2 \models \pi_1 \wedge \cdots \wedge \pi_k[\bar{f}, \bar{a}]$ and we get $S_2 \models h(\pi)[\bar{f}, \bar{a}]$. As $h(\alpha)[\bar{f}, \bar{a}]$ holds, we have $S_2 \models h(\pi) \wedge h(\alpha)[\bar{f}, \bar{a}]$ and hence $S_3 \models h(\psi)[\bar{f}, \bar{a}]$. $\qquad\square$

Lemma 19.10 *If $(S_1, S_3) \in [\![\mathscr{M}_{13}]\!]$ with a witnessing valuation $\bar{f}$, there exists an intermediate instance S_2 such that $(S_1, S_2) \in [\![\mathscr{M}_{12}]\!]$ and $(S_2, S_3) \in [\![\mathscr{M}_{23}]\!]$ with the same witnessing valuation $\bar{f}$.*

Proof Consider

$$S_2 = \left\{ R(t_1, \ldots, t_\ell)[\bar{f}, \bar{a}] \;\middle|\; \begin{array}{l} \varphi \longrightarrow \pi \in \Sigma_{12}, S_1 \models \varphi[\bar{f}, \bar{a}], \\ R(t_1, \ldots, t_\ell) \text{ is an atom in } \pi \end{array} \right\},$$

where $R(t_1, \ldots, t_\ell)[\bar{f}, \bar{a}]$ is the tuple obtained from $R(t_1, \ldots, t_\ell)$ by interpreting the function symbols according to $\bar{f}$ and the variables according to $\bar{a}$. Obviously, $(S_1, S_2) \in [\![\mathscr{M}_{12}]\!]$ with the witnessing valuation $\bar{f}$, so it remains to see that $(S_2, S_3) \in [\![\mathscr{M}_{23}]\!]$ with the witnessing valuation $\bar{f}$.

Suppose that $S_2 \models \pi \wedge \alpha[\bar{f}, \bar{a}]$ for some $\pi \wedge \alpha \longrightarrow \pi' \in \Sigma_{23}$ and let $\pi = A_1 \wedge \cdots \wedge A_k$ with $k \leq m$. By definition of S_2, $A_1[\bar{f}, \bar{a}], \ldots, A_k[\bar{f}, \bar{a}]$ are equal to

$$B_1[\bar{f}, \bar{c}_1], \ldots, B_k[\bar{f}, \bar{c}_k],$$

where B_i is an atom of some π_i such that $\varphi_i \longrightarrow \pi_i \in \Sigma_{12}$ and $S_1 \models \varphi_i[\bar{f}, \bar{c}_i]$ for $i = 1, 2, \ldots, k$ (we can assume the rules use disjoint sets of variables).

Since π uses no function symbols, nor reuses variables, we can define a homomorphism

$$g \colon \pi \to \pi_1 \wedge \cdots \wedge \pi_k$$

as follows: if $A_i = R(y_1, \ldots, y_p)$ and $B_i = R(t_1, \ldots, t_p)$ for some R, let $g(y_j) = t_j$. In consequence, Algorithm 19.1 eventually extends Σ_{13} with

$$\varphi_1 \wedge \cdots \wedge \varphi_k \wedge g(\alpha) \longrightarrow g(\pi').$$

Note that g is defined so that for each variable x used in π, $g(x)[\bar{f}, \bar{c}_1, \ldots, \bar{c}_k]$ is equal to the value assigned to x, $x[\bar{a}]$. In consequence, for each formula ψ, $g(\psi)[\bar{f}, \bar{c}_1, \ldots, \bar{c}_k]$ is the same as $\psi[\bar{f}, \bar{a}]$, as long as ψ only uses variables used in π. In particular, $g(\alpha)[\bar{f}, \bar{c}_1, \ldots, \bar{c}_k]$ is the same as $\alpha[\bar{f}, \bar{a}]$. Since $\alpha[\bar{f}, \bar{a}]$ holds by the initial assumption, we have

$$S_1 \models \varphi_1 \wedge \cdots \wedge \varphi_k \wedge g(\alpha)[\bar{f}, \bar{c}_1, \ldots, \bar{c}_k],$$

which implies

$$S_3 \models g(\pi')[\bar{f}, \bar{c}_1, \ldots, \bar{c}_k],$$

which is equivalent to $S_3 \models \pi'[\bar{f}, \bar{a}]$ (by the assumption that no new variables are introduced on the target sides of dependencies.) □

Algorithm 19.1 can also be used to compute the composition of two mappings specified by finite sets of st-tgds, as every such mapping can be transformed into an equivalent one specified by an SO tgd. It can be shown that exponentiality is unavoidable in such an algorithm, as there exist mappings $\mathscr{M}_{12}$ and $\mathscr{M}_{23}$, each specified by a finite set of st-tgds, such that every SO tgd that defines the composition of $\mathscr{M}_{12}$ and $\mathscr{M}_{23}$ is of size exponential in the size of $\mathscr{M}_{12}$ and $\mathscr{M}_{23}$ (see Exercise 22.3).

Theorem 18.8 also implies that the composition of a finite number of mappings specified by st-tgds can be defined by an SO tgd, as we can compose the mappings one by one.

Theorem 19.11 *The composition of a finite number of mappings, each defined by a finite set of st-tgds, can be defined by an SO tgd.*

Example 19.12 We have already shown in Example 19.7 how SO tgds can be used to express the composition of mappings specified by st-tgds. As a second example, assume that $\mathscr{M}_{12}$ and $\mathscr{M}_{23}$ are the mappings defined in Example 19.2. The composition of these two mappings is defined by $\mathtt{Takes}(n, c) \rightarrow \mathtt{Enrolled}(f(n), c)$. □

Up to this point, we have shown that the language of SO tgds is closed under composition, and that the composition of any finite number of mappings specified by st-tgds can be defined by an SO tgd. Thus, SO tgds are a good language when dealing with the composition operator. But, of course, it is natural to ask whether all the features of SO tgds are necessary, and whether there exists a smaller language that also has these good properties for composition. Interestingly, it can also be proved that all the features of SO tgds are necessary to deal with the composition operator, as every SO tgd defines the composition of a finite number of mappings specified by st-tgds. This fact, which is the converse of Theorem 19.11, shows that SO tgds are exactly the right language for representing the composition of mappings given by st-tgds.

Theorem 19.13 *Every SO tgd defines the composition of a finite number of mappings, each defined by a finite set of st-tgds.*

We do not provide the proof of Theorem 19.13, instead we show the main ideas behind this proof in the following example.

Example 19.14 Let $\mathbf{R_s}$ be a schema consisting of a unary relation P and $\mathbf{R_t}$ a schema consisting of a binary relation R. Furthermore, assume that the relationship between these schemas is given by the following SO tgd σ:

$$P(x) \wedge f(x) = g(x) \rightarrow R\big(f(g(x)), g(f(x))\big). \tag{19.4}$$

We show here the essential steps of an algorithm that, given an SO tgd σ, generates a finite sequence of mappings that are given by st-tgds and whose composition is defined by σ.

For the sake of readability, let $\mathbf{R_1}$ be the schema $\mathbf{R_s}$. The algorithm starts by generating a schema $\mathbf{R_2}$, consisting of binary relations F_1, G_1 and of a unary relation P_1, and a mapping $\mathcal{M}_{12} = (\mathbf{R_1}, \mathbf{R_2}, \Sigma_{12})$ that is specified by a set Σ_{12} of st-tgds consisting of the following dependencies:

$$P(x) \rightarrow P_1(x),$$
$$P(x) \rightarrow \exists y\, F_1(x,y),$$
$$P(x) \rightarrow \exists z\, G_1(x,z).$$

Intuitively, P_1 is a copy of P, $F_1(x,y)$ indicates that $f(x) = y$, and $G_1(x,y)$ indicates that $g(x) = y$. In particular, the second and third dependencies above have the effect of guaranteeing that $f(x)$ and $g(x)$ are defined for every element x in P, respectively. Then the algorithm generates a schema $\mathbf{R_3}$, consisting of binary relations F_2, G_2 and of a unary relation P_2, and a mapping $\mathcal{M}_{23} = (\mathbf{R_2}, \mathbf{R_3}, \Sigma_{23})$ that is specified by a set Σ_{23} of st-tgds consisting of the following dependencies:

$$P_1(x) \rightarrow P_2(x),$$
$$F_1(x,y) \rightarrow F_2(x,y),$$
$$G_1(x,y) \rightarrow G_2(x,y),$$
$$F_1(x,y) \rightarrow \exists u\, G_2(y,u),$$
$$G_1(x,y) \rightarrow \exists v\, F_2(y,v).$$

As in the previous case, P_2 is a copy of P_1, $F_2(x,y)$ indicates that $f(x) = y$ and $G_2(x,y)$ indicates that $g(x) = y$. In particular, all the values of f stored in F_1 are also stored in F_2, by the second dependency above, and all the values of g stored in G_1 are also stored in G_2, by the third dependency above. But not only that, the fourth dependency also guarantees that $g(y)$ is defined for all y in the range of f, and the fifth dependency guarantees that $f(y)$ is defined for all y in the range of g. Finally, let $\mathbf{R_4}$ be the schema $\mathbf{R_t}$. Then the algorithm generates a mapping $\mathcal{M}_{34} = (\mathbf{R_3}, \mathbf{R_4}, \Sigma_{34})$ that uses P_2, F_2 and G_2 to populate the target relation R. More precisely, Σ_{34} consists of the following st-tgd:

$$P_2(x) \wedge F_2(x,y) \wedge G_2(x,y) \wedge F_2(y,z_1) \wedge G_2(y,z_2) \rightarrow R(z_1,z_2).$$

The output of the algorithm is the sequence of mappings $\mathcal{M}_{12}$, $\mathcal{M}_{23}$, $\mathcal{M}_{34}$, which satisfies that $(\mathcal{M}_{12} \circ \mathcal{M}_{23}) \circ \mathcal{M}_{34}$ is defined by SO tgd σ. □

We conclude this section by pointing out that the algorithm sketched in the previous example can be generalized to any SO tgd. In fact, assume that the nesting depth of an SO tgd σ is defined to be the largest depth of the terms that appear in σ. For instance, the nesting depth of SO tgd (19.4) is 2 as the depth of the terms $f(x)$, $g(x)$ is 1 and the depth of the terms $f(g(x))$, $g(f(x))$ is 2. Then the generalization of the algorithm generates a sequence of $r+1$ mappings when the input is an SO tgd of nesting depth r.

19.4 Complexity of XML composition

Complexity analysis gave us a key to relational composition, suggesting the formalism of SO tgds. Is the XML case similar? Are SO tgds sufficient as well? If not, is there another formalism we could use?

A complexity argument gives a negative answer to these questions: there is no reasonable formalism at all, unless additional restrictions are imposed. Theorem 19.15 below states that the composition problem for XML mappings can be undecidable if data comparisons are allowed. This means that there is no decidable formalism capable of expressing compositions of XML mappings.

Of course later we shall present a class that is not only closed under compositions but also makes it possible to compute compositions within reasonable time bounds. This, however, will require restrictions on axes used in mappings, as well as schemas for source and target documents.

For now, we present the negative result.

Theorem 19.15 *There are mappings $\mathcal{M}_{12}^\star$ and $\mathcal{M}_{23}^\star$ in $\mathrm{SM}(\downarrow,\downarrow^+,=)$ such that* COMPOSITION$(\mathcal{M}_{12}^\star, \mathcal{M}_{23}^\star)$ *is undecidable. The same holds for the classes* $\mathrm{SM}(\downarrow,\downarrow^+,\neq)$, $\mathrm{SM}(\downarrow,\rightarrow,=)$ *and* $\mathrm{SM}(\downarrow,\rightarrow,\neq)$.

Proof Our argument relies upon a particular property of the reductions used to show undecidability in the proof of Theorem 18.4: halting of a two-register machine M is there reduced to consistency of a mapping $\mathcal{M}_M = (D_s, D_t, \Sigma_{st})$ all of whose dependencies had only a conjunction of equalities or inequalities on the target side. For such dependencies, the target side's satisfaction does not depend on the target tree.

Now we need two fixed mappings for which the composition problem is undecidable. It is well known that there exists a universal two-register machine U, such that it is undecidable if for a given n the machine accepts with registers initialized to $(n,0)$. We shall construct mappings $\mathcal{M}_{12}^\star$ and $\mathcal{M}_{23}^\star$ and trees T_n so that $(T_n, r) \in [\![\mathcal{M}_{12}^\star]\!] \circ [\![\mathcal{M}_{23}^\star]\!]$ iff and only if U accepts with registers initialized to $(n,0)$.

For $\mathcal{M}_{23}^\star$ we can take $\mathcal{M}_U$, except that we skip the dependency

$$r[I_1(x,y), //R/R(x)] \longrightarrow \bot$$

as we want to allow arbitrary initial values of the first register.

The mapping $\mathcal{M}_{12}^\star$ ensures that the first register is initialized with the number encoded in the source tree T_n. Recall that $\mathcal{M}_U$ uses the data values stored in subsequent R-nodes as values of the registers: n is encoded as the nth data value in this path, counting from the root. Therefore, to encode the value of the first register properly in T_n, we enforce concrete values in the initial n nodes of this path. The source DTD of $\mathcal{M}_{12}^\star$ is $\{r \to R; R \to R \mid \sharp\}$ where R has a single attribute. For T_n we take the tree given by the pattern $r/R(a_1)/R(a_2)/\ldots/R(a_n)/\sharp$ where $a_1, a_2, \ldots, a_n$ are arbitrary pairwise different data values. The dependencies say that the initial segment of register values is copied correctly,

$$r/R(x) \longrightarrow r/R(x),$$
$$r//R(x)/R(y) \longrightarrow r//R(x)/R(y),$$

and that the first register is initialized to the nth value of this segment,

$$r//R(x)/\sharp \longrightarrow \exists y\, r/I_1(x,y).$$

To see that the copying dependencies work as intended, recall that $\mathcal{M}_U$ contains a dependency $r//R(x)//R(x) \longrightarrow \bot$, which ensures that the values copied from T_n are stored in the initial segment of the path.

The remaining reductions can be obtained analogously, by modifying corresponding reductions to the consistency problem (see Exercise 22.3)   □

Theorem 19.15 suggests one possible way of expressing compositions of XML mappings: restrict the use of data comparisons. The following result shows that without data comparisons the composition problem is decidable, but the complexity goes up compared to the relational case.

Theorem 19.16 COMPOSITION$(\mathcal{M}_{12}, \mathcal{M}_{23})$ *is in* EXPTIME *for all mappings* $\mathcal{M}_{12}, \mathcal{M}_{23} \in$ SM$(\Downarrow, \Rightarrow)$.

Proof Let $\mathcal{M}_{12} = (\mathscr{S}_1, \mathscr{S}_2, \Sigma_{12})$ and $\mathcal{M}_{23} = (\mathscr{S}_2, \mathscr{S}_3, \Sigma_{23})$, with $\Sigma_{12} = \{\varphi_i \to \psi_i \mid i = 1, 2, \ldots, n\}$ and $\Sigma_{23} = \{\gamma_j \to \delta_j \mid j = 1, 2, \ldots, m\}$. Given trees $S \models \mathscr{S}_1$ and $T \models \mathscr{S}_3$, we have to check if there is an interpolating tree U.

For a start, consider a variable-free situation. What are the constraints on the interpolating tree? Clearly, what is imposed by S is that some of the target sides of st-tgds from Σ_{12} have to be satisfied in U. In contrast, what is imposed by T, is that some source sides of st-tgds from Σ_{23} are *not* satisfied in U: indeed, $U \models \gamma \implies T \models \delta$ is equivalent to $T \not\models \delta \implies U \not\models \gamma$. Therefore, the existence of an interpolating tree U is equivalent to nonemptiness of

$$\mathscr{A}_2 \times \prod_{i:\, S\models\varphi_i} \mathscr{A}(\psi_i) \times \prod_{j:\, T\not\models\delta_j} \bar{\mathscr{A}}(\gamma_j),$$

where $\mathscr{A}_2$ is the UNFTA underlying $\mathscr{S}_2$, $\mathscr{A}(\psi_i)$ recognizes the language of trees satisfying ψ_i, and $\bar{\mathscr{A}}(\gamma_j)$ recognizes the language of trees that do not satisfy γ_j. By Lemma 18.2, all these automata are at most exponential, which gives an EXPTIME algorithm for the case without data values.

Let us now consider the general case, with variables. Still, neither equality nor inequality is allowed. In particular, no variable can be used more than once in any tree pattern. The main idea is simply to throw in every data value used in S to the alphabet. A tentative set of positive constraints imposed on U by S would then be

$$\Delta = \{\psi(\bar{a},\bar{z}) \mid \varphi(\bar{x},\bar{y}) \longrightarrow \exists\bar{z}\,\psi(\bar{x},\bar{z}) \in \Sigma_{12} \text{ and } S \models \varphi(\bar{a},\bar{b})\}.$$

Patterns in Δ can still contain free variables, but one can simply ignore them, as without repetitions and data comparisons, the variables merely state that some data value is there, which is already enforced by the schema.

For the set of negative constraints enforced by T we would like

$$\{\gamma(\bar{a},\bar{y}) \mid \gamma(\bar{x},\bar{y}) \longrightarrow \exists\bar{z}\,\delta(\bar{x},\bar{z}) \in \Sigma_{23} \text{ and } T \not\models \delta(\bar{a},\bar{z})\},$$

but this yields a potentially infinite set. How do we limit the domain from which the entries of $\bar{a}$ are taken? Let A be the set of data values used in S or in T. It is not difficult to see that in an intermediate tree U each data value not in A can be safely replaced by any fixed data value, in particular, by a fixed data value from A. This holds because we do not use $=$ nor $\neq$. Hence, we can assume that U only uses data values from A and take

$$\Phi = \{\gamma(\bar{a},\bar{y}) \mid \gamma(\bar{x},\bar{y}) \longrightarrow \exists\bar{z}\,\delta(\bar{x},\bar{z}) \in \Sigma_{23},\ \bar{a} \in A^{|\bar{x}|},\ T \not\models \delta(\bar{a},\bar{z})\}$$

with the free variables ignored just like for Δ.

The composition membership algorithm should construct the set Δ (at most $|\Sigma_{12}||S|^{\|\Sigma_{12}\|}$ polynomial checks) and Φ (at most $|\Sigma_{23}|(|S|+|T|)^{\|\Sigma_{23}\|}$ polynomial checks). Then it is enough to check nonemptiness of

$$\mathscr{A}_2 \times \prod_{\psi\in\Delta} \mathscr{A}(\psi) \times \prod_{\gamma\in\Phi} \bar{\mathscr{A}}(\gamma),$$

which can be done in time exponential in the size of Δ and Φ (which are polynomial in the size of S). This gives an EXPTIME algorithm. $\qquad\square$

Theorem 19.15 shows that in principle there could be a suitable formalism for compositions of $SM(\Downarrow,\Rightarrow)$, but most likely it is not SO tgds. Indeed, as we show below, the composition problem can be EXPTIME-hard for some mappings in $SM(\Downarrow,\Rightarrow)$. Note that this does not prove that SO tgds are incapable of expressing XML compositions, as it is not known whether $NP \subsetneq EXPTIME$. However, it is generally believed that $NP \subsetneq PSPACE$, and

PSPACE is contained in EXPTIME. Thus, most likely (barring some unexpected collapse results in complexity theory), compositions of mappings that do not use data comparisons still cannot be expressed with SO tgds.

Theorem 19.17 *There are mappings $\mathcal{M}_{12}^\star$ and $\mathcal{M}_{23}^\star$ in $\mathrm{SM}(\Downarrow, \Rightarrow)$ such that* COMPOSITION$(\mathcal{M}_{12}^\star, \mathcal{M}_{23}^\star)$ *is* EXPTIME-*complete.*

Proof We will reduce from the nonuniversality problem for bottom-up nondeterministic automata on binary trees, modifying the reduction given in Proposition 18.3.

First, define D_3 over $\{\texttt{r}, \texttt{label}, \texttt{state}, \texttt{nontr}, \texttt{reject}\}$ as

$$\texttt{r} \to \sharp\,\texttt{state}^*\,\natural\,\texttt{label}^*\,\flat\,\texttt{nontr}^*$$

$$\texttt{state} \to \texttt{reject}?$$

$$\texttt{label}, \texttt{state} : \texttt{@attr}$$

$$\texttt{nontr} : \texttt{@left}, \texttt{@right}, \texttt{@label}, \texttt{@up}.$$

A tree conforming to D_3 is meant to encode an automaton. It stores the alphabet in the `label`-nodes, state space in the `state`-nodes (we assume that the initial state is stored as first, just after $\sharp$), and the *complement* of the transition relation. The reason we store the complement is that we do not have negation. We do not have to enforce anything on such a tree, since we will be constructing it ourselves based on a given automaton, when preparing input for the composition membership algorithm. In particular, we will make sure that all states, labels, and nontransitions are stored correctly.

Next, let D_2 over $\{\texttt{r}, \texttt{node}, \texttt{label}, \texttt{state}, \texttt{leaf}, \texttt{yes}, \texttt{no}\}$ be given by

$$\texttt{r} \to \texttt{node}$$

$$\texttt{node} \to \texttt{label}\,\sharp\,\texttt{state}^*\,\natural\,(\texttt{node}\,\texttt{node}\,|\,\texttt{leaf})$$

$$\texttt{state} \to \texttt{yes}\,|\,\texttt{no}$$

$$\texttt{state}, \texttt{label} : \texttt{@attr}.$$

A tree conforming to D_2 is meant to encode a rejecting run of the corresponding power set automaton. This time we will need to ensure that it really is a correct rejecting run with the st-tgds, since this is precisely the tree that will be produced by the composition membership algorithm.

Finally, we define D_1 simply as $\texttt{r} \to \varepsilon$. The only tree conforming to D_1 will be used as a stub.

Let us now describe Σ_{23}, which will enforce the correctness of the run. First, we make sure that `label`-nodes store labels,

$$//\texttt{label}(x) \longrightarrow \texttt{r}/\texttt{label}(x).$$

Second, we need to check that for each `node`-node, each state is stored in exactly one `state`-node, and that nothing else is stored there,

$$//\texttt{node}[\texttt{state}(x) \to^+ \texttt{state}(y)] \longrightarrow \texttt{r}[\texttt{state}(x) \to^+ \texttt{state}(y)].$$

This ensures that for each state we either have a yes-node or a no-node.

Next, we make sure that the yes/no nodes are properly assigned in the leaves, and then properly propagated up the tree,

$$//\texttt{node}[\texttt{state}(x)/\texttt{no}, \texttt{label}(u), \texttt{leaf}] \longrightarrow$$
$$\longrightarrow \exists y\,\texttt{r}[\sharp \to \texttt{state}(y), \texttt{nontr}(y,y,u,x)],$$
$$//\texttt{node}[\texttt{state}(x)/\texttt{no}, \texttt{label}(u),$$
$$\texttt{node}/\texttt{state}(y)/\texttt{yes} \to \texttt{node}/\texttt{state}(z)/\texttt{yes}] \longrightarrow$$
$$\longrightarrow \texttt{r}/\texttt{nontr}(y,z,u,x).$$

Finally, check that the run is rejecting,

$$\texttt{r}/\texttt{node}/\texttt{state}(x)/\texttt{yes} \longrightarrow \texttt{r}/\texttt{state}(x)/\texttt{reject}.$$

Let us see that membership in the composition of $\mathscr{M}_{12}^{\star} = (D_1, D_2, \emptyset)$ and $\mathscr{M}_{23}^{\star} = (D_2, D_3, \Sigma_{23})$ is indeed EXPTIME-hard. Take an automaton $A = \langle \Gamma, Q, \delta, q_0, F \rangle$ with $\Gamma = \{a_1, a_2, \ldots, a_m\}$ and $Q = \{q_0, q_1, \ldots, q_n\}$. Without loss of generality we may assume that $F = \{q_k, q_{k+1}, \ldots, q_m\}$. Let $Q \times Q \times \Gamma \times Q \setminus \delta = \{(p_1, r_1, b_1, s_1), (p_2, r_2, b_2, s_2), \ldots, (p_\ell, r_\ell, b_\ell, s_\ell)\}$. Encode A as a tree T_A defined as

$$\texttt{r}[\sharp, \texttt{state}(q_0)/\texttt{reject}, \texttt{state}(q_1)/\texttt{reject}, \ldots, \texttt{state}(q_{k-1})/\texttt{reject},$$
$$\texttt{state}(q_k), \texttt{state}(q_{k+1}), \ldots, \texttt{state}(q_n), \natural,$$
$$\texttt{label}(a_1), \texttt{label}(a_2), \ldots, \texttt{label}(a_m), \flat,$$
$$\texttt{nontr}(p_1, r_1, b_1, s_1), \texttt{nontr}(p_2, r_2, b_2, s_2), \ldots, \texttt{nontr}(p_\ell, r_\ell, b_\ell, s_\ell)].$$

Proving that A rejects some tree if and only if $(\texttt{r}, T_A) \in [\![\mathscr{M}_{12}^{\star}]\!] \circ [\![\mathscr{M}_{23}^{\star}]\!]$ is straightforward.

$\square$

Summing up, if we want to guarantee that the composition is expressible with SO tgds, we need to further restrict the class of mappings. In the following section we shall investigate this issue in more detail and isolate a fairly natural class of mappings closed by composition.

19.5 Tractable XML composition

Finding a formalism capable of expressing compositions of XML mappings is much harder than for relational mappings. We have seen that allowing data comparisons in mappings can lead to undecidable compositions, and even if we forbid data comparisons altogether, we cannot hope to show that SO tgds can express XML compositions without disproving a long-standing conjecture in complexity theory. In this section we pursue a dual goal: we shall try to find out when a composition of mappings can be expressed with SO tgds.

Let us first formally define SO tgds in the XML context. Recall that in XML data exchange, we used dependencies of the form

$$\pi \wedge \alpha \longrightarrow \exists \bar{z}\, \pi' \wedge \alpha',$$

where π and π' are patterns, and α and α' are conjunctions of equalities and inequalities (see Definition 11.3 on page 146 and Definition 11.10 on page 154).

Now, just like in the relational case we write SO tgds as rules using function symbols. This means that in a rule $\pi \wedge \alpha \longrightarrow \exists \bar{z} \, \pi' \wedge \alpha'$, the patterns π, π' can contain expressions of the form

$$\ell(t_1, t_2, \ldots, t_k)$$

where $t_1, t_2, \ldots, t_k$ are terms over some set of function symbols and variables. Similarly, α and α' can contain equalities and inequalities between terms.

For a valuation of function symbols $\bar{f}$ and a valuation of variables (a tuple) $\bar{a}$

$$T, v \models \ell(t_1, t_2, \ldots, t_k)[\bar{f}, \bar{a}]$$

if v has the label ℓ and stores the tuple $t_1[\bar{f}, \bar{a}], t_2[\bar{f}, \bar{a}], \ldots, t_k[\bar{f}, \bar{a}]$ where $t_i[\bar{f}, \bar{a}]$ is the value of the term t_i when the function symbols are interpreted according to $\bar{f}$ and the variables according to $\bar{a}$. The general notion of satisfaction for patterns,

$$T \models \pi[\bar{f}, \bar{a}],$$

is obtained just like for the case without function symbols.

For a mapping $\mathcal{M} = (\mathcal{S}_s, \mathcal{S}_t, \Sigma_{st})$ using function symbols, $(T, T') \in [\![\mathcal{M}]\!]$ if there exist functions $\bar{f}$ such that for each $\varphi \longrightarrow \psi \in \Sigma_{st}$ and each $\bar{a}$, if $T \models \varphi[\bar{f}, \bar{a}]$ then $T' \models \psi[\bar{f}, \bar{a}]$. We indicate the availability of function symbols in the mappings by including FUN in the signature in the SM(σ) notation, e.g., SM($\Downarrow$, FUN).

When is XML mapping composition problematic?

We now give a few examples showing that some features of XML schema mappings cause problems when we try to compose them. The first such feature is disjunction in schemas, as illustrated by the following example.

Example 19.18   Let

$$D_1 = \{r \to \varepsilon\}, \ D_2 = \{r \to b_1 \,|\, b_2; \ b_1, b_2 \to b_3\}, \ D_3 = \{r \to c_1? c_2? c_3?\}$$

with no attributes present and let

$$\Sigma_{12} = \{r \longrightarrow r/\_/b_3\}, \quad \Sigma_{23} = \{r/b_i \longrightarrow r/c_i \mid i = 1, 2\}.$$

Note that the source tree is just a single root node labeled r. Then $[\![\mathcal{M}_{12}]\!] \circ [\![\mathcal{M}_{23}]\!]$ consists of pairs of trees (r, T), where T matches either r/c_1 or r/c_2. It is intuitively clear, and can be proved formally, that such a mapping cannot be defined without disjunction over the target: a disjunction is encoded in the intermediate schema D_2 as the alternative $b_1 \,|\, b_2$, and if this schema is removed, the disjunction should be somehow expressed with dependencies. Note that c_3? is necessary in D_3: with the production $r \to c_1? c_2?$ the composition would be definable by $r \longrightarrow r/\_$.   □

Not only disjunction in DTDs is problematic. As another illustration of difficulties in composing XML schema mappings, look at the following example.

Example 19.19 Consider

$$D_1 = \{r \to a^*\}, \quad D_2 = \{r \to bb\}, \quad D_3 = \{r \to \varepsilon\}$$

with a and b having an attribute each, and

$$\Sigma_{12} = \{r/a(x) \longrightarrow r/b(x)\}, \quad \Sigma_{23} = \{r \to r\}.$$

Here the target trees are single-node trees with label r. In the composition we have pairs (T, r) such that in T at most two different data values are present. This again requires disjunction, e.g., $r[a(x), a(y), a(z)] \longrightarrow (x = y \lor y = z \lor x = z)$. Intuitively, what causes the problem here is a fixed number of repetitions of a label in the DTD (i.e., bb). □

There is also a variety of features in patterns that can lead to compositions that cannot be defined with SO tgds. The example below shows that the use of the wildcard should be restricted.

Example 19.20 Consider

$$D_1 = \{r \to \varepsilon\}, \quad D_2 = \{r \to a_1^* a_2^*; a_1 \to b; a_2 \to b\}, \quad D_3 = \{r \to c_1?c_2?c_3?\}$$

with no attributes and

$$\Sigma_{12} = \{r \longrightarrow r/\_/b\}, \quad \Sigma_{23} = \{r/a_1 \longrightarrow r/c_1; r/a_2 \longrightarrow r/c_2\}.$$

Just like in Example 19.18, $[\![(D_1, D_2, \Sigma_{12})]\!] \circ [\![(D_2, D_3, \Sigma_{23})]\!]$ contains exactly pairs (r, T), where T matches r/c_1 or r/c_2. □

The mappings in Example 19.20 can be modified to use either of $\downarrow^+, \to, \to^+, \neq$ instead of the wildcard (see Exercise 22.3). In other words, the following features take us out of the class of mappings definable with SO tgds:

- disjunction or multiple (bounded) repetitions of labels in the productions of DTDs,
- wildcard, descendant, next-sibling, following-sibling, and inequalities in st-tgds.

Well-behaved composition

Now that we understand which features cause problems with XML composition, just eliminate them all. We are then left with vertical navigation, equality comparisons, Skolem functions, and nested-relational DTDs that rule out disjunctions and repetitions of labels. That is, we are left with mappings from

$$\text{SM}^{\text{nr}}(\downarrow, =, \text{FUN}).$$

The good news is that this class is closed under composition.

Theorem 19.21 *The class of mappings* $\mathrm{SM}^{\mathrm{nr}}(\downarrow,=,\mathrm{FUN})$ *is closed under composition. Moreover, the composition of two given mappings can be computed in single-exponential time.*

The composition procedure is given in Algorithm 19.2. We use the notation $X \hookleftarrow Y$ for $X := X \cup Y$ and for a homomorphism $h \colon \pi \to \pi'$ we write $h(\varphi)$ to denote the substitution of π's variables in φ with their images under h.

In this algorithm we also use two operators from Chapter 13: the completion operator cpl_D and the merge operator mrg_D, defined on page 191.

Algorithm 19.2 Composing XML schema mappings

Require: $\mathcal{M}_{12} = (D_1, D_2, \Sigma_{12}), \mathcal{M}_{23} = (D_2, D_3, \Sigma_{23}) \in \mathrm{SM}^{\mathrm{nr}}(\downarrow,=,\mathrm{FUN})$
Require: no variables introduced on target sides
Require: pure patterns on the source side use only variables
    $\widehat{\Sigma}_{12} := \left\{ \varphi \longrightarrow \bot \mid \varphi \longrightarrow \psi \in \Sigma_{12} \text{ and } \psi \text{ not satisfiable wrt } D_2 \right\}$
2: $\widehat{\Sigma}_{12} \hookleftarrow \left\{ \varphi \longrightarrow \mathrm{cpl}_{D_2} \psi \mid \varphi \longrightarrow \psi \in \Sigma_{12} \text{ and } \psi \text{ satisfiable wrt } D_2 \right\}$
    $\{$Skolemize to remove variables introduced by $\mathrm{cpl}_{D_2}\}$
4: $\Sigma_{13} := \left\{ \varphi \longrightarrow \bot \mid \varphi \longrightarrow \bot \in \widehat{\Sigma}_{12} \right\}$
    $m := \max_{(\varphi \to \psi) \in \Sigma_{23}} \|\varphi\|$
6: **for all** $\varphi_1 \longrightarrow \psi_1, \varphi_2 \longrightarrow \psi_2, \ldots, \varphi_k \longrightarrow \psi_k \in \widehat{\Sigma}_{12}$, $k \leq m$ **do**
    $\{$in case of repetitions, rename variables$\}$
8:     $\rho \wedge \eta := \mathrm{mrg}_{D_2}(\psi_1 \wedge \cdots \wedge \psi_k)$
    $\Sigma_{13} \hookleftarrow \left\{ \varphi_1 \wedge \cdots \wedge \varphi_k \longrightarrow \eta \right\}$
10:    **for all** $\pi \wedge \alpha \longrightarrow \psi \in \Sigma_{23}$ **and all** homomorphisms $h \colon \pi \to \rho$ **do**
      $\Sigma_{13} \hookleftarrow \left\{ \varphi_1 \wedge \cdots \wedge \varphi_k \wedge h(\alpha) \longrightarrow h(\psi) \right\}$
12:    **end for**
    end for
14: **return** (D_1, D_3, Σ_{13})

The procedure is similar to the one for relational mappings (Algorithm 19.1), but there are several important differences:

- some preprocessing replaces Σ_{12} with $\widehat{\Sigma}_{12}$ (lines 1–3);
- Σ_{13} is initialized differently (line 4);
- ρ is not just the conjunction of the target sides of dependencies from Σ_{12} (line 8); and
- additional dependencies are inserted to Σ_{13} (line 9).

Let us briefly discuss these differences.

One aim of the preprocessing phase is to ensure that in $\widehat{\Sigma}_{12}$ the target side patterns are either satisfiable with respect to D_2 or are equal to $\bot$. In the relational case, we have this for free, as each conjunctive query without constants is satisfiable. Observe that a dependency $\varphi \to \bot$ in $\mathcal{M}_{12}$ imposes a restriction on source instances rather than solutions. Indeed, if T has a solution with respect to $\mathcal{M}_{12}$, then T must not satisfy φ. Clearly, if T is to have a solution with respect to the composition of $\mathcal{M}_{12}$ and $\mathcal{M}_{23}$, it should also not satisfy φ. This explains why all such dependencies are included into Σ_{13} (line 4).

Another aim of the preprocessing phase is to include in the target patterns all information that can be inferred from the schema D_2. For instance, if D_2 declares that each a-labeled node has a b-labeled child, we include this information into a target pattern $r/a(x)$ by replacing it with $r/a(x)/b(y)$, where y is a fresh variable. In the relational case, there is no information to infer, so this step is not needed. In general, we use the operation cpl_{D_2} from Chapter 13. The operation was designed for patterns without function symbols, but it can be directly applied to patterns with function symbols. The obtained pattern will often contain new variables (e.g., y in the example above). We eliminate them by standard Skolemization, replacing variables with fresh function symbols. As in Lemma 13.13, which generalizes naturally, the resulting set of st-tgds is equivalent to the original. Thus, without loss of generality we can assume that the algorithm starts with $\Sigma_{12} = \widehat{\Sigma}_{12}$. In particular, we assume that no new function symbols are introduced by Algorithm 19.2.

The operation cpl_{D_2} only adds information about the nodes that are enforced by D_2, but are not mentioned in the target side patterns of $\mathcal{M}_{12}$. Another kind of information that one can infer from D_2 is that some nodes of the pattern are always matched in the same node of the tree. For instance, if D_2 says that the root has exactly one a-labeled child, then $r[a(x)/b, a(y)/c]$ can be replaced with a more informative pattern $r/a(x)[b,c] \wedge x = y$. This kind of information is extracted by the merge operation, mrg_{D_2}, defined in Chapter 13. Just like cpl_{D_2}, the merge operation can be applied to patterns with function symbols without any modifications, and Lemmas 13.14 and 13.15 generalize in a straightforward way. By defining $\rho \wedge \eta$ as $\mathrm{mrg}_{D_2}(\psi_1 \wedge \cdots \wedge \psi_k)$ in line 8, we ensure that $\rho \wedge \eta$ expresses all the information that can be extracted from $\psi_1 \wedge \cdots \wedge \psi_k$ and D_2.

Note that in the example above not only is the structure of the pattern changed, but also a new equality $x = y$ is introduced. This equality, just like any equality present in $\psi_1 \wedge \cdots \wedge \psi_k$, imposes a restriction on source instances that have solutions, and needs to be included in the composition. It is done in line 9. Such new equalities enforced by the intermediate schema can occur even if the original patterns do not use equalities. This shows that without equality on the target side, XML schema mappings are not closed by composition.

In the following two lemmas we show formally that Algorithm 19.2 is correct.

Lemma 19.22 *If $(T_1, T_2) \in [\![\mathcal{M}_{12}]\!]$ and $(T_2, T_3) \in [\![\mathcal{M}_{23}]\!]$ with a witnessing valuation of function symbols $\bar{f}$, then $(T_1, T_3) \in [\![\mathcal{M}_{13}]\!]$ with the same witnessing valuation $\bar{f}$.*

Proof Pick a constraint from Σ_{13}. Suppose first that it is of the form

$$\varphi \longrightarrow \bot,$$

then it is also present in Σ_{12}. Hence, T_1 does not satisfy φ for any valuation, and so (T_1, T_3) satisfies the constraint.

Next, suppose the constraint is of the form

$$\varphi_1 \wedge \cdots \wedge \varphi_k \longrightarrow \eta \,,$$

where $\varphi_1 \longrightarrow \psi_1$, $\varphi_2 \longrightarrow \psi_2$, ..., $\varphi_k \longrightarrow \psi_k \in \Sigma_{12}$ and $\rho \wedge \eta = \mathrm{cpl}_{D_2}(\psi_1 \wedge \cdots \wedge \psi_k)$. Pick $\bar{a}$ such that $T_1 \models \varphi_1 \wedge \cdots \wedge \varphi_k[\bar{f}, \bar{a}]$. Then $T_2 \models \psi_1 \wedge \cdots \wedge \psi_k[\bar{f}, \bar{a}]$, and by Lemma 13.14 (1), $\eta[\bar{f}, \bar{a}]$ holds.

Finally, assume the constraint is of the form

$$\varphi_1 \wedge \cdots \wedge \varphi_k \wedge h(\alpha) \longrightarrow h(\psi) \,,$$

where $\varphi_i \longrightarrow \psi_i$ and $\rho \wedge \eta$ are like above, $\pi \wedge \alpha \longrightarrow \psi \in \Sigma_{23}$, and h is a homomorphism from π into ρ. Pick $\bar{a}$ such that $T_1 \models \varphi_1 \wedge \cdots \wedge \varphi_k \wedge h(\alpha)[\bar{f}, \bar{a}]$. Then $T_2 \models \psi_1 \wedge \cdots \wedge \psi_k[\bar{f}, \bar{a}]$ and by Lemma 13.14 (1) we get $T_2 \models \rho[\bar{f}, \bar{a}]$. Hence $T_2 \models h(\pi)[\bar{f}, \bar{a}]$. As $h(\alpha)[\bar{f}, \bar{a}]$ holds, we have $T_2 \models h(\pi) \wedge h(\alpha)[\bar{f}, \bar{a}]$ and hence $T_3 \models h(\psi)[\bar{f}, \bar{a}]$. $\qquad\square$

Lemma 19.23 *If $(T_1, T_3) \in [\![\mathcal{M}_{13}]\!]$ with a witnessing valuation $\bar{f}$, there exists an intermediate tree T_2 such that $(T_1, T_2) \in [\![\mathcal{M}_{12}]\!]$ and $(T_2, T_3) \in [\![\mathcal{M}_{23}]\!]$ with the same witnessing valuation $\bar{f}$.*

Proof Let

$$\Delta = \{\psi(\bar{a}) \mid \varphi(\bar{x}, \bar{y}) \longrightarrow \psi(\bar{x}) \in \Sigma_{12} \text{ and } T_1 \models \varphi(\bar{a}, \bar{b})[\bar{f}] \text{ for some } \bar{b}\} \,.$$

By $\psi(\bar{a})$, $\varphi(\bar{a}, \bar{b})$ we mean formulae where variables $\bar{x}, \bar{y}$ are substituted by $\bar{a}, \bar{b}$, but the functions are not evaluated. In other words, these formulae contain ground terms. By $\varphi(\bar{a}, \bar{b})[\bar{f}]$ we denote the formula where functions are evaluated according to $\bar{f}$. Recall that a tree $T_2 \models D_2$ is a solution for T_1 with witnessing valuation $\bar{f}$ if and only if $T_2 \models (\bigwedge_{\delta \in \Delta} \delta)[\bar{f}]$ (Lemma 12.1). We shall construct T_2 from $\mathrm{mrg}_{D_2}(\bigwedge_{\delta \in \Delta} \delta)$ and check that it has the desired properties. The proof essentially relies on the simple observation that for each pattern $\xi(\bar{z})$ and each tuple $\bar{c}$

$$\mathrm{mrg}_{D_2} \xi(\bar{c}) = \big(\mathrm{mrg}_{D_2} \xi(\bar{z})\big)(\bar{c}) \,. \tag{19.5}$$

First, we need to see that $\mathrm{mrg}_{D_2}(\bigwedge_{\delta \in \Delta} \delta)$ is not $\bot$. This can only happen if the pure pattern underlying $\bigwedge_{\delta \in \Delta} \delta$ is not satisfiable wrt to D_2 even when attributes are ignored. But then, using the fact that D_2 is nested-relational, we conclude easily that there exists a pattern $\delta \in \Delta$ which is not satisfiable wrt D_2 even when attributes are ignored. Thanks to the preprocessing phase, we then have $\delta = \bot$. In this case there is a dependency $\varphi(\bar{x}, \bar{y}) \longrightarrow \bot$ in Σ_{12} such that $T_1 \models \varphi(\bar{a}, \bar{b})[\bar{f}]$. As Σ_{13} also contains $\varphi(\bar{x}, \bar{y}) \longrightarrow \bot$, we get $T_3 \models \bot$, which is a contradiction. Hence, the pure pattern underlying $\bigwedge_{\delta \in \Delta} \delta$ is satisfiable (up to the values of attributes).

Next, we check that $\bar{f}$ satisfies all the equalities in $\mathrm{mrg}_{D_2}(\bigwedge_{\delta \in \Delta} \delta)$. Pick an equality $t = t'$. If it was already present in some $(\pi \wedge \alpha)(\bar{a}) \in \Delta$, then there exists $\varphi \longrightarrow \pi, \alpha \in \Sigma_{12}$ such that $T_1 \models \varphi(\bar{a}, \bar{b})[\bar{f}]$ for some $\bar{b}$, and some iteration of the outer loop adds constraint $\varphi \longrightarrow \alpha$ to Σ_{13}. Since the pair (T_1, T_3) satisfies Σ_{13}, we have $T_3 \models \alpha(\bar{a})[\bar{f}]$, which means that $t = t'$ holds.

If $t = t'$ was introduced as a result of merging some nodes of $\psi(\bar{a}), \psi'(\bar{a}') \in \Delta$, then

- $\psi(\bar{a})$ has a subformula $\sigma(t)$ and $\psi'(\bar{a}')$ has a subformula $\sigma(t')$,
- the path from r to this subformula in $\psi(\bar{a})$ and in $\psi'(\bar{a}')$ is the same, $\sigma_1 \sigma_2 \ldots \sigma_n$, with $\sigma_n = \sigma$,
- for all j either $\sigma_j \to \ldots \sigma_{j+1} \ldots$ or $\sigma_j \to \ldots \sigma_{j+1}? \ldots$ in DTD D_2.

In one of the iterations of the outer loop the algorithm processes $\varphi \longrightarrow \psi$, $\varphi' \longrightarrow \psi' \in \Sigma_{12}$ such that $T_1 \models \varphi(\bar{a}, \bar{b})[\bar{f}]$ and $T_1 \models \varphi'(\bar{a}', \bar{b}')[\bar{f}]$ for some $\bar{b}, \bar{b}'$. By merging ψ and ψ' with respect to D_2, the algorithm introduces an equality $\hat{t} = \hat{t}'$ such that by substituting variables of $\hat{t}$ according to $\bar{a}$ we get t, by substituting variables of $\hat{t}'$ according to $\bar{a}'$ we get t', and a constraint of the form $\varphi \wedge \varphi' \longrightarrow \hat{t} = \hat{t}' \wedge \ldots$ is added to Σ_{13}. Like before, we conclude that $t = t'$ holds.

Thus $\bar{f}$ satisfies all the equalities in $\mathrm{mrg}_{D_2}(\bigwedge_{\delta \in \Delta} \delta)$ and we can construct a tree T_2 from $\mathrm{mrg}_{D_2}(\bigwedge_{\delta \in \Delta} \delta)$ in the usual way by evaluating the terms according to $\bar{f}$. Since each $\delta \in \Delta$ is complete, so is $\bigwedge_{\delta \in \Delta} \delta$. Hence, by Lemma 13.15, $T_2 \models D_2$ and $T_2 \models (\bigwedge_{\delta \in \Delta} \delta)[\bar{f}]$. This implies that $(T_1, T_2) \in [\![\mathcal{M}_{12}]\!]$.

It remains to verify that $(T_2, T_3) \in [\![\mathcal{M}_{23}]\!]$. Pick a dependency $(\pi \wedge \alpha)(\bar{x}, \bar{y}) \longrightarrow \psi(\bar{x})$ from Σ_{23}. Suppose that $T_2 \models (\pi \wedge \alpha)(\bar{a}, \bar{b})[\bar{f}]$ and let $g \colon \pi \to T_2$ be a witnessing homomorphism. Recall that π uses each variable exactly once, and it does not use function symbols. In consequence, g can be interpreted as a homomorphism from π to the pure pattern underlying $\mathrm{mrg}_{D_2}(\bigwedge_{\delta \in \Delta} \delta)$, such that for each variable z in π, the value $g(z)$ under $\bar{f}$ is equal to the value of z according to $\bar{a}, \bar{b}$. Examining the definition of mrg_{D_2}, it is easy to see that g can also be seen as a homomorphism into ρ, where $\rho \wedge \eta = \mathrm{mrg}_{D_2}(\psi_1(\bar{a}_1) \wedge \cdots \wedge \psi_k(\bar{a}_k))$ for some $\psi_1(\bar{a}_1), \ldots, \psi_k(\bar{a}_k) \in \Delta$, $k \leq \|\pi\|$. By the definition of Δ, there exist $\varphi_1 \longrightarrow \psi_1$, $\varphi_2 \longrightarrow \psi_2$, $\ldots$, $\varphi_k \longrightarrow \psi_k \in \Sigma_{12}$ such that for some $\bar{b}_1, \ldots, \bar{b}_k$, $T_1 \models \varphi_i(\bar{a}_i, \bar{b}_i)[\bar{f}]$ for all i. By (19.5), we have $\rho \wedge \eta = (\hat{\rho} \wedge \hat{\eta})(\bar{a}_1, \ldots, \bar{a}_k)$ for $\hat{\rho} \wedge \hat{\eta} = \mathrm{mrg}_{D_2}(\psi_1 \wedge \cdots \wedge \psi_k)$. Using again the fact that π uses each variable exactly once and does not use function symbols, we lift $g \colon \pi \to \rho$ to a homomorphism $\hat{g} \colon \pi \to \hat{\rho}$ such that

$$\hat{g}(z) \text{ evaluated according to } \bar{f}, \bar{a}_1, \ldots, \bar{a}_k \text{ equals } z \text{ evaluated according to } \bar{a}, \bar{b}. \quad (19.6)$$

Consequently, Σ_{13} contains the dependency $\varphi_1 \wedge \cdots \wedge \varphi_k \wedge \hat{g}(\alpha) \to \hat{g}(\psi)$. Recall that $T_1 \models \varphi_i(\bar{a}_i, \bar{b}_i)[\bar{f}]$ for $i = 1, 2, \ldots, k$ and $\hat{g}(\alpha)[\bar{f}, \bar{a}_1, \ldots, \bar{a}_k]$ holds by (19.6) and by the assumption that $\alpha(\bar{a}, \bar{b})$ holds under $\bar{f}$. Hence, $T_3 \models \hat{g}(\psi)[\bar{f}, \bar{a}_1, \ldots, \bar{a}_k]$, which implies $T_3 \models \psi(\bar{a})[\bar{f}]$. $\square$

20

Inverting schema mappings

The inverse operator is another important operator that naturally arises in the development of a framework for managing schema mappings. Once the data has been transferred from the source to the target, the goal of the inverse is to recover the initial source data; if a mapping $\mathcal{M}'$ is an inverse of a mapping $\mathcal{M}$, then $\mathcal{M}'$ should bring the data exchanged through $\mathcal{M}$ back to the source.

In the study of this operator, the key issue is to provide a *good* semantics for this operator, which turned out to be a difficult problem. In this chapter, we present and compare two main approaches to inverting schema mappings. One of them, leading to an inverse operator, simply defines an inverse of a mapping $\mathcal{M}$ as a mapping that produced the identity mapping when composed with $\mathcal{M}$. A different proposal is to look for the maximum amount of information that can be inferred from the exchanged data: this approach leads to an alternative notion of maximum recovery. We define, study, and compare these notions.

20.1 A first definition of inverse

We start by considering the first notion of inverse for schema mappings proposed in the literature, which we call inverse in this chapter. Roughly speaking, the definition of this notion is based on the idea that a mapping composed with its inverse should be equal to the identity schema mapping. Thus, given a schema $\mathbf{R}$, an identity schema mapping $\overline{\mathrm{Id}}_{\mathbf{R}}$ is first defined as $\{(S_1, S_2) \mid S_1, S_2 \text{ are instances of } \mathbf{R} \text{ and } S_1 \subseteq S_2\}$. The subset relation used here emphasizes that we continue to follow the open-world assumption, that lets us extend instances with arbitrary facts. In fact, this identity is appropriate for the class of mappings specified by st-tgds (and, more generally, for the class of mappings that are total and closed-down on the left, which is defined in the following section).

Using this notion of identity mapping, we can then defined the inverse as follows.

Definition 20.1 (Inverse)   Let $\mathcal{M}$ be a mapping from a schema $\mathbf{R}_1$ to a schema $\mathbf{R}_2$, and $\mathcal{M}'$ a mapping from $\mathbf{R}_2$ to $\mathbf{R}_1$. Then $\mathcal{M}'$ is an *inverse* of $\mathcal{M}$ if

$$\mathcal{M} \circ \mathcal{M}' = \overline{\mathrm{Id}}_{\mathbf{R}_1}.$$

If such an inverse exists, then we say that $\mathcal{M}$ is *invertible*.   □

Example 20.2 Let $\mathbf{R}_1$ be a schema consisting of a unary relation S, let $\mathbf{R}_2$ be a schema consisting of unary relations U and V, and let $\mathcal{M}$ be a mapping from $\mathbf{R}_1$ to $\mathbf{R}_2$ specified by st-tgds $S(x) \rightarrow U(x)$ and $S(x) \rightarrow V(x)$. Intuitively, $\mathcal{M}$ is invertible since all the information in the source relation S is transferred to both relations U and V in the target. In fact, the mapping $\mathcal{M}'$ specified by dependency $U(x) \rightarrow S(x)$ is an inverse of $\mathcal{M}$ since $\mathcal{M} \circ \mathcal{M}' = \overline{\mathrm{Id}}_{\mathbf{R}_1}$. But not only that, the mapping $\mathcal{M}''$ specified by the dependency $V(x) \rightarrow S(x)$ is also an inverse of $\mathcal{M}$, which shows that there need not be a unique inverse. $\qquad\square$

When is a mapping invertible?

The first basic question about any schema mapping operator is for which class of mappings it is defined. In particular, for the case of the inverse operator, one would like to know for which classes of mappings it is guaranteed to exist. We now present existence conditions for the inverse operator, and use them to show that inverses are not guaranteed to exist for all the mappings specified by st-tgds.

Let $\mathcal{M}$ be a mapping from a schema $\mathbf{R}_1$ to a schema $\mathbf{R}_2$. Then:

- $\mathcal{M}$ satisfies the *unique-solutions property* if for every pair of instances S_1, S_2 of $\mathbf{R}_1$, we have

$$\mathrm{SOL}_{\mathcal{M}}(S_1) = \mathrm{SOL}_{\mathcal{M}}(S_2) \implies S_1 = S_2.$$

- $\mathcal{M}$ is *closed-down on the left* if

$$(S_1, S_2) \in \mathcal{M} \text{ and } S_1' \subseteq S_1 \implies (S_1', S_2) \in \mathcal{M}.$$

- $\mathcal{M}$ is *total* if $\mathrm{SOL}_{\mathcal{M}}(S) \neq \emptyset$ for every instance S of $\mathbf{R}_1$.

We can use these properties to give a necessary condition for the existence of inverses.

Proposition 20.3 *Let $\mathcal{M}$ be a mapping that is total and closed-down on the left. If $\mathcal{M}$ is invertible, then $\mathcal{M}$ satisfies the unique-solutions property.*

Proof Assume that $\mathcal{M}$ is a mapping from a schema $\mathbf{R}_1$ to a schema $\mathbf{R}_2$, and let $\mathcal{M}'$ be a mapping from $\mathbf{R}_2$ to $\mathbf{R}_1$ such that $\mathcal{M} \circ \mathcal{M}' = \overline{\mathrm{Id}}_{\mathbf{R}_1}$ (such a mapping exists since $\mathcal{M}$ is invertible). Moreover, assume that S_1 and S_2 are instances of $\mathbf{R}_1$ such that $\mathrm{SOL}_{\mathcal{M}}(S_1) = \mathrm{SOL}_{\mathcal{M}}(S_2)$. We need to show that $S_1 = S_2$.

Given that $\mathrm{SOL}_{\mathcal{M}}(S_1) = \mathrm{SOL}_{\mathcal{M}}(S_2)$, we have that $\mathrm{SOL}_{\mathcal{M} \circ \mathcal{M}'}(S_1) = \mathrm{SOL}_{\mathcal{M} \circ \mathcal{M}'}(S_2)$. Thus, given that $\mathcal{M} \circ \mathcal{M}' = \overline{\mathrm{Id}}_{\mathbf{R}_1}$, we conclude that $\mathrm{SOL}_{\overline{\mathrm{Id}}_{\mathbf{R}_1}}(S_1) = \mathrm{SOL}_{\overline{\mathrm{Id}}_{\mathbf{R}_1}}(S_2)$. Therefore, from the fact that $S_1 \in \mathrm{SOL}_{\overline{\mathrm{Id}}_{\mathbf{R}_1}}(S_1)$ and $S_2 \in \mathrm{SOL}_{\overline{\mathrm{Id}}_{\mathbf{R}_1}}(S_2)$, we conclude that $S_1 \in \mathrm{SOL}_{\overline{\mathrm{Id}}_{\mathbf{R}_1}}(S_2)$ and $S_2 \in \mathrm{SOL}_{\overline{\mathrm{Id}}_{\mathbf{R}_1}}(S_1)$. But this implies that $(S_2, S_1) \in \overline{\mathrm{Id}}_{\mathbf{R}_1}$ and $(S_1, S_2) \in \overline{\mathrm{Id}}_{\mathbf{R}_1}$ and, hence, we conclude from the definition of $\overline{\mathrm{Id}}_{\mathbf{R}_1}$ that $S_2 \subseteq S_1$ and $S_1 \subseteq S_2$. This concludes the proof of the proposition. $\qquad\square$

Proposition 20.3 tells us that the spaces of solutions for distinct source instances under an invertible mapping must be distinct. Thus, one can prove that a mapping does not admit an inverse by showing that it does not satisfy the preceding condition.

Example 20.4   Let $\mathbf{R_1}$ be a schema consisting of a binary relation R, $\mathbf{R_2}$ a schema consisting of a unary relation T, and $\mathscr{M}$ a mapping from $\mathbf{R_1}$ to $\mathbf{R_2}$ specified by st-tgd $R(x,y) \rightarrow T(x)$. Intuitively, $\mathscr{M}$ has no inverse since $\mathscr{M}$ only transfers from source to target the information about the first component of R. In fact, it can be formally proved that this mapping is not invertible as follows. Let S_1 and S_2 be instances of $\mathbf{R_1}$ such that:

$$R^{S_1} = \{(1,2)\} \quad \text{and} \quad R^{S_2} = \{(1,3)\}.$$

Then we have that $\mathrm{SOL}_{\mathscr{M}}(S_1) = \mathrm{SOL}_{\mathscr{M}}(S_2)$, which implies that $\mathscr{M}$ does not satisfy the unique-solutions property since $S_1 \neq S_2$.   □

From the preceding example, we obtain that:

Corollary 20.5   *There exists a mapping $\mathscr{M}$ specified by a finite set of st-tgds that does not admit an inverse.*

Although the unique-solutions property is a useful tool for establishing noninvertibility, it can be shown that it does not characterize this notion. In fact, the following example shows that the unique-solutions property is not a sufficient condition for invertibility even for the class of mappings specified by st-tgds.

Example 20.6   Let $\mathbf{R_1}$ be a schema consisting of unary relations A and B, $\mathbf{R_2}$ a schema consisting of a binary relation R and a unary relation C, and $\mathscr{M}$ a mapping from $\mathbf{R_1}$ to $\mathbf{R_2}$ specified by st-tgds:

$$A(x) \rightarrow R(x,x),$$
$$B(x) \rightarrow \exists y R(x,y),$$
$$A(x) \wedge B(x) \rightarrow C(x).$$

Next we show that $\mathscr{M}$ satisfies the unique-solutions property but it is not invertible. Assume that S_1 and S_2 are distinct instances of $\mathbf{R_1}$. We show that $\mathrm{SOL}_{\mathscr{M}}(S_1) \neq \mathrm{SOL}_{\mathscr{M}}(S_2)$ by considering the following cases.

1. Assume that there exists $a \in A^{S_1}$ such that $a \notin A^{S_2}$, and let T_2 be the canonical universal solution for S_2 under $\mathscr{M}$. Then we have that $(a,a) \notin R^{T_2}$ and, therefore, T_2 is not a solution for S_1 under $\mathscr{M}$. We conclude that $\mathrm{SOL}_{\mathscr{M}}(S_1) \neq \mathrm{SOL}_{\mathscr{M}}(S_2)$.
2. Assume that there exists $a \in A^{S_2}$ such that $a \notin A^{S_1}$. Then it can be shown that $\mathrm{SOL}_{\mathscr{M}}(S_1) \neq \mathrm{SOL}_{\mathscr{M}}(S_2)$ as in the previous case.
3. Assume that $A^{S_1} = A^{S_2}$, and that there exists $b \in B^{S_1}$ such that $b \notin A^{S_1}$ and $b \notin B^{S_2}$. Then let T_2 be the canonical universal solution for S_2 under $\mathscr{M}$. Given that $b \notin A^{S_2}$, we have that R^{T_2} does not contain any tuple of the form $R(b,c)$ and, therefore, T_2 is not a solution for S_1 under $\mathscr{M}$. We conclude that $\mathrm{SOL}_{\mathscr{M}}(S_1) \neq \mathrm{SOL}_{\mathscr{M}}(S_2)$.
4. Assume that $A^{S_1} = A^{S_2}$, and that there exists $b \in B^{S_2}$ such that $b \notin A^{S_1}$ and $b \notin B^{S_1}$. Then we conclude that $\mathrm{SOL}_{\mathscr{M}}(S_1) \neq \mathrm{SOL}_{\mathscr{M}}(S_2)$ as in the previous case.
5. Assume that $A^{S_1} = A^{S_2}$, and that there exists $b \in B^{S_1}$ such that $b \in A^{S_1}$ and $b \notin B^{S_2}$. Then let T_2 be the canonical universal solution for S_2 under $\mathscr{M}$. Given that $b \notin B^{S_2}$, we

have that $b \notin C^{T_2}$ and, therefore, T_2 is not a solution for S_1 under $\mathcal{M}$. We conclude that $\text{SOL}_{\mathcal{M}}(S_1) \neq \text{SOL}_{\mathcal{M}}(S_2)$.

6. Finally, assume that $A^{S_1} = A^{S_2}$, and that there exists $b \in B^{S_2}$ such that $b \in A^{S_1}$ and $b \notin B^{S_1}$. Then we conclude that $\text{SOL}_{\mathcal{M}}(S_1) \neq \text{SOL}_{\mathcal{M}}(S_2)$ as in the previous case.

Now, for the sake of contradiction, assume that $\mathcal{M}$ is an invertible mapping, and let $\mathcal{M}'$ be a mapping from $\mathbf{R_2}$ to $\mathbf{R_1}$ such that $\mathcal{M} \circ \mathcal{M}' = \overline{\text{Id}}_{\mathbf{R_1}}$. Then for every pair S_1, S_2 of instances of $\mathbf{R_1}$ such that $\text{SOL}_{\mathcal{M}}(S_1) \subseteq \text{SOL}_{\mathcal{M}}(S_2)$, it holds that $S_2 \subseteq S_1$. To see why this is the case, first notice that if $\text{SOL}_{\mathcal{M}}(S_1) \subseteq \text{SOL}_{\mathcal{M}}(S_2)$, then $\text{SOL}_{\mathcal{M} \circ \mathcal{M}'}(S_1) \subseteq \text{SOL}_{\mathcal{M} \circ \mathcal{M}'}(S_2)$. Thus, given that $\mathcal{M} \circ \mathcal{M}' = \overline{\text{Id}}_{\mathbf{R_1}}$, we have that $\text{SOL}_{\overline{\text{Id}}_{\mathbf{R_1}}}(S_1) \subseteq \text{SOL}_{\overline{\text{Id}}_{\mathbf{R_1}}}(S_2)$. Hence, from the fact that $S_1 \in \text{SOL}_{\overline{\text{Id}}_{\mathbf{R_1}}}(S_1)$, we conclude that $S_1 \in \text{SOL}_{\overline{\text{Id}}_{\mathbf{R_1}}}(S_2)$ and, therefore, $S_2 \subseteq S_1$.

Next we use the property shown above to obtain a contradiction. Assume that S_1 and S_2 are instances of $\mathbf{R_1}$ such that:

$$A^{S_1} = \{1\} \qquad A^{S_2} = \emptyset$$
$$B^{S_1} = \emptyset \qquad B^{S_2} = \{1\}$$

Then we have that $\text{SOL}_{\mathcal{M}}(S_1) \subseteq \text{SOL}_{\mathcal{M}}(S_2)$, which contradicts the property shown above since $S_2 \not\subseteq S_1$. $\square$

In Example 20.6, we introduced a second condition that invertible mappings satisfy, and that is stronger that the unique-solutions property. Formally, a mapping $\mathcal{M}$ from a schema $\mathbf{R_1}$ to a schema $\mathbf{R_2}$ is said to satisfy the *subset property* if for every pair S_1, S_2 of instances of $\mathbf{R_1}$, we have

$$\text{SOL}_{\mathcal{M}}(S_1) \subseteq \text{SOL}_{\mathcal{M}}(S_2) \implies S_2 \subseteq S_1.$$

It turns out that this condition is a necessary and sufficient condition for the existence of inverses for the class of mappings specified by st-tgds.

Theorem 20.7 *Let $\mathcal{M}$ be a mapping specified by a finite set of st-tgds. Then $\mathcal{M}$ is invertible if and only if $\mathcal{M}$ satisfies the subset property.*

The previous result does not extend to the entire class of mappings that are total and closed-down on the left. In fact, a characterization of invertibility requires a stronger condition, which is defined as follows. Let $\mathcal{M}$ be a mapping from a schema $\mathbf{R_1}$ to a schema $\mathbf{R_2}$, S be an instance of $\mathbf{R_1}$ and T be an instance of $\mathbf{R_2}$. Then T is a *strong witness* for S under $\mathcal{M}$ if for every instance S' of $\mathbf{R_1}$ such that $T \in \text{SOL}_{\mathcal{M}}(S')$, it holds that $S' \subseteq S$. Moreover, T is a strong witness solution for S under $\mathcal{M}$ if T is both a solution and a strong witness for S under $\mathcal{M}$.

To give some intuition about the notion of strong witness, we show in the following proposition a way to construct strong witnesses for invertible mappings that are specified by st-tgds.

Proposition 20.8 *Let $\mathcal{M}$ be an invertible mapping from a schema $\mathbf{R_1}$ to a schema $\mathbf{R_2}$ that is specified by a set of st-tgds. Then for every instance S of $\mathbf{R_1}$, each universal solution T for S under $\mathcal{M}$ is a strong witness solution for S under $\mathcal{M}$.*

Proof Let S be an instance of $\mathbf{R_1}$ and T a universal solution for S under $\mathcal{M}$ (such a solution exists since $\mathcal{M}$ is specified by a set of st-tgds). Assume that S' is an instance of $\mathbf{R_1}$ such that $T \in \text{SOL}_{\mathcal{M}}(S')$. Next we show that $S' \subseteq S$.

Given that $T \in \text{SOL}_{\mathcal{M}}(S')$, we have that $\text{SOL}_{\mathcal{M}}(S) \subseteq \text{SOL}_{\mathcal{M}}(S')$. To see why this is the case, let T' be a solution for S under $\mathcal{M}$. Given that T is a universal solution for S under $\mathcal{M}$, we have that there exists a homomorphism from T into T'. Thus, given that $T \in \text{SOL}_{\mathcal{M}}(S')$ and $\mathcal{M}$ is closed under target homomorphisms (see Proposition 21.1 in Section 21.1), we conclude that $T' \in \text{SOL}_{\mathcal{M}}(S')$.

Since $\mathcal{M}$ is invertible, we know that $\mathcal{M}$ satisfies the subset property. Thus, given that $\text{SOL}_{\mathcal{M}}(S) \subseteq \text{SOL}_{\mathcal{M}}(S')$, we have that $S' \subseteq S$, which concludes the proof of the proposition. $\qquad\square$

In the following theorem, it is shown that the notion of strong witness can be used to characterize invertibility for the class of mappings that are total and closed-down on the left.

Theorem 20.9 *Let $\mathcal{M}$ be a mapping from a schema $\mathbf{R_1}$ to a schema $\mathbf{R_2}$, which is total and closed-down on the left. Then $\mathcal{M}$ is invertible if and only if every instance of $\mathbf{R_1}$ has a strong witness solution under $\mathcal{M}$.*

The complexity of invertibility

Given that inverses are not guaranteed to exist for the class of mappings specified by st-tgds, a second basic question about this notion of inverse is whether invertibility is a decidable condition for this class of mappings. If it is decidable, we would like to know its complexity.

The subset property we have seen earlier can be used to prove that this is indeed a decidable condition: if a mapping $\mathcal{M}$ specified by a set of st-tgds does not have an inverse, then there exists a polynomial-size counter-example showing that $\mathcal{M}$ does not satisfy the subset property. This leads to the following complexity result.

Theorem 20.10 *The problem of checking, given a mapping $\mathcal{M}$ specified by a set of st-tgds, whether $\mathcal{M}$ is invertible is CONP-complete.*

Proof We show here the membership of the problem in CONP, and leave CONP-hardness as an exercise for the reader (see Exercise 22.3). Given a mapping $\mathcal{M} = (\mathbf{R_1}, \mathbf{R_2}, \Sigma_{12})$ that is not invertible, a pair (S_1, S_2) of instances of $\mathbf{R_1}$ is said to be a witness for the noninvertibility of $\mathcal{M}$ if $\text{SOL}_{\mathcal{M}}(S_1) \subseteq \text{SOL}_{\mathcal{M}}(S_2)$ but $S_2 \not\subseteq S_1$ (notice that such a pair shows that $\mathcal{M}$ does not satisfy the subset property). Then it is shown here that for every mapping $\mathcal{M}$ specified by a set of st-tgds, if $\mathcal{M}$ is not invertible, then there exists a witness (S_1, S_2) for the noninvertibility of $\mathcal{M}$ such that $\|S_1\| + \|S_2\|$ is $O(\|\Sigma_{12}\|^2)$, from which the membership of the problem in CONP immediately follows.

Let $\mathcal{M} = (\mathbf{R_1}, \mathbf{R_2}, \Sigma_{12})$, where Σ_{12} is a set of st-tgds, and assume that $\mathcal{M}$ is not invertible. Then we have by Theorem 20.7 that there exist instances S_1, S_2 of $\mathbf{R_1}$ such that $\text{SOL}_{\mathcal{M}}(S_1) \subseteq \text{SOL}_{\mathcal{M}}(S_2)$ but $S_2 \not\subseteq S_1$. Thus, there exist P in $\mathbf{R_1}$ and $t_0 \in P^{S_2}$ such that

$t_0 \notin P^{S_1}$. Let $S_2^\star$ be an instance of $\mathbf{R_1}$ consisting only of the fact $P(t_0)$, that is, $P^{S_2^\star} = \{t_0\}$ and $R^{S_2^\star} = \emptyset$ for all the other relations R in $\mathbf{R_1}$. Since Σ_{12} is a set of st-tgds, we have that:

$$\text{SOL}_{\mathcal{M}}(S_2) \subseteq \text{SOL}_{\mathcal{M}}(S_2^\star).$$

Hence, $\text{SOL}_{\mathcal{M}}(S_1) \subseteq \text{SOL}_{\mathcal{M}}(S_2^\star)$ and $S_2^\star \nsubseteq S_1$, which shows that $(S_1, S_2^\star)$ is also a witness for the noninvertibility of mapping $\mathcal{M}$. Now let T_1, $T_2^\star$ be the canonical universal solutions for S_1 and $S_2^\star$ under $\mathcal{M}$, respectively. Given that $T_1 \in \text{SOL}_{\mathcal{M}}(S_1)$, we have that $T_1 \in \text{SOL}_{\mathcal{M}}(S_2^\star)$ and, therefore, there exists a homomorphism h from $T_2^\star$ to T_1. We use h to construct the desired quadratic-size witness for the noninvertibility of mapping $\mathcal{M}$. More precisely, let $S_1^\star$ be an instance of $\mathbf{R_1}$ defined as follows. For every R in $\mathbf{R_2}$ and tuple $t \in R^{T_2^\star}$, choose a st-tgd $\varphi(\bar{x}) \to \exists \bar{y} \, \psi(\bar{x}, \bar{y})$ and tuples $\bar{a}$, $\bar{b}$ such that (1) $\varphi(\bar{x}) \to \exists \bar{y} \, \psi(\bar{x}, \bar{y})$ is a st-tgd in Σ_{12}, $\bar{a}$ is a tuple of values from $\text{DOM}(S_1)$ and $\bar{b}$ is a tuple of values from $\text{DOM}(T_1)$, (2) $\varphi(\bar{a})$ holds in S_1, (3) $\psi(\bar{a}, \bar{b})$ holds in T_1, and (4) $R(h(t))$ is a conjunct in $\psi(\bar{a}, \bar{b})$. It should be noticed that such a tuple exists since (S_1, T_1) satisfies Σ_{12} and $R(h(t))$ is a fact in T_1 (given that h is a homomorphism from $T_2^\star$ to T_1). Then include all the conjuncts of $\varphi(\bar{a})$ as facts of $S_1^\star$. Next we show that $(S_1^\star, S_2^\star)$ is a witness for the noninvertibility of $\mathcal{M}$ and $\|S_1^\star\| + \|S_2^\star\|$ is $O(\|\Sigma_{12}\|^2)$.

Let $T_1^\star$ be the canonical universal solution for $S_1^\star$ under $\mathcal{M}$. By definition of $S_1^\star$, we have that the homomorphism h mentioned above is also a homomorphism from $T_2^\star$ to $T_1^\star$. Thus, given that $T_1^\star$ is a universal solution for $S_1^\star$ under $\mathcal{M}$ and $\mathcal{M}$ is closed under target homomorphisms (see Proposition 21.1 in Section 21.1), we conclude that $\text{SOL}_{\mathcal{M}}(S_1^\star) \subseteq \text{SOL}_{\mathcal{M}}(S_2^\star)$. Moreover, given that $S_1^\star \subseteq S_1$, we also have that $S_2^\star \nsubseteq S_1^\star$ and, hence, $(S_1^\star, S_2^\star)$ is a witness for the noninvertibility of $\mathcal{M}$. Finally, given that $S_2^\star$ consists of only one fact, we have that $\|T_2^\star\|$ is bounded by $\|\Sigma_{12}\|$. Therefore, given that the number of tuples that are included in $S_1^\star$ for each fact $R(t)$ in $T_2^\star$ is bounded by $\|\Sigma_{12}\|$, we have that $\|S_1^\star\|$ is bounded by $\|\Sigma_{12}\|^2$. Thus, it holds that $\|S_1^\star\| + \|S_2^\star\|$ is $O(\|\Sigma_{12}\|^2)$, which concludes the proof of the theorem. $\qquad \square$

A problem related to checking invertibility is to check, for mappings $\mathcal{M}$ and $\mathcal{M}'$, whether $\mathcal{M}'$ is an inverse of $\mathcal{M}$. Somewhat surprisingly, this problem is undecidable even for the class of mappings specified by st-tgds.

Theorem 20.11 *The problem of verifying, given mappings $\mathcal{M} = (\mathbf{R_1}, \mathbf{R_2}, \Sigma_{12})$ and $\mathcal{M}' = (\mathbf{R_2}, \mathbf{R_1}, \Sigma_{21})$ with Σ_{12} and Σ_{21} finite sets of st-tgds, whether $\mathcal{M}'$ is an inverse of $\mathcal{M}$ is undecidable.*

A fundamental, and arguably the most important, issue about any notion of inverse is the problem of computing an inverse for a given mapping. We shall handle this problem in Section 20.3.

A relaxation of inverses: quasi-inverse

The notion of inverse is rather restrictive as there are many mappings that do not possess an inverse. Thus, there is a need for weaker notions of inversion. We now briefly outline one, known as quasi-inverses of schema mappings.

The idea behind quasi-inverses is to relax the notion of inverse by not differentiating between source instances that are equivalent for data-exchange purposes. More precisely, let $\mathcal{M}$ be a mapping from a schema $\mathbf{R}_1$ to a schema $\mathbf{R}_2$. Instances S_1 and S_2 of $\mathbf{R}_1$ are *data-exchange equivalent* with respect to $\mathcal{M}$, denoted by $S_1 \sim_{\mathcal{M}} S_2$, if $\text{SOL}_{\mathcal{M}}(S_1) = \text{SOL}_{\mathcal{M}}(S_2)$. For instance, for the mapping $\mathcal{M}$ specified by st-tgd $R(x,y) \rightarrow T(x)$, we have that if S_1 is an instance consisting of the fact $R(1,2)$ and S_2 is an instance consisting of the fact $R(1,3)$, then $S_1 \sim_{\mathcal{M}} S_2$.

The quasi-inverse of a mapping $\mathcal{M}$ is then obtained by not differentiating between source instances S_1 and S_2 such that $S_1 \sim_{\mathcal{M}} S_2$. Formally, given a schema $\mathbf{R}$ and a mapping $\mathcal{N}$ from $\mathbf{R}$ to $\mathbf{R}$, the mapping $\mathcal{N}[\sim_{\mathcal{M}}, \sim_{\mathcal{M}}]$ is defined as:

$$\{(S_1, S_2) \in \text{INST}(\mathbf{R}) \times \text{INST}(\mathbf{R}) \mid \text{there exist } S_1', S_2' \in \text{INST}(\mathbf{R}) \text{ such that}$$
$$S_1 \sim_{\mathcal{M}} S_1', \ S_2 \sim_{\mathcal{M}} S_2' \text{ and } (S_1', S_2') \in \mathcal{N}\},$$

and then the notion of quasi-inverse is defined as:

Definition 20.12 (Quasi-inverse)   Let $\mathcal{M}$ be a mapping from a schema $\mathbf{R}_1$ to a schema $\mathbf{R}_2$, and $\mathcal{M}'$ a mapping from $\mathbf{R}_2$ to $\mathbf{R}_1$. Then $\mathcal{M}'$ is a quasi-inverse of $\mathcal{M}$ if $(\mathcal{M} \circ \mathcal{M}')[\sim_{\mathcal{M}}, \sim_{\mathcal{M}}] = \overline{\text{Id}}_{\mathbf{R}_1}[\sim_{\mathcal{M}}, \sim_{\mathcal{M}}]$.   □

Example 20.13   Let $\mathbf{R}_1$ be a schema consisting of a binary relation R, $\mathbf{R}_2$ a schema consisting of a unary relation T, and $\mathcal{M}$ a mapping specified by st-tgd $R(x,y) \rightarrow T(x)$. It was shown in Example 20.4 that $\mathcal{M}$ does not have an inverse, as it does not satisfy the unique-solutions property. However, mapping $\mathcal{M}'$ specified by tgd $T(x) \rightarrow \exists z R(x,z)$ is a quasi-inverse of $\mathcal{M}$. To see why this is the case, consider first the inclusion:

$$\overline{\text{Id}}_{\mathbf{R}_1}[\sim_{\mathcal{M}}, \sim_{\mathcal{M}}] \subseteq (\mathcal{M} \circ \mathcal{M}')[\sim_{\mathcal{M}}, \sim_{\mathcal{M}}]. \tag{20.1}$$

If $(S_1, S_2) \in \overline{\text{Id}}_{\mathbf{R}_1}[\sim_{\mathcal{M}}, \sim_{\mathcal{M}}]$, then there exist instances S_1', S_2' of $\mathbf{R}_1$ such that $S_1 \sim_{\mathcal{M}} S_1'$, $S_2 \sim_{\mathcal{M}} S_2'$ and $(S_1', S_2') \in \overline{\text{Id}}_{\mathbf{R}_1}$. Thus, we have that $S_1' \subseteq S_2'$. Let T_1' be the canonical universal solution for S_1' under $\mathcal{M}$. Then we have that $(S_1', T_1') \in \mathcal{M}$, and also that $(T_1', S_2') \in \mathcal{M}'$ by the definitions of $\mathcal{M}$ and $\mathcal{M}'$, and given that $S_1' \subseteq S_2'$. Hence, we conclude that $(S_1', S_2') \in (\mathcal{M} \circ \mathcal{M}')$, which implies that $(S_1, S_2) \in (\mathcal{M} \circ \mathcal{M}')[\sim_{\mathcal{M}}, \sim_{\mathcal{M}}]$ since $S_1 \sim_{\mathcal{M}} S_1'$ and $S_2 \sim_{\mathcal{M}} S_2'$. Thus, we have shown that inclusion (20.1) holds, and it only remains to prove that the following inclusion holds to show that $\mathcal{M}'$ is a quasi-inverse of $\mathcal{M}$:

$$(\mathcal{M} \circ \mathcal{M}')[\sim_{\mathcal{M}}, \sim_{\mathcal{M}}] \subseteq \overline{\text{Id}}_{\mathbf{R}_1}[\sim_{\mathcal{M}}, \sim_{\mathcal{M}}]. \tag{20.2}$$

If $(S_1, S_2) \in (\mathcal{M} \circ \mathcal{M}')[\sim_{\mathcal{M}}, \sim_{\mathcal{M}}]$, then there exist instances S_1', S_2' of $\mathbf{R}_1$ such that $S_1 \sim_{\mathcal{M}} S_1'$, $S_2 \sim_{\mathcal{M}} S_2'$ and $(S_1', S_2') \in (\mathcal{M} \circ \mathcal{M}')$. Thus, we have that there exists an instance T of $\mathbf{R}_2$ such that $(S_1', T) \in \mathcal{M}$ and $(T, S_2') \in \mathcal{M}'$, from which we conclude that:

$$\{a \mid (a,b) \in R^{S_1'}\} \subseteq \{a \mid (a,b) \in R^{S_2'}\}. \tag{20.3}$$

Let $S_2^{\star}$ be an instance of $\mathbf{R}_1$ defined as:

$$R^{S_2^{\star}} = \{a \mid (a,b) \in R^{S_2'}\} \times \{d \mid (c,d) \in R^{S_1'}\}.$$

By definition of the mapping $\mathcal{M}$, we have that $S_2' \sim_{\mathcal{M}} S_2^{\star}$, from which we conclude that $S_2 \sim_{\mathcal{M}} S_2^{\star}$. Furthermore, from the definition of instance $S_2^{\star}$ and inclusion (20.3), we have that $S_1' \subseteq S_2^{\star}$. Hence, we conclude that $(S_1', S_2^{\star}) \in \overline{\mathrm{Id}}_{\mathbf{R}_1}$, which implies that $(S_1, S_2) \in \overline{\mathrm{Id}}_{\mathbf{R}_1}[\sim_{\mathcal{M}}, \sim_{\mathcal{M}}]$ since $S_1 \sim_{\mathcal{M}} S_1'$ and $S_2 \sim_{\mathcal{M}} S_2^{\star}$. Thus, we have shown that inclusion (20.2) holds, which proves that $\mathcal{M}'$ is a quasi-inverse of $\mathcal{M}$. $\square$

We have seen that quasi-inverses may exist when inverses do not exist. But is it the case that the notion of quasi-inverse strictly generalizes the notion of inverse? If we focus on the class of mapping for which the notion of inverse is appropriate (see Section 20.1), then the answer is positive.

Proposition 20.14 • *There exists a mapping specified by a finite set of st-tgds that is not invertible but has a quasi-inverse.*
• *For every mapping $\mathcal{M}$ that is total, closed-down on the left and invertible, a mapping $\mathcal{M}'$ is an inverse of $\mathcal{M}$ if and only if $\mathcal{M}'$ is a quasi-inverse of $\mathcal{M}$.*

When do quasi-inverses exist? We previously used the subset property to characterize invertibility (see Theorem 20.7). It turns out that a relaxation of this property obtained by not differentiating between source instances that are equivalent for data-exchange purposes characterizes quasi-invertibility. Formally, a mapping $\mathcal{M}$ from a schema $\mathbf{R}_1$ to a schema $\mathbf{R}_2$ is said to satisfy the $(\sim_{\mathcal{M}}, \sim_{\mathcal{M}})$-*subset property* if for every pair S_1, S_2 of instances of $\mathbf{R}_1$, if $\mathrm{SOL}_{\mathcal{M}}(S_1) \subseteq \mathrm{SOL}_{\mathcal{M}}(S_2)$, then there exist instances S_1', S_2' of $\mathbf{R}_1$ such that $S_1 \sim_{\mathcal{M}} S_1'$, $S_2 \sim_{\mathcal{M}} S_2'$ and $S_2' \subseteq S_1'$.

Theorem 20.15 *Let $\mathcal{M}$ be a mapping specified by a finite set of st-tgds. Then $\mathcal{M}$ is quasi-invertible if and only if $\mathcal{M}$ satisfies the $(\sim_{\mathcal{M}}, \sim_{\mathcal{M}})$-subset property.*

Still, not every mapping specified by st-tgds has a quasi-inverse. In fact, a rather strong negative statement is true.

Proposition 20.16 *There exists a mapping $\mathcal{M}$ specified by a single st-tgd that has no quasi-inverse.*

The mapping is quite simple. The source schema $\mathbf{R}_1$ consists of a binary relation E, the target schema $\mathbf{R}_2$ consists of a binary relation F and a unary relation G, and there is a single st-tgd

$$E(x,z) \wedge E(z,y) \to F(x,y) \wedge G(z). \tag{20.4}$$

One can then show that $\mathcal{M}$ does not satisfy the $(\sim_{\mathcal{M}}, \sim_{\mathcal{M}})$-subset property, and thus is not quasi-invertible.

As for the case of inverses, the problem of checking, given mappings $\mathcal{M}$ and $\mathcal{M}'$, whether $\mathcal{M}'$ is a quasi-inverse of $\mathcal{M}$ is undecidable. In fact, it is undecidable even for the most common mappings.

Theorem 20.17 *The problem of verifying, given mappings $\mathcal{M} = (\mathbf{R}_1, \mathbf{R}_2, \Sigma_{12})$ and $\mathcal{M}' =$*

($\mathbf{R_2}, \mathbf{R_1}, \Sigma_{21}$) *with* Σ_{12} *and* Σ_{21} *finite sets of st-tgds, whether* $\mathcal{M}'$ *is a quasi-inverse of* $\mathcal{M}$ *is undecidable.*

20.2 Bringing exchanged data back: the recovery of a schema mapping

As we mentioned before, a drawback of the notions of inverse and quasi-inverse is that not every mapping specified by a set of st-tgds is guaranteed to have an inverse under these notions. In this section, we present the concepts of recovery and maximum recovery, that were introduced to overcome this limitation.

The notion of recovery is defined by following a different approach to that of inverses and quasi-inverses. In fact, the main goal behind this notion is not to define an inverse operator, but instead to give a formal definition for what it means for a mapping $\mathcal{M}'$ to recover *sound information* with respect to a mapping $\mathcal{M}$. Such a mapping $\mathcal{M}'$ is called a recovery of $\mathcal{M}$. But given that, in general, there may exist many possible recoveries for a given mapping, it is also necessary to introduce a way to compare alternative recoveries. This naturally gives rise to the notion of maximum recovery, which is a mapping that brings back the maximum amount of sound information.

Let $\mathcal{M}$ be a mapping from a schema $\mathbf{R_1}$ to a schema $\mathbf{R_2}$, and $\mathrm{Id}_{\mathbf{R_1}}$ the identity schema mapping over $\mathbf{R_1}$, that is, $\mathrm{Id}_{\mathbf{R_1}} = \{(S,S) \mid S \in \mathrm{INST}(\mathbf{R_1})\}$. When trying to invert $\mathcal{M}$, the ideal would be to find a mapping $\mathcal{M}'$ from $\mathbf{R_2}$ to $\mathbf{R_1}$ such that $\mathcal{M} \circ \mathcal{M}' = \mathrm{Id}_{\mathbf{R_1}}$; if such a mapping exists, then we know that if we use $\mathcal{M}$ to exchange data, the application of $\mathcal{M}'$ gives as a result exactly the initial source instance. Unfortunately, in most cases this ideal is impossible to reach (for example, for the case of mappings specified by st-tgds). But then at least one would like to find a schema mapping $\mathcal{M}_2$ that does not forbid the possibility of recovering the initial source data. This gives rise to the notion of recovery.

Definition 20.18 (Recovery)   Let $\mathcal{M}$ be a mapping from a schema $\mathbf{R_1}$ to a schema $\mathbf{R_2}$, and $\mathcal{M}'$ a mapping from $\mathbf{R_2}$ to $\mathbf{R_1}$. Then $\mathcal{M}'$ is a *recovery* of $\mathcal{M}$ if for every instance $S \in \mathrm{DOM}(\mathcal{M})$, it holds that $(S,S) \in \mathcal{M} \circ \mathcal{M}'$.   □

Being a recovery is a sound but mild requirement. Indeed, a schema mapping $\mathcal{M}$ from a schema $\mathbf{R_1}$ to a schema $\mathbf{R_2}$ always has as recoveries, for example, mappings $\mathcal{M}_1 = \mathrm{INST}(\mathbf{R_2}) \times \mathrm{INST}(\mathbf{R_1})$ and $\mathcal{M}_2 = \mathcal{M}^{-1} = \{(T,S) \mid (S,T) \in \mathcal{M}\}$. If one has to choose between $\mathcal{M}_1$ and $\mathcal{M}_2$ as a recovery of $\mathcal{M}$, then one would probably choose $\mathcal{M}_2$ since the space of possible solutions for an instance S under $\mathcal{M} \circ \mathcal{M}_2$ is smaller than under $\mathcal{M} \circ \mathcal{M}_1$. In general, if $\mathcal{M}'$ is a recovery of $\mathcal{M}$, then the smaller the space of solutions generated by $\mathcal{M} \circ \mathcal{M}'$, the more informative $\mathcal{M}'$ is about the initial source instances. This naturally gives rise to the notion of maximum recovery.

Definition 20.19 (Maximum recovery)   Let $\mathcal{M}$ be a mapping from a schema $\mathbf{R_1}$ to a schema $\mathbf{R_2}$, and $\mathcal{M}'$ a mapping from $\mathbf{R_2}$ to $\mathbf{R_1}$. Then $\mathcal{M}'$ is a *maximum recovery* of $\mathcal{M}$ if:

1. $\mathcal{M}'$ is a recovery of $\mathcal{M}$, and
2. for every recovery $\mathcal{M}''$ of $\mathcal{M}$, it holds that $\mathcal{M} \circ \mathcal{M}' \subseteq \mathcal{M} \circ \mathcal{M}''$.   □

Example 20.20   Let $\mathbf{R_1}$ be a schema consisting of a binary relation E, $\mathbf{R_2}$ a schema consisting of a binary relation F and a unary relation G, and $\mathcal{M} = (\mathbf{R_1}, \mathbf{R_2}, \Sigma)$ with Σ a set of st-tgds consisting of the following dependency:

$$E(x,z) \wedge E(z,y) \rightarrow F(x,y) \wedge G(z). \tag{20.5}$$

Let $\mathcal{M}_1$ be a mapping from $\mathbf{R_2}$ to $\mathbf{R_1}$ specified by tgd:

$$F(x,y) \rightarrow \exists z\, (E(x,z) \wedge E(z,y)). \tag{20.6}$$

It is straightforward to prove that $\mathcal{M}_1$ is a recovery of $\mathcal{M}$. In fact, if S is an instance of $\mathbf{R_1}$ and T is the canonical universal solution for S under $\mathcal{M}$, then we have that $(S,T) \in \mathcal{M}$ and $(T,S) \in \mathcal{M}_1$, from which we conclude that $(S,S) \in \mathcal{M} \circ \mathcal{M}_1$. Similarly, if $\mathcal{M}_2$ is a mapping from $\mathbf{R_2}$ to $\mathbf{R_1}$ specified by tgd:

$$G(z) \rightarrow \exists x \exists y\, (E(x,z) \wedge E(z,y)), \tag{20.7}$$

then we also have that $\mathcal{M}_2$ is a recovery of $\mathcal{M}$. On the other hand, if $\mathcal{M}_3$ is a mapping from $\mathbf{R_2}$ to $\mathbf{R_1}$ specified by tgd:

$$F(x,y) \wedge G(z) \rightarrow E(x,z) \wedge E(z,y), \tag{20.8}$$

then we have that $\mathcal{M}_3$ is not a recovery of $\mathcal{M}$. To see why this is the case, consider an instance S of $\mathbf{R_1}$ such that:

$$E^S = \{(1,1),(2,2)\}.$$

Next we show that $(S,S) \notin \mathcal{M} \circ \mathcal{M}_3$. By the sake of contradiction, assume that $(S,S) \in \mathcal{M} \circ \mathcal{M}_3$, and let T be an instance of $\mathbf{R_2}$ such that $(S,T) \in \mathcal{M}$ and $(T,S) \in \mathcal{M}_3$. Given that (S,T) satisfies st-tgd (20.5), we have that $(1,1)$, $(2,2)$ are elements of F^T and $1, 2$ are elements of G^T. But then given that (T,S) satisfies tgd (20.8), we conclude that the tuples $(1,2)$, $(2,1)$ are elements of E^S, which leads to a contradiction.

   Finally, let $\mathcal{M}_4$ be a mapping from $\mathbf{R_2}$ to $\mathbf{R_1}$ specified by tgds (20.6) and (20.7). In this case, it is possible to prove that $\mathcal{M}_4$ is a maximum recovery of $\mathcal{M}$. In fact, next we introduce some characterizations of the notion of maximum recovery that can be used to prove this fact.   □

To check whether a mapping $\mathcal{M}'$ is an inverse of a mapping $\mathcal{M}$, a condition that depends only on $\mathcal{M}$ and $\mathcal{M}'$ needs to be checked, namely that the composition of $\mathcal{M}$ with $\mathcal{M}'$ is equal to the identity mapping. A similar situation holds for the case of the notion of quasi-inverse. On the other hand, verifying whether a mapping $\mathcal{M}'$ is a maximum recovery of a mapping $\mathcal{M}$ requires comparing $\mathcal{M}'$ with every other recovery of $\mathcal{M}$. Given that such a test is more complicated, it would be desirable to have an alternative condition for this notion that depends only on the input mappings. The next proposition gives one such condition.

Proposition 20.21   *Let $\mathcal{M}$ be a mapping from a schema $\mathbf{R_1}$ to a schema $\mathbf{R_2}$, and $\mathcal{M}'$ a recovery of $\mathcal{M}$. Then $\mathcal{M}'$ is a maximum recovery of $\mathcal{M}$ if and only if:*

(1) for every $(S_1, S_2) \in \mathcal{M} \circ \mathcal{M}'$, it holds that $S_2 \in \text{DOM}(\mathcal{M})$, and

(2) $\mathcal{M} = \mathcal{M} \circ \mathcal{M}' \circ \mathcal{M}$.

Proof ($\Rightarrow$) Assume that $\mathcal{M}'$ is a maximum recovery of $\mathcal{M}$. We first prove that condition (1) holds. For the sake of contradiction, assume that there exists $(S_1, S_2) \in \mathcal{M} \circ \mathcal{M}'$ such that $S_2 \notin \text{DOM}(\mathcal{M})$. Then define the mapping $\mathcal{M}'' \subseteq \mathcal{M}'$ as $\mathcal{M}'' = \{(T, S) \in \mathcal{M}' \mid S \in \text{DOM}(\mathcal{M})\}$. Given that $\mathcal{M}'$ is a recovery of $\mathcal{M}$, we have that $\mathcal{M}''$ is a recovery of $\mathcal{M}$. Moreover, $\mathcal{M} \circ \mathcal{M}'' \subsetneq \mathcal{M} \circ \mathcal{M}'$ since $\mathcal{M}'' \subseteq \mathcal{M}'$ and $(S_1, S_2) \notin \mathcal{M} \circ \mathcal{M}''$. Thus, we obtain a contradiction since $\mathcal{M}'$ is assumed to be a maximum recovery of $\mathcal{M}$.

We continue by showing that condition (2) holds. Given that $\mathcal{M}'$ is a recovery of $\mathcal{M}$, we have that $(S, S) \in \mathcal{M} \circ \mathcal{M}'$ for every $S \in \text{DOM}(\mathcal{M})$, which implies that $\mathcal{M} \subseteq \mathcal{M} \circ \mathcal{M}' \circ \mathcal{M}$. Thus, we only need to show that $\mathcal{M} \circ \mathcal{M}' \circ \mathcal{M} \subseteq \mathcal{M}$. By the sake of contradiction, assume that there exists $(S_1, T_1) \in \mathcal{M} \circ \mathcal{M}' \circ \mathcal{M}$ such that $(S_1, T_1) \notin \mathcal{M}$. Then, there exist instances S_2 and T_2 such that $(S_1, T_2) \in \mathcal{M}$, $(T_2, S_2) \in \mathcal{M}'$, and $(S_2, T_1) \in \mathcal{M}$. Note that $T_1 \neq T_2$ and $S_1 \neq S_2$, because we are assuming that $(S_1, T_1) \notin \mathcal{M}$. Let $\mathcal{M}^\star$ be a mapping from $\mathbf{R_2}$ to $\mathbf{R_1}$ defined as:

$$\mathcal{M}^\star = \{(T, S) \in \mathcal{M}' \mid S \neq S_2\} \cup \{(T_1, S_2)\}.$$

Given that $\mathcal{M}'$ is a recovery of $\mathcal{M}$ and $(S_2, T_1) \in \mathcal{M}$, we have that $\mathcal{M}^\star$ is a recovery of $\mathcal{M}$. Now, consider the pair (S_1, S_2). We know that $(S_1, S_2) \in \mathcal{M} \circ \mathcal{M}'$, but given that $(S_1, T_1) \notin \mathcal{M}$ and (T_1, S_2) is the only tuple in $\mathcal{M}^\star$ where S_2 appears as the second component, we have that $(S_1, S_2) \notin \mathcal{M} \circ \mathcal{M}^\star$. Thus, we conclude that $\mathcal{M} \circ \mathcal{M}' \not\subseteq \mathcal{M} \circ \mathcal{M}^\star$. Hence, we obtain a contradiction since $\mathcal{M}'$ is assumed to be a maximum recovery of $\mathcal{M}$.

($\Leftarrow$) We first notice that if $(S_1, S_2) \in \mathcal{M} \circ \mathcal{M}'$, then we have that $\text{SOL}_{\mathcal{M}}(S_2) \subseteq \text{SOL}_{\mathcal{M}}(S_1)$. To see why this is the case, let $T \in \text{SOL}_{\mathcal{M}}(S_2)$. Then given that $(S_1, S_2) \in \mathcal{M} \circ \mathcal{M}'$, we have that $(S_1, T) \in \mathcal{M} \circ \mathcal{M}' \circ \mathcal{M}$. Thus, given that $\mathcal{M} = \mathcal{M} \circ \mathcal{M}' \circ \mathcal{M}$, we have that $(S_1, T) \in \mathcal{M}$ and, hence, $T \in \text{SOL}_{\mathcal{M}}(S_1)$. Next we use this property to prove that if $\mathcal{M}'$ satisfies (1) and (2), then $\mathcal{M}'$ is a maximum recovery of $\mathcal{M}$.

For the sake of contradiction, assume that $\mathcal{M}'$ is not a maximum recovery of $\mathcal{M}$. Then given that $\mathcal{M}'$ is a recovery of $\mathcal{M}$, there exists a recovery $\mathcal{M}''$ of $\mathcal{M}$ such that $\mathcal{M} \circ \mathcal{M}' \not\subseteq \mathcal{M} \circ \mathcal{M}''$. We have then that there is a tuple $(S, S') \in \mathcal{M} \circ \mathcal{M}'$ such that $(S, S') \notin \mathcal{M} \circ \mathcal{M}''$. Given that $\mathcal{M}'$ satisfies condition (1), we have that S' is an instance in $\text{DOM}(\mathcal{M})$. Hence, given that $\mathcal{M}''$ is a recovery of $\mathcal{M}$, we have that (S', S') is a tuple in $\mathcal{M} \circ \mathcal{M}''$ and, therefore, there exists an instance T of $\mathbf{R_2}$ such that $(S', T) \in \mathcal{M}$ and $(T, S') \in \mathcal{M}''$. By the observation in the previous paragraph, we know that $\text{SOL}_{\mathcal{M}}(S') \subseteq \text{SOL}_{\mathcal{M}}(S)$, so if $(S', T) \in \mathcal{M}$ then $(S, T) \in \mathcal{M}$. Therefore, we conclude that $(S, T) \in \mathcal{M}$ and $(T, S') \in \mathcal{M}''$, which implies that $(S, S') \in \mathcal{M} \circ \mathcal{M}''$ and leads to a contradiction. This concludes the proof of the proposition. $\square$

Next we use Proposition 20.21 to prove that the claims in Example 20.20 are indeed correct. But before doing this, we give some intuition about the conditions in Proposition 20.21. The first such condition tells us that if an instance S is not in the domain of a mapping $\mathcal{M}$, then a maximum recovery of $\mathcal{M}$ should not recover information about this instance. The second condition in Proposition 20.21 is a desirable property for an inverse mapping. Intuitively, given a mapping $\mathcal{M}$ from a schema $\mathbf{R_1}$ to a schema $\mathbf{R_2}$ and a mapping $\mathcal{M}'$ from $\mathbf{R_2}$ to $\mathbf{R_1}$, mapping $\mathcal{M}'$ does not lose information when bringing back the data exchanged by $\mathcal{M}$, if the space of solutions of every instance of $\mathbf{R_1}$ does not change after computing $\mathcal{M} \circ \mathcal{M}'$. That is, for every instance S of $\mathbf{R_1}$, it should hold that $\text{SOL}_{\mathcal{M}}(S) = \text{SOL}_{\mathcal{M} \circ \mathcal{M}' \circ \mathcal{M}}(S)$ (or more succinctly, $\mathcal{M} = \mathcal{M} \circ \mathcal{M}' \circ \mathcal{M}$). In general, recoveries do not satisfy this condition, but Proposition 20.21 shows that maximum recoveries satisfy it. And not only that, it also shows that the notion of maximum recovery can be characterized in terms of this condition.

Example 20.22 (Example 20.20 continued) Recall that the mapping $\mathcal{M}$ in Example 20.20 is specified by the following st-tgd:

$$E(x,z) \wedge E(z,y) \rightarrow F(x,y) \wedge G(z),$$

while recovery $\mathcal{M}_4$ of $\mathcal{M}$ is specified by the following tgds:

$$F(x,y) \rightarrow \exists z\,(E(x,z) \wedge E(z,y)),$$
$$G(z) \rightarrow \exists x \exists y\,(E(x,z) \wedge E(z,y)).$$

Next we use Proposition 20.21 to show that $\mathcal{M}_4$ is a maximum recovery of $\mathcal{M}$. Given that $\mathcal{M}_4$ is a recovery of $\mathcal{M}$, we have that $\mathcal{M} \subseteq \mathcal{M} \circ \mathcal{M}_4 \circ \mathcal{M}$. Thus, given that $\text{DOM}(\mathcal{M}) = \mathbf{R_1}$, we conclude from Proposition 20.21 that to prove that $\mathcal{M}_4$ is a maximum recovery of $\mathcal{M}$, we only need to show that $\mathcal{M} \circ \mathcal{M}_4 \circ \mathcal{M} \subseteq \mathcal{M}$.

Let $(S,T) \in \mathcal{M} \circ \mathcal{M}_4 \circ \mathcal{M}$. To prove that $(S,T) \in \mathcal{M}$, we need to show that (S,T) satisfies the st-tgd that specifies $\mathcal{M}$, that is, we have to prove that for every pair of tuples (a,b), (b,c) in E^S, where a, b, c are not necessarily distinct elements, it holds that $(a,c) \in F^T$ and $b \in G^T$. To prove this, first notice that given that $(S,T) \in \mathcal{M} \circ \mathcal{M}_4 \circ \mathcal{M}$, there exist instances S_1 of $\mathbf{R_1}$ and T_1 of $\mathbf{R_2}$ such that $(S,T_1) \in \mathcal{M}$, $(T_1,S_1) \in \mathcal{M}_4$ and $(S_1,T) \in \mathcal{M}$. Thus, given that (a,b), (b,c) are elements of E^S, we conclude that $(a,c) \in F^{T_1}$ and $b \in G^{T_1}$. Hence, from the definition of $\mathcal{M}_4$ and the fact that $(T_1,S_1) \in \mathcal{M}_4$, we conclude that there exist elements d, e and f such that:

$$\{(a,d),(d,c),(e,b),(b,f)\} \subseteq E^{S_1}.$$

Therefore, given that $(S_1,T) \in \mathcal{M}$, we conclude that $(a,c) \in F^T$ and $b \in G^T$, which was to be shown.

On the other hand, it is claimed in Example 20.20 that the mapping $\mathcal{M}_1$ specified by the dependency $F(x,y) \rightarrow \exists z\,(E(x,z) \wedge E(z,y))$ is not a maximum recovery of $\mathcal{M}$ (although it is a recovery of $\mathcal{M}$). To see why this is the case, let S, T be instances of $\mathbf{R_1}$ and $\mathbf{R_2}$, respectively, such that:

$$E^S = \{(1,2),(2,3)\} \qquad F^T = \{(1,3)\}$$
$$G^T = \{4\}.$$

It is clear that $(S,T) \notin \mathcal{M}$ as element 2 is not in G^T. However, $(S,T) \in \mathcal{M} \circ \mathcal{M}_1 \circ \mathcal{M}$ since for the instances T_1, S_1 of $\mathbf{R}_2$ and $\mathbf{R}_1$, respectively, such that:

$$
\begin{aligned}
F^{T_1} &= \{(1,3)\} & E^{S_1} &= \{(1,4),(4,3)\} \\
G^{T_1} &= \{2\}
\end{aligned}
$$

we have that $(S,T_1) \in \mathcal{M}$, $(T_1,S_1) \in \mathcal{M}_1$ and $(S_1,T) \in \mathcal{M}$. Thus, we conclude that $\mathcal{M}_1$ does not satisfy condition (2) in Proposition 20.21, from which we conclude that $\mathcal{M}_1$ is not a maximum recovery of $\mathcal{M}$. $\qquad\square$

As we pointed out before, the main motivation for the introduction of the notion of maximum recovery is to have an inverse operator that is defined for every mapping specified by st-tgds. Here, we identify the class of mappings for which this operator is defined by providing a necessary and sufficient condition for the existence of maximum recoveries. In particular, we use this condition to show that every mapping specified by a finite set of st-tgds admits a maximum recovery.

Recall that in Section 20.1 we introduced the notion of a strong witness to characterize invertibility for the class of mappings that are total and closed-down on the left. More precisely, given a mapping $\mathcal{M}$ from a schema $\mathbf{R}_1$ to a schema $\mathbf{R}_2$ and instances S, T of $\mathbf{R}_1$ and $\mathbf{R}_2$, respectively, T is a strong witness for S under $\mathcal{M}$ if for every instance S' of $\mathbf{R}_1$ such that $T \in \text{SOL}_{\mathcal{M}}(S')$, it holds that $S' \subseteq S$. It turns out that by weakening this condition, one can characterize the existence of maximum recoveries. Formally, given a mapping $\mathcal{M}$ from a schema $\mathbf{R}_1$ to a schema $\mathbf{R}_2$ and instances S, T of $\mathbf{R}_1$ and $\mathbf{R}_2$, respectively, T is a *witness* for S under $\mathcal{M}$ if for every instance S' of $\mathbf{R}_1$ such that $T \in \text{SOL}_{\mathcal{M}}(S')$, it holds that $\text{SOL}_{\mathcal{M}}(S) \subseteq \text{SOL}_{\mathcal{M}}(S')$. Moreover, T is a witness solution for S under $\mathcal{M}$ if T is both a solution and a witness for S under $\mathcal{M}$.

The notion of a witness is indeed weaker than the notion of a strong witness, as the next result shows.

Proposition 20.23 *Let $\mathcal{M} = (\mathbf{R}_1, \mathbf{R}_2, \Sigma)$ be a mapping, where Σ is a finite set of st-tgds, S an instance of $\mathbf{R}_1$ and T an instance of $\mathbf{R}_2$. Then every strong witness for S under $\mathcal{M}$ is a witness for S under $\mathcal{M}$.*

Proof The proposition is a corollary of the fact that if $\mathcal{M} = (\mathbf{R}_1, \mathbf{R}_2, \Sigma)$, with Σ a set of st-tgds, and S_1, S_2 are instances of $\mathbf{R}_1$ such that $S_1 \subseteq S_2$, then $\text{SOL}_{\mathcal{M}}(S_2) \subseteq \text{SOL}_{\mathcal{M}}(S_1)$. $\qquad\square$

Proposition 20.24 *Let $\mathcal{M} = (\mathbf{R}_1, \mathbf{R}_2, \Sigma)$ be a mapping, where Σ is a finite set of st-tgds, and S an instance of $\mathbf{R}_1$. If T is a universal solution for S under $\mathcal{M}$, then T is a witness solution for S under $\mathcal{M}$.*

Proof In the proof of Proposition 20.8, we show that if T is a universal solution for S under $\mathcal{M}$ and $T \in \text{SOL}_{\mathcal{M}}(S')$, then $\text{SOL}_{\mathcal{M}}(S) \subseteq \text{SOL}_{\mathcal{M}}(S')$ (this is a corollary of the fact that a mapping specified by a finite set of st-tgds is closed under target homomorphisms, as shown in Proposition 21.1 in Section 21.1). Thus, we have already provided a proof of the proposition. $\qquad\square$

We now show that the notion of witness solution can be used to characterize the existence of maximum recoveries.

Theorem 20.25 *Let $\mathcal{M}$ be a mapping from a schema $\mathbf{R_1}$ to a schema $\mathbf{R_2}$. Then $\mathcal{M}$ has a maximum recovery if and only if every instance $S \in \mathrm{DOM}(\mathcal{M})$ has a witness solution under $\mathcal{M}$.*

Proof ($\Rightarrow$) Let $\mathcal{M}'$ be a maximum recovery of $\mathcal{M}$, and S an instance in $\mathrm{DOM}(\mathcal{M})$. Then given that $\mathcal{M}'$ is a recovery of $\mathcal{M}$, we have that there exists an instance T of $\mathbf{R_2}$ such that $(S,T) \in \mathcal{M}$ and $(T,S) \in \mathcal{M}'$. Next we show that T is a witness solution for S under $\mathcal{M}$. We already know that T is a solution for S under $\mathcal{M}$, so we only need to show that if $T \in \mathrm{SOL}_{\mathcal{M}}(S')$, then it holds that $\mathrm{SOL}_{\mathcal{M}}(S) \subseteq \mathrm{SOL}_{\mathcal{M}}(S')$. Thus assume that $T' \in \mathrm{SOL}_{\mathcal{M}}(S)$. Given that $(S',T) \in \mathcal{M}$, $(T,S) \in \mathcal{M}'$ and $(S,T') \in \mathcal{M}$, we have that $(S',T') \in \mathcal{M} \circ \mathcal{M}' \circ \mathcal{M}$. But from Proposition 20.21 we have that $\mathcal{M} = \mathcal{M} \circ \mathcal{M}' \circ \mathcal{M}$ and, therefore, $(S',T') \in \mathcal{M}$. We conclude that $\mathrm{SOL}_{\mathcal{M}}(S) \subseteq \mathrm{SOL}_{\mathcal{M}}(S')$ and, hence, T is a witness solution for S under $\mathcal{M}$.

($\Leftarrow$) Assume that every $S \in \mathrm{DOM}(\mathcal{M})$ has a witness solution under $\mathcal{M}$, and let $\mathcal{M}^\star$ be a mapping from $\mathbf{R_2}$ to $\mathbf{R_1}$ defined as:

$$\{(T,S) \mid T \text{ is a witness solution for } S \text{ under } \mathcal{M}\}.$$

By hypothesis, we have that $\mathcal{M}^\star$ is a recovery of $\mathcal{M}$. Next we use Proposition 20.21 to show that $\mathcal{M}^\star$ is a maximum recovery of $\mathcal{M}$.

By definition of $\mathcal{M}^\star$, we have that this mappings satisfies condition (1) in Proposition 20.21. Moreover, given that $\mathcal{M}^\star$ is a recovery of $\mathcal{M}$, we have that $\mathcal{M} \subseteq \mathcal{M} \circ \mathcal{M}^\star \circ \mathcal{M}$. Thus, we have from Proposition 20.21 that if $\mathcal{M} \circ \mathcal{M}^\star \circ \mathcal{M} \subseteq \mathcal{M}$, then $\mathcal{M}^\star$ is a maximum recovery of $\mathcal{M}$. Let $(S,T) \in \mathcal{M} \circ \mathcal{M}^\star \circ \mathcal{M}$. Then there exist instances T_1, S_1 of $\mathbf{R_2}$ and $\mathbf{R_1}$, respectively, such that $(S,T_1) \in \mathcal{M}$, $(T_1,S_1) \in \mathcal{M}^\star$ and $(S_1,T) \in \mathcal{M}$. Thus, by definition of $\mathcal{M}^\star$, we have that T_1 is a witness solution for S_1 under $\mathcal{M}$. Hence, given that $T_1 \in \mathrm{SOL}_{\mathcal{M}}(S)$, we have that $\mathrm{SOL}_{\mathcal{M}}(S_1) \subseteq \mathrm{SOL}_{\mathcal{M}}(S)$. We conclude that $T \in \mathrm{SOL}_{\mathcal{M}}(S)$ since $T \in \mathrm{SOL}_{\mathcal{M}}(S_1)$ and, thus, we have that $(S,T) \in \mathcal{M}$, which was to be shown. This concludes the proof of the theorem. □

As a corollary of Proposition 20.24 and Theorem 20.25, we obtain the desired result that every mapping specified by a finite set of st-tgds admits a maximum recovery. It should be noticed that this result is in sharp contrast with the nonexistence results for the notions of inverse and quasi-inverse and the class of mappings specified by st-tgds (see Corollary 20.5 and Proposition 20.16).

Theorem 20.26 *Every mapping specified by a finite set of st-tgds admits a maximum recovery.*

Up to this point, we have introduced three alternative inverse operators for schema mappings: inverse, quasi-inverse and maximum recovery. In the previous section, we showed that there is a tight connection between the first two operators (see Proposition 20.14), and, thus, it is natural to ask what is the relationship between them and the notion of maximum recovery. We first answer this question for the notion of inverse and the class of mappings that are total and closed-down on the left, for which the notion of inverse is appropriate (see Section 20.1).

Proposition 20.27 *(1) There exists a mapping specified by a finite set of st-tgds that is not invertible but has a maximum recovery.*

(2) For every mapping $\mathcal{M}$ that is total, closed-down on the left and invertible, a mapping $\mathcal{M}'$ is an inverse of $\mathcal{M}$ if and only if $\mathcal{M}'$ is a maximum recovery of $\mathcal{M}$.

Proof (1) Let $\mathbf{R_1}$ be a schema consisting of a binary relation E, $\mathbf{R_2}$ a schema consisting of a binary relation F and a unary relation G, and $\mathcal{M} = (\mathbf{R_1}, \mathbf{R_2}, \Sigma)$ with Σ a set of st-tgds consisting of the following dependency:

$$E(x,z) \wedge E(z,y) \rightarrow F(x,y) \wedge G(z).$$

In Proposition 20.16, we show that $\mathcal{M}$ is not quasi-invertible. Thus, we have that this mapping is not invertible by Proposition 20.14. On the other hand, we show in Examples 20.20 and 20.22 a maximum recovery of $\mathcal{M}$. This proves that condition (1) of the proposition holds.

(2) Let $\mathcal{M}$ be a mapping from a schema $\mathbf{R_1}$ to a schema $\mathbf{R_2}$ and $\mathcal{M}'$ a mapping from $\mathbf{R_2}$ to $\mathbf{R_1}$. Moreover, assume that $\mathcal{M}$ is total, closed-down on the left and invertible. Next we prove the two directions of this part of the proposition.

($\Rightarrow$) If $\mathcal{M}'$ is an inverse of $\mathcal{M}$, then we have that $(S_1, S_2) \in \mathcal{M} \circ \mathcal{M}'$ if and only if $S_1 \subseteq S_2$. Thus, we know that $\mathcal{M}'$ is a recovery of $\mathcal{M}$ and, therefore, given that $\mathcal{M}$ is a total mapping, we have from Proposition 20.21 that $\mathcal{M}'$ is a maximum recovery of $\mathcal{M}$ if $\mathcal{M} \circ \mathcal{M}' \circ \mathcal{M} \subseteq \mathcal{M}$ (we already know that $\mathcal{M} \subseteq \mathcal{M} \circ \mathcal{M}' \circ \mathcal{M}$ since $\mathcal{M}'$ is a recovery of $\mathcal{M}$). Assume that $(S,T) \in \mathcal{M} \circ \mathcal{M}' \circ \mathcal{M}$. Then there exists an instance S' of $\mathbf{R_1}$ such that $(S,S') \in \mathcal{M} \circ \mathcal{M}'$ and $(S',T) \in \mathcal{M}$. Thus, we have that $S \subseteq S'$, from which we conclude that $\text{SOL}_{\mathcal{M}}(S') \subseteq \text{SOL}_{\mathcal{M}}(S)$ since $\mathcal{M}$ is closed-down on the left. Hence, given that $(S',T) \in \mathcal{M}$, we have that $T \in \text{SOL}_{\mathcal{M}}(S)$ and, therefore, $(S,T) \in \mathcal{M}$. Thus, we have that $\mathcal{M} \circ \mathcal{M}' \circ \mathcal{M} \subseteq \mathcal{M}$, which was to be shown.

($\Leftarrow$) Assume that $\mathcal{M}'$ is a maximum recovery of $\mathcal{M}$. In order to show that $\mathcal{M}'$ is an inverse of $\mathcal{M}$, we need to show that $(S_1, S_2) \in \mathcal{M} \circ \mathcal{M}'$ if and only if $S_1 \subseteq S_2$. First, assume that $S_1 \subseteq S_2$. Given that S_2 is an instance of $\mathbf{R_1}$, $\mathcal{M}'$ is a recovery of $\mathcal{M}$ and $\mathcal{M}$ is total, we know that $(S_2, S_2) \in \mathcal{M} \circ \mathcal{M}'$. Thus, given that $\mathcal{M}$ is closed-down on the left, we have that $(S_1, S_2) \in \mathcal{M} \circ \mathcal{M}'$. Second, assume that $(S_1, S_2) \in \mathcal{M} \circ \mathcal{M}'$. Given that $\mathcal{M}$ is invertible, there exists an inverse $\mathcal{M}''$ of $\mathcal{M}$. Then $\mathcal{M}''$ is a recovery of $\mathcal{M}$ and, thus, given that $\mathcal{M}'$ is a maximum recovery of $\mathcal{M}$, we have that $\mathcal{M} \circ \mathcal{M}' \subseteq \mathcal{M} \circ \mathcal{M}''$. We infer that $(S_1, S_2) \in \mathcal{M} \circ \mathcal{M}''$ since $(S_1, S_2) \in \mathcal{M} \circ \mathcal{M}'$, which implies that $S_1 \subseteq S_2$ since $\mathcal{M}''$ is an inverse of $\mathcal{M}$. This concludes the proof of the proposition. $\square$

We now consider the second part of our question, namely what is the relationship between the notions of quasi-inverse and maximum recovery. As shown in the following proposition, the situation is a bit more involved than for the case of the notion of inverse.

Proposition 20.28 *(1) There exists a mapping specified by a finite set of st-tgds that is not quasi-invertible but has a maximum recovery.*

(2) For every mapping $\mathcal{M}$ that is total, closed-down on the left and quasi-invertible, there exists a mapping that is a maximum recovery of $\mathcal{M}$ and, moreover, $\mathcal{M}'$ is a maximum recovery of $\mathcal{M}$ if and only if $\mathcal{M}'$ is a quasi-inverse and recovery of $\mathcal{M}$.

Note that part (1) of this proposition has already been proved in Proposition 20.27.

Given that inverses and quasi-inverses are not guaranteed to exist for the class of mappings specified by st-tgds, we study in Sections 20.1 and 20.1 the decidability of invertibility and quasi-invertibility for this class of mappings. On the other hand, the problem of verifying whether a mapping $\mathcal{M}$ has a maximum recovery becomes trivial in this context, as every mapping specified by this class of dependencies admits a maximum recovery. Thus, we only consider here the fundamental problem of verifying, given mappings $\mathcal{M}$ and $\mathcal{M}'$ specified by st-tgds, whether $\mathcal{M}'$ is a maximum recovery of $\mathcal{M}$. Somewhat surprisingly, not only is this problem undecidable, but also the problem of verifying whether a mapping $\mathcal{M}'$ is a recovery of a mapping $\mathcal{M}$.

Theorem 20.29 *The problem of verifying, given mappings $\mathcal{M} = (\mathbf{R}_1, \mathbf{R}_2, \Sigma_{12})$ and $\mathcal{M}' = (\mathbf{R}_2, \mathbf{R}_1, \Sigma_{21})$ with Σ_{12} and Σ_{21} finite sets of st-tgds, whether $\mathcal{M}'$ is a recovery (maximum recovery) of $\mathcal{M}$ is undecidable.*

As we have mentioned in the previous sections, we are still missing the algorithms for computing the inverse operators introduced in this chapter. In the next section, we present a unified algorithm for computing these operators, which uses some query rewriting techniques, and takes advantage of the tight connections between the notions of inverse, quasi-inverse and maximum recovery shown in Propositions 20.14, 20.27 and 20.28.

20.3 Computing the inverse operator

Up to this point, we have introduced and compared three notions of inverse proposed in the literature, focusing mainly on the fundamental problem of the existence of such inverses. Arguably, the most important problem about these operators is the issue of how to compute them for the class of mappings specified by st-tgds. This problem has been studied for the case of the notions of inverse, quasi-inverse and maximum recovery. In this section, we present an algorithm for computing maximum recoveries of mappings specified by st-tgds, which by the results of the previous sections can also be used to compute inverses and quasi-inverses for this type of mapping. Interestingly, this algorithm is based on *query rewriting*, which greatly simplifies the process of computing such inverses.

We start by introducing the notion of query rewritability over the source, which is similar to the notion of rewritability introduced in Section 7.5. Let $\mathcal{M}$ be a mapping from a schema $\mathbf{R}_1$ to a schema $\mathbf{R}_2$ and Q a query over schema $\mathbf{R}_2$. Then a query Q' is said to be a *rewriting of Q over the source* if Q' is a query over $\mathbf{R}_1$ such that for every $S \in \text{INST}(\mathbf{R}_1)$, it holds that $Q'(S) = certain_{\mathscr{M}}(Q,S)$. That is, it is possible to obtain the set of certain answers of Q over S under $\mathscr{M}$ by just evaluating its rewriting Q' over the source S.

The computation of a source rewriting of a conjunctive query is a basic step in the algorithm presented in this section. This problem has been extensively studied in the database area and, in particular, in the data integration context. In fact, it is well known that:

Proposition 20.30 *There exists an algorithm* QUERYREWRITING *that, given a mapping* $\mathscr{M} = (\mathbf{R_1}, \mathbf{R_2}, \Sigma)$, *with* Σ *a finite set of st-tgds, and a conjunctive query* Q *over* $\mathbf{R_2}$, *computes a union of conjunctive queries with equality* Q' *that is a rewriting of* Q *over the source. The algorithm runs in exponential time and its output is of exponential size in the size of* Σ *and* Q.

Example 20.31 We give here some intuition of why the algorithm QUERYREWRITING uses union and equalities in its output language. Let $\mathbf{R_1}$ be a schema consisting of a unary relation P and a binary relation R, $\mathbf{R_2}$ be a schema consisting of a binary relation T and $\mathscr{M} = (\mathbf{R_1}, \mathbf{R_2}, \Sigma)$, where Σ is a set of dependencies consisting of the following st-tgds:

$$P(x) \rightarrow T(x,x),$$
$$R(x,y) \rightarrow T(x,y).$$

Assume that Q is the target query $T(x,y)$. What is a source rewriting of Q? To answer this question, we need to consider all the possibles ways of generating target tuples from a source instance. Let S be an instance of $\mathbf{R_1}$. If S contains a fact $P(a)$, then all the solutions for S under $\mathscr{M}$ will contain the fact $T(a,a)$. Thus, every answer to the query $P(x) \wedge x = y$ over S will be in $certain_{\mathscr{M}}(Q,S)$. In the same way, if S contains a fact $R(a,b)$, then all the solutions for S under $\mathscr{M}$ will contain the fact $T(a,b)$ and, hence, every answer to the query $R(x,y)$ over S will be in $certain_{\mathscr{M}}(Q,S)$. Given the definition of $\mathscr{M}$, the previous two queries consider all the possible ways to generate target tuples according to $\mathscr{M}$, from which one can formally prove that the following is a source rewriting of query Q (see Exercise 22.3):

$$(P(x) \wedge x = y) \vee R(x,y).$$

It is important to notice that the above query is a union of two conjunctive queries, and that the use of union and equality in this rewriting is unavoidable.   □

We finally have all the necessary ingredients to present the algorithm for computing maximum recoveries. In this procedure, $\mathbf{C}$ refers to the unary predicate introduced in Section 7.4 that distinguishes between constant and null values ($\mathbf{C}(a)$ holds if and only if a belongs to CONST). Moreover, if $\bar{x} = (x_1, \ldots, x_k)$, then $\mathbf{C}(\bar{x})$ is used in the algorithm as a shorthand for $\mathbf{C}(x_1) \wedge \cdots \wedge \mathbf{C}(x_k)$.

Theorem 20.32 *Algorithm* MAXIMUMRECOVERY *runs in exponential time, and on input* $\mathscr{M} = (\mathbf{R_1}, \mathbf{R_2}, \Sigma)$, *where* Σ *is a finite set of st-tgds, it computes a maximum recovery of* $\mathscr{M}$.

Algorithm 20.1 MAXIMUMRECOVERY

Require: $\mathcal{M}_{12} = (\mathbf{R_1}, \mathbf{R_2}, \Sigma)$ with Σ a finite set of st-tgds

Ensure: $\mathcal{M}_{21} = (\mathbf{R_2}, \mathbf{R_1}, \Gamma)$ is a maximum recovery of $\mathcal{M}$

1: $\Gamma := \emptyset$

2: **for all** $\varphi(\bar{x}) \to \exists \bar{y} \, \psi(\bar{x}, \bar{y})$ in Σ **do**

3: $\quad$ $Q(\bar{x}) := \exists \bar{y} \, \psi(\bar{x}, \bar{y})$

4: $\quad$ let $\alpha(\bar{x})$ be the output of algorithm QUERYREWRITING with input $\mathcal{M}_{12}$ and Q

5: $\quad$ $\Gamma := \Gamma \cup \{ \psi(\bar{x}, \bar{y}) \wedge \mathbf{C}(\bar{x}) \to \alpha(\bar{x}) \}$

6: **end for**

Proof From Proposition 20.30, it is straightforward to conclude that algorithm MAXIMUMRECOVERY runs in exponential time. Assume that $\mathcal{M}' = (\mathbf{R_1}, \mathbf{R_2}, \Gamma)$ is the output of the algorithm MAXIMUMRECOVERY with input $\mathcal{M}$. In order to prove that $\mathcal{M}'$ is a maximum recovery of $\mathcal{M}$, we first show that $\mathcal{M}'$ is a recovery of $\mathcal{M}$, that is, we prove that for every instance S of $\mathbf{R_1}$, it holds that $(S, S) \in \mathcal{M} \circ \mathcal{M}'$.

Let S be an instance of $\mathbf{R_1}$ and let T be the canonical universal solution for S under $\mathcal{M}$. Next we show that $(T, S) \in \mathcal{M}'$, from which we conclude that $(S, S) \in \mathcal{M} \circ \mathcal{M}'$ since $(S, T) \in \mathcal{M}$. Let $\sigma \in \Gamma$. We need to show that $(T, S) \models \sigma$. Assume that σ is of the form $\psi(\bar{x}, \bar{y}) \wedge \mathbf{C}(\bar{x}) \to \alpha(\bar{x})$, and that $\bar{a}$ is a tuple of values from T such that $T \models \exists \bar{y} (\psi(\bar{a}, \bar{y}) \wedge \mathbf{C}(\bar{a}))$. We need to show that $S \models \alpha(\bar{a})$. Consider the conjunctive query $Q(\bar{x})$ defined by the formula $\exists \bar{y} \, \psi(\bar{x}, \bar{y})$. Since $\mathbf{C}(\bar{a})$ holds and $T \models \exists \bar{y} \, \psi(\bar{a}, \bar{y})$, we obtain that $\bar{a} \in Q(T)$. Thus, from the results about query answering proved in Chapter 7 and the fact that T is the canonical universal solution for S under $\mathcal{M}$, we obtain that $\bar{a} \in certain_{\mathcal{M}}(Q, S)$. Consider now the query $Q'(\bar{x})$ defined by formula $\alpha(\bar{x})$. By the definition of algorithm MAXIMUMRECOVERY, we have that Q' is a rewriting of Q over schema $\mathbf{R_1}$, and then $certain_{\mathcal{M}}(Q, S) = Q'(S)$. Thus, we have that $\bar{a} \in Q'(S)$, and then $S \models \alpha(\bar{a})$, which was to be shown.

Given that $\mathcal{M}'$ is a recovery of $\mathcal{M}$ and $\text{DOM}(\mathcal{M}) = \text{INST}(\mathbf{R_1})$, we know from Proposition 20.21 that $\mathcal{M}'$ is a maximum recovery of $\mathcal{M}$ if $\mathcal{M} \circ \mathcal{M}' \circ \mathcal{M} \subseteq \mathcal{M}$. Next we show that if $(S_1, S_2) \in \mathcal{M} \circ \mathcal{M}'$, then $\text{SOL}_{\mathcal{M}}(S_2) \subseteq \text{SOL}_{\mathcal{M}}(S_1)$, from which we conclude that $\mathcal{M} \circ \mathcal{M}' \circ \mathcal{M} \subseteq \mathcal{M}$. To see why this is the case, let $(S, T) \in \mathcal{M} \circ \mathcal{M}' \circ \mathcal{M}$. Then there exist instances T_1, R_1 of $\mathbf{R_2}$ and $\mathbf{R_1}$, respectively, such that $(S, T_1) \in \mathcal{M}$, $(T_1, S_1) \in \mathcal{M}'$ and $(S_1, T) \in \mathcal{M}$. Then given that $(S, S_1) \in \mathcal{M} \circ \mathcal{M}'$, we have by hypothesis that $\text{SOL}_{\mathcal{M}}(S_1) \subseteq \text{SOL}_{\mathcal{M}}(S)$. Thus, from the fact that $(S_1, T) \in \mathcal{M}$, we conclude that $(S, T) \in \mathcal{M}$, which was to be shown.

Let $(S_1, S_2) \in \mathcal{M} \circ \mathcal{M}'$, and $T^{\star}$ an instance of $\mathbf{R_2}$ such that $(S_1, T^{\star}) \in \mathcal{M}$ and $(T^{\star}, S_2) \in \mathcal{M}'$. We need to prove that $\text{SOL}_{\mathcal{M}}(S_2) \subseteq \text{SOL}_{\mathcal{M}}(S_1)$. To this end, assume that $T \in \text{SOL}_{\mathcal{M}}(S_2)$. Next we show that $T \in \text{SOL}_{\mathcal{M}}(S_1)$. Let $\sigma \in \Sigma$ be a dependency of the form $\varphi(\bar{x}) \to \exists \bar{y} \, \psi(\bar{x}, \bar{y})$, and assume that $S_1 \models \varphi(\bar{a})$ for some tuple $\bar{a}$ of constant values. We show next that $T \models \exists \bar{y} \, \psi(\bar{a}, \bar{y})$. Given that $S_1 \models \varphi(\bar{a})$, we have that for every $T' \in \text{SOL}_{\mathcal{M}}(S_1)$, it holds that $T' \models \exists \bar{y} \, \psi(\bar{a}, \bar{y})$. In particular, it holds that $T^{\star} \models \exists \bar{y} \, \psi(\bar{a}, \bar{y})$.

By the definition of algorithm MAXIMUMRECOVERY, we know that there exists a dependency $\psi(\bar{x},\bar{y}) \wedge \mathbf{C}(\bar{x}) \rightarrow \alpha(\bar{x})$ in Γ such that $\alpha(\bar{x})$ is a rewriting of $\exists \bar{y}\, \psi(\bar{x},\bar{y})$ over $\mathbf{R}_1$. Then since $T^\star \models \exists \bar{y}\, \psi(\bar{a},\bar{y})$, $\bar{a}$ is a tuple of constant values, and $(T^\star, S_2) \models \Gamma$, we know that $S_2 \models \alpha(\bar{a})$. Now consider the queries $Q(\bar{x})$ and $Q'(\bar{x})$ defined by formulae $\exists \bar{y}\, \psi(\bar{x},\bar{y})$ and $\alpha(\bar{x})$, respectively. Since $S_2 \models \alpha(\bar{a})$, we know that $\bar{a} \in Q'(S_2)$. Furthermore, we know that $Q'(S_2) = certain_{\mathcal{M}}(Q,S_2)$, and then $\bar{a} \in certain_{\mathcal{M}}(Q,S_2)$. In particular, since $T \in \mathrm{SOL}_{\mathcal{M}}(S_2)$, we know that $\bar{a} \in Q(T)$, from which we conclude that $T \models \exists \bar{y}\, \psi(\bar{a},\bar{y})$. We have shown that for every $\sigma \in \Sigma$ of the form $\varphi(\bar{x}) \rightarrow \exists \bar{y}\, \psi(\bar{x},\bar{y})$, if $S_1 \models \varphi(\bar{a})$ for some tuple $\bar{a}$, then $T \models \exists \bar{y}\, \psi(\bar{a},\bar{y})$. Thus, we have that $(S_1,T) \models \Sigma$ and, therefore, $T \in \mathrm{SOL}_{\mathcal{M}}(S_1)$. This concludes the proof of the theorem. $\qquad\square$

Example 20.33 Let $\mathbf{R}_1$ be a schema consisting of a unary relation P and a binary relation R, $\mathbf{R}_2$ be a schema consisting of a binary relation T and $\mathcal{M} = (\mathbf{R}_1, \mathbf{R}_2, \Sigma)$, where Σ is a set of dependencies consisting of the following st-tgds:

$$P(x) \rightarrow T(x,x),$$
$$R(x,y) \rightarrow T(x,y).$$

In order to compute a maximum recovery $\mathcal{M}' = (\mathbf{R}_2, \mathbf{R}_1, \Gamma)$ of $\mathcal{M}$, algorithm MAXIMUMRECOVERY first computes a source rewriting of target query $T(x,x)$:

$$P(x) \vee R(x,x),$$

and it adds dependency

$$T(x,x) \wedge \mathbf{C}(x) \rightarrow P(x) \vee R(x,x) \tag{20.9}$$

to Γ. Then it computes a rewriting of target query $T(x,y)$ (see Example 20.31):

$$(P(x) \wedge x = y) \vee R(x,y),$$

and it finishes by adding dependency

$$T(x,y) \wedge \mathbf{C}(x) \wedge \mathbf{C}(y) \rightarrow (P(x) \wedge x = y) \vee R(x,y) \tag{20.10}$$

to Γ. Given that (20.10) logically implies (20.9), we conclude that the mapping specified by dependency (20.10) is a maximum recovery of $\mathcal{M}$. $\qquad\square$

From Theorem 20.32 and Propositions 20.27 and 20.28, we conclude that algorithm MAXIMUMRECOVERY can also be used to compute inverses and quasi-inverses.

Corollary 20.34 Let $\mathcal{M} = (\mathbf{R}_1, \mathbf{R}_2, \Sigma)$, where Σ is a finite set of st-tgds. If $\mathcal{M}$ is invertible (quasi-invertible), then on input $\mathcal{M}$, algorithm MAXIMUMRECOVERY computes an inverse (quasi-inverse) of $\mathcal{M}$.

One of the interesting features of algorithm MAXIMUMRECOVERY is the use of query rewriting, as it allows us to reuse in the computation of the inverse operator the large number of techniques developed to deal with the problem of query rewriting. However, one can identify two drawbacks in this procedure. First, algorithm MAXIMUMRECOVERY returns mappings that are specified by dependencies that extend st-tgds with disjunctions in the right-hand side. Unfortunately, these types of mappings are difficult to use in the data exchange context. In particular, it is not clear whether the standard chase procedure could be used to produce a single canonical target database in this case, thus making the process of exchanging data and answering target queries much more complicated. Second, the output mapping of MAXIMUMRECOVERY can be of exponential size in the size of the input mapping. Thus, a natural question at this point is whether simpler and smaller inverse mappings can be computed. In the rest of this section, we show an effort to lower the complexity in a restricted case, and we briefly study what are the languages needed to express inverses, quasi-inverses and maximum recoveries.

Recall that a st-tgd is called full if it does not include any existential quantifiers in its right-hand side. Full st-tgds have been widely used in practice, and extensively studied in the data integration and exchange contexts. For this reason, the issue of computing inverses for the class of mappings specified by full st-tgds is considered to be a fundamental problem. Interestingly, next we show a modification of the algorithm MAXIMUMRECOVERY that works in quadratic time and computes maximum recoveries for this type of mapping. It is important to notice that we assume in this procedure, without loss of generality, that every full st-tgd has a single atom in its right-hand side. Besides, given tuples of variables $\bar{x} = (x_1, \ldots, x_k)$ and $\bar{y} = (y_1, \ldots, y_k)$, we use the notation $\bar{x} = \bar{y}$ as a shorthand for $x_1 = y_1 \wedge \cdots \wedge x_k = y_k$.

Algorithm 20.2 MAXIMUMRECOVERYFULL

Require: $\mathscr{M}_{12} = (\mathbf{R}_1, \mathbf{R}_2, \Sigma)$ with Σ a finite set of full st-tgds, and each dependency in Σ having a single atom in its right-hand side

Ensure: $\mathscr{M}_{21} = (\mathbf{R}_2, \mathbf{R}_1, \Gamma)$ is a maximum recovery of $\mathscr{M}$

1: $\Gamma := \emptyset$

2: **for all** predicate symbol $P \in \mathbf{R}_1$ **do**

3:     let $\bar{u}$ be a fresh tuple of pairwise distinct variables containing as many variables as the arity of P

4:     $\Delta := \emptyset$

5:     **for all** $\varphi(\bar{x}) \to P(\bar{x})$ in Σ **do**

6:         $\Delta := \Delta \cup \{\exists \bar{x}(\varphi(\bar{x}) \wedge \bar{x} = \bar{u})\}$

7:     **end for**

8:     let $\alpha(\bar{u})$ be the disjunction of all the elements in Δ

9:     $\Gamma := \Gamma \cup \{P(\bar{u}) \to \alpha(\bar{u})\}$

10: **end for**

Theorem 20.35 *Algorithm* MAXIMUMRECOVERYFULL *runs in quadratic time, and on input* $\mathscr{M} = (\mathbf{R}_1, \mathbf{R}_2, \Sigma)$, *where* Σ *is a finite set of full st-tgds with each dependency in it having a single atom in its right-hand side, it computes a maximum recovery of* $\mathscr{M}$.

Algorithm MAXIMUMRECOVERYFULL can be considered as a specialization of algorithm

MAXIMUMRECOVERY for the case of full st-tgds, as the formula $\alpha(\bar{u})$ computed in line 8 of this algorithm is a source rewriting of target query $P(\bar{u})$. We leave to the reader the proof of this fact, and also the proof that procedure MAXIMUMRECOVERYFULL is correct (see Exercise 22.3).

Example 20.36 Let $\mathbf{R_1}$ be a schema consisting of a unary relation A and a binary relation B, $\mathbf{R_2}$ be a schema consisting of binary relations D and E, and $\mathcal{M} = (\mathbf{R_1}, \mathbf{R_2}, \Sigma)$, where Σ is a set of dependencies consisting of the following st-tgds:

$$A(x) \rightarrow D(x,x) \tag{20.11}$$
$$B(x,y) \rightarrow D(y,y) \tag{20.12}$$
$$B(x,x) \rightarrow E(x). \tag{20.13}$$

In order to compute a maximum recovery $\mathcal{M}' = (\mathbf{R_2}, \mathbf{R_1}, \Gamma)$ of $\mathcal{M}$, algorithm MAXIMUMRECOVERYFULL first considers the predicate symbol D from $\mathbf{R_1}$. For this symbol, it generates a fresh tuple (u_1, u_2) of variables. Let Δ be the empty set. Then it considers the two dependencies in Σ mentioning the predicate symbol D in its right-hand side. In the case of st-tgd (20.11), it adds $\exists x\,(A(x) \wedge x = u_1 \wedge x = u_2)$ to Δ. In the case of st-tgd (20.12), it first notices that this dependency has to be read as $\exists x B(x,y) \rightarrow D(y,y)$, and then it adds $\exists y \exists x\,(B(x,y) \wedge y = u_1 \wedge y = u_2)$ to Δ. Thus, once the dependencies with predicate symbol D in its right-hand side have been processed, it holds that:

$$\Delta = \{\exists x\,(A(x) \wedge x = u_1 \wedge x = u_2),\ \exists y \exists x\,(B(x,y) \wedge y = u_1 \wedge y = u_2)\}.$$

Therefore, the following dependency is added to Γ:

$$P(u_1, u_2) \rightarrow$$
$$\exists x\left(A(x) \wedge x = u_1 \wedge x = u_2\right) \vee \exists y \exists x\left(B(x,y) \wedge y = u_1 \wedge y = u_2\right). \tag{20.14}$$

In the same way, algorithm MAXIMUMRECOVERYFULL considers all the dependencies in Σ mentioning predicate E in its right-hand side, and computes the following dependency:

$$E(u_3) \rightarrow \exists x\,(B(x,x) \wedge x = u_3). \tag{20.15}$$

Given that $\mathbf{R_1}$ consists only of predicate symbols D and E, we conclude that the mapping specified by dependencies (20.14) and (20.15) is a maximum recovery of $\mathcal{M}$.   □

As for the case of algorithm MAXIMUMRECOVERY, from Theorem 20.32 and Propositions 20.27 and 20.28, we conclude that algorithm MAXIMUMRECOVERYFULL can also be used to compute inverses and quasi-inverses.

Corollary 20.37 *Let $\mathcal{M} = (\mathbf{R_1}, \mathbf{R_2}, \Sigma)$, where Σ is a finite set of full st-tgds with each dependency in it having a single atom in its right-hand side. If $\mathcal{M}$ is invertible (quasi-invertible), then on input $\mathcal{M}$, algorithm MAXIMUMRECOVERYFULL computes an inverse (quasi-inverse) of $\mathcal{M}$.*

It is important to notice that, as for the case of procedure MAXIMUMRECOVERY, algorithm MAXIMUMRECOVERYFULL returns mappings that are specified by dependencies that extend st-tgds with disjunctions in their right-hand sides. As we have mentioned before, these types of mappings are difficult to use in the data exchange context and, thus, it is natural to ask whether the use of disjunction in the output languages of algorithms MAXIMUMRECOVERY and MAXIMUMRECOVERYFULL can be avoided, and, in particular, whether the maximum recovery of a mapping specified by st-tgds can be specified in the same mapping language. We conclude this section by given a negative answer to this question not only for the notion of maximum recovery, but also for the notions of inverse and quasi-inverse.

Proposition 20.38   *There exists a mapping $\mathcal{M} = (\mathbf{R_1}, \mathbf{R_2}, \Sigma)$ specified by a finite set Σ of full st-tgds that is invertible, but has no inverse specified by a finite set of tgds.*

Proof   We only present the mapping, and leave the proof as an exercise. Let $\mathbf{R_1}$ be a schema consisting of a unary predicate A and a binary predicate B, $\mathbf{R_2}$ a schema consisting of unary predicates D, E and a binary predicate F, and Σ be a set consisting of the following full st-tgds:

$$A(x) \rightarrow D(x),$$
$$A(x) \rightarrow F(x,x),$$
$$B(x,y) \rightarrow F(x,y),$$
$$B(x,x) \rightarrow E(x).$$

The mapping $\mathcal{M}$ is invertible; in fact its inverse is a mapping $\mathcal{M}' = (\mathbf{R_2}, \mathbf{R_1}, \Sigma')$, where Σ' consists of the following dependencies

$$D(x) \rightarrow A(x),$$
$$F(x,y) \wedge x \neq y \rightarrow B(x,y),$$
$$E(x) \rightarrow B(x,x).$$

The reader is invited to verify that $\mathcal{M}'$ is indeed an inverse, and that it cannot be specified by a finite set of tgds.   □

Proposition 20.38 shows that the language of tgds is not closed under the notion of inverse. By combining this result with Propositions 20.27 and 20.28, we conclude that the same holds for the notions of quasi-inverse and maximum recovery.

Corollary 20.39   *There exists a mapping $\mathcal{M} = (\mathbf{R_1}, \mathbf{R_2}, \Sigma)$ specified by a finite set Σ of full st-tgds that is quasi-invertible, but has neither a quasi-inverse nor a maximum recovery specified by a finite set of tgds.*

20.4 Inverses under extended semantics

So far we have assumed that source instances do not contain null values. However, null values in the source may naturally arise when using inverses of mappings to exchange data. Indeed, we apply inverses to databases containing exchanged data, which, of course, contains nulls. Thus, when we handle inverse operators, it seems natural to let databases contain both constants and nulls, i.e., values from $\text{CONST} \cup \text{VAR}$.

In this section, we introduce two appropriate notions for the scenario of whether source instances may contain nulls, namely *extended recovery* and *maximum extended recovery*, and compare them with the previously proposed notions of recovery and maximum recovery.

The first observation to make is that since null values are intended to represent *missing* or *unknown* information, they should not be treated naïvely as constants. In fact, if null values are treated as constants when verifying the satisfaction of a set of dependencies, then the existence of maximum recoveries for mappings given by tgds is no longer guaranteed.

Proposition 20.40 *If null values are treated as constants, then there exists a mapping specified by a finite set of tgds and containing null values in sources instances that does not admit a maximum recovery.*

Proof Let $\mathcal{M} = (\mathbf{R_1}, \mathbf{R_2}, \Sigma)$, where $\mathbf{R_1}$ is a schema consisting of unary relations A and B, $\mathbf{R_2}$ is a schema consisting of a unary relation E and Σ is a set consisting of the following tgds:

$$A(x) \rightarrow E(x)$$
$$B(x) \rightarrow \exists y E(y).$$

Moreover, assume that the instances of $\mathbf{R_1}$ may contain null values. Next we show that $\mathcal{M}$ does not admit a maximum recovery if nulls are treated as constants when verifying the satisfaction of Σ.

For the sake of contradiction, assume that $\mathcal{M}$ admits a maximum recovery, and let S_1 be an instance of $\mathbf{R_1}$ such that $A^{S_1} = \emptyset$ and $B^{S_1} = \{a\}$, where a is a constant. Then we have from Theorem 20.25 that S_1 has a witness solution under $\mathcal{M}$, say instance T_1 of $\mathbf{R_2}$. Given that the empty instance of $\mathbf{R_2}$ is not a solution for S_1 under $\mathcal{M}$, we have that $E^{T_1} \neq \emptyset$. Thus, we have to consider two cases.

- Assume first that there exists a constant b such that $E(b)$ is a fact in T_1, and let S_2 be an instance of $\mathbf{R_1}$ such that $A^{S_2} = \{b\}$ and $B^{S_2} = \emptyset$. Then we have that $(S_2, T_1) \models \Sigma$ and, therefore $T_1 \in \text{SOL}_{\mathcal{M}}(S_2)$. Thus, from the fact that T_1 is a witness for S_1 under $\mathcal{M}$, we conclude that $\text{SOL}_{\mathcal{M}}(S_1) \subseteq \text{SOL}_{\mathcal{M}}(S_2)$. But this leads to a contradiction since the instance of $\mathbf{R_2}$ consisting of fact $E(c)$, where $c \neq b$ is a constant, is a solution for S_1 under $\mathcal{M}$, but it is not a solution for S_2 under $\mathcal{M}$.
- Second, suppose that there exists a null value n such that $E(n)$ is a fact in T_1, and let S_3 be an instance of $\mathbf{R_1}$ such that $A^{S_3} = \{n\}$ and $B^{S_3} = \emptyset$ (notice that S_3 is an instance of $\mathbf{R_1}$ containing null values). Then given that we are treating null values as constants, we

have that $(S_3, T_1) \models \Sigma$ and, therefore $T_1 \in \text{SOL}_{\mathcal{M}}(S_3)$. Thus, from the fact that T_1 is a witness for S_1 under $\mathcal{M}$, we conclude that $\text{SOL}_{\mathcal{M}}(S_1) \subseteq \text{SOL}_{\mathcal{M}}(S_3)$. But this leads to a contradiction since the instance of $\mathbf{R_2}$ consisting of fact $E(n')$, where $n' \neq n$ is a null value, is a solution for S_1 under $\mathcal{M}$, but it is not a solution for S_3 under $\mathcal{M}$ (since null values n, n' are treated as constants). This concludes the proof of the proposition. $\square$

To distinguish handling nulls from handling constants, we shall consider closing mappings under homomorphisms. The intuition behind this approach is that nulls are intended to represent unknown data and, thus, it should be possible to replace them by arbitrary values. Formally, given a mapping $\mathcal{M}$ from a schema $\mathbf{R_1}$ to a schema $\mathbf{R_2}$, define $e(\mathcal{M})$, the *homomorphic extension* of $\mathcal{M}$, as the mapping:

$$\{(S, T) \mid \text{there exists } (S', T') \in \mathcal{M} \text{ and}$$
$$\text{homomorphisms from } S \text{ to } S' \text{ and from } T' \text{ to } T\}.$$

Thus, for a mapping $\mathcal{M}$ that has nulls in source and target instances, one does not have to consider $\mathcal{M}$ but $e(\mathcal{M})$ as the mapping to deal with when exchanging data, and computing mapping operators, since $e(\mathcal{M})$ treats nulls in a meaningful way.

Example 20.41 Assume that $\mathcal{M}$ is a mapping specified by tgd $A(x) \rightarrow B(x)$, and let S_1 be a source instance consisting of fact $A(n)$, where n is a null value. What should be the solutions for S_1 under $\mathcal{M}$? Given that null values represent missing information, from the fact that $A(n)$ holds in S_1, we can infer that there exists a tuple in table A in this instance, but we cannot infer what this value is. Thus, if T is a solution for S_1 under $\mathcal{M}$, then one should be able to infer from the information in T that there exists a tuple in table B. In particular, if T is an instance of $\mathbf{R_2}$ containing a fact $B(a)$, where a is either a constant or a null value, then T should be a solution for S_1 under $\mathcal{M}$. This intuition is correctly taken into consideration in the definition of $e(\mathcal{M})$, as we have that:

$$\text{SOL}_{e(\mathcal{M})}(S_1) = \{T \mid T \text{ is an instance of } \mathbf{R_2} \text{ and } B^T \neq \emptyset\}.$$

Now let S_2 be a source instance consisting of facts $A(n_1)$ and $A(n_2)$, where n_1 and n_2 are distinct null values. What should be the solutions for S_2 under $\mathcal{M}$? Given that one cannot infer from the name of a null value any information about the constant value represented by it, one cannot infer that two distinct null values represent two distinct constants. Thus, since S_2 is given by facts $A(n_1)$ and $A(n_2)$, we only know that there exists a tuple in table A in this instance and, thus, it should be the case that $\text{SOL}_{e(\mathcal{M})}(S_2) = \text{SOL}_{e(\mathcal{M})}(S_1)$. The intuition behind the definition of $e(\mathcal{M})$ takes this into consideration, as the space of solutions for an instance S under $e(\mathcal{M})$ is constructed by considering an instance S' of $\mathbf{R_1}$ such that there exists a homomorphism from S to S'. In fact, if two instances are homomorphically equivalent, like S_1 and S_2, then they have the same space of solutions under $e(\mathcal{M})$. $\square$

The following theorem shows that with this new semantics, one can avoid anomalies such as the one shown in Proposition 20.40. In fact, the theorem shows that maximum recoveries are guaranteed to exist when considering the extended semantics for mappings given by tgds, and containing null values in source and target instances.

Theorem 20.42 *For every mapping $\mathcal{M}$ specified by a finite set of tgds and containing null values in source and target instances, $e(\mathcal{M})$ admits a maximum recovery.*

The notion of a homomorphic extension gives rise to the notion of maximum extended recovery.

Definition 20.43 (Maximum extended recovery)   Let $\mathcal{M}$ be a mapping from a schema $\mathbf{R_1}$ to a schema $\mathbf{R_2}$ and $\mathcal{M}'$ a mapping from $\mathbf{R_2}$ to $\mathbf{R_1}$. Then

1. $\mathcal{M}'$ is an *extended recovery* of $\mathcal{M}$ if for every instance S of $\mathbf{R_1}$, it holds that $(S,S) \in e(\mathcal{M}) \circ e(\mathcal{M}')$;
2. $\mathcal{M}'$ is a *maximum extended recovery* of $\mathcal{M}$ if $\mathcal{M}'$ is an extended recovery of $\mathcal{M}$, and for every extended recovery $\mathcal{M}''$ of $\mathcal{M}$, we have $e(\mathcal{M}) \circ e(\mathcal{M}') \subseteq e(\mathcal{M}) \circ e(\mathcal{M}'')$. □

At first glance, one may be tempted to think that the notions of maximum recovery and maximum extended recovery are incomparable. However, the following theorem shows that there is a tight connection between these two notions and, in particular, shows that the notion of maximum extended recovery can be defined in terms of the notion of maximum recovery. It is important to notice that a mapping $\mathcal{M}$ admits a (maximum) extended recovery only if the domain of $e(\mathcal{M})$ is the set of all source instances. Thus, it is only meaningful to compare the notions of (maximum) extended recovery and (maximum) recovery under this restriction and, therefore, the following theorem considers a mapping $\mathcal{M}$ from a schema $\mathbf{R_1}$ to a schema $\mathbf{R_2}$ such that $\mathrm{DOM}(e(\mathcal{M})) = \mathrm{INST}(\mathbf{R_1})$.

Theorem 20.44 *Let $\mathcal{M}$ be a mapping from a schema $\mathbf{R_1}$ to a schema $\mathbf{R_2}$ such that $\mathrm{DOM}(e(\mathcal{M})) = \mathrm{INST}(\mathbf{R_1})$. Then*

1. *$\mathcal{M}$ admits a maximum extended recovery if and only if $e(\mathcal{M})$ admits a maximum recovery.*
2. *A mapping $\mathcal{M}'$ is a maximum extended recovery of $\mathcal{M}$ if and only if $e(\mathcal{M}')$ is a maximum recovery of $e(\mathcal{M})$.*

Proof We first introduce some notation to simplify the exposition. Consider a binary relation $\rightarrow$ defined as follows:

$$\rightarrow \; = \{(S_1, S_2) \mid \text{there exists a homomorphism from } S_1 \text{ to } S_2\}.$$

The introduction of relation $\rightarrow$ allows us to simplify the definition of the extended semantics of a mapping. In fact, given a mapping $\mathcal{M}$, we have that

$$e(\mathcal{M}) = \; \rightarrow \circ \; \mathcal{M} \circ \rightarrow .$$

Notice that the relation $\rightarrow$ is *idempotent*, that is, it holds that $(\rightarrow \circ \rightarrow) \;=\; \rightarrow$. In particular, we have that

$$\rightarrow \circ\, e(\mathcal{M}) = e(\mathcal{M}), \tag{20.16}$$

$$e(\mathcal{M}) \circ \rightarrow \;=\; e(\mathcal{M}). \tag{20.17}$$

Thus, if S_1, S_2, T are instances such that $(S_1, S_2) \in \,\rightarrow$ and $(S_2, T) \in e(\mathcal{M})$, then $(S_1, T) \in e(\mathcal{M})$. Hence, if $(S_1, S_2) \in \,\rightarrow$, then it holds that $\mathrm{SOL}_{e(\mathcal{M})}(S_2) \subseteq \mathrm{SOL}_{e(\mathcal{M})}(S_1)$. We use this property in the proof.

(1) We first show that $\mathcal{M}$ admits a maximum extended recovery if and only if $e(\mathcal{M})$ admits a maximum recovery.

($\Leftarrow$) Let $\mathcal{M}'$ be a maximum recovery of $e(\mathcal{M})$. We show next that $\mathcal{M}'$ is also a maximum extended recovery of $\mathcal{M}$. Since $\mathcal{M}'$ is a recovery of $e(\mathcal{M})$, we have that $(S, S) \in e(\mathcal{M}) \circ \mathcal{M}'$ for every instance S of $\mathbf{R}_1$. Moreover, from (20.17) we have that $e(\mathcal{M}) \circ \mathcal{M}' = e(\mathcal{M}) \circ \rightarrow \circ \mathcal{M}'$ and, thus, $(S, S) \in e(\mathcal{M}) \circ \rightarrow \circ \mathcal{M}'$ for every instance S of $\mathbf{R}_1$. Thus, given that $(S, S) \in \,\rightarrow$ for every instance S of $\mathbf{R}_1$, we obtain that $(S, S) \in e(\mathcal{M}) \circ \rightarrow \circ \mathcal{M}' \circ \rightarrow \;=\; e(\mathcal{M}) \circ e(\mathcal{M}')$ for every instance S of $\mathbf{R}_1$, which implies that $\mathcal{M}'$ is an extended recovery of $\mathcal{M}$.

Now, let $\mathcal{M}''$ be an extended recovery of $\mathcal{M}$. Then we have that $(S, S) \in e(\mathcal{M}) \circ e(\mathcal{M}'')$ for every instance S of $\mathbf{R}_1$, and, hence, we have that $e(\mathcal{M}'')$ is a recovery of $e(\mathcal{M})$. Recall that $\mathcal{M}'$ is a maximum recovery of $e(\mathcal{M})$ and, hence, we have that $e(\mathcal{M}) \circ \mathcal{M}' \subseteq e(\mathcal{M}) \circ e(\mathcal{M}'')$, which implies that $e(\mathcal{M}) \circ \mathcal{M}' \circ \rightarrow \;\subseteq\; e(\mathcal{M}) \circ e(\mathcal{M}'') \circ \rightarrow$. Therefore, given that $e(\mathcal{M}) = e(\mathcal{M}) \circ \rightarrow$ and $e(\mathcal{M}'') \circ \rightarrow \;=\; e(\mathcal{M}'')$ by (20.17), we have that $e(\mathcal{M}) \circ \rightarrow \circ \mathcal{M}' \circ \rightarrow \;\subseteq\; e(\mathcal{M}) \circ e(\mathcal{M}'')$, which implies that $e(\mathcal{M}) \circ e(\mathcal{M}') \subseteq e(\mathcal{M}) \circ e(\mathcal{M}'')$. Thus, we have shown that $\mathcal{M}'$ is an extended recovery of $\mathcal{M}$, and that for every other extended recovery $\mathcal{M}''$ of $\mathcal{M}$, it holds that $e(\mathcal{M}) \circ e(\mathcal{M}') \subseteq e(\mathcal{M}) \circ e(\mathcal{M}'')$, which implies that $\mathcal{M}'$ is a maximum extended recovery of $\mathcal{M}$.

($\Rightarrow$) Let $\mathcal{M}'$ be a maximum extended recovery of $\mathcal{M}$. Next we show that $e(\mathcal{M}')$ is a maximum recovery of $e(\mathcal{M})$.

Given that $\mathcal{M}'$ is an extended recovery of $\mathcal{M}$, we have that $(S, S) \in e(\mathcal{M}) \circ e(\mathcal{M}')$ for every instance S of $\mathbf{R}_1$, which implies that $e(\mathcal{M}')$ is a recovery of $e(\mathcal{M})$. Thus, by Proposition 20.21, to prove that $e(\mathcal{M}')$ is a maximum recovery of $e(\mathcal{M})$, it is enough to show that $\mathrm{SOL}_{e(\mathcal{M})}(S_2) \subseteq \mathrm{SOL}_{e(\mathcal{M})}(S_1)$ for every $(S_1, S_2) \in e(\mathcal{M}) \circ e(\mathcal{M}')$, since this fact implies that $e(\mathcal{M}) \circ e(\mathcal{M}') \circ e(\mathcal{M}) \subseteq e(\mathcal{M})$. Let $(S_1, S_2) \in e(\mathcal{M}) \circ e(\mathcal{M}')$. To prove that $\mathrm{SOL}_{e(\mathcal{M})}(S_2) \subseteq \mathrm{SOL}_{e(\mathcal{M})}(S_1)$, we make use of the following mapping $\mathcal{M}^\star$ from $\mathbf{R}_2$ to $\mathbf{R}_1$:

$$\mathcal{M}^\star = \{(T, S) \mid S \text{ is an instance of } \mathbf{R}_1 \text{ and } (S_1, T) \notin e(\mathcal{M})\} \,\cup$$
$$\{(T, S) \mid (S_1, T) \in e(\mathcal{M}) \text{ and } \mathrm{SOL}_{e(\mathcal{M})}(S) \subseteq \mathrm{SOL}_{e(\mathcal{M})}(S_1)\}.$$

We show first that $\mathcal{M}^\star$ is an extended recovery of $\mathcal{M}$, that is, we show that for every instance S of $\mathbf{R}_1$, it holds that $(S, S) \in e(\mathcal{M}) \circ e(\mathcal{M}^\star)$. First, assume that $\mathrm{SOL}_{e(\mathcal{M})}(S) \subseteq \mathrm{SOL}_{e(\mathcal{M})}(S_1)$, and consider an arbitrary instance $T^\star$ such that $(S, T^\star) \in e(\mathcal{M})$. Notice that $(S_1, T^\star) \in e(\mathcal{M})$ since $\mathrm{SOL}_{e(\mathcal{M})}(S) \subseteq \mathrm{SOL}_{e(\mathcal{M})}(S_1)$. Thus, we have that $(T^\star, S) \in \mathcal{M}^\star$ and, hence, $(T^\star, S) \in e(\mathcal{M}^\star)$. Therefore, given that $(S, T^\star) \in e(\mathcal{M})$ and $(T^\star, S) \in e(\mathcal{M}^\star)$, we conclude that $(S, S) \in e(\mathcal{M}) \circ e(\mathcal{M}^\star)$. Second, assume that $\text{SOL}_{e(\mathcal{M})}(S) \not\subseteq \text{SOL}_{e(\mathcal{M})}(S_1)$. Then there exists an instance $T^\star$ such that $(S, T^\star) \in e(\mathcal{M})$ and $(S_1, T^\star) \notin e(\mathcal{M})$. By definition of $\mathcal{M}^\star$, we have that $(T^\star, S) \in \mathcal{M}^\star$ and, thus, $(T^\star, S) \in e(\mathcal{M}^\star)$. Thus, we also conclude that $(S, S) \in e(\mathcal{M}) \circ e(\mathcal{M}^\star)$ in this case.

We are now ready to prove that for every $(S_1, S_2) \in e(\mathcal{M}) \circ e(\mathcal{M}')$, it holds that $\text{SOL}_{e(\mathcal{M})}(S_2) \subseteq \text{SOL}_{e(\mathcal{M})}(S_1)$. Let $(S_1, S_2) \in e(\mathcal{M}) \circ e(\mathcal{M}')$. Given that $\mathcal{M}'$ is a maximum extended recovery of $\mathcal{M}$ and $\mathcal{M}^\star$ is an extended recovery of $\mathcal{M}$, we have that $e(\mathcal{M}) \circ e(\mathcal{M}') \subseteq e(\mathcal{M}) \circ e(\mathcal{M}^\star)$ and, therefore, $(S_1, S_2) \in e(\mathcal{M}) \circ e(\mathcal{M}^\star)$. Thus, given that $e(\mathcal{M}) \circ e(\mathcal{M}^\star) = e(\mathcal{M}) \circ \mathcal{M}^\star \circ \to$ by (20.17), we conclude that there exist instances T of $\mathbf{R_2}$ and S_2' of $\mathbf{R_1}$ such that $(S_1, T) \in e(\mathcal{M})$, $(T, S_2') \in \mathcal{M}^\star$ and $(S_2', S_2) \in \to$. Hence, by definition of $\mathcal{M}^\star$, we have that $\text{SOL}_{e(\mathcal{M})}(S_2') \subseteq \text{SOL}_{e(\mathcal{M})}(S_1)$ (since $(S_1, T) \in e(\mathcal{M})$). But we also have that $\text{SOL}_{e(\mathcal{M})}(S_2) \subseteq \text{SOL}_{e(\mathcal{M})}(S_2')$ since $(S_2', S_2) \in \to$, and, therefore, we conclude that $\text{SOL}_{e(\mathcal{M})}(S_2) \subseteq \text{SOL}_{e(\mathcal{M})}(S_1)$, which was to be shown.

(2) Up to this point, we have shown that $\mathcal{M}$ admits a maximum extended recovery if and only if $e(\mathcal{M})$ admits a maximum recovery. In fact, we conclude from the preceding proof that:

- if $e(\mathcal{M})$ has a maximum recovery $\mathcal{M}'$, then $\mathcal{M}'$ is a maximum extended recovery of $\mathcal{M}$, and
- if $\mathcal{M}$ has a maximum extended recovery $\mathcal{M}'$, then $e(\mathcal{M}')$ is a maximum recovery of $e(\mathcal{M})$.

Next we prove the second part of the proposition, that is, we prove that a mapping $\mathcal{M}'$ is a maximum extended recovery of $\mathcal{M}$ if and only if $e(\mathcal{M}')$ is a maximum recovery of $e(\mathcal{M})$. It should be noticed that the "only if" direction corresponds to the second item above and, thus, we only need to show that if $e(\mathcal{M}')$ is a maximum recovery of $e(\mathcal{M})$, then $\mathcal{M}'$ is a maximum extended recovery of $\mathcal{M}$.

Assume that $e(\mathcal{M}')$ is a maximum recovery of $e(\mathcal{M})$. Then we have that $e(\mathcal{M}')$ is a recovery of $e(\mathcal{M})$ and, thus, $\mathcal{M}'$ is an extended recovery of $\mathcal{M}$. Now let $\mathcal{M}''$ be an extended recovery of $\mathcal{M}$. Then we have that $e(\mathcal{M}'')$ is a recovery of $e(\mathcal{M})$ and, hence, $e(\mathcal{M}) \circ e(\mathcal{M}') \subseteq e(\mathcal{M}) \circ e(\mathcal{M}'')$ since $e(\mathcal{M}')$ is a maximum recovery of $e(\mathcal{M})$. Therefore, we conclude that $\mathcal{M}'$ is an extended recovery of $\mathcal{M}$, and for every extended recovery $\mathcal{M}''$ of $\mathcal{M}$, it holds that $e(\mathcal{M}) \circ e(\mathcal{M}') \subseteq e(\mathcal{M}) \circ e(\mathcal{M}'')$, which means that $\mathcal{M}'$ is a maximum extended recovery of $\mathcal{M}$. This completes the proof of the proposition. $\square$

From Theorems 20.42 and 20.44, we obtain as a corollary that every mapping specified by a finite set of tgds and containing nulls in the source has a maximum extended recovery.

Corollary 20.45 *If $\mathcal{M}$ is a mapping specified by a finite set of tgds and containing null values in source and target instances, then $\mathcal{M}$ admits a maximum extended recovery.*

Finally, another conclusion that can be drawn from Theorem 20.44 is that the machinery developed for the notion of maximum recovery in Section 20.2 can be applied over maximum extended recoveries, and the extended semantics for mappings, thus helping in the study of mappings with null values in the source.

21

Structural characterizations of schema mapping

Mappings are logical specifications of the relationship between schemas. In data exchange, one typically restricts the kind of dependencies allowed in mappings, either to be able to find more efficient procedures for constructing solutions and answering target queries, or to make mappings have desirable properties, such as closure under composition. These two tasks could be contradictory. For instance, the mapping language of SO tgds ensures closure under composition, but such mappings include a form of second-order quantification that can be difficult to handle in practice. Thus, it is desirable to replace an SO tgd by an equivalent set of st-tgds whenever possible.

In this chapter, we consider the problem of simplifying schema mappings by providing characterizations of the most common classes of mappings in terms of the structural properties they satisfy. The main goal for studying these properties is to isolate the features that different classes of mappings satisfy, and to understand what one can lose or gain by switching from one class of mappings to another. We present basic structural properties and then we use them to characterize the class of mappings specified by st-tgds, both generally, and in LAV and GAV scenarios. We also show that the structural characterizations can be used to derive complexity-theoretical results for testing definability of a mapping into some class of mappings.

21.1 Structural properties

In this chapter, we restrict our attention to mappings that do not make use of target dependencies. We now view mappings in a purely semantic way: we think of them as binary relations. Formally, in this section a mapping $\mathcal{M}$ from a source schema $\mathbf{R_s}$ to a target schema $\mathbf{R_t}$ is a set of pairs (S, T) in $\text{INST}(\mathbf{R_s}) \times \text{INST}(\mathbf{R_t})$. The only restriction we impose on them is that they must be closed under isomorphisms. By isomorphisms we mean isomorphisms in the usual mathematical sense: in particular, they do not distinguish between constants and null values, thus they can map a constant to a null value and vice versa. For example, if a pair of instances with the source $\{(\perp, 1)\}$ and the target $\{(1, \perp)\}$ is in the mapping, then a pair of instances with the source $\{(5, \perp')\}$ and the target $\{(\perp', 5)\}$ is in the mapping too, since they represent the same transformation: swapping the elements.

However, the isomorphism between the two sends null $\perp$ to constant 1, and constant 5 to null $\perp'$.

Likewise, in this section, homomorphisms are not necessarily the identity on constants (and can, for instance, send constants to nulls), unless they are explicitly required to be such.

We say that $\mathcal{M}$ is *defined* by a finite set Σ_{st} of st-tgds if for each pair $(S, T) \in \text{INST}(\mathbf{R_s}) \times \text{INST}(\mathbf{R_t})$, we have

$$(S, T) \in \mathcal{M} \iff (S, T) \models \Sigma_{st}.$$

There are several desirable structural properties that one would like the mappings to satisfy. A prototypical example of such a desirable property for a schema mapping is the existence of universal solutions. In this chapter, we consider this property together with some other desirable features. More precisely, assume that $\mathcal{M}$ is a mapping from a source schema $\mathbf{R_s}$ to a target schema $\mathbf{R_t}$. Then

- $\mathcal{M}$ *admits universal solutions* if every source instance S of $\mathbf{R_s}$ has a universal solution under $\mathcal{M}$;
- $\mathcal{M}$ is *closed under target homomorphisms* if for every $(S, T) \in \mathcal{M}$ and every homomorphism $h : T \to T'$ that is the identity on constants, we have $(S, T') \in \mathcal{M}$;
- $\mathcal{M}$ *reflects source homomorphisms* reflecting if for every pair S, S' of instances of $\mathbf{R_s}$, and every pair T, T' of instances of $\mathbf{R_t}$ such that T, T' are universal solutions for S, S' under $\mathcal{M}$, respectively, every homomorphism $h : S \to S'$ can be extended to a homomorphism $h' : T \to T'$.

Notice that in the third property above, neither h nor h' are required to be the identity on constants. For the class of mappings specified by st-tgds, the following holds.

Proposition 21.1 *Every mapping specified by a finite set of st-tgds admits universal solutions, is closed under target homomorphisms, and reflects source homomorphisms.*

Clearly, every mapping specified by a finite set of st-tgds admits universal solutions and is closed under target homomorphisms. We leave it as an exercise for the reader to prove that these mappings also reflect source homomorphisms (see Exercise 22.3). In the following section, we study the problem of characterizing the class of mappings defined by st-tgds by using the above structural properties.

21.2 Schema mapping languages characterizations

Proposition 21.1 shows three fundamental properties satisfied by all mappings given by st-tgds. Thus, it is natural to ask whether these properties characterize this class of mappings. We give a negative answer to this question in the following proposition, where we also identify another fundamental property that mappings given by st-tgds satisfy.

Proposition 21.2 *There exists a mapping $\mathcal{M}$ that is closed under target homomorphisms,* *admits universal solutions, reflects source homomorphisms, but cannot be defined by a finite set of st-tgds.*

Proof Let $\mathbf{R_s}$ be a source schema consisting of a binary predicate U, $\mathbf{R_t}$ be a target schema consisting of a binary predicate V and $\mathscr{M}$ be a mapping from $\mathbf{R_s}$ to $\mathbf{R_t}$ specified by the following dependency:

$$\varphi = \forall x \exists y \forall z \, (U(x,z) \rightarrow V(y,z)).$$

We leave it as an exercise for the reader to prove that $\mathscr{M}$ is closed under target homomorphisms, admits universal solutions and reflects source homomorphisms (see Exercise 22.3). Next we show that $\mathscr{M}$ cannot be defined by a finite set of st-tgds.

For the sake of contradiction, assume that $\mathscr{M}$ is defined by a finite set Σ_{st} of st-tgds, and let n be the maximum number of variables occurring in the left-hand side of an st-tgd in Σ_{st}.

Claim 21.3 *If S, T are instances of $\mathbf{R_s}$ and $\mathbf{R_t}$, respectively, such that $(S,T) \notin \mathscr{M}$, then it has a subinstance $S' \subseteq S$ such that $|\mathrm{DOM}(S')| \leq n$ and $(S',T) \notin \mathscr{M}$.*

Proof Given that $\mathscr{M}$ is defined by Σ_{st}, we need to prove that if S, T are instances of $\mathbf{R_s}$ and $\mathbf{R_t}$, respectively, such that $(S,T) \not\models \Sigma_{st}$, then there exists a subinstance $S' \subseteq S$ such that $|\mathrm{DOM}(S')| \leq n$ and $(S',T) \not\models \Sigma_{st}$. Notice that if $(S,T) \not\models \Sigma_{st}$, then there exists an st-tgd $\varphi(\bar{x},\bar{y}) \rightarrow \exists \bar{z} \, \psi(\bar{x},\bar{z})$ in Σ_{st} and tuples $\bar{a}$, $\bar{b}$ of elements from $\mathrm{DOM}(S)$ such that $S \models \varphi(\bar{a},\bar{b})$ and $T \not\models \exists \bar{z} \, \psi(\bar{a},\bar{z})$. Let S' be the subinstance of S induced by the elements in $\bar{a}$, $\bar{b}$. Clearly, $S' \models \varphi(\bar{a},\bar{b})$. Thus, we have $|\mathrm{DOM}(S')| \leq n$ since $|\bar{a}| + |\bar{b}| \leq n$, and $(S',T) \not\models \Sigma_{st}$ since $S' \models \varphi(\bar{a},\bar{b})$ and $T \not\models \exists \bar{z} \, \psi(\bar{a},\bar{z})$. □

Let $\perp_1$, ..., $\perp_{n+1}$ be a sequence of pairwise distinct null values, S be the following instance of $\mathbf{R_s}$:

$$U^S = \{(1,i) \mid 1 \leq i \leq n+1\},$$

and T be the following instance of $\mathbf{R_t}$:

$$V^T = \{(\perp_i, j) \mid 1 \leq i \leq n+1, \ 1 \leq j \leq n+1 \text{ and } i \neq j\}.$$

Then we have $(S,T) \not\models \varphi$, as for every $i \in \{1,\dots,n+1\}$, it holds that $(1,i) \in U^S$ but $(\perp_i, i) \notin V^T$. Furthermore, for every subinstance $S' \subseteq S$ such that $|\mathrm{DOM}(S')| \leq n$, we have $(S',T) \models \varphi$. To see this, notice that if $S' \subseteq S$ and $|\mathrm{DOM}(S')| \leq n$, then there is $k \in \{1,\dots,n+1\}$ such that $(1,k) \notin U^{S'}$. But then $(S',T) \models \varphi$ as for every tuple $(1,i) \in U^{S'}$, it holds that $(\perp_k, i) \in V^T$. Thus, we have obtained a contradiction, since φ defines $\mathscr{M}$ and instances S, T do not satisfy the statement of Claim 21.3. □

In the proof of Proposition 21.2, we identified the following structural property:

- **n-modularity:** Assume that $\mathscr{M}$ is a mapping from a source schema $\mathbf{R_s}$ to a target schema $\mathbf{R_t}$. Then $\mathscr{M}$ is n-modular, $n \geq 1$, if for every instance S of $\mathbf{R_s}$ and every instance T of

R$_t$, if $(S,T) \notin \mathcal{M}$, then there exists a subinstance $S' \subseteq S$ such that $|\text{DOM}(S')| \leq n$ and $(S',T) \notin \mathcal{M}$.

In fact, what we showed in the proof of Proposition 21.2 is that if a mapping $\mathcal{M}$ is specified by a finite set of st-tgds, then $\mathcal{M}$ is n-modular, where n is the maximum number of variables occurring in the left-hand side of a dependency in Σ_{st}. Interestingly, it can be shown that n-modularity, together with the basic properties presented in the previous section, precisely characterize the mappings that can be defined by finite sets of st-tgds.

Theorem 21.4 *A mapping can be defined by a finite set of st-tgds if and only if it is closed under target homomorphisms, admits universal solutions, reflects source homomorphism, and is n-modular for some $n \geq 1$.*

Proof We have already shown that if a mapping $\mathcal{M}$ is defined by a finite set of st-tgds, then it satisfies the four properties mentioned in the statement of the theorem. Thus, we only need to prove one direction of the theorem.

Assume that $\mathcal{M}$ is a mapping from a source schema **R$_s$** to a target schema **R$_t$** that satisfies the four properties in the statement of the theorem. Then for every instance S of **R$_s$**, choose an arbitrary universal solution T for S under $\mathcal{M}$ (it exists since $\mathcal{M}$ admits universal solutions), and define a st-tgd $\theta_{S,T}$ as follows. Assume that ρ is a one-to-one function that associates to each element in $(\text{DOM}(S) \cup \text{DOM}(T))$ a fresh variable, and assume that $\bar{x} = (\rho(a_1),\ldots,\rho(a_i))$, where $\{a_1,\ldots,a_i\} = (\text{DOM}(S) \cap \text{DOM}(T))$, $\bar{y} = (\rho(b_1),\ldots,\rho(b_j))$, where $\{b_1,\ldots,b_j\} = (\text{DOM}(S) \smallsetminus \text{DOM}(T))$, and $\bar{z} = (\rho(c_1),\ldots,\rho(c_k))$, where $\{c_1,\ldots,c_k\} = (\text{DOM}(T) \smallsetminus \text{DOM}(S))$.

It is important to notice that every element in the set $(\text{DOM}(T) \smallsetminus \text{DOM}(S))$ is a null value. Indeed, assume otherwise, and let a be a constant that occurs in $(\text{DOM}(T) \smallsetminus \text{DOM}(S))$. Since $\mathcal{M}$ is closed under isomorphisms, any instance T' in which a is replaced by a null $\perp$ not occurring elsewhere in T is also a solution for S. But then we have a homomorphism (in the usual data-exchange sense) from T' to T (sending $\perp$ to a) but not the other way around. This contradicts our assumption that T is universal. Thus, indeed, $(\text{DOM}(T) \smallsetminus \text{DOM}(S))$ contains only nulls.

We define $\varphi_S(\bar{x},\bar{y})$ as the conjunction of all atomic formulae $U(\rho(u_1),\ldots,\rho(u_\ell))$ such that $U(u_1,\ldots,u_\ell)$ holds in S, and $\psi_T(\bar{x},\bar{z})$ as the conjunction of all atomic formulae $V(\rho(v_1),\ldots,\rho(v_m))$ such that $V(v_1,\ldots,v_m)$ holds in T. Then $\theta_{S,T}$ is defined as the st-tgd $\varphi_S(\bar{x},\bar{y}) \rightarrow \exists \bar{z}\, \psi_T(\bar{x},\bar{z})$.

Let $S_1, \ldots, S_k$ be a sequence of pairwise nonisomorphic instances of **R$_s$** such that for every instance S of **R$_s$** satisfying $|\text{DOM}(S)| \leq n$, it holds that S is isomorphic to S_i for some $i \in \{1,\ldots,k\}$. Then define Σ_{st} as the following set of st-tgds:

$$\{\theta_{S_i,T_i} \mid 1 \leq i \leq k\}.$$

Next we show that mapping $\mathcal{M}$ is defined by Σ_{st}, that is, we prove that given instances S, T of **R$_s$** and **R$_t$**, respectively, it holds that $(S,T) \in \mathcal{M}$ if and only if $(S,T) \models \Sigma_{st}$. Notice that given that Σ_{st} is a finite set of st-tgds, we conclude that the theorem holds.

($\Rightarrow$) Assume that $(S,T) \in \mathscr{M}$ and that $\varphi_{S_i}(\bar{x}, \bar{y}) \rightarrow \exists \bar{z}\, \psi_{T_i}(\bar{x}, \bar{z})$ is a dependency in Σ_{st} such that $S \models \varphi_{S_i}(\bar{a}, \bar{b})$ for some tuples $\bar{a}$, $\bar{b}$ of values from $\mathrm{DOM}(S)$. We need to prove that $T \models \exists \bar{z}\, \psi_{T_i}(\bar{a}, \bar{z})$.

Given that $S \models \varphi_{S_i}(\bar{a}, \bar{b})$, we have by definition of $\varphi_{S_i}(\bar{x}, \bar{y})$ that there exists a homomorphism h from S_i to S. In particular, if $\bar{c}$, $\bar{d}$ are the tuples of elements from $\mathrm{DOM}(S_i)$ such that $\rho(\bar{c}) = \bar{x}$ and $\rho(\bar{d}) = \bar{y}$, then we have $h(\bar{c}) = \bar{a}$ and $h(\bar{d}) = \bar{b}$. Given that $\mathscr{M}$ reflects source homomorphisms, there exists a homomorphism $h^\star$ from T_i to $T^\star$ that extends h, where $T^\star$ is an arbitrary universal solution for S under $\mathscr{M}$ (such a solution exists since $\mathscr{M}$ admits universal solutions). Thus, given that $T_i \models \exists \bar{z}\, \psi_{T_i}(\bar{c}, \bar{z})$ by the definition of ψ_{T_i}, we conclude that $T^\star \models \exists \bar{z}\, \psi_{T_i}(\bar{a}, \bar{z})$ since $h^\star$ is a homomorphism from T_i to $T^\star$ that extends h (hence, $h^\star(\bar{c}) = h(\bar{c}) = \bar{a}$). Since $T^\star$ is a universal solution for S under $\mathscr{M}$ and $(S,T) \in \mathscr{M}$, there exists a homomorphism g from $T^\star$ to T that is the identity on constants. Therefore, given that $\bar{a}$ is a tuple of constants, we conclude that $T \models \exists \bar{z}\, \psi_{T_i}(\bar{a}, \bar{z})$ since $T^\star \models \exists \bar{z}\, \psi_{T_i}(\bar{a}, \bar{z})$, which was to be shown.

($\Leftarrow$) Assume that $(S,T) \notin \mathscr{M}$. Then we need to prove that $(S,T) \not\models \Sigma_{st}$.

Given that $(S,T) \notin \mathscr{M}$ and $\mathscr{M}$ is n-modular, there exists a subinstance $S' \subseteq S$ such that $|\mathrm{DOM}(S')| \leq n$ and $(S',T) \notin \mathscr{M}$. Thus, by the definition of Σ_{st} there exists an instance $S^\star$ of $\mathbf{R_s}$ such that S' and $S^\star$ are isomorphic and $\theta_{S^\star,T^\star} \in \Sigma_{st}$. Assume that $f : \mathrm{DOM}(S^\star) \to \mathrm{DOM}(S')$ is an isomorphism between $S^\star$ and S', and that $\bar{a}$, $\bar{b}$ are the tuples of elements from $S^\star$ used in the construction of $\varphi_{S^\star}(\bar{x}, \bar{y})$, that is, $\rho(\bar{x}) = \bar{a}$ and $\rho(\bar{y}) = \bar{b}$. Moreover, let T' be an instance of $\mathbf{R_t}$ obtained from $T^\star$ by replacing every element a in $\bar{a}$ by $f(a)$, and leaving the other elements unchanged. Notice that every element in $(\mathrm{DOM}(T') \setminus \mathrm{DOM}(S'))$ is a null value, as every element in $(\mathrm{DOM}(T^\star) \setminus \mathrm{DOM}(S^\star))$ is a null value given that $T^\star$ is a universal solution for $S^\star$ under $\mathscr{M}$ (by definition of $\theta_{S^\star,T^\star}$) and $\mathscr{M}$ is assumed to be closed under isomorphisms. Also notice that $(S',T') \in \mathscr{M}$, since $(S^\star,T^\star)$ is isomorphic to (S',T'), the pair $(S^\star,T^\star)$ is in $\mathscr{M}$ and $\mathscr{M}$ is closed under isomorphisms.

We claim that $(S',T) \not\models \theta_{S^\star,T^\star}$. To the contrary, assume that $(S',T) \models \theta_{S^\star,T^\star}$. Given that $S' \models \varphi_{S^\star}(f(\bar{a}), f(\bar{b}))$, we conclude that $T \models \exists \bar{z}\, \psi_{T^\star}(f(\bar{a}), \bar{z})$. Thus, by the definition of T' and given that every element in $(\mathrm{DOM}(T') \setminus \mathrm{DOM}(S'))$ is a null value, we conclude by the definition of $\psi_{T^\star}$ that there exists a homomorphism from T' to T that is the identity on constants. Therefore, given that $(S',T') \in \mathscr{M}$, we conclude that $(S',T) \in \mathscr{M}$ as this mapping is closed under target homomorphisms (that are the identity on constants). This obviously leads to a contradiction.

We have shown that $(S',T) \not\models \theta_{S^\star,T^\star}$. Since $S' \subseteq S$ and $\theta_{S^\star,T^\star}$ is a st-tgd, we have that $(S,T) \not\models \theta_{S^\star,T^\star}$. Hence, given that $\theta_{S^\star,T^\star} \in \Sigma_{st}$, we conclude that $(S,T) \not\models \Sigma_{st}$, which was to be shown. $\square$

A natural question at this point is whether any of the conditions introduced in this chapter can be withdrawn when characterizing LAV or GAV mappings. We show next that, indeed,

n-modularity can be removed in the LAV case, but at the cost of adding the following new structural property:

- **Closure under union:** A mapping $\mathcal{M}$ is *closed under union* if $(\emptyset, \emptyset) \in \mathcal{M}$, and $(S \cup S', T \cup T') \in \mathcal{M}$ whenever $(S, T) \in \mathcal{M}$ and $(S', T') \in \mathcal{M}$.

Notice that in the previous definition, instances S, S' are not assumed to be disjoint, and likewise for T, T'. It is easy to see that every LAV mapping is closed under union. On the other hand, as the following example shows, mappings defined by arbitrary sets of st-tgds do not have this property. Consider a mapping $\mathcal{M}$ defined by the following st-tgd:

$$L(x,y) \wedge L(y,x) \rightarrow E(x,y).$$

Then for the source instances $S = \{L(1,2)\}$, $S' = \{L(2,3)\}$, we have that $(S, \emptyset) \in \mathcal{M}$ and $(S', \emptyset) \in \mathcal{M}$. However, $(S \cup S', \emptyset)$ does not belong to $\mathcal{M}$, as fact $E(1,3)$ holds in every solution for $S \cup S'$ under $\mathcal{M}$, which shows that $\mathcal{M}$ is not closed under union. Notice that the previous st-tgd is full, and, therefore, we also conclude that GAV mappings are not closed under union.

Removing n-modularity and adding closure under union in the statement of Theorem 21.4 yields a characterization of the class of LAV mappings:

Theorem 21.5 *A mapping can be defined by a finite set of LAV st-tgds if and only if it is closed under target homomorphisms, admits universal solutions, reflects source homomorphisms, and is closed under union.*

Proof We have already shown that if a mapping $\mathcal{M}$ is defined by a finite set of LAV st-tgds, then it satisfies the four properties mentioned in the statement of the theorem. Thus, we only need to prove one direction of the theorem.

Assume that $\mathcal{M}$ is a mapping from a source schema $\mathbf{R_s}$ to a target schema $\mathbf{R_t}$ that satisfies the four properties in the statement of the theorem. Moreover, assume that $\mathbf{R_s} = \langle R_1, \ldots, R_m \rangle$, with each R_i having arity n_i, and suppose that $n = \max\{n_1, \ldots, n_m\}$. Then let $d_1, \ldots, d_n$ be a sequence of pairwise distinct constants, and for every $i \in \{1, \ldots, m\}$, let S_i be an instance of $\mathbf{R_s}$ such that:

$$R_j^{S_i} = \begin{cases} \{(d_1, \ldots, d_{n_i})\} & i = j \\ \emptyset & i \neq j. \end{cases}$$

For every instance S_i ($1 \leq i \leq m$) choose an arbitrary universal solution T_i for S_i under $\mathcal{M}$ (such an instance exists since $\mathcal{M}$ admits universal solutions), and define st-tgd θ_i as follows. Assume that ρ is a one-to-one function that associates to each element in $(\text{DOM}(S_i) \cup \text{DOM}(T_i))$ a fresh variable, and assume that $\bar{x} = (\rho(a_1), \ldots, \rho(a_j))$, where $\{a_1, \ldots, a_j\} = (\text{DOM}(S_i) \cap \text{DOM}(T_i))$, $\bar{y} = (\rho(b_1), \ldots, \rho(b_k))$, where $\{b_1, \ldots, b_k\} = (\text{DOM}(S_i) \smallsetminus \text{DOM}(T_i))$, and $\bar{z} = (\rho(c_1), \ldots, \rho(c_\ell))$, where $\{c_1, \ldots, c_\ell\} = (\text{DOM}(T_i) \smallsetminus \text{DOM}(S_i))$. Then, as in the proof of Theorem 21.4, define $\varphi_i(\bar{x}, \bar{y})$ as the conjunction of all atomic formulae $U(\rho(u_1), \ldots, \rho(u_j))$ such that $U(u_1, \ldots, u_j)$ holds in S_i, define $\psi_i(\bar{x}, \bar{z})$

as the conjunction of all atomic formulae $V(\rho(v_1),\ldots,\rho(v_k))$ such that $V(v_1,\ldots,v_k)$ holds in T_i, and define θ_i as the st-tgd $\varphi_i(\bar{x},\bar{y}) \to \exists \bar{z}\, \psi_i(\bar{x},\bar{z})$.

Let $\Sigma_{st} = \{\theta_1,\ldots,\theta_m\}$. We have that Σ_{st} is a finite set of LAV st-tgds, so to conclude the proof it is enough to show that $\mathcal{M}$ is defined by Σ_{st}, that is, it is enough to show that given instances S, T of $\mathbf{R_s}$ and $\mathbf{R_t}$, respectively, the pair (S,T) is in $\mathcal{M}$ if and only if $(S,T) \models \Sigma_{st}$. This proof follows exactly the same lines as the proof of Theorem 21.4, so we leave it as an exercise for the reader (see Exercise 22.3). □

We conclude this section by presenting a characterization of GAV mappings, in which we use all the properties mentioned in Theorem 21.4 together with the following new structural condition:

- **Closure under target intersection:** A mapping $\mathcal{M}$ is *closed under target intersection* if $(S,T_1 \cap T_2) \in \mathcal{M}$ whenever $(S,T_1) \in \mathcal{M}$ and $(S,T_2) \in \mathcal{M}$.

It is easy to see that every GAV mapping is closed under target intersection. On the other hand, as the following example shows, mappings defined by arbitrary sets of st-tgds do not have this property. Consider a mapping $\mathcal{M}'$ defined by the following st-tgd:

$$R(x) \to \exists y\, E(x,y).$$

Let $S = \{R(1)\}$ be a source instance, and let $T_1 = \{E(1,2)\}$ and $T_2 = \{E(1,3)\}$ be target instances. Clearly, both (S,T_1) and (S,T_2) belong to $\mathcal{M}$, but $(S,T_1 \cap T_2)$ does not as $T_1 \cap T_2 = \emptyset$, which shows that $\mathcal{M}$ is not closed under target intersection. Notice that the previous st-tgd is a LAV st-tgd, and, thus, LAV mappings are not closed under target intersection.

Theorem 21.6 *A mapping can be defined by a finite set of GAV st-tgds if and only if it is closed under target homomorphisms, admits universal solutions, reflects source homomorphisms, is closed under target intersection, and is n-modular for some $n \geq 1$.*

This theorem can be proved by using exactly the same construction as in the proof of Theorem 21.4, but relying instead on the following fact:

Proposition 21.7 *If a mapping is closed under target homomorphisms, admits universal solutions and is closed under target intersection, then every source instance admits a universal solution containing only constants.*

Proof Assume that $\mathcal{M}$ is a mapping from a source schema $\mathbf{R_s}$ to a target schema $\mathbf{R_t}$ satisfying the three conditions in the proposition, and let S be an instance of $\mathbf{R_s}$. Given that $\mathcal{M}$ admits universal solutions, there exists a universal solution T for S under $\mathcal{M}$. Let h be a homomorphism that maps every constant in T to itself and every null value in T to a fresh constant. Then given that $\mathcal{M}$ is closed under target homomorphisms and h is the identity on constants, the instance T' obtained from T by replacing every element a by $h(a)$ is a solution for S under $\mathcal{M}$. Since $\mathcal{M}$ is closed under target intersection, $T^\star = T \cap T'$ is a solution for S under $\mathcal{M}$. It is a universal solution since $T^\star \subseteq T$ and T is a universal solution. Also it contains only constants since $T^\star \subseteq T'$. This proves the proposition. □

Notice that, as opposed to the case of LAV mappings, n-modularity is used in the characterization of GAV mappings. We conclude this section by presenting an example showing that n-modularity is indeed needed in this characterization.

Example 21.8   Assume that $\mathcal{M}$ is a mapping from a source schema $\mathbf{R_s}$ consisting of a binary relation E to a target schema $\mathbf{R_t}$ consisting of a binary relation G. Moreover, assume that $\mathcal{M}$ is defined by the following *infinite* set of st-tgds:

$$\Sigma_{st} = \{E(x_1, x_2) \wedge \cdots \wedge E(x_{n-1}, x_n) \rightarrow G(x_1, x_n) \mid n \geq 2\}.$$

It is not hard to see that $\mathcal{M}$ is closed under target homomorphisms, admits universal solutions, reflects source homomorphisms and is closed under target intersection (see Exercise 22.3). On the other hand, $\mathcal{M}$ is not n-modular for any $n > 0$, which implies that $\mathcal{M}$ cannot be defined by a finite set of GAV st-tgds (by Theorem 21.6). To see why this is the case, notice that if S, T are instances of $\mathbf{R_s}$ and $\mathbf{R_t}$, respectively, then $(S, T) \in \mathcal{M}$ if and only if for every $a, b \in \mathrm{DOM}(S)$ such that (a, b) belongs to the transitive closure of E^S, it holds that $(a, b) \in G^T$. Thus, if S_n, T_n are the following instances of $\mathbf{R_s}$ and $\mathbf{R_t}$:

$$E^{S_n} = \{(i, i+1) \mid 1 \leq i \leq n\},$$
$$G^{T_n} = \{(i, j) \mid 1 \leq i < j \leq n+1\} \smallsetminus \{(1, n+1)\},$$

then we have that: (1) $(S_n, T_n) \notin \mathcal{M}$ since $(1, n+1)$ is in the transitive closure of E^{S_n} and $(1, n+1) \notin G^{T_n}$, and (2) for every instance S'_n of $\mathbf{R_s}$ such that $S'_n \subseteq S_n$ and $|\mathrm{DOM}(S'_n)| \leq n$, it holds that $(S'_n, T_n) \in \mathcal{M}$ since $(1, n+1)$ is not in the transitive closure of $E^{S'_n}$.   □

21.3 An application: simplifying schema mappings

In this section, we study the problem of transforming a mapping given by st-tgds into an equivalent mapping specified by simpler dependencies. More specifically, we apply the characterizations presented in the previous section to pinpoint the exact computational complexity of this problem for GAV and LAV st-tgds.

We start by considering the following problem:

PROBLEM:	GAV-EQUIVALENCE
INPUT:	Mapping $\mathcal{M}$ given by st-tgds
QUESTION:	Is $\mathcal{M}$ equivalent to a mapping $\mathcal{M}'$ given by GAV st-tgds?

GAV mappings are particularly easy, as they essentially provide queries that compute the target. Thus, if we get a positive answer to the equivalence question, it is well worth transforming the mapping and operating with a simpler one. Of course by equivalence of $\mathcal{M}$ and $\mathcal{M}'$ we mean $[\![\mathcal{M}]\!] = [\![\mathcal{M}']\!]$ or, equivalently, that for every source S, solutions under $\mathcal{M}$ and solutions under $\mathcal{M}'$ are the same.

A priori we do not even know whether GAV-EQUIVALENCE is decidable. However, the characterizations presented in the previous section give us a way of analyzing the problem:

we know that the answer to GAV-EQUIVALENCE is positive if and only if $\mathcal{M}$ is closed under target intersection.

We use this observation to analyze GAV-EQUIVALENCE. As a first useful step, we need the following result.

Lemma 21.9   *The problem of verifying, given finite sets Σ, Σ' of st-tgds from a source schema $\mathbf{R_s}$ to a target schema $\mathbf{R_t}$, whether Σ logically implies Σ' is NP-complete.*

The proof of this lemma is left as an exercise for the reader (see Exercise 22.3). We now move to the proof of the main result of this section for the case of GAV mappings.

Theorem 21.10   *The problem GAV-EQUIVALENCE is NP-complete.*

Proof   Given that every full st-tgd can be transformed in polynomial time into an equivalent set of GAV st-tgds, and every GAV st-tgd is a full st-tgd, to prove the theorem it is enough to show that the problem of checking, given a mapping $\mathcal{M}$ specified by a finite set of st-tgds, whether $\mathcal{M}$ can be specified by a finite set of full st-tgds is NP-complete. In this proof, we focus into the latter problem.

Assume that $\mathcal{M}$ is a mapping from a source schema $\mathbf{R_s}$ to a target schema $\mathbf{R_t}$ defined by a finite set Σ_{st} of st-tgds. Let us define Σ'_{st} as the "full" part of Σ_{st}. Formally, Σ'_{st} is the mapping obtained from Σ_{st} by dropping the existential quantifiers and the conjuncts with existentially quantified variables from the right-hand side of each dependency in Σ_{st}. We show next that $\mathcal{M}$ can be defined by a set of full st-tgds if and only if Σ'_{st} and Σ_{st} define the same mapping from $\mathbf{R_s}$ to $\mathbf{R_t}$.

Clearly, if Σ'_{st} and Σ_{st} define the same mapping from $\mathbf{R_s}$ to $\mathbf{R_t}$, then $\mathcal{M}$ can be defined by a finite set of full st-tgds. To prove the opposite direction, assume that $\mathcal{M}$ can be defined by a finite set of full st-tgds, and let $\mathcal{M}'$ be the mapping from $\mathbf{R_s}$ to $\mathbf{R_t}$ defined by Σ'_{st}. Clearly, $(S,T) \in \mathcal{M}$ implies $(S,T) \in \mathcal{M}'$. For the converse, assume that $(S,T) \in \mathcal{M}'$, and let $T^\star$ be the canonical universal solution for S under $\mathcal{M}'$ (see Section 6.3 for the definition of this universal solution). Moreover, let T_1 be the canonical universal solution for S under $\mathcal{M}$, let h be a function that maps every constant in T_1 to itself and every null value in T_1 to a fresh constant, and let T_2 be an instance of $\mathbf{R_t}$ obtained by replacing every value a in T_1 by $h(a)$. Then, from the fact that h is the identity on the constants and $(S,T_1) \in \mathcal{M}$, we obtain $(S,T_2) \in \mathcal{M}$ since $\mathcal{M}$ is closed under target homomorphisms that are the identity on constants (by Theorem 21.6). Thus, given that $T^\star = T_1 \cap T_2$ by definition of these instances and of Σ'_{st}, we conclude that $(S,T^\star) \in \mathcal{M}$ since $\mathcal{M}$ is closed under target intersection (by Theorem 21.6). Therefore, given that there exists a homomorphism from $T^\star$ to T that is the identity on constants (as $T^\star$ is a universal solution for S under $\mathcal{M}'$ and $(S,T) \in \mathcal{M}'$) and $(S,T^\star) \in \mathcal{M}$, we conclude that $(S,T) \in \mathcal{M}$ by using again the fact that $\mathcal{M}$ is closed under target homomorphisms that are the identity on constants.

We show next that the problem of verifying, given a finite set Σ_{st} of st-tgds, whether Σ_{st} and its full part Σ'_{st} define the same mapping is NP-complete. From this proof and the previous discussion, we conclude that the theorem holds as Σ'_{st} can be constructed in polynomial time from Σ_{st}.

Membership in NP is a corollary of Lemma 21.9. Thus, we only need to prove that this problem is NP-hard, for which we reduce from the problem of Boolean conjunctive query containment. Let $\exists \bar{x}\, \varphi(\bar{x})$ and $\exists \bar{y}\, \psi(\bar{y})$ be two Boolean conjunctive queries, and assume that U is a fresh relation symbol whose arity is equal to the number of variables in $\bar{x}$. Moreover, let $\mathcal{M}$ be the mapping defined by a set of st-tgds consisting of the following dependencies:

$$U(\bar{x}) \to \varphi(\bar{x})$$
$$U(\bar{x}) \to \exists \bar{y}\, \psi(\bar{y}).$$

We claim that $\mathcal{M}$ is definable by a finite set of full st-tgds if and only if $\exists \bar{x}\, \varphi(\bar{x})$ is contained in $\exists \bar{y}\, \psi(\bar{y})$. First, assume that $\exists \bar{x}\, \varphi(\bar{x})$ is contained in $\exists \bar{y}\, \psi(\bar{y})$. Then it is easy to see that $\mathcal{M}$ is defined by $U(\bar{x}) \to \varphi(\bar{x})$. Second, assume that $\exists \bar{x}\, \varphi(\bar{x})$ is not contained in $\exists \bar{y}\, \psi(\bar{y})$. In this case, we need to show that $\mathcal{M}$ cannot be defined by a finite set of full st-tgds. Given that $\exists \bar{x}\, \varphi(\bar{x})$ is not contained in $\exists \bar{y}\, \psi(\bar{y})$, there exists an instance T such that $\exists \bar{x}\, \varphi(\bar{x})$ holds in T and $\exists \bar{y}\, \psi(\bar{y})$ does not hold in T. Thus, we have that $T \models \varphi(\bar{a})$, for some tuple $\bar{a}$ of constants, but $T \not\models \exists \bar{y}\, \psi(\bar{y})$, from which we conclude that $(S,T) \notin \mathcal{M}$ for a source instance S such that $U^S = \{\bar{a}\}$. Let T_1, T_2 be two isomorphic copies of the canonical universal solution for S under the mapping defined by st-tgd $U(\bar{x}) \to \exists \bar{y}\, \psi(\bar{y})$ such that $\mathrm{DOM}(T_1) \cap \mathrm{DOM}(T_2) = \emptyset$. Then given that T_1 and T_2 mention only null values, we also have that $\mathrm{DOM}(T_1) \cap \mathrm{DOM}(T) = \emptyset$ and $\mathrm{DOM}(T_2) \cap \mathrm{DOM}(T) = \emptyset$. But then we have that $(T \cup T_1)$ and $(T \cup T_2)$ are solutions for S under $\mathcal{M}$, but $(T \cup T_1) \cap (T \cup T_2)$ is not a solution for S under $\mathcal{M}$ as this intersection is equal to T. We conclude that $\mathcal{M}$ is not closed under target intersection and, hence, we conclude by Theorem 21.6 that $\mathcal{M}$ cannot be defined by a finite set of full st-tgds, which was to be shown. $\square$

We conclude this chapter by considering a similar problem but this time with LAV st-tgds. That is, we deal with the problem defined below.

PROBLEM:	LAV-EQUIVALENCE
INPUT:	Mapping $\mathcal{M}$ given by st-tgds
QUESTION:	Is $\mathcal{M}$ equivalent to a mapping $\mathcal{M}'$ given by LAV st-tgds?

Again, a priori it is not even clear whether the problem is decidable, but now we can use the characterizations presented in the previous section to see that this problem reduces to the problem of checking whether $\mathcal{M}$ is closed under union. This gives us the desired complexity bound.

Theorem 21.11 *The problem* LAV-EQUIVALENCE *is* NP-*complete.*

Proof Assume that $\mathcal{M}$ is a mapping from a source schema $\mathbf{R_s}$ to a target schema $\mathbf{R_t}$ defined by a finite set Σ_{st} of st-tgds. Then define a set Σ'_{st} of LAV st-tgds as follows. For every st-tgd $\varphi(\bar{x},\bar{y}) \to \exists \bar{z}\, \psi(\bar{x},\bar{z})$ in Σ_{st}, if $\varphi(\bar{x},\bar{y})$ mentions exactly one predicate symbol U, then do the following. First, assume that U has arity ℓ and that $U(\bar{u}_1), U(\bar{u}_2), \ldots, U(\bar{u}_n)$ is the sequence of atomic formulae mentioned in $\varphi(\bar{x},\bar{y})$. Moreover, the i-th component of a tuple $\bar{u}$ of variables is denoted by $\bar{u}^i$, and for a variable substitution ξ and variables

u, v, the notation $\xi[v/u]$ is used for a variable substitution such that $(\xi[v/u])(w) = v$ if $\xi(w) = u$, and $(\xi[v/u])(w) = \xi(w)$ otherwise. Now compute a variable substitution ρ by using the procedure below.

1: $D := \{\bar{u}_1, \bar{u}_2, \ldots, \bar{u}_n\}$
2: $V :=$ set of variables mentioned in $\varphi(\bar{x}, \bar{y})$
3: $\rho :=$ identity variable substitution with domain V
4: **while** there exist $i \in \{1, \ldots, \ell\}$ and $\bar{u}, \bar{v} \in D$ such that $\bar{u}^i \neq \bar{v}^i$ **do**
5:      $\rho := \rho[\bar{v}^i / \bar{u}^i]$
6:      $D := \{\rho(\bar{w}) \mid \bar{w} \in D\}$
7: **end while**

It is straightforward to prove that ρ can be computed in polynomial time, that ρ unifies $\{\bar{u}_1, \bar{u}_2, \ldots, \bar{u}_n\}$ in the sense that $\rho(\bar{u}_1) = \rho(\bar{u}_2) = \cdots = \rho(\bar{u}_n)$, and that ρ is the most general unifier for $\{\bar{u}_1, \bar{u}_2, \ldots, \bar{u}_n\}$, in the sense that for every variable substitution ξ that unifies $\{\bar{u}_1, \bar{u}_2, \ldots, \bar{u}_n\}$, there exists a variable substitution λ such that $\lambda \circ \rho = \xi$. Finally, include in Σ'_{st} the following LAV st-tgd:

$$\varphi(\rho(\bar{x}), \rho(\bar{y})) \to \exists \bar{z} \, \psi(\rho(\bar{x}), \bar{z}).$$

Notice that the previous dependency is a LAV st-tgd as ρ unifies $\{\bar{u}_1, \bar{u}_2, \ldots, \bar{u}_n\}$ and $\varphi(\bar{x}, \bar{y})$ mentioned only the predicate symbol U.

We show next that $\mathcal{M}$ can be defined by a set of LAV st-tgds if and only if Σ'_{st} and Σ_{st} define the same mapping from $\mathbf{R}_s$ to $\mathbf{R}_t$. Clearly, if Σ'_{st} and Σ_{st} define the same mapping from $\mathbf{R}_s$ to $\mathbf{R}_t$, then $\mathcal{M}$ can be defined by a finite set of LAV st-tgds. To prove the opposite direction, assume that $\mathcal{M}$ can be defined by a finite set of LAV st-tgds, and let $\mathcal{M}'$ be the mapping from $\mathbf{R}_s$ to $\mathbf{R}_t$ defined by Σ'_{st}. Clearly, $(S, T) \in \mathcal{M}$ implies $(S, T) \in \mathcal{M}'$. For the converse, assume that $(S, T) \in \mathcal{M}'$, and for every fact $U(\bar{a})$ mentioned in S, let $S_{U(\bar{a})}$ be an instance of $\mathbf{R}_s$ consisting only of the fact $U(\bar{a})$. Then given that $\mathcal{M}$ is definable by a set of LAV st-tgds, we have that $\mathcal{M}$ is closed under union by Theorem 21.5 and, hence, to prove that $(S, T) \in \mathcal{M}$, it is enough to prove that $(S_{U(\bar{a})}, T) \in \mathcal{M}$ for every fact $U(\bar{a})$ mentioned in S. In order to prove that $(S_{U(\bar{a})}, T) \in \mathcal{M}$, we have to show that $(S_{U(\bar{a})}, T) \models \Sigma_{st}$. Thus, assume that $\varphi(\bar{x}, \bar{y}) \to \exists \bar{z} \, \psi(\bar{x}, \bar{z})$ is a st-tgd in Σ_{st} and that σ is a variable assignment such that $S_{U(\bar{a})} \models \varphi(\sigma(\bar{x}), \sigma(\bar{y}))$. Then we have to prove that $T \models \exists \bar{z} \, \psi(\sigma(\bar{x}), \bar{z})$. Given that $S_{U(\bar{a})} \models \varphi(\sigma(\bar{x}), \sigma(\bar{y}))$, we have by definition of $S_{U(\bar{a})}$ that:

$$\varphi(\bar{x}, \bar{y}) = U(\bar{u}_1) \wedge U(\bar{u}_2) \wedge \cdots \wedge U(\bar{u}_n),$$

and that $\sigma(\bar{u}_1) = \sigma(\bar{u}_2) = \cdots = \sigma(\bar{u}_n) = \bar{a}$. Let ρ be defined as shown previously for the st-tgd $\varphi(\bar{x}, \bar{y}) \to \exists \bar{z} \, \psi(\bar{x}, \bar{z})$, and f be a one-to-one function that assigns a fresh variable to each constant. Then we have that $(f \circ \sigma)$ is a unifier for $\{\bar{u}_1, \bar{u}_2, \ldots, \bar{u}_n\}$ and, hence, there exists a variable substitution λ such that $(\lambda \circ \rho) = (f \circ \sigma)$ (since ρ is a most general unifier for $\{\bar{u}_1, \bar{u}_2, \ldots, \bar{u}_n\}$). We conclude that $(f^{-1} \circ \lambda) \circ \rho = f^{-1} \circ (\lambda \circ \rho) = f^{-1} \circ (f \circ \sigma) = \sigma$. Thus, given that $S_{U(\bar{a})} \models \varphi(\sigma(\bar{x}), \sigma(\bar{y}))$, we have that

$$S_{U(\bar{a})} \models \varphi((f^{-1} \circ \lambda)(\rho(\bar{x})), (f^{-1} \circ \lambda)(\rho(\bar{y}))).$$

But we have $(S_{U(\bar{a})}, T) \models \Sigma'_{st}$ (given that $(S, T) \models \Sigma'_{st}$, where Σ'_{st} is a set of LAV st-tgds and $S_{U(\bar{a})} \subseteq S$), and also that $\varphi(\rho(\bar{x}), \rho(\bar{y})) \to \exists \bar{z} \, \psi(\rho(\bar{x}), \bar{z})$ is a LAV st-tgd in Σ'_{st}, from which we conclude that $T \models \exists \bar{z} \, \psi((f^{-1} \circ \lambda)(\rho(\bar{x})), \bar{z})$. Therefore, by using again the fact that $(f^{-1} \circ \lambda) \circ \rho$ equals σ, we conclude that $T \models \exists \bar{z} \, \psi(\sigma(\bar{x}), \bar{z})$, which was to be shown.

We show next that the problem of verifying, given a finite set Σ_{st} of st-tgds, whether Σ_{st} and Σ'_{st} define the same mapping is NP-complete. From this proof and the previous discussion, we conclude that the theorem holds as Σ'_{st} can be constructed in polynomial time from Σ_{st}.

The membership of the problem mentioned in the previous paragraph in NP is a corollary of Lemma 21.9. Thus, we only need to prove that this problem is NP-hard, for which we reduce from the problem of Boolean conjunctive query containment. Let $\exists \bar{x} \, \varphi(\bar{x})$ and $\exists \bar{y} \, \psi(\bar{y})$ be two Boolean conjunctive queries, and assume that U, V are fresh unary relation symbols. Moreover, let $\mathcal{M}$ be the mapping defined by a set Σ_{st} of st-tgds consisting of the following dependencies:

$$U(z) \to \exists \bar{x} \, \varphi(\bar{x})$$
$$U(z) \wedge V(z) \to \exists \bar{y} \, \psi(\bar{y}).$$

We claim that $\mathcal{M}$ is definable by a finite set of LAV st-tgds if and only if $\exists \bar{x} \, \varphi(\bar{x})$ is contained in $\exists \bar{y} \, \psi(\bar{y})$. First, assume that $\exists \bar{x} \, \varphi(\bar{x})$ is contained in $\exists \bar{y} \, \psi(\bar{y})$. Then it is easy to see that $\mathcal{M}$ is defined by $U(z) \to \exists \bar{x} \, \varphi(\bar{x})$. Second, assume that $\exists \bar{x} \, \varphi(\bar{x})$ is not contained in $\exists \bar{y} \, \psi(\bar{y})$. In this case, we need to show that $\mathcal{M}$ cannot be defined by a finite set of LAV st-tgds. Given that $\exists \bar{x} \, \varphi(\bar{x})$ is not contained in $\exists \bar{y} \, \psi(\bar{y})$, there exists a target instance T such that $\exists \bar{x} \, \varphi(\bar{x})$ holds in T and $\exists \bar{y} \, \psi(\bar{y})$ does not hold in T. Then let S_1, S_2 be source instances such that:

$$U^{S_1} = \{a\} \qquad V^{S_1} = \emptyset$$
$$U^{S_2} = \emptyset \qquad V^{S_2} = \{a\}.$$

We have that $(S_1, T) \models \Sigma_{st}$ and $(S_2, T) \models \Sigma_{st}$, since $T \models \exists \bar{x} \, \varphi(\bar{x})$ and neither S_1 nor S_2 satisfies $U(a) \wedge V(a)$. However, we have that $(S_1 \cup S_2, T) \not\models \Sigma_{st}$, since $S_1 \cup S_2 \models U(a) \wedge V(a)$ and $T \not\models \exists \bar{y} \, \psi(\bar{y})$. We conclude that $\mathcal{M}$ is not closed under union and, hence, we conclude by Theorem 21.5 that $\mathcal{M}$ cannot be defined by a finite set of LAV st-tgds, which was to be shown. $\qquad \square$

22

Endnotes to Part Four

22.1 Summary

- A reasonable mapping should be consistent, i.e., there should be at least one source instance admitting a solution. A stronger notion of consistency, called *absolute consistency*, demands a solution for every source instance.

- For relational mappings specified by st-tgds, both consistency and absolute consistency are trivial problems, as every source instance admits a solution in this case.

- In the XML setting consistency problems are difficult. Even in the absence of data comparisons, checking consistency requires exponential time, and if data comparisons are allowed, the problem is undecidable. Consistency is only tractable when the schema language is restricted to nested-relational DTDs, and mappings use only vertical order.

- The absolute consistency problem is decidable for the class of all XML schema mappings. The problem can be solved in exponential space, but a single-exponential time algorithm is unlikely. For schemas admitting only trees of some bounded depth, the complexity is within the polynomial hierarchy, so the problem can be solved by a single-exponential time algorithm.

- Two of the most important operations on mappings are composition and inversion.

- Composition of mappings maps an instance I to an instance J, if I is mapped by the first mapping to an intermediate instance K, which is then mapped by the second mapping to J.

- To express syntactically a composition of schema mappings, one needs to state that a null value in the target only depends on some particular values in the source. This can be achieved by enriching the mapping language with function symbols that are quantified existentially (Skolem functions).

- Composition of relational mappings specified by st-tgds can be specified with SO tgds (st-tgds extended with function symbols).

- Composition of XML schema mappings is problematic as soon as disjunction is allowed in schemas.

- For mappings between nested-relational DTDs, a syntactic representation of the composition is guaranteed only if the mappings use no wildcard, descendant, sibling order and data inequalities. Under these assumptions, a syntactic representation can be computed in exponential time.

- Some alternative semantics for the inverse operator for schema mappings have been proposed. A first such semantics is based on the idea that a mapping $\mathcal{M}'$ is an inverse of a mapping $\mathcal{M}$ if the composition of $\mathcal{M}$ with $\mathcal{M}'$ is equal to the identity schema mapping.

- A different approach to define an inverse operator is followed when defining the notions of recovery and maximum recovery. The underlying idea of the notion of maximum recovery is to give a formal definition for what it means for a mapping $\mathcal{M}'$ to recover a maximal amount of sound information with respect to a mapping $\mathcal{M}$.

- There exists a mapping specified by st-tgds that does not admit an inverse, but every mapping specified by these dependencies admits a maximum recovery.

- Maximum recoveries for mappings specified by st-tgds can be computed by an exponential-time algorithm based on query rewriting.

- There exist structural characterizations for the classes of mappings specified by st-tgds, LAV st-tgds and GAV st-tgds. These structural characterizations can be used to prove the NP-completeness of the problem of verifying whether a mapping specified by st-tgds can be specified by LAV st-tgds, or by GAV st-tgds.

22.2 Bibliographic comments

Consistency problems for XML schema mappings were first considered by Arenas and Libkin (2008) in the absence of sibling order and data comparisons. In the general setting, consistency was studied by Amano et al. (2009), who also gave a partial solution to the absolute consistency problem. A general algorithm for absolute consistency was designed by Bojańczyk et al. (2011).

A general framework for metadata management, where mapping operators such as composition and inversion play a central role, was proposed by Bernstein (2003). Mapping composition in the relational setting was first studied by Fagin et al. (2005b), who proved that the problem COMPOSITION$(\mathcal{M}_{12}, \mathcal{M}_{23})$ is in NP for every pair of mappings $\mathcal{M}_{12}$, $\mathcal{M}_{23}$ specified by st-tgds, and showed that there exist mappings $\mathcal{M}_{12}^{\star}$, $\mathcal{M}_{23}^{\star}$ specified by st-tgds such that COMPOSITION$(\mathcal{M}_{12}^{\star}, \mathcal{M}_{23}^{\star})$ is NP-complete. They also proved that the class of mappings specified by st-tgds is not closed under composition, proposed the language of SO tgds, proved that the class of mappings specified by SO tgds is closed under composition, provided an exponential-time algorithm for computing the composition of two mappings specified by SO tgds, and showed that every SO tgd defines the composition of a finite number of mappings specified by st-tgds. Interestingly, it was proved by Arocena et al. (2010) that the composition of two LAV mappings can be defined by a LAV mapping. The equivalence problem for SO tgds was studied by Feinerer et al. (2011). Some extensions of the framework proposed by Fagin et al. (2005b) have been studied in the literature. In particular, Nash et al. (2007) and Bernstein et al. (2008) considered the problem of computing the composition of mappings defined by dependencies that need not be st-tgds, Arenas et al. (2011a) considered the problem of composing mappings that are specified by st-tgds, target egds and weakly acyclic sets of target tgds, and Libkin and Sirangelo (2011) proposed the language of CQ-SkSTDs, that slightly extends the syntax of SO-tgds, and studied the composition problem under the closed-world semantics presented in Section 8.2 for mappings specified by CQ-SkSTDs.

Composability of XML mappings was considered by Amano et al. (2009), but the exact formulation of the result and the proof come from David et al. (2010).

The first notion of inversion for schema mappings specified by st-tgds was proposed by Fagin (2007), who proved that there exist mappings specified by these dependencies that do not admit an inverse. A necessary and sufficient condition for the existence of an inverse for a mapping specified by st-tgds was proposed by Fagin et al. (2008b), and a more general necessary and sufficient condition for the class of mappings that are total and closed-down on the left was proposed by Arenas et al. (2009b). The coNP-completeness of the problem of deciding whether a mapping specified by st-tgds has an inverse was proved by Fagin and Nash (2010), and the undecidability of the problem of verifying, given mappings $\mathcal{M}$, $\mathcal{M}'$ specified by st-tgds, whether $\mathcal{M}'$ is an inverse of $\mathcal{M}$ was proved by Arenas et al. (2009b).

The notion of quasi-inverse was introduced by Fagin et al. (2008b). They proved that it strictly generalizes the notion of inverse proposed by Fagin (2007), provided a necessary and sufficient condition for the existence of a quasi-inverse for a mapping specified by st-tgds, and used this condition to prove that there exist mappings that do not admit a quasi-inverse. The undecidability of the problem of verifying, given mappings $\mathcal{M}$, $\mathcal{M}'$ specified by st-tgds, whether $\mathcal{M}'$ is a quasi-inverse of $\mathcal{M}$ was proved by Arenas et al. (2009b).

The notions of recovery and maximum recovery were introduced by Arenas et al. (2009b). They proposed a necessary and sufficient condition for a mapping $\mathcal{M}'$ to be a maximum recovery of a mapping $\mathcal{M}$, provided a necessary and sufficient condition for the existence of a maximum recovery for a mapping, proved that every mapping specified by st-tgds admits a maximum recovery, showed that the notion of maximum recovery strictly generalizes the notion of inverse proposed by Fagin (2007) for the class of mappings that are total and closed-down on the left, established the relationship with the notion of quasi-inverse for the class of mappings that are total and closed-down on the left, and proved the undecidability of the problem of verifying, given mappings $\mathcal{M}$, $\mathcal{M}'$ specified by st-tgds, whether $\mathcal{M}'$ is a recovery (maximum recovery) of $\mathcal{M}$.

The exponential-time algorithm for computing maximum recoveries presented in Chapter 20, which can also be used to compute inverses and quasi-inverses, was proposed by Arenas et al. (2009b). The same paper also gave a quadratic-time algorithm for computing maximum recoveries for the case of full st-tgds. The fact that there exists an invertible mapping specified by st-tgds that does not admit an inverse specified by st-tgds was proved by Fagin et al. (2008b).

The notions of extended recovery and maximum extended recovery were proposed by Fagin et al. (2011), who showed that there exists a mapping specified by tgds that does not admit a maximum recovery if source instances are allowed to contain nulls, and proved that every mapping specified by these dependencies has a maximum extended recovery even if source instances are allowed to contain nulls. The characterization of the notion of maximum extended recovery in terms of the notion of maximum recovery was given by Arenas et al. (2009a).

Other schema mapping operators such as extract, merge, match, union and intersection have been studied by Melnik (2004); Bernstein and Melnik (2007); Arenas et al. (2010a); and Pérez et al. (2012).

The problem of characterizing the class of mappings specified by st-tgds in terms of their structural properties was studied by ten Cate and Kolaitis (2009). They also provided structural characterizations of the classes of mappings specified by LAV st-tgds and GAV st-gds, and used them to establish NP-completeness of LAV-EQUIVALENCE and GAV-EQUIVALENCE. The problems of simplifying and refining schema mappings were considered by Fagin et al. (2008a); Calvanese et al. (2011); Alexe et al. (2011); and Pichler et al. (2011).

22.3 Exercises

1. Show that the exponential blow-up in the translation of patterns to UFTA(DFA) in Lemma 18.2 cannot be avoided.

2. (Source: Amano et al. (2009))
   Assume that schemas are given by disjunction-free DTDs (productions use concatenation, ?, ∗, +, but no disjunction). Give PTIME algorithms for: (a) satisfiability of $\Downarrow$-patterns; and (b) CONS($\Downarrow$). Hint for consistency: There exists an easiest source tree.

3. (Source: Amano et al. (2009))
   Show that CONS($\Downarrow$) is PSPACE-hard. Hint: Give a reduction from QSAT. Use $t_i, f_i \to \sharp t_{i+1} f_{i+1} \natural$ to encode universally quantified variables, and $t_i, f_i \to \sharp t_{i+1}? f_{i+1}? \natural$ for existentially quantified variables.

4. (Source: Amano et al. (2009))
   Show that CONS($\downarrow, \to, \to^+, =$) is undecidable. Hint: Rotate the encoding used in Theorem 18.4 by 90°.

5. (Source: Amano et al. (2009))
   Modify the reduction above to show that CONS($\downarrow, \to, =$) is undecidable. Hint: A finite sequence contains no repetitions iff every occurrence of an item has the same same successor, different from itself.

6. (Source: Amano et al. (2009))
   Show that CONS($\downarrow, \downarrow^+, \neq$) and CONS($\downarrow, \to, \neq$) are undecidable. Hint: In the reduction above replace = on the target side with $\neq$ on the source side and vice versa.

7. (Source: Amano et al. (2009))
   Show that CONS($\downarrow, \to, \sim$) is undecidable over nested-relational DTDs. Hint: Modify again the two-register machine reduction. Encode the configurations entirely in data values, keeping separately a list of values encoding states of the machine.

8. (Source: Amano et al. (2009))

    Show that $\text{CONS}(\downarrow,\_,=)$ is NEXPTIME-hard over nested-relational DTDs. Hint: Use the proof of hardness of solution existence and enforce that all data values in the source tree are different.

9. (Source: Amano et al. (2009))

    Show that $\text{ABCONS}^{\circ}(\downarrow,\_)$ is Π_2^p-hard. Hint: Recall the reduction used in the proof of Theorem 11.7.

10. (Source: Bojańczyk et al. (2011))

    Give a formal definition of the class $\Pi_2\text{EXP}$ in terms of Turing machines and prove that 2^n-UNIVERSALITY is hard for this class (see page 242).

11. (Source: Bojańczyk et al. (2011))

    Modifying the reduction from the proof of Theorem 18.9, show that ABCONS is $\Pi_2\text{EXP}$-hard for $\text{SM}^{\text{nr}}(\downarrow,\_,\sim)$ and $\text{SM}^{\text{nr}}(\downarrow,\_,\rightarrow,=)$, and NEXPTIME-hard for $\text{SM}^{\text{nr}}(\downarrow,\_,=)$.

12. (Source: Fagin et al. (2005b))

    Let $\mathcal{M}_{12}$ and $\mathcal{M}_{23}$ be the mappings in Example 19.2, and σ_{13} be the following FO dependency:

    $$\forall n \exists y \forall c\, (\texttt{Takes}(n,c) \rightarrow \texttt{Enrolled}(y,c)).$$

    Show that σ_{13} defines the composition of $\mathcal{M}_{12}$ and $\mathcal{M}_{23}$.

13. (Source: Fagin et al. (2005b))

    Let $\mathcal{M}_{12} = (\mathbf{R}_1, \mathbf{R}_2, \Sigma_{12})$ and $\mathcal{M}_{23} = (\mathbf{R}_2, \mathbf{R}_3, \Sigma_{23})$, where Σ_{12} and Σ_{23} are finite sets of st-tgds. Prove that $\text{COMPOSITION}(\mathcal{M}_{12}, \mathcal{M}_{23})$ is in NP.

14. (Source: Fagin et al. (2005b))

    Show that for each SO tgd σ from a schema $\mathbf{R_s}$ to a schema $\mathbf{R_t}$ there exists a polynomial p, with the following property. Assume that S is an instance of $\mathbf{R_s}$, T is an instance of $\mathbf{R_t}$, U is a set such that $\text{DOM}(S) \cup \text{DOM}(T) \subseteq U \subseteq \text{CONST} \cup \text{VAR}$ and $|U| \geq p(\|S\| + \|T\|)$. Then $(S,T) \models \sigma$ if and only if (S,T) satisfies σ with witnessing valuations whose domain and range is U.

15. (Source: Fagin et al. (2005b))

    Let $\mathcal{M}_{12}$ and $\mathcal{M}_{23}$ be the mappings in Example 19.2. Use the composition algorithm for SO tgds to calculate an SO tgd σ_{13} defining the composition of $\mathcal{M}_{12}$ with $\mathcal{M}_{23}$.

16. (Source: Arenas et al. (2009a))

    An SO tgd σ is said to be *equality-free* if it does not contain any atomic formula of the form $t_1 = t_2$, where t_1 and t_2 are terms built from some variables and function symbols. Show that if a mapping $\mathcal{M}$ is defined by an equality-free SO tgd, then $\mathcal{M}$ is closed under target homomorphisms.

17. (Source: Fagin et al. (2005b))

    Here you will show that equalities in SO tgds are strictly necessary for the purposes of composition. More precisely, let $\mathbf{R}_1$ be a schema consisting of a unary predicate Employee, $\mathbf{R}_2$ a schema consisting of a binary predicate Manager and $\mathbf{R}_3$ a schema consisting of a binary predicate `Manager'` and a unary predicate `SelfManager`. More-over, assume that $\mathcal{M}_{12} = (\mathbf{R_1}, \mathbf{R_2}, \Sigma_{12})$ and $\mathcal{M}_{23} = (\mathbf{R_2}, \mathbf{R_3}, \Sigma_{23})$, where Σ_{12} consists of the following st-tgd:

$$\text{Employee}(x) \rightarrow \exists y \text{Manager}(x,y),$$

and Σ_{23} consists of the following st-tgds:

$$\text{Manager}(x,y) \rightarrow \text{Manager}'(x,y),$$

$$\text{Manager}(x,x) \rightarrow \text{SelfManager}(x).$$

Use the property shown in Exercise 22.3 to prove that the composition of $\mathcal{M}_{12}$ and $\mathcal{M}_{23}$ cannot be defined by an equality-free SO tgd.

18. (Source: Fagin et al. (2005b))

    Let $\mathbf{R_1}$ be a schema consisting of unary predicates $P_1, \ldots, P_n, R_1, \ldots, R_n$, $\mathbf{R_2}$ a schema consisting of unary predicates $S_1, \ldots, S_n$ and $\mathbf{R_3}$ a schema consisting of unary predicate T. Moreover, let $\mathcal{M}_{12} = (\mathbf{R_1}, \mathbf{R_2}, \Sigma_{12})$ and $\mathcal{M}_{23} = (\mathbf{R_2}, \mathbf{R_3}, \Sigma_{23})$, where Σ_{12} consists of the following st-tgds:

    $$\begin{aligned} P_i(x) &\rightarrow S_i(x), & i &= 1, \ldots, n, \\ R_i(x) &\rightarrow S_i(x), & i &= 1, \ldots, n, \end{aligned}$$

    and Σ_{23} consists of the following st-tgd:

    $$S_1(x) \wedge \cdots \wedge S_n(x) \rightarrow T(x).$$

    Prove that if $\mathcal{M}_{13}$ is a mapping specified by an SO tgd and defining the composition of $\mathcal{M}_{12}$ with $\mathcal{M}_{23}$, then $\mathcal{M}_{13}$ has at least 2^n conjuncts.

19. (Source: Amano et al. (2009))

    Show that there are mappings $\mathcal{M}_{12}^{\star}$ and $\mathcal{M}_{23}^{\star}$ in $\text{SM}(\downarrow, \downarrow^+, \neq)$ such that COMPOSITION($\mathcal{M}_{12}^{\star}, \mathcal{M}_{23}^{\star}$) is undecidable. Prove the same for $\text{SM}(\downarrow, \rightarrow, =)$ and $\text{SM}(\downarrow, \rightarrow, \neq)$. Hint: Use the idea from Theorem 19.15

20. (Source: Amano et al. (2009))

    CONSCOMP(σ) is the following decision problem: Given mappings $\mathcal{M}, \mathcal{M}' \in \text{SM}(\sigma)$, decide if the composition of $\mathcal{M}$ and $\mathcal{M}'$ is consistent. Show that CONSCOMP($\Downarrow, \Rightarrow$) is in EXPTIME.

21. (Source: Amano et al. (2009))

    Show that the complexity of CONSCOMP(σ), defined in Exercise 22.3, is at least as high as that of CONS(σ). (In particular CONSCOMP($\Downarrow, =$) and CONSCOMP($\downarrow, \rightarrow, =$) are undecidable and CONSCOMP($\Downarrow, \Rightarrow$) is EXPTIME-hard.) Show that the same holds even if both input mappings for CONSCOMP(σ) are assumed to be consistent.

22. (Source: Amano et al. (2009))

    Let $D_1 = \{r \rightarrow \varepsilon\}$ and $D_3 = \{r \rightarrow c_1?c_2?c_3?\}$ with no attributes. For each of the classes $\text{SM}^{\text{nr}}(\downarrow, \downarrow^+)$, $\text{SM}^{\text{nr}}(\downarrow, \rightarrow)$, $\text{SM}^{\text{nr}}(\downarrow, \rightarrow^+)$, $\text{SM}^{\text{nr}}(\downarrow, \neq)$ give an example of two mappings whose composition is the mapping between D_1 and D_3 consisting of pairs of trees (r, T), where T matches either r/c_1 or r/c_2.

23. Generalize the PTIME-algorithm for certain answers given in Part THREE so that it handles mappings in $\text{SM}^{\text{nr}}(\downarrow, =, \text{FUN})$ and queries in $\textbf{CTQ}(\downarrow, =)$.

24. (Source: Fagin et al. (2008b))
    Prove that the mapping $\mathcal{M}$ specified by the set $\{P(x) \to T(x), R(x) \to T(x)\}$ of st-tgds does not have a Fagin-inverse.

25. (Source: Fagin et al. (2008b))
    Prove that the mapping $\mathcal{M}$ specified by st-tgd $P(x,y,z) \to R(x,y) \wedge T(y,z)$ does not have a Fagin-inverse.

26. (Source: Fagin and Nash (2010))
    Prove that the problem of verifying, given a mapping $\mathcal{M}$ specified by a set of st-tgds, whether $\mathcal{M}$ is Fagin-invertible is CONP-hard.

27. (Source: Fagin et al. (2008b))
    Let $\mathcal{M}$ be an arbitrary mapping. Prove that if $\mathcal{M}$ is quasi-invertible, then $\mathcal{M}$ satisfies the $(\sim_{\mathcal{M}}, \sim_{\mathcal{M}})$-subset property.

28. (Source: Fagin et al. (2008b))
    Let $\mathcal{M}$ be the mapping in Exercise 22.3. Prove that the mapping $\mathcal{M}'$ specified by tgd $R(x,y) \wedge T(y,z) \to P(x,y,z)$ is a quasi-inverse of $\mathcal{M}$.

29. (Source: Fagin et al. (2008b))
    Find a quasi-inverse for the mapping in Exercise 22.3.

30. (Source: Arenas et al. (2009b))
    Show that in Example 20.20, mapping $\mathcal{M}_2$ is not a maximum recovery of mapping $\mathcal{M}$.

31. Find a quasi-inverse of the mapping $\mathcal{M}$ specified by st-tgd $P(x,y,z) \to R(x,y) \wedge T(y,z)$ that is neither a recovery nor a maximum recovery of $\mathcal{M}$.

32. Let $\mathcal{M}$ be the mapping in Example 20.31 and Q be the target query $T(x,y)$. Prove that $(P(x) \wedge x = y) \vee R(x,y)$ is a source rewriting of Q under $\mathcal{M}$.

33. Prove that the formula $\alpha(\bar{u})$ computed in line 8 of algorithm MAXIMUMRECOVERYFULL is a source rewriting of target query $P(\bar{u})$. Use this fact to conclude that this algorithm is correct.

34. Use algorithm MAXIMUMRECOVERYFULL to find a maximum recovery for the mapping $\mathcal{M}$ specified by st-tgd $P(x,y,z) \to R(x,y) \wedge T(y,z)$.

35. Let $\mathcal{M} = (\mathbf{R_1}, \mathbf{R_2}, \Sigma)$, where Σ is a finite set of tgds, and assume that the instances of $\mathbf{R_1}$ can contain null values. Prove that every instance of $\mathbf{R_1}$ has a universal solution under $e(\mathcal{M})$. Use this fact to conclude that $e(\mathcal{M})$ admits a maximum recovery.

36. (Source: Arenas et al. (2009a))
    This exercise is about recoveries under the universal solution semantics. For a mapping $\mathcal{M} = (\mathbf{R_1}, \mathbf{R_2}, \Sigma)$, let $u(\mathcal{M})$ be defined as the set of pairs: $\{(S,T) \mid T$ is a universal solution for S under $\mathcal{M}\}$. Prove that the mapping $(u(\mathcal{M}))^{-1} = \{(T,S) \mid (S,T) \in u(\mathcal{M})\}$ is a maximum recovery of $u(\mathcal{M})$.

37. (Source: ten Cate and Kolaitis (2009))
    Let $\mathcal{M}$ be a mapping specified by a finite set of st-tgds. Prove that $\mathcal{M}$ reflects source homomorphisms.

38. Let $\mathscr{M} = (\mathbf{R_s}, \mathbf{R_t}, \Sigma)$, where $\mathbf{R_s}$ is a source schema consisting of a binary predicate U, $\mathbf{R_t}$ is a target schema consisting of a binary predicate V and $\Sigma = \{\forall x \exists y \forall z (U(x,z) \to V(y,z))\}$. Prove that $\mathscr{M}$ is closed under target homomorphisms, admits universal solutions and reflects source homomorphisms.

39. (Source: ten Cate and Kolaitis (2009))
    Complete the proof of Theorem 21.5.

40. (Source: ten Cate and Kolaitis (2009))
    Let $\mathscr{M}$ be the mapping defined in Example 21.8. Prove that $\mathscr{M}$ is closed under target homomorphisms, admits universal solutions, reflects source homomorphisms and is closed under target intersection.

41. (Source: ten Cate and Kolaitis (2009))
    Prove Lemma 21.9.

References

Abiteboul, S., Hull, R., and Vianu, V. 1995. *Foundations of Databases*. Addison-Wesley.

Abiteboul, S., Segoufin, L., and Vianu, V. 2006. Representing and querying XML with incomplete information. *ACM Transactions on Database Systems*, **31**(1), 208–254.

Afrati, F., and Kolaitis, P. 2008. Answering aggregate queries in data exchange. Pages 129–138 of: *ACM Symposium on Principles of Database Systems (PODS)*.

Alexe, B., ten Cate, B., Kolaitis, P. G., and Tan, W. C. 2011. Designing and refining schema mappings via data examples. Pages 133–144 of: *Proceedings of the ACM SIGMOD International Conference on Management of Data (SIGMOD)*.

Amano, S., Libkin, L., and Murlak, F. 2009. XML schema mappings. Pages 33–42 of: *ACM Symposium on Principles of Database Systems (PODS)*.

Amano, S., David, C., Libkin, L., and Murlak, F. 2010. On the tradeoff between mapping and querying power in XML data exchange. Pages 155–164 of: *International Conference on Database Theory (ICDT)*.

Amer-Yahia, S., Cho, S., Lakshmanan, L., and Srivastava, D. 2002. Tree pattern query minimization. *VLDBJ*, **11**, 315–331.

Arenas, M., and Libkin, L. 2004. A normal form for XML documents. *ACM Trans. Database Syst.*, **29**(1), 195–232.

Arenas, M., and Libkin, L. 2008. XML data exchange: Consistency and query answering. *Journal of the ACM*, **55**(2).

Arenas, M., Pérez, J., Reutter, J. L., and Riveros, C. 2009a. Composition and inversion of schema mappings. *SIGMOD Record*, **38**(3), 17–28.

Arenas, M., Pérez, J., and Riveros, C. 2009b. The recovery of a schema mapping: Bringing exchanged data back. *ACM Transactions on Database Systems*, **34**(4), 22:1–22:48.

Arenas, M., Pérez, J., Reutter, J. L., and Riveros, C. 2010a. Foundations of schema mapping management. Pages 227–238 of: *Proceedings of the 29th ACM Symposium on Principles of Database Systems (PODS)*.

Arenas, M., Barceló, P., Libkin, L., and Murlak, F. 2010b. *Relational and XML Data Exchange*. Morgan&Claypool Publishers.

Arenas, M., Fagin, R., and Nash, A. 2011a. Composition with target constraints. *Logical Methods in Computer Science*, **7**(3).

Arenas, M., Perez, J., and Reutter, J. 2011b. Data exchange beyond complete data. Pages 83–94 of: *Proceedings of the 30th ACM Symposium on Principles of Database Systems (PODS)*.

Arenas, M., Barceló, P., and Reutter, J. L. 2011c. Query languages for data exchange: Beyond unions of conjunctive queries. *Theory of Computing Systems*, **49**(2), 489–564.

Arenas, M., Barceló, P., Fagin, R., and Libkin, L. 2013. Solutions and query rewriting in data exchange. *Information and Computation*, **228**(1), 28–61.

Arocena, P. C., Fuxman, A., and Miller, R. J. 2010. Composing local-as-view mappings: Closure and applications. Pages 209–218 of: *Proceedings of the 13th International Conference on Database Theory (ICDT)*.

Barceló, P. 2009. Logical foundations of relational data exchange. *SIGMOD Record*, **38**(1), 49–58.

Barceló, P., Libkin, L., Poggi, A., and Sirangelo, C. 2010. XML with incomplete information. *Journal of the ACM*, **58**(1).

Benedikt, M., Fan, W., and Geerts, F. 2008. XPath satisfiability in the presence of DTDs. *Journal of the ACM*, **55**(2).

Bernstein, P. A. 2003. Applying model management to classical meta-data problems. Pages 209–220 of: *Conference on Innovative Data Systems Research (CIDR)*.

Bernstein, P. A., and Melnik, S. 2007. Model management 2.0: Manipulating richer mappings. Pages 1–12 of: *ACM SIGMOD Conference*.

Bernstein, P. A., Green, T. J., Melnik, S., and Nash, A. 2008. Implementing mapping composition. *VLDB J.*, **17**(2), 333–353.

Bex, G. J., Neven, F., and den Bussche, J. V. 2004. DTDs versus XML Schema: A practical study. Pages 79–84 of: *Proceedings of the WebDB Workshop*.

Björklund, H., Martens, W., and Schwentick, T. 2008. Optimizing conjunctive queries over trees using schema information. Pages 132–143 of: *Proceedings of Mathematical Foundations of Computer Science*.

Björklund, H., Martens, W., and Schwentick, T. 2011. Conjunctive query containment over trees. *Journal of Computer and System Sciences*, **77**(3), 450–472.

Bojańczyk, M., Kołodziejczyk, L. A., and Murlak, F. 2011. Solutions in XML data exchange. Pages 102–113 of: Milo, T. (ed), *International Conference on Database Theory (ICDT)*. ACM.

Calvanese, D., Giacomo, G. D., Lenzerini, M., and Vardi, M. Y. 2011. Simplifying schema mappings. Pages 114–125 of: *Proceedings of the 14th International Conference on Database Theory (ICDT)*.

Chirkova, R., Libkin, L., and Reutter, J. 2012. Tractable XML data exchange via relations. *Frontiers of Computer Science*, **6**(3), 243–263.

Comon, H., Dauchet, M., Gilleron, R., Löding, C., Jacquemard, F., Lugiez, D., Tison, S., and Tommasi, M. 2007. *Tree Automata Techniques and Applications*. Available on: http://www.grappa.univ-lille3.fr/tata. Released October, 12th 2007.

David, C. 2008. Complexity of data tree patterns over XML documents. Pages 278–289 of: *Proceedings of Mathematical Foundations of Computer Science*.

David, C., Libkin, L., and Murlak, F. 2010. Certain answers for XML queries. Pages 191–202 of: *ACM Symposium on Principles of Database Systems (PODS)*.

de Rougemont, M., and Vieilleribière, A. 2007. Approximate data exchange. Pages 44–58 of: *International Conference on Database Theory (ICDT)*.

Deutsch, A., and Tannen, V. 2003. Reformulation of XML queries and constraints. Pages 225–241 of: *International Conference on Database Theory (ICDT)*.

Deutsch, A., Nash, A., and Remmel, J. 2008. The chase revisited. Pages 149–158 of: *ACM Symposium on Principles of Database Systems (PODS)*.

Doan, A., Halevy, A., and Ives, Z. 2012. *Principles of Data Integration*. Morgan Kaufmann.

Fagin, R., Kolaitis, P. G., Miller, R. J., and Popa, L. 2005a. Data exchange: Semantics and query answering. *Theoretical Computer Science*, **336**, 89–124. Preliminary version in *Proc. 2003 International Conference on Database Theory*, pp. 207–224.

Fagin, R., Kolaitis, P., Nash, A., and Popa, L. 2008a. Towards a theory of schema-mapping optimization. Pages 33–42 of: *Proceedings of the 27th ACM Symposium on Principles of Database Systems (PODS)*.

Fagin, R., Haas, L., Hernandez, M., Miller, R., Popa, L., and Velegrakis, Y. 2009. Clio: Schema mapping creation and data exchange. Pages 198–236 of: *Conceptual Modeling: Foundations and Applications, Essays in Honor of John Mylopoulos*. Lecture Notes in Computer Science, vol. 5600. Springer-Verlag.

Fagin, R. 2007. Inverting schema mappings. *ACM Transactions on Database Systems*, **32**(4).

Fagin, R., and Kolaitis, P. G. 2012. Local transformations and conjunctive-query equivalence. Pages 179–190 of: *Proceedings of the 31st ACM Symposium on Principles of Database Systems (PODS)*.

Fagin, R., and Nash, A. 2010. The structure of inverses in schema mappings. *Journal of the ACM*, **57**(6), 31.

Fagin, R., Kolaitis, P. G., Popa, L., and Tan, W. C. 2005b. Composing schema mappings: Second-order dependencies to the rescue. *ACM Transactions on Database Systems*, **30**(4), 994–1055.

Fagin, R., Kolaitis, P., and Popa, L. 2005c. Data exchange: Getting to the core. *ACM Transactions on Database Systems*, **30**(1), 174–210.

Fagin, R., Kolaitis, P. G., Popa, L., and Tan, W. C. 2008b. Quasi-inverses of schema mappings. *ACM Trans. Database Syst.*, **33**(2), 11:1–11:52.

Fagin, R., Kimelfeld, B., and Kolaitis, P. 2010. Probabilistic data exchange. Pages 76–88 of: *International Conference on Database Theory (ICDT)*.

Fagin, R., Kolaitis, P. G., Popa, L., and Tan, W. C. 2011. Reverse data exchange: Coping with nulls. *ACM Trans. Database Syst.*, **36**(2), 11.

Feinerer, I., Pichler, R., Sallinger, E., and Savenkov, V. 2011. On the undecidability of the equivalence of second-order tuple generating dependencies. In: *Proceedings of the 5th Alberto Mendelzon International Workshop on Foundations of Data Management (AMW)*.

Fuxman, A., Kolaitis, P., Miller, R., and Tan, W.-C. 2006. Peer data exchange. *ACM Transactions on Database Systems*, **31**(4), 1454–1498.

Garcia-Molina, H., Ullman, J., and Widom, J. 2001. *Database Systems: The Complete Book*. Prentice Hall.

Garey, M., and Johnson, D. 1979. *Computers and Intractability: A Guide to the Theory of NP-Completeness*. W. H. Freeman and Company.

Gheerbrant, A., Libkin, L., and Tan, T. 2012. On the complexity of query answering over incomplete XML documents. Pages 169–181 of: *International Conference on Database Theory (ICDT)*.

Giacomo, G. D., Lembo, D., Lenzerini, M., and Rosati, R. 2007. On reconciling data exchange, data integration, and peer data management. Pages 133–142 of: *ACM Symposium on Principles of Database Systems (PODS)*.

Gottlob, G., and Nash, A. 2008. Efficient core computation in data exchange. *Journal of the ACM*, **55**(2).

Gottlob, G., Koch, C., Pichler, R., and Segoufin, L. 2005. The complexity of XPath query evaluation and XML typing. *Journal of the ACM*, **52**(2), 284–335.

Gottlob, G., Koch, C., and Schulz, K. U. 2006. Conjunctive queries over trees. *Journal of the ACM*, **53**(2), 238–272.

Gou, G., and Chirkova, R. 2007. Efficiently querying large XML data repositories: A survey. *IEEE Trans. Knowl. Data Eng.*, **19**(10), 1381–1403.

Grahne, G., and Onet, A. 2012. Representation systems for data exchange. Pages 208–221 of: *Proceedings of the 15th International Conference on Database Theory (ICDT)*.

Haas, L. M. 2007. Beauty and the beast: The theory and practice of information integration. Pages 28–43 of: *International Conference on Database Theory (ICDT)*.

Hell, P., and Nešetřil, J. 1992. The core of a graph. *Discrete Mathematics*, **109**(1-3), 117–126.

Hernich, A. 2011. Answering non-monotonic queries in relational data exchange. *Logical Methods in Computer Science*, **7**(3).

Hernich, A., and Schweikardt, N. 2007. CWA-solutions for data exchange settings with target dependencies. Pages 113–122 of: *ACM Symposium on Principles of Database Systems (PODS)*.

Hernich, A., Libkin, L., and Schweikardt, N. 2011. Closed world data exchange. *ACM Transactions on Database Systems*, **36**(2).

Hidders, J. 2003. Satisfiability of XPath expressions. Pages 21–36 of: *Database Programming Languages*.

Hopcroft, J., and Ullman, J. 1979. *Introduction to Automata Theory*. Addison-Wesley.

Housel, B., Taylor, R., Ghosh, S., and Lum, V. Y. 1977. EXPRESS: A data extraction, processing, and restructuring system. *ACM Transactions on Database Systems*, **2**(2), 134–174.

Imieliński, T., and Lipski, W. 1984. Incomplete information in relational databases. *Journal of the ACM*, **31**(4), 761–791.

Klarlund, N., Schwentick, T., and Suciu, D. 2003. XML: Model, schemas, types, logics, and queries. Pages 1–41 of: Chomicki, J., van der Meyden, R., and Saake, G. (eds), *Logics for Emerging Applications of Databases*. Springer.

Kolaitis, P. G. 2005. Schema mappings, data exchange, and metadata management. Pages 61–75 of: *ACM Symposium on Principles of Database Systems (PODS)*.

Kolaitis, P. G., Panttaja, J., and Tan, W. C. 2006. The complexity of data exchange. Pages 30–39 of: Vansummeren, S. (ed), *ACM Symposium on Principles of Database Systems (PODS)*. ACM.

Lenzerini, M. 2002. Data integration: A theoretical perspective. Pages 233–246 of: *Proceedings of the 21st ACM Symposium on Principles of Database Systems (PODS)*.

Libkin, L. 2006a. Data exchange and incomplete information. Pages 60–69 of: *ACM Symposium on Principles of Database Systems (PODS)*.

Libkin, L. 2006b. Logics for unranked trees: An overview. *Logical Methods in Computer Science*, **2**(3).

Libkin, L., and Sirangelo, C. 2011. Data exchange and schema mappings in open and closed worlds. *J. Comput. Syst. Sci.*, **77**(3), 542–571.

Marnette, B. 2009. Generalized schema-mappings: from termination to tractability. Pages 13–22 of: *ACM Symposium on Principles of Database Systems (PODS)*.

Marnette, B., Mecca, G., and Papotti, P. 2010. Scalable data exchange with functional dependencies. *PVLDB*, **3**(1), 105–116.

Marnette, B., Mecca, G., Papotti, P., Raunich, S., and Santoro, D. 2011. ++Spicy: An OpenSource tool for second-generation schema mapping and data exchange. *PVLDB*, **4**(12), 1438–1441.

Mądry, A. 2005. Data exchange: On the complexity of answering queries with inequalities. *Information Processing Letters*, **94**(6), 253–257.

Mecca, G., Papotti, P., and Raunich, S. 2009. Core schema mappings. Pages 655–688 of: *ACM SIGMOD Conference*.

Meier, M., Schmidt, M., and Lausen, G. 2009. Stop the chase: Short contribution. In: Arenas, M., and Bertossi, L. E. (eds), *AMW*. CEUR Workshop Proceedings, vol. 450. CEUR-WS.org.

Melnik, S. 2004. *Generic Model Management: Concepts and Algorithms*. Lecture Notes in Computer Science, vol. 2967. Springer.

Miller, R. J., Hernndez, M. A., Haas, L. M., Yan, L.-L., Ho, C. T. H., Fagin, R., and Popa, L. 2001. The Clio project: Managing heterogeneity. *SIGMOD Record*, **30**(1), 78–83.

Nash, A., Bernstein, P. A., and Melnik, S. 2007. Composition of mappings given by embedded dependencies. *ACM Trans. Database Syst.*, **32**(1), 4:1–4:51.

Neven, F. 2002. Automata, Logic, and XML. Pages 2–26 of: Bradfield, J. C. (ed), *CSL*. Lecture Notes in Computer Science, vol. 2471. Springer.

Papadimitriou, C. 1994. *Computational Complexity*. Addison-Wesley.

Pérez, J., Pichler, R., Sallinger, E., and Savenkov, V. 2012. Union and intersection of schema mappings. Pages 129–141 of: *Proceedings of the 6th Alberto Mendelzon International Workshop on Foundations of Data Management (AMW)*.

Pichler, R., Sallinger, E., and Savenkov, V. 2011. Relaxed notions of schema mapping equivalence revisited. Pages 90–101 of: *Proceedings of the 14th International Conference on Database Theory (ICDT)*.

Schwentick, T. 2007. Automata for XML – A survey. *Journal of Computer and System Sciences*, **73**(3), 289–315.

Sipser, M. 1997. *Introduction to the Theory of Computation*. PWS Publishing Company.

ten Cate, B., and Kolaitis, P. 2009. Structural characterizations of schema-mapping languages. Pages 63–72 of: *International Conference on Database Theory (ICDT)*.

ten Cate, B., Chiticariu, L., Kolaitis, P. G., and Tan, W. C. 2009. Laconic schema mappings: Computing the core with SQL queries. *PVLDB*, **2**(1), 1006–1017.

ten Cate, B., Dalmau, V., and Kolaitis, P. G. 2012. Learning schema mappings. Pages 182–195 of: *Proceedings of the 15th International Conference on Database Theory (ICDT)*.

Ullman, J. 1988. *Principles of Database and Knowledge-Base Systems, Volume I*. Computer Science Press.

Vianu, V. 2001. A Web odyssey: From Codd to XML. Pages 1–15 of: *ACM Symposium on Principles of Database Systems (PODS)*.

Index